Successful Small Business Management

Successful Small Business Management

CURTIS E. TATE, JR.
The University of Georgia

LEON C. MEGGINSON
University of South Alabama

CHARLES R. SCOTT, JR.
The University of Alabama

LYLE R. TRUEBLOOD
The University of Tulsa

1978   Revised Edition

BUSINESS PUBLICATIONS, INC.
Dallas, Texas   75243

Irwin-Dorsey Limited
Georgetown, Ontario   L7G 4B3

ISBN 0-256-02074-4
Library of Congress Catalog Card No. 77–91317
Printed in the United States of America

3 4 5 6 7 8 9 0 K 5 4 3 2 1 0 9

Preface

In the contemporary world, the need for the independent business (that is, small business, entrepreneurship, private enterprise) is seen more vividly than ever in the economic and social environments. The opportunity to supply needed products or services for which there is a void in the marketplace provides both the opportunity and challenge. In the population, there are those who, for a variety of reasons, need employment opportunities and entry into a business of their own will satisfy this employment and aspiration need. Independent business provides an opportunity for the technically displaced, the physically disabled, and those unhappy with their present work situation, with problems of relocation, and with higher aspiration levels.

At the time of preparing the first edition of this book, and on a continuing basis since, we have been studying the world of independently-owned businesses. This has made us continuously aware of the problems and needs of the business owner-manager. From the inception, our intent has been to formulate a comprehensive body of material that will provide you the reader with a complete concept of owning-managing a business. The basic premise is to make the material thorough, simple, and addressed to you.

Our academic and practitioner experience attests to our knowledge of the requisites for successful small business management. The success achieved by many of our former students in starting and operating their own businesses is further proof of our expertise.

We have been evaluating the approach of the first edition and its reception by students and faculty. This revision reflects the combination of our continuous study of the independent business environment and the evaluation of our personalized approach to the student. We have reorganized the material to better reflect what we perceive to be a more appropriate sequencing of the information. In addition, we have made minor adjustments to reflect the contemporary changes in the business environment.

All of us today are interested in being active participants in the game of living rather than being merely passive observers. Doing our own thing and searching for a sense of meaning, identity, creativity, and achievement are important to all of us.

One of the best ways of accomplishing these things is to become the owner-manager of an independent business. While the management of all types of economic activity is becoming increasingly more complex and difficult, this is especially true of small and independent businesses.

Because of this trend, the purpose of this book is to help you "do your own thing." This does not mean that you will be successful just because you have read and studied this text, but this should help improve your chances of succeeding. Operating a small business is a very practical but challenging occupation. It involves desire, theoretical knowledge, practical experience, hard work, and even some element of luck.

This book is designed to provide you with a combination of theoretical and practical knowledge. The text material presents the ideas, concepts, and philosophies of each subject area. The cases give you the opportunity to apply that knowledge to actual situations.

Our objectives in developing this book have been to:

1. Show you, as a student, a prospective owner and manager of a small or independent firm, or a person interested in the subject, some of the advantages and disadvantages of those businesses.
2. Indicate to you how to become involved in your venture.
3. Demonstrate how to avoid some of the mistakes in conceiving, initiating, organizing, and operating a small firm that have been economically fatal to others.
4. Enable you to achieve the optimum benefit from the limited economic and human resources available to you.
5. Assist you in succeeding in managing and operating your own business.

We have tried to present a truly readable approach to the subject of management and entrepreneurship. The presentation of ideas is made more alive by using current examples of actual business applications. Materials were selected on the basis of their fundamental contribution to learning and their ability to stimulate interest and involvement. Many cases place you in the position of being an owner-manager of a small business facing a difficult decision-making situation.

In order to aid your learning process, we have divided the book into

7 parts and 25 chapters. Some of the unique characteristics of small businesses and the persons who own and operate them are discussed in Part I.

Once you decide you want to own and manage a small business, you must choose the kind of business to engage in and select the specific firm you will enter. These challenges are explored in Part II.

Staffing your organization, producing your product or service, marketing it, and planning and controlling your finances to make a profit—these are the most important business activities you will need to perform effectively if you want to succeed. These are discussed in relative detail in Parts III, IV, V, and VI. The practical aspects of these activities are emphasized. Finally, some special considerations in managing a small or independent business are brought into perspective in Part VII.

Changes from the first edition include expansion and rewriting the section on franchising; re-ordering of parts and chapters; reduction of the total number of cases; replacement of some of the cases; addition of incidents and casettes, *management audit* and *personal evaluation* checklists, and inclusion of a glossary of terms. While doing this, an effort was made to keep the book to its original length. During the revision process, we made a complete review of the writing of all sections of the book.

We believe that this revised edition of *Successful Small Business Management* will fill the needs of students interested in small businesses. It is hoped that those using the text will identify with the individuals included in the cases and will learn to be better managers.

Our thanks to those contributing the cases used in this revised edition. As well as, our thanks to John Ryan, Corporate Finance Department, Robinson-Humphrey Company; Woodrow Stewart, attorney, Telford, Stewart, and Stephens; John Sewell and John Lattimer, Small Business Administration; and Will Hattendorf, Economic Development Administration, our thanks for their advice and assistance in keeping this book reality-oriented.

Thanks are due for the contributions made through the years by the many researchers, entrepreneurs and managers, and professional people and members of the Southern Case Research Association.

Also, a special thank you to Mary Combs Tate, Jayne Megginson, Addie M. Scott, and Wyn Trueblood for their unfailing support.

We would be remiss if we failed to acknowledge the assistance of those who provided secretarial assistance in the preparation of the manuscript and the Teacher's Manual, and who patiently proofed the material. To Janice Glab, Jo Anne Martin, and Renee Langlois, thank you.

February 1978

Curtis E. Tate, Jr.
Leon C. Megginson
Charles R. Scott, Jr.
Lyle R. Trueblood

List of Case Contributors

Robert L. Anderson
Janelle C. Ashley
Harvey J. Brightman
Howard Chamberlain
Robert Crayne
Dennis M. Crites
Emit A. Deal
Lynn E. Dellenbarger, Jr.
Donald DeSalvia
Robert Gatewood
John Hand
M. M. Hargrove
Richard S. Harrigan
Fred Ingerson
Rudolph L. Kagerer
Peter R. Kensicki
Philip W. Ljungdahl
Robert McGlashan
Joseph Barry Mason
Morris L. Mayer
Terrence A. Oliva
Kenneth W. Olm
B. D. Perkins

Larry Gene Pointer
Harold Prasatik
Sydney C. Reagan
Robert A. Rentz, Jr.
William V. Rice, Jr.
Ed D. Roach
James F. Russell
Donald W. Scotton
Arthur D. Sharplin
A. Michael Sibley
A. W. Smith
Burnard Sord
Calvin W. Stevens
Alonzo J. Strickland, III
Jeffrey C. Susbauer
Arthur A. Thompson
Howard A. Thompson
James M. Todd
Thomas F. Urban
Louis C. Wagner
Stephen L. Woehrle
Allan Young
Thomas W. Zimmerer

Contents

standing the Uniqueness of Small Firms. Adaptability to Change. Accurate Operating and Market Information. Using Human Resources Effectively. Obtaining Investment Capital. Handling Government Regulations. The Increasing Competence and Growing Involvement of Females and Minorities. An Introspective Personal Analysis: *What Is Your Philosophy of Life? What Are Your Mental Abilities? What Are Your Attitudes?* Appendix: Performing a Personal Self-Analysis.

PART II
PLANNING AND ORGANIZING A NEW BUSINESS

Selecting the Type of Business You Would Like to Enter: *Review Your Abilities. Eliminate Undesirable Businesses. Use a Checklist. How You Can Classify the Types of Business. How You Can Choose the Business to Enter.* Studying the Economic Environment: *Studying the Economic Environment for the Business. Studying the Market for Your Business.* Deciding Whether to Start a New Business or Buy an Existing One: *Entering an Established Business. Starting a New Business of Your Own.* Appendix: Deciding Whether to Start a New Business or Buy an Existing One.

To Buy or Not to Buy: *Determining Why the Business Is Available. Analysis of Accounting Information. Analysis of Pricing Formula. Appraisal of Operations, Plant, and Equipment. Preparing an Economic Feasibility Study.* Implementing Your Plans.

Developing a Timetable. Establishing Your Business Objectives. Setting up the Organizational Structure. Determining Personnel Requirements. Determining Your Physical Plant Needs: *Location. Buy or Lease.* Planning Your Approach to the Market: *Building an Image. Channels of Distribution. Pricing Policies.* Preparing Your Budgets: *Types of Budgets.* Anticipating Difficulties. Locating Source of Funds: *Your Own Funds. Funds of Other Individuals. Trade Credit. Commercial Banks. Investment Banks. Major Nonfinancial Corporations. Insurance Companies. Small Business Administration. Small Business Investment Corporations. Industrial Development Corporations. Economic Development Administration (EDA). State Employment Agencies. Agricultural Loans.* Implementing Your Plans: *Capital Procurement. Corporate Charter and*

Permits. Contracting and Purchasing Facilities and Supplies. Personnel Selection and Training. Beginning Your Operations. Appendix: An Example of a Mini-Proposal and a Business Plan.

PART III
STAFFING YOUR BUSINESS

Rates of Pay. Other Aspects of the Wage and Salary Administration Program. Rewarding Management Personnel. Directing Your Employees' Activities: *Exercising Leadership. Communicating. Motivating.* Using Management by Objectives. Appraising Your Employees' Performance.

PART IV
PRODUCING YOUR PRODUCT OR SERVICE

Work to Be Done in the Near Future. Installing an Information System to Direct the Activities. Controlling Production: Quantity and Quality.

Cases for Part V

PART VI
PROFIT PLANNING AND CONTROL

19. **Evaluating Your Financial Position and Operations** **377**

How You Can Evaluate Your Financial Operations and Position. Financial Accounts of the Firm: *Assets. Liabilities. Owners' Equity. Revenue and Expenses. Profit.* Methods of Evaluating the Firms' Financial Condition: *Values of Each Ratio in the Past. Values of Other Like Companies.* Important Ratios and Their Meanings.

20. **Maintaining Adequate—and Accurate—Records** **389**

Importance of Records Keeping. What Information Is Needed: *Records of Service to Customers. Records of Services Performed for You.* Recording the Information: *Sales. Cash Income and Outgo. Accounts Receivable. Accounts Payable. Inventory. Expenses. Financial Statements.* Processing and Storing Information. Job Costs.

21. **Planning for a Profit** **404**

How to Plan for Profit: *Steps for Profit Planning. An Example of Profit Planning.* Step 1: Establishing Your Profit Goal. Step 2: Determining Your Planned Volume of Sales. Step 3: Estimating Your Expenses for Planned Volume of Sales. Step 4: Determining Your Profit from Steps 2 and 3. Step 5: Comparing Your Estimated Profit with Your Profit Goal. Step 6: Listing Possible Alternatives to Improve Your Profits. Step 7: Determining How Changes in Costs Vary with Sales Volume Changes. Step 8: Determining How Profits Vary with Changes in Sales Volume. Step 9: Analyzing Alternatives from a Profit Standpoint. Step 10: Selecting Changes in Your Plans.

22. **Controlling the Financial Structure and Operations of Your Firm** . **417**

What Is Involved in Control? *The Role of Control. Steps in Control.* Characteristics of Control Systems: *Controls Should Be Timely. Controls Should Not Be Costly. Controls Should Provide the Accuracy Needed. Controls Should Be Quantifiable and Measurable. Controls Should Show Causes, When Possible. Controls Should Be Assigned to One Individual.* Causes of Poor Performance. Establishing Standards of Performance. Obtaining Information on Actual Performance: *Indirect Control by Means of Reports. Effective Cost Control.* Comparing Actual Performance with Standards. The Design and Use of Budgets: *Sales Budget. Cash Budget. Credit, Collections, and Accounts Receivable. Other Budgets.*

Safeguarding Your Assets with Insurance: *The Nature of Insurance and Its Limitations. Alternatives to Commercial Insurance. Types of Coverage. Guides to Buying Insurance. Product Liability.* Safeguarding Your Assets with Security Systems: *Nature of the Problem. Preventive Measures. Document Security.*

Cases for Part VI

PART VII
SOME SPECIAL CONSIDERATIONS IN MANAGING AN INDEPENDENT BUSINESS

Importance of Franchising. What Can a Franchise Do for Me? What Classification of Franchise Will You Choose? *Fast Foods. Motel. Automotive Franchises. Service Stations. Auto Tune-Ups. Convenience Markets. Real Estate Franchising.* What Franchise for Me? *Some Pitfalls. Some Pertinent Questions to Ask.* Some Conclusions Concerning Franchising.

Need for Management Succession: *An Overlooked Problem. What Is the* Real *Problem?* Some Problems in Managing a Family-Owned Business: *Individuals' Interests Conflict with Firm Objectives. Difficulty of Making* Rational *Decisions. Incompetence of Family Members—or Worse. Definite Authority. Sharing of Profits. Some Sources of Help for You.* Some Difficult Problems with Managers: *Incompetence. Replacing a Key Executive.* Taxes, Estate Planning, and the Future of Your Business. Preparing Your Successor: *Providing Him or Her with Adequate Information. Starting Early! The "Moment of Truth."* A Management Audit. Appendix A: Inventory of Information Used to Manage and Operate a Company. Appendix B: General Management Audit.

part I

Characteristics of Small Businesses and Their Owner-Managers

About 95 percent of all business enterprises in the United States are classified as small. Because these small businesses are so prevalent and perform such an important function in our economic system, it is desirable to start this book by showing the unique challenges involved in managing one of them. Owners and managers of these independent enterprises usually believe in individual freedom, initiative, and the free-enterprise system.[1] Most people consider it important to keep this part of our business society healthy.

The first thing you should do if you are considering entering a small business is to decide whether owning or managing such an enterprise is the "right" thing for you to do. The material in this part should help you make that important decision.

If you are already a small business executive, this material should permit you to sit back and take a hard look at where you now are and where you are going. (In order to have a consistent presentation and avoid needless repetition, we will assume that you are planning to enter a small business for the first time.)

The role of small business in our economy and the challenges it affords are put into perspective in Chapter 1. Then, considerable attention is given in Chapter 2 to the characteristics, attitudes, and objectives of owner-managers of independent firms.

You, as one of these individuals, have been our pri-

---

[1] While there is a distinction between a "small" business and an "independent" business enterprise, we will use the terms interchangeably.

mary consideration in presenting this material. In essence, you may enter business for yourself because you want to attain the objectives of financial profits, independence, a chance to engage in creative and challenging activities, and other benefits. In order to achieve these objectives, however, you must give up security and other benefits achieved through working for someone else and assume the risks inherent in ownership. These thoughts are covered in Chapter 3.

1

The Challenge of Owning
and Managing an Independent
Business

In managing any business, there must usually be a conscious choice between the desirable alternatives and the undesirable ones. There must
be a weighing of the advantages against the disadvantages of each of
these. The resulting decisions tend to be based upon the individual's
evaluation of the relative merits of the available alternatives. This relationship should also be present in a person's mind when he* or she is deciding whether to become the owner of a business or to work as a manager for someone else.

This chapter is designed to help you evaluate intelligently the alternatives of becoming the owner of a small business or of going into some
other activity.

DISTINCTION BETWEEN MANAGING SMALL AND
BIG BUSINESS

In distinguishing between big business and small business, some of the
criteria used are relative size, type of customers, financial strength, and
number of employees. For example, in the Small Business Act of 1953,
Congress defined a small business as one that "is independently owned
and operated and which is not dominant in its field of operation."[1] The

---

* The commonly used pronoun "he" is used in this book to refer to persons of
either sex. Its use is not intended to imply that the person being referred to is either
masculine or feminine.

[1] W. B. Barnes, *First Semi-Annual Report of Small Business Administration*
(Washington, D.C.: Small Business Administration, January 31, 1954), p. 7ff.

3

specific criteria to be used in determining size would be set by the Small Business Administration.

Distinction According to Size

There is no generally accepted definition of a "small business." The definitions vary all the way from that of one government office, which defines it as "one with $9 million or less in assets, a net worth under $4.5 million, and earnings in the last two years of no more than $450,000"[2] to ours, which is "an organization with a name, a place of operations, an owner, and one or more workers other than the owner." Complicating the search for a usable definition is the large number of "invisible" businesses, such as people working out of their own homes.

FIGURE 1–1
Percentage Distribution of Firms by Business Receipts and Assets, 1973

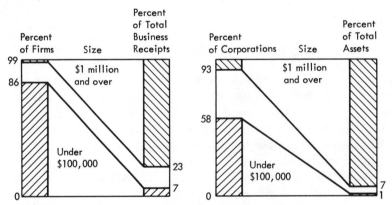

Source: *Statistical Abstract of the United States, 1976*, pp. 508, 515.

A different definition is used by the Federal Reserve Bank. It says a small business is one which "is independently owned and operated but is not dominant in its field."[3] The United States Employment Service estimates that the average manufacturing firm has 60 employees; the average wholesaler has nine; the average retailer has four; and the average service establishment has two. Over 70 percent of small business involves distribution.[4]

---

[2] "Small Business: Washington Begins to Take It More Seriously," *U.S. News & World Report*, August 8, 1977, p. 77.

[3] Small Business Administration, *Strengthening Small Business Management* (Washington, D.C.: U.S. Government Printing Office, 1971), p. 42.

[4] Ibid.

In 1973, there were over 2.9 million partnerships and corporations and over 10.6 million proprietorships in this country. About 86 percent of the firms had business receipts of less than $100,000, and about 58 percent of the corporations had assets of less than $100,000 (see Figure 1–1).

Regardless of the definition used, the Small Business Administration is charged with the responsibility for looking out for the interests of around 10 million small firms and around 3 million family farms.[5] Therefore, for purposes of this book, we will assume that there are around 13 million small or independent businesses in the United States.

Distinction According to Intentions

An important distinction to be made is that the *intentions* of the owners and managers of small firms tend to be different from those of professional managers of large enterprises.

Intentions of Managers of Large Enterprises.   The intentions of managers of large businesses are many and varied. Yet, they can probably be summarized as: the desire for job security; the desire for place, power, and prestige; and the desire for high income.

Those managers who are in the field for the extra income admit that managing a company is filled with responsibilities and worries, but they are willing to sacrifice other pleasures in order to have the benefits that go with a high income (including the large number of fringe benefits, such as expense accounts and the availability of company facilities for personal use).

Intentions of Owners of Small Businesses.   While these same motives might impel someone to become the owner of a small business, it must be recognized that there is a vast difference, which can be summarized by the word "independence." This distinction was made by a recent graduate of one of our larger universities, who had majored in Business Administration, when he wrote to one of us explaining why so few college graduates want to go into business for themselves.

> I believe that at least part of the answer is that the new graduates just don't know where to start and what to expect in the business world. With this lack of knowledge, they just don't have the "guts" to try it on their own. In my own case, I decided when I was in undergraduate school that I did not want to work for the other man. I always said that if I were going to make anyone rich, it was going to be myself. (Unfortunately, it has not worked out that way—yet.) Even with this burning desire to be my own boss, I was very hesitant and almost afraid to go into business for myself. However, I'm still glad I did.

---

[5] "Small Business: Washington Begins to Take It More Seriously," p. 77.

This letter illustrates the objective of those who become managers of small businesses. That goal is the freedom from interference or control by "superiors." Those individuals desire autonomy in exercising their initiative and ambition, which often results in innovations and leads to great flexibility, which is one of the virtues of small business.

UNIQUE ADVANTAGES OF A SMALL BUSINESS

The small business has many advantages over its larger competitors. It is usually in closer touch with its customers, employees, and suppliers. The small business tends to have better employee relations than larger firms. It can do a more individualized job for customers and thereby can attract them on the basis of specialty product, quality, and personal services rather than on the impersonal factors of price or mass production of largely identical products.

Because of the small percentage of income that goes for overhead and nonrevenue producing activities, there are still some activities that can be performed more efficiently by small organizations than large ones.

Source of Innovation

The small enterprise is often a source of new materials, processes, ideas, services, and products that larger firms are reluctant to provide. The big company is usually committed by its investment in tools, inventory, and personnel to producing the same product in large quantities or for long periods of time, and is not as flexible as a smaller firm.

Keep Larger Firms "On Their Toes"

Smaller companies have become a controlling factor in the American economy by keeping the bigger concerns "on their toes." With the introduction of new products, methods, services, and so forth, the small businesses help check the development of monopolies, which is sometimes the tendency in larger organizations. Therefore, small businesses encourage competition, if not in price, at least in design and efficiency.

Produces People

Small local businesses usually have a more intimate knowledge of their communities, and therefore take more personal interest in them. Their owners and managers are mainstays of community projects. Another unique advantage of the small business is that *it produces people as well as goods and services.* Small companies enable their people to achieve a more well-rounded, balanced development than they could achieve in larger organizations. This development is accomplished by providing them a greater variety of learning experiences in work activities not open to individuals holding more specialized jobs in larger organizations. People have greater freedom in making decisions as well as in performing a greater variety of activities. This freedom, in turn, lends zest and interest to their work. In addition, it trains people to become better leaders and to use their talents and energies most effectively.

Develops Risk Takers

It has been said that the small business is a manifestation of one of the basic freedoms of American life, namely, risk taking—with its consequent rewards and punishments. The entrepreneur has *relative* freedom to enter or leave a business at will, to start small and grow big, to expand or contract, and to succeed or fail. This freedom is the basis of our economic system. Yet, the freedom to enter and leave is not absolute. Certain legal and other requirements must be met before one can start a new business. The same is true of closing a firm. The manager may have responsibilities to customers, employees, investors, and/or the community that prevent leaving at will.

This characteristic has forced the small business to be flexible. Therefore, it can switch its production readily to meet changing market conditions and can adapt itself quickly to changing demands within its field and capacity. It can even change fields. The small business is a center of initiative where experiments may be conducted, where innovations may be initiated, and where new ventures are started. Many of the new products of today originated in small business concerns. Particularly is this true in the electronic computer field, where the initial developments were carried on in small companies; e.g., the Univac computer.

UNIQUE DISADVANTAGES OF A SMALL BUSINESS

Probably more has been written concerning the disadvantages of small business than any other aspect of this area of study. Usually, the discussions boil down to three things: inadequate management ability, inadequate financing (including "unfair" taxation), and a poor competitive position.

One study showed the pitfalls facing small business managers and what can be done about them. The results are shown in Figure 1–2.

What are the specific disadvantages of small businesses? The problems of effective management of a small business have multiplied during recent years. During World War II, the Korean Conflict, and the Vietnam War, many independent enterprisers started in business and showed unusual profits. However, as the "seller's market" ended each time and a "buyer's market" developed, the problems confronting them began to multiply in character and intensity.

FIGURE 1–2
Pitfalls Facing Small Businessmen

Pitfalls
1. Lack of experience
2. Lack of money
3. The wrong location
4. Inventory mismanagement
5. Too much capital going into fixed assets
6. Poor credit granting practices
7. Taking too much out for yourself
8. Unplanned expansion
9. Having the wrong attitudes

What can be done about these pitfalls?
1. Recognize limitations
2. Plan properly
3. Keep records
4. Watch the balance sheet—not just the profits
5. Investigate
6. Cooperate with suppliers and banks
7. Learn
8. Utilize professional assistance
9. Watch your health

Source: W. H. Kuehn, *The Pitfalls in Managing a Small Business* (New York: Dun & Bradstreet, March 1973).

Inadequate Management

During these periods, many small business managers *relied on one-person management.* They tended to guard their positions very jealously and seldom selected effective subordinates. If they did, they failed to give them enough authority and responsibility to manage adequately. Often, the problem of "inbreeding" existed; members of the family who were not capable were brought into the firm in positions of authority.

Managers of small businesses *cannot be specialized* in one area. As they must make their own decisions and are forced to live with those choices, whether they are good, bad, or indifferent, the managers are faced with a dilemma. Because of the business's limited resources, it cannot afford to make costly mistakes; but because the organization is so small, it cannot afford to hire assistance to help prevent managers from making mistakes. Lack of sufficient time to give attention to the various managerial functions accounts for the vast majority of failures among small businesses.

Shortage of Working Capital

A related specific limitation of small businesses is the *shortage of working capital*. This leads to the inability to keep up with their larger competitors in new facilities, equipment, tools, and methods. Many efforts have been made to overcome this difficulty by making loans available to small businesses and by trying to obtain favorable tax laws to assist them.

Lack of Balance

Another disadvantage is the *lack of coordination between production and marketing*, that is, the lack of adequately balancing and coordinating these two important functions. It is important for a small business to keep a judicious balance between (1) having too few products so that sales are lost, and (2) diversifying too fast. This means that there should be a balancing between the advantages of diversification and the advantages of product specialization.

Some other disadvantages are: a lack of proper records keeping; lack of effective selling techniques especially market research, specialty advertising and personal selling; too rapid and unplanned expansion; and the increasing complexity of internal management as the organization grows in size. These disadvantages, although real and of significance to the small business, cannot be adequately treated here. They are covered elsewhere throughout this book.

THE PROBLEM OF "FAILURE"

The threat of failure is ever present for small businesses. Discontinuances result from many factors, including health, changes in family situations, and the apparent advantages of working for someone else. These are voluntary decisions to quit.

There are, however, other discontinuances which are the result of inability or failure to make the business "go." Things just don't work out as planned. These are "failures."

There are two types of failures. One ends up in court with some kind of loss to the creditors. There are relatively few of these failures. In fact, there were only 11,432 such failures in 1975, as shown in Table 1–1.

The underlying causes of these "formal failures" are shown in Figure 1–3.

The overall failure figures don't tell the whole story. As can be seen from Table 1–2, the chances of failure are greater in some regions and

TABLE 1-1

Formal Business Failures Classified by Year and Size of Liability

Year	Under $5,000	$5,000 to $25,000	$25,000 to $100,000	$100,000 to $1 million	Over $1 million
1972	394	2,497	4,149	2,236	290
1973	285	2,434	3,908	2,375	343
1974	304	2,150	4,279	2,755	427
1975	292	2,226	4,986	3,459	469

Source: *The Business Failure Record, 1975* (New York: Business Economics Department, Dun & Bradstreet, 1976).

states than in others. It is evident from the chart—Table 1–2 that your chance of failing in the mountain states is less than along the Pacific Coast; while Wyoming is the best state in which not to fail, your chance of failing is the greatest in California.

The other kind of failure is more important, numerically, and probably emotionally as well. This *personal* failure involves situations where individuals have put their savings—or income—into a business only to see losses wipe out their investment. Creditors don't suffer, for the owner has put up the funds to absorb the losses and pay off the debts. The owner is the one who packs up, closes the door, and says, "That's it! I'll never try starting a business of my own again."

The Service Corps of Retired Executives (SCORE), a group of retired business executives who perform the public service of aiding and advising

FIGURE 1-3

Causes of 9,915 Business Failures in 1974

Overall Causes	Percentage	Underlying Causes
Neglect	1.9	Bad habits, poor health, marital difficulties, and so on
Fraud	0.9	Misleading name, false financial statement, premeditated overbuy, irregular disposal of assets, and the like
Lack of experience in the line	15.6	Inadequate sales, heavy operating expenses, receivables difficulties, excessive fixed assets, poor location, competitive weakness, and others
Lack of managerial experience	14.1	
Unbalanced experience	22.3	
Incompetence	40.7	
Disaster	0.9	Fire, flood, burglary, employee fraud, strike, etc. Some of these occurrences could have been provided for through insurance
Reason unknown	3.6	

Source: *The Business Failure Record*, 1974 (New York: Business Economics Department, Dun & Bradstreet, 1975).

TABLE 1–2
Failure Rate by States—Rate per 10,000 Listed Concerns 1974

Region and State	Rate	Region and State	Rate
New England		Missouri	10.6
Maine	25.5	North Dakota	41.2
New Hampshire	50.4	South Dakota	10.3
Vermont	18.0	Nebraska	17.0
Massachusetts	39.5	Kansas	20.7
Connecticut	24.2	Total West North Central	22.8
Rhode Island	11.1		
Total New England	32.0	East South Central	
		Kentucky	36.6
Middle Atlantic		Tennessee	31.2
New York	61.9	Alabama	23.3
New Jersey	73.4	Mississippi	29.1
Pennsylvania	39.8	Total East South Central	30.0
Total Middle Atlantic	57.5		
		West South Central	
South Atlantic		Arkansas	20.2
Maryland	55.5	Oklahoma	28.3
Delaware	19.6	Louisiana	22.9
District of Columbia	41.6	Texas	39.3
Virginia	34.4	Total West South Central	33.2
West Virginia	7.3		
North Carolina	12.6	Mountain	
South Carolina	6.5	Montana	18.9
Georgia	41.8	Idaho	15.2
Florida	25.6	Wyoming	—
Total South Atlantic	27.6	Colorado	21.4
		New Mexico	30.2
East North Central		Arizona	19.3
Ohio	35.4	Utah	6.6
Indiana	26.2	Nevada	18.1
Illinois	40.3	Total Mountain	18.0
Michigan	68.4		
Wisconsin	23.5	Pacific	
Total East North Central	41.4	Washington	34.2
		Oregon	61.9
West North Central		California	76.4
Minnesota	49.6	Total Pacific	69.4
Iowa	14.3		

Note: Data for Alaska and Hawaii not available.
Source: *The Business Failure Record, 1974* (New York: Business Economics Department, Dun & Bradstreet, 1975).

small business managers, has estimated that around 400,000 small firms go out of business each year in the United States, and 100,000 of these fail in the first year of existence.[6] The causes of failure, in descending order, are: (1) lack of business records, (2) lack of business experience, (3) insufficient stock turnover, (4) uncollected accounts receivable, (5) inventory shrinkage, (6) poor inventory control, (7) lack of finances, (8) improper markup, and (9) lack of sales.

---

[6] "Failing Businesses," *Parade,* September 8, 1974, p. 24.

THE PROBLEM OF GROWTH

The problem of growth appears to be a built-in dilemma facing many small businesses. First, if the owners are inefficient and if their initiative or abilities are not sufficient, their organizations flounder and eventually become included among the casualties called "business failures," as just mentioned.

Second, if the owners are mediocre, their organizations continue to be small businesses and are constantly plagued with the problems associated with smallness.

Third, if the owner-managers are efficient and capable, and their organizations succeed and grow, they run the risk of losing the very things they seek from their business firms. The very act of growing means losing some of the autonomy and control the owners seek. If nothing else, the owners now must please a larger number of people, including customers, the public, and their employees. They also have the problem of con-

FIGURE 1–4
Stages in the Development of a Small Business

First Stage--One-person operation, where owner does all the activities.

Owner - Manager - Worker

Second Stage--Separation of management and nonmanagement functions; hired subordinates to do some of the manual and/or mental activities while owner manages.

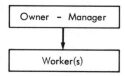

Third Stage--Separation of ownership and management functions; owner begins to relinquish the responsibilities for the day-to-day running of the business activities to a professional manager.

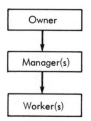

Source: Adapted from L. C. Megginson, *Providing Management Talent for Small Business* (Small Business Management Research Reports; Baton Rouge: College of Business Administration, Louisiana State University, 1961), p. 7.

trolling other people, exercising the very power they resented in others. All too frequently, owner-managers are not equipped to control other people well, and they begin to have interpersonal problems in their firms. If they become large enough and require outside capital for future success and growth, they may lose autonomy and control over their organizations. Even if they lose control, however, they may still retain a sense of achievement for what they have been able to create within their "own" organization. They can still say, "This is something I've built."

Historically, the ownership and management of small businesses have tended to follow the growth pattern shown in Figure 1–4. During the first stage, the owner both manages the company and performs all the work himself. As the organization grows into the second stage, the owner hires one or more employees to help perform the manual and/or mental activities. Later, as the organization begins to get larger, it enters the third stage, in which the owner hires a manager to run the business. Thus, the business takes on the form, characteristics, and many of the problems of a big business.

An insurance firm began in the late 1920s with a husband and wife selling policies during the day and doing the paper work at night. As chairman of the firm, the man described the process of growth in this way:

> A company's success and growth is a chain reaction. First, there is the growth which leads to new responsibilities. This, in turn, leads to a search for executive talent to undertake the new responsibilities. If the search is successful, the effective management leads to better business, which leads to more profits. Then, the decision must be made to expand again. Thus, the cycle is repeated.
> ꞏ However, the chain reaction can be broken at any point in the cycle. For instance, if the attempt to find another manager is unsuccessful, the growth may stop. Somewhere along the line, the founder ceases being the owner-manager of a small company with its unique problems and rewards and becomes the manager of a large company with all of its problems.

In this connection, it should be emphasized that the length of service of professional managers (as opposed to owner-managers) in small organizations *tends* to be relatively short. They move from one company to another as they progress. Often, owners must give managers an interest in the company to hold them.

SOME CURRENT PROBLEMS WORRYING SMALL BUSINESSES

Whether small businesses are growing, stabilizing, or failing, they tend to have some common problems that bother them. For many years, the federal government made a point of exempting small businesses from

FIGURE 1–5
Top Problems Worrying Small Businessmen in 1976

1. Government regulations in general.	7. High interest rates.
2. Inflation.	8. Environmental restrictions.
3. Taxes.	9. Lack of available capital.
4. Government paper work.	10. Minimum-wage laws.
5. Labor unions.	11. Insufficient depreciation allowances.
6. Federal deficits.	12. Crime.

Source: Survey conducted by U.S. Chamber of Commerce, as reported in *U.S. News & World Report*, December 20, 1976, p. 24.

many laws, rules, regulations, and regulatory interpretations. Now, it seems that the businesspeople themselves perceive that this attitude has changed, as reflected by a survey conducted by the U.S. Chamber of Commerce. Figure 1–5 lists the 12 top complaints voiced by these independent businesspeople.

SUMMARY

The most valid distinction between small and big business is based on the *intentions, aims, goals,* or *objectives* of the owner-managers. Small business managers primarily crave independence and freedom from control. They enjoy the autonomy they have in the exercise of their initiative and ambition.

This type of enterprise is often faced with a dilemma, for if the owners are inefficient or mediocre, they fail; but if the businesses are too successful, they become so large that their founders may lose the independence that they sought in the first place. You should recognize that remaining small *is not a sign of failure.* You can remain small, successful, satisfied, and still find a niche for yourself in the business world. In other words, there is a place for the small business if the owner works at making it effective and successful.

Finally, small businesses provide the dynamism, innovation, and effectiveness that has led to our productive economic system.

QUESTIONS FOR FURTHER DISCUSSION

1. What would you say is the most valid distinction between small and big business? Explain.
2. Discuss the unique advantages of a small business.
3. Briefly discuss some of the primary disadvantages of a small business.
4. Explain the phrase, "The problem of growth appears to be a built-in dilemma for the small business manager."

5. Briefly discuss the stages in the development of a small business. Have you seen any examples of this growth pattern? Explain.
6. What are some *overall* causes of failures? Explain.
7. Distinguish between the two types of failure.
8. Discuss the current problems worrying small business managers.
9. What would you say are the intentions of managers of large businesses?
10. What is the principal difference between the intentions of managers of large businesses and of small businesses?

2

What Are Your Objectives?

After presenting to you the challenges afforded by owning and operating a small business, we would like to explore the role you could play as the owner of one of these important units. In this chapter we discuss (1) your personal objectives, (2) the objectives of small businesses, and (3) the importance of meshing together these objectives.

YOUR PERSONAL OBJECTIVES

Your occupation represents much more to you than just a set of skills and functions; it represents a way of life. It largely provides and determines the environment—both physical and psychological—in which the individual lives; it selects, and often strengthens, the traits that the person most frequently uses. The occupation usually carries with it a status in the community and provides the individual's social roles and patterns for living. Since it largely determines the sorts of person with whom one spends much of one's life, it greatly influences value judgments and ethical standards. Occupational preference and personality traits are also usually related. Consequently, the ultimate objective in choosing your occupation should be the satisfaction of individual needs.

Theoretical Needs

Many efforts have been made to classify and explain human needs. The more popular efforts are summarized for the readers who have studied them elsewhere, or as an introduction to those who have not.

Maslow's Needs Hierarchy. Abraham Maslow, a psychologist, said that human needs could be ranked in an increasing order, or hierarchy, from the bottom up.[1] As one need is satisfied, the next higher need comes into play. The needs, which were modified by McGregor, are:

5. Self-fulfillment.
4. Ego satisfaction.
3. Social acceptance.
2. Safety.
1. Physiological needs, such as hunger.

Herzberg's Motivators and Maintenance Factors. Frederick Herzberg, another psychologist, said there are two sets of factors present in every job situation.[2] One set of factors is necessary in order to *maintain a good working relationship,* but they *do not motivate the individual to produce at a higher level.* They are:

1. Supervision.
2. Company policies and administration.
3. Employee benefits.
4. Job security.
5. Working conditions.
6. Salary.
7. Relationships with others.

The other factors, if present, *motivate people to produce at a high level.* They are:

1. Achievement.
2. Recognition.
3. Responsibility.
4. Creative and challenging work.
5. Advancement.

These needs or motives primarily pertain to managerial and non-managerial employees. They are not necessarily those of owners or entrepreneurs. In fact, they tend not to be. They are included here, though, for your use in evaluating the needs and motives of small business owners.

Motives of Small Business Owners

The above discussion of human needs will provide you the background for further study. As the owner of a small business, you have the potential

---

[1] Douglas McGregor, *The Human Side of Enterprise* (New York: McGraw-Hill Book Co., 1960), pp. 36–39.

[2] Frederick Herzberg et al., *The Motivation to Work,* 2d ed. (New York: John Wiley & Sons, Inc., 1959).

for fulfilling all of these needs through managing your own firm. The manner in which your needs are fulfilled depends upon the knowledge, skills, and personality traits you bring to your business. Your personal objectives express the type of life you wish to lead.

A great deal depends on the type of person you are and your dedication to your business. Owning your own business can be very rewarding in the following ways:

1. You can make a great deal of money, including certain expense account benefits. Be sure to bear in mind the legality and tax accountability of these!
2. You can perform a satisfying service to your community.
3. You can obtain prestige in your community.
4. You can find the challenges and new experiences many and varied.
5. You can be proud of what you have built.

There is a certain satisfaction in managing something you have built that does not come to you from directing a business that others have built. But before you decide upon this course, questions must be answered—if you are to succeed. Ambition, desire, capital, and willingness are not enough. You still need:

1. Technical and managerial know-how.
2. Preparation.
3. Experience.
4. Ability.
5. Perseverance.
6. Willingness to work.
7. Outgoing personality.
8. Judgment.
9. Competitive spirit.
10. Health to use all of these.

Now, one last time, before you consider risking your money, time, and effort to become an entrepreneur, ask yourself the following questions:

Am I willing to make the necessary personal and family sacrifices?
What is more important—to make a lot of money or to perform a useful service?
Do I have the patience and tenacity required for this type of activity?
Do I have the skills and knowledge so that I can collect the resources needed; can I convert those resources so that customers will want them; and can I organize and direct the activities needed to succeed?
How much of me do I want to put into the business?
How much money do I need to get started and where do I get it?

There are many other questions that you should raise, but we will discuss these later.

OBJECTIVES OF A SMALL BUSINESS

Since the most valid distinction between small and big business is based on the *intentions, aims, goals,* or *objectives* of the owner-manager and the firm itself, these factors deserve considerable attention on your part at the very beginning of your interest in small business. One of the most important functions you—as the owner-manager—will perform is setting these goals and objectives. *The objectives are the ends toward which all the activities of your organization will be aimed.* Essentially, they determine the "character" of the firm and are the purposes toward which all the activities of your organization—including plans, policies, and programs—will be directed. They are the focal point of all your entrepreneurial functions.

An important distinction should be made between the objectives of the organization itself and those of its owner(s), managers, and employees. This distinction is important because the two sets of objectives are not necessarily the same. We will now look at some organizational objectives that should be considered along with the personal objectives which have just been mentioned.

As for the business itself, there are at least two sets of objectives—the *overall enterprise objectives* and the *subsidiary goals* of the individual parts of the organization. There must be overall objectives, for without them there is the danger that individual goals may not be consistent with each other. The enterprise's objectives give unity of direction to the organization and provide standards by which actions of members of the firm can be measured. Each part of the firm will then set its objectives in order to contribute to the objectives of the enterprise.

Among the *overall enterprise objectives* that are important for you to consider are those of:

1. Service.
2. Profit.
3. Community participation.
4. Growth.

Service Objective

The overall objective of any business organization must be to perform a useful *service* for society by producing and distributing goods or services (or the satisfactions associated with them) to the public. Even in a profit-oriented organization the primary objective is *service* to the public in the form of producing goods or services at a cost that will ensure a "fair" price to the consumer and "adequate" profits to the owners. Thus, the person who aspires to operate a small business must keep uppermost in mind the necessity for having service as his primary objective, but with profit as a natural consequence. If the enterprise ceases to give service, people will not accept the organization and it will go out of business. On the other hand, if profits do not result, the owners will cease operating the firm.

When you make decisions concerning the type of business you desire to establish or enter, your firm's products, and the type(s) of customers you will serve, you will be considering the service objective.

Profit Objective

A private organization is expected to receive a profit for its operations. In a capitalistic free-enterprise economy, profit is acceptable and considered to be in the public interest. The *profit motive* is not always understood, so a word of explanation may be needed by some readers. The production of profits is the reward for taking risks—such as investing your funds in an untried business and trying to anticipate the needs and wants of the public—and they are required if any private business is to survive. Profits are needed to create new jobs, acquire new facilities, and develop new products or services. The making of profit is fundamental to a capitalistic society. Profits are not self-generating, however: they are residual and come into existence through satisfying the demand for a product or service. Products and services must be produced efficiently and effectively. In turn, the types of goods and services demanded are so numerous and varied that multiple objectives must be formulated if the product or service is to satisfy those demands.

In summary, profits compensate you for your acceptance of business risks and for performance of economic service. They are needed to assure continuity of your business.

Social Objectives

Your firm also has *social objectives* for people in the community other than customers—employees, suppliers, the government, and the community itself. All of these groups should be served effectively. You—as owner—therefore, have a social responsibility. You occupy a trusteeship position and should act to protect the interests of your customers, employees, suppliers, and the general public, as well as to make profit. Your personal moral code should have a sound basis if you are to act fairly and honestly in your relationships with all these groups.

Speaking from a social viewpoint, the small organization offers a sense of belonging that is missing in larger groups. There is a feeling of *esprit de corps* that cannot be duplicated in a large company. According to the sales manager of a small distribution company:

> A small business is both an economic and a social system. There is a sense of belonging that is hard to find in a big company. Also, in a small company, the job carries with it a position which gives the person a sense of prestige that he would lose if he went to a larger company.

Growth Objective

You should be concerned with your firm's *growth* and select a growth objective early in your career. Some of the questions you need to answer in setting this objective are:

Do I seek relative stability or merely survival?

Do I seek a rate of profit which is "satisfactory," considering my efforts and investment?

Do I seek to maximize profits?

Will I be satisfied to remain small?

Do I want to grow and challenge larger firms?

Walter Barnett is a local contractor specializing in commercial construction.[3] He has had many offers to expand locally, regionally, and even statewide. He has consistently chosen to remain small, bid on the jobs he wants, have few labor problems, earn a comfortable living, and "enjoy life." He appears to be succeeding in achieving these objectives.

Ray Williams, who built residential housing, had an excellent reputation for quality at a reasonable price. He received an offer to associate with a firm in an adjoining state, and he accepted. When the economy slackened 18 months later, construction declined, money became "tight," and he found himself overextended. He is now back working for another contractor.

Subsidiary Goals

The primary function of the small business manager is to direct the activities of the business toward attaining its overall objectives. Subsidiary objectives should be set for each functional unit of the organization (such as production, marketing, finance, personnel, and research) to

---

[3] The names in these incidents and illustrations and in the cases at the end of the parts are fictitious, although the events are real.

provide guidelines in meeting the overall objectives of the business. In addition, the personal objectives of all individuals performing tasks within each functional unit must be considered and directed toward the organization's overall objectives.

This process is not as simple as it may appear, for each level of objectives may consist of several related objectives. In a practical business situation, the attainment of two or more objectives on any given level is often achieved only at the expense of other objectives on the same level or between levels. Consequently, conflict sometimes arises between objectives. This conflict must be resolved or minimized if productivity and profitability are to be achieved.

MESHING OF OBJECTIVES

A survey of 97 small, owner-managed firms in the San Antonio area revealed a correlation between profitability, customer satisfaction, manager satisfaction, and psychic rewards.[4] It also showed that the chances of success are greatly increased when the objectives of the business— service at a profit—are meshed with owners' personal objectives. The results of the study indicate that it is possible for you to integrate multiple objectives into a unified whole.

Questions arise as to whether this integration of objectives can actually be accomplished and to what extent it can be achieved in small business establishments. An integration of objectives can be accomplished if the emphasis is directed toward *optimizing objectives* and *minimizing company and personal conflicts.* Communication plays an important part in the process. The close interpersonal relationships between owners of small businesses and their subordinates, customers, and others speed up communications and make integration easier.

One thing that may appeal to persons interested in a small or independent business is to observe the manner and kind of business that seems to come forth from a simple beginning, yet provides a good income.

An example of this was Susan Jones' chicken debeaking business. Susan was married to Tim Jones, who at one time was in the poultry supply business. She was a college graduate with a major in home economics and wanted to supplement the family income while using her education.

The beaks of young baby chicks have to be trimmed to prevent them from pecking other chicks and injuring them. Susan used a

---

[4] Hal B. Pickle and Brian S. Rungeling, "Empirical Investigation of Entrepreneurial Goals and Customer Satisfaction," *The Journal of Business,* vol. 46, no. 2 (April 1973), pp. 268–73.

machine that debeaks and cauterizes the cut in a single operation when the chick is five or six days old.

She trained several young women to work with her each day she was in the field. The day normally started for Susan and four to six members of her crew when they climbed into her station wagon about 4:00 A.M. and departed for the poultry farm to be worked that day. After debeaking 100,000 birds (usually eight hours' work), they were finished for the day.

The work was done under terms of a contract with the poultry farmer at a rate of five cents per chick. Though the work was not continuous, Susan's income was substantial for the year. Tim Jones took great pride in his wife's business and the income it generated.

SUMMARY

In this chapter, we have discussed the objectives of small businesses, some personal objectives of business owners and managers, and the importance of meshing together those objectives.

In choosing objectives for your small business, there are at least four important ones. These are *service, profit, social,* and *growth.* The two overriding objectives are *service* and *profit.* Profit is your reward for accepting business risks and performing an economic service. *It is necessary if you are to continue doing those two things.*

A primary objective of your firm should be that of providing a direct *service.* A privately owned business is an economic institution that has the purpose of producing and distributing goods or services or, more basically, the satisfactions associated with them. If your firm fails to fulfill the service objective, it will go out of business.

Next, you must decide upon your own objectives, which motivate you to become a small business manager. The most important ones are *achievement, challenge, stimulation* of new experiences, *growth* and *advancement,* a seeking for *identity, recognition,* and *esteem* of others.

Business objectives must be integrated with your personal objectives for the most successful operation of a small business.

In summary, the personal rewards to proprietors of small businesses are many and varied. However, they can be summarized by saying that the owners can see clearly the cause-effect relationships between their enterprise, ability, and energy and the material rewards they receive as a result of exercising those talents in running a small firm. The owners determine their own rewards and do not have to wait for someone above them to approve (or disapprove) an increase in their rewards. Thus, they are responsible for their own achievement, advancement, the feeling of pride that comes from creating and building something to pass on to one's family, and the inherent satisfaction of being part of a dynamic, growing entity.

QUESTIONS FOR FURTHER DISCUSSION

1. What are some of the more important objectives that seem to motivate small business managers?
2. Explain the interrelationship between the *service* and *profit* objectives.
3. Why is it that one of the most important functions of the owner-manager is setting objectives?
4. Is it necessary to distinguish between the objectives of the organization and those of its members? Why?
5. What is the purpose of *enterprise objectives?* Briefly discuss those objectives.
6. What is the relationship between enterprise objectives and subsidiary goals?
7. Explain the statement: "A person's occupation represents much more than just a set of skills and functions; it means a way of life."
8. The small business person is a classic example of Theory X or Theory Y. Why?
9. Is an integration of objectives possible? When and how?
10. What do you feel your objectives would be if you went into business for yourself at this time?

3

You Are the Owner of
a Small Business

In the first chapter, some of the characteristics, advantages, and disadvantages of small business enterprises were pointed out. One's personal and business objectives were looked at in Chapter 2. Now, you should look at some unique characteristics of successful small business managers, some personal requirements for success in small business, and an introspective personal analysis you can make in order to see whether you have the characteristics needed for success in managing a small firm.

As one studies the behavior of people who choose careers in small business, one is made acutely aware that, all too often, failure resulted from one or more of the following weaknesses:

1. Too much was left to chance.
2. The crucial obstacles went unnoticed through ignorance.
3. The amounts of time and physical effort demanded of the small business manager were not recognized and planned for.
4. The amount of capital required for a particular business was not determined, or—as is more often true—was grossly underestimated, and therefore not provided for.
5. Too many decisions were made by "hunch" or through intuition, without adequate background and experience upon which to base vital judgments.

Helping you avoid these pitfalls is what this chapter is all about.

CHARACTERISTICS OF SUCCESSFUL SMALL BUSINESS MANAGERS

The skills, abilities, and personal characteristics of owner-managers exert a more powerful influence on the fortunes of small companies than they do on those of larger firms. Whether you have these characteristics or not should then weigh heavily in determining whether or not you enter a small firm. Also, the kinds of methods and procedures you adopt in a small firm should be designed not only to offset any personal deficiencies you may have but also to build upon your strengths.

What, then, are the characteristics of successful owners of small enterprises? There are at least five unique characteristics of such individuals, namely:

1. A great sense of independence.
2. A strong sense of enterprise.
3. Domination as much by personal and family considerations as by professional choices.
4. High valuation of his/her time.
5. Expectation of quick and concrete results.

No individual will have all these characteristics to be sure, but they are the ones we have found to be present most frequently in owner-managers of the smaller firms.

There are two other characteristics of small businessmen that do not necessarily lead to success. They are: small business owners tend to enter the business more by chance than by design, and they tend to have limited formal education. This latter point is obviously not true for all businesses, as some of the technologically oriented businesses of today require higher levels of education and competence than is required in larger nontechnical businesses.

A Great Sense of Independence

Successful small business managers have *a highly developed sense of independence* and they have *a strong desire to be independent of outside control,* whether this control is financial, governmental, or any other type of restraint on their initiative. They are the unreconstructed rebels of the business world who enjoy the feeling of freedom which comes from being "captain" of their own fate.

> Robert Smith worked his way through college sweeping floors in a lighting fixture store. Later, he set up a wholesale division for his boss. He believed that success depended upon "never working for a company that you can't own," and building a firm of moderate size that "you can control completely." Seven years ago, at age 23, he borrowed $75,000, purchased some metalworking equipment, and set up shop, producing and selling modern lighting fixtures. Now, he sells several million dollars worth of lamps each year.

A Sense of Enterprise

The managers of small businesses have a strong sense of enterprise, which gives them a desire to use their ideas, abilities, ambitions, aspirations, and initiatives to the greatest degree possible. They are able to conceive new ideas, plan them, see them carried out, and profit from the results of those plans. This is not always true in a larger organization where different specialists do different phases of the work.

> George Martin was born in Europe under Nazi domination. His goal, from the time he came to the United States at age 16, was to become a millionaire. During college and while in the Army, he dabbled in buying and selling securities. This activity provided him with the savings to start a service putting together tax-sheltered investments for wealthy people. At 31 years of age, he attributes his millions to "hard work, intuitive skills, persistence—and luck."

Another aspect of enterprise that is almost always present in small businessmen is their drive for achievement and their willingness to work long hard hours to reach their goal.

> Dick Crowe, from a middle-class New York neighborhood, worked his way through college doing odd jobs. After graduation, he became a real estate agent and later bought a weight-watchers' franchise. According to his own appraisal, he is totally committed to the firm, works long hours, and doesn't know how to enjoy himself. "I can't relax, for my mind is always working, thinking, calculating."

Personal and Family Considerations

Small business managers are probably dominated as much by personal and family considerations as by the profit-making motive. Quite frequently, our students tell us they are returning home to start a business because that is what their family expects them to do. Even more frequent is the comment that they are going back to run the family business rather than go somewhere else and work for another company. In both cases, the person is doing it from a sense of obligation to his family rather than from the desire for profit.

Other examples are:

> A young man resigned a regular commission in the U.S. Army, where he was quite satisfied to make a career, in order to return to the wholesale distributorship and replace his father, whose health was failing.

Another young man gave up a promising career as a professional personnel administrator in order to replace his father in his family's automobile agency. His father had died and his mother either had to sell out or get the son to run the firm.

A third man resigned from college in his senior year to run the family-owned picture-framing business when his father died.

Perception of the Value of Time

Time is very valuable, because of the many duties that must be performed in a small business. The position of a small business manager is to be differentiated from that of the manager of a large corporation, who is expected to give a certain percentage of his time to "public relations," and have someone else perform his duties while he is away. The small business manager must still perform all the duties even if he engages in outside activities. He is very jealous of his time and appears irritable if someone infringes upon that time.

Dudley Moore has an insurance agency. He tries very hard to protect his time so as much as feasible can be used for his business purposes. For example, even when engaged in nonbusiness activities, he takes steps to conserve his time. He accepts only those positions where his expertise is really needed and he feels he can make a contribution. Also, he is usually the last one to arrive at a committee meeting—only after the "chitchat" is over—and leaves as soon as the business activities are over.

Expectation of Quick Results

Entrepreneurs expect quick and concrete results from an investment, whether it is an investment of time or capital. They seek a quick turnover of a relatively small amount invested in the firm rather than engaging in the long-range planning that is common in large businesses.

In general, small business managers are free and wish to remain free from the artificial conformity required in the larger organizations. They are rugged individuals who are willing to take risks and who have the determination and perseverence to capitalize upon those risks.

Some Other Characteristics of Small Business Owners

In addition to these characteristics, which tend to lead to success, owners of small businesses tend to enter the business by chance and to have limited formal education.

Chance versus Design.   Many people have gravitated by chance into a position of ownership or management of the small firm rather than having prepared for it by design. This is especially true when you have grown up in the business, have lived with it from day to day, and then one day find yourself in the position of having to take over the business. These are the owners or managers who quite frequently ask for assistance in the form of management training and development. This type of individual differs sharply from one who comes to college with the ambition to become a professional manager and gears his whole program toward that end.

> Joe Ditta graduated from college in music and sought a career in the music profession. He had worked in the family restaurant while attending school. Soon after he became a professional singer, his father died, and he returned home to manage the restaurant for the family.

Limited Formal Education.   Small business managers are apt to have only limited formal education. Yet, they tend to supplement this learning with informal learning through reading, "picking the brains" of more learned friends, and through extension and correspondence courses.

EFFECTS OF EXTERNAL FACTORS

While we accept these characteristics of successful small business managers, there is another theory developed from several small-sample studies at Harvard and MIT.[1] The researchers examined entrepreneurs who were involved in substantial ventures. They found that while very successful entrepreneurs may ultimately stand apart, at the beginning (when they make the decision to become entrepreneurs), they are in most respects very much like other ambitious, striving individuals. It was also found that the entrepreneurial interests for those who became small business managers were a function more of external differences than of internal ones. Their decisions were the result more of practical readiness and financial constraints than of individual psychology or personality.

REQUIREMENTS FOR SUCCESS IN SMALL BUSINESS

Although it is impossible to determine or state *all* the requirements for success in small business, at least we know that the following are important:

1.   A sensitivity to internal and external changes affecting the business.
2.   The ability to react quickly to those changes.

---

[1] Be sure to read Patrick R. Liles, "Who Are the Entrepreneurs?" *MSU Business Topics,* vol. 22, no. 1 (Winter 1974), pp. 5–14.

3. Access to accurate and useful operating and marketing information.
4. The effective, but humane, use of human resources.
5. Acquisition of sufficient investment capital, at a reasonable price.
6. The effective handling of government laws, rules, and regulations.

Understanding the Uniqueness of Small Firms

As the owner-manager of a small business, you should have a thorough understanding of the peculiarities of the size of your business. You should not seek to duplicate or copy the management techniques of larger firms. Rather, you should develop your own techniques to meet the needs of your business.

Adaptability to Change

An important characteristic of small business enterprises is their vulnerability to technological and environmental changes. Because they are small, such changes have a greater effect upon their operations and profitability. Yet, small businesses can have an advantage over larger firms in this respect, for they can react faster to change because they have fewer people making decisions. It is extremely important that you *be sensitive to the changes taking place both inside and outside your firm and that you be ready to react quickly to these changes.*

Accurate Operating and Marketing Information

Gathering *accurate and useful information concerning the operations of your business and its market* is extremely important. You must keep informed—on a regular and frequent basis—of the financial position and market position of the business. You must know how to analyze this information and develop plans to maintain or improve your position.

Using Human Resources Effectively

The *effective, but humane, use of your human resources* is extremely important to a small business enterprise, because its owner-managers have a close and more personal association with their employees. These workers can be an economical source of information and ideas and their productivity greatly increased if you allow them to share ideas with you—and if you are *willing to recognize and reward their contribution.*

Obtaining Investment Capital

One of the most difficult problems facing small business managers is *obtaining sufficient investment capital—at a reasonable price.* This requires that you plow back more of the profits into your business. You must be willing and able to delay fulfillment of your desire for dividends in favor of the best long-run interest of the business. You must develop a strong credit rating and pay your debts promptly.

Handling Government Regulations

You need to be able to *handle "red tape" effectively*, for the day when small business firms enjoyed an exemption from governmental legislation and regulation has passed. It is now even argued that small businesses are taxed disproportionately higher than larger businesses. Recent civil rights, occupational safety and health, and environmental legislation no longer exempts small business establishments, but frequently adds tremendously to their costs of operation.

Environmental regulations and compliance directives are of major concern to small business owners. Their response is varied and often rebellious.

Such was the case of the independent sawmill operator, a man who had spent 30 to 40 years of his life in this business, having found it economically rewarding and self-fulfilling. He burned the sawdust and bark in a special incinerator, which emitted smoke that wafted about, depending on the wind. While there had been occasional complaints from people in the surrounding area, they had never been taken too seriously until a complaint was filed with the air pollution control section of the Department of Human Resources. This group had the responsibility for policing complaints and assuring compliance with air quality standards.

The premises were inspected to determine the validity of the complaint, and a directive was issued calling for the installation of new burning equipment that would better control smoke emission. The capital cost of this new installation was estimated to be between $35,000 and $40,000.

At this point, the owner, who was 72 years old, picked up his phone and called a son, who was also in the lumber business. His terse statement was, "I want you to have this sawmill. I am quitting. I am too old to put up with this environmental stuff. There is no way that I can spend the kind of money they want me to spend."

He quit, and six months later he died.

What can you, as a small businessman, do about this government involvement? There are several things that you may want to do. They include:

1. Learn as much as you can about the laws, particularly if it is possible that the law can aid you.

2. Challenge detrimental or harmful laws, either by yourself, appearing before a congressional small business committee, or joining organizations such as the National Federation of Independent Businesses.
3. Become involved in the legal-political system to elect representatives of your choosing and change the laws.
4. Find a better legal environment, if possible, even if it means moving to a different city, county, or state.
5. Learn to live with the laws, rules, or regulations.

The sixth way of coping with this involvement—*which we do not advocate*, but *which is always a possibility*—is to ignore the law and hope it goes away. *This strategy is potentially dangerous and should be used only as a last resort.*

THE INCREASING COMPETENCE AND GROWING INVOLVEMENT OF FEMALES AND MINORITIES

During recent years, females and minorities have increasingly become involved in small and independent businesses. Various government organizations have helped minorities set up businesses of their own, and the Small Business Administration has several programs to help them.

The same is true of females. According to one estimate, there were in 1977 around 1 million female-owned businesses, more than double the number in 1972. According to the director of the American Women's Economic Development Corporation in New York, "The next great group of entrepreneurs will be women."[2] A National Association of Women Business Owners was founded in 1976.

> Susan Sasser and a female partner work ten-hour days in their Washington, D.C., auto-repair shop, named "Wrenchwoman, Inc." They have found it to be a very stimulating and rewarding business. The success they are achieving in their operation has confirmed that being female imposes no restriction in a business of this kind.[3]

AN INTROSPECTIVE PERSONAL ANALYSIS

Now that you have seen some of the characteristics of successful small business managers, as well as the personal requirements needed for success in a small firm, you should be particularly interested in whether you possess a sufficient number of those characteristics and re-

---

[2] "Starting a Business: Women Show It's Not Just a Man's World," *U.S. News & World Report*, August 29, 1977, p. 55.

[3] Ibid.

quirements to be successful. The following personal evaluation should help you decide this important question.

What Is Your Philosophy of Life?

As shown in Chapter 2, your management philosophy will provide a basis for decision making in your company. In order to manage your firm effectively, you need an ethical value system and some basic principles that you believe in and that you can use as guidelines. Among the more important questions related to this ethical value system are the following:

1. What are your true motives?
2. What real objectives do you seek?
3. What psychological and social relations do you consider to be needed for success?
4. What general economic atmosphere do you prefer to operate in?

Need for a Philosophy. To begin with, let us state clearly that everyone has a philosophy, whether it is conscious or unconscious, whether it is well-defined or ill-defined. If you have and use a conscious and well-formed philosophy of management, many major advantages will be yours. Such a philosophy should:

1. *Help you win effective support and followers.* People will know what you stand for and what overall action you are most likely to take. They will know why you act as you do and will therefore have more confidence in your actions.
2. *Provide guidelines for you and provide a foundation for your managerial thinking and decision making.* Your management philosophy should be especially useful because conditions are changing so rapidly that you will face new management challenges to which there are no tailor-made solutions.
3. *Supply a framework within which you can improve your thinking abilities.* Your thinking process will be directed and stimulated so that you achieve more effective and satisfactory developments.

Types of Philosophies. There are many types of people and an infinite variety of philosophies. However, we limit ourselves to contrasts between two pairs of philosophies: rugged individualism versus group-centered managers and activities-oriented versus results-oriented management.

Characteristics associated with these philosophies vary, but in general the *rugged individualist* is highly self-reliant and is a decision-maker. Most of the strong-willed, powerful industrialists in the 1890s and early 1900s—such as Henry Ford—were guided by this philosophy. On the other hand, many present-day managers believe that the group should be considered in all managerial decisions and actions. These *group-centered* individuals rely upon planning and decision-making groups, use committees extensively, and consider the many mutual interests of management and other employees.

The *activities-oriented* manager stresses what must be done, tends to be a "one-person show," prescribes the organization structure, determines the tasks of subordinates, delegates decision-making authority, determines the best methods to perform the work, and exercises tight control over employee performance. The *results-oriented* manager prefers to use the full resources of his people, emphasizes goal-setting, assists in achieving goals, wants himself and his subordinates to develop self-commitment and self-direction for results, has his subordinates play a large part in determining the methods of work, and exercises control by results.

Your philosophy, in turn, depends upon your personal values, or on what you consider to be *right* or *wrong, good* or *bad, desirable* or *not desirable.* Based upon your philosophy and value system, your business objectives and policies are formulated.

Professional versus Personal Approach.   There are two categories into which the philosophy should be divided:

1. An impersonal, professional approach.
2. A personal, moral-ethical approach.

We have found in counseling and consulting with prospective business owners that on occasion it is essential to approach the issues from both viewpoints. For example, an individual may come in to discuss the prospects of opening a bar or tavern. *Impersonally and professionally,* it is pointed out that certain licenses and permits must be obtained. The services of a local attorney familiar with these matters need to be acquired, because certain additional hidden payments may be needed. The approximate capital investment involved for building, fixtures, and inventory and the type of location desirable for this establishment are defined. The consultant may point out certain specific locations that are available and explain why these locations are desirable and other locations undesirable. Also, the amount of net income that may be anticipated will be stated. From a *personal, moral-ethical point of view,* it might be pointed out that there are social implications of being involved with this type of business, such as the local tendency to brand people involved in those businesses with a stigma that becomes a lifetime mark. In addition, it might be pointed out that there are certain local ethical sensitivities that might be offended by such businesses. Therefore, it might be best in the long run, from a personal viewpoint, to avoid those activities that would be in direct conflict with these ethical standards, even though the economic benefits might be substantial.

What Are Your Mental Abilities?

If you still want to become an entrepreneur, then you should make a penetrating analysis of your personal attributes in order to determine the type of business that may satisfy your personal objectives and needs. You might ask yourself questions about *your mental abilities,* such as these:

1. Are you able to conceptualize your choice of a business; in other words, can you visualize it in its entirety, physically and functionally?
2. Are you able to observe things in perspective?
3. Can you generate ideas in a "free wheeling" fashion?
4. Can you generate ideas relating to new methods and new products?
5. Are you technically oriented?
6. Can you interpret and translate activities into a technical framework?
7. Are you sensitive to the human factor?
8. Are you sensitive to the feelings, wants, and needs of others?

What Are Your Attitudes?

If you are still thinking of entering a small business, you should make a self-analysis of your *personal attitudes* in specific areas. Some of these areas are your:

1. Aspiration level.
2. Willingness to accept responsibility.
3. Mental and emotional stability.
4. Commitment to the idea of small business.
5. Willingness to take risks.
6. Ability to tolerate irregular hours.
7. Self-discipline.
8. Self-confidence.

Each of these attitudes is discussed in detail.

Are you able to define your *aspiration level?* Aspiration is the driving or motivational force behind the individual. It is what you want to achieve in life. You may want to express this level in terms of education, marital and parental status, dollars, status in the community, doing physical or mental labor, being of service to others, or other things.

For example, an excellent student wanted to go into the heating and air conditioning pipe-wrapping business, but did not consider the income from the business to be satisfactory. Consequently, he became a manager in a large business.

The degree to which you are willing to accept *responsibility* determines the relationship you will have with the public and the customer.

So far in your life, have you willingly accepted responsibility? Are you willing to assume responsibility in the future? Are you willing to admit the last error you made? Are you an individual whose attitude toward responsibility is to accept it even though this may mean personal sacrifice? Are you willing to be responsible for the actions of others, even if you have delegated to them the authority to act for you?

> Faye Fendley, daughter of a poor restaurant owner, dropped out of school at 14; moved to Manhattan, using $300 saved from baby-sitting; worked part-time in a real estate agency; received her own license at 21 and started her own real estate business; married at 23. She was widowed, with three children, at 29. Spurning chances to sell the bakery she and her late husband owned, she assumed the full responsibility for running and expanding the business.

Are you a *stable person,* or are you a person who is impatient and unwilling to wait for success? If success is not immediately achievable, are you willing to continue to work toward its achievement? Do you seek immediate gratification of your wants, or are you willing to postpone them in order to reinvest in the firm? When given an opportunity that offers a significant potential, but may not be readily achievable, many young people tend to grow weary and move to another activity. These people in their limited progression may, on occasion, generate a "good income" in their chasing after "fast buck" opportunities, but these opportunities may lack stability and security. The successful entrepreneur does not work this way.

> Stan Bernthal, college dropout, worked in a garment factory. In his spare time, he designed clothing out of scraps of material for young people. He and his college roommate organized a firm to provide these good-looking, inexpensive clothes. In spite of initial success, Stan limited himself to $12,000 a year salary until the firm was assured of success.

Are you *committed?* This is the trait that determines whether an individual will endure the trials, tribulations, and personal and family sacrifices necessary to move ahead toward the achievement of one's objectives. How committed are you to your idea for the business you have dreamed of? Unless this commitment is firmly implanted, it is suggested that you forego the idea and seek that vocation to which you can be committed.

Do you enjoy *taking risks?* Are you willing to take the chance of "losing your shirt" to gain other benefits? Or, do you "play it close to your vest" and seek the "sure thing" in life? It does make a difference!

Can you live with an *irregular schedule?* Are you willing to forego regular hours and be worried during your time off? Are you willing to give up your weekends if something goes wrong or it becomes necessary to prepare a proposal for that new contract? Or, would you prefer regular hours, holidays, and vacations?

Are you *self-disciplined?* Are you able to exercise discipline over yourself and your affairs? The old cliche applied to early business owners, "Don't take too much out the front door," still applies. It is important that sufficient resources remain in the business to provide working capital and to provide for growth and contingencies.

> A local home building contractor had a very profitable business. Coming from a low economic background, he began to purchase luxuries he had always wanted for himself and his family. Soon, there were insufficient funds to meet bills, payrolls, taxes, and other business expenses. The end result was bankruptcy.

Are you *self-confident?* Do you have confidence in yourself and can you make decisions alone?

If the answers to these questions are yes, or if you feel that you can make them yes at some time in the near future, you may have the qualities that would make your small business venture a satisfying and rewarding activity.

You are now at the point of deciding whether to go into your own business or not. As you approach the point of making a decision, you are in a position comparable to a person driving an automobile who is approaching a stop light. Just as the light control mechanism is outside the influence of the driver, there are factors beyond your control that should influence your decision about entering a business of your own. These external factors—social, economic, cultural, and natural elements—are beyond your control. In the same manner as the driver approaching a traffic light must be responsive to the control mechanism in observing the status of the light, so must you be responsive to the environmental factors pertinent to the success or failure of your business.

See the appendix at the end of this chapter for a questionnaire to aid you in performing this personal self-analysis.

SUMMARY

We have tried in this chapter to impress you with some characteristics of the successful small businesspeople, and some personal requirements for a successful small business.

Finally, a personal analysis program was suggested whereby you may be able to determine whether you have the attitudes required for success in this area.

Before reaching a final decision on what career you want to follow, you should decide what you want out of life. If your personal objectives and the company objectives are not in harmony, you will not derive the personal satisfaction you seek from your business.

QUESTIONS FOR FURTHER DISCUSSION

1. All too often, certain crucial factors are overlooked when one chooses a career in small business. What are some of these factors?
2. What are some key personal requirements needed for one to succeed in small business? Briefly explain their importance.
3. What is meant by the cliche, "Don't take too much out the front door"?
4. Conduct your own personal analysis by honestly trying to answer the questionnaire in the appendix of this chapter.
5. What characteristics have been found to be present most frequently in owner-managers of smaller firms? Briefly discuss each of these characteristics.
6. How would you summarize the characteristics of small business managers?
7. If one were to ask oneself, "What is my philosophy of life?" or "What are my mental abilities?" what specific types of questions should one ask?
8. Contrast the philosophy of rugged individualism with the group-centered philosophy. Do the same for the activities-oriented philosophy with the results-oriented philosophy.
9. When one is conducting a personal analysis program, one should make a self-analysis of *personal attitudes* in specific areas. Briefly discuss each of these areas.
10. Comment on the sawmill operator's action regarding his sawmill.

APPENDIX: PERFORMING A PERSONAL SELF-ANALYSIS

The purpose of this questionnaire is to aid you in analyzing and evaluating your objectives, abilities, interests, health, economic status, and responsibilities in order to determine whether you would be more effective working for someone else or owning your own business.

You should go through and answer each one of these questions *as conscientiously as possible,* so that you will be able to see whether you have the possibilities of succeeding in a small business. Incidentally, we have been able to develop a profile of people who have answered this questionnaire even when they have not answered a given question. In other words, *the missing answers tend to* be as important as the ones you include in evaluating your possibilities. When you have finished the form, look at the facts revealed by your answers in order to have an insight into your future.

Please indicate your choice by checking the appropriate space.

1. My objective in life is:
   a. To make a lot of money _____
   b. To be my own boss _____
   c. To have a comfortable living _____
   d. To have a business of my own that will allow me leisure time _____
   e. To work for someone else _____
   f. To avoid accepting responsibility:
      (1) For providing employment for others _____
      (2) For providing products/service to others _____
   g. To spend whatever time and effort that is necessary to achieve success _____

2. My marital status is:
   a. Married _____
   b. Single _____
   c. Divorced _____
   d. Children: Yes _____ No _____
      Ages _____
   Given these responsibilities I plan to commit myself to (circle one):
   20   40   60   80   hours per week to the business.

3. My education is:
   a. Elementary _____
   b. High school:
      1 year _____ 2 years _____ 3 years _____ 4 years _____
   c. Technical school _____
      Type of training _____
   d. College:
      1 year _____ 2 years _____ 3 years _____ 4 years _____
      Kind of degree: _____
      Major _____ Minor _____
      Master's degree _____ Kind _____
      Fields _____ _____ _____
      Other: _____

4. My experience is (list in order from latest to earliest):
   a. Last/current job _____
      Employer _____
      Title _____
      Dates of employment _____ to _____
   b. Job _____
      Employer _____

Title _____

Dates of employment _____ to _____

c.   Job _____

Employer _____

Title _____

Dates of employment _____ to _____

Ability I gained from each employment situation:

_____

_____

_____

_____

_____

5.   My expertise is:

| | (check one) | | |
(List)	High	Medium	Low
_____	____	____	____
_____	____	____	____
_____	____	____	____
_____	____	____	____
_____	____	____	____
_____	____	____	____
_____	____	____	____
_____	____	____	____

6.   My hobbies are: _____

_____

_____

_____

_____

_____

7.   I spend my free time doing: _____

_____

_____

_____

_____

_____

_____

8.   My capabilities are:

    a.   Directing the activities of others _____

    b.   Planning an activity in a manner that takes the least time, effort and material _____

  c. Serving people in a pleasing manner _____
  d. Helping people resolve their personal differences _____
  e. Managing money _____
  f. Keeping records _____
  g. Organizing people, money, machines, and things to produce the products/service _____
  h. Effectively following instructions and directions of others _____
  i. Being my own boss _____
  j. Being a self starter _____
  k. Taking initiative _____
  l. Making decisions _____
  m. Creating new ideas for products and services _____

  9. My inadequacies are:
  a. I can't make decisions _____
  b. I postpone making decisions _____
  c. I try to get others to make decisions for me _____
  d. I dislike assuming responsibility _____
  e. I avoid responsibilities whenever possible _____
  f. I do not handle money well _____
  g. I seem unable to keep my checkbook balanced _____
  h. I am generally insecure without someone to guide and support me _____

10. Regarding my health:
  a. I always feel good _____
  b. I can work two jobs without ever getting tired _____
  c. I frequently find it difficult to finish the day _____
  d. I have a headache: Once a week _____
            Once every two weeks _____
            Once or twice a month _____
            Seldom if ever _____
  e. I sleep: 6 hours _____ 7 hours _____ 8 hours _____
     9 hours _____ Less than 6 hours a day _____
  f. I have to take some form of medication to sleep: Yes _____
    No _____
  g. I have bad dreams: A lot _____ Average _____ Seldom _____
  h. I get dizzy: Sometimes _____ Frequently _____ Seldom _____ Never _____
  i. I am absent from work:
    (1) One day a week _____
    (2) One day every two weeks _____
    (3) One to two days per month _____

        (4)   Four to five days a year _____

        (5)   Rarely _____

  j. My last complete physical was _____

                                        (date)

  k. I have these known health problems: _____

  l. I have no known health problems _____

11. My health permits me to (check one):

  a. Travel a great amount   Yes _____ No _____

  b. Engage in a lot of physical work   Yes _____ No _____

  c. Work long hours   Yes _____ No _____

  d. To function well in tense situations Yes _____ No _____

  e. Use my eyes extensively   Yes _____ No _____

12. My health keeps me from: _____

_____

_____

13. Regarding my present economic status:

  a. My net worth is:

      (1)   Equity value of real estate $ _____

      (2)   Cash surrender value of life insurance $ _____

      (3)   Marketable securities $ _____

      (4)   Savings $ _____

      (5)   Other $ _____

  b. My annual income is:

      (1)   Salary $ _____

      (2)   Special income $ _____

      (3)   Investment:

           (a)   Rental income $ _____

           (b)   Stocks $ _____

           (c)   Bonds $ _____

                  Total investment income $ _____

      (4)   Interest $ _____

      (5)   Annuities $ _____

      (6)   Trust $ _____

      (7)   Estate $ _____

      (8)   Other $ _____

              Total annual income $ _____

  c. My annual financial responsibilities are:

      (1)   Mortgage payments $ _____

      (2)   House insurance $ _____

      (3)   Real and personal property taxes $ _____

      (4)   Car payments $ _____

(5)	Life insurance	$ _____
(6)	Utility bills	$ _____
(7)	Other loan repayments	$ _____
(8)	Alimony and child support	$ _____
(9)	Children's education expense	$ _____
(10)	Medical/dental expense	$ _____
(11)	Medical insurance	$ _____
(12)	Household expense	$ _____
(13)	House/lawn maintenance	$ _____
(14)	Auto expense	$ _____
(15)	Food	$ _____
(16)	Business/professional expense	$ _____
(17)	Other	$ _____
	Total annual personal expense	$ _____

14. How much can I afford to risk? $ _____

15. Considering my responsibilities, my interests, my hobbies, my health, and my economic status, I am willing:
    a. To devote _____ hours per week to the business
    b. To invest $ _____ in the business

16. What specific kind of business would I be most happy operating as an owner/manager?
    Answer: _____
    _____
    _____
    _____
    _____
    _____
    _____

17. How would I compensate for my inadequacies? _____
    _____
    _____
    _____
    _____
    _____
    _____

18. After carefully reviewing the answers I have given to the questions above, being honest and frank with myself, I think that I could accomplish my objectives in life, achieve a reasonable level of success and happiness by:
    a. Having my own independent business _____
    b. Working for someone else   _____

WHERE TO LOOK FOR FURTHER INFORMATION

"Are You One of Them?" *MBA*, vol. 7, no. 6 (June–July 1973), p. 5.

Buchan, P. Bruce. "Corporate Risk Policies." *Journal: Management Advisor,* vol. 10, no. 5 (September–October 1973), pp. 45–51.

"For All the Headaches, You Can Still Start Your Own Business." *U.S. News & World Report,* July 26, 1976, pp. 43–46, contains an excellent discussion of how five entrepreneurs took the risk of entering a business and how they coped with the problems that arose.

Henderson, Carter. "What the Future Holds for Small Business." *Nation's Business,* vol. 64, no. 3 (March 1976), pp. 25–28.

Libman, Joan. "Female Entrepreneurs Like Del Goetz Make 'Man's Work' Pay Off." *The Wall Street Journal,* vol. 55, no. 38 (August 22, 1975), p. 1.

Narver, John C., and Preston, Lee E. "The Political Economy of Small Business in the Postindustrial State." *Journal of Contemporary Business* (Spring 1976), reprint.

"Now It's Young People Making Millions." *U.S. News & World Report,* vol. 74, no. 8 (February 25), 1974), pp. 47–50.

Roscow, James P. "Can Entrepreneurship Be Taught?" *MBA*, vol. 7, no. 6 (June–July 1973), pp. 12, 16, 50, and 51.

Schreier, James W. "Is the Female Entrepreneur Different?" *MBA*, vol. 10, no. 8 (March 1976), pp. 40–43.

"Small Business, The Maddening Struggle to Survive." *Business Week,* June 30, 1975, pp. 96–104.

"Some Hints on Small Business Company Success." *The Iron Age,* vol. 199, no. 22 (June 1, 1967), p. 25.

cases for part I*

I–1   Shaffer's Drive Inns[1]

About 20 years ago the Shaffer family (mother, father, and son) decided to open a drive-in in a Midwestern city of about 200,000 people. They figured that the general area was lacking a drive-in that would offer a variety of quality services such as malts, sandwiches, curb service, and modern indoor eating facilities as well, so they built a facility that incorporated all the above features and named it Shaffer's Drive Inn.

The son, Albert Shaffer, put a lot of energy into managing the store and worked harder than most people realized. In fact, he was soon able to buy his mother and father out and gain exclusive control of the store for himself. It was 15 years before Albert Shaffer decided to build another store; four years later, he built a third one. He always issued stock for each store that he built, but controlled at least 51 percent of the stock in each one.

Mr. Shaffer was respected and admired by his employees and had a "great man" image among them. He was an authoritarian leader, and his employees accepted his judgment as law because, in their opinion, he was right 99 percent of the time. Mr. Shaffer, when discussing anything that might arise with his employees, would never "tear into" the people, but would argue the point with them and listen to what they had to say and would then point out where they were either right or

---

* The cases in this book are *actual situations* involving *real people* in *real organizations,* although the names have been disguised. The cases are not designed to present illustrations of either correct or incorrect handling of administrative problems.

[1] This case was prepared by Joe L. Hamilton, formerly at Louisiana State University, but now with Container Corporation.

wrong. Once he had his mind made up though, it usually stayed made up.

The organizational structure used by Shaffer's Drive Inns was compli-cated. There were two managers and an assistant for each store, and assistants were to be trained to become future managers. In addition to these managers in each store, there were other people, including kitchen help, curb boys, and so forth. Not only did this organizational structure have some serious flaws in it, but it led to some personality conflicts, as will be discussed later.

Shaffer's Drive Inns proved to be very popular. A lot of research went into the proper location for each of them, and each was located where it could make its appeal either to college students or to heavy automobile traffic. The Drive Inns became well known for their excellent service. These were specific objectives of Mr. Shaffer and were in tune with his business philosophy.

Shaffer's Drive Inns proved to be so popular that a decision was reached to build three more Drive Inns in a nearby city. These three stores opened during a one month period. It was at this point that Mr. Shaffer realized his business was getting away from him. The people he chose for managers were well trained to go into the stores, but they had very little contact with the main office and consequently were forced to make most of their own decisions. In addition, the two managers in each store were constantly bickering with each other. The tendency to pass the buck was a serious temptation. The employees were quick to realize they could play one manager against the other to achieve desired goals.

Mr. Shaffer believed in personal contact to get his views across. But, as the stores were now becoming geographically separated, he was having a difficult time spending the proper amount of time at each store. He decided he needed an assistant to be his right-hand man and carry on when and where he could not. He wanted someone from inside the or-ganization who knew all the ropes. Mr. Shaffer chose Marc Mason, known as a "self-made man," to be his unofficial assistant. Although Mr. Mason was entirely capable of handling the job, his selection caused serious complaints and criticisms from three of the store managers, Messrs. Denney, Riley, and Nettles.

These three men had been with the organization for a combined time of over 30 years, and each one assumed himself to have certain authority he didn't actually possess. They were described as "completely set in their ways and resisted any and every planned change." When Mr. Mason became Mr. Shaffer's unofficial assistant, they resisted every move he made in every conceivable way.

Mr. Denney had a high school education. He was known "to argue just for the sake of arguing." He was not known as a "go-getter" and was content to work in the slowest store of the chain. He seemed to have an inferiority complex in that he thought he wasn't as good as everyone else. In the opinion of some of his associates, he was not even capable of managing his own money. His strongest feature was his length of service, for he had been with the organization so long that he assumed he had high status. Mr. Denney shared the managership of one store with Mr. Riley.

Mr. Riley was a quiet-spoken man; he seldom raised his voice to anyone. He was "of average intelligence, but was not able to communicate properly with his employees." As a result, he wasn't able to get as much out of his employees as he should have.

Mr. Nettles once shared the management of a store with Mr. Mason. He was an ex-marine, and was considerably older than Mr. Mason. Mr. Nettles was known "to be pretty sharp and to know quite a bit about the business." Mr. Nettles could never bring himself to believe that he had been bypassed by Mr. Mason, and was frequently vocal about his feeling of dissatisfaction.

"Mr. Mason," it was said, "was treated very unfairly in the early days of his career. He was not brought into decisions or taken into the confidence of the man he worked with. However, he was a diligent worker and put in many hours of hard work. He was the type of man who really made a place for himself, and his hours of long, hard work were recognized by Mr. Shaffer."

Despite the growing communications problems, Mr. Shaffer went ahead with plans for another Drive Inn (the eighth one) in still another town. Now the lines of communication were really split. Mr. Shaffer, even with the assistance of Mr. Mason, was not able to devote as much time as he should to each of the stores. This left the store managers to their own discretion in many of their decisions. They started making more and more of their own decisions and started relying less and less on Mr. Shaffer and Mr. Mason. This was much to the displeasure of Mr. Shaffer. The problems that followed the opening of the eighth store caused Mr. Shaffer to seek outside help.

QUESTIONS FOR FURTHER DISCUSSION

1. What does this case show about the problems involved in organizing a small business?
2. What were some of the organizational problems facing the owner?
3. What does it show about the problems resulting from growth of a small firm?
4. What were the objectives of the owner of the business?
5. What does the case show about interpersonal problems in small business?
6. What should Mr. Shaffer do about his problems?

I–2 Bob Jones[1]

A former employer described Bob Jones as "an employee who is personable, very willing to receive supervision and correction, but continually fails to comply with suggestions for improvement and has little regard for established rules, procedures, and policies. It is readily apparent to everyone that the employee's personal attitude, friendliness, and cooperation with other employees is beyond reproach. He seldom has a personality clash or disagreement with other employees in the office."

Bob Jones had been with a state organization for four years. His job required him constantly to come in contact with the public, and a great deal of good (or bad) publicity could result from his actions on the job. The employee was "quite capable as evidenced by his entrance examination, references, and past work experience." However, at frequent intervals Bob had to be told to improve his work habits. During these discussions, he indicated an interest in correcting the various deficiencies as they were pointed out to him by his manager. Each time he was in complete accord with the recommendations made to him and pledged to do a better job. The "payoff" never came, however. A follow-up revealed little or no adherence to established procedures and new suggestions. Bob would fall right back into his old habits.

The principal areas of weaknesses the manager found were "an almost complete disregard for details in every phase of his work. Although Bob was capable, and did the over-all job fairly satisfactorily, he was completely negligent in preparation of the details associated with each job." As time went on, it was noticed that Bob was spending an excessive amount of his office time engaged in personal activities. It was found that he used office time primarily for social purposes rather than for business. When questioned about this, Bob would always promise to improve, but as with the details of his work, he would soon forget his good intentions. It was also noticed that he requested an excessive amount of annual and sick leave, often for one hour or less.

This situation fluctuated over a period of time, would get better and then worse. However, it never reached a point requiring drastic action until Bob bought half interest in a restaurant. The purchase of this business aggravated two already bad practices. First, the amount of time Bob spent in the office to manage his private business increased. Second, and equally bad from the office manager's point of view, he did not get his normal rest because he tried to work at his business between six and eight hours a day after his normal workday at the state office.

His efficiency continued to decline until the office manager decided

---

[1] Prepared by Leon C. Megginson, University of South Alabama.

something should be done. The manager finally told Bob that his private business was interfering with his official duties. He was further told that if he continued to have outside business activities, he must write to the head of the agency at the state capital, describe his business involvement, and obtain the administrator's opinion as to the advisability of continuing in the business.

When the agency head denied Bob the right to operate his private business, he resigned from the organization to devote himself full time to his restaurant business.

QUESTIONS FOR FURTHER DISCUSSION

1. Do you think Bob's personal objectives are compatible with those of a small business? Explain.
2. To what extent are Bob's personal characteristics compatible with those needed to operate a small business successfully?
3. What must Bob do to operate the business successfully? Explain.
4. What future do you predict for Bob in his new venture? Explain.

I–3 The Toy Shop
"I Think I'd Like to Go into Business" [1]

> Nothing is so good as it seems beforehand.
>
> George Eliot

In August 1975, Mr. Robert M. Cummings telephoned the Small Business Institute (SBI) director at Stephen F. Austin State University and said:

> The SBA suggested I call you about getting help with an idea that I have for going into business. I have been a speech and hearing therapist for the Lufkin Treatment Center for the past eight years. In my work with children, I have come to know a lot about toys, including

---

[1] Prepared by Ed D. Roach and Janelle C. Ashley, Stephen F. Austin State University.

what toys children really seem to prefer and like to play with. I am especially interested in educational toys.[2]

My wife was a third-grade teacher for several years, so we both know something first-hand about children—and what they like to play with. I'm calling you because my wife and I think we are ready to try our hand at what thus far has been just an idea: starting our own business, a retail toy store.

I know you've heard stories of this sort before—an idea and an urge to capitalize on it—but without the full knowledge of either the opportunities or the perils. May I come to visit with you?

Mr. and Mrs. Cummings visited the director the following week. The director presented them a "going-into-business packet" and suggested that they review it, especially the materials relating to objectives and planning.

Robert Cummings was 32 years of age, and both he and his wife had received their undergraduate degrees from Stephen F. Austin. Neither of them had any experience in business, but both felt that their vocations —speech therapist and elementary school teacher—had given them an insight into what a successful toy store should be like. They expressed a commitment to learning the business and making it their life's work.

At the time of the first meeting, Mr. Cummings was earning a salary of $15,600 per year. Mrs. Cummings had not worked since their only child was born, but she planned to work full time at the toy store if the venture proved to be feasible. Mr. Cummings stated that he estimated the combined income for him and his wife (assuming a teaching position for her) would be approximately $25,000 per year.

LOCATION AND PLANS FOR THE STORE

The proposed store was to be located in Lufkin, about 120 miles north of Houston and some 20 miles south of Stephen F. Austin State. It had a population of about 30,000 and its trade area, about 80,000. The city was fairly industrialized with four or five industries providing most of the employment.

The couple intended to locate the venture in a new mall called Towne Square to be built on one of the most heavily travelled streets in Lufkin. Groundbreaking was scheduled for January 1976. The mall was designed with the goal of attracting shoppers to the stores that were expected to relocate there from downtown. Downtown Lufkin was very old and most of the stores there were in need of remodeling.

---

[2] Educational toys were envisioned by Cummings as any toys, games, and so forth that aid the learning process. They were not envisioned as replacing the learning process in school, but as aiding the child in learning fundamental concepts while being fun at the same time.

EXHIBIT 1

Proposed Front Elevation

Cummings' plans for the store included approximately 3,000 square feet, with the retail sales area projected to take up 2,500 feet. The remaining area was to serve as stockroom, office, and restroom (see Exhibits 1 and 2 for details).

Cummings foresaw the image of the store as a quality toy store that carried a complete line of toys, crafts, and hobbies at a fair price.

> I will not be competitive with the discount stores, but I feel that the wide assortment of merchandise at a fair price will yield an adequate amount of profit. I expect to appeal to that group of parents who want their children to have a safe, quality toy. I plan to emphasize to this target market the benefit that can be gained from educational toys. My wife and I plan to operate the store with the assistance of my mother.
>
> I want the interior of the store to be designed to make shopping easy and pleasant with bright colors and a comfortable atmosphere.

STATEMENT OF OBJECTIVES

Cummings stated that his objective was to "start from scratch and go into business for myself."

> I expect this goal to yield an annual income of $25,000 to $30,000. My goal for the first year of operation is to have a net income after expenses of $8,000 to $10,000. I want to go into business for myself because I want to be my own boss. I selected the educational toy business because I feel the market for educational toys is large enough to accommodate an additional store and the demand for such toys is currently not being met in the Lufkin area.
>
> I see as an "ideal" store one similar to an educational toy store located in Kent.[3] That shop offers its customers a complete line of merchandise at competitive prices. It presents the image of quality and com-

---

[3] Name disguised. It is a city of approximately 65,000 located 100 miles northwest of Lufkin.

EXHIBIT 2

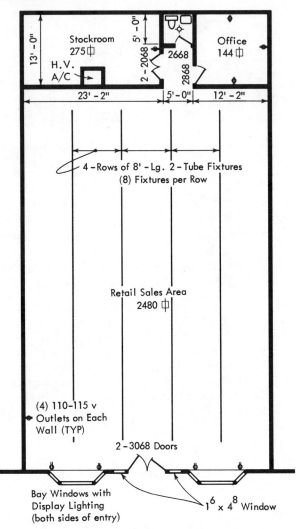

petitiveness in a pleasant atmosphere. That is the kind of store I intend to have. I expect my target market to be parents and children up to the age of 12.

You've heard what I want to do, Professor. Is it feasible? What's our next step?

PARTICIPATION IN THE SMALL BUSINESS INSTITUTE

At the conclusion of the initial discussion, the Cummingses agreed to peruse the "going-into-business packet." In addition, the director assured them of a place in the next SBI program to be held at the University.

Several weeks later, a senior marketing student, accompanied by the SBI director, visited Mr. Cummings in Lufkin. A broad range of topics was discussed, among which were the following: a feasibility study to be conducted for the proposed business, the lines of toys to be carried, and the amount of capital required for start-up of the business. A considerable amount of time was spent discussing Mr. Cummings' rather strong feelings that he should carry a line of bicycles in addition to educational toys.

QUESTIONS FOR DISCUSSION

1. Are there any crucial obstacles the Cummingses appear to be overlooking?
2. What is meant by "building an image" for the store?

part II

Planning and Organizing
a New Business

In Part I, you saw some of the challenges of entering a small business, some personal and business objectives of small businessmen or women, and some characteristics that lead to success in owning or managing that type of business. *We assume that you have now decided that you want to become an independent entrepreneur.* If so, the material in this part should be of great use to you.

Its chapters provide some insights into the types of business you might enter and some assistance in evaluating the business environment in which you will operate or are operating. As a prospective owner of a business, you have these two broad alternatives available: (1) to establish a new business, or (2) to enter an ongoing business. Detailed procedures for each of these alternatives are presented.

Figure II–1 is a graphic presentation of some of the activities involved in starting up a firm. It illustrates how you move from your original idea for a business through the various activities to the final objective, profit. This illustration is intended to assist you in visualizing the nature of your firm and what is needed for it to become a reality.

"Management is getting things done through people," said Lawrence Appley, former president of the American Management Association. We agree with his conclusion, but there is more to managing an independent enterprise than that. As Figure II–2 shows, you must also make decisions and allocate your scarce financial, physical, and human resources so that your business will achieve its objectives, which should, then, help you reach your personal objectives.

The seven functions shown in the center of Figure II–2 must be performed by any person running a business, whether he or she is the owner of the business, or a professional manager running someone else's business. While all the functions are discussed in the text, individual chapters are not organized around them. The *planning* function is found in this part, especially in Chapters 7 and 8. Chapters 6 and 8, as well as other chapters in this part, deal with the *organizing* function. *Staffing* and *directing* are covered in Part III, with *staffing* being covered in Chapters 9 and 10 and *directing* in Chapters 10 and 11. *Coordinating* is implied in most of the chapters in Part VI. Part VI also deals with *controlling*, especially Chapter 22. Other aspects of control are found in Chapters 13 and 14. The *evaluating function* also permeates most of the text, but Chapter 10 deals with evaluating personnel, Chapter 19 covers

FIGURE II–1
Concept of Entering Business

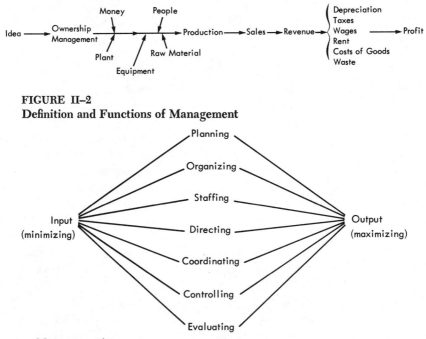

FIGURE II–2
Definition and Functions of Management

Management is:
1. Doing through others;
2. Decision making; and
3. Allocating scarce resources; so that
4. Objectives are reached.

financial evaluation, and Chapter 25 deals with self-evaluation, as does the appendix to Chapter 3.

The material in Chapter 4 will help you study the economic environment of your new business; Chapter 5 explains how to enter an existing business, if you choose that route; otherwise, Chapter 6 will help you establish an entirely new enterprise. The material in Chapter 7 will help you perform the overall planning function, while Chapter 8 will be of assistance in setting up the legal, financial, and administrative structures.

As your new business needs to be managed effectively by someone, you must now answer a most significant question, namely, "Should I be the owner of the firm and hire someone else to manage it for me, or should I both own and manage it myself?" If you choose to be the manager yourself, you should be prepared to become a generalist manager and not try to be a specialist in your own area of interest and competence. The generalist-type manager has conceptual skills that enable her or him to analyze the total situation, detect problems, determine causes, and bring about effective solutions.

Finally, you should not imitate practices and methods used in larger firms because they could produce operating and procedural inefficiencies in your company. Furthermore, the skills and personal characteristics of managers affect the fortunes of small companies more than those of large companies. Therefore, your procedures and methods should utilize your personal strengths and offset your personal deficiencies.

4

Studying the Economic
Environment for Your Business

It is now time for you to give careful consideration to the type of business that satisfies your personal goals and objectives, to study its economic environment, and to decide whether to buy an existing firm or start a new one of your own. These decisions will largely determine whether you will be successful and satisfied during your business career.

The process of choosing the type of business you wish to enter will be influenced by your personal value system, education, training, financial ability, and family situation. Since owning an independent business is such a very personal matter, you should consider as broad a range of options as is feasible. In conducting this survey and analysis of possible business opportunities, however, you should not become so involved in details that you lose sight of your overall objective. Instead, your mission should be to find that business which helps you achieve your objectives while still satisfying your other personal needs.

As the economic environment will play a vital role in the success or failure of your firm, you should study it very carefully. All too frequently, it becomes obvious from later events that little effort was made to determine whether the economic environment was friendly or hostile to the new owner-manager.

Also, people often commit funds to a business without adequate preliminary investigation concerning the venture's feasibility.

Such was the case of the young college graduate. Though he had been involved with several aspects of eating establishments,

he had not actually owned or managed one. Seeing a vacant building, he thought here was the opportunity to open a fancy restaurant.
A contract was signed for the purchase of the property, and funds
were spent for preliminary plans and other related activities.

Then the problems began to appear! The cost of renovation ran
many times his original mental estimate; there existed an old restrictive covenant in the deed that prevented a new owner from having
complete freedom in using the property as desired.

In the end, the project had to be terminated, and the investment
of several thousand dollars produced nothing but another example
of where a feasibility study would have been economically advantageous.

The authors' intent in this chapter is to outline a procedure for you
to use in studying the economic environment for your business. The
material should also help you determine whether your idea for a business
is economically feasible and to aid you in deciding whether to buy an
existing firm or to start one of your own.

SELECTING THE TYPE OF BUSINESS
YOU WOULD LIKE TO ENTER

Probably the best point of departure for you to use in selecting the
type of business to enter is to review the introspective personal analysis
you made of yourself in Chapter 3. The purpose of this reevaluation is
to eliminate those options that are not compatible with your personal
likes and dislikes. You would probably be miserable if you chose an activity that you found to be inconsistent with your abilities and personality. (See the case entitled "Potential High Fashion Shop" at the end
of this part for an example of this.)

Review Your Abilities

The main purpose of that analysis should be to identify what physical,
mental, emotional, and spiritual abilities you have, including:

1. Your intellectual abilities.
2. Your education, training, and experience, which determine the expertise you have for certain types of business. As a rule of thumb,
   you should have a minimum of three years' experience—preferably
   some of it managerial—in the particular line in which your proposed
   company will be engaged. Through this experience, valuable information about the management, operations, and "statistics" of the
   company should have been obtained.
3. Your philosophies and ethical value system, which will keep you
   from being satisfied in many kinds of business.

4. Your attitudes and feelings, which will limit your success to only a small variety of activities.
5. Your physical health and stamina.
6. Your personal goals, which should probably include income desired from your business.

A significant question that you should answer is, "How much profit do I expect to receive from this business as remuneration for my time and investment in it?" Profit potential—at least for the first year, preferably the first two years, of operations should be determined.

Other considerations to be considered are your spouse and his/her likes and dislikes, whether you want to be near your relatives and/or friends, and what would it take to make you a satisfied—and therefore a successful—person.

This analysis is the first culling procedure; it should drastically reduce the number and variety of choices available to you.

If you would feel more comfortable by taking attitude, interest, and aptitude tests to assist you in making your decision, such tests are available through your university, college, junior college, or vocational-technical school. In addition, you may find a professional psychologist to assist you.

Eliminate Undesirable Businesses

The next rejection process is to eliminate the businesses that will not provide you with the challenges, opportunities, and rewards—financial and otherwise—that you are seeking. Be rather ruthless in asking, "What's in it for me?" as well as inquiring, "What can I do to be of help to others?" Ask yourself questions similar to the following about each business you consider:

1. How much capital is required to enter and compete successfully in this business?
2. How long will it take me to recoup my investment?
3. How long will it take me to reach an acceptable level of income?
4. How will I live until that time?
5. What is the degree of risk involved? Am I willing to take that risk?
6. Can I hack it on my own? Or, will I need the help of my family? Others?
7. How much work is involved in getting the business going? In running it? Am I willing to put out that much effort?
8. Do I want to acquire a franchise from an established company, or do I want to "start from scratch" and "go it on my own"?
9. What are the potentials of this type business? What are my chances of achieving that potential?

10. Are sufficient data available for me to reach meaningful decisions? If so, what are the sources of information?

A psychology professor involved with research in learning theory believed he had discovered a phenomenon centered upon the "right" space between the lines and the "right" height of the letters that would simplify and assure the early development of writing and learning skills of children in their early school years. He believed that a series of products such as lined writing paper, with alphabetical letters of the "right" height, incorporated into toys and games, and alphabet cereal could be produced around these ideas.

His initial idea was to work through existing businesses. After some disappointments in trying to interest companies producing writing papers, he turned to one of SBA's SCORE counselors for assistance.

The counselor was impressed with the strong commitment by the professor but was not convinced that the concept had a "proprietary value," since some years earlier he had seen some writing paper with letter examples that seemed almost identical. In an effort to confirm or disprove the value of these ideas, the counselor contacted several authorities, who confirmed the lack of proprietary value.

The professor's commitment would not permit him to accept these judgments. He resigned his university position in order to devote full time to the project in spite of the facts that he had a wife and two children and had no other visible means of economic support.

Upon further questioning, the professor admitted that he had not written for publication any of his research findings, so the counselor suggested—to the chagrin of the professor—that possibly his best approach was to return to an academic post and devote his full energies to gaining professional recognition for his research findings. The last knowledge the counselor had of the professor was his continued dogged determination to establish his own production company—without success.

Use of a Checklist

You might want to prepare yourself a checklist in order to be more methodical and objective in this evaluation. Figure 4–1 shows a list used by a consultant who helps people decide what business to enter. This list may be modified to meet your unique needs.

Where can you find the information needed to make this type of analysis? The first place to look is in the technical section of your nearest library—or the government documents section. The librarians in either of these sections can assist you in finding industry data. You will probably want to study carefully the U.S. census data on population, busi-

FIGURE 4-1
Business Selection Survey Checklist

Capital Required	Degree of Risk Involved	Amount of Work Involved	Independent Ownership or Franchise	Potential of the Business	Source of Data

ness, housing, and possibly even agriculture. The Small Business Administration in Washington or a regional office can be of great help to you. Also, contact:

1. The research division of your local chamber of commerce.
2. The trade association for the industries you are interested in.
3. Local business leaders.
4. Bankers and other financial experts.
5. Your congressman.

How You Can Classify the Types of Business

While there are several ways of classifying the types of business available, we chose to group them as: (1) retailing; (2) service; (3) wholesaling; (4) research and development; (5) consulting; and (6) manufacturing.

A more detailed grouping, showing the options in each group, is shown in Figure 4-2.

How You Can Choose the Business to Enter

The point has now been reached where you need to have an exercise in "brainstorming." Get a group of your friends together and ask them what kinds of products or services they need. Then, ask them if those needs are being met adequately. If not, what would be necessary for their needs to be satisfied? Try to get them to identify not only existing types of business, but also as many new kinds of business as possible. You should then consider the kinds of products and services not now available, but that are needed and could—if available—find a market.

You might also assemble a diversified group of local small business-

FIGURE 4–2
Some Business Options, Classified into Related Groups

I. Retailing
  1. Food
    a. Grocery
    b. Fast-prepared
    c. Convenience
    d. Restaurant
    e. Lounges
    f. Specialty shops
  2. Appliance
  3. Hardware and building material
  4. Specialty
  5. Clothing
II. Service
  1. Service station
  2. Auto repair
  3. Appliance repair
  4. Building repair and renovation
  5. Janitorial
  6. Plumber
  7. Electrician
  8. Floor covering
  9. F.O.B. (fixed base operation-aircraft)
  10. Travel agencies
III. Wholesaling
  1. Jobbers
  2. Brokers
  3. Distributors
  4. Manufacturing agents
IV. Research and development
  1. Materials
  2. Products
  3. Software information systems
  4. Specialized machinery
  5. Manufacturing systems

V. Consulting
  1. Management
  2. Management information systems
  3. Financial
  4. Investment
  5. Marketing
  6. Risk management
  7. Land use and development
  8. Engineering
  9. Economic
  10. Government
  11. Various additional highly specialized areas
VI. Manufacturing
  1. Metals
    a. Sheet metal
    b. Machine shop
      (1) General
      (2) Special equipment
    c. Foundry
    d. Mini-steel mill
  2. Plastics
    a. Extrusion
    b. Applicators
    c. Formulators
  3. Food processing
    a. Meat
    b. Vegetables
    c. Bakery
    d. Specialty items

men to "brainstorm" with you on business opportunities. Another possible source of participants for this exercise might be members of the local ACE (Active Corps of Executives) or SCORE (Service Corps of Retired Executives) chapters.

An example of a business that originated from ideas of local business managers was a sheet metal shop that was established to supply the sheet metal requirement of a machine shop.

When you are obtaining advice from outsiders, always remember that it is your resources that are at stake when the commitment is made. Thus, the ultimate decision must be yours.

After this exercise in free-wheel thinking, the next step is actually to select that business which seems best for you. Your earlier checklist would now come in handy in making your choice.

In fact, you may want to make more than one choice and leave yourself some options. Remember to consider your personal attributes in order best to utilize your capabilities. In the selection process, the business should fit one's reason for being and one's life objectives. Yet, an effort should be made to maintain an attitude of objectivity and let your mind govern—not your emotions.

Once the choice has been made, it is necessary to conduct an economic feasibility study to determine, as best you can, its economic possibilities. As one former student put it, "The time spent in doing these various exercises pays off in the end. It actually helps achieve your purpose in less time by guiding you to do those things you need to do." He has evidenced this by starting three businesses in distinctly different but related fields and achieving success in sales and profits in the first year of operation of each of them.

STUDYING THE ECONOMIC ENVIRONMENT

The method of studying the environment may be carried out rationally and objectively or with little thought. You may either use the analytical and rational approach of a computer or play the odds and rely on chance, as in playing a slot machine, as shown in Figure 4–3. The "game" of business requires the best objective, rational, and reasoned effort from you, if you are to succeed.

FIGURE 4–3
Which Method to Use in Making Your Decisions

Rational Objective   Chance

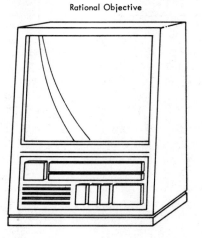 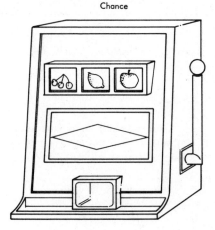

Studying the Economic Environment for the Business

You should begin your study by analyzing the characteristics of the economic environment related to the particular kind of business in which you are interested. An overview of the economic status of the industry —of which your potential business will be a part—may be provided by obtaining answers to these questions:

1. How many firms are there in this type of industry?
2. Do they vary in size, or do they seem to be uniform in size and general characteristics?
3. What is the geographic distribution of the firms in the industry? Are they concentrated in one area, or are they widely distributed? (Rising transportation costs have increased the importance of this factor.)
4. What is the relationship between small firms of this type and larger firms and other industries? There may be adverse features associated with this relationship. As an example, carpet plants solely dependent on the auto industry for customers are subject to the fluctuations of auto sales.
5. Does the firm serve only the domestic market? Or are there opportunities to serve foreign markets as well?
6. What are federal, state, and local government agencies' attitudes toward this type of business?
7. What is society's attitude toward this type of business?

After deciding the overall economic environment in the industry, you need to study the business climate for your business in the area in which you would like to operate. One approach that is frequently used in analyzing an area is to evaluate the objective and subjective factors that influence the region's business climate. Additional data that pertain to your particular type of business may also be obtained.

Studying the Market for Your Business

You should next determine what is happening in the market place, and the possible future your business will have in that market. The size, nature, and other characteristics of the market, as well as your firm's future possibilities, may be derived from answers to questions such as these:

1. What is the relationship of population to the proposed business?
   a. Identify the age and age distribution among the population. Is a specific age group of greater importance to this business than others?

b. Identify the population by sex, race, education, fertility rate, occupations, and other characteristics that affect the demand for goods and services.

c. Define the size of the population and trends in size, age, sex, racial, educational, and occupational distributions. A declining population, or a declining population segment, in a specific geographic area may indicate an unsuccessful future for some businesses. The declining birth rate is affecting many industries oriented toward the baby, teenager, and youth markets.

2. What is the size and distribution of income within the population?
3. Is the sales volume for this kind of business growing, stable, or declining?
4. What is the number and size of competitors?
5. What is the success rate of competing businesses?
6. What are the technical aspects (state of the art)?
7. What are the sources of supply?
8. What are the capital requirements?
9. What is the rate of return on investment?

Estimate Size of the Market. This information should help you estimate the size of your market. Additional data may be obtained from trade associations, chambers of commerce, and various federal, state, and local government agencies. Examples of specific sources are the U.S. Department of Commerce (through its Office of Business Economics) and the Bureau of the Census. The divisions of research of colleges and universities also may be of assistance to you.

Statistical information gathered and tabulated by the Bureau of the Census may be particularly useful in evaluating the following variables, which determine the size and composition of your market:

1. Population characteristics.
2. Employment patterns.
3. Personal income.
4. Business sales and income.

Estimate the Competition. In studying the market area, you should ascertain the number of similar businesses that have been liquidated or merged with a competitor. The latter is usually a sign of economic weakness.

You should determine the kind of technology being applied by other firms in your industry. For example: Are other machine shops using hand equipment? Or, are they using the latest equipment, including numerically controlled devices? The state of technology is significant in determining operating costs.

Estimate Your Share of the Market. Now, you should be able to arrive at a "ball park" figure for your total sales volume and your share of the market. In arriving at this kind of estimate, you should select reasonable and conservative figures. For example, you—as the planner of a new business—should first define the geographic boundaries of the market area and then, from your knowledge of the potential customers in the various communities located in this area, make an estimate of products that might be purchased. It is better to plan for a lower level of sales in order to budget more effectively the business' operation.

Set up a Plan. If you call on your own resources and those of other people who are specialists in your business area, you may be able to develop a detailed plan for your business. This plan would include land, building, equipment, inventory, working capital, and personnel. You should then be able to determine the capital requirements for each of these productive factors, as well as the total of your capital requirements. Some additional capital should be provided for contingencies. The adequacy of the size and cost of inventory is determined by the number and location of suppliers.

Estimate Your Capital Requirements. Information concerning your capital requirements may be obtained from potential competitors. You may even find that owners of existing businesses will cooperate with you by supplying various types of useful information, so long as you approach them in a manner to merit confidence. Some owners play the old game of "I've got a secret," but our experience indicates that these people are in the minority. Other sources of information may include suppliers, wholesalers, and manufacturers.

> A consultant was searching for comprehensive information relating to the opening of a retail fabric shop. He called a major textile manufacturer, who indicated that this information was readily available from "McCall Patterns" and "Simplicity Patterns." Each of the pattern makers maintained comprehensive market research programs, and made such information readily available.

Estimate Your Return on Investment. By using the capital requirements and developing an estimate of your expected profits after taxes, you should be able to estimate the rate of return you can hope to receive on your investment and on each dollar of sales. You will probably want to set a "return on investment" objective that, when added to your estimated value of your own services, should compare favorably with the profit potential for your type of business. There is no generally acceptable guideline as to how much this rate of return should be.

By using the rate of return figure you decide upon, and given the knowledge of the market in which you plan to operate, you can compute what sales will be needed to give you a satisfactory return.

> For example, suppose you invest $25,000 in a small business and your objective is to receive a 12 percent return on your investment.

You also think you could earn $12,000 a year working for someone else. You should then expect to receive an annual income from the business of at least $15,000, which is the equivalent of $12,000 salary plus $3,000 return on investment.

You further estimate your market to consist of 5,000 companies spending an average of $1,000 per year for the items you will sell. This represents a total market potential of $5 million. You know that the typical profit-to-sales ratio for that industry is about 6 percent. By dividing your hoped-for earnings of $15,000 by the profit margin of 6 percent, you find that you must have sales of $250,000 in order to achieve your profit objective. This means you would need at least a 5 percent share of the market for your products.

Use SBA Resources.   In addition to the data sources previously listed, the Small Business Administration has developed a variety of information resources that may be obtained by contacting the nearest Small Business Administration office, one of the U.S. Printing Office retail outlets, or the Superintendent of Documents, Washington, D.C.

After completing all these mental exercises, you should know whether the rate of return for the business you have chosen is acceptable, based on current economic information. Since you want to achieve the highest possible rate of return, you should make fresh comparisons with alternative investment opportunities. You should decide whether this business is the opportunity sought. If it is, then the decision is "Go!"

DECIDING WHETHER TO START A NEW BUSINESS
OR BUY AN EXISTING ONE

You have now decided that you are the entrepreneurial type and that you want to own a business. You have also determined what type of business you want to enter and have found it to be economically feasible. The next step is to choose the specific business that affords you the opportunity you seek. In surveying the situation, you may want to look at the alternatives of either entering an established business or conceiving, planning, organizing, and operating a new business of your own. In this respect, you are like the traveler on the road in Figure 4–4, who must make a decision. You will want to select the alternative that seems to afford you the best opportunity of accomplishing your goals. However, just as the traveler, you may find yourself in the dilemma of not knowing which direction to take. After viewing the options, you must make a decision—a decision that you hope will carry you to success.

The following material should help you make this decision most effectively. Specifically, it presents the reasons for and against entering an existing firm and starting a new one "from scratch."

There are several sources from which you can obtain information on

FIGURE 4–4
Which Road to Take

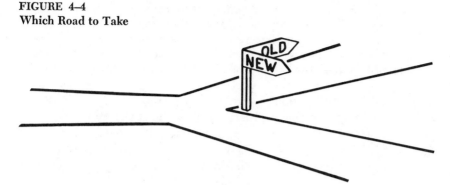

available business opportunities. Included are *The Wall Street Journal,* a list of bankruptcy sales in your local paper, your banker, and chambers of commerce.

One word of caution is important at this point. *The past success or failure of such businesses alone is not enough to justify a decision on whether or not to buy a given business. Instead, you must make a thorough analysis of the present condition of the business and a future appraisal of what it might do.*

Entering an Established Business

Before you are able to make the analysis you desire, you must first locate that business, or those businesses, that are available for purchase. In your search, you will find that some firms are not available at any price, others will become available, but at a high price (as is in the cliche, "I'll sell anything I have for a price"); and there will be those firms whose owners are actively seeking a buyer.

Before you read the following material, let us point out that "buying a business" can mean different things to different people. First, it may mean acquiring the total ownership of an entire business. Second, it may mean acquiring only the assets of a firm, or its name, or only certain parts of the business. While we make no specific definition of what we mean by the term at this time, keep this uncertainty in mind as you study the following material.

Some Considerations in Acquiring an Ongoing Firm.   One important factor is always the *price* asked for the firm. Sometimes a successful ongoing business may be acquired at a bargain price. For some reason, it can be bought at a fraction of the dollar cost, or its replacement value.

For example, a small stone company was owned by a few stockholders who wanted to sell out in a hurry for personal reasons. The company had more assets, including accounts receivable and cash on hand in the bank, than the purchase price the owners were asking. Some outsiders purchased all the outstanding shares. They were able to take the cash on hand and that received from the receivables to reimburse themselves for all the shares they had bought.

You should be ready to grab similar opportunities.

A retailer may be willing to sell his business for the current price of his inventory. However, you should be cautious. You should not purchase his accounts receivable and you should be certain that his payables and other liabilities are established. Be sure to have your own CPA audit the records and verify the inventory and its value.

A grocer who wanted to sell her store reduced her retail prices in order to attract a large number of customers. It mattered little to her that many items were reduced to cost or less. A "sucker," who saw the large number of customers, took the bait and bought the store. About three weeks after assuming ownership and management, he had to replenish his stock. He had to raise his prices, but then his business dropped off, and he was very unhappy over his situation.

Another element of consideration is *your managerial ability*. There are those who have a talent for acquiring businesses that are in economic difficulty or are not achieving the results possible. These persons are able to come into a business and initiate changes that turn the business around. Once the business prospers, the new owner looks for another buyer to purchase the successful business from him. The seller then seeks another similar opportunity.

Reasons for Acquiring an Established Business. While it is difficult to discuss this subject intelligently without knowing the specific details of each situation, at least there are some generalizations that can be made. Some advantages of acquiring an established business are:

1. The facilities—building, equipment, inventory, and personnel—are in a functioning status.
2. A product or service is already being produced and distributed.
3. A market has been established and exists.
4. Revenue and profits are being generated.
5. The location may be very desirable.
6. Financial relationships have been established with banks and trade creditors.

An experienced small businessman recently sold one of his businesses. He searched for an existing business in which he might become involved. His interests were managerial challenge, economic growth, and profit. After viewing several possibilities, he acquired a small company that manufactured a top quality airport service vehicle. The company needed additional capital and more effective management. The new owner was able to bring these two ingredients.

Reasons against Acquiring an Established Business.   Buying an on-going business may also have these disadvantages:

1.   The physical facilities (building and equipment) and product line may be old and obsolete.
2.   The personnel may be stagnant and have a poor production record.
3.   Union-management relations may be poor.
4.   The inventory may contain an excessive amount of "dead stock."
5.   Too high a percentage of the assets may be in poor-quality accounts receivable.
6.   The location may be bad.
7.   The financial condition, and relations with financial institutions, may be deteriorating.
8.   There may be some poor customers who are draining the assets of the firm.

A firm in the extractive industry had failed. The owners were seeking new financial assistance in order to reactivate its operation. While a favorable market environment existed, the inferior quality of the firm's raw material made it unacceptable in the marketplace. Had the principals sought a new site with a better quality material, the business could probably have been reactivated. Substantial quantities of acceptable material were available near the existing property, but the owners did not choose to use them.

Starting a New Business of Your Own

In considering the possibilities of establishing a new enterprise, you should recognize that you have more freedom of choice in defining the nature of the business than if you purchase an existing firm. Remember that there are both pluses and minuses in choosing this alternative. You should view a particular business in terms of whether it will enable you to achieve your personal objectives. Also, how do the advantages and disadvantages of this option compare with those of entering the on-going business? Is there—on this basis—a reasonable opportunity for success?

As previously stated, some people have as their goal in life the initiation of new businesses. They find pleasure in establishing new ventures, getting them operating at a profit, and then finding a buyer for them. Then they start the process over again.

Other people enjoy the challenge and sense of accomplishment that come from creating something new. They feel that they have been useful, and will probably keep the business and run it themselves. Yet, they may later start and operate other firms.

Businesses are started in a variety of ways. The Chapman family business originated by accident. In the early days of the automobile, two nationally prominent industrialists were touring the hinterlands by auto. During one day's travels, they found themselves many miles from a restaurant or hotel. They had their driver take them to a farm house that stood some distance from the main road. When greeted by the lady of the house, they inquired if she might prepare a meal for them, for which they would gladly pay. A short time later she fed them a meal that had an "outstanding quality of palatability."

The word spread, and others came with a similar request in an ever increasing frequency. In time, the farm house became a familiar friendly place for the wayworn traveler, known far and wide as "Chapman House."

The years passed, the children grew into adulthood, married, and had children of their own. In the meantime, Chapman House's activities continued to expand to include a motel—as well as an expanded restaurant—where textile and food products prepared by the local citizens were sold.

Reasons for Establishing a New Business.   Some of the reasons for starting a new business of your own may include the opportunities to:

1. Define the nature of your business.
2. Create the type of physical facilities you prefer.
3. Take advantage of the latest technology in selecting equipment, materials, and tools.
4. Utilize the most recent processes and procedures.
5. Obtain fresh inventory.
6. Have a free hand in selecting, training, developing, and motivating personnel.
7. Design your own management information system.
8. Select your competitive environment—within limits.

A young entrepreneur wanted to enter the food, beverage, and lodging business. He could purchase one or more of a number of existing facilities. Each had a community image. His other option was to restore a historic building, which had earlier served as a hotel, into a superior-quality facility.

Reasons against Establishing a New Business.   Some of the disadvantages of starting a new business "from scratch" are:

1. Problems of selecting the right business.
2. Unproven performance records in sales, reliability, service, and profits.
3. Problems associated with assembling the resources—including location, building, equipment, material, and people.
4. Necessity of selecting and training a new work force.
5. Lack of an established product line.
6. Production problems associated with the start up of a new business.
7. The lack of an established market and channels of distribution.
8. Problems in establishing basic accounting system and controls.
9. Difficulty in working out the "bugs" that develop in the initial operation.

A new restaurant, catering to a high-class clientele, was established in a questionable and not very accessible neighborhood. In spite of advertising and the support of influential people, the business failed. Yet, a small business specialist had counseled the potential investors against making an investment in the venture because of the many negative factors.

The questionnaire in the appendix to this chapter should help you in deciding whether to start a new business or to enter an existing one.

SUMMARY

The purpose of this discussion of the environment of small business was to enable you, by following the outlined analysis procedure, to reach a conclusion with which you can be comfortable. You should perform this analysis yourself because it will enhance your probability of success.

Also, in deciding whether to buy an existing business or start a new enterprise, no one can really advise you what to do. Instead, you must "do your own thing." Thus, you must match the available alternatives with your abilities and inclinations.

QUESTIONS FOR FURTHER DISCUSSION

1. Explain how you can investigate the alternatives for starting a business.
2. What are some types of business available to you?
3. How can an exercise in "brainstorming" help you to choose your business?
4. What are the major factors that should be considered in studying the economic environment for a given industry?
5. What are the major factors that should be considered in studying the business climate for the market area?
6. What are the major factors that should be considered in studying the composition of the market for your product?

7. How can capital requirements be investigated?
8. How can the return on investment be estimated?
9. Discuss the importance of price and managerial ability in acquiring an established business.
10. What are the reasons against acquiring an established business?
11. What are the reasons for establishing a new business?
12. What are the reasons against establishing a new business?

APPENDIX: DECIDING WHETHER TO START A NEW BUSINESS OR BUY AN EXISTING ONE

Should I start a new business or buy an existing one?

At this point in your career, this should be a very important question for you. The material in this form should aid you in making this choice.

You might want to reproduce these pages and do the same thing for several businesses you have in mind. We recommend that you go through and answer the questions concerning a business you have in mind as conscientiously as you can.

If, after answering the material in Part A, you decide to enter an established business rather than to establish one of your own, then you should proceed to the material in Part B. You should fill this form out for *each* specific business you are considering entering.

Part A

Before deciding whether you will establish a new business or purchase an established business, you need to give consideration to the positive and negative features of each. More important, you should rate each point a plus or minus as you perceive the significance of the point and its value to you.

1. Define the nature of the business:

   _____

   _____

   _____

2. Favorable points for establishing a new business: Plus (+) or Minus (−)
   a. Opportunity to create the type of physical facilities I prefer   _____
   b. Ability to take advantage of the latest technology in selecting equipment, materials, and tools   _____

    c. Opportunity to utilize the most recent processes and procedures   _____

    d. Opportunity to obtain a fresh inventory   _____

    e. Opportunity to have a free hand in selecting, training, developing, and motivating personnel   _____

    f. Opportunity to design my own management information system   _____

    g. Opportunity to select my competitive environment within limits   _____

3. Favorable points for selecting an established business (plus [+] or minus [−]):

    a. Avoiding the difficulty of a business with an unproved performance record in sales, reliability, service, and profits   _____

    b. Avoiding the problems associated with assembling the composite resources—including location, building, equipment, material, and people   _____

    c. Avoiding the necessity of selecting and training a new work force   _____

    d. Avoiding the lack of an established product line   _____

    e. Avoiding production problems associated with the start-up of a new business   _____

    f. Avoiding the lack of an established market channel of distribution   _____

    g. Avoiding the problems in establishing a basic accounting and control system   _____

    h. Avoiding the difficulty in working out the "bugs" that develop in the initial operation   _____

4. Checking back over the points covered in 2 and 3 above, I conclude:

    a. I want to establish a new business   (   )

    b. I prefer to enter an established business   (   )

5. If your answer in 4 is *b*, then proceed with Part B, which follows.

Part B

Considerations for selecting an established business, your responses, those of the present owner, and the facts concerning the status of the business should guide you to a comfortable decision as to whether this business is for you.

1. Why is the business available for purchase? _____
    _____
    _____
    _____

2. Are the physical facilities worn out or outdated? Yes _____
    No _____

3. Does the inventory contain mostly "dead stock"? Yes _____
    No _____

4. Is the market for the firm's product/service declining?
    Yes _____ No _____
    a. Changing neighborhood? Yes _____ No _____
    b. Declining population? Yes _____ No _____
    c. Technological change? Yes_____ No _____

5. Has the union recently won an election as a bargaining agent
    for the company's employees? Yes _____ No _____

6. Is the business solvent? Yes _____ No _____
    (Have you had a reputable CPA appraise the firm's assets and
    liabilities?) Yes _____ No _____

7. What are the intentions of the present owner? _____
    _____
    _____

8. Does the present owner plan to establish a new business or ac-
    quire another business that would leave him/her in competi-
    tion with you? Yes _____ No _____

9. Is the present owner in good health? Yes _____ No _____

10. Does the present owner wish to retire? Yes _____ No _____

11. Does the present owner wish to continue to be associated
    with the business as minority owner/consultant? Yes _____
    No _____

12. Analysis of accounting information:
    a. Cash position:
        (1) Cash on hand $_____
        (2) Cash in bank $_____
    b. Current ratio: _____
        (current assets/current liabilities)
    c. Quick ratio: _____
        (current assets − Inventories)/(current liabilities)
    d. Debt-to-equity ratio:

(Debt [current liabilities, notes/bonds] ÷ Owner's funds [common stock, preferred stock, capital surplus, and retained earnings]) _____

e. Ratio of net income to sales:
(net income/Net sales) _____

f. Net income to investment ratio:
(net income/investment) _____

g. Amount of debt:
(1) Notes $_____
(2) Bonds $_____
Terms of Debt: _____

h. Validity of financial statements:
Accurate _____ Overstated _____ Understated _____
Warning: Check to see: Relationship of book value of fixed assets to replacement costs; percentage of total accounts receivable over 90 days (_____%); nature of accounts receivable present aging (Yes _____ No _____); dollar amount of bad debts charged off last 6 months ($_____), 12 months ($_____), 36 months ($_____)

i. Adequacy of cost data:
Can you accurately determine the cost of producing the product or service? Yes _____ No _____

j. Is there available data to enable you accurately to break down the price of a product or service into costs and profit? Yes _____ No _____

13. Appraisal of operations, plant and equipment:
a. How effective are the personnel?
(1) What is the rate of labor turnover? _____%
(2) What is the rate of absenteeism? _____%
(3) Is there evidence of deliberate acts of employee sabotage? Yes _____ No _____

b. What is the amount of waste?
(1) Material _____% $_____ per day
(2) Machine time _____% $_____ per day
(3) Personnel time _____% $_____ per day

c. What is the quality of production?
(1) What portion of production or service is completed without defects? _____%
(2) What portion of the rejects may be reworked? _____% If reworked, how much additional time is involved in this process? _____

(3) What portion of production results in rejects that cannot be reworked? _____%

(4) What is the cost of replacement shipments that have to be made because of material that was shipped of unusable quality? $_____

d. What is the physical condition of the plant?

(1) Is the plant of sufficient size and design to meet current and projected requirements? Yes _____ No _____

(2) Does the plant appear to be laid out for the most effective use of people, machines, and material? Yes _____ No _____

(3) Does the material handling system seem to be designed and laid out to accomplish a minimum labor demand and a minimum demand for time in transit? Yes _____ No _____

(4) How does the plant equipment compare with the latest available? _____

_____

_____

(5) What is the maintenance status of plant equipment? Excellent _____ Good _____ Fair _____ Poor _____

5

How to Enter an Existing Business

After having made the choice to enter a small or independent business, after having determined that your business idea is valid and economically feasible, and if you have decided to enter an existing firm, you are now ready to take that important step. The material in this chapter presents a plan of action for helping you achieve that goal.

By this time, you should be aware of the many problems and challenges awaiting individuals moving into small business ownership and management. There are times when the pitfalls that exist in entering an established business may be well concealed. It is the intent of this chapter to aid you in seeing an established business in true perspective—its strengths as well as its weaknesses.

While there is some similarity between establishing a new business—which is discussed in the next chapter—and entering an ongoing enterprise, there are several significant differences. These are covered in this chapter. The procedures and analyses that follow are intended to provide you with an overview of how to evaluate an existing firm and to aid you in determining: (1) whether or not to purchase a given business, and (2) if you do buy it, what you should do to implement your plans and begin operations.

TO BUY, OR NOT TO BUY?

In considering your options in selecting an established business, it is likely that you will narrow them down to a single choice. At that point, you should check the business out before making your final decision. It

FIGURE 5–1
To Go or Not to Go

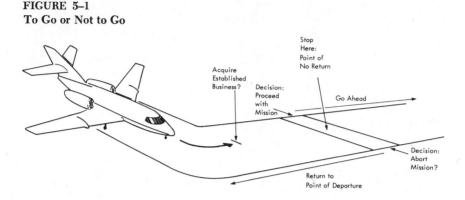

might be compared to the steps involved in moving an aircraft from the boarding gate of the terminal to the taxiway, to the runway, and into the air. Certain items must be checked off at each step of the way, with the pilot having the right to abort the flight—up to the point where he is committed to taking the aircraft into the air. So it is with you and your purchase of an established business; up to a given time, you may cancel out, but at that point you are committed to take over the business. Figure 5–1 is intended to illustrate this comparison.

Determining Why the Business Is Available

You should determine why the firm is available for purchase, as this—in itself—is a "red flag" warning that something may be wrong. You need to determine whether something is wrong and, if so, what and why and what can be done about it.

The following discussion is designed to help you determine whether a particular business, which is available, is right for you.

Why Available? The question, "Why is this business available for purchase?" should help you establish the validity of the owner's stated purpose for selling the business. Maybe it is in accordance with the old cliche, "Anything I have is for sale—at a price, that is, for the *right* price." Some reasons provide a positive opportunity, while others may be negative opportunities for you. The following analysis should help you determine the potential opportunity to be found in a firm.

Does the present owner have "too many irons in the fire"? Too many businesses are run by one individual who is unable to allocate sufficient time to successfully manage all of them.

Bob Bleckley had dropped out of college in his senior year for financial reasons. After working several years for a building supply firm, he went to work for a partnership engaged in diversified construction of commercial buildings. He was made manager of the metal door division. The partners were so busy with their other activities that they gave him little assistance or interest. Bob was running the division.

He offered to buy the division from the partners and they accepted. He now is the owner-manager of that firm and two other small activities.

What Is the Present Condition of the Business?   You should seek specific, detailed answers to the following questions.

Are the Physical Facilities Worn Out?   If the plant, equipment, tools, and furniture are worn out, it is likely that the business' maintenance costs will be excessive. It is also likely that the firm can no longer effectively compete in the marketplace.

A druggist and his wife had been running their drugstore for 40 years—largely without making changes and improvements in their physical plant. After the death of his wife, the druggist, who was approaching 70, decided to sell the business. He was unable to find a buyer, for the equipment was so antiquated and in such poor condition that it was practically useless. He finally sold his stock, including his prescription file, to another pharmacist, who moved them to another place of business.

Does the Inventory Contain Mostly "Dead Stock"?   The firm's inventory may be unsalable at any price because it is no longer in demand, or has deteriorated.

The owner of a hardware store decided to sell it in 1970. The prospective buyer found 200 horse collars among the antiquated stock.

Is the Market for the Firm's Product Declining?   The demand for a business' product may be declining for one or more of the following reasons:

1. Changing neighborhood—There may be a change in the residents' economic status; there may be a change from one ethnic group to another, from one age group to another, or in the life-style of the inhabitants.
2. Declining population—The outward movement of the population in both urban and agrarian areas has had a devastating economic effect on some firms.
3. Technological change—The advent and installation of new technology may immediately cause the firm to become obsolete.

The owners of a company in Florida processing large cans of grapefruit juice decided to build a new, more efficient plant. As soon as it was completed, they found themselves competing with a new plant producing fresh-frozen juice concentrates.

Is the Business Solvent?   The business may be insolvent. Unfortunately, there have been instances when people have discovered all too late that the firm they purchased had less assets than liabilities.

A building contractor sold 150 homes for down payments of over $500,000. Because of *abysmally inadequate financing,* he was unable to complete the houses. The firm was sold, but the new owners had to either return the money or give title to their property to the purchasers.

An audit by a reputable accounting firm could be effective in uncovering such information. Another protective measure is the use of escrows, whereby part of the purchase price is put in safe keeping until all aspects of the sale have been completed.

What Are the Present Owner's Intentions?   *Will the Present Owner Remain in Competition?* Sometimes, for reasons of location, the age of the facility or equipment, an owner decides to dispose of his firm, open another one, and compete with the purchaser of his old firm. For protection, you should have an attorney draw up an agreement that the present owner will not re-enter a similar business in the community or market area for a reasonable period of time. These agreements are sometimes difficult to enforce, but most businessmen do live up to their agreement.

The owner of a pest control franchise needed to change locations for family reasons. The new location was within the franchise area, so the purchasers required him to sign an agreement that he would not re-enter the business for five years.

In the meantime, he opened a restaurant and related business and became quite successful. At the end of five years, he opened an independent pest control business in his new location.

Is the Present Owner in Good Health?   If the owner is in poor health, you should determine that it is physical and not economic.

Bob Howard was interested in owning his own business. One Sunday, he was reviewing the want ads in the newspaper, when he spotted an item of interest.

FOR REASONS OF HEALTH, OWNER WILLING TO SACRIFICE SUCCESSFUL, PROFITABLE SANDWICH SHOP. PRICED FOR IMMEDIATE SALE.

Bob grabbed his coat and dashed over to "Easy Sandwich Shop." The place was full and business looked great. (All the owner's friends just needed a sandwich that day.) After some delay, Bob was able to engage the owner in serious negotiation. After some haggling, the principals shook hands, and Bob wrote a check from his savings for $10,000.

A month later, Bob was chagrined to learn that the business was "ready to fold" when he took the bait. The former owner's friends were gone and business was "lousy." The $10,000 received by the former owner had worked a "fast cure" for his ill-health.

Does the Present Owner Desire to Retire?   The owner may have reached the age where he wishes to retire, which is a valid reason for offering a business for sale. Because of taxes, the owner may want to be paid for the business over a number of years, In addition, he may want to contract for a specified number of years to serve as a consultant or to fill some managerial role.

A word of caution is appropriate. Sometimes the continued association of a former owner may be detrimental to the welfare of the new owner. By continued association with the firm, the former owner may cause the new owner to be unsuccessful, thereby regaining ownership of the business.

At least, the presence of the old owner restricts the freedom of action of the new man and can otherwise inhibit his actions.

Joe Jones, an experienced insurance man, became the controlling partner in an insurance firm, which also owned a savings and loan association. The previous owner, 75 years old, remained as chairman of the board of the savings and loan association and active partner in the insurance company.

The next 10 years were miserable for Joe, for he was treated as a junior clerk by the minority partner. He finally sold his interest to someone else.

The following procedure should be helpful in uncovering undesirable economic conditions in a firm you are considering purchasing.

Analysis of Accounting Information

The reason for analyzing the firm's accounting data is to determine its economic health. You should take a physical inventory to determine the accuracy of the recorded information and make a quantitative analysis of the economic value of the assets and liabilities.

In performing your analysis, there are innumerable items you should check. The most important of these are now presented in general terms. (The specific details and examples will be discussed in Part VI.)

Cash Position.   Is the firm's cash position high or low, considering the industry, location, and so forth? Due to taxes, a firm may accumulate a strong cash position. The owner may prefer to sell the firm and take advantage of the capital gains benefit over ordinary income. Other reasons for having a strong cash position are to take care of poor funds management, or to provide for flexibility so you can take advantage of any profitable opportunity that presents itself.

Analysis of Ratios.   Many financial ratios can be used in estimating the economic health of a firm. While these are usually used in managing a going concern (as shown in Chapter 18), they can also help you make a purchase decision.

Current ratio is defined as *current assets* divided by *current liabilities* and is a measure of short-term solvency. Current assets normally include cash, marketable securities, accounts receivable, and inventories. Current liabilities are composed of accounts payable, short-term notes payable, income taxes payable, and accrued expenses. A general rule of thumb is that the current ratio should be 2 to 1.

Quick ratio is obtained by dividing *current liabilities* into *current assets minus inventories.* You can use this ratio to estimate the ability of a firm to pay off its short-term obligations without having to sell its inventories. Inventories tend to lose value faster than other assets when sold in a hurry. A rule of thumb for the quick ratio is 1 to 1.

Debt-to-equity ratio shows the firm's obligations to creditors, relative to the owner's funds. Debt includes current liabilities and bonds; owner's funds include common stock, preferred stock, capital surplus, and retained earnings.

Ratio of net income to sales is calculated by dividing *net income* by *net sales.* You may use net income before taxes or after taxes. No set guideline exists, as the ratio varies among industries, and even among companies.

Net income to investment ratio is found by dividing *net income* (before or after taxes) by *investment.* Here, again, there is no convenient rule of thumb.

Determination of Debt.   You need to check both the amount of debt and the terms of debt. The *amount of debt* is important, for it shows your financial obligations. You are primarily concerned with short-term notes (less than one year), term notes (one- to five-year maturities), and long-term debt (anything in excess of five years).

Concerning *terms of debt,* you should learn the rate of interest; the firm's ability to repay the debt in its entirety, without penalty; whether a minimum deposit balance is required by the lender; and whether an acceleration clause would operate in the event of default in payment of interest and principal.

Validity of Financial Statements.   You should determine the validity of the financial statement items. Each item listed on the financial statements should be verified by physically counting the listed items to determine whether they agree with the amount shown. Also, you need to find out whether the items are of the stated value.

You should check on the age of accounts receivable. Some businesses continue to carry accounts receivable that should be charged off to "bad debts," resulting in an overstatement of the firm's profit, income tax liability, and value. A tabular summary classifying them by age, such as 30, 60, 90, 120, 180 or more days, would give some perspective of the effectiveness of the existing management's credit policies and practice. The *age of accounts payable* should also be determined.

Cash Flow Analysis.   Managers often overinvest in inventory without being aware of the total annual cost of carrying it. Yet, when all elements of cost for carrying inventory are considered, the annual cost may range from 25 to 35 percent of the average inventory investment. You should prepare a cash flow analysis in order to determine the effectiveness of management in allocating its resources. In preparing it, you should remember that money has a cost in the form of real or imputed interest. If you consider this cost, you should try to use this resource most advantageously in producing a profit.

It is important that you consider the monthly cycle of cash revenue and cash payout. In addition, you should take into account the yearly cycle of cash inflow and outgo.

Adequacy of Cost Data.   You should determine whether cost data are adequate and accurate. One often finds that the accounting system used, even when supervised by a CPA or by one of the national accounting firms, fails to reveal the actual costs of individual activities. Thus, it is impossible to determine the price for each product or service in order to satisfy a predetermined profit criterion. Nor is it possible to explain undesirable variances.

Analysis of Pricing Formula

You should analyze the pricing formula used by the firm. Be sure that the price for individual products or services includes all elements of costs, including a provision for an adequate profit.

Appraisal of Operations, Plant, and Equipment

The objective of the following discussion is to help you study the total management operations of a firm, and not just that of the chief executive officer.

Management Effectiveness.   How effective is the firm's management? In acquiring an ongoing business, you may decide to keep key management personnel. Therefore, it is desirable to look for performance and behavioral characteristics that may serve as a basis for appraising how effectively each manager performs—as an individual and as a part of the managerial group.

Plant Efficiency.   Some questions to ask in specific production areas are:

1. *How effective are the personnel?* You can approximate the productivity of individual employees, as well as of the total group of workers. You can look for the portion of time spent productively compared to that wasted on nonproductive efforts. Other questions concerning labor cost, waste and scrap, product image, company image, and competitive position are:

a.   What is the rate of labor turnover?
b.   What is the percentage of absenteeism?
c.   Do employees deliberately commit acts of sabotage that reflect on the image of the product and company?

2. *What is the amount of waste?* The amount of waste serves as an important key to profit or loss. By being particularly observant of operations, you can determine the amount of material and supplies being needlessly wasted in the operations.

> A carpet mill was observed to be looping out to the edge of the jute or polypropylene backing. Yet, from one to three inches was sliced off each side after the carpet was finished. It was estimated that the mill was unnecessarily using about $10,000 worth of fiber per day by not stopping the looping process approximately an inch from the edge of the backing.

Machine time that is not being utilized is an important waste. Investment in equipment is usually costly, and this cost must be offset by keeping the equipment operating as much as possible.

3. *What is the quality of production?* The quality of products, or the quality of service produced by the employees, should be graded. The grading may be done by answering questions such as:

a.   What portion of production is completed without defects?
b.   What portion of the rejects may be reworked, and if any, how much time is involved in this process?
c.   What portion of production results in rejects that cannot be reworked?
d.   In terms of cost, how many shipments must be reshipped because some of the shipped material is not of usable quality?

4. What is the physical condition of the plant? You should consider present and future demands made on the plant, as well as:

a. Adequacy of the size and design of the plant. Is it of sufficient size and design to meet current and projected requirements?
b. Efficiency of layout. Optimum results can be attained only if the plant is effectively laid out. Important items to consider are: If the equipment is spaced and laid out in a sequence of productive steps, only a nominal amount of *work-in-process inventory* is needed. The greater the number of operations that require doubling back and crossing over, the greater will be the requirements for this type of inventory.

Materials-handling cost is also important, for the more frequently work-in-process inventory has to be moved, the greater will be the cost of handling it.

The manner in which a plant is laid out has a direct relationship to labor requirements and therefore to *labor costs*.

> A veneer mill and plywood plant was designed and laid out to take advantage of cheap labor. There was a minimum of conveyors and a maximum amount of handling by the workers. The net result was excessive cost and negative profit.

Some other layout considerations are:

What is the age of the equipment?
How does the present equipment compare with the latest equipment in terms of operating costs and rate of production?
What is the state of repair of the present equipment? Is it well-kept, or does it appear that as little effort as possible is spent on maintenance?

Answers to these questions are significant in terms of their relationship to future capital requirements and efficiency of operations. Occasionally, old equipment that is well-maintained, but that has been fully depreciated, offers a cost advantage over newer, more modern equipment. It may be possible that the continued use of older equipment may produce a greater profit, but it also may not. Sometimes, it is necessary to purchase new equipment on an installment basis. The effect of such a step on the cash flow should be carefully analyzed.

Preparing an Economic Feasibility Study

An economic feasibility study for an on-going business is similar in nature to the economic feasibility study for a new enterprise, which was presented in Chapter 4. If you are to avoid being trapped by economic conditions that may result in either economic disaster or stagnation, you should determine the business' feasibility. While most of this material either has been presented or will be presented in later chapters, it is summarized here. The data for the study could be gathered and analyzed under the following classifications:

1. *Population trends of the market.* Is the area experiencing an increase or decrease in population? Is the make-up of the population stable, or is one ethnic, economic, or age group moving out and another moving in?

2. *Age distribution of the population.* If there is a correlation between the demand for a firm's product or service and a particular age group, the size of that group should be identified.

3. *Income levels and distribution of the population.* Sales are affected by both purchasing power and its distribution within the population. You should study the relationship between the income distribution among specific age groups and the demand for goods and services.

4. *Market size.* From the *Journal of Marketing, Sales Management,* census reports, local chambers of commerce data, area planning and development commissions, local newspapers' market data, and other sources, you can obtain information to help you define the size of the firm's market.

5. *Share of market.* By estimating the size of the market, and by defining the amount of competition and its quality, you can search for areas of weakness upon which you can capitalize.

6. *Amount of investment.* The amount of investment may be determined by seeking answers to these questions:

What is the owner's asking price?

Is the asking price favorable?

What is the opinion of an appraiser specializing in this type of business?

7. *Return on investment.* You should consider available investment opportunities to determine whether the return on investment (after-tax profit divided by investment) in this particular business is adequate.

8. *Impact of expected changes.* Changes in the legal, physical, social, cultural, economic, and religious environments can have adverse effects on your chances of success. Some of these are:

a. Zoning changes may have some influence if the business is retail in nature.

Over 30 families deposited $5,000 each for new homes to be constructed. None was finished. According to town officials and engineers, the builder was incompetent and was *unable* or *unwilling to comply with the building code regulations.*

b. Construction of traffic arteries or changes and relocations may cut businesses off from their customers.

> Jo Anne's Dress Shop was located in a small shopping center on a highway leading into and out of Capital City. The street was closed for about 18 months for widening and relocation. Jo Anne's clientele, composed primarily of middle-income housewives, shifted their traffic patterns. By the time the street reopened, Jo Anne's business had declined to the point that she went bankrupt.

c. The emphasis being placed on the environment and ecology has resulted in constraints on some businesses. You should be careful that a confrontation with the environmentalists does not occur. Changes in laws regulating pollution controls have also increased the costs of doing business.

d. Changes in tax laws and other government regulations affect the volume of paper work and the time necessary to prepare the required reports.

e. Labor laws have a direct effect on the cost of doing business. An example is the federal Occupational Safety and Health Act (OSHA), which establishes specific safety standards. (See Chapter 11 for details.)

f. Technological changes may adversely affect you. Innovations in the local newspaper equipment field, such as new and cheaper offset systems, and computers aiding in the composition of the paper, have caused many publishers to abandon their existing equipment.

IMPLEMENTING YOUR PLANS

If you have decided to buy the business, you are ready to activate "operation acquisition." Figure 5–2 indicates the sequence of steps that you will probably follow in moving from the decision to purchase the old business to the point of taking over and running the business' operation. The rooms may be considered as the places where the important designated activities will take place. The sequence of rooms is intended to impress upon you the importance of following the appropriate sequence of activities.

Financing the Business. You are now ready to develop a plan for financing the business. As indicated earlier, financing an existing business will depend to a significant extent on the terms asked by the seller.

Considering Changes in Method of Operations. As a result of the operational analysis suggested earlier in this chapter, you should have developed some ideas concerning the changes you would like to make in the business' existing method of operations.

Developing a Formal Plan.   You should now prepare a formal plan of *change* to be integrated with a formal plan of *action*. You may wish to call this a Manual of Operating Procedures.

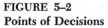

FIGURE 5–2
Points of Decisions

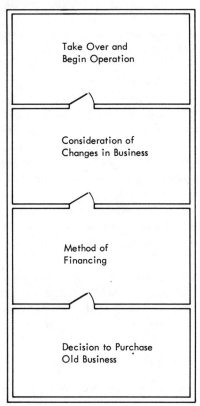

Take Over and
Begin Operation

Consideration of
Changes in Business

Method of
Financing

Decision to Purchase
Old Business

Taking over the Business.   It is now time to start operations. If you have followed the procedures outlined above, the probabilities of your succeeding in your new business will be greatly increased. Yet, you should be prepared for unforeseen contingencies and be ready to react promptly to any difficulties that may arise.

SUMMARY

Well! You are now committed to being a small business manager. You have: (1) found a business you like; (2) determined that the reasons that the present owner wishes to sell are valid; (3) analyzed the accounting information and found it acceptable; (4) determined the accuracy of financial statements; (5) appraised the operations, plant, and equipment; (6) studied the economic feasibility, and found the firm to be needed and potentially profitable; (7) decided to buy it; (8) found, and arranged for, financing; (9) decided on changes you would like to make in the firm's operations; (10) developed a formal plan for acquiring and running the firm; and (11) "taken over the reins" of your firm.

Now, you must manage it. How you can successfully do that is the main topic of the next part.

QUESTIONS FOR FURTHER DISCUSSION

1. Discuss some of the reasons why a business may be available. How could you tell if they are valid?
2. What are the *current ratio* and *quick ratio?*
3. How can you determine the validity of the financial statements?
4. Discuss *cash flow analysis.*
5. Discuss the problem of the amount of waste in considering plant efficiency.
6. Considering plant efficiency, what factors should be considered in studying a firm's lay-out?
7. Briefly discuss the areas that should be considered in an economic feasibility study.
8. If you decide to buy a business, how do you go about implementing your plans?

6

How to Establish Your
New Business

You should have established by now a basic concept of the nature of small business and how you expect to relate personally to a specific type of small business. You should also have decided whether you are going to take over an existing firm—as discussed in the previous chapter—or are going to plan a new one from the beginning. It is the purpose of this chapter to aid you in successfully planning a new small business, if that is your intention. The material should enable you to move in an orderly fashion *from the idea stage to making the new business a reality*. In addition, should the need exist, the formal plan may serve as a mechanism for interesting others to invest in your new venture.

As far as you—the potential new entrepreneur—are concerned, the outlined procedure should aid in avoiding costly blunders. It should conserve time and result in a more polished final product. Insofar as potential investors are concerned, the formal proposal should demonstrate that your idea has been well studied and appropriately structured. Often, the potential new small business owner approaches investors with little more than a dream. The effect is likely to be a negative response. This material should help you avoid these—and other—pitfalls.

In general, the business process involves putting financial, physical, and human resources into an organization in the form of "inputs." These are converted through some form of "operations" or "production" into "goods" or "services." These, in turn, are distributed to other processors, assemblers, wholesalers, retailers, or the final consumer as "outputs." Figure 6–1 presents a generalized chart of such a process.

The specific steps needed to start this process include at least the following:

1. Developing a timetable.
2. Establishing your business objectives.
3. Setting up your organizational structure.
4. Determining your personnel requirements.
5. Determining your physical plant needs.
6. Planning your approach to the market.
7. Preparing your budget.
8. Locating sources of funds.
9. Implementing your plans.

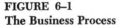

FIGURE 6–1
The Business Process

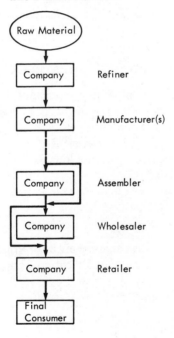

DEVELOPING A TIMETABLE

You should establish a timetable for developing the business in an ordered, coordinated fashion. Data should be developed relating to performing each step in starting the business. Next, a time frame for accomplishing each of the steps should be determined. Many of these steps can be, and often are, performed simultaneously. You, as the owner, have the responsibility of meeting the time schedule.

ESTABLISHING YOUR BUSINESS OBJECTIVES

In order for your enterprise to have purpose and direction, you should establish the objectives you hope to achieve for yourself and your firm. These should be compatible with the objectives discussed in Chapter 2. Examples of some possible categories of objectives are:

	After 1 Year	*After 5 Years*	*After 10 Years*
I. Size			
Physical....................			
Financial...................			
II. Type of products			
Number....................			
Kind of product lines........			
III. Number of employees..........			
IV. Sales........................			
V. Profits.......................			

SETTING UP THE ORGANIZATIONAL STRUCTURE

As previously stated, you must develop a unified organizational structure, taking into consideration the legal, financial, and administrative aspects of your business. Keeping in mind the basic premise that "My business is very personal," it is important that you select those forms that are in *your best interest*. Also, you should organize for the "long run" and not just for the "short run." The outline that follows is intended to aid you in considering the options available to you at each juncture and to assist you in making the best choice.

1. Legal alternatives
    You must choose the form that seems most appropriate to you based upon your needs, objectives, qualifications, and philosophies.
    a. Proprietorship.
    b. Partnership.
    c. Corporation.
    d. Holding company.
2. Capital structure
    The extent to which equity and debt are used will be determined by the interrelationships and the interactions between:
    a. Amount of personal funds you wish to commit to the business.
    b. Amount of personal funds other principals wish to commit.
    c. Amount of leverage desired.
    d. Availability of equity and borrowed capital and at what costs—interest and concessions.
    e. Degree of risk you wish to assume.

3. Administrative structure

You now must develop a formal organizational plan based upon these factors:

   a. The reason for the existence of the business.
   b. Your primary personal and business objectives.
   c. The plans, programs, policies, and practices that will enable you to achieve your objectives.
   d. The authority and responsibility relationships that will permit you to accomplish your mission.

An element often overlooked by the small business manager is the importance of having access to a board of directors (or advisers, if the firm is not a corporation) to evaluate the firm's operation and to make recommendations relating to future activities. You *must* be willing to be responsive to its guidance. You should expect to pay these people a minimum of $100 per meeting, plus expenses, and as the firm prospers, an increased amount. The board should be composed of at least three people from outside the business and an equal number from within.

In selecting outside members, you should look toward a balance of expertise and experience, such as: (1) a business manager with a record of success in business, preferably in a related but different field; (2) another business manager with a different background, but equally successful; and (3) if available, an academic person with a general management background that encompasses the operations of small businesses. (See Chapter 8 for further details on setting up your administrative structure.)

DETERMINING PERSONNEL REQUIREMENTS

The next organizational step is to determine the duties and responsibilities (job descriptions and specifications) needed to perform the activities of your business. Then, the process of estimating your personnel requirements can be undertaken. (See Chapter 9.)

One problem area seems to be more prevalent in smaller firms than in larger organizations. Frequently the business is closely related to the family unit, and this relationship may contribute to morale problems if outsiders are brought in. The small business owner-manager should be aware of these potential problems and take deliberate steps to prevent them.

DETERMINING YOUR PHYSICAL PLANT NEEDS

There are two important decisions you must now make, namely, (1) what location to choose, and (2) whether to buy (build) or lease your physical facilities.

Location

You should seek that location which satisfies your requirements and provides you optimum benefits. For example, if you are going into the retail business and are considering a specific piece of vacant property, it is desirable to determine the reason behind the vacancy. Often, a particular location seems to be a "born loser," experiencing a whole series of failures. Also, you must be concerned about the means of transportation (foot, car, or public transportation), traffic patterns, and traffic volume.

Factors that should be considered in choosing a location are: access to your work force, availability of utilities, the type of business, relationship to your market, and availability of transportation.

Access to Work Force.   The availability of people with the personal attributes and skills your business requires is essential for success. You should consider the possibility of blending part-time with full-time personnel in order to provide more flexibility and a more economic operation. Another consideration is the distances and types of residential areas from which you will draw people. If you can locate where people can walk to work and possibly even go home for lunch, you may have an advantage in pay negotiation, worker loyalty and interest, as well as better job attendance.

Availability of Utilities.   Access to needed utilities, such as electric power, gas, water, sewerage and steam, is also very important. Two other factors to consider are flexibility in operation and economics (not only the initial installation costs, but also operating costs).

Type of Business.   The type of business you are going to operate, such as retail, service, or manufacturing, will also influence your locational decisions. This factor is important as it relates to access to customers, suppliers, work force, utilities, transportation, and compliance with zoning regulations. The *mission* of the business serves as a basic consideration in seeking the "right" location.

Availability of Vendors.   Is there a sufficient number of vendors to supply the needs of your business? In the selection of vendors, you should determine the types of supportive service each seller can provide. The kinds of support that may be derived are: (1) assistance in designing a product or products; (2) aid in the selection of machinery and plant; (3) technical assistance in solving problems; and (4) assistance with pricing and formulating trade credit practices.

Relationship to the Market.   What is the relationship of the location to your market? Is it a central location? Is there an adequate number of customers in the market area to sustain your business? You must identify and focus on the competitive advantages you can offer that will enable you to obtain your target share of the market. Evaluate any "tie ins" that will enable you to expand your business, such as equipment sales, service, gas, and/or supplies.

Access to Transportation. Can the most economical form of transportation for both your in bound and out bound shipments be made? Are there railroad spurs to the location? Truck lines? Buses?

Buy or Lease

The question of whether to buy or lease your physical plant is important. The supply of capital may be the determining factor. Also, the rate and amount of return you can receive on capital invested in other ways will be another consideration. The nature of space requirements and the availability of a structure will also be significant. You should not overlook the role of depreciation and its effect on cash flow. Also, do your building requirements indicate the need for specialized or general-purpose structure? You should be cautious in committing yourself to a special-purpose structure because of the long-range ramifications of disposing of it if you decide to move or go out of business.

PLANNING YOUR APPROACH TO THE MARKET

Three marketing factors you need to consider before opening your business to the public are: (1) building an image; (2) what channels of distribution to use; and (3) pricing. While these factors are discussed in greater detail in Chapters 16, 17, and 18, those facts you should know before starting your business are provided here.

Some years ago, a man living in the New England area conceived an idea for a new kind of dustpan that could be made of rubber and made in a variety of colors. Lacking the production resources, he had a dozen samples of this new product custom-made.

Armed with his dozen multicolored dustpans, he went to Boston to hawk his wares to Filene's and Jordan-Marsh, neither of whom seemed interested in them. He was sure that housewives would buy his product since it could be made to fit any floor irregularities and would not mar the floor. As he was returning home, irritated with the rejection of his product, these things weighed on his mind.

What could he do to prove his idea was good? While he was passing through Pawtucket, Rhode Island, the idea hit him. "Why not market-test it by calling on housewives?" Pulling into a residential street, he parked his car and set out to ring doorbells. Forty-five minutes later, he returned to his car with only 2 of the 12 left.

Convinced that his idea was good, he developed a company to

market the product. In time, the company grew, its product line ever expanding. When retirement came to the man who started with a dozen multicolored dustpans, he was head of a national company whose sales could be counted in the millions and a personal capital base that would afford an affluent retirement.

Building an Image

A number of factors should be considered in building an image for your firm. What segment of the market offers the best potential opportunity? What advertising media will best reach this market?

A radio station operated on both AM and FM frequencies. After a substantial time period, its sales manager evaluated the results of its efforts to sell advertising, and discovered that its advertising customers obtained 45 percent or more of their business volume from the black community. The members of this community, however, made up a meager portion of the station's FM listening audience. The FM had never attracted the desired volume of advertising revenue. A shift to black disc-jockeys and a program format attuned to this community produced a substantial increase in advertising revenues.

Too much money may be spent on the exterior of the building, the decor, billboards, or an ineffective advertising program. Funds spent in these areas often result in a reduction in the quality of service and merchandise. It would be better to reverse the pattern by giving excellent service and good quality merchandise, for these are remembered longest and provide the desired customer appeal and following.

A hotel coffee shop was located in a small town on a major tourist route. The building of an interstate highway on the periphery of the town has not caused a loss of customers. People say, "I have been coming here for 25 years and I enjoy the service and food." Others say, "I have driven an extra 150 miles to get here." While this business has continued to survive and even be successful, one is aware of numerous other instances where quality and service deteriorated and the business ultimately failed.

Channels of Distribution

The nature of the business and the economic characteristics of the industry will partially determine your channels of distribution. There are various classes of business, and each has a number of options for marketing its products. Some alternatives you have are:

I. Industrial products
   A. Direct sales to customers.
   B. Manufacturers' agents.
   C. Distributors (wholesalers–warehouses).

II. Consumer products
   A. Direct sales.
      1. Door-to-door.
      2. Independent retail outlets.
   B. Wholesalers.
   C. Chain retail outlets.
   D. Establishing your own retail outlets.
      1. Direct ownership.
      2. Franchise.

III. Service

Examples of services are: TV, radio, appliance, and automobile repairing; day-care nursery, catering; real estate, insurance; care of aged; and consumer finance. The usual channel is direct to the ultimate consumer.

Pricing Policies

Whatever the business, pricing is important. However, the focus usually should not be on *price*, but on *service*. In pricing your good or service, you should consider *all the relevant factors*, including costs of production and distribution as well as possible market acceptance, then add an additional percentage to provide you with your planned profit. (See Chapter 21.)

Certain rules of thumb are available for use in determining the price in most businesses. For example, in the restaurant industry total food costs generally have not exceeded 33 percent of the sales price. More recently, a price based on food costing from 33 to 44 percent is believed to be more realistic. In the upper range, the owner may elect to go with word-of-mouth advertising rather than spending money on various advertising media.

A restaurant owner in a college town was not sensitive to the relationship between food cost and price. He was in financial difficulty and sought the aid of the Small Business Administration. A SCORE volunteer was assigned as a consultant. His first question was, "What's the most popular item on your menu?" The restaurant owner replied, "Our $2.25 steak." The consultant asked for a scale and a raw steak. He showed the businessman that the raw steak cost $1.85. Obviously, the reason for the steak's popularity was the mark up of less than 22 percent. It was also the reason why the business was in financial difficulties.

PREPARING YOUR BUDGETS

It is now time to pull together all the revenue and cost items for which you have planned. This process is called budgeting and will be discussed in Chapter 24.

The budget should be considered as an instrument of both planning and control. It helps you plan how you will allocate your firm's scarce resources. The main objective is to maximize your revenue, minimize your cost, and increase your profit. Profit should be included in the total budget. Specific profit figures depend upon many factors, including the type industry you enter, your location, and your efficiency.

Concerning "management information," you need to ask yourself these two questions:

1. What decisions do I need to make?
2. What information do I need in order to make those decisions?

Your answers to these questions should serve as guidelines in preparing your budgets. Some of the items you should consider are: expenses, including the cost of the money you will use (remember that money has a cost, whether it is owned or borrowed), depreciation, obsolescence, utilities, maintenance, supplies, personnel, fringe benefits, insurance, material handling, waste, transportation, cost, and start-up cost; revenues, including sales of your product or service, sale of property, and interest on money invested; and the resulting profit—or loss. Records are needed to aid in developing budgets and cost information and to aid in controlling. This is a good time to plan your basic accounting system and records.

Types of Budgets

The most important budgets for a small firm such as yours are:

1. An operating budget.
2. A capital budget.
3. A cash flow budget.

Operating Budget. In preparing the operating budget, you try to anticipate the costs of obtaining and selling your products and the income received from selling them. This budget will serve as a basis for comparing budgeted activities with actual performance and as a basis for determining the cause of variances from your plans.

Capital Budget. The capital budget reflects your plans for obtaining, replacing, and expanding your physical facilities. It assists you in beginning operations and being able to have the needed buildings, tools, equipment, and other facilities.

Cash Flow Budget. The cash flow budget is a statement of how much *cash* will be needed to pay what expenses at what time, as well as indicating from where the cash will come to pay them. The lack of *ready cash* resources is the primary reason that firms get into an illiquid position, causing a forced liquidation. By using the cash flow budget, such a dilemma may be avoided.

Anticipating Difficulties

At the danger of being called "alarmists," we should point out that you should look realistically at the possibility of failure and begin to prepare for it. In preparing the budget for your new business, you must understand and accept the equity risk and investment required. You should look at the costs involved in acquiring assets, using them, and then having to liquidate the business if it fails. Figure 6–2 should help you understand your risks.

FIGURE 6–2
The Value of Assets in a Going Concern and in Case of Liquidation

Items	Going Concern Value	Liquidation Value
Start-up costs............................	0	0
Cash drain until breakeven level of operation is attained............	0	0
Basic working capital investment for a mature level of business (includes cash position adequate to take care of __weeks of payroll and operating expenses)......	Good value	Cash 100% Accounts receivable depends on quality of debtors or depends on inventory market (less handling cost)
Equity in plant, product, and equipment........................	Some value	Some value
Goodwill and other intangible assets............................	No value	No value

LOCATING SOURCE OF FUNDS

After you have budgeted the amount of funds needed for capital expenditures and to begin operations, you must locate the sources from which you can obtain those funds.

Your ability to raise funds is one of the significant determinants of the size and type of business you can enter. You should recognize that methods of financing change and that there is no one best method. While some methods have advantages over others, the attitude and desires of the investors or lenders will determine the sources of financing available to you at a given point in time.

The following discussion should help you find the needed money to begin operations. (See Chapter 7 and the related materials in Parts IV and VI.)

Your Own Funds

Some people have the philosophy of using only their personal funds and that borrowing is to be avoided in any business venture. Other people believe that they should use as little of their personal funds as possible, and instead they should obtain as much leverage as possible by using the funds of others.

Assuming that you either must, or wish to, use funds of others, there are several sources of outside funds. Two documents that can be of great benefit to you in obtaining money to begin operations are the mini-proposal and the business plan. An example of each of these is shown in the appendix at the end of this chapter.

Funds of Other Individuals

You may find other private individuals with excess funds who are interested in investing in a venture opportunity. You may find such a person among your friends, or through your attorney, CPA, banker, or securities dealer. These people often have a specific preference for the type of business in which they are willing to invest. In general, they prefer a business with which they are familiar.

Commercial and industrial financial institutions may provide you with funds. The proportion of funds such institutions make available may range from 25 to 60 percent of the value of the total assets. Usually, the cost of such financing is higher than other alternatives, but such funds may be the most accessible. These institutions may help you through:

1. Loans on your fixed assets.
2. Lease-purchase arrangements.
3. Accounts receivable financing.
4. Factoring arrangements on accounts receivable.

Trade Credit

Trade credit should not be overlooked. This source of credit refers to the purchases of inventory, equipment, and supplies that are made on an open account in accordance with customary terms for this type of business.

Commercial Banks

In the past, commercial banks have been a good source of credit for business managers having funds of their own and with proved successful experience. More recently, because of the higher rate of return, banks have shifted a greater portion of their funds into consumer financing. The large demand for funds in recent years has pushed interest rates and terms of bank loans to higher levels and less favorable terms.

You should also consider the following services offered by commercial banks:

1. General account (demand deposit).
2. Payroll accounting.
3. Income tax service.
4. Various computerized services.
5. Lock box collections to expedite payments and cash flow.
6. More individualized services.

Investment Banks

Investment banks serve to bring together those who need funds and various sources of funds. Many of them are sound and have developed a reputation for integrity and providing their clients with good service.

You should choose from bankers who specialize in regional business, for they are frequently more familiar with the geographic area, the economics of the region, and are accustomed to servicing specialized needs. These bankers also maintain relationships with insurance companies, large individual investors, and investment managers of pension trusts.

The availability of an investment banker and his service are determined by:

1. Your present financial requirements.
2. Your market potential.
3. Your projected status for two years in advance.

Unless you can reasonably anticipate that your firm will be classified as a regional or national firm within two years, you cannot expect to have access to an investment banker.

Major Nonfinancial Corporations

Major producing corporations, through their financial subsidiaries, often play a significant role in financing certain types of activities which are closely related to some phase of their operations. Some examples are:

General Electric, Westinghouse, and others have been active in helping finance mobile homes and apartments. The mobile home manufacturers will install the appliances of a specific supplier, who then helps finance the producer. In addition, the appliance-financing subsidiary often finances the sale of the home to the ultimate consumer.

The "Big Three" auto firms operate through their financial subsidiaries to aid their dealers in financing dealerships, provide a floor plan arrangement for financing the dealers' new car inventories, and finance the sale of cars (including used cars) to customers.

Insurance Companies

Insurance companies may be a source of funds for your firm. You can go directly to the company, or contact its agent, an investment banker, or a mortgage banker.

While insurance companies have traditionally engaged in debt financing, more recently they have demanded that equity purchase warrants be included as a part of the total package.

Small Business Administration

One of the primary purposes of the SBA is to provide financial assistance.[1] The main difference between the SBA and a private lending agency is in the terms of the loan. Though banks may be limited by regulation or law on the terms of their loans, the SBA tends to permit longer periods of repayment and make other concessions to small firms. Yet, as far as credit risks are concerned, the SBA has requisites very similar to banks. The borrower should be a good credit risk.

The SBA has been limited in its financial activities by the constraints imposed by Congress in allocating funds for loan purposes. The types of loans it can provide to you, and the manner of their utilization, are discussed in the following paragraphs.

Direct Loans. Direct loans usually fit into three categories: (1) *ethnic loans*—significant interest has been shown in this type of loan, especially loans ranging up to $25,000; (2) *catastrophe* or *disaster loans* —these loans are made in an area where some form of disaster has struck. The terms are usually three percent interest and an amortization period of 20 years; and (3) *small loans*—made to business firms needing between $1,500 and $3,000. Direct loans have been restricted because of the limited supply of funds.

---

[1] You should understand that Congress periodically enacts new legislation, and this determines the kind of assistance the Small Business Administration provides. We suggest, therefore, that you contact the nearest district office of the SBA to determine what type of assistance you may be able to obtain from this federal agency.

Participating Loans. With participating loans, the SBA takes a portion of the total loan on a direct cash participation basis, and a bank or other lender provides the remainder. In this type of loan, the SBA assumes a subordinated position to the other lender in the event of liquidation. Because funds are limited, only a small number of these loans are made.

Guaranteed Loans. Guaranteed loans have been the most popular in recent years. The SBA guarantees the lender 90 percent of the loan up to a total of $350,000. The borrower may contact the SBA directly or through a bank whose policy is to make SBA guaranteed loans. The practice of using the bank as an intermediary seems to produce more satisfactory results.

The SBA is now formalizing programs to help banks resell some of their guaranteed loans. This is creating an active secondary market in the loans guaranteed by the SBA.[2]

Lease Guaranty Program. The lease guaranty program was initially established to enable small businesses to locate in major shopping centers where a credit rating of AAA is required. Current regulations require:

1. Paying three months' rent at the outset to be placed in escrow.
2. The amount of lease that may be guaranteed is limited to $2.5 million.
3. A 2.8 percent single insurance premium is required for guaranteeing the total rent of the lease.

Small Business Investment Corporations

SBICs are chartered by the SBA and make qualified SBA loans. For each dollar the SBIC put into a loan, the SBA matches.

Loans are usually made for a period of five to ten years. The SBICs may stipulate that they be given a certain portion of stock purchase warrants or stock options, or they may make a combination of a loan and a stock purchase. The latter combination has been preferred.

Industrial Development Corporations

Industrial development corporations have greater freedom in the types of loans they are able to make. They make "501" or "502" loans.

501 Loans. 501 loans are granted from state-chartered industrial development corporations whose initial capital is provided by member commercial banks that also are members of the Federal Reserve System. These corporations make term loans, working capital loans, mortgage

---

[2] "A New Market for SBA Loans," *Business Week*, July 4, 1977, p. 54.

loans, and contract performance loans, and can borrow up to one half of the loan amount from the SBA.

502 Loans. 502 financing is arranged by an industrial development corporation established by an individual community. The amount of equity and number of stockholders required are determined by the community's population. The SBA has a ceiling of $350,000 per individual borrower, and the repayment period may extend for 25 years.

Economic Development Administration (EDA)

The EDA makes a variety of direct loans to industries located in communities in areas classified as economically depressed or in communities that are declared as regional economic growth centers. This financial assistance usually starts where the SBA authority ends, i.e., $350,000.

The direct loans made by the EDA may be used for fixed assets or working capital. In addition, the EDA may extend guarantees on loans to private borrowers from private lending institutions, as well as guarantees of rental payments of leases from qualified lessors for fixed assets.

The agency may lend up to 65 percent of the total cost of the assets for which the loans are made, but the agency prefers to remain in the 50 percent range. A rule of thumb in determining the amount of a loan is from an average of $5,200 to a minimum of $10,000 per employee for each new job the project will create. The rate of interest is reviewed quarterly. While the life of the loan may reach 25 years, the average maturity is 18.

It is suggested that you contact your local planning and development commission or Chamber of Commerce to determine your qualification for EDA financial assistance. Congressional authorization changes from time to time, so you should check to see what types of assistance are available at any given time. Recently, the tendency has been to liberalize the scope of EDA financial assistance.

State Employment Agencies

Grants may be available through your local state employment agency for use in training and developing your employees. Bases for this type of assistance may be: the changing nature of work, training of new employees lacking the needed skills, or for training employees for a new business for which the needed skills are lacking. Changes occur from time to time in the provisions of the authorizing legislation, and it is suggested that you check with your local state employment agency to determine what kinds of assistance may be available.

Agricultural Loans

A number of sources of funds for agricultural loans are federally funded. The Cooperative Extension Service, or one of its local agents, may be checked for information concerning availability and procedures.
Some sources of funds are:

1. Federal Land Bank Association.
2. Production Credit Corporation.
3. Farm Home Administration.

IMPLEMENTING YOUR PLANS

Now you are ready to take the plunge! It is time to obtain your funds, get a charter, purchase your facilities and supplies, hire and train your people, and start operating.

Capital Procurement

Using your capital structure plan and the sources of funds you have developed, obtain the funds, put them in your checking account, and start writing checks.

Corporate Charter and Permits

You should obtain the services of an attorney in acquiring your charter, if you are incorporating. He can also help you obtain any occupational licenses and permits.

Contracting and Purchasing Facilities and Supplies

After the funds, charter, and permits are obtained, you should refer to your timetable and start negotiating contracts and purchasing equipment, products, and supplies needed to run your business.

Personnel Selection and Training

As the time approaches for the beginning of operations, you should refer to your organization chart, job titles, and job specifications in order to determine your personnel requirements. Methods of selecting and procuring personnel will be influenced by local conditions. The presence of a community college, liberal arts college, university, or vocational-technical school will influence your decision to use all full-time employees or to use some full-time and some part-time employees. You can receive assistance in obtaining prospective employees from institutional placement offices, state employment agencies, and private employment agencies. It may be necessary to use local advertising media to attract prospective employees, but this practice usually increases the amount of time required for screening.

The nature of your business and the background of the newly hired employees will influence the amount of time needed, and the methods to be used, in employee training. (See Chapter 10.)

BEGINNING YOUR OPERATIONS

You are now a business manager; you are operating your own firm, you have all the risks and you hope to receive the benefits and rewards of "being on your own." Some unforeseen problems should be anticipated, however, for they will surely occur during the "crank-up" period.

SUMMARY

The material in this chapter has outlined the steps you should follow in establishing a new business of your own. You should by now have:

1. Developed and followed a realistic timetable.
2. Established your business goals and objectives.
3. Set up your organization structure, including the legal, financial, and administrative aspects.
4. Estimated, selected, and trained your people.
5. Determined your physical plant and facility needs, and contracted for, or purchased, them.
6. Planned your marketing activities, including advertising, channels of distribution, and pricing.
7. Prepared budgets.
8. Found sources of funds and obtained the money needed.
9. Secured your charter and the permits needed to begin operating *your own business.*

QUESTIONS FOR FURTHER DISCUSSION

1. Explain how you would determine the organizational structure of your business.
2. Discuss the procedure for estimating your personnel requirements.
3. What are the factors that should be considered in determining the location of your business?
4. What is meant by "building an image" for your firm?
5. Describe how you would set your pricing policy.
6. What is a budget and why is it useful for a business?
7. Explain briefly the major sources from which you might raise capital.
8. Describe the Small Business Administration and how it might help you raise funds.

APPENDIX: AN EXAMPLE OF A MINI-PROPOSAL
AND A BUSINESS PLAN[1]

A. Mini-proposal

The mini-proposal is typically a three- or four-page summary of a business plan sent to potential investors to determine whether there is any interest in the venture. If investors are interested, they will request a complete business plan.

Aspects covered in a mini-proposal are:

1. Amount of capital required—a dollar range of investments is often preferred by investors.
2. Type of industry—investors often are interested, or uninterested, in certain industries.
3. Nature of the enterprise.
4. Sales and profit projections for three to five years.
5. Management—highlights of careers of each founder.

B. Business Plan

A business plan is written by the individual(s) responsible for starting and operating a company. It covers the company objectives and describes the steps necessary to achieve them. It should provide information about the conditions in the industry and provide milestones— for example, completion of product development—against which progress can be determined.

When preparing your business plan, you should consider the information needs of bankers, suppliers, customers, investors, and employees.

Your managers should participate in developing the business plan. This participation should make the plan more "salable" to them, illustrate their interdependence, and build their commitment.

You may desire to obtain the services of others—business consultants, lawyers, CPAs, bankers, stockbrokers, customers, suppliers, and government agencies—to aid in developing a plan.

The important aspects of a business plan are:

1. Brief description of business, including operating history, if any.
2. Directors, including names and corporate affiliations.
3. Management team—brief resumes covering qualifications for attaining company objectives.
4. Management compensation and incentives.
5. Outside professional assistance; e.g., attorney, CPA.

---

[1] Donald M. Dible, *Winning the Money Game* (Santa Clara, Calif.: The Entrepreneur Press, 1975), pp. 87–110.

6. Organization chart.
7. Capital required and its specific uses.
8. Company's current financial condition.
9. Major products:
   a. Detailed description, including photographs and/or drawings.
   b. Uses.
   c. Unique characteristics.
   d. Warranties.
   e. Profit margins.
   f. Costs.
   g. Patent protection.
   h. Technological advantages.
   i. Research and development.
   j. Product liability.
10. Market served:
    a. Overall market.
    b. Market studies.
    c. Ease of entry.
    d. Overall growth rate.
    e. Names of potential customers.
    f. Names of competitors.
    g. Expectations concerning percentage market share.
11. Market strategy:
    a. Market segments.
    b. Channels of distribution.
    c. Advertising plan.
    d. Methods of financing sales.
    e. Pricing.
    f. Sales organization.
12. Manufacturing:
    a. Assembly characteristics.
    b. Vertical integration.
    c. Product cost breakdown.
    d. Tooling cost.
    e. Special or general-purpose equipment.
    f. Economies of scale.
    g. Supplier relationships.
    h. Availability of raw materials.
13. Appendixes:
    a. Pro-forma projections for three to five years.
    b. Legal structure of business.
    c. Founders' resumes and financial statements.
    d. Founders' compensation.
    e. Market surveys.

7

Planning for Your Business

Now that you have studied the economic feasibility of your firm and have decided whether to buy an existing firm or start a new one, you are about ready to begin the planning process. First, though, let us take an overview of the managing process.

Let us assume that you have chosen to manage your prospective business, rather than to hire a professional manager to run it for you. As the owner-manager, you will need to perform certain basic managerial functions effectively in order to have a profitable company. These functions are shown in Figure 7–1.

Although these managerial functions are shown separately and in sequence, they are not so neatly separated in the real world of small business; you often perform them together. For practical purposes, however, we discuss them separately and in the order shown.

The planning and organizing functions are discussed in this chapter and the next; the staffing and directing functions are covered in Part III; and the others are discussed throughout the text.

Planning must be done *both before and after* operations are begun. While no effort is made in this text to separate preliminary planning and planning in an ongoing organization, you should recognize that the two do exist.

The need for effective planning for small business is emphasized— along with some suggestions for making planning more effective—and planning your strategies is covered in this chapter. Then, the steps involved in planning the legal, financial, and administrative structure of your firm are discussed in the next chapter.

FIGURE 7-1

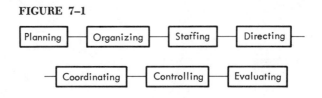

NEED FOR EFFECTIVE PLANNING

Planning is probably the most difficult management function to perform in a small business because the owner-manager is too involved in day-to-day operations, does not see the immediate results from his or her efforts, is fearful about the company's future, and for other reasons mentioned later. Yet, owners and managers in those firms need to plan as thoroughly as—if not more thoroughly than—managers of larger companies. The reasons are that most small firms:

1. Do not always have sufficient resources to overcome their future problems.
2. Cannot afford to underwrite losses that can occur while adjusting to unexpected changes.

You should recognize that changing circumstances will probably affect your plans. A means should be provided for modifying your company's objectives to meet such changes. Activities that are profitable today may not be so in the future.

Your company is especially vulnerable to bold moves by competitors. Besides managing your company well internally, you should keep yourself informed about your competitors and be able to predict closely what they will do.

Planning is especially important during your company's first year of operations. When you approach a banker, one of his first questions will concern a proposed budget.

You should delegate some planning, particularly operational and program planning, because your lower-level managers will be personally involved in carrying out the operational plans and programs while the owner-manager should be free to devote his/her full attention to executive-level planning. Your employees' ideas are often helpful in providing solutions to your firm's problems. In addition, you should consult periodically with an attorney, an insurance agent, and various other specialists (such as a tax accountant).

Too often, small business managers do not analyze popular programs adopted by other companies before adopting them for their own operations. The suitability of such programs should be thoroughly studied to be certain whether they will be beneficial for your company.

Irrespective of how well plans have been formulated, some crises will arise. You should act decisively in these situations.

HOW TO PLAN

You should start planning by getting a complete picture of your operations. The types of information that you need in making adequate plans are:

1. A brief description of your company's present practices in all important areas, including products, purchasing, quality control, labor relations, and sales outlets.
2. A statement of your present organization, procedures, and reports.
3. A list of the principal external factors—such as government regulations, the state of the economy, competition, the community environment, technology, and the labor markets—that affect your company most.
4. A list of changes you expect in any of these factors in the next few years.
5. A list of the main strengths and weaknesses of your present operation (based on items 1 through 4).

You should find that writing these things down clarifies your own thinking and helps you convey your ideas to others who will participate in implementing the plans. You should be able to give objective consideration to the areas being planned, when you plan.

Planning consists of these steps:

1. Recognizing and making a definitive statement of the problem.
2. Collecting and classifying relevant facts.
3. Setting forth alternative courses of action.
4. Evaluating the pros and cons associated with these courses.
5. Selecting the course of action (the plan).

In order to ensure that your plans are complete, you should be able to answer these questions:

1. *Why* must it be done?
2. *What* action is necessary?
3. *Where* will it take place?
4. *Who* will do it?
5. *How* will it be done?
6. *How much* control (including kind and degree) should be exercised?

The sequence of these questions is also important. The "why" of the action should be determined first, while the questions of control should come last.

LEVELS AND TYPES OF PLANNING

As far as *level* of planning is concerned, you should be able to distinguish between "organizational," "executive-level," "operational," and "project" or "program" levels of planning. Then, you need to determine the appropriate *length* of the planning period.

Levels of Planning

Organizational planning occurs before and during the organization of the business. It is involved with determining the objectives of the firm, the legal and financial structure, and administrative aspects, including organizational relationships. This type of planning is necessary before you can begin operating your firm.

Executive level planning is broad in scope, long-range, and abstract. It entails selecting the company's objectives and policies and establishing programs and procedures for achieving them. Long-run trends in income levels, market size, product use, business location, and manufacturing and merchandising operations are involved. This type of planning is neglected by many small business managers. Too often they are engaged in fire-fighting, crisis-type management and are so immersed in daily operations and routines that they cannot perform executive-level planning.

Operational planning is limited to separate departmental or functional activities. It tends to be narrow in scope, short-range, and concrete. It depends to a considerable extent on prior planning decisions made at the executive level. Often, operational plans consist of budgets which are prepared one year in advance with a detailed breakdown by months.

Planning is also concerned with a specific *project* or *program*. However, you should recognize that a particular course of action in implementing a project should conform to the overall operations of your company.

Length of Planning Period

You should also be able to differentiate between long-range and short-range planning.

Long-range planning takes into account trends in income levels, industry developments, growth of population, and mobility of people and how these factors affect product or service usage, market size, business location, production and distribution processes, and operations. The manager of a small business should forecast whether the volume of sales will be adequate to justify high initial costs of a product.

Short-range planning is more immediate in nature, covering a period of three to six months, a forthcoming season, or—at most—one year. In day-to-day operations, this planning is important because it allows the owner or manager to solve specific problems. Short-range plans should contribute to, and be consistent with, long-range plans. Also, small companies should probably strive to excel in this type planning, as flexibility is their strong suit. The following case illustrates this point.

In response to strong competition and reduced profits, a manufacturer, whose background included a career as an outstanding salesman, decided to continually expand sales.[1]

Results: Sales were increased. The need for working capital to carry inventories and receivables was increased. In negotiations with a lender, the latter wanted a high rate of interest, which practically eliminated the net profit on the increased sales.

Failure: Proper planning was not performed, since other functions than sales—production and financing—were not considered.

Solution: The manufacturer posed and answered these questions:

a.   What is the business goal?
b.   Can it be achieved, and if so, how?
c.   What is the future of the business?

An emphasis on short-term planning does not mean that long-range planning *can be ignored*. The following illustrates this truth.

The management of a consumer durable goods manufacturing company set a goal of industry leadership for its company. A 35 percent share of the market within five years was specified.

Results: The company attained only a 15 percent share.

Cause: Quality products were priced competitively and marketed aggressively, but were styled above consumer tastes.

Failure: Market research was not undertaken to determine consumers' tastes.

Solution: Replanning of products, which included a market study of potential customers, was accomplished.[2]

---

[1] Adapted from Bruce E. DeSpelden, "Management Planning for Sound Growth," *Management Aids Annual no. 9* (Washington, D.C.: Small Business Administration, 1963), pp. 8–15.

[2] Adapted from T. Stanley Gallagher, "Sound Objectives Help Build Profits," *Management Aids Annual no. 11* (Washington, D.C.: Small Business Administration, 1965), pp. 1–7.

Why do so many small business owner-managers neglect long-range planning? Certain barriers, such as the following, tend to discourage them:

1. Fear—Some believe that careful thought about their companies' future will reveal new trouble or problems.
2. Inexactness—Many believe that planning is so inexact that it does not seem worth doing, for no matter how carefully they plan, things do not work out according to the plan.
3. Changeability—Some complain that plans change too rapidly to make planning worthwhile.
4. Lack of planning knowledge—You should consider this approach:
   a. Set goals and objectives.
   b. Develop plans to achieve goals.
   c. Assess the progress being made to achieve the objectives.
5. Lack of proper time and place—You should first do the things that should be done, not the things you like to do.

Planning to Use Your Time Wisely

Do you know how to use your time wisely? Its proper use can help you to run your business more effectively. Daily problems tend to keep you from planning properly. It might be revealing for you or your secretary to record how you spend your time during, say, 5-, 10-, or 15-minute intervals for a week. By totaling your time by categories, you may find that you spend too much time on activities such as solving production problems, talking on the telephone and/or talking to people, and too little on more important activities.

In planning your use of time, you should survey the time you normally spend on various activities. For a period of time, say four weeks, record every minute of time spent on every activity during the day. Then, analyze these data to determine those projects and tasks involving the greatest expenditure of time and the factors responsible for any waste of time. You should then plan your workday based upon this analysis. Perhaps you should deliberately arrange for planning by using evenings and weekends.

To help you analyze your own activities and their relative usefulness to achieving your firm's objectives, you should ask these questions:

1. Can this activity be eliminated or delegated?
2. Can this activity be combined with others?
3. Can the time required to perform the activity be reduced?
4. Can the sequence of activities be changed?

Some other methods of saving your valuable time are:

1. Organizing the work, including delegation of as many duties as feasible to your subordinates.
2. Selecting a competent secretary to sort out unimportant mail, screen incoming calls, and keep a schedule of appointments and activities.
3. Using dictating equipment.
4. Adhering to appointment and business conference times.
5. Preparing an agenda for meetings, and confining discussions to only those items on the agenda; making "follow-up" assignments to specific subordinates.

SOME SELECTED PLANNING FUNCTIONS AND TYPES OF PLANS

Figure 7–2 shows some of the more important planning functions and types of plans that you—as a small business owner—will probably have to make. The second of these, "objectives," has already been covered in previous chapters. Yet, it should be stated here that the poorest part of planning in many small companies is the setting of overall objectives. Determining a company's objectives in terms of markets or products is extremely difficult because of the problems involved in evaluating the external environment in which the firm is operating. Also, an appraisal of the company's internal resources is not always easy!

The third, "strategies," will now be discussed in detail. The others will be discussed later in their context in the following chapters.

PLANNING YOUR STRATEGIES

As shown in Figure 7–2, strategies are major objectives or goals *defining what business your company is actually in, the kind of enterprise it is,* and *the plans for achieving your goals and objectives.*

Your company's strategy should be deliberately determined and made known to *all* employees to aid in performing long-range planning and to serve as an inspiration to organizational effort.

As shown in Chapter 4, you begin policy formulating by *studying the economy,* then *the industry,* and then *your own company.* Relative to the *economy,* you try to identify opportunities and problems (risks or threats), such as technological, economic, social, and political changes. For example, some factors are changes in population, government, or social mores; inflation; war; and others.

Industry refers to the one that you are entering. The purpose of an industry analysis is to predict growth, profitability, and key factors affecting success.

A comparison of *your company's* strengths and weaknesses with your competitors' strengths and weaknesses should be made. Also, your com-

FIGURE 7-2
Planning Function and Types of Plans

Planning Functions	Examples

Planning
  Selection from among alternatives
    of future courses of action for
    the firm as a whole and for each
    department.	

Objectives
  Purposes, goals, results of the firm
    and its parts.
	Company Objectives—Overall objective is to perform useful service for society.
	Product Line—Manufactures and distributes high-quality, custom-made, special living room and dining room furniture.
	Scope of Market—Markets its furniture in the states of Georgia, Florida, Alabama, and Louisiana.
	Personal Objectives—Statement of the type of life you wish to lead.

Strategies
  Major objectives or goals defining
    what business the company is in
    and the kind of company it is;
    plans for achieving these goals.	

Policies
  Overall guides to action which
    provide some consistency in
    decision making, particularly in
    repetitive situations.
	Personnel Policy—Promoting from within, whereby preference for promotion is given to present employees.

pany's strengths should be matched with key factors for success in the industry as shown by the analysis you performed earlier.

Your company strategy should:

1. Identify the product-market scope of your firm—the particular products or services that it will promote.
2. Select the basic ways in which those products or services will be created.
3. Determine the major steps necessary for your company to assume the desired course of action.
4. Establish the standards used to measure achievement.

Your company's strategies should provide central direction to the activities of your organization and to your people. The public or market

FIGURE 7–2 (*continued*)

Planning Functions	*Examples*
Standards Values to be used as norms; these are necessary for control, because they assist in measurement.	*Specifications*—Machines and materials should be arranged in order and close together in order to produce economically and effectively.
Budgets Plans of income or outgo, or both; including money, sales items, purchased items, etc.	*Sales budgets, cash budgets, pro forma income statements* and *balance sheets.*
Procedure Series of related tasks to be performed in a given sequence, using an established method of performing the work. A procedure includes how and when each task is to take place, and by whom it is to be performed.	*Selection Procedure*—Used in selecting employees with the proper qualifications and placing them in positions in the firm where their talents can best be used.
Method Prescribed manner for performing a given task. A method deals with a task comprising one step of a procedure, and specifies how this one step is to be performed.	*Task*—Performed by a production employee in the machining department.
Program Comprehensive plan which includes objectives, standards, budgets, policies, procedures, and methods. A given program may not necessarily include all of these components.	*Production Program*—Which designates the materials, processes to be followed, machines to be utilized, production schedules to be met, and warehouses to which shipments are made.

should also be informed about your company's particular products or services.

SUMMARY

In this chapter, we assumed that you would run your business yourself and perform the managerial functions of planning, organizing, staffing, directing, coordinating, controlling, and evaluating.

Planning is selecting the future courses of action for the firm as a whole and for each department within it. The types of plans you will need are objectives, strategies, policies, standards, budgets, procedures, methods, and programs.

Small firms are especially adept at doing short-range planning because of their flexibility.

Some barriers to effective planning are fear, inexactness, rapid change, lack of knowledge, and lack of proper time and place. However, these barriers can be partially overcome.

Planning consists of the following steps:

1. Recognizing and making a statement of the problem.
2. Collecting and classifying relevant facts.
3. Setting forth alternative courses of action.
4. Evaluating the pros and cons associated with these courses.
5. Selecting the course of action (the plan).

QUESTIONS FOR FURTHER DISCUSSION

1. Why is the following question critical? "If you own a small company, should you hire someone else to manage it for you or should you manage it yourself?"
2. Cite six questions that should be answered to ensure that plans are complete.
3. Define and illustrate the following types of plans: (a) objectives; (b) policies; and (c) budgets.
4. Why is planning your strategies so important? Explain.
5. List some reasons why many small business managers neglect long-range planning.
6. List the steps in planning.

8

Planning the Legal, Financial, and Administrative Structure of Your Firm

Now that you have planned your strategies for your firm, you are about ready to start managing it. You have at least three more important decisions to make, however. First, you must determine what legal form you wish your enterprise to have. Second, you must decide your financial structure. Third, you must decide how to organize it for effective operations.

The material in this chapter should help you make these important choices. First, though, a word of caution is in order. While we will provide you with a summary of the most important basics in these areas, complete coverage is not feasible—or even desirable. Instead, we recommend that you seek the professional assistance of a lawyer specializing in business and corporate law, a reputable CPA, and/or a banker familiar with local business conditions.

DETERMINING LEGAL FORM

In many small businesses, too little attention is paid to selecting objectively the legal form that best serves the owner's interests. There seems to be an appalling lack of knowledge relating to the advantages and disadvantages of using the various forms of legal organization. Our intent is to provide you with a better understanding of the legal form a business may have. The most popular of these legal forms are the: (1) proprietorship; (2) partnership; (3) corporation; (4) holding company; and (5) trust.[1]

---

[1] If you wish further information on this subject without seeing a lawyer, refer to Harold F. Lusk, et al., *Business Law: Principles and Cases,* 4th U.C.C. ed. (Homewood, Ill.: Richard D. Irwin, Inc., 1978).

Proprietorship

A proprietorship is an enterprise owned by a single individual. It is the easiest and simplest form of business to organize. Many people prefer this type of organization because of its simplicity and their inherent preference for individual control. It does provide for relative freedom of action and control, as well as being simple to enter and leave. In these respects, you may find it an attractive form to use.

You should consider at least two negative factors, though. First, as you and your business are one and the same, you and it cannot legally be distinguished and separated. Consequently, the legal life of the business terminates with your death: some legal action must be taken to reactivate and reinstate it. Second, you have unlimited liability for the debts of the firm. If the firm does not possess sufficient assets to pay for all of its obligations, you must use your personal assets to pay for them. Conversely, if you have unpaid personal debts, the creditors can use the assets of your business to satisfy their demands.

About four out of five of all businesses in the United States are proprietorships. The proportion is even higher for small businesses.

Partnership

A partnership is the joining together of two or more individuals to form an organization. Partnerships are quite popular because of these *advantages:*

1. Pooling of the resources of more than one individual.
2. Specific specialized skills possessed by the individual partners.
3. Division of labor and management responsibility.

Partnerships are more effective than proprietorships in raising financial resources and in obtaining better management.

Yet, there are *disadvantages* inherent in the partnership arrangement, including:

1. Death of any of the partners terminates the life of the partnership. This may be offset by an agreement that states that the remaining partner(s) will purchase the interest of the deceased partner from his estate. Frequently, the partnership itself carries insurance to cover this contingency.
2. Members of a general partnership, or the general partners in a limited partnership, have unlimited liability for the debts of the firm.
3. Partners are responsible for the acts of each and every other partner.
4. A partner cannot obtain bonding protection against the acts of the other partner(s).
5. An impasse may develop when the partners become incompatible.

Because of this last disadvantage, you should include in your partnership agreement a "buy-sell" arrangement to provide for the perpetuation of the business. This clause can be activated in the event of one or more of the following:

1. An impasse develops between the partners in reaching an agreement on an important issue.
2. One or more of the partners develops other interests and wishes to leave the partnership.
3. A partner dies.
4. A conflict of interests develops.

Types of Partnerships. Partnerships may be general or limited. In a *general partnership,* each partner is held liable for the acts of the other partners. A *limited partnership* can be created only by compliance with a state's statutory requirements. Such a partnership is composed of one or more *general partners* and one or more *limited partners.* The firm is managed by the general partners, who have unlimited personal liability for the partnership's debts. The personal liability of the limited partners is limited to the amount of capital contributed by them.

The exemption from personal liability of limited partners is conditional upon their not participating in any way in the management of the firm. The limited partners *are* permitted, however, to be employees of the firm. Unfortunately, legal decisions do not make it very clear as to how far the limited partners can go in giving advice or reviewing management decision making without losing their exemption from personal liability. There is no requirement that a limited partnership so designate itself in its name or otherwise in its dealings, though the surnames of the limited partners may not be used in the firm name.

Tests of a Partnership. It is sometimes difficult to tell whether an enterprise is a proprietorship, partnership, or corporation. There is no simple test for the existence of a partnership, but the major requirements are: the intent of the owners, co-ownership of the business, and carrying on the business for a profit. Also, no formalities are required to create a partnership. You may form one and not realize it.

As a general rule, the sharing of profits, together with having a voice in the management of a business, are sufficient evidence to imply the existence of a partnership.

Rights of the Partners. If there is no agreement to the contrary, each partner has an equal voice in the management of the business. Also, a majority of the partners has the legal right to make decisions pertaining to the daily operations of the business. All partners, however, must consent to the making of fundamental changes in the structure itself. Each partner's share of the profits is presumed to be his or her only compensation and, in the absence of any other agreement, the profits and losses are distributed equally.

Corporation

A corporation is sometimes defined as a legal entity, or an artificial being, whose life exists at the pleasure of the courts of law. The formation of a corporation is more formal and complex than is required for the other legal forms. The minimum number of persons required as stockholders varies with individual state laws. Commonly, the number varies from three to five, and in many cases two of these may be "dummies" who serve as incorporators in name only and remain inactive as far as the activities of the firm are concerned. The procedure for formation is usually legally defined and requires the services of an attorney. Incorporation fees frequently amount to $300 to $1,000.

Advantages and Disadvantages.   The primary *advantages* the corporate form offers you as a small investor are:

1. It is a legal entity separate and distinct from you as an individual.
2. It offers permanence. If you or another one of the owners dies, the shares can be transferred to others without affecting the legal life of the firm.
3. Your liability for the firm's debts is limited to the amount you invest in its stock. Your private resources cannot be touched.
4. You can have representative management.
5. Large amounts of capital can be raised relatively easily. Some authorities would question the validity of this statement.

Some offsetting *disadvantages* that might keep you from using this form of structure are:

1. Taxes and fees are high.
2. The procedures, reports, and statements required become cumbersome and burdensome.
3. Your powers are limited to those stated in the charter.
4. You may have difficulty doing business in another state.
5. The other stockholders may not be interested in the firm.
6. It tends to be a more impersonal form of business.

Because of the limited liability feature, the corporate form is considered superior to all other forms of organization.

Other Considerations.   If other individuals are involved in your venture, and you decide to incorporate, a pre-incorporation agreement should be drawn up and signed by the incorporators. This agreement should provide protection against any member, or members, of the group taking off on their own with the proprietary basis for establishing the organization. It at least provides you the restitution of damages that may have been incurred.

In order to protect you and the other parties involved, a buy-sell arrangement for the major stockholders should be included in the articles of incorporation. Also, if the success of the venture is dependent on your, or certain other individuals', participation in the firm, "key man insurance" should be carried on you and those persons. This type of insurance will protect the resources of the firm in the event of loss of such a person and provide protection during the period of adjustment that follows (see Chapter 24).

Adequate bond and insurance coverage against losses that result from the acts of employees and others should be maintained. Also, liability and Workman's Compensation insurance coverage should be maintained.

Board of Directors. Most state incorporation statutes require that the stockholders elect a board of directors who represent their interests. Several important functions of a board are:

1. Appoint the company president and influence the selection of other company officers, such as vice president, secretary, and treasurer.
2. Meet regularly with the officers to review the company's progress.
3. Assist in the formulation of policy.
4. Establish salaries of company officers.
5. Provide for management succession in the company.
6. Offer good management counseling services during board meetings and in private consultations outside the meetings.
7. Effect changes in the management of the company.[2]

Company officers are responsible to the board of directors for day-to-day operations.

Board members are often "centers of influence" and can assist in increasing company sales. The number of directors should be odd to insure that a majority will exist when votes are taken on key decisions (as long as every member votes). The minimum number of directors specified in many statutes is five.

Sources of effective directors are diverse. Among the possibilities are: experienced businesspeople; investors; college professors representing disciplines relevant to the company's operations; retired bankers; and professionals, such as attorneys, CPAs, or business consultants. The value of these professionals on the board is debatable. Their advice may be valuable. On the other hand, if company officers decided that their services were unsatisfactory, the problem of replacement could be troublesome.

Board members are generally compensated for their services by fixed payments—$25 to $100 or more—for each meeting they attend.

Difficulties are experienced in obtaining outsiders to serve on the boards of small companies because liability suits may be filed against them by disgruntled stockholders, employees, customers, or suppliers.

---

[2] Donald M. Dible, *Up Your Own Organization!* (Santa Clara, Calif.: The Entrepreneur Press, 1971), pp. 140–44.

Holding Company

As your firm grows larger, or as you wish to expand your activities while conserving your own resources, you might consider it desirable to establish a parent corporation to serve as a holding company for your corporation. Under certain conditions, you may gain tax advantages from this arrangement. Furthermore, the assets of the parent company may be protected by limiting the liability.

Trust

For estate and other reasons identified under the tax laws, the trust arrangement established a method of providing the owner of a business with certain tax advantages. A popular one in recent years has been the "real estate investment trust," which gives higher tax-bracket individuals certain income tax advantages.

A trust differs from a corporation in that it is established for a specific period of time—or until certain designated events have occurred. It is administered by a trustee, or a board of trustees. The trust receives specific assets from the person, or persons, establishing it. The trust covenant defines the purpose of the trust, names the beneficiary or beneficiaries, and establishes a formula for the distribution of income and trust assets.

DETERMINING YOUR FINANCIAL STRUCTURE

The nature of the legal structure you choose for your firm will have a direct relationship with the nature of the financial structure. It should be emphasized that the methods of financing a business are varied, although certain patterns do seem to occur more frequently than others. Innovations that work are commonplace. In the material that follows, we attempt to discuss the more popular financial practices and structures.

Proprietorship

Frequently, we think of the proprietorship as being financed from the personal funds of the proprietor. In many instances, however, only a small portion of the funds required are financed from personal sources. A bank loan, a loan from an individual, a loan from or guaranteed by a government agency, or a loan from a business may be obtained. The amount of money that can be obtained in addition to that of the proprietor will be determined by the amount of personal funds possessed and the amount and quality of personal assets that may be pledged for a loan. The amount and percentage of money for a loan to the proprietor will be determined by:

1. The "track record" of the individual proprietor; that is, a record of past performance.
2. The nature of the business venture itself, including the amount of fixed assets, size of inventory, the rate of inventory turnover, market potential, profit potential, and so forth.

The usual proportion of debt ranges from 25 to 60 percent of the owner's equity.

Partnership

In starting a partnership, one of the factors to be considered in selecting your partners is whether the individuals possess adequate financial resources to contribute. The capital contribution made by each partner goes into the "paid-in capital" account.

Occasionally, one or more of the partners may make the partnership a loan after the business has started operating. In such instances, the loan will be evidenced by a note. The loan may be secured by fixed assets of the partnership or unsecured, that is, issued against the general credit of the partnership.

In some instances, additional funds may be obtained from outside sources such as banks, individuals, government agencies, and other businesses. Usually, this type of financing will take the form of short- or intermediate-term loans.

Corporation

In establishing a new business, the amount of equity capital required of the initial stockholders will usually range from 40 to 100 percent. The amount is dependent upon such factors as the nature of the venture, abilities and past performance of the management group, kind of assets involved, and market potential.

Equities. During the period immediately following World War II, more than one class of equity (*common stock*) was frequently used. For example, Class A stock would be made voting, but would be subordinated to Class B stock as far as dividends were concerned. Class B stock would be non-voting.

Debt. A favorite debt device has been the *convertible debenture*, which provides investors with not only the security of a debt instrument, but also an opportunity to shift from debt to equity when the firm's stock appreciates.

Recently, many institutional lenders, because of tight money, demand for funds, and a changing market environment, obtained *stock purchase warrants* of up to 50 percent of the total equity. These warrants give the investors the right to purchase a certain number of shares of the firm's common stock at a stated price. The volume of debt, whether it was debentures or mortgage bonds, was usually about 25 to 50 percent of the total capital structure.

Other Considerations. Under certain conditions, it may be advantageous for the incorporating investors to invest a portion of their funds in equity securities and the remainder in debt because of tax advantages and a more favorable priority position in case the firm liquidates.

Sometimes, *subordinated instruments,* such as *second mortgages, junior notes,* or *bonds,* are used.

Preferred stock, which pays a stated dividend before the common stockholders receive any returns, may be desirable even though it tends to restrict the flexibility of the capital structure.

Warrants, as mentioned above, may be used or required by certain investors as part of the financial package. Examples of investors demanding these are SBICs (Small Business Investment Companies) and insurance companies.

Industrial revenue bonds provide a cheaper means of acquiring funds when your business will be located in an industrial park, community, or region where the use of such an instrument is available.

The use of debt in financing enables you to obtain *leverage* upon your equity investment; in other words, by using debt you are able to expand your income relative to your equity.

You should be careful that the indenture provisions of debt instruments are not restrictive and do not limit your actions too much. You want to have the opportunity to work through any periodic adversity without being "washed out" by covenants in the indenture that fail to provide adequate "running room."

Section 1244 Stock. Your corporation may be made more attractive to investors if you comply with the statutory concept of a "small business corporation," as defined in Section 1244 of the Small Business Tax Revision Act of 1958. For this to happen, (1) the total amount of stock offered under the plan, plus other contributions to capital and paid-in surplus, may not exceed $500,000 and (2) the total amount of the stock that may be offered, plus the equity capital of the corporation, must be less than $1,000,000.

Section 1244 stock is common stock (voting or nonvoting) in a domestic corporation. *Losses* on the sale, exchange, or worthlessness of this stock *are treated as ordinary losses rather than capital losses sustained by an individual.* The total amount that may be treated as an ordinary loss cannot exceed $25,000 or, if a husband and wife are filing a joint return, $50,000. This provision could give you a considerable tax advantage. The stock must be issued to the taxpayer in exchange for a transfer by him or her of money or other property. Stock issued in exchange for stock or securities of another corporation, or for services rendered, does not qualify. Also, only the individual to whom the stock is issued qualifies for the benefits of Section 1244.

Finally, taxpayers who are owner-operators of a closely held corporation should make certain that they qualify a maximum amount of their stock under this special provision. When planning their business, most potential owners are so optimistic that they simply cannot see the need for anticipating tax differences that become important only if their new ventures fail. Historical data does not support this position, however, for many more small businesses fail than succeed. If for some reason your business should fail, the opportunity to obtain a tax refund based on a $50,000 ordinary net operating loss deduction is substantially more valuable to you than the potential use of a $50,000 net capital loss carryforward. This provision should also be of special interest to you in seeking venture capital for your new corporation. High marginal tax bracket investors are attracted by the possibility of investing in a new firm if they know that the government will share their risk of loss on a 70–30 basis, but will only share in the potential profits on a 25–75 basis. Also, except for knowledge of the provision and a little timely action, the cost associated with this tax-saving opportunity is essentially zero.[3]

If outside sources of funds are desired, in addition to equity, there may be convertible preferred stock with warrants and bonds. The nature of the structure under these circumstances is determined by the tenor of the money market.

> At the end of 1973, the slow response of the money market indicated that it might be necessary for the original owners of a company to share ownership interest on a dollar-for-dollar basis. In other words, the securities accepted by the outside investors might have been convertible preferred with warrants and bonds. However, a "sweetener" was necessary for the consummation of the deal. The "sweetener" took the form of partial ownership of the firm.

PLANNING YOUR ADMINISTRATIVE STRUCTURE

You must also set up an administrative structure in order to run your business most effectively.

Organizing involves deciding what activities are necessary to attain your firm's objectives, dividing them into small work groups, and assigning each group to a manager possessing the necessary authority to carry out the activities and reach the objectives. A major problem with many

---

[3] If you desire further information on this important subject, see your tax attorney or refer to Ray M. Sommerfeld, *Federal Taxes and Management Decisions*, rev. ed. (Homewood, Ill.: Richard D. Irwin, Inc., 1978).

small business managers is that they do not organize their activities properly. The material in this chapter should help you be more successful by helping you organize your firm better.

Organizational Principles and Practices

An important principle of organization that you should follow is *unity of command*. Under this principle, each employee should have only one superior to whom he or she is *directly responsible* for certain matters. When subordinates must report to two bosses concerning the same assignment, they may become frustrated if they receive conflicting instructions from the two supervisors.

In assigning work to your subordinates, you should try to arrange for *authority to be coequal with responsibility*, although this is not always possible. Sometimes—in the short run—your managers must assume responsibilities greater than their authority. However, try to give your subordinates sufficient authority to carry out their responsibilities. Otherwise, they lack the means of performing their duties. On the other hand, avoid delegating greater authority to your subordinates than they need to fulfill their responsibilities. Otherwise, they may use that authority unwisely and encroach upon the decision-making power of someone else.

The meaning of delegating and placing responsibility is "letting others take care of the details." Delegation is perhaps the hardest thing owner-managers have to learn. Some never do. Others pay lip service to the idea, but actually run everything themselves.

When you delegate, you should be assured that your subordinates are technically competent in their areas. They should either be managers or be capable of becoming managers.

The owner-manager of a small factory established three departments—a production department, a sales department, and an administrative department—and appointed a manager for each. He specified the following responsibilities:

1. The production manager was responsible for manufacturing, packing, and shipping.
2. The sales manager was responsible for advertising, customer solicitation, and customer service.
3. The administrative manager was responsible for personnel, purchasing, and accounting.
4. The production manager was designated "assistant general manager" and delegated authority to make all operational decisions in the owner's absence.

The owner gave each manager a detailed statement of the function of his department and the extent of his authority. Actions that

the managers could take on their own initiative and actions tha
required approval by the owner-manager were enumerated.

Each department manager was instructed to designate and train
an assistant who could manage the department when the need arose.

The owner coordinated the departments. The sales manager and
production manager set customer delivery dates together.

Control was exercised by holding each subordinate responsible
for his actions and checking the results of those actions. The owner
neither "breathed down his managers' necks," nor lost control of
things. He relied upon reports and periodic staff meetings.

The owner kept his subordinates informed so that they would have
the facts they needed for making their decisions. He tried to communicate effectively with them. He explained the "why" of his
instructions.

His managers were given freedom to do things their way and he
did not evaluate them upon whether they did a particular task exactly as he would have done it. He judged them by their results—
not their methods.

If a manager deviated too much from policy, the owner brought
him back into line. He avoided "second-guessing" his managers.
If the subordinate did not run his department to the owner's satisfaction and if his shortcomings could not be overcome, the owner
replaced the manager.[4]

Another principle you should follow is that *decisions are best made
by the person "closest to the spot."* Also, authority should be exercised by
a single person, usually the one responsible for performing the task. Time
should not be wasted in unnecessary consultation and cross-checking
before acting.

You should watch carefully the *span of control* of each supervisor or
manager. By this span we mean the number of subordinates reporting
to one superior. First-line supervisors may have 10, 15, 25, 30 (or more)
employees reporting to them, because of the similarity of their work.
On the other hand, middle managers may have only 5, 8, or 10 supervisors for whom they are responsible, because of the diversity of their
work. You should be especially careful of how many managers are reporting to you personally. If the number becomes too large, operations
of your business could be severely hampered.

Division of labor, or *specialization,* should be used wherever feasible,
as it leads to increased expertise.

You should provide your employees with a written statement of their
duties, responsibilities, authority, and *relationships.* Inform each of them
what they can and cannot—or should not—do. Remember, though, that

[4] Stanley Wantola, "Delegating Work and Responsibility," *Management Aids for
Small Manufacturers no. 191* (Washington, D.C.: Small Business Administration,
1972).

hority for certain duties, you relinquish the responsi-
e duties are performed. Yet, you cannot relinquish
eir effective performance.

tion, by Types of Authority

You should be familiar with the forms of organization, according to these types of authority:

1. Functional.
2. Line.
3. Line and staff.
4. Informal.

Your business may start as a *functional organization*, in which each supervisor is in charge of a specific function. For example, one supervisor may be assigned repair work; another, inspection; and another, production control. This form of organization is effective only in the very small business, because in larger firms, it is not compatible with the precepts of span of control and unity of command.

Your business may be better organized as a *line organization*. "Command" authority is used in this type of structure. Each supervisor is in charge of a specific operational unit and the employees assigned to work in it.

Further company growth may require *line and staff authority*. "Advisory" authority, specialty, and service characterize the staff. The staff assists line personnel in carrying out its activities.

An *informal organization* will always exist within the formal structure of your business. This organization consists of many interpersonal relations that arise as a result of friendships that develop on and off the job. Two examples are *informal leaders* and the *grapevine* communication system. You should determine who the informal leaders are, obtain their support for your programs, and encourage them to "sell" your programs to the rest of your employees.

Ways of Organizing Your Firm

With respect to your company's formal organization structure, you may choose to group the activities into manageable units by:

1. **Function.** Like skills are grouped together to form an organizational unit, such as *production* or *marketing*. The lowest level of the organization should probably be structured on this basis.
2. **Product.** Production or sales activities may be grouped by product, such as *men's wear, ladies' wear,* and so forth.

3. **Process.**   Small companies often base their organization upon manufacturing processes, such as *welding* and *painting*.
4. **Geographic area.**   If your company requires a strong, local marketing
effort, organizing the sales force by areas or territories can be appropriate.
5. **Type of customers.**   A firm's customers may be classified as *industrial, commercial,* or other designation.
6. **Project.**   To illustrate, a small public accounting firm may be organized on the basis of its clients' projects.
7. **Individual abilities of subordinates.**   You may assign work to people
according to their particular talents. However, a limitation is that
the organization structure tends to change whenever a key employee
is replaced.

Preparing an Organization Chart

You should be forewarned that there is no magical organizational
structure, no one right organization. Instead, we recommend using whatever structure seems to make sense to you in your situation. The test is:
Does it work at an acceptable cost? The people, not the form, should be

FIGURE 8-1

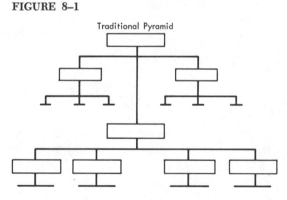

concentrated on, because they are the key factor. While there is truth
in these observations, the following discussion is also relevant.

You should set up a series of authority and responsibility relationships
expressed in a formal organization chart. Even if you have a one-man
business, a chart can be useful as a reminder of how your time might
be most effectively utilized.

You may select a traditional formal organization structure that may
be described as a triangular pyramid. (See Figure 8-1.) This relationship provides for a tighter and narrower span of control. It requires more
centralization of authority and more detailed supervision.

FIGURE 8–2

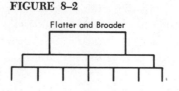

Flatter and Broader

On the other hand, you may select the flatter, broader span of control. (See Figure 8–2.) If so, you will provide your subordinates with less centralized authority and less detailed supervision.

A chart should be not only a useful tool for the present, but also an aid in planning for the future development of your organization and in projecting personnel requirements.

A list of job titles and job specifications should accompany the chart. Job specifications spell out the duties, responsibilities, and working conditions of the work assignment and the qualifications necessary to fulfill the jobs acceptably.

If you (or a partner and you) have a small unincorporated company, there may be no "president" or other management title. Instead, the organization structure might be similar to that shown in Figure 8–3. In fact, a tight, formal organizational structure should not be imposed because it could stifle creativity and reduce initiative.

As your firm grows beyond a certain size, you will often find that some specialized skills are required that you do not possess. You should first attempt to obtain outside, part-time assistance to aid, say, your sales manager, who may lack advertising expertise, or your plant manager, who may lack industrial engineering training. You may also decide that you cannot manage the detailed operations any longer because the size and complexity of your operations are increasing too rapidly. You should preferably seek people in your company to designate as managers. Figure 8–4 portrays an organization in which several managers have been appointed to handle specialized functions.

FIGURE 8–3
Organization for a Small Manufacturing Firm

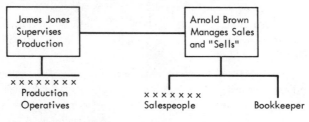

FIGURE 8-4
Organization Structure of a Small
Manufacturing Firm

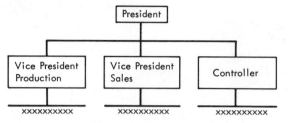

Some Organizational Problems

If they exist in your company, organizational problems are the first, or at least among the first, types of problems that should be solved.

To help you detect organizational problems—and to correct them—see Figure 8–5. This figure describes the symptoms of problems, the possible underlying causes, and some possible actions to remove or correct the problems.[5]

One of the most common weaknesses in the management of small businesses is that the owner is a "one-man show," doing everything and delegating nothing, and his or her people fail to develop.

> A small retailer was a "jack-of-all-trades." He did all jobs in the store as the need arose. He assigned tasks to his employees on a random, unspecialized basis, and did not set up distinct functions or an organization structure.
>
> *Problem:* Many organizational deficiencies existed.
>
> *Solution:* The retailer introduced specialization of tasks and of people. Simple, repetitive routines were introduced. Employees specialized in performing a major function and handling a certain grouping of merchandise.
>
> The store was organized around the functions of merchandising, selling and adjustments, sales promotion, accounting and finance, store operations, merchandise handling, and personnel. Certain functions were combined and delegated to a specific employee.[6]

In some companies, organization structure tends to be loose for the first years of operations. The members of the management team apply

---

[5] Robert G. Murdick, et al., *Business Policy: A Framework for Analysis* (Columbus, Ohio: Grid, 1972).

[6] Adapted from John W. Wingate and Seymour Helfort, *Small Store Planning for Growth* (Washington, D.C.: Small Business Administration, 1966), pp. 27–28.

FIGURE 8–5
Small Business Organizational Problems

Symptoms	Possible Problems	Needed Action
1. Company seems to be drifting aimlessly or trying to go in all different directions.	The organization lacks an effective plan.	The board of directors should recognize these symptoms and formulate 1–3 year plans.
2. Conflicts occur among managers and key personnel. Confusion arises about current objectives and operations.	The manager is not working closely and personally with his people to develop unified objectives and a team approach.	Daily conferences should be held between the manager and his staff to build a working organization.
3. When the manager is not available, the organization is paralyzed.	The manager may believe no one else can make a decision without his being available.	The manager should delegate authority. A committee of the more capable employees may suggest to the manager that they be given more responsibility in decision making.
4. Supervisors make decisions that are reversed by the manager.	The manager has not developed a consistent set of policies.	Some policies and procedures should be put into writing to cover the major repetitive actions and areas of decision making.
5. One activity, such as sales or production, cannot keep abreast of its work.	The manager is incompetent. Personality problems are present.	An immediate objective study is needed. If the manager cannot determine the cause of the problem, he should obtain a business consultant to study the situation and make recommendations.
6. Administrative costs have grown more rapidly than sales.	Big-company organization structure is being imposed upon the small company.	The number of managers should be reduced and the remaining managers' responsibilities broadened.

their skills to the many jobs that are done. For example, one management member will be concerned with overall internal and production management and mechanical engineering. Another will deal with marketing, product development, company image, and systems engineering. A third member may interact with a certain type of customer. A fourth member may be the chief electronic engineer. Considerable overlap often exists between the functions of the management members; for example, the internal manager may sell equipment and develop new product ideas.[7]

SUMMARY

We have tried to show you how to set up your legal, financial, and administrative structure. The usual progression is to determine what legal form you desire (or must have) for your business, decide the sources of your funds and your capital structure, and choose your administrative organization.

We hope you have learned enough from this presentation to permit you to know when to call in an outside expert and to know what questions to ask him when you do.

QUESTIONS FOR FURTHER DISCUSSION

1. What are the negative and positive factors of the proprietorship, partnership, and corporation when it comes to selecting the legal form of business?
2. Considering the financial structure of a business, what are the strong and weak points of proprietorship, partnership, and corporation?
3. Describe the holding company and trust.
4. List the five important functions of a board of directors.
5. Define these organization principles: (a) unity of command, (b) co-equality of authority and responsibility, and (c) span of control.
6. Describe these forms of organization, according to the types of authority: (a) line organization, (b) line and staff organization, and (c) informal organization.
7. Describe five ways in which activities can be grouped into organizational units.
8. Make contact with a small business and report on its legal, financial, and administrative structures.

WHERE TO LOOK FOR FURTHER INFORMATION

Barker, Phyllis A. *"Budgeting in a Small Service Firm." Small Marketers Aids no. 146.* Washington, D.C.: Small Business Administration, 1971.

---

[7] Jeffrey A. Timmons, Leonard F. Smollen, and Alexander L. M. Dingee, Jr., *New Venture Creation: A Guide to Small Business Development* (Homewood, Ill.: Richard D. Irwin, Inc., 1977), p. 508.

Blicksilver, Harold. "Organizational and Financial Planning for New Business Ventures." *The Vital Majority.* Washington,. D.C.: Small Business Administration, 1973, pp. 274–75.

Broom, H. N., and Longenecker, Justin G. *Small Business Management.* Cincinnati, Ohio: Southwestern, 1975, pp. 394–433.

Bunn, Verne A. *Buying and Selling a Small Business.* Washington, D.C.: Small Business Administration, 1969, pp. 3–119. (If you are serious about buying an existing business, this is *must* reading!)

Buskirk, Richard H., and Vaughn, Percy J., Jr. *Managing New Enterprises* (St. Paul, Minn.: West Publishing Co., 1976).

Cohn, Theodore, and Lindberg, Roy A. *How Management Is Different in Small Companies* (New York: American Management Association, Inc., 1972.)

Cornwell, Arthur W. "Sales Potential and Market Share." *Small Marketers Aids no. 112.* Washington, D.C.: Small Business Administration, 1972.

Denton, Charley M. *Franchising in the Economy, 1971–1973.* Washington, D.C.: U.S. Department of Commerce, 1973, pp. 7–16.

Golde, Roger A. "Breaking the Barriers to Small Business Planning." *Management Aids for Small Manufacturers no. 179.* Washington, D.C.: Small Business Administration, 1972, p. 2.

Greene, Gardiner G. *How to Start and Manage Your Own Business* (New York: McGraw-Hill Book Company, 1975).

Klatt, Lawrence A. *Small Business Management: Essentials of Entrepreneurship* (Belmont, Calif.: Wadsworth Publishing Company, Inc., 1973).

Kudrle, Albert E. *Motels.* Washington, D.C.: Small Business Administration, 1970, pp. 4–6. (Small Business Bibliography, No. 66)

Murdick, Rogert G., et al. *Business Policy: A Framework for Analysis.* Columbus, Ohio: Grid, 1972. (For information on organizing *any* type of firm.)

"On the Way: New Round of Help for Small Business," *U.S. News & World Report,* August 30, 1976, pp. 38–40.

Rosenblatt, Samuel M. *Franchising in the Economy, 1972–1974.* Washington, D.C.: U.S. Department of Commerce, 1974, pp. 1–15; 41–42.

Sommer, Howard E. "How to Analyze Your Own Business." *Management Aids for Small Manufacturers no. 46.* Washington, D.C.: Small Business Administration, 1973.

Wantola, Stanley. "Delegating Work and Responsibility." *Management Aids for Small Manufacturers, 1972.* Washington, D.C.: Small Business Administration, 1972.

cases for part II

II-1 Potential High Fashion Shop*

A woman in her middle 40s telephoned a Small Business professor at State University concerning her interest in establishing a "High Fashion Ladies' Wear Shop."

After two or three additional phone calls, she paid a visit to the professor's office. During the ensuing conversation, it seemed to the professor that her client lacked many of the essential ingredients for establishing and successfully operating a high fashion shop. In an effort to maintain a stance of objectivity, the professor handed the client a "personal analysis questionnaire" to take home for study and completion, to be returned to her at a later date.

One of the primary concerns of a professional consultant when dealing with a client who is considering establishing a new business is: "What is the possibility for success?" As the professor analyzed the information, she became concerned about the many negative factors:

a. The potential owner's lack of fashion consciousness that seemed to be so essential in this kind of business.

b. While there had been some exposure to this kind of business through attendance, for a brief time, at a commercial modeling and fashion school, there was no real evidence of the kind of expertise required to successfully manage a high fashion shop.

---

* Prepared by Curtis E. Tate, Jr., University of Georgia.

139

c. The consideration of bringing in a partner who appeared to lack both the skill and the ability to contribute funds to the venture.

d. The limited financial resources of the client, which, at most, amounted to only $18,000–$20,000. The woman was also overconfident of her ability to obtain additional funds from vocational-rehabilitation. (The woman had a physical disability, but she had, until recently, been employed in a clerical position. The "Rehab" counselor did not consider her *eligible* for vocational-rehabilitation financial assistance.)

e. The woman's concern for her personal independence of her husband, who was also physically handicapped and was on the threshold of receiving his doctorate.

The focus seemed to be on her need for achievement, as she appeared to be competing with her husband. "I want to be known as Jayne Snow, not as Mrs. William Snow," she said. While this seemed to be evidence of strong motivation, the professor wasn't sure that this was the appropriate kind of motivation.

In the end, the professor concluded that this business venture had too many strikes against it. The perseverance of the client, however, forced the professor to the conclusion that the best assistance could come from the Small Business Institute and the local SCORE chapter, so she referred the woman to these sources of assistance.

Later, in checking with the director of the Small Business Institute concerning the client, the professor discovered that the woman had not followed her suggestion.

She was sure that it had been in the woman's best interest to drop the project.

QUESTIONS FOR DISCUSSION

1. Evaluate the woman's approach to studying and entering a business.
2. Estimate her chances of success.
3. Would you have advised her any differently? How?

II–2   University Cinemas[1]

Mr. Gary Benjamin, 48, managed the University Cinema for CTW, Inc., a chain owning about 50 theaters in the Midwest. Some, like University

[1] Prepared by Peter R. Kensicki, Cincinnati Financial Corporation, and John Hand, Auburn University.

Cinema, were located in small university towns; others were located in metropolitan areas. CTW had been experiencing severe cash-flow difficulties, and by early 1972 management had decided to sell some of the less profitable theaters. The managers of the theaters to be sold were offered the first opportunity to buy. Since the University Cinema had not been profitable, CTW notified Mr. Benjamin that the theater would be sold, and offered him the opportunity to buy. The asking price for University Cinema was $20,000 for the equipment and $130,000 for the building.

Mr. Benjamin was most anxious to buy the operation. He was convinced that it had the potential to be highly profitable, and that the poor results in the past were due to CTW's tendency to ignore differences in local markets and to the parent firm's poor reputation among film distributors. The distributors were reluctant to release any but the cheapest films to CTW because the firm was consistently late in remitting rental fees for the films. Mr. Benjamin was positive that he could make University Cinema profitable by correcting these problems and by making the building more attractive and comfortable.

Mr. Benjamin did not have the personal wealth to finance the purchase. He had to find one or more partners. Roman Johns expressed an interest. Mr. Johns, 28, was employed as manager of a successful men's clothing store. However, he had previous experience in theater, and Mr. Benjamin fully respected his ability. Unfortunately, he, too, was short of cash. Both Benjamin and Johns were friends of John D. Lundgren. Mr. Lundgren, 38, was a successful local businessman, and was seeking investment opportunities. His knowledge and respect for both Gary Benjamin and Roman Johns convinced him that backing the theater operation would be a sound investment. He agreed to put up $20,000 cash and assume personal liability for the $120,000 mortgage. The remaining $10,000 was contributed by Johns and Benjamin in equal shares. The deal was closed in August of the same year. The company had some second thoughts when these eager buyers appeared in New York, but no major difficulties arose.

With CTW out of the way, the next problem was to establish the structure of ownership. The original proposal was to set up two corporations: Lafayette Corp. would hold the real estate and University Cinemas, Inc. would operate the theater. Initially, Lundgren would own two thirds of Lafayette and the other two men one sixth each; in five years Benjamin and Johns could increase their shares to 20 percent. Lundgren was to own 20 percent of University Cinemas while Benjamin and Johns held 40 percent each.

All three men had misgivings about the structure of ownership. While each was enthusiastic about the prospects of success, each had different objectives and thus preferred a different arrangement. Lundgren's sole interest was in the building. He had little interest in the theater business, and had no time to participate in the management even if he wanted to. Johns wanted to run a movie house; he did not want to be bothered with managing a piece of real estate. All he wanted was a lease so that someone else would pay the taxes and fix the roof. Benjamin also wanted to concentrate on the theater's operation, but he also wanted to own part of the building. His reasons were not clear to the others; perhaps after so many years of taking orders from a distant and unimaginative boss he needed assurance that at last it was really his. These differences were entirely friendly, but they obviously had to be settled before operations could proceed.

QUESTIONS FOR DISCUSSION

1. What are the definitions of the legal types of organizations?
2. What are the advantages and disadvantages of each type of organization?
3. What are the variations of the partnership form of organization?
4. What does each of the following really want: (a) Roman Johns? (b) Gary Benjamin? (c) John D. Lundgren?
5. What unique talents does each of them bring into the proposed business?
6. How would you set the administrative organization?
7. Would you suggest a separate corporation to manage the building and another one to manage the theater operations? Who should own each of them?

II–3   Ski Lodges and Second Houses[1]

Pete had been feeling restless and uneasy about his job and his career for about six months or so. As he looks back on it, this restlessness was probably a normal period in the career of a young executive. An MBA, working for the same company for the 3½ years since graduation, Pete was advancing at the normal pace—and that was the problem. He and several friends at the company discussed their futures frequently. "The glamour of working for a large manufacturing organization had worn off," Pete recalls. "We all had been doing the same thing for about three or four years and couldn't look forward to any significant promotion or change for another three to five years."

[1] Prepared by Curtis E. Tate, Jr., and Robert Gatewood, University of Georgia, Athens, Georgia.

A few of the fellows, including Pete, began looking around for other jobs. Fortunately, the job market was good and some promising positions turned up. Pete had two offers from smaller firms that he considered to offer a definite step up. Another idea, however, also fascinated him. He had been following the progress of a ski slope that was being built in the northern part of the state, where his family had long resided. It was now completed and doing a brisk business. This facility, coupled with the natural recreation spots of the land (lakes, rivers, and mountains), made a highly desirable year-round family vacation area. Pete's family owned a large tract of land near the ski area, and he felt sure it could be developed profitably.

After much internal debate, Pete decided to try his luck with land development, reasoning that if he couldn't get anything going successfully within three years, he would still be young enough to easily find another job in an industrial organization.

From his MBA program, Pete knew all the standard ways of obtaining financial support for business endeavors. Unfortunately, they all involved selling stocks, bonds, property, and so forth, or using them as collateral for loans. Pete had no such holdings. As a matter of fact, he had only enough to sustain himself for a few months while he got started on his ideas. His first action, therefore, was to find himself a job helping to run a lodge and restaurant in the area. He also immediately enrolled in a real estate course being offered locally. Pete reasoned that the best way to gain information about land development and its financing was to gain entrance into the group most likely to be working with such matters.

Within a few months, Pete had completed the course and had passed the state examination "with flying colors." He had also, by this time, re-established some contacts in the area and succeeded in obtaining a position with a real estate firm in his town. He then quit his job at the lodge and was able to devote full time to learning about land transaction and development. Various ideas filtered through his mind during this time, but nothing seemed to be that "right" idea.

Finally, it occurred to him that the best way to capitalize on the recreation value of the area was not to build another amusement facility, but rather to provide the housing that families need in such an area. Consequently, he studied his family's tract of land carefully. It was near enough to the ski facility to provide lodging for the skiers. That seemed like a good idea, but the tract was also large enough to serve other purposes. The best idea seemed to be to divide it up and sell off lots to individuals as sites for second homes. So Pete, with his parents' permission and cooperation, set about creating this dual purpose for the land.

Arranging for the distribution and sale of the second home sites was no problem at all; Pete did that himself. The development of the lodging facilities for skiers was quite a bit more difficult, because it required a good deal of financial support.

Pete determined that he could comfortably build ten chalet type individual units, a trout lake that might be used for ice skating in the winter, a small swimming pool, and picnic areas on the 85 acres allotted for this facility.

Of the ten chalets, three were to be four-bedroom; three, three-bedroom; two, two-bedroom; and two, one-bedroom. All had kitchen and dining facilities. When he questioned contractors in the area about the cost of building such a development, Pete soon learned he was into a high-cost project—about $125,000. Unfortunately, he was no better off financially than he was a few months before when he started this endeavor.

Pete then started around to the various lending institutions for funds. His first stop was a savings and loan association. This institution was very interested in some tangible demonstration of business success or something of marketable value before it would contribute to the project. Needless to say, Pete was forced to look elsewhere. "Who else," he wondered, "would be able to lend large sums?" He answered his own question by looking at his monthly paycheck stub. Why not try the federal government? It certainly had a lot of the money he and his friends earned. Pete's next visit, then, was to the Small Business Administration. They were quite interested in the idea, but Pete decided that their interest rate and repayment schedules were prohibitive.

Pete then went to the more obscure agencies, i.e., the Federal Land Bank and the Production Credit Association. Both were able to lend money under a farm recreation provision in their charters and were quite interested in the project. From the former, Pete borrowed $40,000 for 30 years and from the latter $72,000 for 10 years. Both loans were on a floating interest basis tied to the prime lending rate. The combined amount of $112,000 was a little short of his needed amount, but certainly enough to get started. On further discussion with the contractor, the building cost went up even higher because Pete decided to build very high quality units both to ensure their longevity and also to make them easier to sell individually if renting did not succeed. He made up the difference by raising an additional $20,000 at 8¼ percent for 20 years from the savings and loan he originally talked with and by deciding to do most of the landscaping work himself. With this amount of capital amassed, the construction proceeded quickly and the project was completed within ten months.

Pete figured that to meet loan payments ond operating expenses, the project would have to generate $28,000 income yearly. He then did a survey of the nearby motels and hotels to aid him in setting rates for the chalets. From this survey, he decided upon $150 per week for the four-bedroom units, $125 for the three-bedroom, $115 for the two-bedrooms, and $100 for the one-bedrooms. If the units averaged 35–40 percent occupancy throughout the year, this would generate $21–24,000 income. The difference Pete felt could be made up from the sale of the lots for second homes. Advertisement for the operation was handled through brochures, signs, and mass media in towns within a 125 mile radius.

Once the venture had been set up, Pete turned his attention to another matter. During the construction of his chalets, Pete became more enamoured with the second-home market. The problem was he didn't have any more land and definitely not any more money. He did, however, know of some land that would suit his purposes nicely. His solution to the dilemma was straightforward. Simply take in partners who would purchase the land in return for 60 percent of the profit on the houses and the return of their costs. The reliable savings and loan was quite willing to finance the construction of individual houses to be sold on the open market, so the cost of construction was financed and begun. Pete thus found himself in the land development profession in a short time. Now came the long part—waiting to see if he would be successful.

QUESTIONS FOR DISCUSSION

1. In looking at Pete, what personal attributes seem evident that would cause him to leave the security of corporate employment to assume the risk and insecurity of a new venture?
2. Do the facts seem to indicate that we can label an individual as being an entrepreneurial type, i.e., possessing identifiable personal characteristics that enable the individual to assume the role of business ownership?
3. Evaluate the methods used by Pete in planning and implementing the new business. If you were carrying out an undertaking of this kind, how would you proceed?
4. Would you have attempted to obtain contractual commitments from prospective lessees or purchasers prior to launching these ventures? Explain.
5. What type of presentation would you have prepared to present to the prospective customers?
6. Do you consider Pete assumed too much risk in establishing the business? Please discuss.

II–4   The Mother and Child Shop[1]

As Mick McGregor describes it, "I've never really been the type to devote myself to just one thing for very long. Trying something new has

---

[1] Prepared by Curtis E. Tate and Robert Gatewood, University of Georgia.

always been fascinating for me." Maybe that's why a married man, with a first child due shortly, a full-time job, who is also working on a Ph.D., decides to fill his free moments by starting his own business.

Mick had toyed with the idea of starting a business but had never really done much about it until a friend and neighbor of his, Jack Pollach, mentioned at a Halloween party in 1967 that there was some store space available in a large shopping complex in town. Jack was developing plans for a candy store and discussed his ideas with Mick. He also mentioned that there were a few stores still to be leased.

Mick was intrigued by this idea of starting a store and encouraged by his friend's actions. He had some money set aside for investment and felt that putting this into a small business could be a profitable decision. The problem, however, was deciding what kind of store it should be. What products should be carried? The town Mick lived in was a community of about 40,000 located about 65 miles from one large city and about 150 miles from another. Mick's reasoning was that he needed to find some store or goods that his town didn't have yet, but was ready to have. In other words, he needed something for which there was a market but for which people had to go to the larger cities to buy at the present time.

Off and on during November, Mick pondered this problem. There really wasn't a specific thing that he was interested in selling; he was just trying to maximize his chances of success by coming up with a "sure-thing" stock of merchandise. After all this effort, it was actually Mick's wife, Cathy, who wasn't very interested at all in going into business at that particular time, who gave him the idea. Cathy was due to have their first child late in November. During that last week, she commented to Mick that she would certainly be happy when her pregnancy was over if for no other reason than that she would be able to buy clothes again.

Maternity clothes were sold only as a sideline by a few of the larger stores in town. Their selection was, at best, limited. The comment didn't register immediately with Mick, but later that evening the full impact hit him. It seemed like the very idea he had been looking for. He didn't have much time to act on the idea in the next days, however, for four days later their first child was born.

Once mother and child were home and as settled as possible, Mick began to pursue his idea vigorously. He first spent several evenings at the local library reading about manufacturers and suppliers of maternity clothing and specifically about their marketing. His main concern was deciding whether or not his town was large enough to support a maternity shop. He thought that the best way to do this was to first develop a list, from within his state and three adjacent states, of cities that were approximately the same size as his. Then he would determine how many of these had maternity clothing shops. This would give him an idea of how active the market was in similar, nearby cities and whether such a store in a city of his size was, in fact, possible. To do this Mick first went to the latest census information and listed those cities within his four-state sample that had populations 35–45,000. To get the names of merchants in these towns, he first went to the trade journals and noted the stores in the towns on his list and the lines they carried. He also was able to find telephone books for most of the cities and determine whether any maternity clothing shops were indexed. From this he found that nearly 80 percent of the cities on his list had at least one shop like the one he was considering, and about 25 percent had two or more shops. Mick concluded from these findings that his idea was at least generally sound.

He next wanted to find out some specific information about his own community in order to decide if the store was practical in his own city. He was able to find data on both the per-family income and the amount of money spent on mothers' and children's clothing each year for his area and other areas on his list. His area compared very favorably with the others on this basis. Finally, from the county planning commission, Mick obtained information on the estimated population increase over the next five and ten years and the areas of projected growth within the county. These data told him that the county would grow by 10–15 percent for the next five years and by 15–25 percent over the next ten. In addition, areas near his tentative site were projected to increase in population. From all these data, Mick was greatly encouraged. He felt that he had a sound idea that was indeed supported by all the marketing information he could find.

It also occurred to him during this time that a better bet might be to have a combination maternity and baby store. Women who had become familiar with the store and its merchandise during their pregnancy might thus be influenced to come back afterward to buy clothing for their babies. The combination seemed natural and was quickly adopted.

By mid-December of 1967, then, Mick had the idea for a combination maternity-children's store which appeared to have very little competition in town and which tentatively could be located in one of the largest and busiest shopping centers in town. That all seemed fine. The next question was, "Who's going to run this thing?" Mick wasn't confident enough in his idea to quit his job and his graduate education to go into it full-time. The logical choice, at least to him, seemed to be Cathy. Cathy, having been a mother for all of two weeks, was less than wildly enthusiastic about the prospects of managing a store too. But she agreed if two conditions were met: (1) that a full-time sales clerk would be hired, and (2) that a room in the back of the store could be designed for the baby.

That problem solved, Cathy and Mick moved on to the next one— finding out something about how to run a business like this. In mid-

December, while they were visiting Cathy's parents in one of the nearby large cities, they decided that the best way to find this information might be to talk with someone in the business. So they selected a maternity store that Cathy and her mother knew, and drove over to talk to the owner. In retrospect Mick describes that afternoon as perhaps the most important of that time period, both informationally and psychologically. The owner and his wife were extremely helpful and encouraging, discussed many financial and managerial details, and sent Mick and Cathy on their way feeling very confident of their decision to start this business. The effect of the visit was so positive that in early January Mick and Cathy signed a three-year rental lease with the owners of the shopping complex for a 1,000-square-foot store.

Among other things that they found out from the friendly store owner was that the next buying show for the region was to be held on January 28 and 29. This show was the main opportunity for comparing all the clothing lines' styles and prices for the coming spring and summer. The shortness of the time until the show was disconcerting. If they went to the show and bought merchandise, that meant they would have to open for business in a few months to sell the spring and summer clothing. If they didn't buy merchandise at this show, they most likely would have to wait several months for the fall-winter show. They decided to take the risk and try to open their store with the spring clothing.

To have a chance of meeting this deadline, Mick and Cathy decided to divide responsibilities. Cathy, because of her recent experience with maternity clothing, was in charge of selecting manufacturers' lines and styles and buying the inventory. Mick, calling on his undergraduate background of industrial engineering and his graduate training in business, took responsibility for designing and preparing the store layout and deciding on the financial and managerial aspects of the store.

Cathy suggested that the store stock high-quality, name-brand merchandise. She would pick styles and particular items at the show, depending mostly on her own tastes and advice gathered from product salesmen.

Mick's immediate problem before the show was to decide how much inventory to carry initially. From his estimates of per family income and amount of money spent on mothers' and children's clothing, and mainly from his discussion with the store owner, Mick estimated that first year sales would be about $19,500. He also decided that he would be happy if the store broke even for the first year. So he figured total expenses should be kept to $19,500 for that year. From this figure, Mick subtracted fixed costs (personnel, rent, utilities, licenses, and estimated remodeling costs), which were about $7,500, to determine how much could be spent on inventory. This figure was $12,000. Knowing from his business courses that inventory should turn over about four times a year, it was simple to estimate an initial inventory cost of about $3,000. However, after estimating the amount of merchandise he could buy for $3,000, Mick realized how little clothing that would actually be. He was concerned about the image such a sparse inventory might project. So he totaled up his projected initial expenditures to see whether he could afford to start with a larger inventory. Remodeling, rent, utilities, and personnel salaries for the first two months would come to about $2,500. If Mick increased his starting inventory to $4,500, that would mean an initial outlay of about $7,000. This figure was within the amount of money Mick had set aside for investment, so he decided that he would take the chance and increase his inventory to $4,500.

He then categorized the various items the store would be carrying into the following groups: maternity casual wear, maternity dresses, lingerie, and children's wear. Again going back to his previous discussion with the store owner, he decided to divide his inventory among these categories in the proportions 30 percent, 30 percent, 7 percent, and 33 percent respectively. This information on total inventory and how it should be divided among product groups was then given to Cathy, who would have to work out the number of each size, etc., that should be bought. She estimated this through talks with salesmen and the store owner they had visited previously.

This task completed, Mick, from the middle of January to the middle of March, turned his attention to decorating the store. Drawing from his experience as an industrial engineer and ideas he gathered from visiting other stores, he designed the layout himself and did most of the work. Tasks such as the wiring and the counter and cabinet construction, he hired others to do but was able to specify exactly what he wished done. He was also careful not to omit the special room in the back of the store for the baby.

Everything went very smoothly at the merchandise show for the two prospective merchants. They were able to meet the salesmen they wished and purchase clothing they liked. Deliveries of almost all articles were promised within six weeks.

February was spent working on the store, obtaining the necessary city and state licenses, selecting a full-time saleswoman, and becoming very nervous at the thought of actually opening the store. The person hired was an experienced saleswoman who had been recommended by a friend of Mick and Cathy.

By the beginning of March, almost all was ready for an opening. The only advertising that had been done up until this time was a large paper sign across the front windows. Also, Mick belonged to several civic organizations in town and informally passed the word about the store to other members. News traveled fast in town, and quite a few people knew about the proposed opening. Mick and Cathy decided that it might be better to hold other advertising until a few weeks after the store actually opened. This would give them some time to get a feel for operating the store. So it was decided to have the grand opening in mid-April, with newspaper and radio advertising to precede the opening by two weeks. The actual opening would be as soon as the store was completed and a majority of the inventory in stock. This turned out to be March 17, 1968 —less than four months after Cathy's comments about the difficulty of finding maternity clothes.

QUESTIONS FOR DISCUSSION

1. How might the owners have changed their procedure in planning the business?
2. Do you think their method of researching the business was adequate? What changes would you have made?
3. Do you think adequate effort was devoted to determining capital requirements?
4. After some individual research on your part, would you accept their inventory allocation?
5. What weight would you give the special knowledge of the wife? the husband?
6. Do you think an adequate effort was made to determine the feasibility of the market? Give reasons for your answer.
7. What have you gained from studying this case?
8. Do you note any apparent personality characteristics that seem to indicate Mick to be the entrepreneurial type?

II–5   Metal Fabricators[1]

Metal Fabricators, Inc., was a small firm engaged in the fabrication of metal products. Practically all its income came from small subcontracts from general contractors in the area. However, since its incorporation in early 1970, the two owner-managers had been attempting to develop and market a sand-blasting machine with a new type of control mechanism, which they had conceived. Only two of the sand-blasting machines or "pots," as they are called, had been sold, although most of the company's efforts had been directed at this part of the business.

---

[1] Prepared by Arthur D. Sharplin, Louisiana State University.

The two owner-managers, Jerry Rogers and Joe Benson, had similar education and work experience, including about three years of college, with several engineering courses. They were both competent welders, and both had served as construction superintendents on several medium-sized projects. Jerry's work experience had been much broader and more successful than Joe's, and he was still much in demand as a construction superintendent. He had turned down several job offers during the last year. Jerry came from a low-income, small-town family, while Joe was from a relatively well-to-do family.

Larry Ford, who owned 51 percent of the stock in the firm, was a local businessman who devoted little of his time to Metal Fabricators. But it was Larry Ford's initiative that had brought Metal Fabricators into existence. Jerry and Joe were temporarily unemployed, as construction superintendents often are, when Larry asked them if they could build a special type of hopper for Ford's construction company. Jerry and Joe rented a building and a welding machine and constructed the hopper. This job led to others, and the firm was incorporated in March, 1970. Larry Ford, who purchased most of the stock, appointed Joe president and Jerry general manager, with the mutual consent of the two men.

Regardless of their titles, Jerry and Joe worked side by side to complete the small contracts they obtained. Within about a month there was more work than Jerry and Joe could do; they hired two or three welders on a part-time basis.

During its first ten months of operation, the firm encountered difficulties similar to those normally encountered by small, new firms. Cash-flow problems occurred and there were times when Jerry and Joe felt obligated not to draw their salaries so that funds would be available to purchase required materials and to pay the welders. Organizational difficulties were also encountered. It didn't matter at first that Joe was president and Jerry was general manager, but when there were employees to be supervised, areas of responsibility and authority had to be established.

At first, Jerry and Joe discussed each new problem and usually arrived at a mutual conclusion as to what to do about it. Later on, though, Joe began to handle more and more of the "business end of the operation" and Jerry began to run the shop. As the responsibilities of the two men became more clearly defined, they began to take unilateral action—often without informing each other.

The result of all these trends was that there were often disagreements as to whether the action taken was proper. When the men were together, they often argued about one thing or another. Several of the arguments were quite heated.

One day in November when Joe was at the shop for one of his almost daily visits, the following interchange took place:

JERRY: Joe, there are several things I'd like to talk to you about. I think we should get together for an hour or so right away.

JOE: What's bothering you, buddy? Looks like things are going pretty well on your end of the operation.

JERRY: I'd rather not discuss it now. Can we get together Wednesday night at about 7:00?

JOE: Yes, I suppose that'll be all right.

When the men arrived for their meeting, each had made up a list of items he wanted to discuss. They went to the small, cluttered office that was built into one corner of the fabrication shop and started to talk:

JOE: We need to work out a plan and market our pots so that we can get them moving as soon as I get this valve ready. That should be within about two weeks.

JERRY: I don't want to discuss what we are going to do. I want to discuss what we have done and what mistakes we've made and how we are going to keep from making the same ones in the future.

JOE: Okay. Well, what's on your mind?

JERRY: Well, to begin with, you're handling the business end of this operation. You've prepared monthly financial statements but you didn't seem to know that we had a shortage of cash until we had no money to pay our salaries. You should have anticipated the shortage so that we could do something about it.

JOE: You saw the financial statements, too, and you thought they were okay.

JERRY: Anyway, Joe, I wish you would try to have a little more foresight and let me know about these things before they get serious. Another thing, you've only been here about two hours a day recently. You spend the rest of the time working on our new control system. So I'd rather you not give the men any directions when you are here without my approval.

JOE: Jerry, when I see the men doing something wrong I'm going to feel free to correct them with or without your approval. Anyway, the things that I've told them have been pretty obvious.

The conversation went on in this vein for about 30 minutes with Jerry bringing up points that had been bothering him and Joe commenting on those points. After Jerry had completed his list of items the session proceeded as follows:

JOE: Now, I have several things that I'd like to mention. Particularly, you seem to be so concerned about my end of the business, I think you should pay more attention to running the shop.

JERRY: Running the shop! Why, everything is running perfectly in the shop. The men are happy and we get every job out within the estimated time. All we need is a little better financial management and a few more sales calls on your part.

JOE: Jerry, I've also been concerned because you keep pushing to make the company bigger. You want to hire more welders, and take on more of these humdrum little fabrication jobs. I'd rather we just do enough of that to get by. We are never going to be successful unless we do something really big. And, if we can develop this sand-blast machine and get just a few sales I think we might really hit pay dirt.

JERRY: I'm not trying to make a killing, Joe, and I don't have a lot of faith in long shots anyway. I'd rather just sit back and build the things that we know how to build, and just do it a little cheaper and better than the next fellow.

JOE: Well, we are not going to settle that tonight! There was one other thing I wanted to ask you to do and that is to set up a wage allocation system so that we'll know how much of the men's wages are expended on each job. Several times in the past you haven't been able to tell me whether we even made money on a job or not.

JERRY: Sometimes we haven't made money, and that's because you keep changing the amount of the bids after we've agreed upon a figure. Last week on the Enjay job I spent an hour convincing you that we ought to bid $4,500 and you said "okay." But yesterday I found out that you bid the job at $4,000. We are not going to make a cent on that contract, Joe. Sam said that he even called you and asked if you had left something out because our bid was so much lower than any of the others. But, rather than admit that you had made a mistake, you stuck with the original bid.

JOE: We disagree about that, but I'm president of this company and I have to be able to make decisions.

JERRY: We've talked for 45 minutes and I don't think we've settled a thing.

JOE: Sure we have, you are going to set up a labor schedule for each job and I hope you are going to try keep your nose a little more out of my business. I'm going to have the control system ready for the sand-blast pot week after next. Also, I'm not going to give any more orders directly to the men.

JERRY: You said, too, that you would make 35 sales calls within the next 60 days.

JOE: Yes, I said that, and I will.

JERRY: Well I still don't think we've accomplished much, but I suppose we've about talked it out. I'll see you tomorrow.

As the work load increased, Joe and Jerry soon found that they either had to hire some more welders or turn down some contracts. At first, students at a near-by trade school were hired on a part-time basis. Also, for a while, two experienced welders, who had full-time jobs elsewhere, were hired to work evenings and week-ends. It soon became clear that the work load was sufficiently dependable to support at least three full-time employees, and the following conversation ensued between Jerry and Joe in early 1972:

JOE: I'll call Mr. Smith who teaches over at the trade school tomorrow and ask him to recommend three of his new graduates.

JERRY: Joe, this is rather ticklish work and these trade school boys just don't have the savvy to do the job. We have to watch them every second.

And we are spending more time training them than we are actually performing the work.

JOE: Jerry, a good welder will cost us $5.00 an hour. We can get these boys from the trade school for $3.50 an hour.

JERRY: Sure, we pay them about 70 percent as much as we would a good welder, but you give me one good, experienced welder and I can put out more work than I can with all three of those kids. Besides, when we get one of these kids halfway trained, we'll have to pay him $4.50 an hour to keep him.

JOE: We'll still save money while we're paying him $3.50. You and I can do the complicated work and, if we plan and schedule the work right, all the other men will have to do is weld.

JERRY: Well I'm still not convinced, but I'll sure try to make it work. Go ahead and call Mr. Smith tomorrow.

Three young men who had been at the top of their class at the vocational-technical school were hired on the recommendation of Mr. Smith. They started at about 70 percent of the going rate for experienced welders. During the weeks that followed one of the welders found a better job elsewhere and failed to show up for work one morning. Another decided he did not really like welding and quit his job to go to work on a pipeline. When the second welder left, Joe and Jerry had to decide how to obtain replacements.

QUESTIONS FOR DISCUSSION:

1. What does the case indicate about the need for organization?
2. What does it suggest about the need for planning?
3. What does it imply about control?
4. How do you explain the shortage of finances? How could this problem be overcome?
5. What does the case show about the differing objectives of the two owner-managers? The silent partner, Mr. Larry Ford?
6. What do you think of the selection procedure of the firm? Explain your answer.
7. How would you improve the procedure?
8. What is your reaction to hiring students directly out of the vocational-technical school rather than recruiting experienced employees?
9. What is your analysis of the wage policy of the firm?
10. What would you do now?

II–6   Panther Inn[1]

In October 1972, Midland University became a member of the Small Business Institute (SBI), program operated under the auspices of the Small Business Administration (SBA). The objective of the SBI was to provide management assistance to small businesses by university students. The student consultants, in turn, had an opportunity to complement their academic experience through exposure to "real world" problems.

One of the 20 cases assigned to the students at Midland University was the Panther Inn, a family restaurant and lounge located at the intersection of I-88 and State Route 127. The Inn was located in the Panther Valley with a scenic view of rolling farmland from the lounge and restaurant serving area. It was geographically located in Midland County about 40 miles from Midland University.

The project was assigned to a team of three MBA students: Dave, Harold, and Jim. All three of the consulting team were a little older than the average student, having served in the military prior to continuing their education. All three had prior small business experience. Their faculty adviser was Professor Urman.

The Inn was originated by Harvey Adams, who had secured a loan of $300,000 from the SBA. The loan was 90 percent guaranteed by the SBA, with an interest rate of 8 percent on the unpaid balance. Four months later, he secured a loan of $350,000 from the SBA. The first $300,000 of this loan was to cancel the original note, while the remaining $50,000 was for additional financing. An additional $10,000 was borrowed from relatives to provide working capital. The restaurant and surrounding property had a current net worth of $700,000, but the worth was expected to reach over $1,000,000 at completion.

Since Mr. Adams was involved in other business activities, he handed the business over to his son, Chuck, who became owner and manager. Chuck was 22 years old, married, and a high school graduate with no prior business education or experience.

In their initial meeting, both Mr. Adams and Chuck enthusiastically welcomed the proposed team counseling. Chuck admitted that he knew nothing about a restaurant and that he originally wanted to be just the bartender for the lounge. Since the restaurant was entering the operational phase, Dave, Harold, and Jim outlined their approach to its problems. They initially concluded that special attention should be directed

---

[1] Prepared by Thomas F. Urban, of Texas A&M University, and Harvey J. Brightman, Miami University (Ohio).

toward market research, inventory control, financial and accounting operations, and overall management of the restaurant and the lounge.

In touring the facility, the team noted that there were two distinct operations. The *restaurant* was on the main floor and the *lounge* was on the lower level. Seating capacity for the restaurant included two counters with 15 seats and tables with a capacity of 175 customers.

At the time of the case, the party rooms were not operating at full capacity (approximately 200 persons). The lounge area was operating at 100-person capacity, but when fully completed, two bars would be operating with a capacity of 200 customers.

Chuck stated that they had 24 full-time and part-time employees. Because of the constant turnover and anticipated increases in personnel needs, Chuck had been spending a lot of time interviewing prospective employees and filling positions.

After touring the restaurant, the team began to discuss the specific needs of Panther Inn. Chuck stated again that he didn't know much about business. He thought he should be making a profit because a lot of customers came in, but there didn't seem to be any money left over. He was too busy hiring people and tending bar "to look into money matters." Chuck wasn't sure where the customers were coming from, but many seemed to be tourists. He also wanted to know how to order the supplies needed for the restaurant. Sometimes they ran out of food, while at other times the employees had to eat it in order to keep it from going to waste. Chuck concluded his difficulties by stating, "I want to be a good manager, but how? I never have any time left over to take care of anything. Just tell me what to do and I'll do it."

The team told Chuck that they needed to develop a cost analysis of the restaurant and lounge as well as an analysis of the current wage structure. Since Chuck had no idea as to whether the restaurant or the lounge was making a profit, he relied on his accountant to provide these figures. The team indicated that they would need more data and figures to analyze the situation. Chuck said that they could get these from the accountant if he had them. He stated that the accountant was an old family friend of his father and was a "nice guy."

In addition, the team recommended a market research program in order to determine the extent of his market segmentation. Finally, Chuck wanted an analysis of his parking lot layout and facilities in order to ensure efficient parking for the customers. The first meeting closed on a friendly note as Chuck had to return to the lounge to tend bar. He promised to get all the records from the accountant and said, "You guys can do anything you want. I just don't know that much about business and you're the experts. I'm glad the SBA put you in to do the work for me."

Several weeks later, Dr. Urman was grading papers when he was interrupted by Dave, Harold, and Jim. "We're quitting Panther Inn," said

Jim, "He's not going to get any more cheap labor from us. He never does anything and now he took off for Florida—a two-week vacation because he 'had to get away'."

"Yeah!" said Harold, "We drove all the way up there and he's in Florida. That's it! He never does anything we want him to."

"Hold on a second," said Dr. Urman, "We just can't drop a case because it's too tough. We have a contract with the SBA and that's one of our cases. Let's start at the beginning."

"OK," said Jim, "The first time we went out, we told him what we were going to do and what we needed. He never did anything. He wanted us to do everything. When we went back a few days later, he hadn't gotten the records from the accountant. In fact, the accountant hadn't even filed a tax return for the Inn. We told him to place a register at the door to have people sign in. We could get our market information from this as to where the customers come from—tourists, families, and so forth. We drew up a plan for his parking lot. He wanted us to go out and paint the lines for parking spaces for him. Us—MBAs!"

"Yeah!" said Harold, "Look at our progress reports. We tell him to do something and it's never done. The only way we get him to do anything is to do it ourselves. Look at that accounting mess! We finally drove out to his accountant's and got the books. That dumb bookkeeper! He even wears green eye shades! He still uses a single entry system. We analyzed the books and he didn't have any of the data we needed. We finally worked up a cost analysis by collecting the data ourselves. Then, we found he made a $2,300 error. He didn't post figures in the ledger, and when he did post, he put the figures in the wrong places. We finally broke the figures down into separate listings for the lounge and restaurant. When we told Chuck to get rid of him, he said that he couldn't because the accountant was a friend of his father's."

"I took care of his personnel problems," said Dave, "We prepared a wage analysis. Then I wrote ads for the papers and went to the employment agencies myself. I made up an organization chart and a job description for each position. All Chuck wants to do is tend bar. He keeps saying 'Do what you guys want to do. The SBA sent you in. You're the experts.' He just thinks that everything will work out. He doesn't have any experience and wants us to take care of everything. He doesn't want to be a manager!"

"I had to take care of his marketing," said Jim, "I wrote the ads and put them in the paper. He can't rely on tourists all year. We designed the billboard for him and he never put it up. We have to do everything for him. We advertise low prices and he raises everything on his menu by $1.00 to $2.50. He didn't need to do that without asking us. Then, we advertise a family restaurant and he still won't put in a kids' menu. We wanted him to give out balloons or panthers or something and he still hasn't even looked into it. Chuck apologizes to us for not carrying through and he admits that he's lazy. All he wants to do is tend bar.

"If we can't quit this case, Dr. Urman, how can we get him to do the things we want him to? We've done more work on this than any of our other courses and we don't have anything to show for it. He just wants us to do the busy work—and now he goes to Florida."

QUESTIONS FOR DISCUSSION:

1. What does this case show about outside assistance for a small firm?
2. What should be the role of the owner-manager and the team in this type of situation?
3. What should the team do now? Dr. Urman?
4. How could Chuck be induced to do a better job of managing his firm?
5. Evaluate each of the suggestions made by the team as to feasibility, applicability, and expected effectiveness.

II–7   Tanner's Grocery Store[1]

Star City is a southern town of 50,000 people located in a primarily rural area. There are several small industrial plants and a great deal of farming, but the identifying characteristic of the city is the major state university located within it. This, coupled with a relatively large number of impoverished blacks, enabled the city to obtain federal funds in the form of a Model Cities Program to aid the city in providing assistance in the areas of housing, recreation, education, and employment to the blacks.

One of the efforts initiated under the program was directed at preparing a group of blacks in the fundamentals of small business operation. Faculty members of the university were employed to provide instruction in management, marketing, and accounting to a group that had been selected on the basis of overall ability, motivation, and potential to succeed. The major emphasis in the training was placed on providing the fundamental skills needed in making business decisions. In addition, the effort included assistance in researching business opportunities, preparation of loan applications, and consultative assistance once the business has been acquired, if an ongoing one, or started, if a new one. These

---

[1] Written by Rudolph L. Kagerer and James F. Russell, University of Georgia.

services were provided by graduate students in business under the guidance of the director, who was primarily an administrator.

William Tanner was one of the blacks selected for the training. A native of Star City, he was 25 years old, married, and the father of one child. He had completed two years of college and served in the U.S. Army as a medical technician. Soft spoken and intelligent, Tanner showed great enthusiasm for the opportunity the program represented, but did not continue his enthusiasm, attending only 21 of more than 100 class sessions in a period of a year. He had worked for two years as an inventory clerk and timekeeper for a manufacturing firm, and for one year as an employment interviewer for the state employment service. He had held several smaller jobs as a teenager, but none of them was long lasting or responsible in nature. His record in the jobs he had held appeared to be good, such that he was offered a promotion when he considered leaving his last job to undertake his own business. Tanner was a faithful church attender, a junior deacon and choir member, and had shown some organizational ability in that he had taken part in the formation of a local chapter of a national black fraternity in college and had served as the first president of the chapter. He did have some financial resources, in the form of $1,000 in savings, but obviously not enough to launch a business of any substantial size. In short, Tanner appeared to have the educational qualifications and interpersonal skills for operating a small business. Little could be inferred concerning his motivation, except that he stated that he wanted to "make it," so that young blacks could view him as a model and see that they, too, might have a chance. He believed that the blacks would support him because he, too, was black, and so did not concern himself with many of the more onerous aspects of business training such as financial management and accounting.

An opportunity presented itself to Tanner in Greenwaite's Grocery Store. John Greenwaite and his partner, James Slater, both white, had been operating the store for the past three years. They had started out in a smaller store and had moved to their present location when the need arose for more floor space to allow for expansion. Both stores were in the same, primarily black neighborhood. The partners operated the store daily from 7:00 A.M. until 11:00 P.M., carried a limited inventory of name-brand products and operated a cut-to-order meat department specializing in less expensive cuts of pork and beef. They managed to draw "reasonable profits" from the business by sharing the work load, minimizing extra labor costs, and by maintaining a 25 to 30 percent markup on their shelf products, justified by the convenience aspect of the hours of operation and made possible by the judicious granting of credit. By virtue of their long stay in the neighborhood, they had eliminated many of the bad credit risks and granted credit only to those who were known by them to be prompt payers. In addition, they were known to grant small, high-interest loans to good customers to meet emergencies, although the repayment terms were not generally known. When Tanner came around and began asking whether they wished to sell the business, the partners felt pleased at the possibility of turning a profit on the sale.

William Tanner decided to buy Greenwaite's Grocery Store, and the partners agreed to sell it to him. Tanner applied for a loan to the Small Business Development Corporation, a wholly owned subsidiary of a national bank that had several branches in Star City. The Corporation had been formed specifically to make relatively high-risk minority small business loans, provide loan capital primarily to minority group members with "good character" but no cash to facilitate house purchasing, and to grant property improvement loans on an extended term basis to persons who might ordinarily be termed "marginal" applicants. The officers of the Corporation were also officers of the bank, and loan officers were ordinarily "officers in training," relatively new bank employees who served temporarily in the Corporation as a part of their initial officer training.

When an applicant applies for a small business loan five major steps are taken in the initial processing. The character of the applicant is evaluated by means of a careful check with credit and character references and a personal, in-depth interview. The applicant is asked to prepare a personal financial statement, and is given assistance if necessary. He or she is asked to make projections, both personal and business, and to detail personal and business goals so that his or her financial management capability and grasp of reality can be assessed. The ability of the applicant to conduct the proposed business and his or her experience and ideas about the business are evaluated. Finally, assistance is given in an attempt to determine the real value of the business the applicant intends to initiate or assume.

If a loan is granted, a follow-up team consisting of one officer of the corporation and one management associate (ordinarily a bank officer trainee) works with the account, requiring a monthly profit and loss statement and annual balance sheet and giving financial guidance to the borrower.

During this period, there was considerable federal, state, and local pressure to place minority group members into business. The Corporation, which had been in business for three years, had granted several loans for this purpose. In fact, the president of the bank, who was extremely public minded, had stated that "the greatest untapped resource of the state is in the black race." As a result, the Corporation aggressively sought such loans, and was quite eager for Tanner to negotiate a loan for assumption of a business that seemed to be successful.

In Tanner's case, Mr. Bowden, the loan officer, reported a book value of assets in excess of $30,000, including accounts receivable, inventory, equipment, and good will. Greenwaite and Slater's unaudited profit and loss statements had shown a steady profit for the past year. Inventory was estimated by adding up shelf prices for all items in the store, and subtracting 25 percent of the total, since Greenwaite and Slater had marked up their items 25 to 30 percent. The equipment was priced at replacement value, even though some of the equipment had outlived its depreciation value. Tanner was granted a loan in the amount of $30,000, with which he paid $28,000 to Greenwaite and Slater. He retained $2,000, and added $1,000 from his savings to serve as liquid capital.

QUESTIONS FOR DISCUSSION

1. What were Mr. Tanner's objectives in wanting to go into business for himself?
2. What personal characteristics did he have that favored his becoming a small businessman?
3. What does the case illustrate about the university's role in small business development?
4. What does it show about the government's role?
5. What does the case show about entering an existing business?
6. What does it show about the sources of credit?
7. Discuss the basis used by the Corporation to evaluate an applicant's credit worthiness.
8. Discuss the method used in evaluating the assets of the store.

part III

Staffing Your Business

Lawrence Appley, former president of the American Management Association, said "Management is the development of people and not the direction of things. . . . Management is personnel administration."[1] This statement indicates that the primary duty of all managers is the proper selection, placement, development, and utilization of the talents of their personnel. How well—or how poorly—they do this is a major factor in the success or failure of the business.

Of all the resources of a company, only people have the ability to vary their own productivity. While a machine can perform only the tasks for which it was designed and within the limits of its capacity, employees have many productive capabilities, can be motivated, can be innovative, and can adapt to changing circumstances.

You, as an owner-manager, should understand that the personnel function is important in either establishing a new business or entering an ongoing business. It is also involved in performing the general management and business functions described throughout this book.

Every small business manager is a "personnel manager" in the sense that work is done through people, with people, and for people. Consequently, you should be personally capable of handling employee relations

---

[1] Lawrence A. Appley, "Management Is Personnel Administration," *Personnel*, vol. 46, no. 2 (March–April 1969), p. 8.

until your company becomes large enough to afford a personnel manager.

This part of the text looks into the most important aspects of the personnel function. It contains some valuable insights that can help you be effective as the manager of your business. It contains information about planning your personnel requirements, developing sources from which you can recruit new employees, recruiting them, choosing the people you need, training and developing them into productive workers, evaluating their performance, compensating them, and dealing with various personnel relationships, including industrial relations.

The relationship between these activities is shown in Figure III–1.

FIGURE III–1

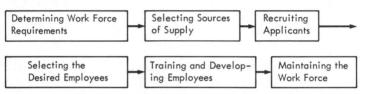

The first four of these functions are discussed in Chapter 9, while the last two are covered in Chapters 10 and 11, respectively.

It may seem to you that many of these functions are of limited value to you in owning-managing a small independent firm. Yet, as your organization grows, you will find these functions becoming increasingly important. Also, while we recognize that even some of the larger firms do not use formalized programs for handling these functions, *we are not trying to do a survey of what is done*. Instead, *we are trying to visualize what you could do in order to operate your business more successfully*. We strongly feel that if you pursue either an informal or a formal program for handling these functions in an effective manner, it will improve the operations of your firm and lead to greater profitability.

9

Selecting Your Employees

You can be successful in your business only if you have the right kind and number of people to help you, for you cannot do everything yourself. As with your other managerial activities, finding and hiring the people who have the productive qualities you need is not easy. Yet, it can be done successfully if you use the same care with, and give the same attention to, this activity as you do others.

The ideal procedure for selecting your people is to determine what jobs are to be performed, decide what qualities you are looking for in the people to be hired, search for individuals with those qualities, select the best persons available, and properly introduce them to your organization and their particular jobs. These subjects will be covered in this chapter under the headings:

1. Planning your personnel requirements.
2. Finding new employees.
3. Recruiting new employees.
4. Selecting employees for given jobs.
5. Introducing new employees to their job.

PLANNING YOUR PERSONNEL REQUIREMENTS

Personnel planning is one of the most frustrating situations that the typical small business manager will encounter. Perhaps the primary reason for this is that the small business is not big enough to hire the exact type and number of people needed. Typically, it does not have the proper means to recruit, select, develop, and utilize its personnel. Lack of economies of scale—so far as record keeping and administration of a systematic personnel program are concerned—may also exist. Another problem may be personality conflicts. One disgruntled person represents a much larger percentage of the total work force in the small firm than in the larger one. Therefore, it is important for the small business manager to try to keep from hiring the wrong employee. A related aspect of this problem is the fact that because of the usual practice of promoting from within, an incompetent worker may rise to higher levels in the organization.

How to Conduct Employee Planning

When you plan your work force, you are concerned with the type and quality of personnel your firm has and what it will need in the future. Therefore, you should:

1. Determine the jobs to be performed and the qualities needed to perform them—that is, assemble job specifications.
2. Forecast the total number of people needed in each category by collecting and analyzing industry growth data and by studying your firm's growth data.
3. Develop employee plans for a given period—perhaps one year—for each job classification or skill.
4. Inventory the skills of all your present personnel—their education, training, and experience; their talents, abilities, skills, and trades; and their potential for growth.
5. Compare your employee plans with your personnel inventory to identify shortages.
6. Determine the sources of supply from which you can recruit extra people as needed.

How to Prepare Job Specifications

Because the quality and quantity of your work force are both important, your personnel plans should be complete and detailed, but flexible and updated at least semi-annually. The statement is frequently made that one should organize around "what is to be done" rather than "who is to do it." The use of *job specifications* will enable you as a small business manager to follow this principle of matching the person to the job to be filled.

A retailer's business was growing rapidly. While he was busy with customers, the telephone was ringing and correspondence was piling up. He believed he needed a secretary. But did he? Secretaries and stenographers are scarce and expensive. Perhaps a typist would fill the bill. Finding a qualified typist would probably be easier, and the salary savings would be substantial. While the retailer might find it a chore to write out letters rather than dictate them, he would probably not be skilled at dictation anyway, and he could probably compose a letter more effectively by seeing how it appeared before typing.[1]

Job specifications are written statements covering the duties, authority, responsibilities, and working conditions of the job and of the *personal qualifications* required of a person to perform the job successfully. A typical job specification includes at least the following types of information:

1. The physical demands of the job and the minimum physical requirements of the individual to fill the job.
2. The working conditions—including physical conditions and psychological conditions such as relationships with others and responsibilities for other people, money, equipment, etc.
3. A summary of the duties and responsibilities of the job.
4. Educational background and knowledge, skills and techniques, and training and experience required to perform the job, as well as special training and development needed.
5. Days and hours of work.
6. Machines, tools, formulas, and other equipment used.
7. The pay classification and promotional opportunities.
8. Desirable personal characteristics.

The specifications should provide a statement of the minimum acceptable standards the person should meet in order to perform the job satisfactorily. For dead-end, routine, and low-level jobs, it may also be desirable to state the maximum acceptable standards in order to prevent an overqualified person from taking the job and being dissatisfied.

Many methods are used to gather data for the job specifications, but the most popular ones are observation, the questionnaire, and the interview.

Job specifications provide the foundation for performing the personnel function effectively. They will aid greatly in recruiting, selecting, and placing employees in your firm and in deciding what wages and salaries to pay. They will also be valuable in personnel training and development and in deciding transfers and promotions.

A service station dealer wanted to hire an "experienced attendant." He believed it was unnecessary to specify the attendant's

---

[1] Rudolph Ralphelson, "Finding and Hiring the Right Employee," *Small Marketers Aids no. 106.* (Washington, D.C.: Small Business Administration, 1972).

FIGURE 9–1
Sample Job Description

Job title: Office and credit manager
Supervisor: Store manager

Job Summary

Responsible for all office and credit functions of the store. Has control of store's assets and expenditures. Helps manager administer store's policies and methods. Exercises mature judgment and initiative in carrying out duties.

Duties

1. Inspects sales tickets for accuracy and completeness of price, stock classifications, and delivery information. (Daily)
2. Prepares bank deposits, listing checks and cash, and takes deposit to bank. (Daily)
3. Keeps sales and expenses record sheets, posting sales and expenses, and accumulating them for the month. (Daily)
4. Processes credit applications: analyzes financial status and paying record of customers, checks references and credit bureau to determine credit responsibility. (Daily)
5. Sends collection notices to past-due accounts, using mail, telephone calls, and personal visits (if necessary) to collect. (Daily)
6. Sells merchandise during rush hours of the store. (Daily)
7. Checks invoices of outside purchases to verify receipt, quantity, price, etc. Gets store manager's approval. (Weekly)
8. Does all bookkeeping and prepares financial and profit-and-loss statements of store. (Monthly)

Duties	Approximate Time Spent on Each Duty (percent)
Bookkeeping	40
Credit and collection	20
Selling on retail floor	20
Inventories and stock control	10
Miscellaneous functions	10

Source: *Personnel Management,* Administrative Management Course Program, Topic 6 (Washington, D.C.: Small Business Administration, 1965), p. 56.

duties because, "He'll know what the job is." But is this true? Service station attendants have different kinds of duties, including working at the pumps selling gasoline, lubricating cars, changing tires, and doing repair work during slack times at the pumps. If the dealer needed a repair man but did not so indicate, he could waste considerable time interviewing men who were qualified only for driveway work.

If you do not want to go to the extreme of preparing job specifications, you should at least establish *job descriptions* for the most important positions. These are merely statements of duties and responsibilities of the job itself, and do not include personal characteristics and qualifications. (See Figure 9–1 for a sample job description.)

FINDING NEW EMPLOYEES

Once you have decided what type(s) of employees you need for a given job, the next step is to decide where to seek them. There are only two basic sources: from *within the firm* through promotion, upgrading, or transfer; and from *outside the company* through recruitment and selection. More specifically, there are four sources usually used by managers of independent businesses. They are:

1. Qualified people from within the organization.
2. Personnel from competing firms in the same industry.
3. Organizations outside the industry.
4. Educational institutions.

A *balanced program* of using people from each source is superior to using either the internal source or the external source exclusively. You should have a balanced policy of promoting from within and recruiting from outside when the need arises.

Filling Jobs from within the Firm

There are three methods of securing employees internally: *upgrading* the employee now holding the position; *promoting* an employee from a lower level job; and *transferring* an employee from a similar position elsewhere in the organization.

Some companies use the outside recruitment device instead of training their own personnel. They permit the larger companies who can afford the expensive costs of the formal training programs to develop the individual employees. Then, the smaller companies pay the higher price, in the form of higher wages, to attract the individuals to work for them.

> An independent insurance company wanted to introduce a new kind of policy, but there was no one in the firm who knew this activity. One of the salesmen, realizing the opportunities involved, left the company and went to work for a national company to learn that type of insurance.
> Later, he rejoined his original employer—as the manager of that activity—at a much higher salary.

Reason for using Internal Source

There are many reasons for and against using internal sources. You should be familiar with these arguments and then make your own decision.

Advantages of using the internal source for your personnel include knowledge concerning the person's capabilities, strengths, and weaknesses. Promotion from within will probably also build the morale of all employees (except, perhaps, the individual who is jealous because of being bypassed).

Disadvantages of the internal source may be the lack of anyone capable of filling the vacant job or willing to take it, and the possible inbreeding produced by excessive reliance on this source.

You should first decide what kind of personal qualifications you are seeking and then choose the sources most likely to produce people with such qualifications. Some of these sources are expensive in terms of your time and money, while others are free. Also, the results are not always worth the cost of using the method.

Upgrading.   Increasing skill requirements in various areas have led to technological unemployment, a situation in which an employee can no longer perform their jobs because educational or skill demands have increased beyond their capacity. Such virtually vacant positions can be filled by upgrading present employees. This involves retraining unskilled or semiskilled workers in their present positions so that they will be able to perform the increasingly complex functions. This method was very effective during World War II, but at present there are two limitations on it: a lack of motivation on the part of the technologically unemployed and a lack of adequate and pertinent procedures by which to select candidates for upgrading. If these restrictions can be overcome, this procedure results in improving and enhancing the individual's productive abilities.

Promoting.   Although increases in salaries are sometimes misconstrued as promotions, this is not necessarily true. For there to be a promotion, there must be movement of the worker to a higher position in which responsibilities are increased and in which there is greater status or prestige. Frequently, promotions result in higher titles or job classifications.

Bases for Promotion.   There are three bases for promotion: *seniority* or the individual's length of service; *merit,* which refers to the individual's ability and capability to perform the job better than others; or a *combination* of the two. In theory, promotions based upon merit are more desirable from an incentive point of view, for they induce employees to produce more in order to demonstrate their "merit." For lower level jobs, however, particularly where unions are involved, seniority is becoming the more common basis for promotion. The reason for this trend is that seniority is objective, does not involve value judgments, and does not lead to as many personal conflicts as do the other bases for promoting.

Transferring. Positions can also be filled internally by transferring an employee from the same organizational level elsewhere in the organization without promoting him. This is usually done when a person has greater capabilities than those required by the position he holds or when the transfer puts him in line for greater potential advancement. Essentially, a transfer involves a change in responsibilities and duties, either with or without a change in pay.

Job Posting. If a union represents your employees, you will probably be required to post available job openings on a bulletin board to give present employees a chance to bid on them. This method has also been found to be a good method of complying with equal employment opportunities laws.

Methods of Improving Internal Sources. To utilize internal sources most effectively, you might want to consider using the currently popular process of "job enlargement," or, preferably, "job enrichment." By means of job enrichment, the duties of a few different jobs may be combined into one job.

> One of your machine operators, in addition to handling regular production runs, might also be assigned to set up the machine, inspect the completed work, service the machine, or perform other duties.

Job interest and satisfaction may be increased for some of your employees by rotating them among a few to several jobs, or by rearranging their work places to permit them to enjoy more group interaction.

Filling Jobs from outside the Firm

Ultimately, all jobs must be filled from outside the organization, unless the company is reducing its work force. As individual positions are filled through upgrading, promoting, or transferring employees, the vacated positions must be filled externally.

Reasons for Using External Sources. A growing organization must go outside to obtain personnel for at least its lowest level jobs. But there are also reasons for going outside for high-level personnel. Inevitably, there needs to be an infusion of "new blood" into an organization to prevent "inbreeding," conformity, and stagnation.

A more valid justification for external hirings is found in problems caused by mechanization and automation. Because of the new skills that are often needed in a hurry, it is sometimes necessary to go outside the organization to find an individual with the education, training, and experience that provide you with the required skill level. It should be added, however, that companies are beginning to assume the responsibility of first trying to upgrade their own employees.

When internal promotion policy is followed too rigidly, there are inevitable mistakes in filling higher job requirements. The personnel may have either too much or too little education, and there may be excessive emphasis on social acceptability, level of anticipation, experience, and so forth. It is practically impossible to anticipate the skills that will be needed in the future, to hire someone with those requirements who will enter at the bottom, and to expect that person to progress all the way through the organization.

Some Sources You Can Use.   Some of the specific outside sources from which you can recruit new employees are:

1. Former employees.
2. Friends and relatives of employees by means of "referrals."
3. Personal applications received in person or through the mail.
4. Competing firms.
5. Labor organizations.
6. Employment agencies, either public or private.
7. Educational institutions, including high schools, business schools, vocational-technical schools, junior colleges, colleges, and manufacturers' training schools.
8. Leased manpower.

RECRUITING NEW EMPLOYEES

After you have decided the specifications for the job(s) to be filled and the source from which you are going to recruit prospective employees, someone must set the selection procedure in motion. This really involves two things, namely, *recruiting*, or attracting a group of prospective employees, then *selecting* the one(s) you need and want.

The more effective firms use some form of requisition to initiate the procedure. In essence, this tells the manager responsible for the personnel function how many employees are needed, what qualifications they need, when they will be needed, and how much they will be paid.

There are many methods you can use in recruiting new people. These include:

1. School and college scouting.
2. Advertising, using newspapers, trade journals, radio, billboards, and window displays.
3. Private and public employment agencies.
4. Employee referrals.

The following is an example of using an external source and two methods of recruiting:

> A retail store manager put a Help Wanted sign in the window. He found this practice to be time-consuming, because many unqualified applicants inquired about the job. Furthermore, when he disapproved an applicant, he stood the risk of losing the business of the applicant plus his friends and family. The manager also found that newspaper advertising reached large groups of job seekers. But it also brought in many unqualified people. If the store's telephone number was included in the ad, calls tied up his line and customers could not reach the store.
>
> In order to fill his vacancy, the manager should have considered using the services of either a public or a private employment agency, or he should have obtained leads from his present employees.

SELECTING EMPLOYEES FOR GIVEN JOBS

Mistakes in selecting and placing personnel in your firm can be greatly reduced if you use an orderly and systematic procedure for choosing the right people. While no one method is generally acceptable, the following procedure illustrates one effective method that can be used in filling a position.

1. Review the job specifications for this position.
2. Consider your present employees, for one of them may be able to perform the job acceptably, or become qualified if his abilities are upgraded.
3. Look outside the company and recruit applicants if none of your present employees can fill the job.
4. Use an application blank in gathering information from applicants.
5. Prepare for interviews with applicants by listing the points you need to cover.
6. Conduct the interviews.
7. Bring the supervisor of the prospective employee into the act; you may even want him to do the interviewing.
8. Use psychological tests to determine the applicant's knowledge, skills, and attitudes.
9. Check on qualified applicants with their previous employers.
10. Arrange for the applicant to take a physical examination.
11. Decide whether the applicant should be hired on a trial basis.
12. Conduct an orientation program for the new employee.
13. Decide whether the employee should be retained after a prearranged probationary period.

FIGURE 9–2
Flowchart of Selection Procedure

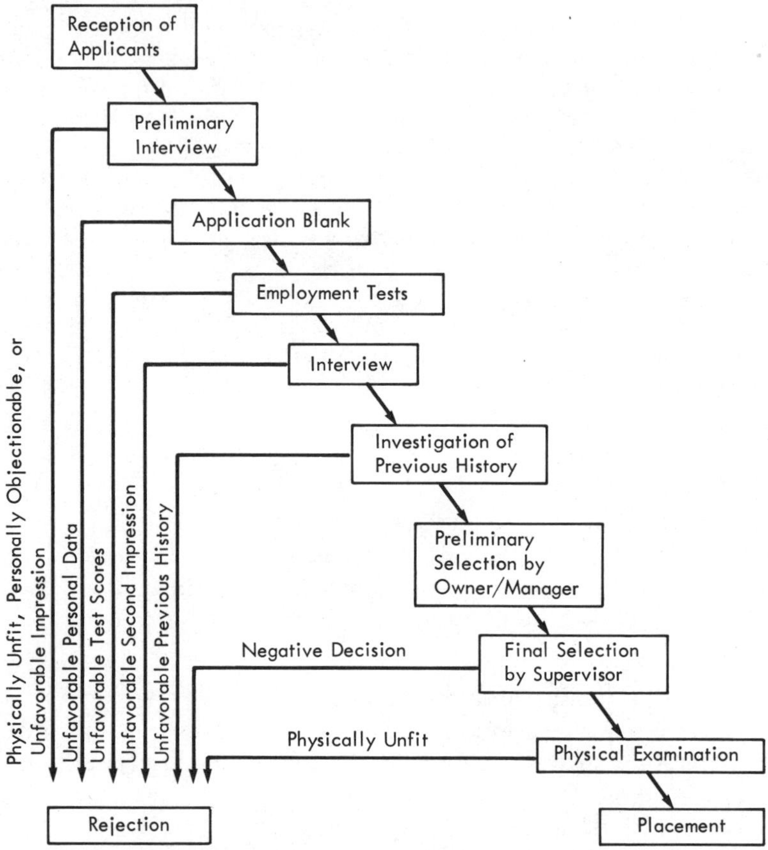

Source: Based on L. C. Megginson, *Personnel: and Human Resources Administration*, 3d ed. (Homewood, Ill.: Richard D. Irwin, Inc., 1977), pp. 195 and 202.

Figure 9–2 shows this suggested selection procedure in graphic form. A word of caution is in order at this point, 1978. The Civil Rights Act of 1964, the Age Discrimination in Employment Act of 1967, the Vietnam Era Veterans' Readjustment Assistance Act of 1972, the Rehabilitation Act of 1973, and other Federal laws, as well as Executive Orders 10,925; 11,246; 11,375; 11,491; 11,616; and others, prevent discrimination against prospective employees on grounds of race, creed, color, sex, nation of origin, physical condition, or age. In fact, you should have an *affirmative action program* of hiring people from various groups. You should be certain that your selection procedure conforms to national and local laws and customs. (See Chapter 11 for more details.) Since Congress, the courts, and administrative interpretations continue to undergo change in the area of employee selection, it is suggested that you keep current on the present status of those things that apply to you and your business.

Application Blank

Application blanks are used at the time a candidate applies for employment, and may be submitted in person or by mail. The candidate lists employers for whom he has worked, titles of jobs he has held, and the length of employment with each company. He describes his background, education, marital status, military status, and other useful data. The blank should be carefully designed to provide information that you need about the candidates, but it should not be a "hodge-podge" of irrelevant data. The completion of the blank by the applicant will provide you a sample of his neatness, thoroughness, and ability to answer questions. Since many states have restrictions concerning the kinds of questions that may be included on an application blank, you should check any laws that your state may have governing such practices.

Figure 9–3 is one of the best application blanks we have seen. Although it is used by one of the largest firms in the country, *it can be used by you as a model of completeness, conciseness, clarity, and legality.* (Notice the *lack* of questions that would violate equal employment opportunities laws.) You could use this form as a model to design your own form to provide you with the necessary information to make employment decisions, and yet not run afoul of the law.

Interviewing

In preparing for the interview, you should use the information in the application blank to learn about the applicant. You should prepare beforehand the questions you need to ask to get the other information you need. Your personal experience with the job may provide some questions. In order not to overlook anything significant during the interview, you should list the points that should be covered. You should ask the applicant specific questions, such as:

1. What did you do on your last job?
2. How did you do it?
3. Why did you do it?
4. What job did you like best? Least?

Compare your list of questions with the job specification to see that you are matching the individual's personal qualifications with the job requirements.

If you are observant and perceptive during the interview, you can obtain some impressions about the candidate's abilities, personality, and attitudes toward work, as well as evaluate appearance and speech. You

FIGURE 9–3
Example of an Effective Application Blank

991-0002H
APPLICATION FOR EMPLOYMENT

EXXON

PLEASE PRINT

Exxon Corporation and affiliates

EQUAL OPPORTUNITY EMPLOYERS

PERSONAL

NAME (LAST, FIRST, MIDDLE)

CONTACT PHONE NO. (GIVE AREA CODE) — A.M. — P.M. — TIME

PRESENT ADDRESS — ALTERNATE PHONE NO. (GIVE AREA CODE) — TO

PERMANENT ADDRESS (IF DIFFERENT FROM ABOVE) — CONTACT PHONE NO. (GIVE AREA CODE) — CALL

SOCIAL SECURITY NO. — DO YOU HAVE RELATIVES WITH EXXON? (NAME, WHERE, RELATIONSHIP) ☐YES ☐NO — HAVE YOU APPLIED TO EXXON BEFORE? (WHICH COMPANY - WHEN)

U.S. CITIZEN ☐YES ☐NO — NON-U.S. CITIZEN — PLEASE INDICATE U.S. VISA STATUS ☐PERMANENT VISA ☐STUDENT VISA — EXCHANGE STUDENT VISA — VISITORS VISA — OTHER VISA EXPLAIN

ALIEN REGISTRATION NO. — HAVE YOU EVER BEEN DEPORTED FROM THE U.S.? ☐YES ☐NO

EDUCATION

NAME AND LOCATION OF HIGH SCHOOL					GRAD. DATE	(MO./YR.)	YOUR CLASS STANDING IN YOUR MAJOR	YOUR OVERALL GRADEPOINT AVERAGE

COLLEGE NAME AND LOCATION	DATE (MO./YR.)		FIELDS OF STUDY		GRADUATION		MY STDG. IS 1ST IN CLASS OF 60 EXAMPLE: 1/60	MY AVG. 3.7 ALL A'S 4.0 EXAMPLE: 3.7/4.0
	FROM	TO	MAJOR	MINOR	DEGREE*	DATE (MO./YR.)	/	/
							/	/
							/	/

*INSERT NUMBER OF COLLEGE CREDIT HOURS COMPLETED IF NO DEGREE OBTAINED.

COLLEGE FINANCING — % G.I. BILL — OWN % WORK — % SCHOLARSHIP EXPLAIN- — % OTHER EXPLAIN-

EMPLOYMENT

EMPLOYMENT DESIRED ☐PERMANENT ☐SUMMER — DATE AVAILABLE FOR WORK — LOCATION PREFERENCE (IF ANY) — SALARY EXPECTED

TYPE OF WORK DESIRED INITIALLY — TYPE OF WORK DESIRED EVENTUALLY

IS THERE SOME DIVISION OR FUNCTION IN WHICH YOU ARE ESPECIALLY INTERESTED? — IS THERE A SPECIFIC PROJECT OR STUDY THAT YOU WOULD LIKE TO DO?

EMPLOYER NAME, ADDRESS & PHONE NO. (INCLUDE GRADUATE ASSISTANTSHIP & SUMMER JOBS)	DATE (MO./YR.)		YOUR JOB TITLE AND DUTIES	SUPERVISOR'S NAME AND JOB TITLE
	FROM	TO		

U.S. MIL.

BRANCH OF SERVICE — FROM (MO./YR.) — TO (MO./YR.) — RANK ON ENTRY — RANK ON DISCHARGE — TYPE OF DUTY (ESPECIALLY IF PROFESSIONAL)

ACTIVITIES

SUBJECTS OF SPECIAL STUDY OR RESEARCH, COLLEGE OR OTHER

HONORS, HONOR SOCIETIES, SCHOLARSHIPS, EXTRA CURRICULAR ACTIVITIES - OFFICES HELD OR RESPONSIBILITIES (EXCLUDE THOSE WHICH INDICATE RACE, COLOR, RELIGION, SEX, OR NATIONAL ORIGIN)

ADDITIONAL INFORMATION

Have you been convicted under any criminal law within the past 5 years? (Excluding minor traffic violations) ☐YES ☐NO

Have you ever been imprisoned as a result of a criminal conviction? ☐YES ☐NO
If the answer to either of the above questions is "YES", please give details on back.

Are you or have you ever knowingly been a member of the Communist Party or any organization which advocates overthrow of the United States Government by force or any illegal or unconstitutional method?

☐YES ☐NO   If "YES", please give details on back.

ARE YOU UNDER TECHNICAL CONTRACT OR RESTRICTION WITH A FORMER EMPLOYER? ☐NO ☐YES – WITH WHOM?

MAY WE CALL YOUR PRESENT EMPLOYER? NOW – ☐YES ☐NO — AFTER VISIT – ☐YES ☐NO — COMMENTS

I authorize investigation of all statements contained in this application for employment. I understand that misrepresentation or omission of facts called for hereon will be sufficient cause for cancellation of consideration for employment or dismissal from the Company's service if I have been employed. I understand that employment is subject to a physical examination in which my health is found to be satisfactory to the Company. I understand that if I am employed evidence of U.S. citizenship or U.S. resident status or a birth certificate or other evidence of date of birth will be required.

X SIGNATURE   DATE SIGNED

This is to inform you that as part of our procedure of processing your employment application it is understood that an investigative report may be made whereby information is obtained through personal interviews with third parties. This inquiry includes information as to your character, general reputation, personal characteristics, and mode of living, whichever may be applicable. You have the right to make a written request within a reasonable period of time for a complete and accurate disclosure of additional information concerning the nature and scope of the investigation.

(PLEASE GIVE US ANY ADDITIONAL INFORMATION ON SCHOLASTIC ACHIEVEMENT OR EXPERIENCE ON A SEPARATE SHEET OF PAPER)

Source: Exxon Company.

can also provide information about your company and the job. Remember, the applicant needs facts to decide whether to accept or reject the job, just as you need information to decide whether or not to offer it. The interview may be individual or group, and may be structured or nondirective in nature.

The supervisor of the prospective employee should have an important role in this procedure. In fact, you may want the supervisor to conduct the interview as well as evaluate the application blank. If you are the interviewer, however, you should at least have the supervisor meet the applicant and show him the job and the work area. Failure to let the supervisor participate can lead to unfavorable attitudes later.

The interviewing may occur in one or two stages. Some firms have a *preliminary interview,* during which the application is completed and general observations of the applicant are made. A *more penetrating interview* may be held later to probe his attitudes, belief system, and willingness and desire to work. The method you choose will depend upon the time available and the importance of the position to be filled.

Employment Tests

Through using employment tests, you can determine the candidate's intelligence quotient (IQ), skill, aptitude, vocational interest, and personality. *IQ tests* are designed to measure one's capacity to learn and solve problems and to comprehend complex relationships, and are particularly useful in selecting employees for managerial positions. *Proficiency and skill tests* are tests of ability to perform a particular trade, craft, or skill, and are useful in selecting operative employees. *Aptitude tests* are used to predict how a person might perform on a given job, and are most applicable to operative jobs.

Vocational interest tests are designed to determine the areas of major interests of the applicant, as far as work is concerned. Interest does not guarantee competence, but it can result in the employee working and trying harder. A limitation of the test is that certain persons are adept at faking the answers.

Personality tests are designed to measure whether the applicant is an "introvert" or an "extrovert," the total personality structure, and emotional adjustment and attitudes. These tests, along with inventories of emotional maturity, are often used to evaluate interpersonal relationships and see how the person might fit into your organization. Faked answers can also arise in using these tests. In addition to their use in selection, these tests are valuable in evaluating present employees for promotion and as a basis for consulting with employees.

Aptitude tests are, by far, the most reliable indicators of an applicant's skill level. On the other hand, intelligence and personality tests should be interpreted by professionals. You may be able to obtain some testing assistance from your state employment service.

If tests are used as a basis for making any personnel decision, they must be *valid*, that is, there must be a high degree of correlation between the test scores and objective measures of performance on the job; *designed and administered by a professional; culturally unbiased;* and *in complete conformity with EEOC guidelines.*[2]

Checking References

The small business manager is often victimized by employees whose credentials are not checked thoroughly. The importance of your checking applicants' references carefully cannot be overemphasized.

Reference checks provide answers to questions concerning the candidate's performance on previous jobs. They are helpful in verifying information on the application blank and statements made during interviews. They are also useful in checking on possible omissions of information and clarifying specific points. Three sources of reference are:

1. Academic.
2. Personal.
3. Previous employers.

Checks made by telephone or in person with business references are preferred to written responses. The writer of a letter of reference may have little or no idea of your job requirements. Also, past employers are sometimes reluctant to write uncomplimentary letters of reference. Be sure to ask specific questions about the candidate's performance, as well as determining whether former employers would consider rehiring the person.

Physical Examination

The applicant's health and physical condition should be matched to the physical requirements of the job. You should require that each applicant be examined by a physician before hiring. The examination could reveal physical limitations that would limit job performance. Also, it will help you comply with your state's workmen's compensation laws by providing a record of the employee's health at the time of hiring. Compensation claims for an injury that occurred prior to his employment with you could be prevented. This step is usually last, as it is ordinarily the most expensive one.

---

[2] See L. C. Megginson, *Personnel and Human Resources Administration,* 3d ed. (Homewood, Ill.: Richard D. Irwin, Inc., 1977), pp. 206–8 and 226–33, for further information on this subject.

Decision to Hire

After completion of the selection procedure, you are in a position to decide whether the applicant should be hired on a trial basis or rejected. The final decision whether the employee matches the job requirements should be made only at the end of a probationary period. Furthermore, by that time, the employee should know your company sufficiently well to decide whether to stay. Probationary periods should be set for the various jobs in your company, with length depending upon the type of work. Some jobs may require six weeks, and others six months—depending on how long it takes to learn to perform the job acceptably.

INTRODUCING NEW EMPLOYEES TO THEIR JOBS

Frequent discussions should be held with a new employee during the orientation program. Several should be held during the first day and during the first week. The purpose of these talks is to determine that the new employee has the necessary facts about you and your firm and about your objectives, policies, and rules. You should also inform the employee of your ideas of what performance is expected.

A formal interview with the employee may be appropriate at some point during the first month. Its purpose would be to correct any mistaken ideas that the employee may have about the job, and to determine whether the employee feels that you and your people are fulfilling your commitments.

During the orientation and follow-up period, you should compare the new employee's performance with your expectations. You can also start to point out any shortcomings, as well as strong points. Another formal meeting should also be held at the end of the probationary period. You will then state whether you are going to keep the employee or not.

During the probationary period, you can depend upon personal observations of the new employee. You can also check with the supervisor concerning progress and receive volunteer comments from co-workers.

When you make the final decision concerning retention or dismissal, again refer to the job specification. Review it item by item. The new employee's supervisor should do the same. The two evaluations should be compared. If your decision is to keep the new employee, discuss both strong points and weak ones. Encourage the employee to keep trying to improve. State when to expect a merit increase in pay. If you decide the employee is to be rejected, the parting should be as graceful as possible.

SUMMARY

Some ideas on selecting people to help you operate your business are offered in this chapter. You may not be able to use all these ideas in your firm, especially when it is new and small. And yet, you may be able to use some of the thoughts in an informal way, even if you don't have formal programs.

This chapter has covered (1) personnel planning, (2) source of new employees, (3) recruiting new people, (4) selecting people for given jobs, and (5) introducing new people to the job.

In doing *personnel planning*, you should (1) develop job specifications, (2) forecast the total number of people needed in each category, (3) develop employee plans, (4) inventory the skills of all your present personnel, (5) compare your plans with your inventory so you can identify shortages, and (6) determine the sources of supply from which you can recruit the extra people needed.

Some specific sources from which you might be able to recruit new personnel were given.

In *recruiting* people, you can use (1) school and college scouting, (2) advertising, (3) private and public employee agencies, and (4) employee referrals.

In *selecting* people, you need to (1) review the job specifications for the position, (2) consider your present employees, (3) recruit applicants from outside the company if none of your employees can fill the job, (4) use an application blank in gathering information from applicants, (5) prepare for interviews with applicants by listing the points that you need to cover, (6) conduct the interviews, (7) bring the supervisor of the prospective employee into the act, (8) use psychological tests, (9) check on qualified applicants with their previous employers, (10) arrange for a physical examination, (11) decide whether the applicant should be hired on a trial basis, (12) conduct an orientation program for the new employee, and (13) decide whether the employee should be retained after a definite probationary period.

After the person is hired, it is important that you *introduce him to the job* properly, for this is where most labor turnover begins.

QUESTIONS FOR FURTHER DISCUSSION

1. According to Lawrence Appley, what is the primary duty of every manager?
2. What does manpower planning entail in the small company?
3. Explain some possible effects of equal employment opportunities laws on a small firm.
4. What specific sources for finding new employees are usually used in small businesses?
5. Give some of the advantages and disadvantages of using the internal source of labor supply.

6. What methods can be used by small business managers in recruiting new people?

7. What are some possible alternatives to using tests?

8. How would you prepare for, and conduct, an effective interview with an applicant?

9. What are some sources of references that the small business manager may use in investigating applicant?

10. Why should a physical examination be required of an applicant?

11. Why is a probationary period needed for new employees?

12. How should new people be introduced to their jobs?

10

Developing and Maintaining Your Personnel

In the last chapter, you learned about planning your personnel requirements, selecting the sources from which you would recruit your employees, determining how to recruit them, and doing the actual selection of people. Now that you have selected and placed your people, you need to be concerned with:

1. Training and developing them into productive workers.
2. Setting their wages and salaries.
3. Directing their activities.
4. Evaluating their performances.

This chapter covers these topics in depth.

TRAINING AND DEVELOPING YOUR EMPLOYEES

The ultimate efficiency of your business will be determined by the interaction of two related factors:

1. The caliber of the people you hire, including their inherent abilities, and their development through training, education, experience, and motivation.
2. The effectiveness of their personal development by you after they are hired.

The process called *personnel development* may be defined as an attempt to increase the employee's productive capacity up to the highest level of the job to be performed.

Need for Training

Not only must your new employees be trained, but also the present ones must be retrained and upgraded in order to adjust to rapidly changing job requirements. Some of the more general reasons for you to emphasize growth and development are:

1. Readily available and adequate replacements for present personnel who may leave or move up.
2. Freedom to use advancements in technology because of a more highly trained staff.
3. A more efficient, effective, and highly motivated work team, which increases the company's competitive position.
4. Adequate manpower resources for expansion programs.

More specific results that you will probably receive from training and developing your workers include:

1. Increased productivity.
2. Reduced turnover.
3. Increased financial rewards.
4. Decreased costs of materials and equipment.
5. Less supervision required.
6. Higher morale.

Your employees also have a stake in development, for they acquire a greater sense of worth, dignity, and well-being as they become more valuable to society. They will receive a greater share of the material gains that result from their increased productivity. These two factors will give them a sense of satisfaction in the achievement of personal and company goals.

Methods of Training

You, as the small business manager, have access to various methods of training nonmanagerial employees. These methods include:

1. On-the-job training (OJT).
2. Apprenticeship.
3. Internship.
4. Outside training.

On-the-job training is a program in which the employees receive training while they perform their regular jobs. Thus, they are both producers and learners. An effective program consists of these steps:

1. Planning what is to be taught the employee.
2. Informing the employee of the details of the plan.

3. Establishing a time schedule for the employee to follow.
4. Periodically advising the trainee about his/her progress.

The purpose of *apprenticeship training* is to develop well-rounded individuals who are capable of performing a variety of jobs. It usually involves learning a group of skills that, when combined, qualify one to practice a trade. The program is usually a long-term process, covering from two to seven years, and a union is often involved in administering it.

Internship training is a combination of school and on-the-job training. It is usually used with employees who are prospects for marketing or clerical positions, or who are being prepared for management positions.

In *outside training*, the employees receive training at schools outside the company. Usually, the company reimburses the employees for all or part of their tuition expenses.

Other forms of development that you probably can use on a limited basis are *programmed instruction* (sometimes called "learning machines"), *educational television, extension courses,* and *correspondence courses.*

Outside Assistance You Can Use in Training

There are many outside programs available to help you train employees. You can probably use some of the following.

All states have *vocational-technical education* programs whereby vocational-technical schools assist firms by conducting regular or special classes where potential employees can become qualified for skilled jobs, such as machinist, lathe operator, power-machine operator, and so forth.

Another training activity for new employees is the *vocational rehabilitation* programs sponsored by the U.S. Department of Health, Education, and Welfare in cooperation with state governments. These programs provide counseling, medical care, and vocational training for physically and mentally handicapped individuals.

The Manpower Development and Training Act of 1962, as amended, provides a program of federal assistance in training unemployed and underemployed workers. You would hire these individuals and pay their wages. The government reimburses you for part of those wages, instruction fees, and materials and supplies used and provides advice and consultation on training problems and in developing training programs. You do the actual training yourself.

Title V of the Economic Opportunity (Antipoverty) Act of 1964 authorizes state welfare departments to provide training programs for welfare recipients or members of their families. The individual is hired by you and you do the training, with the government paying the cost of training.

These last two programs—and many others—have been incorporated into the Comprehensive Employment and Training Act of 1973, but are still available to help you train minority members and the disadvantaged.

The JOBS (Job Opportunities in the Business Sector) Program, which was launched several years ago by NAB (the National Alliance of Businessmen), encourages you—the employer—to submit proposals for contracts to provide on-the-job training for the disadvantaged, hard-core unemployed. You are paid for any additional costs incurred because of limited qualifications of those hired and trained. The state *public employment offices* are used for recruiting, selecting, and counseling the trainees.

The National Apprenticeship Act of 1937, which is administered by the Bureau of Apprenticeship and Training in the Labor Department, sets policy for apprenticeship programs. Write to this Bureau for help in conducting such a program.

Some Guidelines for Developing People

Some specific basic guidelines that can be of great help to you in developing and conducting your training and development programs are:

1. The objectives of the development activities should be established.
2. Trainees should be carefully selected.
3. Qualified instructors and proper instructional techniques should be used. Be aware that good managers are not necessarily effective trainers.
4. Some method of evaluating the results of the training program should be established.
5. Trainees should not be brought along faster than they can absorb the training and demonstrate the skills. On the other hand, they should not be permitted to stagnate in the program.
6. Feedback on performance should flow from both trainers and trainees. The former should periodically report results to trainees and to you, and the latter should also submit written reports periodically to you on their progress.
7. Learning is stimulated by motivation. When trainees finish the program, they should be given new and challenging assignments with appropriate increases in compensation or advances in position.

Developing employees for your competitors should be avoided! Yet, your firm will probably experience some degree of personnel turnover. People die, become disabled, retire, or quit. Voluntary separations, or quits, are a key indicator. If these separations occur often, you should determine the reason. Among the reasons may be poor supervision, dead-end jobs, or poor training or motivation of employees.

SETTING WAGES AND SALARIES

Another important duty you have is setting wages and salaries for your people. Their earnings must be high enough to motivate them to be good producers, yet low enough for your firm to maintain a satisfactory earnings level.

Effects of Governmental Factors

As with selection and training, there are many state and federal laws, executive orders, rules, and regulations with which your wage policy must comply.

One of the first things you must be concerned with is the *Fair Labor Standards Act of 1938* (sometimes called the Wage and Hour law), which currently requires that you pay your employees a *minimum* wage of $2.65 per hour (at January 1, 1978, up to $3.35 in 1981) plus one and one-half time their hourly rate for all hours over 40 per week. As these rates are subject to change, by action of Congress, you should check with the local Wage and Hour Division of the Department of Labor for the latest figures. While certain managerial and professional personnel are exempt from the provisions of the act, you should also check with the Division for specific details, as they are too numerous and involved to present in a summary such as this.

The Equal Pay Act of 1963 requires you to pay females the same rate you pay males for doing the same "general" type of work.

If you have a contract involving federal funds, you may be subject to the Public Construction Act of 1931, the Service Contract Act of 1965, or the Public Contracts Act of 1936. You should check with the Labor Department to see whether you are legally liable under any of these acts.

Rewarding Nonmanagerial Employees

There are two aspects of wage and salary administration that are particularly relevant to small business. People work for monetary and nonmonetary rewards. *Nonmonetary* rewards are a form of psychic income, and they often motivate us even when monetary income fails to do so.

As for monetary rewards, you should understand that both the *absolute* and *relative* amounts of income received are important to employees. They are concerned with their *absolute* level of pay so far as it is adequate to meet their needs. However, they are also concerned about their *relative* level of income when compared with what their fellow workers are making. In fact, an employee could be quite satisfied with the amount of absolute pay, but highly disgruntled because an associate at an equal or lower status is receiving higher pay.

Setting Rates of Pay

Some important factors to consider when setting rates of pay are:

1. Effort: Employees like to believe they are paid in proportion to their physical and mental expenditures.
2. Time: The time spent performing a job should be directly related to the amount of pay.
3. Your ability to pay.
4. The standard and cost of living in the area.
5. Legislation, including laws establishing minimum wages and hours for which overtime is paid.
6. Unions, including wage patterns established through collective bargaining—whether or not your firm is unionized.
7. Supply and demand for workers, which are reflected in the wages received by employees with similar skills in the area.

One way you can provide more equitable wages and salaries is to use either formal or informal *job evaluation,* whereby the relative worth of each job to your firm is determined. The job evaluation process can be done in a number of ways, but the *ranking system* and the *point system* are the two most commonly used. Managers of independent firms who perform their own job evaluation generally rank jobs in some ascending or descending order, depending upon their relative values to the company. Professional consultants performing job evaluation programs for small businesses generally use the point system.

In actual practice, *prevailing rates and classifications* are used extensively by small business managers. In other words, managers pay greater attention to the so-called going rates in the community, as determined by wage and salary surveys or word of mouth, for similar jobs in establishing their companies' wage and salary structures.

Other Aspects of the Wage and Salary Administration Program

Some other aspects you should consider in compensating your employees are:

1. The manner in which the employees will be paid: by wage or by salary.
2. The wage and salary structure in your firm.
3. Adoption of a wage incentive system.
4. The extent of employee benefits—such as life insurance; hospitalization, sickness, and accident insurance; and pension plans—you will provide your workers.

A *wage incentive system* may be an effective motivational tool, particularly in a small manufacturing plant. Purposes of the plan can include increased production, reduced waste, and better use of machinery. Employees' productivity, skill, effort, and attitudes can then be rewarded on a more equitable basis. The oldest and most frequently used plan is a straight piece-rate system, whereby a given rate is paid for each unit produced.

Another plan is a *cash bonus based on profit.* Often, young employees prefer "cash-in-hand" because of their need for cash and the effects of inflation.

A company reviewing its employee benefit program was considering a pension program. A detailed analysis proved that the existing plan of a monthly cash bonus based on company profits and a year-end cash bonus based on 11 months' profits provided the best incentive.

You may also want to consider *bonus awards* for outstanding performance. A certain sum of money or a gift is given to outstanding employees.

The owner-manager of a small company decided to eliminate paid vacations and sick leave. Instead, all employees were given 30 days annual leave to use as they saw fit. At the end of the year, they were paid at regular rates for the leave not used. Employees had previously had to prove they were actually ill when sick leave was taken, and they had to apply for personal leave in advance. The results attained from the new program were reduced unscheduled absences and overtime pay, and happier, more productive employees.[1]

Other motivational possibilities are:

1. Using bonuses as morale boosters, particularly during seasonal slacks or other "slow" periods.
2. Controlling absenteeism through incentive compensation.
3. Using profit-sharing plans to stimulate productivity.

Whatever plan you use should be simple and easy to administer. Also, it should be clearly understood and accepted by the employees.

Some Special Considerations in Granting Pensions. You could also consider using one or more of the following employee benefit programs: money-purchase pension plan, pension plan, and bonus awards. Most small businesses can afford these deferred-compensation programs, which are intended to help attract and hold quality employees. The Internal Revenue Service has approved model plans that contain all the forms

---

[1] Jack H. Feller, Jr., "Keep Pointed toward Profit," *Management Aids for Small Manufacturers no. 206* (Washington, D.C.: Small Business Administration, 1972).

and agreements needed to establish a comprehensive, simple, and flexible program. You can choose from a wide variety of plans—from mutual funds, banks, insurance companies, and others—in tailoring a program to your company's needs.

If you desire to give your employees a retirement income based on a fixed dollar contribution by the company, the *money-purchase pension plan* is appropriate. Deposits for all employees in the plan must be the same percentage of pay. You should consider this plan only if your company has relatively stable earnings.

Under a *pension plan,* you can provide your employees with retirement benefits that can be computed at any time. The plan is dependent neither on profits nor on pension-fund investments. It will necessitate an actuarial study.

Requirements for a successful employee benefit plan are:[2]

1. Your company's plan should be the right type for your purpose.
2. Generally, your company's contribution should be at least eight percent of the employee's salary or wages.
3. Your company needs an average annual return of at least six to eight percent from investment of the plan's funds in order to underwrite the benefits.
4. You should remind and inform your employees about the benefits and value of their plan at least annually.[3]
5. Your plan should be reviewed periodically and kept up to date in its benefits.

The Employee Retirement Income Security Act (Pension Reform Act) of 1974 is profoundly affecting small firms; its main provisions are shown in Figure 10–1. Because the law proved difficult for many small businesses to conform to, many decided to give up their program and permit their employees to have their own private retirement program. (See the seventh item—Individual Retirement Accounts—in the figure.)

Other Financial Benefits. There are two other financial programs that you should know about. If you use them, by all means call in experts to aid you!

The Keogh Plan (HR 10) permits you as a self-employed person or a partner in a partnership to have a tax-deferred retirement program. Up to $7,500, or 15 percent of earned income, whichever is lower, may be withheld from your current income and invested.

---

[2] Harold A. Hobson, Jr., "Selecting Employee Benefit Plans, *Management Aids for Small Manufacturers no. 213* (Washington, D.C.: Small Business Administration, 1972).

[3] This is now required by the Pension Reform Act of 1974. See Rudolph Kagerer, "Do Employees Understand Your Benefits Program?" *The Personnel Administrator,* vol. 20, no. 6 (October 1975), pp. 29–31, for details.

FIGURE 10–1
The Pension Reform Law

Major Provisions	Effective Dates*	
	Existing Plans	New Plans
Eligibility .... Prohibits plans from establishing eligibility requirements of more than 1 year of service, or an age greater than 25, whichever is later.	January 1, 1976	Date of enactment (September 2, 1974)
Vesting .... Establishes new minimum standards; employer has three choices: 1. 100 percent vesting after 10 years of service. 2. 25 percent vesting after 5 years of service, grading up to 100 percent after 15 years. 3. 50 percent vesting when age and service (if the employee has at least 5 years of service) equal 45, grading up to 100 percent vesting 5 years later.	January 1, 1976	Date of enactment
Funding .... Requires the employer to fund annually the full cost for current benefit accruals and amortize past service benefit liabilities over 30 years for new plans and 40 years for existing plans.	January 1, 1976	Date of enactment
Plan termination insurance .... Establishes a government insurance fund to insure vested pension benefits up to the lesser of $750 a month or 100 percent of the employee's average wages during his highest paid 5 years of employment; the employer pays an annual premium of $1 per participant and is liable for any insurance benefits paid up to 30 percent of the company's net worth.	Benefits: July 1, 1974; other provisions: Date of enactment	Phased in over 5 years
Fiduciary responsibility .... Establishes the "prudent man" rule as the basic standard of fiduciary responsibility; prohibits various transactions between fiduciaries and parties-in-interest; prohibits investment of more than 10 percent of pension plan assets in the employer's securities.	January 1, 1975	January 1, 1975

		Date of enactment	Date of enactment
Portability	Permits an employee leaving a company to make a tax-free transfer of the assets behind his vested pension benefits (if the employer agrees) or of his vested profit-sharing or savings plan funds to an individual retirement account.	January 1, 1975	January 1, 1975
Individual retirement accounts (IRAs)	Provides a vehicle for transfers as noted above and permits employees of private or public employers that do not have qualified retirement plans to deduct 15 percent of compensation, up to $1,500, each year for contributions to a personal retirement fund. Earnings on the fund are not taxable until distributed.	January 1, 1975	January 1, 1975
Reporting and disclosure	Requires the employer to provide employees with a comprehensive booklet describing plan provisions and to report annually to the secretary of labor on various operating and financial details of the plan.	January 1, 1975	January 1, 1975
Lump-sum distributions	Changes the tax rules to provide capital gains treatment on pre-1974 amounts and to tax post-1973 amounts as ordinary income, but as the employee's only income and spread over 10 years.	January 1, 1974	January 1, 1974
Limits on contributions and benefits	1. Increases the maximum deductible annual contributions that can be made by self-employed people to H.R. 10 or Keogh plans to the lesser of $7,500 or 15 percent of earned income.	January 1, 1974	January 1, 1974
	2. Limits benefits payable from defined benefit pension plans to the lesser of $75,000 a year or 100 percent of average annual cash compensation during the employee's 3 highest paid years of service.	January 1, 1975	January 1, 1975
	3. Limits annual additions to employee profit-sharing accounts to the lesser of $25,000 or 25 percent of the employee's compensation that year.	January 1, 1976	January 1, 1976

* Applicable to single employer plans; multiemployer plans are given more time to comply with some of the new standards.
Source: Donald G. Carlson, "Responding to the Pension Reform Law," *Harvard Business Review*, vol. 52, no. 6 (November–December 1974), p. 134.

Under the *keyman deferred compensation plan,* a contract is drawn between you and your employee. Your firm agrees to invest annually a specified dollar amount or percent of wages. Your firm holds title to these assets until the retirement, disability, or death of the employee, when the benefit becomes payable to the named beneficiary.

Don't be misled into believing that employee benefits are not expensive. As desirable and necessary as they are in attracting and holding employees, they constitute one of your major costs of production. According to the U.S. Chamber of Commerce, the amount of these benefits paid by the average firm (large, medium, *and* small) in 1975 was $3,984 per employee per year, or 26 to 38 percent of total payroll.[4]

You may want to consider using the "cafeteria" or "smorgasbord" approach when determining what employee benefits to provide. Under this system, all employees receive a statement of the amount (in dollars) they are entitled to receive for such benefits. Each person then tells you how to allocate the money between a variety of programs available. Advantages of this system are increased employee awareness of the value of the fringe benefits, freedom of choice, and personalized approach.

Rewarding Management Personnel

A well-conceived and effectively operated management compensation plan can help you motivate your top assistants. It can also help you know your employment costs for these assistants.

Determining Level and Form of Reward. The level of pay for these managers depends on many factors. Some of the more important of these variables are:

1. The kind of industry you are in.
2. The size of your firm.
3. The company's geographic location.
4. The responsibilities of each position.
5. The pay method used (bonus or nonbonus).
6. Growth (rapid or steady) of your company.

You should establish a salary range, adjust present salaries to that range, and periodically review your conpensation plan. The salary range for each position should have a minimum for beginners, intermediate figures for advancement, and a maximum. Responsibility should be the determining factor for the required spread in a range. For example, at the vice presidential level, a 60 percent spread may be needed, while for lower management positions, a 40 percent spread might be sufficient.

---

[4] *Employee Benefits, 1975* (Washington, D.C.: Economic Analysis and Study Group, Chamber of Commerce of the United States, 1976).

In defining a salary range, you could establish the competitive salary as the midpoint. Examples of percentage spread are shown below:

Percentage Spread	Range of Salaries		
	Minimum	Midpoint	Maximum
40................	$10,000	$12,000	$14,000
50................	15,000	18,750	22,500
60................	20,000	26,000	32,000

After you have established salary ranges, you should compare the salaries you are currently paying your managers with the ranges. Provided that your assistants' performances merit adjustment, and if your company has the ability to pay, you should adjust current salaries to the appropriate place in the ranges.

A vital question is: What should you do when a substantial difference exists between the manager's current salary and what his salary should be? You should consider these guidelines:

1. Do not take any hasty action, but consider carefully possible effects of your actions.
2. If the current salary is greater than what it should be, try to upgrade the manager's performance. A promotion may be a possible solution, but a promotion should not be created in order to justify an excessive salary.
3. If the current salary is less than what it should be, determine the cost of bringing the salary into line and develop a plan for raising it to the desired level.

Since pay levels and practices are constantly changing, you should compare your compensation plan with competitive practices at least annually. Information on competitive salaries may be obtained from local surveys, including those done by chambers of commerce; informal contacts at service clubs or industry conventions; and national surveys conducted by trade associations.

Using Financial Rewards to Motivate. If your business is growing rapidly, your compensation program normally should be designed for the type of manager who is willing to take risks. Even if the salary is less than he could receive elsewhere, if a substantial bonus is paid for results and if good opportunities for promotion exist, he will be motivated to produce for you. On the other hand, if your firm's sales and profits are growing slowly, your compensation plan probably should emphasize salary and perhaps an attractive retirement plan.

One effective bonus plan is to use *profit sharing*. Such plans usually have four features:

1. The bonus payments are directly related to company profits, and a predetermined formula is used to determine the amount of profits that will be provided for bonuses.
2. Participation in the plan is reserved for managers whose performance significantly affects profits.
3. Payments are based on each manager's performance.
4. Bonuses are paid promptly.

The bonus formula usually consists of a percentage of the company's profits before taxes, but after providing a normal return to the owner(s). For top assistants, bonuses for superior performance are commonly 50 to 60 percent of their salaries.

DIRECTING YOUR EMPLOYEES' ACTIVITIES

Directing is guiding and supervising the performance of duties and responsibilities by your subordinates. It consists of:

1. Exercising leadership.
2. Communicating ideas, orders, and instructions.
3. Motivating performance.

Exercising Leadership

Effective leadership involves democratic directing rather than autocratic commanding. Leadership depends upon your interpersonal influence. To exercise effective leadership, you should create a good work climate that contributes materially to motivation of better work performance. You should then be skillful in communicating your orders down the chain of command, using formal and informal channels.

You should have empathy—the ability to put yourself into the shoes of other individuals and consider matters from their point of view.

Do you understand your personal leadership characteristics? It is probably more important for you to find subordinates who will respond to your style of management than it is for you to attempt to reorient your own personality, attitudes, and self-image.

Once you have chosen good subordinates, you should try to build effective supervisory relationships into your company. The following factors are significant in doing this:

1. Your attitude toward your supervisors.
2. Your choices for supervisors.
3. Training given to them.

4. Opportunities for their job satisfaction.
5. Rewards for work well done.

Your *attitude toward supervisors* is at the heart of the matter. It can make them believe that they are either errand runners, police, or leaders. If you consider them as errand runners, they will tend to follow instructions without question or suggestion. Since they have little authority, independence, or prestige, they will be resentful and avoid responsibility. If you consider them to be police, they will see that rules are obeyed and that the work is carried out. If you consider them to be leaders, however, they will probably see that company policies are followed and that the work gets done in an efficient manner.

Supervisors are expected to be your management representatives in dealing with nonmanagement employees. You should treat them as members of your management team with responsibilities for human relations, training, and liaison in addition to work performance. You should listen to their ideas and respect their opinions.

You should consult all your subordinates for their ideas. They have some good ideas, because they look at a problem from a special point of view. Also, asking them for their ideas will give them a sense of importance.

Communicating

You should recognize that most workers understand only about 20 percent of what you think and hope they understand. Communication should be two-way. You should be able to communicate your ideas to subordinates, and they should be able to communicate ideas to you. You should be an effective listener.

To be most effective in communicating ideas, orders, and instructions, you should understand these principles of effective communication:

1. Know what is to be communicated to subordinates and the most appropriate communication medium that will reach them.
2. Understand the subordinates' expectations and hopes.
3. Understand your own motives and objectives, and what you intend to gain from the communication.
4. Follow up to determine whether subordinates clearly understand the message.

Another part of communicating is counseling. In order to counsel effectively with subordinates, you should have this information:

1. What your subordinates are doing.
2. What unsolved work problems they have.
3. What suggestions they have for improvement.

4. How they feel about their jobs, their fellow employees, and their company.

Motivating

In motivating your employees, you should understand Maslow's hierarchy of needs and Herzberg's motivators and maintenance factors, which are mentioned in Chapter 2.

Motivation is rather complex and difficult to understand, at best. Understanding has been further complicated by the use of jargon by

FIGURE 10–2
Practical Approach to Motivating Your Employees

You, the Owner		Incentives You Can Use to Motivate Your Subordinates	Your Subordinates	
Your Objective	*What Is Needed to Achieve Your Objectives*	*Incentives You Can Use to Motivate Your Subordinates*	*What Needs Must Be Satisfied for Their Objectives to Be Achieved*	*Their Objective(s)*
Service and profit	Performance and productivity	Challenging work	Self-esteem	Self-satisfaction
		Merit increases and promotions		
		Praise and recognition		
		Personal publicity		
		Responsibility		
		Job enrichment	Social	
		Status systems		
		Suggestion system		
		Communications system		
		Staff meetings		
		Training and development	Security	
		Wage incentive plans		
		Savings plans		
		Profit sharing		
		Seniority systems		
		Insurance		
		Pensions		
		Other employee benefits		
		Money, or sustenance for survival	Survival	

some writers and speakers. We will try a simplified approach to help you stimulate your workers, from a *practical, not a theoretical approach.*

In essence, motivation is applying an incentive that will *promise* to satisfy the predominant need of the worker at the moment of time. Once that need is satisfied, however, it will no longer motivate the worker; another need must be appealed to.

A practical approach to motivating your employees might be viewed as in Figure 10–2. In general, you should know what the employees need in order for them to have self satisfaction; then you must try to find an incentive to apply in order to unlock their springs to motivation.

Motivation requires skill, for you always motivate—either positively to produce, or negatively to withhold production, as shown by the following example.

> A man went into an ice cream shop and ordered a banana split. When it came, something was obviously wrong. There was about twice as much of the goodies as there should have been.
>
> The man asked the young man who was serving him, "What's the matter?"
>
> The young man replied, with a shrug, "I'm mad at the boss."

USING MANAGEMENT BY OBJECTIVES

To be most effective in motivating your employees, you should probably practice Management by Objectives (MBO) in your firm. If you do, the first step you should take is to set overall objectives for the firm. These objectives should be specific and understandable; quantifiable in order that progress can be measured; and realistic, meaning that they are attainable—with difficulty.

An objective of "increasing sales" should not be set, because it is not clear what is meant. Instead, a definite objective should be set, say, "to increase sales by a minimum of 5 percent and a maximum of 15 percent over the next fiscal year at prices that will provide a gross profit of 35 percent."

Desirable objectives to be accomplished should probably involve profitability, competitive position, productivity, and employee relations, and be stated specifically, as *how much* profit, *what percentage* of the market, *how much* cost of production, *how much* labor turnover, and during what period.

All of your subordinates should be asked to set objectives for themselves, their people, their material, and so forth. You should meet with each of them to reach agreement on those objectives, how they can be accomplished, and how they relate to achieving the overall company objectives. You should review their objectives with them and make suggestions for how those objectives can be achieved.

Each subordinate should be provided a continual feedback of the results being attained, and these should be compared with the objectives. You should help each person overcome obstacles that stand in the way of reaching the objectives.

Near the end of the period, each subordinate should prepare a brief statement concerning how the performance compares to the objectives. Each subordinate's report should be reviewed in detail and then discussed.

An agreement should be reached with each subordinate on how good performance has been. If the objectives were not achieved, an effort should be made to find out why.

An MBO program can be operated on a daily, weekly, or monthly basis. If it is working effectively, quick feedback, immediate weighing of measures of success, and good results for your company should follow.

Other applications of MBO on a *daily basis* may pertain to your production supervisor and office manager. For example:

An order may be received by your supervisor for 1,000 widgets. This order sets a goal, and performance leads to its accomplishment.

The office manager may be assigned ten contracts to be processed. This assignment also sets a goal.

In essence, we are saying you should be concerned with survival of your company, not only five or ten years from now, but also next week. You should act and react quickly in order to keep your firm alive—now!

Your MBO program can also be used as an effective training tool for your employees and as the base of a critique of their efforts, on a continuing basis.

APPRAISING YOUR EMPLOYEES' PERFORMANCE

Your firm should have an effective personnel appraisal or employee evaluation system to enable you to answer the question: How well are my people performing? Under such a system, each employee's performance and progress are evaluated and rewards are given for above-average performance. Often, this method is used in determining merit salary increases.

If a Management by Objectives program or its equivalent is not being used, *merit rating* is based upon the following commonly used factors:

1. Quantity and quality of work performed.
2. Cooperativeness.
3. Initiative.
4. Dependability.
5. Attendance.

6. Job knowledge.
7. Ability to work with others.
8. Safety.
9. Personal habits.

Each of these factors can be evaluated, for example, as *superior, above-average, average, below-average,* or *poor.* The person's wage or salary is then determined from this evaluation.

Relationships should exist also between merit rating and promotions. The appraisal system can also help you identify marginal employees, as well as point up areas of improvement and possible training and development needs for all your people. The system can also be a valuable ingredient in the Management by Objectives program in determining the degree of success with which objectives are achieved. Under such a plan, each individual manager should be held responsible for establishing written performance criteria used for promotion.

SUMMARY

In this chapter, we have discussed (1) training and developing your people, (2) setting wages and salaries for them, (3) directing their activities, and (4) appraising their performance.

The need for developing employees, methods of training, sources of outside assistance, and some guidelines to follow in developing people were also discussed.

The most frequently used *training methods* are on-the-job training, apprenticeship, and internship. Less frequently used methods of training include programmed instruction, educational television, extension courses, and correspondence courses.

Some basic *guidelines* to follow in developing people are:

1. Have clearly defined objectives.
2. Select trainees carefully.
3. Use only qualified instructors and materials.
4. Evaluate results of development activities.
5. Don't rush the trainees.
6. Provide trainees—and trainers—feedback on their progress.
7. Provide motivation for growth, such as wage or salary increase or promotion.

In setting wages and salaries for nonmanagerial personnel, you should consider such factors as effort, the time spent, your ability to pay, the standard and cost of living, legislation, the role of unions, and the supply of—and demand for—workers in your area.

Two other important considerations in the compensation picture are (1) whether to use a wage incentive system, profit-sharing plan, or bonus system to motivate employees; and (2) the type and extent of employee benefits.

In compensating your managerial personnel, you should establish salary scales, decide where a given manager fits on the scale, and use bonuses or profit sharing to motivate them.

Government laws, rules, regulations, and administrative decisions affect most of these wage considerations. Of especial importance is the Pension Reform Act, because of its reporting requirements.

An important aspect of personnel management is directing the activities of your employees. Included are: exercising leadership, communicating with, and motivating your employees. One effective method of accomplishing these is using an MBO program.

An important part of developing and maintaining your work force is appraising your employees' performance. This involves evaluating their performance relative to some standard, telling them how they are doing, and explaining how they can improve their performance.

QUESTIONS FOR FURTHER DISCUSSION

1. Why should personnel development be emphasized in a small business?
2. Discuss briefly some specific results that are usually received from training and developing employees.
3. Describe briefly the methods of training nonmanagerial employees.
4. Give some guidelines that may be used in developing and conducting training and development programs.
5. Explain some of the factors that should be considered in setting rates of pay.
6. What are some of the possible effects of governmental factors on wage problems of a small business?
7. What are some possible considerations in deciding whether to provide your own pension program or pay your employees cash and let them set up their own IRAs?
8. What are the purposes of a wage-incentive system?
9. Describe three employee-benefit programs.
10. Describe the "cafeteria" or "smorgasbord" approach in determining what employee benefits to provide.
11. What is an effective personnel appraisal (or employee evaluation) system? In the absence of MBO, list five factors that are evaluated.
12. Define the following terms:
     a. Leadership.
     b. Empathy.
13. Cite three principles of effective communication.
14. In a Management by Objectives (MBO) program, what criteria should the objectives meet?

11

Improving Your Relationships with Your Employees

In the last two chapters you studied how to handle some of your more important staffing, development, directing, and compensation problems. Suggestions were made for planning your personnel requirements, recruiting applicants, selecting the most capable people from those available, evaluating your selection procedure, training and developing your employees, compensating them appropriately, directing them, and evaluating their performance.

But you should also be familiar with some of the other important phases of the personnel function, including:

1. Understanding legislation that affects your business.
2. Handling employees' grievances.
3. Exercising discipline.
4. Dealing with labor unions.

This chapter provides an overview of these topics.

HANDLING LEGISLATION THAT AFFECTS YOUR BUSINESS

The whole area of personnel relations in your business is affected by labor legislation, as shown in previous chapters. Some of these laws and their effects on you are now explained in greater detail.

Equal Employment Opportunities

In 1964, Congress passed the *Civil Rights Act. Title VII* of this Act, as amended by the *Equal Employment Opportunities Act of 1972*, prohibits discrimination because of race, color, religion, sex, or national origin in hiring, upgrading, and all other conditions of employment. It applies to employers of 15 or more persons.

As shown in Chapter 9, other groups affected by this type legislation are older workers, the handicapped, and Vietnam veterans. All of these have special laws, rules, and regulations for their protection, but space permits only some generalizations concerning the most significant ones.

Some Special Aspects of Sex Discrimination.   Generally, all jobs must be open to both men and women unless the employer can prove that sex is a bona fide occupational qualification (BFOQ) necessary to the normal operations of that particular business.

Advertisements cannot be run by a company for "male only" or "female only" employees. This practice may be discriminatory unless sex can be shown as a BFOQ. Disqualifying female employees from jobs requiring heavy lifting, night shifts, and dirty work is often illegal unless justification exists for these restrictions. Automatic discharge of pregnant women and refusal to reinstate them after childbirth, requiring retirement at different ages, or not hiring women with small children constitute discrimination.

According to the Equal Pay Act of 1963, you must also pay males and females the same rate of pay for performing the same general type of work.

Some Laws Pertaining to Age.   The Fair Labor Standards Act and many state statutes prescribe the minimum age for employees. Typically, these laws specify a minimum of 14 to 16 years with a higher minimum often set for hazardous occupations. On the other hand, the Age Discrimination in Employment Act of 1967 says you cannot discriminate against present or potential employees aged 40–64. This includes not only hiring, but also retiring and other aspects of employment.

Some Practical Applications of the Laws.   In recruiting applicants for employment, companies no longer may be allowed to rely completely on "walk-ins" or word-of-mouth advertising of job openings, especially if their own work force is predominantly of one race. Friends or relatives of present employees cannot be recruited if a company has a disproportionate amount of a certain class of employees. A company cannot set hiring standards with respect to test results, high school diplomas, height, arrest records, manner of speech, or appearance, which result in discrimination on the basis of race, color, sex, religion, or national origin.

Seniority systems should not result in "locking" minorities into unskilled and semi-skilled jobs without providing them lines of progression to better jobs. Equal opportunity for promotions should be provided. Training and performance appraisals should be conducted on a nondiscriminatory basis. Discrimination should not exist relative to hourly rates and deferred wages including pensions or other deferred payments.

Recreational activities—bowling teams, softball teams, Christmas parties, etc.—should be open to all employees on a nondiscriminatory basis. So far as facilities of a "personal nature" are concerned, an employer should make every "reasonable accommodation" for employees covered by these laws.

All employees are entitled to equality in all conditions of employment, including:

1. Hiring.
2. Layoff.
3. Recall.
4. Discharge.
5. Recruitment.
6. Compensation.
7. Overtime.
8. Promotional opportunities.
9. Paid sick leave time.
10. Paid vacation time.
11. Insurance coverage.
12. Training and development activities.
13. Retirement privileges and pension benefits.
14. Rest periods, lunch periods, etc.

FIGURE 11–1
Agencies That Enforce Equal Employment Opportunity Laws

Equal Employment Opportunity Commission
   Handle complaints of bias against women, blacks, religious groups, other minorities. Can file suits against employers with 15 or more employees and against labor unions with more than 15 members, after efforts at conciliation.

Office of Federal Contract Compliance
   Part of Department of Labor, this office monitors job policies of companies holding federal contracts or subcontracts valued at more than $10,000. Contractors are required to take affirmative action to end—or prevent—job discrimination and other civil rights violations.

Employment Standards Division
   This unit, a part of the Department of Labor, is responsible for setting employment standards, including programs dealing with job discrimination against older workers.

U.S. Civil Service Commission
   Reviews employment policies of federal agencies to attack discrimination in government jobs. Consults with state and local governments to establish and improve merit hiring systems.

Civil Rights Division of Justice Department
   Files lawsuits against either private employers or labor unions charged with engaging in a pattern or practice of discrimination. Also, can bring individual or "pattern" suits against state and local governments for job discrimination against women, minorities, religious groups, or the elderly.

Source: Leon C. Megginson, *Personnel and Human Resources Administration*, 3d ed. (Homewood, Ill.: Richard D. Irwin, Inc., 1977), p. 73.

The *Equal Employment Opportunity Commission* (EEOC) was established by Title VII, and it receives and investigates charges of employment discrimination. In order to stop violations, the Commission may take action itself or go to a U.S. District Court. The Commission promotes *affirmative action programs* (AAPs) to put the principle of equal employment (AAPs) opportunity into practice. The EEOC and some of the other agencies regulating and enforcing these laws are shown in Figure 11–1 on page 203.

Social Security

As a small business manager, you are both a taxpayer and a tax collector. To finance Old Age, Survivors, and Disability Insurance, you must pay a tax on each employee's earnings and deduct a comparable amount from the employee's salary. Since tax laws are subject to change, you should check the rate and base amount applicable. As the proportion of the aged in the total population rises, it may be anticipated that both taxes and benefits will increase.

At present, (January 1, 1978), the program is financed by 6.05 percent contributions on the first $17,700 of an employee's income, paid by both the employer and employee. The rate for self-employed individuals is 8.1 percent. The contribution percentage—as well as the income base—are ever changing, depending upon actions of Congress. Consequently, *extreme care should be used in order to keep current on the law and its applications.*

An unemployment insurance tax is also provided under the *Social Security Act of 1936.* The state government receives most of this tax. It may be as high as 3.2 percent of the first $4,200 of each employee's pay. If you stabilize employment in your firm, you can have lower rates under merit rating provisions. Maintaining the validity of your tax trust funds is important because of the legal liability associated with them.

Workers' Compensation[1]

Accidents and occupational diseases are covered under state workers' compensation statutes. You are required to pay insurance premiums either to a state fund or to a private insurance carrier. Funds accumulated in this fashion are used to compensate victims of industrial accidents or occupational illness. Your premiums will be affected by hazards in your company and the effectiveness of your safety program.

---

[1] Formerly called "workmen's compensation."

Unions and Collective Bargaining

You are required by the National Labor Relations Act of 1935, as amended by the Labor Management Relations Act of 1947 and the Labor-Management Reporting and Disclosure Act of 1959, to bargain with the union if a majority of your employees desire unionization. You are forbidden to discriminate in any way against your employees for union activity.

The purpose of the Act was to facilitate the process of collective bargaining, not necessarily to prevent or settle disputes. Under the Act, both you and the union are required to bargain in good faith in order that difficulties may be resolved and an agreement reached.

The National Labor Relations Board serves as a labor court, and its general counsel investigates charges of unfair labor practices, issues complaints, and prosecutes cases. The Board can issue direct orders, but only the courts can levy fines or penalties. You can appeal a ruling of the Board through a Circuit Court.

Under right-to-work laws in some states, the union shop is outlawed. A union shop clause provides that all employees must join the recognized union within 30 days after being hired.

The appendixes at the end of this chapter contain checklists that will help you evaluate what you can legally do when a union tries to organize your firm.

Environmental Protection

In 1970, the Environmental Protection Agency was created under an Act of the same title to help protect and improve the quality of the nation's environment. Areas covered are:

1. Solid waste disposal.
2. Clean air.
3. Water resources.
4. Noise.
5. Pesticides.
6. Atomic radiation.

Industrial pollution can be prevented or controlled either through waste treatment or process changes or both. Much oil pollution is also preventable. Builders, developers, and contractors—many of them small businesses—can help prevent and control water pollution. Soil erosion, wastes from feedlots, improper or excessive use of pesticides and fertilizers, and careless discarding of trash and junk are among the causes of water pollution.

Because of the actions of the Agency in requiring pollution-control equipment to be installed in "marginal" plants, many of these plants are closing and employees are losing their jobs. If you face this situation as a small business manager you should assist your employees as much as possible in obtaining other jobs. You should work together with community agencies—such as chambers of commerce and industrial development corporations—in trying to attract other businesses and industries to absorb your former employees.

Occupational Safety and Health

The Occupational Safety and Health Act, which created OSHA (the Occupational Safety and Health Administration), was passed in 1970. Its purpose is to assure so far as possible safe and healthful working conditions for every employee and to preserve our human resources. An employee—or representative—has these five important rights:

1. If he believes that a violation of job safety or health standards threatens physical harm, he may request an inspection by sending a signed, written notice to the U.S. Department of Labor. He may not be discharged or discriminated against for filing the complaint.
2. When the Department of Labor inspector arrives, usually unannounced, the employee's representative may accompany the inspector on the visit.
3. If the employer is cited by the OSHA and protests either the fine or the abatement period, the employee can participate at the hearing and object to the length of the abatement period.
4. Concerning exposure to toxic materials or other physically harmful agents, the employee may observe the company's monitoring processes. If an OSHA standard covers the substance, the worker is entitled to information about his exposure record.
5. The employee's authorized representative may request that the Secretary of the Department of Health, Education, and Welfare (HEW) determine whether any substance found in the place of employment has potentially toxic effects. If HEW makes this finding, the Secretary of Labor may institute a procedure to set a safe exposure level for that substance.

Supporters of OSHA claim reductions in lost time and in workers' compensation, decreases in lost wages, lowered medical costs, and higher productivity. Critics believe that the Act has been implemented too rapidly and restrictively, and that compliance costs are so high that a company's competitive position is threatened.[2]

---

[2] Since January 1973, businesses with fewer than eight employees are no longer required to maintain injury and illness records. Still, these firms must report fatalities and accidents that hospitalize five or more persons, and small business accident and illness reports are still reflected in BLS statistics.

Even though many accidents are caused by the employees' own carelessness and lack of safety consciousness, they usually do not receive citations. Instead, employers are responsible that their employees wear safety equipment. Furthermore, employers are subject to fines for unsafe practices irrespective of whether any accidents actually occur. You should provide safety training for your supervisors and employees and discipline employees for noncompliance with safety work rules. The Act has encouraged increased examination and questioning of management's manning decisions and equipment selection. To illustrate, a union could claim that a crew size is unsafe or that a machine fails to provide a safe work place. The Act makes compulsory training in forklift truck driving and respirator-wearing.

Five industries in which small businesses predominate—roofing and sheet metal; meat and meat products; lumber and wood products; manufacturers of mobile homes, campers, and snowmobiles; and stevedoring—have relatively high injury and illness rates.

"Dry-run" inspections are not permitted by OSHA inspectors because if they do come to your premises, they are obligated by law to inspect fully, to cite, and to fine. You can request a free health hazard evaluation by the National Institute of Occupational Safety and Health in the HEW. Training may be obtained from OSHA and National Safety Council chapters. Your workmen's compensation insurance carrier may be helpful. However, its approval does not guarantee the same from OSHA. You may also obtain useful information from equipment manufacturers, other employers who have had an inspection, trade associations, and your local fire department. You should provide effective coordination among manufacturing, safety, medical, industrial relations, and so forth.

Occasionally, there is some frustration in attempting to comply with OSHA regulations and standards due to a lack of clarity. In addition, while an OSHA inspector may present you with a citation for noncompliance or may reject the procedure or protective measures being used, definitive corrective information may not be forthcoming. OSHA inspectors are not allowed to offer this type assistance. As this book goes to press, efforts are being made by Congress to satisfy various complaints registered against the OSHA program. You should recognize that the newness of the program and its very nature will keep it in a state of transition for some time. Therefore, you are advised to utilize the resources suggested above, as well as your local chamber of commerce, area planning and development commission, and the office of the Small Business Administration serving your area. Small Business Administration loans could be available to help you meet safety and health standards.[3]

---

[3] Fred W. Foulkes, "Learning to Live with OSHA," *Harvard Business Review,* vol. 51, no. 6 (November–December 1973), pp. 57–67.

HANDLING YOUR EMPLOYEES' GRIEVANCES

Complaints and grievances will inevitably occur. You should encourage your employees to inform you when they think something is wrong and needs correcting. Also, you should instruct your supervisors how to handle the complaints and grievances. An effective grievance procedure should have these characteristics:

1. Assurance to employees that expressing their complaints will not prejudice their relationships with their immediate supervisors.
2. A clear method from the employees' viewpoint of presenting their grievances, and a description of how those complaints will be processed.
3. A minimum of red tape and time in processing their complaints and determining solutions.
4. An effective method for employees who cannot express themselves well to present grievances.

Unresolved grievances can lead to strikes. You should listen patiently and deal with a grievance promptly even though you believe an employee's grievance is without foundation. You should thank the employee for bringing the grievance to your attention. Before you render judgment on the grievance, you should think about it carefully and gather pertinent facts. You should inform the employee of your decision on the grievance and follow up later to determine whether the cause of the grievance has been corrected.

You should maintain written records of all grievances (and disciplinary actions) in employees' files. These records are beneficial in your defense against any charges of unfair labor practices that may be brought against you.

EXERCISING DISCIPLINE

One of the findings resulting from behavioral science research is that employees like to work in a disciplined environment—in the sense of having a system of rules and procedures and having them enforced equitably.[4]

There are two ways of obtaining an orderly, disciplined environment, either through getting your employees to exercise self-control or by imposing external discipline.

Self-Discipline

You should encourage self-discipline by your employees rather than using direct control. As owner-manager, your personal example will be

---

[4] See Megginson, *Personnel and Human Resources Administration,* pp. 467–83, for some of the research findings and the discussion of practical applications of discipline.

important. Your employees should have confidence in their abilities to perform their jobs, believe that their performance is compatible with their own interests, and believe that you will provide support if they run into difficulties.

Externally Imposed Discipline

Regarding discipline, you will probably find that 95 percent of your employees conduct themselves reasonably; they rarely cause any problems. If you do not deal effectively with the few who violate rules and regulations, however, employees' disrespect will likely become widespread. In order to be effective in administering discipline, you should:

1. Know the rules.
2. Act promptly on violations.
3. Gather pertinent facts.
4. Allow employees an opportunity to explain their positions.
5. Set up tentative courses of action and evaluate them.
6. Decide what action to take.
7. Apply the disciplinary action, observing labor contract procedures.
8. Set up and maintain a record of actions taken.

You should also be able to distinguish between major and minor offenses and consider extenuating circumstances, such as the employee's length of service, prior performance record, and duration of time since the last offense. You should never be vindictive with an employee for violating a rule.

DEALING WITH LABOR UNIONS

Many small business managers have rather strong personal anti-union feelings because they believe: (1) they have "made it on their own," and employees want to take something away from them; and (2) an individual's drive and initiative are more productive than group-set norms. You should recognize, however, that employees join unions because of their needs, as they perceive them, for a union.

If your company is unionized, you have more constraints on what you can and cannot do in your relations with your people. Your employees may view you more as an economic opponent than as a person with whom cooperation can be expected to obtain mutual benefits. Improving personnel performance is more difficult in a unionized company than in a nonunionized company.

If a union does try to organize your firm, there are certain things you can and cannot do. See the appendixes at the end of this chapter for the things you *can* and *cannot* do.

The purpose of labor unions is to bargain on behalf of their members as a counterbalance to the economic power of the employer. Your employees, through their elected representatives, negotiate with your company for wages, fringe benefits, working conditions, and so forth. The union's principal role is collective bargaining.

If your company is unionized, you should be prepared for the possibility that certain difficulties may occur. Many of your actions and statements may be reported to union officials. You may be harassed by the union's filing unfair labor practice notices with the National Labor Relations Board. Your best defense is to know your management rights under the Labor Management Relations Act.

Bargaining with a labor union involves preparation, negotiation, and agreement. The bargaining is then followed by another phase, living with the contract. *Preparation* may well be the most important step. You should have obtained facts about wages, hours, and working conditions before you sit down at the bargaining table. You should have information on other contracts in the industry and in the local area. Disciplinary actions, grievances, and other key matters that arose during the day-to-day administration of the current contract should have been noted. Current business literature concerning general business and the status of union-management relations in the nation and in your industry can be useful. A carefully researched proposal should be developed well in advance of negotiation of the contract.

Having done this, you should be in a much more favorable negotiating position than if you use a negative strategy of permitting the union to develop its own ideas for a new contract to which you attempt to offer defensive counterproposals. All too frequently, fear seems to negate the owner's willingness to develop in advance a contract proposal with attractive features that will appeal to the rank-and-file employee. The "I don't want to give away any more than I have to" attitude generally fails to contribute to a viable union-management relationship.

You should recognize the *negotiation* step as being critical, particularly if it is not handled properly. You should consider not only the impact of wages on your company, but also the effects of seniority, discharge rules, and sick leave. You should understand that anything given up now probably can never be regained.

The *agreement* usually consists of ten clauses covering:

1. Union recognition.
2. Wages.
3. Vacations and holidays.
4. Working conditions.
5. Layoffs and rehiring.
6. Management prerogatives.
7. Hours of work.
8. Seniority.
9. Arbitration.
10. Renewal clause.

Specifics are set forth in each of these areas, and rules are established which should be obeyed by you. The management prerogatives clause defines the areas in which you have the right to act, free from questioning or joint action by the union.

Once the agreement is signed, you should *live with the contract* until time to negotiate a new one. All of your management personnel should be thoroughly briefed on the contents. Meanings and interpretations of each clause should be reviewed, and the wording of the contract should be clearly and unambiguously understood. Your supervisors' questions should be answered in order that they will be better prepared to deal with labor matters.

Your company's labor relations and personnel practices should be consistent, uniform in application and interpretation, and based on a sense of fair play. We have observed numerous instances where owners have pursued policies that could be labeled as selfish and greedy; the end product has been unionization, bankruptcy, or both.

To enable you to do the proper thing in a specific labor relations situation, you can obtain advice and reliable information from numerous private groups and some government agencies. The *private sources* consist of employers' associations, trade associations, labor-relations attorneys, labor-relations consultants, leader companies, and professors. *Government sources* are federal and state mediators, wage-hour investigators, National Labor Relations Board regional offices, and state industrial relations departments. Leader companies set labor contract patterns in key bargaining sessions and small companies tend to follow their lead. Often, their labor relations staffs are willing to help you. The wage-hour investigator is not only a law enforcement officer, but also is interested *in helping an owner-manager* avoid violations.

SUMMARY

Many thoughts have been presented in this and the preceding two chapters for performing the personnel function. Your firm's personnel program might be considered progressive if (1) selection, testing, placement, and training of all personnel are conducted on an organized and efficient basis; (2) salary and wage rates are fair and equitable for each employee; (3) incentive plans for all levels of employees are based on an effective set of standards and an active personnel appraisal system; (4) you, or another manager possessing adequate authority, formulate sound industrial relations policies and represent the company in labor negotiations and administer the contract impartially; (5) labor turnover is minimized and employee morale and efficiency maximized; and (6) individual records for each employee are kept current for use in an inventory of qualifications.

In addition, you should review each position in your company periodically, perhaps quarterly. Does duplication of work exist? Is work structured so that employees are encouraged to become involved? Can tasks be given to another employee(s) and a position eliminated? Can a job be filled by a part-time person?

> A procedure observed in one firm which seemed to reduce needless activities and minimize the number of employees was asking each employee this question: "What do you do all day long and why?"

Imagine this hypothetical problem: You must terminate one employee. Who would it be? How would you restructure your jobs? A real solution to this imaginary problem may be to your advantage.

QUESTIONS FOR FURTHER DISCUSSION

1. What are three characteristics of an effective grievance procedure?
2. How should a manager handle grievances effectively?
3. Describe briefly the Labor Management Relations Act and the Labor Relations Act.
4. Describe the preparation for bargaining with a labor union.
5. How is Old Age, Survivors, and Disability Insurance (OASDI) financed?
6. What does the Fair Labor Standards Act prescribe?
7. What does the Equal Employment Opportunities Act provide?
8. What effects may the Environmental Protection Act have upon a small company?
9. What is the purpose of the Occupational Safety and Health Act (OSHA)?
10. Why are many small business managers "anti-union"?

APPENDIX A: TWENTY-SEVEN THINGS YOU *CAN DO* WHEN A UNION TRIES TO ORGANIZE YOUR COMPANY

1. Keep outside organizers off premises.
2. Inform employees from time to time on the benefits they presently enjoy. (Avoid veiled promises or threats.)
3. Inform employees that signing a union authorization card does not mean they must vote for the union if there is an election.
4. Inform employees of the disadvantages of belonging to the union, such as the possibility of strikes, serving in a picket line, dues, fines, assessments, and one-man or clique rule.
5. Inform employees that you prefer to deal with them rather than have the union or any other outsider settle grievances.

6. Tell employees what you think about unions and about union policies.
7. Inform employees about any prior experience you have had with unions and whatever you know about the union officials trying to organize them.
8. Inform employees that the law permits you to hire a new employee to replace any employee who goes on strike for economic reasons.
9. Inform employees that no union can obtain more than you as an employer are able to give.
10. Inform employees how their wages and benefits compare with unionized or nonunionized concerns where wages are lower and benefits less desirable.
11. Inform employees that the local union probably will be dominated by the international union, and that they, the members, will have little to say in its operations.
12. Inform employees of any untrue or misleading statements made by the organizer. You may give employees the correct facts.
13. Inform employees of known racketeering, Communist, or other undesirable elements that may be active in the union.
14. Give opinions on unions and union leaders, even in derogatory terms.
15. Distribute information about unions such as disclosures of the McClellan Committee.
16. Reply to union attacks on company policies or practices.
17. Give legal position on labor-management matters.
18. Advise employees of their legal rights, provided you do not engage or finance an employee suit or proceeding.
19. Declare a fixed policy in opposition to compulsory union membership contracts.
20. Campaign against union seeking to represent the employees.
21. Insist that no solicitation of membership or discussion of union affairs be conducted during working time.
22. Administer discipline, layoff, and grievance procedures without regard to union membership or nonmembership of the employees involved.
23. Treat both union and nonunion employees alike in making assignments of preferred work or desired overtime.
24. Enforce plant rules impartially, regardless of the employee's membership activity in a union.
25. Tell employees, if they ask, that they are free to join or not to join any organization, so far as their status with the company is concerned.
26. Tell employees that their *personal* and *job* security will be determined by the economic prosperity of the company.

APPENDIX B: TWENTY-TWO THINGS YOU *CANNOT DO* WHEN A UNION TRIES TO ORGANIZE

1. Engage in surveillance of employees to determine who is or is not participating in the union program; attend union meetings or engage in any undercover activities for this purpose.
2. Threaten, intimidate, or punish employees who engage in union activity.
3. Request information from employees about union matters, meetings, etc. Employees may, of their own volition give such information without prompting. You may listen, but not ask questions.
4. Prevent employee union representatives from soliciting memberships during nonworking time.
5. Grant wage increases, special concessions or promises of any kind to keep the union out.
6. Question a prospective employee about his affiliation with a labor organization.
7. Threaten to close up or move the plant, curtail operations, or reduce employee benefits.
8. Engage in any discriminatory practices, such as work assignments, overtime, lay-offs, promotions, wage increases, or any other actions that could be regarded as preferential treatment for certain employees.
9. Discriminate against union people when disciplining employees for a specific action and permit nonunion employees to go unpunished for the same action.
10. Transfer workers on the basis of teaming up nonunion employees to separate them from union employees.
11. Deviate in any way from company policies for the primary purpose of eliminating a union employee.
12. Intimate, advise, or indicate, in any way, that unionization will force the company to lay off employees, take away company benefits or privileges enjoyed, or make any other changes that could be regarded as a curtailment of privileges.
13. Make statements to the effect that you will not deal with a union.
14. Give any financial support or other assistance to employees who support or oppose the union.
15. Visit the homes of employees to urge them to oppose or reject the union in its campaign.
16. Be a party to any petition or circular against the union or encourage employees to circulate such a petition.
17. Make any promises of promotions, benefits, wage increases, or any other item that would induce employees to oppose the union.

18. Engage in discussions or arguments that may lead to physical encounters with employees over the union question.
19. Use a third party to threaten or coerce a union member, or attempt to influence any employee's vote through this medium.
20. Question employees on whether or not they have or have not affiliated or signed with the union.
21. Use the word "never" in any predictions or attitudes about the unions or its promises or demands.
22. Talk about tomorrow. You can talk about yesterday or today, when you give examples or reasons, instead of tomorrow, to avoid making a prediction or conviction which may be interpreted as a threat or promise by the union or the NLRB.

WHERE TO LOOK FOR FURTHER INFORMATION

Cass, E. L., and Zimmer, F. G., eds. *Man and Work in Society.* New York: Van Nostrand Reinhold Co., 1975.

Cheek, Logan M. "Cost Effectiveness Comes to the Personnel Function." *Harvard Business Review,* vol. 51, no. 3 (May–June 1973), p. 97.

Chung, Kae H. *Motivational Theories and Practices.* Columbus, Ohio: Grid, Inc., 1977.

Drucker, Peter F. *People and Performance: The Best of Peter Drucker on MBO Management.* New York: Harper's College Press, 1977.

Feller, Jack H., Jr. "Keep Pointed toward Profit." *Management Aids for Small Manufacturers no. 206.* Washington, D.C.: Small Business Administration, 1972.

Fels, Lipman G. "15 Questions You Dare Not Ask Job Applicants." *Administrative Management,* vol. 53, no. 6 (June 1974), pp. 20, 21, 80, 82.

Foulkes, Fred K. "The Expanding Role of the Personnel Function." *Harvard Business Review,* vol. 53, no. 2 (March–April 1975), pp. 71–84.

Harris, O. Jeff. *Managing People at Work: Concepts and Cases in Interpersonal Behavior.* Santa Barbara, Calif.: Wiley/Hamilton, 1976.

Hobson, Harold A., Jr. "Selecting Employee Benefit Plans." *Management Aids for Small Manufacturers no. 213.* Washington, D.C.: Small Business Administration, 1972.

Megginson, L. C. *Personnel: A Behavioral Approach to Administration.* 2d ed. Homewood, Ill.: Richard D. Irwin, Inc., 1972, for a presentation of the philosophical and theoretical aspects of personnel.

Megginson, L. C. *Personnel and Human Resources Administration.* 3rd ed. Homewood, Ill.: Richard D. Irwin, Inc., 1977, for a technical, legal, and professional approach to personnel.

Mitchell, Howard M. "Selecting and Developing Personnel Professionals." *Personnel Journal,* vol. 49, no. 7 (July 1970), pp. 583–89.

Mitchell, James M., and Schroeder, Rolfe.   "Future Shock for Personnel Administration." *Public Personnel Management,* vol. 3, no. 4 (July–August 1974), pp. 265–69.

Murdick, Robert G., et al.   *Business Policy: A Framework for Analysis.* Columbus, Ohio: Grid, Inc., 1972. Credit is given to the authors of this text for many of their ideas which are included in this chapter.

Patten, Thomas H., Jr.   "Personnel Management in the 1970s: The End of Laissez Faire." *Human Resource Management,* vol. 12, No. 3 (Fall 1973), pp. 7–19.

Sanford, Aubrey C.   *Human Relations: The Theory and Practice of Organizational Behavior.* 2d ed. Columbus, Ohio, Charles E. Merrill, 1977.

Siegel, Lawrence, and Lane, Irving M.   *Psychology in Industrial Organizations.* 3d ed. Homewood, Ill.: Richard D. Irwin, Inc., 1974.

Smith, Leonard J.   "Checklist for Developing a Training Program." *Management Aids for Small Manufacturers no. 186.* Washington, D.C.: Small Business Administration, 1967.

Summer, Howard E.   "How to Analyze Your Own Business." *Management Aids for Small Manufacturers no. 46.* Washington, D.C.: Small Business Administration, 1973.

Warren, E. Kirby, Ference, Thomas P., and Stoner, James A. F.   "Problems in Review." *Harvard Business Review,* vol. 53, no. 1 (January–February 1975), pp. 30–38, 146–48.

cases for part III

III-1 The Harassed Contractor[1]

A contractor purchased a mobile concrete mixer and sent it to the site of one of his jobs. Those responsible for the mixer left it outside of the fenced-in area that night and it was stolen. Subsequently, the contractor found that a subordinate had failed to record it for insurance coverage.

Recently he had had an increase in thefts occurring between the time material had been delivered and its intended use. He had tightened up on his scheduling so that material would arrive when needed. For example, he had made special arrangements for material to be delivered at 6:00 A.M. on the day it was needed, instead of the afternoon before.

Recently, OSHA personnel had been in for two different functional inspections of his plant. He met the OSHA standards in the first inspection, but not in the second one. He said he had been following the standards as he interpreted the rulings, but was fined following the second visit with no warning. He found these visits time-consuming and unreasonable in that he had no recourse except through costly legal action.

The owner was concerned about some of the recent court rulings with regard to product responsibility. He pointed to a bent leg of a metal scaffolding stand. He said past practice was to use a torch to cut the leg off and weld a new one on. He now discards the item because of

---

[1] Prepared by Charles R. Scott, Jr., University of Alabama.

problems of product liability. He cited the report of an accident that had occurred in a structure 16 years after installation, with the installer recently being sued and losing the case. He said industry liability insurance normally warrants the product for about 18 months. He now wondered if he was building up a liability over the years against which he would have to pay very large premiums or absorb heavy losses.

During the past year, the NLRB had held an election among the workers in the plant. The contractor had spent many hours during the month before the vote working on planning his strategy, meeting with lawyers, and talking to employees. The employees voted not to unionize. This did not affect his outside workers, who were already unionized.

QUESTIONS FOR DISCUSSION

1. Evaluate the legal environment in which the contractor finds himself.
2. What suggestions could you make to him for coping with that environment?

III–2   Jiffy-Burger Restaurant[1]

About a year ago, Bill Northrup came to Mid City and opened a small drive-in restaurant called *Jiffy-Burger*. Bill had previously worked 15 years for International Oil, where he had been in charge of training all new salesmen. The challenge and appeal of managing his own business, however, persuaded him to give up a secure position and invest all his savings in this new venture.

On a recent day, Bill was visiting with his neighbor, Ron. It soon became evident to Ron that his visitor was worried about something, so he asked if Bill was having trouble at the restaurant. The following conversation took place.

BILL: Ron, you just can't imagine the problem I've had since opening that damn restaurant! I never thought it would be this much trouble running my own business. This past year has been a nightmare. Let me tell you about it!

Before opening, I placed an ad in the local paper asking for "hired help." Of the 125 applicants answering the ad, about 100 were high-school dropouts.

---

[1] Prepared by Art Sharplin, Louisiana State University.

Of course, I didn't expect college graduates for this type of work, but half of them couldn't even read. It was quite a shock to discover that so many of our younger generation are going into life illiterate. What kind of future do these kids have? They don't seem to have any ambition or desire to improve themselves. Most of them are completely undependable. I spend half of my time replacing boys who just quit. The average employee stays about two months. As a result, I'm always operating short-handed. Even when they show up, I can't get any cooperation from them.

You know, I thought I understood people pretty well, but these kids are impossible. I guess it can be attributed partly to their family background. Take Steve, for example. He is 17 years old and his parents have separated. Steve dropped out of school last year and is living with his brother, who is on welfare.

RON (*Interrupting*): Can't you do anything to help them?

BILL: I've treated Steve as I would my own son, but he didn't appreciate it. He worked for two months and then just stopped coming. He didn't even tell me he was quitting. If you treat them nice they think you're a 'sucker' and take advantage of you. If you try to reason with them, they resent it. The only thing these kids understand is force. I have to watch them every minute to get any work out of them.

RON: I don't know. It seems that if they were given some responsibility they would show more interest.

BILL: I've tried that. But they won't accept responsibility. In the first place, if I put one in charge, the others resent having to take orders from someone their own age. The petty jealousies are ridiculous. When business is good, I sometimes ask one of the boys to help the man at the grill. The 'grill' man then gets 'huffed up' because someone is taking his job away from him. I just can't get them to work as a team.

RON: Don't they ever become friends? I understand one of the basic needs of restaurant workers is a friendly relationship among themselves.

BILL: Yeah, several of them will pal around together for awhile, but within a week they're fighting among themselves. That's the problem that bothers me. If they could become more cohesive in their informal relationships, they would work together more efficiently. But they aren't even loyal to each other. Every time I walk in, one of them meets me at the door to "rat" on another. The friction resulting from all the conflict usually ends with several quitting. Even when I hire a good worker, within two weeks the group pressures bring him into line. It's just one vicious cycle. I'm afraid to leave them alone for fear of what will happen.

RON: I thought you had a night manager to take charge when you left.

BILL: I did until last week. He was an older fellow and he did a fairly good job. However, I caught him stealing from me.

RON: Did you file charges?

BILL: What good would that do? I'd never get the money back and I would have a hard time proving it was him. I estimated the loss at over $200. When I mentioned it, he just disappeared. This isn't the first time that's happened. I've fired three others for the very same reason.

RON: How could he take that much without your knowing it?

BILL: I thought I had controls to prevent that. We work on a ticket system. Each item is accompanied by a prenumbered ticket. When the cashier fills an order he removes the ticket and puts it in the cash register. Some days we are short-handed and the manager has to assist with two jobs. When this happened he merely reused some of the tickets and extracted an equivalent amount of cash. By the time I caught on the damage was already done. The other three I caught were taking food, all of which I know they couldn't use.

RON: The way you tell the story, its a pretty hopeless case.

BILL: You haven't heard the worst of it. This, I think tops them all. Last month, in one of my futile attempts to improve the situation, I gave them all a bonus. Beforehand, I carefully explained that the money would be distributed on the basis of hours worked. They all agreed readily that this was fair. However, after I handed it out, half of them became disgruntled and started griping. As a result, the room was in a chaotic state for a week and two employees quit.

RON: Why don't you raise the pay rate and get more qualified workers?

BILL: I can't do that! I'm already paying above the standard rates. I'm having enough trouble breaking even as it is.

RON: Yes, but if you improved the working conditions wouldn't business pick up enough to overcome the added cost? The present situation certainly affects the customers.

BILL: I'm not at all sure that raising the wages would improve the service. The jobs are still the same and adding a few cents to the wage rate won't attract much better people. The only solution is to get out. As soon as the lease expires I'm going to sell the business to some other fool and let him try to make a go of it.

QUESTIONS FOR DISCUSSION

1. What does this case show about the hiring practices of a small business?
2. What does it show about wage and salary problems?
3. What does it indicate about the need for definite personnel policies?
4. What suggestions for improvement could you make to Bill if you were Ron?

III–3   The Pepper Bush[1]

Sherman Kent, an electrical engineer and a graduate of one of the foremost universities in the Southwest, determined that his future lay in

[1] Prepared by William V. Rice and Robert McGlashan, University of Houston at Clear Lake City.

operating a restaurant. This idea evolved by accident over a period of time when Sherman did the cooking for hunting and fishing trips with friends. He used jalapeno pepper liberally to flavor the food and combined it with cheese to form a spread to enhance the flavor of meat.

His hunting and fishing companions suggested that he should market his product. As the discussions became more serious, they agreed to back him financially if he would establish and manage a restaurant specializing in hamburgers with the special recipe jalapeno cheese sauce. Thus, the Pepper Bush was born.

Sherman opened the small restaurant in a suburban community of approximately 15,000 near a large metropolitan area in the spring of 1973. While he was the operating partner, two other partners helped finance the business by securing a small loan from a local bank. He secured a building with a seating capacity of 50 and equipped it to serve the usual line of short-order food items. Though he specialized in hamburgers with the special jalapeno and cheese sauce, he also served the usual line of hamburgers, french fries, beverages, and so forth. His principal competition was franchise food operations such as McDonald's and Burger King.

By the summer of 1975, business had increased to an expected gross of $125,000, and Sherman was thinking of expanding. Financing could be secured from the bank, and a newer and larger site could be found in the vicinity of the present restaurant.

The personnel policies of the Pepper Bush could be described as highly unstructured. When Sherman opened the restaurant, he hired a cook, three waitresses, and a dishwasher by running ads in the local papers. He did much of the cooking himself and performed all of the management functions. In 1975, his employees consisted of two cooks, five full-time waitresses, two part-time waitresses, and three dishwashers.

One of the cooks, Alvin Marsh, also served as assistant manager. Alvin was one of the first employees hired and had been with Sherman throughout the two-and-a-half-year existence of the Pepper Bush. He served as manager in Sherman's absence and for the previous six months had been actively involved with Sherman in hiring new employees. When a vacancy occurred, one of the employees would bring a friend to Sherman to be interviewed, or Sherman would run an ad in the local paper.

The interview was relatively brief, no formal application was required, and the applicant was either hired on the spot or told immediately that he would not be hired. Turnover of employees had been remarkably small. Two of the waitresses had been at the Pepper Bush since it opened. Sherman stated that the low turnover rate was due to the fact that he took a personal interest in each of his employees and took into account individual differences. For example, he did not require any uniform dress. Most of the waitresses wore jeans and a blouse, and the male help could wear their hair as long as they desired. He also allowed a "very flexible schedule of work," with the various classes of employees working out their own substitutions, as long as each category was covered during the appropriate hours.

Sherman had no formal job descriptions and his training consisted of on-the-job training. For example, all waitresses were expected to be able to work the cash register, wait tables, clean the tables, and, if on the last shift, clean up for the night. But, if the waitresses were too busy, the cook might also work the cash register or clean the tables. All employees were expected to do whatever needed doing.

The proposed expansion would complicate Sherman's personnel problems. The "personal touch," the paternalistic attitude that Sherman had taken toward his employees (the average age of the ten full-time employees was 21), was a luxury he could afford. But, if he expanded, and he expected at least to double the number of employees within the next six months, would he need a more formalized organizational structure? Sherman and Alvin also discussed the overall personnel problems.

QUESTIONS FOR DISCUSSION

1. Should Sherman and Alvin continue the present unstructured informal personnel policy if they did not expand?
2. How would the proposed expansion affect this policy?

III–4   Holly Springs Foods[1]

Holly Springs Foods, producer of special food products for food processors, began in the early 1950s as a partnership. In 1956, because of product difficulties and personal problems of the partners, the partnership was dissolved. At that time, George Bobo formed a corporation and became president and major stockholder, and his brother, Bill, holder of a very significant block of the company stock, became treasurer and office manager. George was in his early 50s and Bill was some two or three years younger.

The company had its next crisis in early 1962, when the market for

---

[1] Prepared by Curtis E. Tate, Jr., University of Georgia, and James M. Todd, Memphis State University.

its major product line suddenly disintegrated. In response to this, two new product lines were developed that seemed to offer greater potential. Sales increased over the next two to three years to approximately $1 million per year. This level of sales continued throughout the 1960s.

The company experienced another crisis, however, as a result of its effort to expand its sales and that failed. Through an all-out effort by George Bobo and Ken Irby, the sales manager, the company was able to salvage its situation and turn around toward increased sales and profitability. Much of the increased sales could be attributed to a greater emphasis on proprietary products and increased sales effort. By the mid-1970s, sales exceeded $3 million a year with an above-average profit margin.

In the late 1960s, Janie Snow came to Holly Springs to do general clerical work, take dictation, and keep company records. She was in her early 20s, divorced, and had the responsibility of a three-year-old daughter.

At the outset, she gave the appearance of being a loyal, dedicated worker. Her workplace was located adjacent to George Bobo's office, and there soon developed "a very close working relationship between them." Many times, when Janie was unable to complete all of her book work during the day, she carried it home at night to continue. During the second crisis period, she seemed always to give the needed extra push to help accomplish the work that had to be done.

As the clerical work began to increase with increased sales, it became necessary to add additional help. Pat was brought in to act as the receptionist and assist the production people with their paperwork. Pat was in her middle 30s, divorced, and the mother of a number of teenage children. She, too, was a loyal, dedicated worker, but on occasion, family problems kept her from work.

Later, Betty and Sally were brought in to accommodate the added marketing paperwork requirements. Betty, in her late 30s or early 40s, was married, and her years of work experience in a variety of circumstances had given her the perceptive maturity to function effectively in the new environment. Sally was in her late 40s. The work activities of Sally and Betty were related.

About this time, Janie began to have some health and personal problems. Since she had always been given favored treatment, she adopted the practice of working her own schedule and frequently was absent during the week, saying she would make it up on Saturday and Sunday, which she frequently did.

Shortly after Betty and Sally's arrival, it became apparent that the two seemed to form an informal coalition, along with Pat, in opposition to Janie. From time to time, there were momentary outbursts, which George Bobo ignored.

Two years ago, George decided to move Janie into an office some distance from his own. He told her that she would be directly responsible to Bill Bobo instead of to him. She became quite upset over this change of events and rebelled at every opportunity—with little results.

A short time later, the company consultant was working with George and asked to review the firm's profit bonus records. When George went to Janie to get them, he discovered that she had them at home. George was quite upset because he saw no reason for those particular records to have been taken to her home.

Following this incident, George called her into his office and told her that she was not to take any company records away from the plant in the future. From time to time, however, when the work load became excessive, she continued to take work home.

While Janie's health seemed to improve, her personal problems continued to exist and frequently led to absenteeism. She continued to believe that she should be permitted to work her own schedule, considering her own personal convenience only. After a series of absences, she was called in and told that she must work from 8:00 A.M. to 5:00 P.M. in the same fashion as other members of the clerical staff and that her recent practices of writing her own work schedule would no longer be tolerated.

Whether by coincidence or not, the question of bonus records came up again last summer, and Janie again had them at home. George was visibly upset by this circumstance and indicated that some action would result. A week later, the consultant learned that Janie had been terminated.

After Janie's termination, the consultant discovered that Betty was taking work home with her.

QUESTIONS FOR DISCUSSION

1. Discuss the legal aspects of Janie's treatment and discharge.
2. What does this case illustrate about the consequences of favorable treatment of employees?
3. Evaluate the firm's hiring policies.
4. What would you suggest now if you were the consultant?

III–5   Where Do We Get Workers for a Third Shift[1]

Petro Manufacturing, located in the Houston area, was an independent machine shop specializing in production metal working. The firm op-

---

[1] Prepared by Howard Chamberlain and A. W. Smith, Texas A&M University.

erated 13 automatic screw machines, 5 numerical control machining centers, numerous conventional machine tools, and an extensive grinding shop. The typical shift employed 25–40 workers, depending on the work available. Most of these workers were skilled machinists. A proposed expansion of Petro Manufacturing sales had become effective during the summer and fall of 1974, to the point that the typical shop work week had stretched to two ten-hour shifts a day, six days a week. Sunday work was not unusual.

At this point, management was giving serious thought to the possibility of starting a third shift.

Several advantages of a third shift were evident to management:

1. Wages would be paid at regular rates rather than overtime rates.
2. Employees would work fewer hours with less fatigue and perhaps higher overall efficiency.
3. There would be maximum utilization of existing machine tools and equipment.

Even with a third shift, however, the need for overtime could still be satisfied, at least partly, by working Saturday and possibly part of Sunday. If the ten-hour shift that workers were accustomed to ceased, some workers would look for additional moonlighting jobs in other plants. In this particular industry, during busy times, it was not unusual for workers to work eight hours at one plant and an additional four hours at another plant.

At the same time, the move to a third eight-hour shift would likely incur several difficulties and disadvantages:

1. Some of the better workers, accustomed to a high level of overtime, would become dissatisfied as the amount of overtime pay would be reduced.
2. Current slack in work schedules, which could be taken up by working more than ten hours a shift on a machine, would no longer be available because the machines would be scheduled to run continuously 24 hours a day. The only time available for catch-up, or extra work, would be during Saturday or Sunday.

It was decided that the biggest stumbling block would be in obtaining sufficient skilled personnel. The Houston area had lower unemployment rates than other cities in the nation. In fact, there were practically no unemployed workers of the type Petro Manufacturing needed.

Petro's personnel people described their workers this way:

> Machine shop workers are a nomadic group, tending to move from one shop to another and back again as the work load in the individual shops varies. Many of these workers actively seek situations that require much overtime. If they are working for a shop that can support them

only eight hours a day, five days a week, they will keep their ear to the grapevine to find out who is busy and attempt to hire on in a shop that is working five ten-hour shifts, or possibly even six ten-hour shifts, per week. If that is not available, they may well take moonlighting work in shops with a higher work demand. A fair percentage of these employees have less loyalty to their company than to their trade. A significant proportion of Petro Manufacturing production workers was in their second or third—in a few cases, their fourth—employment period with Petro in the last few years.

While the Houston area was experiencing a very tight labor market, other areas in the United States were in a general recession. Larger cities —Los Angeles, Detroit, and Cleveland—were identified as areas where Petro could obtain unemployed workers for use in their operation. The aerospace industry had experienced a severe cutback, causing widespread unemployment in the Los Angeles area. The automobile industry had also experienced a cutback, causing unemployment in the Detroit area. It was also felt that each of these industries would employ machinists with the skills necessary to help Petro meet its demand.

The personnel manager's problem was how to visit the three cities in order to make the most effective use of Petro people's time and to try to produce the greatest number of potential employees.

QUESTIONS FOR DISCUSSION

1. How should Petro go about recruiting employees in a distant area?
2. How could Petro convince prospective employees to move up to two thousand miles to go to work for an unknown employer?

III–6   Kellog Motors[1]

Kellog Motors was an automobile agency in Pleasantville, a small rural community in the Mississippi delta. Historically, agriculture had been the area's primary economic base with "cotton the king." However, in 1971 growing welfare receipts represented a major portion of the county's income.

Pleasantville had a population of about 6,500 in 1960 and 7,000 in 1970.

---

[1] Prepared by Robert A. Rentz, Jr., Scottsdale Memorial Hospital, and Leon C. Megginson, University of South Alabama.

It was the only town within a county of about 15,000 people, of whom around 40 percent were black. The population of the county declined more than 10 percent from 1960 to 1970. It was estimated that most of the loss was from outmigration, especially from the farms in the surrounding countryside.

Like many small towns, Pleasantville had only three automobile agencies—a General Motors dealership; a Ford dealership; and a Chrysler dealership, owned and operated by Mr. J. A. Kellog.

Mr. Kellog was originally from a city near Pleasantville. As a youth he was a good student with natural mechanical inclinations. Upon graduation from high school, Kellog was encouraged by his family, especially an aunt who was a college professor, to enter college and pursue an education in engineering, but he refused. His interest was not in school, he said, but in automobiles.

Starting as a mechanic's helper when 16, he quickly built a reputation as a good mechanic. Three years later he founded his own business. Actually, Pleasantville had no one who knew about automobile repairs until Kellog came there and established his business. After about a year of doing almost all the work himself, he went back to his home town and encouraged two mechanics to come work for him in Pleasantville, as business was good.

Five years later Mr. Kellog became a Chrysler dealer. Before that time, he had handled Chevrolet, but he dropped the franchise when General Motors tried to force more cars upon him than he wanted immediately before a major model change. He rapidly sold his remaining stock and made room for his new stock of Chryslers, while 12 Chevrolets which General Motors said he must take sat refused and in demurrage in railroad cars.

In 1962, the Dodge automobile and truck agency was obtained to increase the firm's market potential. Until that time Kellog had been without a truck line. This addition gave the dealership a full line of products with the Valiant in the compact field, Plymouth and Dodge in both the intermediate and standard-size car class, Chrysler in the medium to luxury car class, and the Dodge in the truck market. Kellog Motors also had a profitable Texaco dealership.

Competing dealerships in Pleasantville have come and gone throughout the lifespan of the firm. The Ford agency has changed hands four times in the past 12 years, and Chevrolet three times. The agencies were more highly organized and formally structured than the Chrysler dealership.

Kellog's only son had a bachelor's degree in business administration and was currently enrolled at State University studying toward an MBA degree. Respecting his son's education, Kellog often asked him his opinion on various problems of the business. Kervin, the son, who was considering managing the business someday, was interested in its affairs, and attempted to find ways to apply what he had learned in his formal education to the betterment of the business.

One of the problems facing the son was the fact that the dealership was in a small town and was a small sized business, while the young man's education had been directed mostly toward big business. This difference caused conflict between Kervin and his father as the son attempted to apply his knowledge to the affairs of the business. The following exchange is an example:

KERVIN: Dad, I think Brick is mad again about having to grease those cars. He doesn't think a mechanic should have to do that type of work.

MR. KELLOG: I can't help that, Kervin. What should I do when there are several wash and lube jobs to be done and he doesn't have anything to do in the shop? Should I let him sit down back there and pull a laborer off the front to grease cars, or let the wash man both wash and grease them when we are rushed like this?

KERVIN: Well, I don't know. But I've learned that each man should have his own job with distinct duties, and that he should be entirely responsible for them and only them.

MR. KELLOG: Well, that's all right for a big organization, but it will not work for a small business such as this. I don't want anyone to think he has only one job; he is to do anything that needs doing, when it needs doing.

KERVIN: Perhaps you're wrong. I also noticed something else. You don't let the men help make decisions that affect them. Maybe they would be happier and produce more if you let them have their say in the management of the business; after all, they are a part of it, aren't they?

MR. KELLOG: Now, wouldn't that be fine. What the hell? Do you think those jerks out there know anything about running this place?

KERVIN: Maybe they don't, but if they aren't the right people, then get the right people.

MR. KELLOG: That's easier said than done. That is one of the big problems, and perhaps the biggest problem for a small business today. Where are the right personnel to be found? Today, a good mechanic is almost as hard to find as gold at the end of the rainbow. A good mechanic can make as much as $250 to $300 per week, and yet, no one wants to become a mechanic. Ask boys in high school what they want to be. Practically all of them want to be doctors, business executives, lawyers, engineers, teachers, or perhaps football coaches. I bet you that not a single one answers that he wants to be a mechanic. Who is going to maintain the automobiles of those doctors, lawyers, and engineers? Here is a problem for you, your teachers, and the politicians of the nation. But right now I am looking at the situation from my own point of view.

Mr. Kellog went on to explain that a business man becomes successful by hiring good people and then building an organization around them. A doctor or lawyer is limited to only what he can turn out personally, but the business man is different, for his managerial abilities constitute a creative force within himself. He can multiply his productivity many fold. But to do this, he must have the right personnel; he must surround himself with capable men so that he can multiply the amount of production that can be achieved. If the right workers are not to be found, however, he is limited to only what he, individually, can produce.

Kervin knew these facts to be true, for there were very few mechanics available. Also, during the previous ten years, very few young men had entered the skilled fields. However, it seemed that the problem was even more severe for Kellog Motors than for the larger concerns. Since Mr. Kellog was a skilled mechanic, his customers could depend on him to see to it that their automobiles were repaired when they were supposed to be. If Kervin were in charge, he would not be able to guide the mechanics and ensure that they did the job correctly, as his father had been able to do. Kervin was not accustomed to doing mechanical work.

Another drawback in the small company was that if it were lucky enough to find a good mechanic, he would probably not want to come to a small town and leave a shop where he had established customers. As this question particularly disturbed the young college man, he asked his dad one day:

KERVIN: Dad, what can be done to solve this problem of mechanics? There are many young men who are unemployed, or their folks are on welfare. Why can't they be trained to become craftsmen?

MR. KELLOGG: The factories realize the problem and are offering training programs for mechanics. The arrangement is for the dealer to send the mechanic to school for several days at a time to learn to repair specific parts of the auto. The problem is that when you train a mechanic and he becomes good and starts attracting customers, he usually quits and opens a small shop of his own. So you lose the time and money you invested in his training. In Brick's case this would be easy with the emphasis upon "black capitalism," and the government's emphasis upon "civil rights."

KERVIN: If you would put them on a commission basis instead of paying them salary, it would perhaps solve this problem.

MR. KELLOG: Maybe it would. There is one bad thing about the commission method, though. It would perhaps encourage mechanics to be crooked. For instance, he will do jobs on automobiles that don't actually need to be done, or he will make parts replacements when they aren't necessary. Mechanics often make what is called a double charge," too. That is, if he pulls a wheel off to fix a wheel cylinder and while he has it off he also replaces the brake shoe, he charges for each of them as a separate job, as if he had to take the wheel off for each job separately.

The son had been studying "democratic leadership" versus "authoritarian management" at school. One of his professors had often said that the manager must create within his subordinates a love for him, which is admittedly hard to do. Otherwise he must create a healthy fear, or respect, among his followers towards him. This problem was acute in the agency, as shown in the following example:

MR. KELLOG: I sent James back to the shop this afternoon with a pair of chains for one of the men to put on a car. He came back and said there wasn't anyone there. So, I walked around the corner and there stood Charley and Brick at the bar on the corner drinking. I said, 'What the hell do you mean coming around here during working hours? I ought to pay you both off right now.' They both left the bar and walked ahead of me all the way back, with me telling them what I thought of them every step of the way.

KERVIN: I can't understand why they would do a thing like that. Maybe you have been too hard on them.

MR. KELLOG: Bull! You have to be hard; you can't be nice to them. Yesterday, during the snow, they had had a hard day putting anti-freeze in cars. Around ten minutes before quitting time we had everything ready to close up and another car drove in for anti-freeze. I told the driver he would have to wait until the next day, as we were closing. I thought I would be nice to the labor considering how hard they had worked. What I should have done was tell them to open up the shop again and put the anti-freeze in that car. They just don't appreciate what you do for them. You can't be considerate and nice to them—they will take advantage of you every damn time they have an opportunity.

The lack of good mechanics was enough of a problem by itself; however, it had side effects. As a result of the great demand for their services and the relatively few good ones available, they became hard to manage. They knew they were in demand, and did things they would not do otherwise. This may be an example of the problem:

MR. KELLOG: In addition to the shortage of mechanics, the government's ruining the ones who are working. Brick's attitude has certainly changed now that he has so many opportunities to do other things. He's getting hard to live with. In fact, I'm reasonably sure that he has stolen oil from this place to go in his own automobile. The reason I believe this is that he never buys oil for that car of his, yet he buys gasoline and other things for it. I know it doesn't run without oil.

KERVIN: He could buy his oil somewhere else.

MR. KELLOG: Why would he do that when he buys other things here? It doesn't make sense. Anyway, he should buy oil here once in a while.

KERVIN: I will go along with you on that.

MR. KELLOG: We started keeping a closer check on our oil inventory and James came up five quarts short on Havoline #20, exactly the oil Brick's car requires. I know it went into his automobile.

KERVIN: Well, are you going to fire him?

MR. KELLOG: No, I will just have to watch him closer. He is a good mechanic, and is making me money. What's wrong?

KERVIN: Nothing, I was just thinking.

QUESTIONS FOR DISCUSSION

1. How can a small firm like this find and keep capable employees?
2. Should Mr. Kellog have a more formal organization structure with separate job specifications for each employee? Explain your answers.
3. How would you motivate these employees?
4. With this business, and with these employees, which leadership style would be best? Explain your answer.
5. What would you do about the missing oil? Explain.
6. What does the case show about the problems of manning a small business?

part IV

Producing Your Product or Service

Previous parts of this text have been concerned with planning for and managing the business you have inherited, bought, or organized. The previous part dealt extensively with selecting, developing, and maintaining your work force.

Now, it is time to look at the process of producing your good or service. This may not be an easy or simple task, for many and diverse activities are required to carry on the production function.

You must be concerned with determining what products to sell; deciding whether to buy them from someone else or produce them yourself; planning, acquiring, laying out, and maintaining the physical facilities required for operations; procuring and producing the right quantity of the right products, at the right time, and at the right cost; controlling the quality and quantity of your inventory; maintaining a work force; and *doing all of this as efficiently and economically as possible!*

All these activities make the production function interesting, challenging, and rewarding, but also quite frustrating. In order to help you meet this challenge, this part will cover:

1. Changing inputs to outputs, including acquiring your physical facilities.
2. Designing and controlling work.
3. Purchasing and controlling your materials.

The first of these functions is covered in Chapter 12; the second, in Chapter 13; and the third and final one, in Chapter 14.

12

Operations: Converting Inputs to Outputs

All business organizations produce something, either a product or a service. Thus, all firms are engaged in some form of operations, which can be called "production." Yet, this term itself may be misleading, as you will soon see.

In this chapter, we will discuss "operations," or converting inputs into outputs. Among the many inputs are personnel, money, machines, materials, and methods. Among the outputs are the product(s) produced, or service(s) performed, for your customers.

An immediate response to the material in this chapter may be that it applies only to a fabricating or manufacturing type business. When examined more closely, however, it should become apparent that the principles and procedures detailed here are of such a nature that they provide you with the opportunity to utilize them in a broad spectrum of activities.

SYSTEMS FOR CONVERTING INPUTS TO FINISHED PRODUCTS

The term *production* often refers to manufacturing, because production methodology was first developed and applied in manufacturing industries. Yet, in reality, *production* can be defined as *the creation of value or wealth by producing goods and services.* This definition includes other activities, as well as manufacturing. As indicated above, all companies receive inputs and convert them to outputs, as do industrial companies. Managers must have a system to do this. Figure 12–1 shows the trans-

FIGURE 12–1
Examples of Production Systems

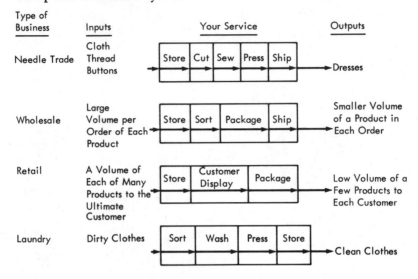

formation or movement of goods for a number of types of companies. Note that the conversion of the inputs to outputs represents the major activity of the business—the reason for the company's existence—and may be a transforming of form, place, or time.

Other examples of inputs and outputs, which must have conversion processes, are shown in Figure 12–2.

Productive Elements

How can the production methodology used by industrial firms be applied to all types of small businesses? The processes of changing inputs to outputs have some characteristics that are common to all situations, and have the following common elements:

1. Systems to transform the input as to form, place, or time.
2. A sequence of steps or operations to convert the inputs into outputs.
3. Special skills and often tools, machinery, or equipment to make the transformation or conversion.
4. Some time frame in which the work is to be done.
5. Instructions to identify the work to be performed and the units being produced.
6. Standards and maximum rates of input and output.
7. Exceptions and errors that must be handled.

FIGURE 12–2
Examples of Inputs and Outputs

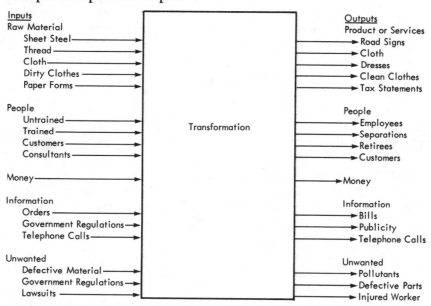

Inputs
Raw Material
  Sheet Steel
  Thread
  Cloth
  Dirty Clothes
  Paper Forms

People
  Untrained
  Trained
  Customers
  Consultants

Money

Information
  Orders
  Government Regulations
  Telephone Calls

Unwanted
  Defective Material
  Government Regulations
  Lawsuits

Transformation

Outputs
Product or Services
  Road Signs
  Cloth
  Dresses
  Clean Clothes
  Tax Statements

People
  Employees
  Separations
  Retirees
  Customers

Money

Information
  Bills
  Publicity
  Telephone Calls

Unwanted
  Pollutants
  Defective Parts
  Injured Worker

Productive Elements Applied to Different Industries

Not only do the inputs and outputs within a company have many common characteristics, but the transformation processes within different classifications of businesses have common characteristics. Let us look at some of these different applications to firms in different industries.

A Manufacturing Company. To *manufacture* means to *make,* or process, a raw material into a finished product. "Raw material" may be the outputs from other companies, such as synthetic rubber, resistors, or plastic powder, which are changed in form and/or assembled. Usually, a series of operations is commonly performed by machines in the conversion process. Formerly, these operations were usually performed by blue-collar workers using tools and machines. Now, manual labor has largely been replaced by machines, some of which are either automatically controlled or controlled by other machines. These devices can turn out more uniform products, with greater precision, in greater volume, and with less skill required than manual production.

Manufacturing companies may produce only one standard product, while others, at the other extreme, produce each product to special order, with no product ever being repeated. The former type of process, called *continuous production,* operates automatically. The production system, once established, keeps performing the same actions. Also, the outputs can be stored with little chance of obsolescence or loss of value because of style or use changes.

Companies producing goods for customers requesting nonstandard products must produce these when the customer wants the product. These companies are called *job shops*—they produce to the customer's order, or by the job. Seasonal and other variations in demand cause production to vary up and down considerably, and tend to result in idle time and varying employment levels.

In both processes, planning and controls must be exercised. The product is usually designed by an engineer, who usually not only executes the design, but also converts it into production specifications. The operations to be performed, the machines to use, the skills of workers needed, and the material inputs needed are determined for each product or order. The time to produce is set, and instructions for workers and tools to use are designated. The information is used in performing and checking the work to assure output conformance with specifications. Thus, a procedure is set to guide and check production.

A Service Company with Manufacturing Characteristics.   Many small businesses fall into this category. Cleaning and laundering, cabinet making, short-order food processing, patient processing, printing, and machining organizations are examples. The inputs are converted to finished products through one or a series of operations. The required operations are repeated with variations for special orders. Firms of this kind differ from manufacturers in the emphases placed on the design of the system of transformation.

The service company usually receives smaller orders, with some variation in the input and the desired output. For example, a customer may bring into a laundry different items, such as sheets, clothing, rags, and linens. These, in turn, are made from different combinations of white, colored, natural, and synthetic cloth. Greater emphasis is put on individual handling and contact. This extra activity results in higher unit costs than for single-product, high-volume processes. Also, the related systems needed to plan, identify, and control are relatively more complex.

These companies fit the job shop classification, but when they are designed properly, they may take on the characteristics of continuous production. In the laundry, for example, all clothing is sorted into different types of cloth. Then, each type of cloth follows a set process.

Certain businesses, such as short-order food processors, can reduce the supporting systems needed by building into the physical facilities controls over the process. The amount of communication is reduced by limiting the variety and fixing the procedures to a small number. A hamburger stand with high volume works on an inventory replenishment basis, and hamburgers follow set variations on the same pattern.

Wholesalers. This group of companies receives large volumes of many items and distributes them in smaller quantities. The transformation process involves converting large packages of like items into large and small packages of a variety of items. The sequence of operations can be planned and controlled in the same manner as for the manufacturing process. The emphasis moves from transforming by machinery to storing, materials handling, and packaging.

Retailing. Again, the process within a store has subprocesses, but the organization includes movements of customers, as well as the materials. The primary emphasis is directed toward convenience to the customers and only secondarily toward material flow. The placing of goods in the store and the movement of customers in relation to the goods are important contributors to or detractors from the sale of goods.

Other Types of Companies. Many other small businesses not included in the prior classifications can benefit from the same type of internal analyses as those discussed. Automobile repairing, home building, and accounting firms have similar flows of material, people, or forms.

The set of processes in each organization tends to reflect its reason for existence. For example, materials and parts are converted to finished goods in a manufacturing company; patients are processed through treatments in a hospital; and goods are moved to the proper place, the customer is guided to that place, and the transaction is completed at another point in a self-service store. All other processes, including paperwork, are supportive and designed to assure achieving the objectives of the firm.

DECIDING WHETHER TO MAKE OR BUY

The process of changing raw material to a finished product that is delivered to the customer is a long process, usually involving many companies performing different productive functions. Figure 6–1 showed the sequence of steps raw materials go through to become a finished product you use as a consumer. One company may refine the raw materials, several may perform manufacturing processes, another may assemble the parts into the finished product, and so on. A given company may perform a large or small part of this process. Fixing the place and the size of the segment is an important decision.

Deciding to Specialize or Generalize

Part II discussed how you would decide your place in the chain and what segment you wanted for yourself. Now, let us look at how the size of each segment is determined. Such determination depends on what you decide to buy and process, and to whom you decide to sell. The following two examples will illustrate this point.

If you were producing birdhouses made of wood, you could:

1. Buy wood and cut the parts, or buy precut pieces.
2. Assemble the birdhouse, or sell the packaged pieces to be assembled by the customer.
3. Sell to a wholesaler, retailer, or the final user.

A food processor can:

1. Grow or buy its vegetables.
2. Sell its output to a wholesaler, retailer, or directly to the consumer.

For best results, you should try to specialize in the segment of the total process where you have the greatest expertise.

The *advantages of specializing* and concentrating in a small area that the company performs best are:

1. Less capital investment is needed for machinery and for people with differing capabilities.
2. Management can concentrate better on a small segment.
3. Planning, directing, and controlling are less complex.

The *advantages of a larger segment* are:

1. More control of the process.
2. Less idle machine and personnel time.
3. Greater potential for growth.

The Economics of Your Decision

The decision as to what segment you will seek is usually based on the economics of the situation. It might be advantageous for you to make some of the parts you normally buy in order to use idle time of the machines and people. You might drop some of the early or late operations instead of buying more machinery when you do not have enough capacity. Remember, though, that any additions or reductions must be evaluated from a cost viewpoint, and that some of these costs may vary with changes in volume, while others do not.

Having decided on the segment of the total transformation process you wish to perform, you can now begin to plan, obtain, and install your producing unit.

The physical facilities of your company—including the building itself, machines and equipment, furniture and fixtures, and others—must be designed to aid the employees in producing the desired product or service at a low cost. The design function includes the layout and selection of machines and equipment and the determination of the features desired in the building. For purposes of discussion, the function is divided into two parts: (1) planning and (2) implementation.

STEPS IN PLANNING YOUR PHYSICAL FACILITIES

Good selection and arrangement of your physical facilities can pay dividends. Planning your physical facilities requires the following steps:

1. Determine the services you plan to perform (discussed in earlier chapters).
2. Break the production into *parts, operations,* and *activities.*
3. Determine the times required to perform each operation.
4. Using these time figures as a guide, estimate the number of machines and workers you need.
5. Decide the type of arrangement you feel is best for the sequence of operations.
6. Determine the general layout, using blocks for sections of the plant.
7. Plan the detailed layout that will provide the most effective use of your personnel, machines, and materials.

Step 1: Determine Your Services

This step was discussed in earlier chapters, but in general the business you are in will determine what good(s) you will need to produce or what service(s) you will perform.

Step 2: Break the Product or Service into Parts, Operations, and Activities

Assuming you are going to produce a product to sell to customers, you need to break the product down into:

1. Parts going into it.
2. Operations needed to produce it.
3. Activities surrounding its production.

Parts are the divisions of the product that, when assembled, form the output. Some outputs have only one part; others, such as radios and hamburgers, have many. The part or parts must be identified.

Operations are the steps or segments of work performed to accomplish the conversion of the inputs into outputs. The segments are often identified by the specialized work of a machine, as for example drilling, typing, or wrapping. The conversion process usually requires a series of

FIGURE 12-3

Operation Process Chart and Calculations for Making a Typical Metal Sign

Operations	Symbols for Sequence	Machine	Hours Required per Machine	Forecast Volume per Hour	Number of Machines Needed
Cut Sides	①	Shear	.12/100 Cuts	500 Cuts	1
Cut Corners	②	Press	.17/100 Corners	600 Corners	2
Punch Holes	③	Press	.10/100 Holes	500 Holes	1
Wash	④	Tank	.005/Sign	300 Signs	10 Ft.*
Dry	⑤	Oven	.01/Sign	300 Signs	15 Ft.*
Phosphate Coat	⑥	Tank	.008/Sign	300 Signs	12 Ft.*
Dry	⑦	Oven	.02/Sign	300 Signs	30 Ft.*
Paint Metal	⑧	Spray Gun	.28/100 Signs	300 Signs	1
Bake	⑨	Oven	.10/Sign	300 Signs	150 Ft.*
Print Sign	⑩	Silk Screen	Varies (see table)	300 Signs	2
Bake	⑪	Oven	.10/100 Signs	300 Signs	1
Box Signs	⑫	Bench	1.00/100 Signs	300 Signs	3 Workers

* Conveyors are used to move signs into, through, and out of tanks and ovens at 10 feet per minute. Tanks and ovens are measured in feet.

operations. Figures 12–3 and 12–4 show the operations for making metal signs and collecting groceries. The circles indicate operations.

Activities, such as moving materials, are necessary for the performance of the operations. Nonactivities, including delays, are caused by imbalance of the times of the operation. Activities and nonactivities may not be identified fully until the final layout planning is performed. The number and extent of nonactivities should be minimized.

To determine the parts and operations, you start with the output and work backward to the inputs. In an assembled product, the disassembly process is called *exploding.* The process identifies the parts. Then, the operations on each part and their sequence can be identified, and the type of machine(s) selected. The sequence may be fixed or rigid, as the cutting of boards precedes their assembly as a bookshelf. Or, the sequence may not be important, as in the order of cutting the boards. In other cases, the proper sequence of operations is important to obtain a high volume of sales, as in a cafeteria or a supermarket. Flexible sequences of operations are desirable to facilitate efficient utilization of machines and personnel.

FIGURE 12–4
Operation Process Chart for a Customer in a Supermarket

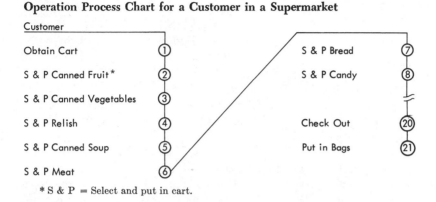

* S & P = Select and put in cart.

Step 3: Determine the Times to Perform the Operations

Each operation required to produce a good or perform a service consumes the time of machines and personnel. The times can be obtained by making an estimate, or by using one of the several time measurement methods discussed in the next chapter. The total time includes the time to perform the operation plus time for unavoidable delays and personal needs. Some operations are routine and are easily measured; others are more variable and not so easily measured. The times obtained are used to determine the number of machines and the number of people needed to perform the work and the speed of conveyors.

Step 4: Estimate the Number of Machines and Workers Needed

Knowing the time that a machine takes to perform an operation on a product, and knowing your planned production, you can determine the number of machines needed. Figure 12–3 shows the number of machines required to make 300 signs per hour. Operation 3, punching holes, requires half the time of a press [$(.10 \div 100) \times 500$ holes]. Either one machine can be purchased for this operation, or it can be combined with Operation 2, cutting corners, which requires less than half the time of a second machine. Similar studies are made in supermarkets to determine the number of check-out stations.

Step 5: Decide the Best Arrangement for the Sequence of Operations

You should try to obtain the least movement of product and people. However, people and machines should not be idle and space should not be wasted. The plant can be planned according to either, or a combination of both, of the following two types of layout:

1. Product, or service.
2. Process, or function.

The *product layout* places the machines or serving units in such a way that the product moves along a line as it passes through its sequence of operations. Assembly lines in the automobile industry are the best-known examples of this type of layout. As the automobile frame moves on a conveyor, the engine, axles, steering mechanism, and other components are added until a finished car comes off the conveyor. A cafeteria line is another example.

This type layout has been spreading from the large manufacturing operations to nonmanufacturing and small businesses as more standardized routines have been developed and as demand volume and the capacities of machines and people have been better matched. Some examples of small businesses using this layout are the short-order line in a cafeteria, packing materials for an order in a warehouse, and one-product companies. In fact, all layouts should generally conform to this concept, as shown in Figure 12–5.

FIGURE 12–5
Product Layout

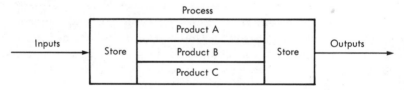

With this type of layout, materials or people move forward from operation to operation with little backtracking. A supermarket could set up this type of layout if it knew that a large enough number of customers wanted the same items. The customers could move down the line picking up the items as they went, and be through in a short time. If the customer selects purchases according to the order in which the goods are displayed, there is no need to backtrack. The advantages of this type of layout plan include:

1. Specialization of workers and machines.
2. Less inventory.
3. Fewer instructions and controls.
4. Faster movement.
5. Less space for aisles and storage.

The second type of layout, *process,* is based on keeping the machines and workers busy, thus keeping the idle time to a minimum. Machines performing the same type of work are grouped together, and the same is true of workers with like skills. Some examples of this type layout include presses grouped together so that each press can keep busy and typists put in a "pool" to perform typing for many offices. This type of layout increases the movement of material or people, and necessitates higher inventory. The *advantages* of the process layout include:

1. Its flexibility to take care of change and variety.
2. Its use of general-purpose machines and equipment.
3. Its more efficient use of machines and personnel.

Few layout plans are confined to either the one type or the other. Instead, they consist of combinations of the two to take advantage of the situation. Idle time created by differing production rates is more than compensated for by decreased inventory.

Layouts can be planned to move material, people, tools, or machines. Thus, in some stores the customers move through self-service lines; in others, the sales person moves about to bring the goods to the customer. Products move through some production processes; in others, people and tools move to the product. For part of the physical examination in a clinic, doctors and nurses move to the patient; for others, the patient moves from room to room.

Some of the factors to be considered in planning for movement are:

1. Size of goods and machines.
2. Safety requirements.
3. Volume of input and output.
4. Type of service.

Step 6: Determine the General Layout

The next step is to determine the general layout, using blocks for sections of the layout. A block can be a machine, a group of machines, a group of products on display, or a department. This step is intended to establish the general arrangement of the plant, store, or office before spending much time on details. Estimates are made of the space needed in each block using past layouts; summation of space for machines, men, aisles, and other factors; or the best judgment available. The intent is to plan the general arrangement before planning the detailed layout.

Figure 12–6 is an illustration of a block layout. The dashed lines and solid lines show the general block areas for presses, painting, shipping, and so forth. Blocks can be used for planning the layout of an office building or residence.

Besides the activities directly concerned with the main activities of the company, space for maintenance, planning, food, personal needs, and

FIGURE 12–6
Plant Layout for Metal Sign Company

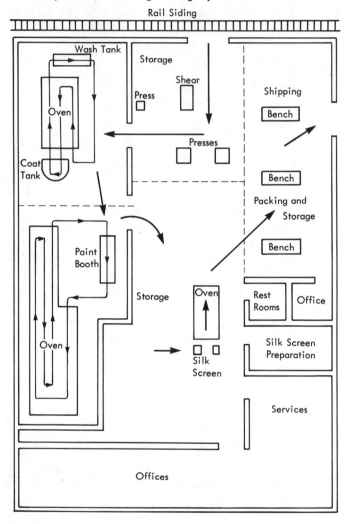

other services, is provided. These should be placed conveniently near the units being serviced. Estimates of the space required can be obtained from books, pamphlets, trade associations, and past experience.

If you are replanning the layout of an existing building, or are planning to move into one, the location of outside walls is predetermined. The size and shape of the land may be confining.

On the other hand, if you are planning a new building, you have greater flexibility. This allows you to design it so that changes can be made easily in the future. Buildings are usually designed to provide space for several years, while the number of machines planned is for only the near future—as machines can be added at a later date. In most operations, single-story, square, and columnless buildings with movable utility outlets are preferred. The building is designed from the inside out.

Entrance locations are important in the layout, particularly for service establishments. Customers enter downtown stores from the street and goods usually enter from the back. These entrances may be fixed, setting the flow of goods from back to front. Some producing plants use the same transportation units for delivering supplies and materials as for shipping the finished goods. The flow is thus U-shaped. Other—usually less important—external factors are:

1. Entrances for employees.
2. Connections to utilities.
3. Governmental restrictions.
4. Weather factors.

Included in the layout should be plans for expansion and other future conditions.

Step 7: Plan the Detailed Layout for Efficiency and Effectiveness

You must plan in detail the layout of your people, machines, and materials if you are to have efficient performance. Each machine and piece of equipment is located, and space allocated for its use. As with blocks, templates—or models—of the machines, equipment, and workers help you perform this step. These templates can be moved about to obtain your best plan. Figure 12–6 shows machine locations for the metal sign plant determined by using templates for placing machines.

In manufacturing, many methods are used to move materials. Conveyors, carts, by hand, trucks, and cranes are examples. For example, the materials shown in Figure 12–3 could be moved by fork-lift truck, carts, and overhead and belt conveyors. Notice that, as shown, the conveyor carries the metal plates through washing, drying, coating, and drying without stopping. Wholesale warehouses are faced with many types of materials handling problems. The objective is to minimize materials handling and its cost without increasing other costs.

Each operation should be examined to assure easy performance of work. If the worker spends too much time standing, walking, turning, and twisting, the work will take longer and be more tiring. Frequently used items or tools should be located close at hand for quick service. A short study of location of tools in a garage illustrates this point. An understanding of methods study is helpful in planning workers' activities.

Some specific matters that you should include in your final layout planning are:

1. *Space for movement.* Are aisles wide enough for one- or two-way traffic? Is there enough room if a queue forms? Can material be obtained easily and is space available when it is waiting?
2. *Utilities.* Have adequate provisions been made for incoming wiring and gas or for disposal of water at each machine? Will any future moves be necessary?
3. *Supply of equipment.* Can shelves be restocked conveniently?
4. *Safety.* Has equipment using flammable material been properly isolated and proper fire protection been provided? Are moving parts and machines guarded and the operators protected from accidents?
5. *Working conditions.* Does the worker have enough working space and light? Have you provided for low noise levels, proper temperature, and elimination of objectionable odors? Is the worker safe; can he socialize and take care of his personal needs?
6. *Cleanliness and maintenance.* Is the layout designed for good housekeeping at low cost? Can machinery, equipment, and building be maintained easily?
7. *Product quality.* Are provisions made to protect the product as it moves through the plant or sits in storage?

Although we have been talking about manufacturing facilities, many of the same generalizations hold true for retail and wholesale establishments.

IMPLEMENTING YOUR PLANS

The first step in implementing your plans is to test them to see whether they are sound. There are many ways you can do this. One method is to have employees—or other persons who can give some experienced opinions—review the plans and give you their suggestions. Another method is to simulate the process by moving templates or models of the goods or people through the process so that you can analyze their movements. You might deliberately include some mishaps to see what happens. It might be well to use the processing plans that will be discussed in Chapter 13 to see how the production plan works with your layout.

The actual implementation of your plans will depend on whether this is a brand new venture, a layout for an existing building, or a rearrangement of the present layout. Construction of a new building requires further steps in the design of the building and its surroundings. These steps include consideration of at least the following factors:

1. Type and method of construction.
2. Arrangements for parking.

3. Roads and transportation of goods.
4. Landscaping.

The installation of a new or rearranged layout plan requires careful planning and scheduling to minimize delays and costs. Some of the techniques in Chapter 13 will be useful in this planning.

SUMMARY

This chapter has shown you how to organize your productive system in order to transform your inputs of personnel, money, machines, methods, and materials into the outputs of goods and/or services. The systems to do this have many common elements, regardless of the type industry involved.

Some illustrative industries and their use of these elements were discussed. Then, some factors for you to consider in deciding to buy your materials from outside or produce them yourself were presented. The decision should be based upon the relative costs of the alternatives.

After making these decisions, you are able to plan for, purchase, and install your physical facilities. Some principles of laying out these facilities were also presented.

QUESTIONS FOR FURTHER DISCUSSION

1. List the parts and operations needed for a set of shelves for your study room.
2. Can you add other inputs and outputs to those in Figure 12–2? What are the transformation processes that occur for selected items in Figure 12–2?
3. Analyze the layout of a kitchen. Can you make some recommendations for an improved layout?
4. Describe the differences among the layouts of several stores. List the good and bad points of each.
5. Do you think the layout of the metal sign plant, Figure 12–6, is a good one? Explain.
6. How would you move the material in the metal sign plant?
7. What advantages would the metal sign factory gain if it purchased cut and punched metal plates? What disadvantages would it suffer?

13

Designing and Controlling Work

So far, you have selected the good(s) and/or service(s) you plan to produce or perform, estimated what physical facilities you need, and decided how those facilities should be laid out. Now, you are ready to start producing the good(s) and/or service(s). This requires designing work methods, measuring work, providing instructions, and directing and controlling the activities. (Some of these activities have been designed into the systems already described and will only be referred to as the total system is described.)

The planning and control process is a communications system designed to convey to employees the *what, how, where, who, when,* and *why* of the work to be done. It is also a check on what has been done to correct and adjust the work and process to assure that the customer receives good service—in terms of both time and quality.

The specific topics that will be covered in this chapter are:

1. Work design.
2. Work measurement.
3. Planning—the forecast.
4. Planning—converting sales plan to a production plan.
5. Scheduling—setting the time for work to be done.
6. Information to direct activities.
7. Controlling production—quantity and quality.

WORK DESIGN

In Chapter 12, we showed how to plan the layout of a plant, but we did not study the detailed movement of materials and the layout of the workplace. These topics now need to be studied. For example, in the metal sign plant, are the metal plates properly placed so that the operator cutting the corners has short and easy moves? How many machines can one man operate? Are there new methods of moving materials? The following steps are used in work design and improvement:

1. State the problem.
2. State the function of the work.
3. Collect information.
4. List alternatives.
5. Analyze and select alternatives.
6. Formulate, review, and test the selected changes.
7. Install and follow up the changes.

Each of these steps will be discussed briefly.

State the Problem

As usual, you should begin by stating the problem. Why study the work? Is the cost of the work too high? Is the work delaying other work? Is the quality of the service low? Is the service to the customer delayed? The reason(s) for making a study of the work should be clearly understood and stated in order to provide direction.

State the Function of the Work

Often a given production function appears obvious, as for example to sew a seam, to drill a hole, or to sell to a customer. However, you should begin by asking questions. Is this operation necessary? Is it the only alternative? A clear statement of the reason for the operation starts you toward finding the best method to perform the function.

Collect Information

Collecting information breaks the work into parts and establishes appropriate relationships. The purposes are twofold—training and informing.

The reason for *training* is to develop your ability to observe work as a series of activities. For example, a description of a machine operation might include statements such as "prepare material," "do the work," and "remove finished product." The term "prepare material" might include reaching for material, selecting material, grasping material, moving material to the machine, and positioning the material. This type of training, combined with the use of some common-sense principles, develops your ability to identify inefficiencies.

FIGURE 13–1
Flow Process Chart for Making Metal Signs

Item Description	Operation / Transportation / Inspection / Delay / Storage	Distance in Feet	Pick-Ups Lay-Downs	Time in $MIN.$	Quantity	Why?	What?	Where?	When?	Who?	How?	Notes
IN STORAGE AREA	O ⇨ □ D ▽											
TO SHEARS BY CART	O ⇨ □ D ▽	15'	1	2	1	√					√	FORK TRUCK CONVEY
IN STACK	O ⇨ □ D ▽			10	1	√						
CUT SIDES, SHEAR	O ⇨ □ D ▽		1	2								
IN STACK	O ⇨ □ D ▽			10	3	√						CONVEYOR-ROLL TO PRESS
TO PRESS, CART	O ⇨ □ D ▽	10	1		6			√		√		"
IN STACK	O ⇨ □ D ▽			3	3							
CUT CORNERS, PRESS	O ⇨ □ D ▽		1	1	1							

The reason for *informing* is to aid you in recording the details of the work being done for later analysis. Several types of charting procedures are shown in Figures 13–1, 13–2, and 13–3, and are discussed.

Figure 13–1 shows a flow process chart for the first and second operations in making a metal sign, as shown in Figure 12–3. Not only does it show the cutting of sides and corners, but it also adds transportations, delays, and storage. Observe the number of delays and transports that occur for each operation. You will want to reduce these, because they are costly. Symbols are used to simplify your understanding of the process. Data are also collected on methods of movement, distances, time, and quantity.

FIGURE 13–2
Motion Study of Assembling Bolt, Washer, and Nut

Left-Hand Description	Activity	Activity	Right-Hand Description
To bolt	→	→	To washer
Grasp bolt	O	O	Grasp washer
To washer	→	→	To bolt
Hold	D	O	Assemble
Hold	D	→	To nut
Hold	D	O	Grasp nut
Hold	D	→	To assemble
Hold	D	O	Assemble
Dispose	→	D	For disposal

Legend: O = Operation; → = Movement; D = Delay.
Note the large percentage of delay.

Figure 13–2 presents a motion study of a simple operation of assembling a bolt, washer, and nut. Note that the assembler is holding the bolt well over half the time. His/her hand is a very expensive vise.

Figure 13–3 shows the relationship between an operator and a machine. The operator loads and unloads the machine and the machine performs its operations automatically. Note that the idle time for the operator amounts to over half the time.

Figure 13–4 can be used to analyze your decisions involved in getting up in the morning.

FIGURE 13–3
Operator Running an Automatic Printing Machine

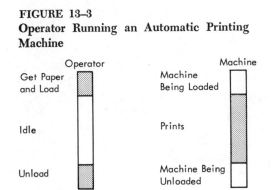

List Alternatives

Listing of alternatives is the core of any analysis and is a critical step in decision making. All work and services can be performed in many ways, and products can be made from many different materials. For example, your pencil can be made of wood, metal, or plastic; it can have an eraser and clip, or not have them; and it may be cylindrical or hexagonal. A hole can be punched, drilled, burned, or cut. You should question the whole process, parts of the process, and each individual activity by recording all alternatives. The following questions are helpful.

1. Why is the activity being performed?
2. Can it be eliminated?
3. What and where is the activity, and who is performing it?
4. Can it be combined with another operation or operations?
5. When is the activity performed?
6. Can the work sequence be changed to reduce the volume of work?
7. How is the activity performed?
8. Can it be simplified?

How many alternatives can you list for the bolt and washer assembly in Figure 13–2? Why assemble? Can you devise a holder to eliminate the *hold* and *dispose* activities? Can the operator in Figure 13–3 run

FIGURE 13–4
Computer Diagram on How to Get up in the Morning

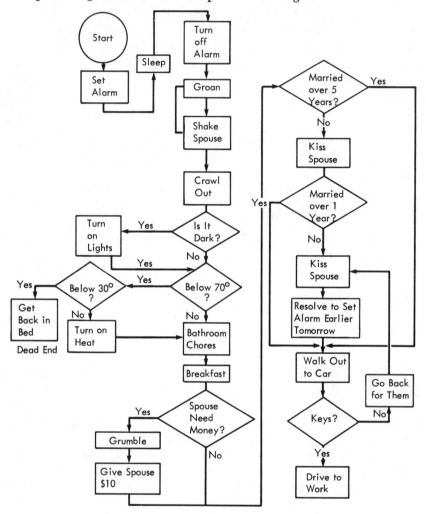

another machine also? Or inspect? Or perform the next operation? The objective is to remove or otherwise simplify as many activities as possible without reducing the quality and quantity of output.

Analyze and Select Alternatives

This step is the evaluation of the alternatives based on practicality, cost, acceptance by workers, and the effect on output. In a good list of alternatives, a small percentage will be finally acceptable. However, the extra time invested in exploring alternatives improves your chances of finding the best design.

Formulate, Review, and Test the Selected Changes

This step converts ideas into reality, checks for any errors or missed possibilities, and makes sure the proposed procedures will perform as expected.

Install and Follow up the Changes

Installation includes placing the physical equipment (as for example a foot pedal), gaining acceptance by the people involved with the operation, and training workers. The objective is to improve performance to its optimum level.

WORK MEASUREMENT

One of the most difficult problems is the measurement of work. We have few precise tools for these measurements, but rely heavily on the fallible judgment of people to make the measurements. Physical work can be measured more precisely than mental work, but it still requires judgment.

This section is concerned with measuring the time for doing physical work. Once time standards are set, they can be used to:

1. Determine how many people or machines are needed for a desired output.
2. Estimate the cost of sales and other orders.
3. Determine the standard output for incentive systems.
4. Schedule production.
5. Measure performance.

The time to perform can be divided into: (1) the time to perform the work, and (2) the time for personal needs and irregular activities.

Time for Work Performance

The methods that can be used to determine the time to perform the work are:

1. Estimates by people experienced in the work.
2. Time study, using a watch or other timing device.
3. Synthesis of the elemental times obtained from tables.

Time Standards Set by Experienced People. This is the simplest and least costly method of obtaining a time for work, but it is also the least precise. No breakdown of the work is made, and the standards often include past inefficiencies. These standards are often adequate if the person setting the standards is careful.

Time Study. This is probably the best method. Yet it has the poorest reputation, because time studies have often not been properly done or used. A time study is made by a person—usually an industrial engineer—actually observing the work being done. The observer uses a stop watch; makes many recordings of the time for each segment of the work; evaluates the worker's performance against the observer's standard of normal speed and effort; adjusts the time values; selects the *normal* time, using some averaging method; and adds a certain amount of time for personal needs and irregular activities.

Synthesis of Elemental Times. This is a pencil-and-paper method based on the accumulation of data from research studies. Tables of manual times have been developed for a wide range of activities used by workers, including reaching, moving, grasping, positioning, turning, walking, and bending. A synthetic time can be set for assembling the bolt, washer, and nut shown in Figure 13–2. Tables are also available to compute times for machining operations. By analyzing the work into the proper elements, times from the tables can be applied to obtain a *normal* time for an operation.

Adding Time for Personal Needs

Personal and irregular time allowances are added to normal time to obtain the total time in which an operation should be performed under "normal" conditions. Allowances for personal needs in time-study and synthesis methods include times for use of the rest room, poor working conditions, and fatigue. Tables are available for these times. The time for irregular activities, as for example getting material, receiving instructions, repairing minor breakdowns, and cleanup can be determined by work sampling or by estimating the frequency and length of time for each type of activity.

Work sampling is based on making a large number of observations at random times. For each observation, you record whether a worker is producing, idle, or doing irregular work. The percentage of observations in each category is the estimate of the percentage of the total time the worker spends in that activity.

Work output is usually expressed in *standard allowed hours* (SAH) per unit of output. Workers on incentive plans, who are paid on the number of SAH they produce, usually will earn five percent to 30 percent more SAH than their actual hours. Research indicates that the introduction of a good incentive system will increase production by about 30 percent.

PLANNING: THE FORECAST

Sales forecasting and marketing research will be discussed in Chapter 16. Converting those forecasts into a sales plan is the starting point for your production plan. Before the sales plan can be fixed, your production capacity must be checked. The best sales plan from a marketing viewpoint may not be the best plan for the company as a whole. It may require too much overtime, too much idle time, or some combination of the two.

The optimum plan from a production standpoint is to maintain a constant level of production—near capacity for both machine and person—of one product, with inputs arriving as needed and outputs taken by customers as they are completed. This is an ideal to shoot for, and the concept provides the direction toward which you should move.

If the sales plan does not keep production busy, what can be done? Should the company advertise more heavily, reduce prices, or redesign its product to increase the volume? The loss in income from these actions may be more than made up by more efficient operation of the plant. Should another product, or a variation of your product, be added to the company's service? Or would this increase the change-over costs and cause such confusion in production that it would cost more than the value received from the added sales?

Maybe the sales plan calls for more output than the capacity of the production process. If so, the plan can be satisfied by expanding the capacity, by producing on overtime, or by subcontracting. Each of these can be very expensive and is capable of causing you more problems than benefits.

PLANNING: CONVERTING A SALES PLAN TO A PRODUCTION PLAN

You will be told that it is impossible to predict the sales of a small business with any reasonable degree of accuracy. This may be true, but even crude estimates are usually better than none at all. Time is required to purchase, produce, and deliver an item if it is not in stock when the customer orders it. On the other hand, the company incurs extra cost when material is held in inventory. As will be mentioned in Chapter 14, inventory is used to give flexibility to a production process. While this practice results in savings, it also adds to the cost. These costs and savings should be balanced.

The largest inventories are planned for the beginning and end of the process, where the company has the minimum of control over its environment. The sales plan is affected primarily by the customer. Sales volume fluctuates from one time period to another. How can the production plan and sales plan be aligned for optimal results?

Planning starts with the longer periods and proceeds backward to the day-to-day operations. Chapter 1 discussed the long-range planning needed to plan for and install physical facilities. The next step is to plan for the next shorter time period, which may be one year. The sales plan, which is usually done for the year ahead, is broken down into months (or perhaps by quarters for the last six months). The production plan should be prepared for these same periods.

Some alternative *production plans* (PP) that you may consider are:

PP-1.   Produce what is demanded by your customers at the time they need the goods.

PP-2.   Produce at a constant level equal to the average monthly demand for the year. Inventories will increase when the volume of demand is lower than the production volume, and will decrease when demand is higher.

PP-3.   Produce complementary products, which balance out increases and decreases in the volume of demand for individual products. The sum of the monthly demands should result in a constant production level.

PP-4.   Subcontract production that is in excess of a certain level.

PP-5.   Decide not to expand production to meet demand.

PP-6.   Employ special sales inducements, perhaps extra advertising and lower prices, when your sales volume is expected to be low.

One of the major causes of predictable variations in demand is the yearly cycle of seasons. Examples of this variation include demands for sports equipment, heating and cooling facilities, and landscaping. Alternative production plans will be discussed using seasonal variations in the examples.

Figure 13–5 shows a possible monthly plot of the sales plan for your company for the year ahead. The measure of sales volume can be dollars,

FIGURE 13–5
Sales and Production Plans with Seasonal Changes in Demand

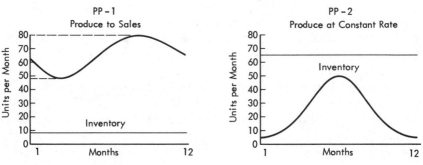

standard allowed hours (SAH), tons, or other units, whichever best measures production capacity; inventory level; and sales demand.

Under Production Plan One (PP–1), shows output and sales volume lines are the same, and the inventory of finished goods can be held at a constant minimum level. As plant capacity is large—equaling 80 units—overtime work can be avoided. Production requires full plant capacity during only a small part of the year, and the plant is idle up to 30 units per month during another part of the year. With the trend to increase fringe benefits, annual wage systems, and severance pay, this type of production plan is becoming outdated.

Production Plan Two (PP–2) shows a constant level of production with a heavy build-up of inventory. The advantages of this plan are:

1. Decrease in capacity needed.
2. Constant level of personnel, with a minimum of hiring and layoff costs.
3. Reduction in paper work needed in running the production system.

This type of production is ideal from the production viewpoint.

The major disadvantage of PP–2 is the large inventory cost, which can bankrupt your company if it is not evaluated carefully. (See Chapter 14.) Companies ordinarily do not attempt to level production completely, but try to find some compromise between PP–1 and PP–2. An analysis can be made by finding the minimum cost plan, using the following formula:

$$\text{Annual added costs} = \text{Inventory costs} + \text{Overtime costs} + \text{Change in level costs.}$$

Production Plan Three (PP–3)—producing complementary products—might be likened to producing both furnaces and air conditioners. The furnaces are produced for winter and the air conditioners for summer. If the same machines and skills can be used in producing both products, and if the volumes produced and sold can be balanced, the sales and production forces will be kept working at a constant rate the year round. This is one of the reasons many companies have a variety of products in their product lines.

Production Plan Four (PP–4)—subcontracting excess production—has several variations. You might make more of the parts yourself during slack periods, and subcontract to others during peak periods.

Production Plan Five (PP–5)—not expand production to meet sales—is often rejected without much thought, as this means a loss of sales. However, these extra sales may be so expensive to produce that they are unprofitable. Extra capacity and/or overtime may be required.

Production Plan Six (PP–6)—offer special sales inducements—is a marketing activity that will be covered in Part V.

After you have established your production plan for the year, other plans or budgets can be developed. The amount of materials, parts, and goods; the employees required; and the financing needed can be determined.

SCHEDULING: SETTING THE TIME FOR WORK TO BE DONE IN THE NEAR FUTURE

The previous section discussed the development of the general production plan for a period of one year. This section covers day-to-day scheduling. As orders are received, they are either filled from inventory or ordered into production.

Most companies keep an inventory of standard items in order to give quick service. They stock the items for which they have forecasted sufficient demand and for which the value of fast service is greater than the added cost of carrying the inventory. These are the types of items that are produced to stock when the plant would otherwise be idle.

Orders are scheduled into production:

1. On a preplanned schedule.
2. When inventory is reduced to a certain low level.
3. When orders are received and inventory is not available.

The preplanned schedule works best for standard items, the demand for which can be forecast. The number of units in a production order is determined by balancing the costs involved. A large order increases inventory costs per unit; a small order increases the planning, machine set up, handling, and paper-work costs per unit. Producing to customer order, specialty items, usually sets the size of a production order, except when future orders of the same item are expected. (A further consideration of these costs is included with the discussion of purchase order sizes in Chapter 14.)

Schedules set the times to produce specified goods. A company producing the same units continuously can automatically set how many units to produce by setting the total number of operator and machine hours per week. Job shops, on the other hand, must schedule each order.

FIGURE 13–6

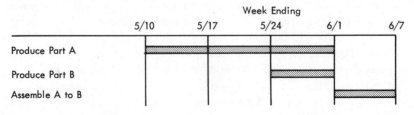

This scheduling can be done by one of the following methods:

1. Sending orders into the shop in sequence. The shop processes the jobs through the operations on a first-come, first-served basis.
2. Setting priorities, and processing orders accordingly. "Rush" orders have top priority.
3. Using either 1 or 2 for each operation.
4. Setting a specific time for each operation for each job.

Note the following relationships:

Method	Scheduling Cost	Idle Time	Processing Time	Inventory Level
1............	Low	High	High	High
4............	High	Low	Low	Low

In doing all your scheduling, an effort should be made to keep inventory as low as practical. A long-time sequence of operations on a part that is to be assembled to a short-time sequenced part should be started early. This can be illustrated by the often used bar, or Gantt, chart, shown in Figure 13–6.

By scheduling Part A to start on May 10 and Part B to start on

FIGURE 13–7
PERT Chart for Putting in a Pipeline

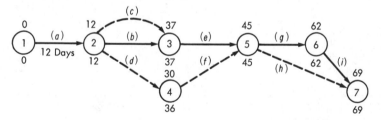

				Completion Date		
Legend:			Days	Earliest	Latest	Slack
(a)	Survey ditch....................		12	12	12	0
(b)	Dig ditch.......................		25	37	37	0
(c)	Order and receive rock..........		3	15	37	22
(d)	Order and receive pipe and fittings.................		18	30	36	6
(e)	Rock ditch.....................		8	45	45	0
(f)	Assemble valves and fittings......................		9	39	45	6
(g)	Lay pipe.......................		17	62	62	0
(h)	Install fittings.................		13	58	69	11
(i)	Cover ditch....................		7	69	69	0
	Earliest day estimated to be completed..........	12				
	Latest day can be completed.	12				
	Critical path...............	—				

May 24, the two parts are expected to be completed at the time they are needed for assembly. If the delivery date for the order is June 7, the delivery may be made soon after the work is completed.

A chart has been developed for scheduling networks—sequences of operations, each of which may be dependent upon the completion of several other activities. This chart, called the *critical path method* (CPM) or *program evaluation and review technique* (PERT), is used by many companies in the construction industry. Figure 13–7 shows a chart for the installation of an underground pipe.

The circles represent the start and end of activities, and lines show activities (the length of the line has no meaning). The times at the circles give the earliest and latest times for the end of the prior operation and the beginning of the next one; the difference is called "slack." The circles with zero slack time are on the "critical path," and the sum of the times for all the activities between those circles determines how long the whole process will take. The times are usually the best estimates of knowledgeable people.

INSTALLING AN INFORMATION SYSTEM TO DIRECT THE ACTIVITIES

Orders received and plans made must be communicated to those doing the work. The information is provided by written or oral instruc-

FIGURE 13–8
Route Sheet Used in Garment Plant

	SKIRT	SCH.NO. LOT NO. AMT.	7732 24	SKIRT	
	.NR–24–7732 Thread bkle.on tab.tack to fnt. ****			.060–24–7732 Reverse	
					1:00
11:00	.448–24–7732 Hem Waist & Btm. BS			.132–24–7732 Serge Btm.	
					3:00
3:00	.128–24–7732 SS 2d Side Seam ***			.196–24–7732 Serge Elastic to Waist	
					5:00
4:00	.164–24–7732 SS One Side Seam T&L			1.134–24–7732 Topst.fnt.pleats bste.across top **	27:00

tions, by training workers, and/or by having a fixed flow of material. Each worker must know what and how many items he is to produce, when and where he is to produce them, and what he needs in order to perform the job satisfactorily. You should design a simple, yet adequate, system to do this in your firm.

The route sheet shown in Figure 13–8 is used in a garment plant and travels with a bundle of cut cloth. This form tells the workers what to sew, the type of operation, the time for the operation, and what the next operation is. The size of bundle sets the quantity. As each operator completes an operation, the proper tab is clipped to be returned to the office. More complex systems are needed for other processes.

CONTROLLING PRODUCTION: QUANTITY AND QUALITY

Even if the best of plans are made, the information is communicated, and the best work is performed, controls are still needed. If no control is exercised over the operations, the process will fail. The *principle of exception* should be followed.

Controlling by exceptions involves comparing your plans with the plant's performance. In simple systems, this comparison can be made informally by personally observing the performance. Usually, though, a system of formal checks is needed.

Orders may be filed by due dates, work to be completed in each department may be recorded each day, or bar charts or graphs may be used. The record of performance is obtained through feedback, or by having forms returned with information on work performed. For example, press operators clock their time in and out on the edge of a job envelope carrying instructions; workers in a garment plant clip off pieces of the route sheet and return it pasted on their time ticket; a garage repairman enters his time on the order form.

You need not make changes when performance equals or exceeds your plans. An exception arises when performance does not reach the level desired. Then you need to decide what to do to improve future performance.

One example of an important control system is that used for quality control. The methods used in quality control have been developed further than those for other control systems, and are used in many other systems, including cost control. The system begins with setting the level of quality desired. The quality level is based on:

1. The value of quality to the customer.
2. The cost of the quality.

Customers want high quality, but are often willing to pay only a limited price for the product. Production costs rise rapidly as the demand for quality rises beyond a certain point. Therefore, you should ask the following questions:

1. Who are my customers, and what quality do they want?
2. What quality of product or service can I obtain, and at what costs?

Then you need to establish controls to obtain that quality. Do not try to exceed that level, for your costs will increase. But do not allow quality to go below that level, for you will lose customers. Design your process so that it will produce products or services within the desired quality range. Then, design your quality control system to check performance.

The steps needed in any system of control are:

1. Set standards for your quality range.
2. Measure your actual performance.
3. Compare performance with standards.
4. Make corrections when needed.

Standards of quality may be set for dimension, color, strength, content, weight, service, and other characteristics. Some standards may be measured by instruments, as for example rulers or gauges for length, but color, taste, and other standards must be evaluated by skilled individuals. Measurement may be made by selected people at certain places in the process—usually upon the receipt of material, and always before it goes to the customer. You can spot check (sample), or check each item.

Inspection reduces the chances of a poor-quality product being passed through your process and to your customer. But not all defective work is eliminated by inspection. By recording the number of defective units per 100 units, you can observe the quality performance of the process and make needed corrections. The final check might be to keep a record of the number of complaints received per 100 sales made.

SUMMARY

Planning and controlling a company's internal operations involve the following:

1. Analyzing individual steps of the processes to eliminate inefficiencies.
2. Setting time and quality standards.
3. Planning the work and informing the workers.
4. Checking performance.

Some of the techniques for implementing these activities have been presented in this chapter.

QUESTIONS FOR FURTHER DISCUSSION

1. Make a process flowchart of registering yourself for classes.

2. List alternatives for the process charted above. Do you see any improvements that can be made?

3. How would you determine how many tables a waitress should handle?

4. Recall a secretary you have observed in the past. What percentage of time was spent typing, talking on the telephone or to people in person, etc.? How did you measure these times? Might this be a form of work sampling?

5. In some parts of the country, building construction varies seasonally. Is this a problem for company management? What decisions must management make concerning these variations?

6. How can a building contractor schedule the building of a house so as to keep idle time and inventory to a minimum?

7. Newspapers have reported a variety of complaints about the quality of service from automobile garages and other shops. If you were managing a shop, how would you control the quality of your service?

14

Purchasing and Controlling Materials

It is not unusual to find that the profitability of a small business depends upon the ability of the owner-manager to exercise effective purchasing and materials control. The absence of "know-how" in these areas many times is revealed only during the postmortem of the failed business.

The intent of the authors in this chapter is to emphasize the importance of these areas. In addition, another objective is to aid you by providing information that leads you to adopt sound procedural practices. The specific topics covered are:

1. Materials (or goods) planning and control.
2. Inventory.
3. Quantities per order.
4. Ordering procedure.
5. Sources of supply.
6. Receiving materials.

MATERIALS (OR GOODS) PLANNING AND CONTROL

In the previous chapters, we discussed the flow of materials in a business and the use of inventory to take care of seasonal variations in demand. Now, we need to consider the decisions regarding materials planning and control, including:

1. Amount of material needed for the output desired.
2. Amount of inventory and its storage and recording.

3. Quantity and time of order.
4. Vendor relations.
5. Quality of materials and price per unit.
6. Methods of receiving and shipping.
7. Handling of defective materials and stock-outs.

Policies and procedures should be established so that most of these decisions become routine in nature. When exceptions occur, they should be handled by you or someone to whom you delegate the decision. These policies and procedures should minimize the total cost of materials to the company. But remember that total cost includes more than just the price of the materials themselves. It includes costs that are charged to the goods, as well as other costs that are hidden in other expenses— usually in overhead. Overhead consists of expenses that cannot be charged directly to the product or service.

Trade-offs must be made to obtain the best cost. Materials are a form of investment, and until they are sold and produce revenue, the money cannot be used for other income-producing purposes. Consequently, you want to buy in small quantities and sell them rapidly in order to obtain income. But if the quantities you have on hand are too small, you may miss income-producing opportunities and may lose customers. Also, purchasing in small quantities usually results in higher prices. Another problem concerns the controls established to keep losses from theft to a minimum. While increasing controls may reduce the cost from losses, it also increases the control cost. The problem is to find the optimum balance between the two costs.

In materials planning and control, you should recognize that most of your income will come from a small percentage of your products or services, and that some of your materials will be of high value and some of lower value. About 80 percent of the average firm's income comes from 20 percent of its products. Materials planning and control should be directed mainly toward the 20 percent. You may want to classify the goods in categories and set a procedure for each category. Thus, for the 20 percent, you may set standards and procedures for each item; for the next, say, 30 percent, you may handle items in groups; and for the last 50 percent, you consider all items as a single group. The percentages given are only guides for your consideration. You will need to analyze your product line in the light of the procedures discussed in the rest of this chapter.

Another important area is the study of products and services to determine whether all the particular inputs are needed. This is called *value analysis,* and is based on relating the purpose of each part to its cost or value. It determines the best material or design for each part or input.

INVENTORY

The inventory of materials, parts, goods, and supplies represents a high investment in all businesses. Many companies have failed because their inventories tied up too much money, or the items in inventory became obsolete, impaired, or lost. You should have an appropriate set of policies concerning the items to carry in inventory, the level of inventory, and control of the stock.

The purpose of an inventory is to disconnect one segment of a process from another, so that each segment can operate at its optimum level of performance. A process composed of several operations, with inventory between them, might be diagrammed as in Figure 14–1.

FIGURE 14–1

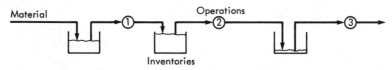

Note that the inventories are shown at different levels at different stages of the process. The level depends on the prior activities of the supplier to, and the user of, the inventory. For example, operation 1 may have been running recently and operation 2 may have been shut down. Also notice that operation 3 may not have enough material if operation 2 does not start up soon.

Types of Inventories

Inventories exist in various places in the business, and in different stages of production, as:

1. Purchased materials, parts, and products.
2. Goods in process or between operations.
3. Finished goods at the factory, warehouse, or store.
4. Repair parts for machines.
5. Supplies for the office, shop, or factory.
6. Patterns and tools.

Each of these types of inventory is performing basically the same function and can be studied in the same way. Some of the inventories, however, represent a much greater investment, cause more serious trouble if the items are not in stock, and are more costly to restock than others. The amount of attention and time spent on these should be greater than on the others.

Determining Economic Inventory Levels

Even a small company may have thousands of items in stock. The total investment should be kept in a proper relation to the finances of the company. This relationship will be discussed in Chapter 20 when the financial analysis of the company is considered. The detailed analysis made to determine the economical inventory level must consider the total inventory so as not to jeopardize the company's financial position. The total investment in inventory should not be so great that it deprives you of enough cash to pay your current bills.

FIGURE 14–2
Graph of the Changing Level of Inventory of an Item

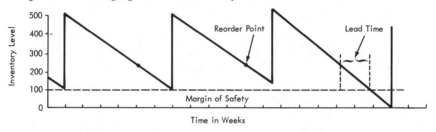

Figure 14–2 shows how the number of units of a *purchased item* varies over a period of time. When a purchased item is received, the inventory increases instantly. The units are removed from inventory as they are demanded. At certain intervals, or when the inventory falls to a given level, a purchase order is sent to the vendor for a certain quantity. The order will be received some time later. In the meantime, more units may be drawn from inventory. This cycle is repeated for each item purchased.

For items *in process* and *in finished goods,* the inventory builds up over a period of time as goods are produced, so the vertical line in Figure 14–2 would be sloping upward to the right. The inventory builds up because production is greater than demand. The following discussion pertains to purchased items, but with minor adjustments it would apply to "in process" and finished goods also.

Determining when to Order

The level of inventory at which an order should be issued is based on:

1. The quantity to be used between the time an order is issued and the items are received.
2. A quantity needed to provide a margin of safety.

The time to be allowed in (1) is determined by the sum of the times for:

1. Order to be processed in your company.
2. Order to be transported to the vendor.
3. Vendor to make and package the items.
4. Items to be transported to your company.

The total delay varies from time to time, so a margin of safety is added to obtain the quantity at the reorder point. The margin of safety, in turn, depends upon:

1. Variability of the time to obtain the items from the vendor. A higher variability requires a higher margin of safety.
2. Variability of usage.
3. Cost of not having inventory—losses from stock-outs.
4. Cost of carrying inventory, estimated for each item or group of items. These inventory costs include:
   a. Space charges.
   b. Insurance and taxes.
   c. Profits lost because money is tied up in inventory.
   d. Obsolescence of items.
   e. Deterioration.
   f. Theft.

Estimates of the costs of carrying inventory range from 15 percent to over 100 percent of the average inventory investment for a year. Values of 20 percent to 25 percent are often used.

You can compute, or estimate, the reorder point quantity by trying various levels and reordering points and adding the cost of carrying the inventory and the cost of running out of goods multiplied by the probability of running out. The lowest total cost is the best reorder point. Note that more attention should be focused on some items than on others.

QUANTITIES PER ORDER

The quantity you include on each order affects the level of inventory and the time between orders. You may place your orders:

1. At certain intervals, such as once a week, month, or quarter, when you order an amount that brings the level of the inventory up to a predetermined standard amount.
2. When the inventory reaches a certain quantity, such as 250 units in Figure 14–2. The quantity ordered is a fixed amount called the *economic order quantity* (EOQ).

The quantity to order in (1) and (2) can be computed or estimated in the same manner, but in (1) it is used only as an expected average. The economic order quantity is determined by balancing:

1. The cost of the order, which includes
   a. The costs of processing and handling the order.
   b. The costs of the item, realizing that larger orders usually warrant price discounts.
   c. Transportation costs.
2. The inventory carrying costs.

Figure 14–3 shows the way the costs per unit vary as the quantity ordered is changed. The point of lowest cost is the EOQ. This can be found by using a formula or by comparing the unit costs for different order quantities. Note how a discount affects the curve and that a range in quantities has approximately the same low cost.

FIGURE 14–3
Changes in Purchase Unit Costs

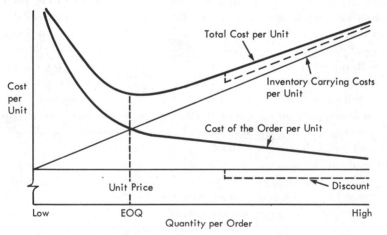

ORDERING PROCEDURE

Many items can be ordered on a routine basis. The procedure starts with the need as reflected by the reorder point and requires keeping a:

1. Perpetual inventory, which records when the inventory has reached the reorder point. Figure 14–4 shows a perpetual inventory card.
2. Quantity set aside that will not be used without making out a purchase order.
3. Method of calling attention to the need for the order, such as a gauge for a tank of oil.

The amount to reorder is shown on the inventory card or on some other form. The vendor and method of packaging and transporting are also recorded.

FIGURE 14-4
Inventory Record Form

| Date | Received | | Issued | | Balance |
	Order No.	Units	Req. No.	Units	on Hand
7/13	3401	400			450
7/17			1075	10	440
7/22			1090	10	430

Reorder Point: 70 Bags   Reorder Quantity: 400 Bags
Item No.   Description   Unit
315   Zinc Oxide (3Z33)   50# Bags

Items Requiring Special Analysis

The major items of purchase require more analysis as their cost and quality can have a greater effect on your company. You, or someone else in authority in your firm, should be involved in these purchases. A number of the considerations that require higher-level decisions are:

1. Expected changes in price. Short delays in buying for expected decreases in price or increased quantities for expected increases in price can result in savings. However, stock-outs or too heavy inventory costs should be guarded against.
2. Expected changes in demand. Seasonal products fall into this category.
3. Orders for a demand for specialty goods. The quantity ordered should match the amount demanded so that no material is left over. When the quantity of the demand is known, estimates of losses in process are added to the order. When the quantity of the demand is not known, you must depend on the forecasts plus the estimates of losses.
4. Short supply of materials.

Speculative buying should be avoided unless you are in that business. While all business decisions have a certain element of speculation, a small businessman cannot afford to gamble with money required in their business. The procedure for processing a purchase order and receiving the goods is flow-charted in Figure 14-5.

FIGURE 14–5
Purchase Order Procedure

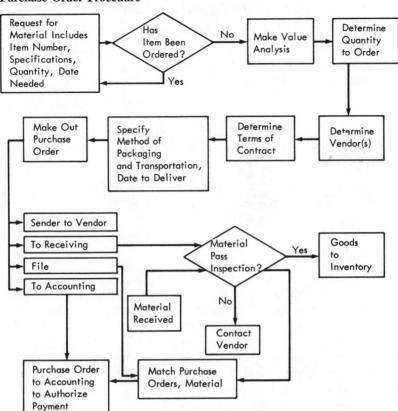

Placing Responsibility for Ordering

One person should have the responsibility for ordering all materials, but that person should obtain the help of those people knowledgeable in the area where the goods are needed. By having a single person responsible, duplicate orders for the same material are avoided, the specialized skills needed for purchasing can be used, and responsibility for improvements in the buying process is localized.

The number of forms needed for obtaining and controlling products, and the number of copies of these forms, depend on the amount of formality desired. A simple requisition form can be forwarded to the purchasing agent who, in turn, reviews the requisitions, issues the purchase order to the vendor, follows up on orders when needed, checks the receipt of the material, takes corrective action when needed, and sees that the material is delivered to the proper place.

SOURCES OF SUPPLY

Sources from which you obtain your inputs are important because:

1. Price of purchased goods is a major cost in your outputs.
2. Reliability in delivery and quality affects your operations.
3. Vendors can be valuable sources of information.
4. Vendors can provide valuable service.

Considering Various Aspects of Price

The prices from different vendors are not the same. Higher prices may be charged for:

1. Higher quality.
2. More reliable and faster delivery.
3. Better terms for returning goods.
4. More services, such as in advertising, type of packaging, and information.
5. Better, or delayed, payment plan.

You may be able to purchase an item at a lower price, but your total cost of processing the item may be higher. For example, the price plus transportation cost from a distant source may be less than from a local source, but the faster service from the local source may allow you to carry less inventory. The reduction in inventory may more than compensate for higher local price. One source may be able to supply you a wide assortment of goods you need, reducing the expense of ordering from many sources.

Your sources of supply may be brokers, jobbers, wholesalers, manufacturers, or others. Each of these sources provides a type of service that may be valuable to you. For example, the wholesaler stocks many items so that he can give fast delivery of a wide variety of items. A manufacturer ships directly with no intermediate handler, but it is restricted in the product it can supply. However, the manufacturer may have sales representatives or agents who can help the small business. Regional and national trade shows and private trade associations provide valuable information and services for keeping up-to-date on sources and their products and services.

Using Few or Many Sources

Should you buy from one or many sources? The argument for a single source is that a closer and more individual relationship can be established. When shortages occur, you probably can obtain better service than if you have many sources. Discounts may be obtained with larger volume buying. On the other hand, multiple sources allow you to find the source with a greater variety of goods and, often, better terms. Some companies put out requests for bids, and negotiations can result in better arrangements.

Care should be exercised on the ethics of the supplier and your relationship to it. Many unethical practices exist and should be guarded against, including gifts, entertainment, misrepresentation, and reciprocity. A small company should try to maintain a good image in its dealings with vendors in order to obtain good service.

RECEIVING MATERIALS

The receipt and forwarding of materials to inventory constitute the last step in acquiring inputs. This step is performed to check that the material is what has been ordered, is in the proper condition, and is the proper quality. The purchasing agent is informed that the goods have been received, and are ready for processing.

A copy of the purchase order and other desired specifications are sent to those receiving the material. The material is checked for damage in transportation; for specified characteristics such as color, size, and the item specified; and for the proper quantity and price. Those processing the materials are delayed if they do not find the right kind and quantity of material in inventory. Proper receiving procedures can eliminate these discrepancies.

Materials can be stored in the containers in which they are received, in separate containers, or by individual item. The receiving agent prepares the material for storing.

SUMMARY

In this chapter, we have tried to present a helpful discussion of the importance of obtaining the proper materials, in the right quantity, of the right quality, at the right time, and for the right price.

In an era of shortages, the success of firms will depend upon their skill—and luck—in finding and acquiring adequate supplies of goods, materials, and supplies.

If you are to succeed, you will need to manage efficiently and effectively the planning and controlling of materials, including inventories, ordering points, sources of supply, and receiving and storing merchandise.

QUESTIONS FOR FURTHER DISCUSSION

1. In what ways can inventories serve to reduce costs? To increase costs?
2. How would you make an economic study to determine the quantity of

a food item to buy for your family on each trip to the store? How often should purchases be made?

3. Discuss the advantages and disadvantages of having a food freezer in your home.

4. What are the advantages and the disadvantages of shopping at a single store rather than at several?

5. How would a hardware store be affected by running out of a stock item (stocking-out)?

6. Discuss the advantages and the disadvantages of buying locally versus buying from a distant seller.

WHERE TO LOOK FOR FURTHER INFORMATION

Buffa, E. S. *Modern Production Management*. 5th ed. New York: John Wiley and Sons, 1977.

Hedrick, F. D. *Purchasing Management in the Small Company*. New York: American Management Association, Inc., 1971.

Hopeman, R. J. *Production: Concepts, Analysis, and Control*. 3rd ed. Columbus, Ohio: Charles E. Merrill, 1976.

"Improving Materials Handling in Small Business." 3d ed. *Small Business Management no. 4*. Washington, D.C.: Small Business Administration, 1969.

Kline, J. B. "Pointers on Scheduling Production." *Management Aids for Small Manufacturers no. 207*. Washington, D.C.: Small Business Administration, 1970.

Mayer, R. R. "The Equipment Replacement Decision." *Management Aids for Small Manufacturers no. 212*. Washington, D.C.: Small Business Administration, 1970.

Miles, L. *Techniques of Value Analysis and Engineering*. 2d ed. New York: McGraw-Hill Book Company, 1972.

Moore, F. G. *Production/Operations Management*. 7th ed. Homewood, Ill.: Richard D. Irwin, Inc., 1977.

cases for part IV

IV–1   Drake Printers
IV–2   Bobby Rivers Sportswear, Inc.
IV–3   Franklin Electric Co.

IV–1   Drake Printers[1]

"Do I have any problems? I have plenty of them," said Bill Strickland, owner and president of Drake Printers. "You are interested in the production area? Let me start with the space problem. We do not have enough space on the first floor and only stairs to the second. H. J. thinks he can find an elevator to help us. Also, we cannot move our machines because special flooring was placed under each machine when we moved into this rented building 15 years ago. It would take too much money to fix the floors or to move to another building."

Mr. Strickland continued: "Let me describe our system. We did about half a million dollars of business last year. The jobs range from a few dollars for some personal calling cards to several thousand for multicolored booklets—averaging about $100 per order. Jobs are phoned in or the customer comes to the office. Either Will or I put the information for the order on a three-part order form (Exhibit 1). The top copy we keep in the office, filed by customer. Each day, I receive a list of these orders and lists of jobs to be processed in each of the press and bindery departments so that I can set the priority for processing (Exhibit 2). These schedules are sent to the shop.

"The second copy is the stockman's copy. However, it is used for making a purchase order when I judge that we do not have an item for the order. Most of the time the paper will be delivered in time for printing. The third copy, an envelope, is the shop processing order. We put any aids needed for processing in it and send it to the shop. The envelope moves through the shop with the material. When the

---

[1] Prepared by Charles R. Scott, Jr., University of Alabama.

277

EXHIBIT 1
Customer Order

/ MAY 21 1974

GALLEY PROOF ; REVISED GALLEY ; PAGE PROOF ; REVISED PAGE ; VELOX

PROOF Yes ( ) No ( ) | Proof OK with Corrections | Letterpress (set change
No. 25188

TO | Proof OK

DATE | Give Revised | OFFSET (X)

JOB BY — DATE May 14, 1974

NAME Brewer State Junior College

ADDRESS

JOB PROMISED Friday Morning PURCHASE ORDER NO.

JOBS IN SHOP MAKE-UP MAN

Deliver (X) UPS Will Call ( ) Paid ( ) Collect ( )

QUANTITY	DESCRIPTION		PRICE
		Last Price	3805/1M - $74
1500	Fight Inflation	Art	40.40
	Flyers	Cuts	
		Printing	2.46
		TOTAL 1.43 —	T.E.

Printed on Back ( ) Head to Head ( ) Tumble Head ( ) 42.86

SPECIAL INSTRUCTIONS — 2 folds for mailing - Punking In | FOLDER PAGES | SADDLE STITCHED | SIDE STITCHED

ORIGINAL DUP. TRIP. QUAD. QUINT. INVOICED

COLOR OF INK (BLACK) (RED) (BLUE) OTHER: MAY 29 1974

PADDED TAGBOARD MARBLEBOARD BOX

PUNCHING: NO. OF HOLES SLOT Invoice No. 19530

PERFORATIONS: Across Up and Down On Press Round Hole Slit

BEGIN NUMBER END NUMBER (Hand) ROUND CORNER

CARBONS: Pencil ( ) Typewriter ( ) SNAPOUT: Black ( ) Blue ( )

FINISHED SIZE 8½ x 11 SHEET SIZE

NO. OUT CUT FROM QUAN. No. 25188

GRADE & WT. 50 lb Offset White

RETURN: ART WORK ☐ PICTURES ☐ ENGRAVINGS ☐

TO DATE RETURNED

envelope is returned with the delivery time stamped on it, Will or I figure the price. We use our knowledge of our operations and, sometimes, the Franklin catalogue, which is a pricing book for the printing trade. We plan to set up systems for obtaining the time and material used on each job. At present, we do not have these.

EXHIBIT 2
Priority List

	Dept. _TYPESETTING_		Page _1_		Date _5/15_	
Priority	Job No.	Description	In	Out		Progress
6	24655	SELA/COP. SO EAST LATIN AMER.	5/6	5/29		
3	24952	CONT. ED. U OF A/COMM AFF. SEM.	5/10	5/17	✓	
2	24955	" " " /5TH ANN. NAT. GAS	5/10	5/16	✓	
1	20519	CHAMBER OF COMM./MAPS	5/10			
25	25038	TUSC. ACADEMY/ENVELOPES	5/9	5/16	✓	
27	25030	FOR REPORT	5/9			

"We figure the price for about 30 percent of the orders at the time of ordering and, on the others, give a ball park figure."

Just then, a worker came in about a rush job. When he had left, Mr. Strickland said, "Here's another question. How do you charge overtime?"

"Yes, we are having the problems with getting paper. It is not so much how much but more the type of paper. Now, we are having to keep six to eight weeks of paper inventory. Except for special orders, we order at least four cartons of paper on each order in order that transportation costs will not be too high. We have Jimmy, a business administration student, listing all our stock on this form (Exhibit 3)— his list will include from 400 to 500 items. We hope to design a good inventory system to eliminate taking physical inventory each four months. We estimate our profits monthly but, now, we must estimate our inventory.

EXHIBIT 3
Inventory List

Quantity	Size	Wt.	Kind	Color	Price (Unit)	Price (Total)
17500	17x22	16 lb	SPRING-HILL BOND	WHITE		
3700	17x28	16 lb	"	"		
8000	19x24	16 lb	"	"		
8000	17x22	20 lb	"	"		
0	17x28	20 lb	"	"		
7500	19x24	20 lb	"	"		
21000	17x22	16 lb	"	COLORS		
16,000	17x28	16 lb	"	"		

EXHIBIT 4
Shop Layout

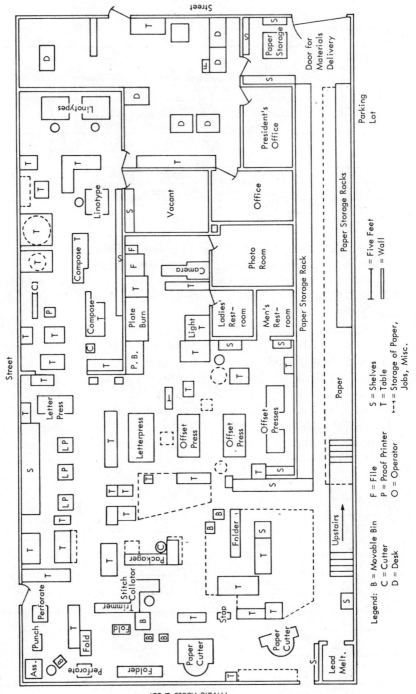

Legend: B = Movable Bin
C = Cutter
D = Desk

F = File
P = Proof Printer
O = Operator

S = Shelves
T = Table

├──┤ = Five Feet
═══ = Wall
├──┤ = Storage of Paper, Jobs, Misc.

"A stockman is watching the stock level constantly to determine when to place an order for more stock. We have the paper stored in racks behind this office (Exhibit 4), but we have so much paper and so little room that it is now stored in the aisle. Sometimes, we have to move the paper outside the building to get it to the presses.

"We have paper, jobs in process, and clutter in the plant. About once a week, I go around with an employee to point to material for him to throw away. We need more space. Oh, yes, we have type set for repeat orders stored on the tables in the type-setting room. Storage of plates is becoming a problem. Also, we have about 100 file drawers upstairs full of past job orders.

"We need more productivity—more volume. Our paper cost has increased from 33 to 38 percent of our cost, and labor has risen from 33 to 43 percent. We have seven employees setting and composing type and preparing the plates, six press operators, seven in the bindery area, and five in the office."

Exhibit 4 shows the shop layout. The second floor is not shown. (It is the same size as the first floor and is an open attic except for the art office above the downstairs offices and past-order files in a hall at the top of the stairs.)

The process starts with typesetting, lines of metal letters, or offset plate making. After the proofreading, the printing is performed on the presses. Paper is moved from storage to the paper cutter, then to the presses, and on to the bindery. The bindery has many operations—collating, drilling holes, cutting, stapling, stitching, and several methods of binding. Supervisors direct the workers concerning the jobs and their sequence. The shop has machines for most operations, but some operations are done manually. Completed jobs are returned to the front office. Material is moved by hand, by dolly, and by hand-hydraulic lift of pallets along narrow aisles.

QUESTIONS

1. Make a process chart (1) following the order forms and (2) following the paper. Show on your layout the general movement of the form and paper through the shop.
2. Does the company appear to have a good flow of material through the plant? Explain.
3. Does the company appear to have space problems? If so, list them.
4. What are the alternative methods Mr. Strickland might use to solve the space problems?
5. Which of these methods do you believe are the best? List the advantages and disadvantages of each.

6. Make specific recommendations for Question 5 that can be given to Mr. Strickland for him to implement.

7. Do you believe that the one form is adequate for instructing the workers and for scheduling? Explain.

8. How can you determine the productivity of the workers? Is this necessary? Explain.

9. Do inventory problems exist? If so, what are your recommendations to Mr. Strickland?

IV–2   Bobby Rivers
Sportswear, Inc.[1]

Bobby Rivers Sportswear had prospered from its first year of operation. First year (1953) sales of $275,000 were followed by a steady growth in sales until they were at the $1 million level. Financial and operating results were considered highly confidential. Bobby Rivers Sportswear was admittedly operating profitably, and the rate of profit was generally comparable to that of other garment firms in the state. Whenever sales were in the 8,300 dozen garment range annually, profits were comparable to the industry average of approximately 3.5 percent margin on sales, after taxes.

All capital stock in the company was owned by the three founders. Mr. H. H. Fancher, owner of 65 percent of the stock, assumed responsibility as president and general manager, and supervised all activities related to design, production, sales, finance and personnel. Mr. Dunning, with a 25 percent ownership, was responsible for miscellaneous activities in the plant, including shipping, receiving, and maintenance. Mr. Archer, a brother-in-law of Mr. Fancher and a son of the former owner, held 10 percent of the stock but took no part in the management of the company.

The company attempted to serve only a limited segment of the ladies' ready-to-wear market. Its goal was to produce dresses and suits using basic, popular fabrics and designed to sell in the medium-low price range. No high-style garments were included in the line, hence the styles produced tended to have more permanency, which in turn resulted in greater emphasis on cost and quality.

---

[1] Prepared by Kenneth W. Olm and Fred Ingerson, University of Texas at Austin.

Fancher felt that much of his success was due to his ability to supply quality goods within specified time deadlines. The laxity of many manufacturers in the industry in meeting contractual agreements sometimes resulted in costly delays or gaps in the product lines of retailers.

The designing process began with the selection of a retail price for the garment. The selected retail price thus determined the wholesale price and the target cost of the garment. The designer then selected materials, style details, zippers, buttons, and other features to conform to the cost limitation previously established.

The production process started when the designer made the style and drew up the original pattern. Then a pattern girl graded the pattern up or down for different sizes and made different-size patterns. The marker girls fitted the pattern to cloth to obtain the least yardage per garment. Fancher stressed that "that's what makes your money." Fancher made out *cut sheets* which were used to order the correct number of cuts to fill the size and color requirements for a particular style. These cut sheets were given to a cutter who stacked piece goods in alternate colors (to prevent shading), stapled markers to piece goods to prevent shifting, and cut out pieces with an electric cutting knife. A stack of piece goods could be cut out for 100 to 500 dresses at once.

Goods were bundled by size and color (all 8s, all 10s, etc. of one color together), and the correct cuts of interlining were included for that number of dresses. Each bundle was numbered, and these bundles were issued to sewing operators. The supervisor had a master book in which she recorded the bundles as they were given to sewers. The employee number, bundle number, part number, amount, style number and color were recorded in the master book, which also logged each bundle through each operation. Each worker maintained record cards of what work had been done, and these cards were checked with the master book. All operations had part numbers (e.g., sleeves #6, blouses #7, etc.). The master book provided a record of who did what work, and what rate they were to get per garment or per dozen garments. Operations were highly specialized in that one operator performed one operation only, such as pinking, hemming, making buttonholes, etc.

At an output level of approximately $1 million, employment varied from 90 to 100 employees, with 90 percent of the employees residing within a five mile radius of the factory and the remaining 10 percent living in rural settlements within 15 miles of the factory. Mr. Fancher estimated there were fewer than 25 persons available for employment in the immediate area who were capable of being trained.

Standard output was not determined from formal time studies. Because of his own long experience and because the basic operations performed changed very little from one year to the next, Mr. Fancher was confident that he could estimate standards to a satisfactory degree of accuracy. Any discrepancies would likely be noticed by the one experienced sewing-line supervisor.

Bottlenecks in the flow of work tended to occur on occasion, because of the absence of a key worker for whom there was no fully trained substitute or because of the breakdown of a critical machine. Mr. Fancher felt that the company was not large enough to support a fully trained specialist mechanic, so when complicated machines like the buttonholer required servicing, either the machine was rushed to Dallas (a two-hour drive) for service, or a specially trained mechanic was called from Dallas. Simple jobs could be handled by the firm's general maintenance mechanic.

Inspection was performed at four points in the production process. Bolts of material were inspected visually at the time they were laid out in layers on the cutting tables preliminary to the cutting operation. After sewing, seams were inspected when trimmed and threads were clipped. Later, the pressers were expected to check for spots, stains, or other flaws. A final inspection was performed by the packer preparing garments for shipping.

Flawed garments were seldom reworked. Instead, in conformity with industry practice, they were sold as "seconds" or "rejects" at cut-rate prices. Judging from the very few returned garments and the relatively small percentage of rejects, Mr. Fancher considered his quality control and inspection procedures quite satisfactory. Less than 1 percent of units produced were faulty.

Problems encountered in the scheduling of production could be divided into three types. Fancher alone handled all scheduling, basing his decisions upon his personal experience and "feel" for the problem.

The master production schedule was decided by Fancher twice a year for each season. Because of his intuitive feel of the market, developed from 22 years of selling experience plus 10 years of general management, he felt that he could estimate the total demand for garments, even if he could not guess the individual colors and sizes. Because their key customer was primarily interested in a fixed quality level at a fixed, minimum price, and ordered fairly large quantities at one time, Fancher was able to set his production schedule with considerable assurance as far as basic styles were concerned. Changes had to be made, of course, as reports of sales established which styles were the better sellers and which were poorer. Detailed schedules were then altered to reflect demand for specific styles, colors, and sizes.

Frequent changes in schedules, combined with layout and cutting mistakes, sometimes resulted in fabric shortages. Difficulty was encountered in reordering specific patterns or weaves from suppliers, because most fabrics were produced on a one-run basis. To compensate for possible fabric shortages, Fancher formerly had ordered more of each type of fabric than he expected to need. The costs of such overpurchases became prohibitive and, although Fancher took pride in the company's reputation for meeting all promised orders, a policy was adopted to fall short on certain orders and refuse some reorders rather than to continue incurring the extra cost of buying excess fabrics.

In setting weekly schedules for particular styles, care had to be exercised to maintain a balance because certain styles required more time on particular operations than others. For example, a shirtwaist required many more buttonholes than most other dresses. Fancher attempted to balance the scheduling of particular styles in any one day so far as to keep everyone working at approximately the same pace. Rescheduling also was necessary occasionally to avoid disruptions caused by the absence of a key worker or a key machine, or because materials were delayed in transit to the plant at Maryhill.

On at least one occasion, when Fancher was on an out-of-state trip, the company was unable to accept a large reorder because the minority stockholders lacked authority to make decisions concerning large purchases of fabrics. In this case, the supplier had the desired fabric in stock.

The third type of scheduling problem faced by Fancher occurred only when current sales exceeded an annual rate of 8,300 dozen dresses, which was the normal capacity of the plant on a one-shift basis. Translated into dollars, an annual sales volume of $1 million was the capacity of the plant. Because Fancher was not inclined to expand the facilities or add a second shift, he chose to subcontract sewing to two nearby independent contract shops. The company delivered the necessary piece goods and patterns, and received the garments in a finished condition. All subcontract work was inspected, invoiced, and shipped from Maryhill to customers.

Inspection of contract work often showed a much lower quality of workmanship than was considered acceptable at the Bobby Rivers plant. For this reason, Fancher tried to keep orders within the capacity of the Maryhill factory. The lack of suitable facilities to produce over $1 million worth of garments caused Fancher to reject feelers for a large contract business with a second dry goods chain rather than chance sacrificing the quality image of his goods.

Mr. Fancher often wondered about the future course the company was going to take. While he was not disappointed in the progress that had been made to date, the fact that his sales had stabilized at a $1 million annual volume disturbed him a little whenever he found time to reflect on the situation.

QUESTIONS FOR DISCUSSION

1. What production advantages did Bobby Rivers obtain from staying away from high-style garments? Disadvantages?

2. What do you think of Fancher's scheduling procedure? Recommend changes if you feel some should be made.

3. Evaluate Fancher's decision to subcontract. What alternatives does he have?

4. What effect would an increase in sales have on production? What might be the effect of automating part of the operations?

5. Make an analysis of the record keeping for work performed.

6. Do you feel that the lost order incident due to Mr. Fancher's being out-of-state is serious? If so, how would you recommend the company guard against its recurrence?

7. Evaluate the designing process. Should production people be included in the process? How?

IV–3   Franklin Electric Co.[1]

In March 1975, Norman Jackson, President of Franklin Electric Co., called in a business consultant, Dave Broadway, for advice about solving Franklin's problem of monthly fluctuations of sales. (See Exhibit 1.) In order to provide Mr. Broadway with the necessary background, Mr. Jackson summoned the leading personnel in this small company to assist

EXHIBIT 1
Monthly Sales for Fiscal 1975

Month	Bookings	Shipments	Backlog
1974			
April.............	$ 8,446	$21,607	$ 69,115
May.............	22,774	19,554	77,243
June.............	31,728	16,477	92,494
July.............	4,392	15,762	81,061
August..........	17,748	19,953	78,848
September.......	25,221	21,327	82,741
October.........	23,349	20,889	85,201
November.......	6,135	19,927	71,409
December.......	41,998	21,033	92,369
1975			
January.........	70,368	20,536	142,200
February........	9,596	18,175	133,593
March..........	6,370	17,002	122,941

[1] Prepared by Richard S. Harrigan and Burnard Sord, University of Texas at Austin.

in briefing Mr. Broadway. Among those present were Frank Jeffries, engineer; John Lennox, general manager; Laura Cole, bookkeeper and secretary; and John Range, vice president.

Mr. Jackson explained that Franklin manufactured several specialized electronic components—crystal oscillators, temperature-controlled crystal oscillators, tuning fork oscillators, and tuning fork filters. (See Exhibit 2). These products were used in systems that required precise timing—particularly military systems and electronic test equipment. Mr. Jackson stressed that Franklin did quality work and held patents on two manufacturing processes, which led him to believe that his company had significant growth potential. The problem, as expressed by Mr. Jackson, was how to reach this market and thereby establish a clear upward trend rather than experience the random variations that had characterized the past year.

EXHIBIT 2
Sales by Product, Fiscal 1975

Product	Number of Units	Revenue
Crystal oscillators	816	$ 63,861.14
Temperature controlled crystal oscillators (TCXO)	487	35,347.00
Tuning fork filters	349	29,154.00
Tuning fork oscillators	1,324	98,759.60
Total	2,976	227,121.74

COMPANY HISTORY

Mr. Jackson and several associates had purchased Franklin in 1973, with Mr. Jackson owning 40 percent of the stock. Franklin was originally a wholly owned subsidiary of Amatron, Inc., an intermediate-size producer of electronic instrumentation whose manufacturing facilities were situated in the Southwest. Mr. Jackson was to assume the responsibility as chairman of the board and president. He held a degree in chemistry from a local college and currently served as plant supervisor in a local manufacturing plant. He planned to retain this position after assuming his new responsibilities with Franklin, but would be available for consultation when needed. Shortly after the purchase, the production manager left, and primary responsibility for day-to-day operations fell on the shop foreman, John Lennox. Lennox handled customer calls concerning products, managed the inventory, and coordinated work schedules.

In September 1973, Mr. Lennox became general manager. He had to assume the purchasing responsibilities and several other chores formerly performed by the Amatron manager. These duties kept him in the front office and made it difficult for him to render assistance to the technicians. In January 1974, with Mr. Jackson's approval, Mr. Lennox hired Frank Jeffries, a graduate of Virginia Polytechnic Institute, who had worked in related product lines at Amatron for several years. Mr. Jeffries began handling much of the telephone contact with customers, did some purchasing, supervised the technicians closely, and redesigned some of the products.

PRODUCT LINES

Frequency-sensitive instruments such as computers and simple digital counters usually rely upon ordinary line power for a frequency reference. Where line power is unreliable (shipboard), missing (airborne applications), or not sufficiently stable, internal frequency references must be provided. Franklin manufactured such frequency generating components, called oscillators, and filters. The oscillators could be classified into three groups—crystal, temperature compensated crystal (TCXO), and tuning fork. The crystal oscillators were used for high stability, high frequency requirements for such applications as computing machines, industrial controls, radar, and navigation systems. The TCXO was simply a crystal oscillator capable of operating over a wide temperature range—for planes flying in the stratosphere or in arctic zones. Noncrystal tuning fork oscillators were used for low frequency, moderate stability requirements such as in barometric pressure indicators and underwater timers. Active tuning fork filters had capabilities of allowing one frequency to pass while rejecting others. The tuning fork filter had applications in radar systems, tone signaling devices, and submarine sonar. Franklin was the sole producer of tuning fork filters, owned a patent on the manufacturing process, and, according to Mr. Jeffries, had a large potential growth in demand.

Mr. Jeffries performed the design work for these products and was particularly optimistic about the future of the filters. He stated, "The devices we produce are state-of-the-art devices," and claimed his designs were of superior quality to those currently in use.

PROCESSING AN ORDER

Customers generally telephoned Franklin to provide needed specifications and to request a price. Those receiving a reasonable price ordered from one to two prototypes. Mr. Jeffries would design a circuit, lay it out on a pegboard, and send the board to a company specializing in the design of smaller boards for production. On return of the board, Jeffries added necessary components and sent it to a nearby computer for testing. Unacceptable boards were reworked. Good boards were sent to customers for approval or disapproval for rework. On their approval, Mr. Jeffries wrote the assembly procedure for mass production of the product.

The production process for crystal oscillators and TCXOs consisted of assembling various electrical units on a PCB board by three assemblers, visual inspection by quality control, electronic testing by technicians and oscilloscopes, and placing in a can and labeling. Some models, such as TCXOs, made as many as five trips between assembly and technical testing before completion and meeting the tests.

Ninety-five percent of the tuning fork oscillators were built from scratch by Todd Ramber, a technician. He ground the forks himself and did all of the assembly work. The machinists did much of the painting and also ground the tuning forks that were used in the tuning fork filters and made the cans. Mr. Lennox believed that the good appearance of the label was critical to the product. Because he was dissatisfied with the quality of labeling done by the assembly people, he frequently did the labeling himself. He explained, "It is simply easier for me to take four or five hours to label them myself than it is to try to teach the workers how to label."

Franklin offered a one-year guarantee on parts and labor for all products. Mr. Jeffries estimated the per-unit cost of repairing a returned product to be equal to about one half the profit margin for that unit. During 1974, the monthly percentage of returns on total sales varied between 2 and 10 percent.

When the return rate approached 10 percent, it generally indicated a particular production problem that warranted special attention such as Jeffries' trip to a large West Coast customer which resulted in a change in Franklin's testing procedure.

ORGANIZATION

An organization chart of Franklin Electric is shown in Exhibit 3. Mr. Jackson and Mr. Range had other full-time positions. Mr. Broadway's comments on Mr. Lennox: "It is impossible to get the needed cost information from Mr. Lennox. It is clear that only Jeffries has a comprehensive understanding of the operation. Lennox is merely a glorified foreman. It is ludicrous to consider him the manager who will launch this company into a growth era. It is clear that Lennox represents a poor allocation of funds. You pay him $14,000 a year. You could get a University of Arizona MBA for $13,000. Lennox is only a high school graduate who spent several years in the Air Force." It was reported that Lennox "was on the phone telling potential customers who were looking for quotes that we were too busy and couldn't consider their orders."

Mr. Broadway suggested to Mr. Jackson and Mr. Range that Mr. Jeffries be sent on several more sales trips in the near future to increase

EXHIBIT 3
Organization Chart

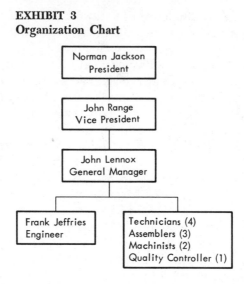

the contact between Franklin and potential customers. Mr. Jackson replied, "I agree, but we really need Frank at the shop."

"I tend to think that Franklin is overly dependent on Frank," Broadway rejoined. "He appears to do all the engineering, supervising of production, and whatever selling Franklin conducts. I believe you must work toward ending this overdependence on one man."

"Frank has made a very valuable contribution to our company," Mr. Jackson replied. "We certainly worry about something happening to him. We have taken out life insurance on him."

Mr. Range observed, "We do not have clear job descriptions at Franklin. I admit that Lennox's potential is limited, but we need written job descriptions because without descriptions people are confused about the true lines of authority."

CONCLUSION

On April 1, special advertisements were sent to 250 customers resulting, ostensibly, in a backlog of orders of over $200,000 by April 20. At a meeting on May 2, Jeffries assured Mr. Jackson that Franklin would produce $30,000 in May, even after a dismal $18,000 in April.

By May 25, it was clear to Mr. Jackson that maximum production for the month would be $20,000. He wanted desperately to take whatever action was necessary to make Franklin grow. Mr. Broadway had informed him about international markets that Franklin could tap.

Mr. Jackson was concerned about the growth and the future of the company. He was reviewing the recommendations made by the consultant and pondering what actions he should take and what priorities he should establish.

QUESTIONS FOR DISCUSSION

1. From your analysis, was Mr. Jackson looking at the right problem? Justify your answer.

2. List the major problems facing Franklin. For each, analyze the situation and list alternative decisions.

3. Can production meet the demand generated by the special advertising? If so, how?

4. Chart the activities that occurred from the receipt of an order until the products are sent to the customer. Can this procedure be improved?

5. What would you do about Lennox? Is he a problem? How about Jeffries? Ramber?

6. Do you believe job descriptions are needed? Explain.

7. Was the special advertising wise?

part V

Marketing Your Product or Service

Staffing, production, marketing, and financing are all essential business functions. Each of them should be performed economically and effectively in order for your firm to be successful. The following chapters should help you perform the marketing function better.

Marketing denotes the distribution of your firm's product or service to your customers in order to satisfy their needs and to accomplish your firm's objectives. Marketing includes developing the product or service, pricing, distributing the product, advertising, merchandising, doing personal selling, promoting, and directing the sales and service people. It is an essential function because unless your firm has a market, or can develop a market, for its product or service, the other functions of staffing, producing, and financing are futile.

The marketing function and the philosophy that underlies its performance are presented in Figure V–1.

This logical approach to the performance of the marketing function is covered in this part. Chapter 15 will cover the subject of developing marketing strategies. Specifically, it will deal with the marketing concept, strategic marketing policies, and developing the "what-to-do" marketing strategies you plan to use. This chapter is followed by three chapters dealing with the "how-to-do-it" marketing operations.

Chapter 16 covers sales forecasting and promoting.

FIGURE V–1
Schematic of Marketing Function

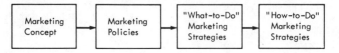

It specifically includes the subjects of marketing research, sales fore-casting, advertising, and sales promotion.

In Chapter 17, personal selling through agent middlemen or your own sales force is discussed.

Finally, Chapter 18 covers some of the other marketing problems, including setting up sales territories, planning and controlling the activities of your salespeople, determining your marketing mix.

15

Developing Marketing Strategies

An area that frequently seems to be neglected by the independent business owner is the marketing activity. Yet, in the final analysis, what occurs in the marketplace determines the success or failure of the firm. Therefore, we have attempted to lay out in this chapter in a step-by-step fashion what you must do to succeed in marketing. Attention is focused on the marketing concept, strategic marketing policies, and "what-to-do" strategies.

Concerning the marketing concept, the aspects covered are: determining what customers' needs are and how you can satisfy them; specifying the market to be served—called market segmentation; and deciding the advantage(s) that your company has—called its competitive edge.

The strategic marketing policies described are: morality and public service, products, markets, profits, personal selling, customer relations, promotion, credit policies, and credit cards.

The chapter concludes with a discussion of the following "what-to-do" marketing strategies: expanding sales into new markets; increasing penetration into present market; and making no marketing innovation, but rather emphasizing product design and manufacturing innovations.

THE MARKETING CONCEPT

The marketing concept is based upon the importance of the customers to a firm. If you decide to use this approach in your firm, you will need to: (1) determine what your customers' needs are, and how those needs can be satisfied; (2) select the market you will try to serve; and (3) decide what advantage you have that will give you a competitive edge over other firms.

Meeting Customers' Needs

The underlying principle of the marketing concept, as it applies to your business, is that your firm should seek to meet the needs of customers—at a profit to you. Customers' needs are your firm's primary focus, and your resources should be organized to satisfy those needs. The marketing concept should guide the attitude of all employees in your firm. They should be devoted to stimulating and satisfying the wants and needs of customers. Too often, only the salespeople in a company observe the concept, while other employees (say, delivery people, cashiers, or clerks) are rude and create customer ill will.

Learning Customers' Need

You should learn your customers' likes and make them feel that you are interested in them. You should give them extra service, because your customers will remember it and inform others. You should be an expert on your products and tell the truth about them even if sales are lost. You should build your trade around existing customers.

You should possess an ability to "read" customers—that is, to determine what they want and how you can best fulfill their needs and desires. In other words, you should want to know what "turns them on."

> The owner of a small ladies ready-to-wear store in a rural community had a good business going. It was discovered that most of the store's customers lived in a city 50 miles away. Some wondered why people shopped at her store when they could have patronized a store in their own city.
>
> Answer: She knew her customers by name, understood their needs, and bought with them in mind as individuals. "This dress should please Mrs. Adams." She then called each customer to inform her of the special purchases.[1]

You should sell your customers only as much as they can afford. An "over-sold" customer will not be a "repeat." You should encourage your sales people to build personal followings among customers. One retail salesperson built his following by writing 20 letters each day to

---

[1] Irving Schwartz, "Personal Qualities Needed to Manage a Store" *Small Marketers Aids no. 145* (Washington, D.C.: Small Business Administration, 1970).

them. Each letter described new stock that would appeal to the personal preference of the customer.

You should have a customer policy whereby sales personnel give the benefit of doubt to customers who return merchandise.

> When the new owner of a men's clothing store checked the records, he found that the last purchase made by one of his close friends had occurred more than six years ago. He asked the friend why. The latter replied that the previous owner had refused to make an adjustment on a tuxedo that did not fit.
>
> This policy probably lost the store about $2,000 at retail because the customer would probably have bought about 15 suits plus accessories during that period of time. The new owner assured the friend that he would make future adjustments when needed. He regained a customer.[2]

Be Conscious of Your Image. You should rate your business periodically in order to determine what kind of image your firm has. You can do this by trying to think about your firm as your customers would. Looking at your firm from their standpoint, ask yourself:

1. Is my firm doing all that it can to be customer-oriented?
2. Can customers find what they want, when they want it, and where they want it at a competitive price?
3. Do my employees and I make sure that they leave with their needs satisfied and with a feeling toward our company that will bring them back again?

Customers want a business to be helpful! The American Institute of Banking makes this observation: "The easiest way to make money is to learn what people want and sell it to them. The fastest way to lose money is to offer something, regardless of what people want, and try to make them buy it."[3]

You should do little favors for your customers; they like your thoughtfulness more than any gift, although people dislike receiving big favors that they cannot repay.

In the following examples, the marketing concept was not followed by the salespeople involved:[4]

> The customer asked for a certain kind of fishing rod in a sporting equipment store. The salesman replied, "Sorry, we don't carry that brand," and did not offer to show the store's own brand to the cus-

---

[2] Ibid.

[3] Robert G. Murdick et al., *Business Policy: A Framework for Analysis* (Columbus, Ohio: Grid, 1972), p. 71.

[4] Kenneth Grubb, "Are Your Salespeople Missing Opportunities?" *Small Marketers Aids no. 95.* (Washington, D.C.: Small Business Administration, 1970).

tomer. The store's brand had features which the competing brand did not have, and it cost no more. But the customer never knew it, unless he heard about it elsewhere.

In an appliance store, the salesman's facial expression said, "Make up your mind," as he waited for a customer to decide which washing machine she liked best. His "message" reached her because she did not buy a washer. He said, "I know she must have thought I had all day to wait on her." He did not know that she planned to buy a drier also.

Look for Danger Signals. If you are interested in the marketing concept, you will look for these *danger signals:*

1. Many customers walk out of your store without buying.
2. Many of them no longer visit the store.
3. Customers are not urged to buy additional items or "trade up" to more expensive items.
4. Traffic (pedestrian and vehicle) in front of your store has fallen off.
5. Customers are returning more merchandise than they should.
6. Your company's sales are down this month compared to the same month last year, and sales for the year to date are down from the same period last year.
7. Your employees are slow in greeting customers.
8. Your employees appear indifferent and make customers wait unnecessarily.
9. Your employees' personal appearance is not neat.
10. Your sales people lack knowledge of the store's merchandise.
11. The number of mistakes made by your employees is increasing.
12. Because of high prices, you have the reputation of being greedy.
13. Your better qualified employees leave for jobs with competitors.

All of these signals are evidence that your store is not following the marketing concept.

Market Segmentation

Your firm should specify what market it is attempting to serve. A product or service that fulfills the needs and wants of a specifically defined group of people is preferable to the product or service that is a compromise to suit widely divergent tastes. A marketing segment should be defined in terms of various characteristics such as economic status, age, education, occupation, and location. Your best opportunity is to identify a market segment that is not well served by other firms. One authority has said:

If we are to market successfully, we must in one way or another continually search for "holes" in the market. These holes are nothing but consumer needs and wants that exist because of inadequate or nonexistent products or services.[5]

Another authority states, "Choose a small market and develop it until you dominate. Be a big frog in a small pond."[6]

In determining your segment of the market, there are some fundamental questions you should ask yourself, such as:

1. What is my place in industry, and how can I find my competitive niche?
2. Am I known for my quality or my price?
3. If I sell industrial products, do I sell to more than one customer?
4. What image do the customers and the public have of my firm?
5. I serve only a limited number of customers. Why?

A common error found in many small retailing firms is "straddling the market," or attempting to sell both high-quality and low-quality goods. As a result, the retailer is carrying a limited inventory of everything, but does not have a good selection of anything.

In summary, you should clearly perceive the share of the market—or the percentage of the total market—that your firm can *actually obtain*. This perception is possible only when you have clearly defined your market in specific terms.

Competitive Edge

In order for your firm to be successful, you should seek a "competitive edge." Your business, as well as all other firms, needs some reason for being, something that is desirable from the customers' viewpoint that sets it apart from, and gives it an advantage over, its competition. You should know who your competitors are and how they operate. You should be stressing quality, reliability, integrity, and service rather than lower prices.

The competitive edge should be realistic. To determine whether it is realistic in your firm, you should answer these questions:

1. Is the competitive edge based on facts?
2. Do you know specifically what your customers are seeking?
3. Do you have an edge that is sufficiently important to entice the customer away from his present source of supply?

---

[5] Allan Wickman, Jr., "Marketing Ideas Make or Break a Company," *Marketing Insights* (January 19, 1970), p. 3.

[6] Gardiner G. Greene, *How to Start and Manage Your Own Business* (New York: McGraw-Hill Book Company, 1975), p. 114.

4. Have you used market research to make this determination?
5. Is the competitive edge compatible with your firm's capabilities and constraints?
6. Does your firm have the necessary resources—e.g., personnel—to accomplish it?
7. Is the competitive edge based on conditions that are likely to change rapidly?[7] That is, you should be conscious of, and oriented toward, the future.

Your firm should focus on earning profits instead of increasing the volume of sales. You should not increase sales without considering production costs, adequacy of capital, position of competition, and so forth. Expenses incurred in achieving the increased volume may exceed the revenues achieved and result in losses. You can literally "Sell yourself into bankruptcy." Sales increases should not far exceed your company's well-rounded growth in vital areas such as working capital and productive capacity.

STRATEGIC MARKETING POLICIES

You and the top managers in your firm should formulate strategic marketing policies for certain areas, including:

1. Morality and public service.
2. Products.
3. Markets.
4. Profits.
5. Personal selling.
6. Customer relations.
7. Promotion.
8. Credit policies.
9. Use of credit cards.

Morality and Public Service.   Policies on morality and public service consist of general statements expressing your firm's desire to be honest in its dealing with the public and its customers.

To illustrate, the importance of policies prohibiting collusion with competitors became evident when executives of some turbine-generator suppliers were found guilty of market and price collusion in the 1950s.

Products.   Policies on products will determine the direction in which your firm may grow in the future and may keep your company from "running off in all directions." If you are a manufacturer, you should

---

[7] Murdick et al., *Business Policy*, p. 71.

generally restrict your products to custom, special purpose, low-volume products rather than high-volume, assembly-line products where big companies are competitors and have advantages over you. If you have a small department store, you may deal in either low-quality, low-price goods or high-quality, high-price goods. If you are a retailer, you may specialize in either soft goods or durable goods.

The small firm often finds its most effective competitive weapon in the field of product strategy. It may concentrate upon a narrow product line, develop a highly specialized product or service, or provide a product-service "package" containing an unusual amount of service. Competitors' products, prices, and services should be obtained and examined to determine whether your company can build a better product.

Markets.   Market policies are designed to clarify what geographic areas you wish to serve and other market characteristics appropriate for your firm. Perhaps you desire to remain only a local business. You may decide to market only consumer, industrial, or defense goods. You may decide to sell only at retail, wholesale, or to manufacturers.

Profits.   Profit policies may require that sales goals be specified that will provide your firm a sufficiently large sales volume and a certain dollar profit. Or profit as a percentage of sales may be specified, which calls for low marketing costs.

Personal Selling.   Personal selling policies may range from those guiding the structure of your sales organization to those covering your sales representatives' behavior. For example, you may have a policy stating that only one representative of your company may call upon an account. You may not permit "hard selling." Other sales policies may relate to your representatives' qualifications and compensation and to constraints on your sales managers.

Customer Relations.   Your company's relationship with your customers may be illustrated with this question: Should you have a policy that the customer is always right?

Promotion.   The pattern of your firm's advertisements may reveal your company's promotion policies. You should follow a policy of tasteful advertising at all times. You may restrict your promotion to trade shows, or to industrial publications, or to some other advertising medium.

Credit Policies.   In order to stimulate sales, you should provide credit for your customers. However, an appropriate credit policy is essential if you wish to be successful in granting credit.

Typical problems that face owners of retail and service firms when they get involved in the over-extension or unwise extension of credit are presented below:

Martin's Restaurant, a new business, was located in an area where many families and individuals were receiving public assistance, and its owner-manager gave credit freely. Within the first few weeks of operation, the firm had accounts receivable of $250, more than one fourth its total capital.

Recognizing his predicament too late, the owner declared: "I have been unable to make enough money to pay my bills. I cannot pay my bills if my customers do not pay me. If some money is not received from them soon, I will have to close the restaurant."

The restaurant closed less than one year after it was established.

Mr. Neely and his wife had invested almost $6,000 of their savings in a venture. They paid $4,000 cash for equipment, and allocated the balance for working capital needs.

Sales increased during each of the 13 months they had been in business, and all bills had been paid. Much capital, however, was tied up in accounts receivable that could not be collected. The trouble was that Mr. Neely was soft-hearted. He stated: "I do not want to extend credit to anyone, but the problem is to tell that to my customers so their business will not be lost." The owners stopped giving credit altogether, but the firm's gross profits dropped by almost one-half. Mr. Neely was so discouraged that he sold the firm for only $2,500.[8]

Retailers lose far more from slow accounts than from bad debts. Costs related to slow accounts are the most important item in the total cost of doing credit business. Some adverse effects of slow-paying charge accounts are:

1. Increased bad-debt losses.
2. Increased bookkeeping and collection expenses.
3. Increased interest expense due to greater capital requirements.
4. Reduction of capital turnover and profit.
5. Loss of business because "slow payers" tend to transfer their patronage elsewhere.

The longer a charge account goes unpaid, the more difficult it is to collect. (See Chapter 24.)

You should establish a definite credit policy covering the following factors:

1. To grant or not to grant credit.
2. To require a down payment or not to require one.
3. How much should the typical down payment be.
4. How much time should be allowed on installment sales.

In selecting your credit customers, you can use the three Cs of credit as your guideline:

[8] *Records and Credit in Profitable Management* (Washington D.C.: Small Business Administration), Administrative Management Course, pp. 27–28.

Character: What is the customer's reputation in business and the community?
Capacity: What is the customer's ability to repay?
Capital: What is your customer's financial condition, or how much equity does he have in his company?

You should explain your credit terms to your customers clearly and unmistakably.

The customer's position should be investigated to obtain the following credit information:

1. Address and length of residence in your locality.
2. Occupation and earnings.
3. Marital status and number of dependents.
4. Ownership of property.
5. Amount of debts or payment and other credit accounts.
6. References, including bank references.

Additional questions include: Does your credit applicant change residence frequently? Change jobs often? Pay accounts slowly?

In many retail stores, the initial step in credit investigation is the completion of an application form. The information obtained is used in determining the applicant's financial responsibility.

Your retail credit bureau can be contacted and asked to provide reports on prospective credit customers.

Other credit pointers are:

1. Set definite limits concerning the amount a customer can charge. Keep the credit within bounds.
2. Keep accurate, complete records.
3. Send statements at regular intervals.
4. Watch past-due accounts.
5. Take legal steps when necessary.

A well-planned collection policy is very beneficial to your firm.[9] Such a policy should include specific rules on such matters as:

1. When are accounts to be payable?
2. How soon after the due date shall the first reminder be mailed?
3. How soon after the due date shall the credit privileges be suspended on a past-due account?
4. How many steps shall be in the standard follow-up procedure, and what duration of time shall elapse between the steps?
5. What tools and methods shall be used in the follow-up?
6. When shall past-due accounts be given to a collection agency or an attorney?

[9] Ibid., pp. 32–33.

Use of Credit Cards.   In order to stimulate sales, you, as a retailer, should seriously consider the use of credit cards. Their objectives are to attain more rapid completion of credit sales, reduce customer waiting time and inconvenience, and eliminate certain recordkeeping costs.

Bank credit cards, such as Visa (formerly BankAmericard) and Master Charge, have become important in generating sales. In 1970, there were about 24 million cardholders. Merchants report sales, sales returns and allowances, and other credits; and banks charge and credit their deposit accounts. Retailers pay a joining fee, a fee on sales made, and other fees.

You should recognize the advantages of no bad debt losses; no collection problems; and no personnel, equipment, or space requirements for servicing accounts receivable.

These policies should be examined relative to your company's strategic marketing plans. Are they consistent with your marketing strategies?

APPROACHES TO MARKETING STRATEGY—WHAT TO DO

Marketing strategy relates to how you meet the needs of the market better than your competitors. There are really two problems involved, namely, determining the available strategies and choosing the one to be used by your firm.

Determining Available Marketing Strategies

In determining the available marketing strategies for your firm you should take this approach:[10]

1.   Analyze your present and future market situations.
2.   Shape your product to fit your market.
3.   Evaluate your company's resources.
4.   Keep informed about your competitors.

Analyzing Present and Future Market Situations.   You should determine the opportunities that lie in present and future market situations as well as problems and adverse trends in the environment that will affect your company.

Market size and growth are vital. Growth rate potential should be accurately forecast. For example, a new business should have a market growing at the rate of at least 15–20 percent per year. Factors that affect this growth, such as actions of the federal government, should be evaluated. Your market segments should be determined.

---

[10] Donald M. Dible, *Winning the Money Game* (Santa Clara, Calif.: The Entrepreneur Press, 1975), pp. 114–15.

Relevant questions covered earlier are: "Who are your customers?" and "What are their needs?" You should understand your customers' buying process. For example, concerning consumer products, this process consists of: need, awareness, trial, and repurchase. You should determine which stage(s) of the process that you will address and how to address them.

Shaping Product to Fit Market. You should be concerned with shaping your products to fit your markets and with finding markets that fit your products. A market niche should be selected that is too small to interest large companies.

A small company manufactured and sold truck springs.
Problem: Competition with larger companies was severe.
Solution: The company started manufacturing and selling springs for swimming pool diving boards.

You should select products that offer unique features that differentiate them from your competitors' products.

A calculator manufacturer produced and sold calculators that met the needs of scientists more effectively than competitors' simpler models.

Pricing should be primarily related to your market rather than primarily to your costs. Obviously, your costs should be known and covered; buyers are not interested in your costs, however, but rather the price that they are willing to pay.

Evaluating Company Resources. Your strengths, as well as your limitations, should be determined in an overall fashion and at each stage of the selling process. You should be realistic about your financial pressure, cost pressures, competitive pressures, and timing pressures. Your successes and failures should be understood. Why were you successful? Failures should be viewed as important learning experiences. You should understand your strategy. What do you want to accomplish? What are your market share objectives?

Understanding Competitors. You should understand your competitors as well as you understand yourself and keep informed about them. What are their strengths and limitations, pressures, costs and profitability, market strategies, and corporate strategies?

Determining Your Corporate Strategy

Next, you should identify the strategy you wish to use. Are you pioneering? Do you desire to be a leader in market share? Are you a follower? Your strategy should be written and used by all your managers in sales, advertising, production, and finance.

In order to obtain a competitive edge, your company must innovate in product design, marketing, or manufacturing. You may find it necessary to adopt developments made by others in two of these areas while you innovate in the other. You should determine which of these three "what-to-do" marketing strategies to follow:

1. Expand sales into new classes of customers.
2. Increase penetration in market segments corresponding to existing customers.
3. Make no marketing innovations, but copy new marketing techniques and attempt to hold the present market share by product design and manufacturing innovations.

These strategies are elaborated upon below.

Expanding Sales into New Markets. To reach new markets, you may consider these possibilities:

1. Develop additional related products or models within your product line.
2. Develop completely new products unrelated to your present line.
3. Find new applications in new markets for your product.
4. Develop customized products; perhaps you desire to upgrade from low-quality to medium-quality goods.

In introducing new and improved products, you should recognize their relationships to the existing product line and established channels of distribution, cost of development and introduction, personnel and facilities, and competition and market acceptance.

The new and improved products should be consistent with the existing product line. Otherwise, costly changes in manufacturing methods, channels of distribution, advertising, and personal selling may be necessary.

Significant capital outlays for design and development, personnel and facilities, market research, advertising and sales promotion, patents, and equipment and tooling may be involved. Profits may not be realized for one to three years on the sale of the new product, and financing should be adequate to cover this "breaking-in" period.

Competition should not be too severe. A rule of thumb is that new products can be introduced successfully only if a five percent share of the total market can be obtained. Your small firm may compete effectively with: (1) a nonstandard product, either a higher-priced product or an economy model; (2) fast deliveries or short production runs of special items; or (3) high quality that makes your product superior to products offered by competitors.

The following example pertains to the acquisition of a product or product line to certain specifications.

> The management of a defense-aerospace oriented, precision metal-stamping and machine shop desired to acquire a product or product line that met the following specifications:
>
> *Market*—The product is one for use by industrial or commercial firms of a specific industry, but not by the government or general public except incidentally.
>
> *Product*—The product sought is one on which 60 percent of the total direct manufacturing cost consists of metal stamping and/or machining processes.
>
> *Price range*—The price range is open, but preferably should be $300 to $400.
>
> *Volume*—The volume is open, but preferably should produce $200,000 in sales in the first year with a potential sale of $1 to $2 million annually.
>
> *Finance*—Capital of $50,000 in addition to present plant capacity is available for manufacturing a new product.
>
> *Type of acquisition*—Royalties are preferred to a patent, although purchase of a patent, joint venture, merger, or purchase of a company outright will also be considered.[11]

You should carefully consider diversification, or product line expansion. Advantages may be:

1. Increased profits.
2. Contribution to long-range growth.
3. Stabilization of product, employment, and payrolls.
4. Filling out a product line.
5. Lowering of administrative overhead cost per unit.

Availability of necessary facilities and skill are relevant factors. Diversification costs may exceed increased sales.

Increasing Penetration of Present Market. Perhaps you have been selling replacement parts primarily, but are attempting to expand by selling to original equipment manufacturers. Or, you may reduce the variety of products and models in order to produce substantial operating economies.

Make No Marketing Innovations. The strategy of retaining current marketing practices without trying to innovate is particularly suitable for your firm if its strength lies in its technical competence. In retailing, it is often advisable for store managers to follow this strategy.

---

[11] John B. Lang, "Finding a New Product for Your Company," *Management Aids for Small Manufacturers, no. 216* (Washington, D.C.: Small Business Administration, 1972).

Over the long range, your firm may follow one strategy for several years with the intent to change after certain marketing goals have been achieved.

SUMMARY

We have tried to emphasize the importance of adopting the marketing concept, establishing broad marketing policies, and determining what marketing strategies you will use in selling your goods or services.

The *marketing concept* means you will give special consideration to the needs, desires, and wishes of your prospective and present customers.

Marketing policies will provide the guidelines you and your employees need in satisfying the needs of your customers.

Marketing strategies are the careful plans and methods you need in order to have a competitive advantage over other firms.

Once the what-to-do strategy (objective strategy) has been determined, your next step is to evaluate current "means" strategies. These strategies are described in the next chapter.

QUESTIONS FOR FURTHER DISCUSSION

1. Define the *marketing function.*
2. What is a proper priority of marketing questions for which the management of a small company should seek answers?
3. Define the *marketing concept* and cite three illustrations of its application.
4. Explain *market segmentation.*
5. Explain a *competitive edge.*
6. Describe briefly five strategic marketing policies.
7. Cite three adverse effects of "slow" charge accounts.
8. Briefly describe the three Cs of credit.
9. Give five types of credit information that should be obtained in the investigation of a customer.
10. Cite three advantages of using credit cards in a small company.
11. Describe the approach that should be taken in determining the available marketing strategies for your firm.
12. Cite three "what-to-do" marketing strategies.
13. Cite three methods of expanding sales into new markets.
14. Cite three advantages of diversification, or product line expansion.

16

Sales Forecasting, Pricing, and Promoting

It is not unusual to find people who, when thinking of small businesses and their role in the marketplace, think of market research and sales forecasting as having little or no value. These people think of these activities as applying to larger firms and to be too time-consuming and too complex to be used by the smaller firms.

Yet, our experience with various types of businesses seems to refute that idea. Determining the nature of the market, its location, its potential volume, and the most effective procedure for its penetration are essential elements to small—as well as to larger—organizations. The quality of this endeavor plays a significant role in product design, packaging, display, advertising, sales, and—in essence—the degree of success achieved as measured in dollars of sales and profit.

The intent of this chapter is to present some of the marketing "means," or the "how-to-do-it" strategies. The means strategies covered are: market research and sales forecasting, pricing your product or service, determining your channel(s) of distribution, and conducting advertising, merchandising, and sales promotion.

Concerning market research, we describe its areas, the steps involved in performing it, the sources of marketing information, and some of the difficulties in performing it. Some samples and illustrations of sales forecasts are also presented.

As for pricing, we look specifically at markups, pricelining, and other factors affecting pricing.

We then discuss some of the problems in designing your channel(s) of distribution, as well as suggestions for modifying the channel as necessary.

The types of advertising discussed are product and institutional. Other aspects of advertising emphasized are programs, budgets and expenditures, policies, and measuring its results.

The chapter concludes with a description of sales promotion activities, with particular emphasis on media that may be used effectively by retailers and manufacturers.

MARKET RESEARCH AND SALES FORECASTING

Market research should provide a basis for more effective decisions by you and your marketing managers. It consists of fact-finding and forecasting and reporting the findings to you or your managers, who make the decision whether or not to take the indicated action.

Areas of Market Research

Areas of market research that you should consider are: identification of customers for your firm's products or services, and determination of their needs, evaluation of sales potential for your industry and your firm, selection of the most appropriate channel of distribution, and evaluation of advertising efficiency.

Market research studies may be directed toward the measurement of population, income level, purchasing power, and other indexes of sales potential in your trading area. The establishment of accurate sales quotas and measurement of effectiveness in selling depend upon the determination of sales potential.

To show the importance of researching the customers for a company's products, the following example is presented.

> The manager of a customer durables manufacturing firm set a goal of industry leadership and a target share of the market to be obtained within a certain period of time.
>
> *Problem:* The company did not attain the desired share of the market. The product line was styled above mass tastes. The designer was designing the product line for department store buyers (prestige stores at that), but three fourths of the product was being sold through furniture stores. The manager realized that he had failed to research the customer adequately.
>
> *Solution:* He then arranged for market research, which indicated that many furniture store buyers were seeking products styled quite differently.[1]

---

[1] T. Stanley Gallagher, "Sound Objectives Help Build Profits," *Management Aids for Small Manufacturers, no. 11* (Washington, D.C.: Small Business Administration, 1965).

Market research consists of the following steps:

1. Recognition of a problem.
2. Preliminary investigation and planning.
3. Gathering factual information.
4. Classifying and interpreting the information.
5. Reaching a conclusion.

The real nature of the difficulties facing your firm should be determined by a careful analysis of the situation. A problem creates the need for information. Your next step is to review the facts already known, perhaps through discussions with people inside or outside your firm or by reading trade publications. Once the facts are gathered, their significance, interrelationships, and implications for your firm should be determined.

Sources of Marketing Information

The sources of marketing information consist of: (1) secondary sources of published data, (2) primary sources of published data, and (3) primary sources of unpublished data.

Secondary Sources of Published Data. Secondary sources contain data originally compiled and published elsewhere. Examples of these sources are:

1. Government publications, such as *Survey of Current Business* and *Statistical Abstract of the United States.*
2. Trade association reports.
3. Chambers of commerce studies.
4. University research publications.
5. Trade journals.
6. Newspapers.

The U.S. Bureau of the Census regularly collects data on the number of industrial establishments, their sales volume, and number of employees for many industry groups, broken down by county and Standard Metropolitan Statistical Area (SMSA). An SMSA contains one city of 50,000 or more inhabitants or "twin cities" with a combined population of that size.

The data are reported for Standard Industrial Classification (SIC) Codes, which facilitate research by firms where sales can be related to their customers' type of activity. The Code breakdowns start with broad industrial categories, for example, apparel classifications, such as men's, youths', and boys' furnishings, work clothing, and allied garments; and subclassifications, such as shirts, collars, night wear, underwear, and neckwear.

Many trade associations and other organizations that gather industrial data also use the SIC Code.

Metropolitan newspapers often develop important market data, such as purchasing power information, for their advertising clients. Examples are Scripps-Howard publications and the Memphis *Commercial Appeal.*

Primary Sources of Published Data.   A primary source of published data consists of the compilation and initial publication of the data. The U.S. Census Reports are illustrations.

Primary Sources of Unpublished Data.   Examples of primary sources of unpublished data are your firm's records and external data obtained from your dealers, customers, and competitors.

Sales Forecasting

You should measure your company's potential market in terms of both units and dollars. A sales forecast, both long- and short-range, should be prepared. It is the foundation of budgeting for your firm. Typically, it indicates sales during the last planning period, current sales, and future sales. (See Figure 16–1.)

FIGURE 16–1
Jones Soap Company: Sales Forecast for Atlanta Market

Brand	Sales
Last Year	
Brand A...................	$10,000
Brand B...................	56,000
Brand C...................	37,000
This Year	
Brand A...................	$12,000
Brand B...................	69,000
Brand C...................	42,000
Next Year	
Brand A...................	$15,000
Brand B...................	62,000
Brand C...................	45,000

The Jones Company obtained actual data from its records.
Source: Harry Lipson and John R. Darling, *Introduction to Marketing* (New York: John Wiley, 1971), pp. 184–85, 347.

Using Quotas in Forecasting.   Your firm's sales quotas can be used in sales forecasting. They can be used to set targets for your firm, individual salesmen, departments, or sales territories. They should be realistic. Market sampling studies and a study of census data may be used in deriving the quotas.

A small manufacturer of automobile dashboard accessories had a problem.

Problem: What new sales territories should be added?

Solution: The manufacturer used *Census of Population* data as an aid in making his decision. His first question was: "Where are the high concentrations of automobiles?" Then he determined which of the geographic areas being considered had concentrations of automobile supply stores and variety stores, the most appropriate kinds of retail outlets. He found this information in the *Census* of *Business.*

The manufacturer of paneling and room accessories had franchise arrangements with local contractors who used these materials to convert basements into finished rooms.

Problem: What new areas will be best for franchises?

Solution: From census statistics on housing, he determined: (1) the type of houses that predominated in a particular area; and (2) whether the houses were built on concrete slabs or with a full basement. He eliminated areas where the houses had no basements.

Another question: Could people in the particular areas afford to finish off their basements?

Answer: To answer this question, he examined census data on family income, the number of children, and car ownership—particularly families that owned more than one car, indicating that they had discretionary income that might be spent for home improvement. He granted franchises in areas that had a good market potential.

Problem: An apparel manufacturer wanted to determine trends that might affect his business.

Solution: He used census population data for keeping his company in step with its customers. These data indicated that the areas in which he was selling had a high concentration of teenagers and young adults. He then added new clothing styles appropriate for these groups.[2]

Using Sales Representatives' Knowledge. Sales representatives' knowledge obtained through customer contacts should also be used in establishing sales quotas.

A small company used its salesmen in developing market plans for a new product, an item used by the steel industry.

Problem: The manager needed to estimate the new product's market potential.

---

[2] Solomon Dutka, "Using Census Data in Small Plant Marketing," *Management Aids for Small Manufacturers no. 187* (Washington, D.C.: Small Business Administration, 1972).

Solution: A steel plant's use of the new product would be proportional to the amount of water used by it for cooling purposes. Salesmen, in their regular calls, asked about the amount of water used at each plant.

The water usage data were compared with each plant's known capacity for producing steel, pig iron, and coke. A ratio between production capacity and water usage was calculated. Statistics from the American Iron and Steel Institute were used to calculate the total amount of cooling water used by the steel industry. A list of water usage data was compiled for every steel, iron, and coke plant in the country. With this list, salesmen determined which plants had the best potential.[3]

Using Questionnaires.   When information is needed from a large number of companies, you should consider using mail questionnaires. Sometimes confidential information can be obtained that customers prefer not to give to salesmen. Such information as commission percentages that competitors pay their agents, market shares obtained by competitors, and market potential for your products in various geographic areas may be obtained from these mail surveys.

A small company made a product used by meat packing plants.
Problem: The manager wanted to determine the sales potential for an area consisting of 300 counties.
Solution: From *County Business Patterns* (a series of booklets published by the U.S. Department of Commerce), he determined the total number of meat packing plants and their employment. He mailed questionnaires to these plants. Upon analyzing them, he learned that an average plant bought $200 worth of his product per employee per year. By multiplying the total employment in these plants by $200, he derived the potential annual sales.[4]

Using Personal Contacts.   There are certain kinds of questions that can best be answered by interviews with your customers and distributors. Some of these questions are:

1. Why are you losing business? Because of price?
2. Is something wrong with your product? Your sales personnel?
3. Why don't your distributors push your line harder? Is it your discount schedule? What is the future for your product?
4. Are your customers experimenting with processes that may replace your product? Are they likely to shift to "in-house" manufacturing of your product?

---

[3] Warren R. Dix, "Getting Facts for Better Sales Decisions," *Management Aids for Small Manufacturers, no. 12* (Washington, D.C.: Small Business Administration, 1966).

[4] Ibid.

Sometimes, respondents tell you what they think you want to hear. Some people don't want to hurt your feelings, and they won't tell you if they think that your company is behind the times or that your competitor's new models give better service.

You should consider the extent and intensity of your competition. One way to determine how much merchandise you and your competitors sell is using direct data.

The manager of a furniture store obtained information on total furniture sales for counties A and B, and determined that the store accounted for 25 percent of county A's furniture sales and 10 percent of county B's. For county A, total furniture sales totaled $3 million, and the store's sales were $750,000.

Alternatively, he could have determined the per family expenditure for furniture and multiplied it by the estimated number of families in the area. Population data could have been used (e.g., total population divided by three) in estimating the number of families.

If sales data are not available for your type of goods in your market area, you should *estimate the volume of business* by relating sales of your type of merchandise to other merchandise that is sold in conjunction with yours, or by relating known national data to known local data.

A tire dealer determined that the sales of new cars three years ago had a strong effect on present retail tire sales. National sales of replacement tires in any one year were found to consistently represent 10 percent of auto sales three years earlier. Ten percent of the 1971 automobile sales could have been used as market potential for 1974 in its area.

Using Statistical Analyses and Projections. In analyzing your firm's records, statistical analyses and projections based on past sales may be utilized in developing sales quotas. Also, an accounting analysis of the profitability of selling to particular customers or of selling particular products may be made, and certain low-quality, high-cost customers to whom sales are unprofitable may be identified. Furthermore, analysis of your sales records on profitable credit customers may provide good information for merchandising decisions and sales promotion programs. An analysis of your company's accounts receivable aging data—current, 30-day, 60-day, 90-day, and over 90 days—is beneficial.

If your store sells many varieties of products, market-share should be measured in total dollar volume rather than in product units sold. You should determine the total sales and the rate of growth for the type of goods you offer.

An area with apparel sales of $2,000,000, $2,200,000, and $2,420,-000 in three successive years shows a 10 percent annual rate of growth. Other things being equal, it may be expected that these sales will amount to $2,662,000 in the fourth year. To *match* that growth, a store's volume should increase by 10 percent; to *increase* its market share, it would have to increase by more than 10 percent.

Overcoming Market Research Difficulties

A major disadvantage associated with market research in small businesses is that such businesses lack knowledge of research techniques. However, the services of outside experts—such as the market research consulting firm—may be secured. You may obtain the services of an advertising person who is "moonlighting." Other possibilities include help from trade associations, local chambers of commerce, banks, and field offices of the U.S. Department of Commerce and the Small Business Administration. You should consider cooperative research with other small businesses—say, evaluations of traffic flow and parking availability.

You should not engage in the armchair type of "top-down" market research exemplified by the following: "Of 40 million homes in the United States in 1976, 70 percent of the owners use a power lawn mower, which produces a market of 28 million. My firm is attempting to obtain 5 percent of this market, or sales of 1.4 million mowers." This type of research is too vague. Instead, your market research should consist of detailed field study—specifics pertaining to initial customers; quantities, price, and gross profit margin; specific competitors and their sales and profits; response with first prototypes; and number of orders on hand.[5]

Your firm should closely follow market changes due to shifts in the composition of your customers, their values and preferences, and their locations. "Fad" items and services tend to have a short life cycle. You should plan to "get in and get out" within an appropriate time frame in order to maximize profits.[6]

You cannot afford all the market research you would like, so projects where the payoff is greatest should be selected. The objectives of each research project should be carefully specified. Selection of research techniques should be based upon cost considerations and the value of the decisions to be made. Market tests should be made before the introduction of new products.

---

[5] Donald M. Dible, *Winning the Money Game* (Santa Clara, Calif.: The Entrepreneur Press, 1975), p. 66.

[6] Successful products go through a life cycle. The stages of the cycle are: (1) the introductory period, in which there is low customer acceptance; (2) a growth period, in which gains are rapid; (3) maturity, in which sales level off; and (4) decline, in which sales fall. In general, the average life of products is decreasing because of rapid technological development and business change.

PRICING YOUR PRODUCT OR SERVICE

The importance of pricing is illustrated by the observation that about one half of all the failures in small business can be traced to a product or service that was being sold at the wrong price.[7]

Relating Price to Costs

The first step in setting prices is having an accurate knowledge of costs.

All items should be priced at a level to provide an adequate profit margin. The policy of pricing "to cover costs" has dangerous long-run implications. In periods of rapid inflation, particularly, costs should be constantly monitored and price changes made to provide for continued profitability.

Small companies that base their pricing solely on costs, rather than on the values as seen by their customers, lose profits. Companies selling to a style-conscious market or ones that provide a unique service can set more profitable prices by recognizing the short-lived novelty of their products and the values of their services to their customers.

If your firm has idle facilities, your price may be less than total cost. Provided your price covers the variable costs and makes some contribution toward the fixed costs, this practice may be desirable.

A word of caution is appropriate at this point. You should constantly check the package price structure and profits based on units sold.

A new club lessee of a food-beverage concession decided to adopt a pricing policy of selling food at cost and making profits from the sale of beverages. Overlooked was the fact that a significant portion of customers were either nondrinkers or light drinkers. Therefore, profits were not as anticipated.

Setting a Price Strategy

Your goal should be to find the price-volume combination that will maximize profits. When setting a price strategy, you should consider these factors:

1. The customer and channel of distribution.
2. Competitive and legal forces.
3. Annual volume and life-cycle volume.
4. Opportunities for special market promotions.
5. Product group prices.

---

[7] Theodore Cohn and Roy A. Lindberg, *How Management Is Different in Small Companies* (New York: American Management Association, Inc., 1972), p. 24.

The product, price, delivery, service, and fulfillment of psychological needs form the total package that the customer buys. A price should be consistent with the product image. Since customers often equate the quality of unknown products with price, raising prices may increase sales.

Price cutting should be considered as a form of sales promotion. You should reduce price whenever the added volume resulting from the reduction produces sufficient sales revenue to offset the added costs. However, if an inelastic demand exists for your product, a lower price will not result in a greater number of units being sold. Your competitors' probable reactions should be considered in determining whether to reduce prices. Small firms generally should not consider themselves price leaders.

Other Aspects of Pricing

Markups, price lining, and odd pricing are other aspects of pricing you should consider. In calculating the selling price for a particular product, retailers, wholesalers, and manufacturers should add a *markup* to the purchase or manufacturing costs. An initial markup should cover operating—particularly selling—expenses, operating profit, and subsequent price reductions (e.g., markdowns and employee discounts). An initial markup may be expressed as a percentage of either the sales price or the product cost. A markup of $8 on a product costing $12, say, would produce a selling price of $20. The markup would be 40 percent of the sales price and 66⅔ percent of cost. Although either method is correct, consistency should be followed in the use of either base. Your business should have effective cost analysis by products in order to price the product effectively. You should recognize that modifications or markup percentages may be needed because of factors such as competitors' prices and the use of loss-leaders, or promotional, pricing.

Price lining refers to the offering of merchandise at distinct price levels. To illustrate, women's dresses might be sold at $40, $60, and $80. Income level and buying desires of a store's customers are important factors. Advantages of price lining are the simplification of customer choice and reduction of the store's minimum inventory.

Concerning *odd pricing*, some small business managers believe customers will react more favorably to prices ending in odd numbers. Prices ending with "95," such as $29.95, are common for merchandise selling under $50.

By adding extra service, warranties, or paying transportation costs, your firm may sometimes effectively lower price without incurring the retaliation of lower prices by competitors with no volume gains.

DETERMINING YOUR CHANNEL(S) OF DISTRIBUTION

A marketing channel is the pipeline through which a product flows on its way to the ultimate consumer. The choice of channels of distribution is not a simple one, but is important, as shown in these examples.

A small firm manufactured perishable salads, which were sold direct to retail food stores. The salads required frequent delivery and close control to ensure freshness. The company diversified into two new lines: pickles and jelly. The manager selected the same marketing channel for these lines as for the salads. Because sales increased at the stores, expansion was necessary. As pickles and jelly had a longer shelf life, they could have been put into a separate, less expensive channel of wholesalers and chain warehouses.

A small manufacturer added an infant cereal to its product line, and selected its existing marketing channel of drug stores.
Problem: Consumers considered cereal as a food item and bought it at food stores.
Solution: The manufacturer started using food brokers as a channel.[8]

Design Your Own Channel of Distribution

Channels should be tailor-made to meet the needs of your firm. For example, in order to obtain regional or national coverage of its products, a company may find it productive to use distributors or manufacturers' agents in conjunction with its own sales force.

Factors to Consider. You should establish a distribution plan that includes these factors:

1. Geographical markets and consumer types arrayed in order of importance.
2. The coverage plan: whether distribution will be effected through many outlets, selected outlets, or exclusive distributors.
3. The kind and amount of marketing effort expected of each outlet.
4. The kind and amount of marketing effort you, the manufacturer, will contribute.
5. Policy statements concerning any areas of conflict.
6. Provision for feedback information.
7. Adequate incentives to motivate resellers.

---

[8] Richard M. Clewett, "Checking Your Marketing Channels," *Management Aids for Small Manufacturers, no. 9* (Washington, D.C.: Small Business Administration. 1963), p. 38.

New products commonly require different distribution channels from those needed for products which are well-established and widely accepted.

> A company started selling its new high-priced germicidal toilet soap through drugstores and prestige department stores. When consumer acceptance made the soap a staple, the company selected food stores.[9]

A company may have new markets for its products, and new marketing channels may be required.

> A pneumatic drill manufacturer originally sold directly to the mining industry.
> *Problem:* The volume of sales and profitability were inadequate.
> *Solution:* The manufacturer selected distributors who were able to cater to the construction market.

> A paint manufacturer selected hardware and paint stores, its existing channel of distribution, to distribute a new household floor wax.
> *Problem:* The new product was reaching only a small part of the potential market.
> *Solution:* The manufacturer switched to food stores as the channel.[10]

If you are a manufacturer, your ultimate outlets should be willing to work with you on product promotion. You may arrange cooperative advertising with your dealers to share promotion costs. You should specify in advance criteria for selection of outlets and apply them.

Another problem a manufacturer may face is whether to ship directly from the factory or establish regional warehouses. The latter will provide more rapid service, but likely at higher inventory-carrying costs. However, transshipments between warehouses may permit lower inventories.

Avoid Multiple Channels.   Multiple distribution channels sometimes create conflicts. Distribution can be adversely affected unless these conflicts are resolved.

> A manufacturer introduced a ladder attachment and selected a large mail-order house as the channel.
> *Problem:* The company was incurring high costs by shipping small quantities to many points.
> *Solution:* The manufacturer attempted to distribute the attachments through hardware stores.

---

[9] Ibid.
[10] Ibid.

Results: Hardware stores refused to sell the attachments, because the greater discounts provided the mail-order house left them unable to compete.

In contrast, the manufacturer of do-it-yourself wood-working equipment selected a large mail-order house as the sole channel for a definite period of time. The manufacturer planned to sell through its customary channels later.[11]

When to Change Your Channel

Changes in buyers' locations may dictate a change in marketing channels. Changes in concentration of buyers may also require a change in marketing channels. Because of the rapid growth of markets in the far west and southwest, many manufacturers have stopped using agents and started selling directly to wholesalers and distributors.

The need to change your marketing channels may be revealed through examining the following indicators:

1. Shifting trends in the types of sources from which consumers or users buy.
2. Development of new needs relative to service or parts.
3. Changes in the amount of the distributors' profits.
4. Changes in policies and activities of each type of outlet according to customer types and areas, inventory, and promotion advertising.
5. Manufacturer's own organization relative to change in financial strength, higher or lower sales volume of existing products, and changes in marketing personnel or organization.
6. New objectives concerning customer groups and marketing areas.
7. Items of new products.
8. Changes in competitors' distribution plans.

ADVERTISING, MERCHANDISING, AND SALES PROMOTION

Advertising and sales promotion activities are important for you to consider. Too many owners of small businesses advertise merely to see their names in print, which is an expensive "ego trip."[12]

Advertising

Advertising is used to inform your customers of the availability of your products or services and the uses they can make of them, and

---

[11] Ibid.

[12] Gardiner H. Greene, *How to Start and Manage Your Own Business* (New York: McGraw-Hill Book Company, 1975), p. 157

to convince customers that your products are superior to your competitor's. In order to be successful, advertising should be based upon your firm's providing quality workmanship and efficient service. It should be closely related to changes in your customers' needs and desires. Rather than spend the money available on a random unplanned basis, you should establish an advertising program.

Types of Advertising. The types of advertising are *product* and *institutional.* The first term is self-explanatory, but the latter pertains to the selling of an idea regarding your company. The purpose of institutional advertising is to keep the public conscious of your company and its good reputation. The majority of small business advertising is of the product type. Determinants of the type of advertising are:

1. The nature of the business.
2. Company objectives.
3. Industry practice.
4. Media used.

Developing Your Advertising Program. Your advertising programs should be of a continuous nature. One-shot advertisements that are not part of a well-planned program are usually ineffective. All funds allocated for advertising should usually not be spent on a single medium. The proportion of your advertising budget allocated to each medium will be determined by the nature of your market.

> The owner of three laundromats, which were clean, well-maintained, and had a few loyal customers, could not increase the volume of sales in one of them.
>
> Prior advertising practice was to advertise in newspapers on a one-shot basis every four months at a high expense. Money was wasted because most newspaper readers lived outside the marketing area of the problem unit.
>
> A new advertising plan was tried. Three successive mailings of handbills were sent to potential customers in the immediate vicinity of the problem unit. The desired volume in this unit was soon reached.

On the other hand, noncontinuous advertising could be used to prepare your customers to accept a new product, to suggest to them new uses for established products or to bring to their attention special sales.

The question of *when to advertise* is very important for your business. Advertising media should reach—but not overreach—your present or desired market. Generally, you will have many media available, but you should choose those that will provide the greatest return for your advertising dollar. You should determine whether your advertising and sales promotion will be used to back up your sales representatives or used in place of them. To back up the representative, the ad should "pave the way" so that your company and product are well known.

You should develop an *advertising budget,* a plan for the outlay of funds for advertising. Standard advertising ratios for your line of business or type of industry are effective guides. *Advertising expenditures* vary with:

1. The type of product.
2. The location, age, and prestige of your firm.
3. The extent of its market.
4. The media used.
5. The current stage of the business cycle.
6. The amount of excessive advertising by your competitors.

If the advertising budget is set as a percentage of sales, then the less your company's sales, the less effective the advertising will be when it is needed most. On the other hand, diminishing returns may be realized from your advertising.

Your *advertising policy* may also govern the amount spent for advertising given products.

Advertising should be truthful and in good taste. An advertising agency may be invaluable in designing your firm's advertising program, evaluating and recommending advertising media, attempting an evaluation of the effectiveness of different advertising appeals, performing design and art work for specific advertisements, advising on sales-promotion problems, furnishing mailing lists, and making market-sampling studies to evaluate product acceptance or area sales potentials. Suppliers and trade associations may also be beneficial in the performance of these activities.

When and How to Use An Advertising Agency.   Most small business owner-managers plan and execute their own advertising programs, particularly when they consider the rather high costs of retaining the services of an advertising agency.[13] Often this practice is false economy, however, since significant differences exist between materials prepared by professionals and those prepared by amateurs.

Before considering the use of an advertising agency, you should recognize that most of the money spent for advertising goes to newspaper publishers, and that most newspaper advertising is developed by skilled persons within the newspaper organization.

The following aspects of using an advertising agency are covered below: definition and functions of advertising agency, evaluating agen-

---

[13] See Frederic R. Gamble, "How Advertising Agencies Help Small Businesses," *Management Aids for Small Business Annual no. 2* (Washington, D.C.: Small Business Administration, 1958), for more information on this subject.

cies, selection of agency, agency-client contract, and achieving an effective agency-client relationship.

Functions of Advertising Agencies.   Advertising agencies are organizations of skilled advertising specialists with experience in serving successful business firms in many different industries. Such an agency can help by:

1. Doing a preliminary study and analysis, including
    a.   Making a study of your product or service to determine its advantages and disadvantages relative to competitors' offerings.
    b.   Analyzing your present and potential markets concerning location, season, trade and economic conditions, and nature and amount of competition.
    c.   Studying your distribution channels—wholesalers, dealers, contractors, sales representatives, and so forth.
    d.   Evaluating advertising media that can profitably be used to distribute your product to your customers and distribution channels.
2. Developing, implementing, and evaluating your advertising plan, including
    a.   Developing and presenting for your approval an advertising plan.
    b.   Designing, writing, and illustrating your advertisements.
    c.   Contracting for the advertising space in its own name.
    d.   Writing or obtaining the program and the commercial copy.
    e.   Putting advertisements into appropriate form and forwarding them to the media with proper instructions.
    f.   Arranging for performers to present your message on the air.
    g.   Contracting for advertising time.
    h.   Supervising actual production of program or commercial.
3. Following the appearance of your advertising,
    a.   Checking and verifying insertions, display, or broadcast.
    b.   Handling auditing, billing, and paying for the service and for the space or time.

An advertising agency will also coordinate its work with your other sales activities to insure the greatest effect from the advertising. And if you wish, it can also help you (usually for a special fee) in areas such as package designing, sales research, sales training, preparations of sales and service literature, designing, merchandising displays, preparation of house organs, and public relations and publicity.

Evaluating Agencies.   Advertising agencies are listed in the National Standard Advertising Register and in classified telephone directories. You should find that interviews with business acquaintances, advertising management representatives, media representatives, and trade publications and associations will be helpful in evaluating agencies. You may also consider a third-party approach in evaluating agencies. This approach involves retaining a management or advertising consultant to make the initial contacts.

You should also interview representative clients of several of the agencies. A key question is: What proportion of its advertising success was attributed to its agency's performance? Also, past clients can indicate reasons why they changed agencies.

Agencies that survive the interviewing process are ready for a formal presentation to you and your management. This presentation should consist of:

1. Agency materials designed to show its ability to meet your needs.
2. Agency reaction to the set of standards of performance suggested by you for the advertiser-agency relationship.
3. Agency reaction to the method of compensation suggested by you.

You may request advertising agencies to conduct preliminary research, submit a speculative advertising plan, or create a speculative advertising campaign for your products. These activities may be performed at shared cost, covering direct expenses incurred, or possibly subsidized by you.

In these ways, you should locate bona fide advertising agencies that are qualified to give you the advertising counsel you need.

Selection of Agency.   After you cull the list to only one agency, you should investigate whether it meets these basic qualifications:

1. It should be a bona fide, independent operation, free from undue control by any one advertiser, in order to avoid prejudice or restriction in its service to you.
2. It should be free from control by a medium owner, so that it will give you unbiased advice in the selection of media.
3. It should keep all commissions allowed by media (i.e., not rebate any) and devote them to the service and development of advertising specified in its media contracts.
4. It should possess adequate personnel with the experience and ability to serve your needs.
5. It should be financially able to meet obligations it incurs to media owners.

The size of the agency is less important. You may select a smaller one, believing that it may give you more attention and have smaller overhead costs. You may find it practical to use a local agency because of convenience and the reputation of its personnel. Or, you may need the greater staff and specialization of a large agency.

The Agency-Client Contract. The terms of the contract, or letter of agreement, should be clear, understood, and in writing. Contracts should include at least these four points:

1. Term.
2. Scope of services that the agency will perform.
3. Agency's billing terms—for all forms of advertising, materials and services purchased, and special services performed.
4. Rights and duties of agency and your company if contract should be terminated, including handling of unfinished work and uncompleted contracts.

The people who produce the agency's advertising are important. You should answer the following two questions about them in the affirmative:

1. Are they good?
2. Are they given the freedom to produce the items of which they are capable?[13]

Achieving an Effective Agency-Client Relationship. A productive relationship with the agency requires mutual confidence and a free exchange of information. The agency's understanding of your needs and wants is critical to the success of the relationship. You should take the initiative in specifying requirements and continually obtaining a clear understanding and acceptance of them.

The client should pay the agency promptly in order that it may meet the media's due dates. The two percent cash discount, allowed by most media to stimulate prompt payment, is given to the client when he earns it by paying the agency promptly. The agency is not responsible for the failure of media or suppliers to fulfill their commitments.

Such a relationship is based upon the following principles:

1. The agency will not concurrently handle a product that is directly competitive with yours.
2. You will not engage the services of another agency without the first agency's consent.
3. The agency will secure your approval on all advertising expenditures.
4. You will pay the agency at the medium's published rate, and the agency will retain commissions allowed by the media.

You also need to agree on compensation. The basic methods of compensation may include:

1. Media commission.
2. Media commission subject to a minimum fee.

---

[13] Greene, *How to Start and Manage Your Own Business,* p. 163.

3. Media commission plus percentage charges, retainer fee, incentive fee, as well as new product development, testing, and commercialization fees.

The agency needs to know how its performance will be evaluated—that is, by sales results and/or reaching advertising objectives. It also expects product and company information and knowledge of company objectives, marketing strategies, and the role of advertising.

You should instill in your employees a full understanding of the collaborative relationship with the agency. The latter should be regarded as having a peer relationship with your company.

Copy strategies should be the result of team effort and mutual agreement. These strategies refer to what is stated in the advertising and to whom it is addressed. You know more about your products and their uses, strengths, and limitations than anyone else. You should help the agency to understand this information and match product benefits with consumer needs.

You should regularly and systematically review with the agency its work and tell it where it stands. Evaluation sessions should be held with agency management to identify strengths, outstanding performance, and troubles—if any. These evaluations should lead to mutually agreed upon courses of action designed to improve the relationship and agency performance.

If your company becomes a small account for your agency, you may find that you are not receiving the attention that you need. In that event, you should start looking for a new agency.[14]

Measuring the Results of Advertising. Measuring the results of your advertising—by comparing sales with advertising—is important. Assume that you are the owner of a small retail firm and you desire to determine whether your advertising is doing the job that you intend it to do. Before the advertisement is composed, you should answer this question: "What do you expect the advertising to do for your store?" You should divide your advertising into two kinds: *immediate response* and *attitude* advertising. The purpose of immediate response advertising is to entice the potential customer to buy a particular product from your store within a short period of time—today, tomorrow, the weekend, or next week. This type of advertising should be checked for results daily and at the end of one week, two weeks, and three weeks for appearance. The carry-over effects of advertising are the reason for checking after the first week.

Attitude or "image-building" advertising is the type you use to keep your store's name and merchandise before the public. You continually remind people about your regular products or services or inform them about new or special policies or services. This type of advertising is more

---

[14] Ibid., p. 162.

difficult to measure, because you cannot always attribute a specific sale to it. You can measure some attitude advertising, such as a series of ads about your store's brands, at the end of one month from the ad's appearance or at the end of a campaign.

Your success in measurement depends upon how well the ads have been planned. These pointers are pertinent in planning your ads:

1. Identify your store completely and clearly.
2. Select illustrations that are similar in nature.
3. Select a printing type face and stick to it.
4. Develop easily read copy.
5. Use coupons for direct mail advertising response.
6. Get the audience's attention in the first five seconds of a television or radio commercial.

> For example, a retail monument dealer used a regular TV spot to advertise a $133 monument. Few customers came to purchase that item, but the advertisement proved to be a successful traffic builder for higher-priced items.

In using radio spots, saturation or blitz may prove to be successful techniques. Radio stations usually have a special package of spot rates, for example, 70 spots in seven days. Alternating between saturated coverage and prime-time spots is economical and effective.

You should consider using these tests for immediate response ads:

1. Coupons to be brought to your store.
2. Letter or phone requests referring to the ads.
3. Split runs by newspapers.
4. Sales made of the particular item.
5. Checks on store traffic.

Record keeping is essential in testing attitude advertising, because you want to compare ads and sales for an extended time. You may make your comparisons on a weekly basis.

When ads appear concurrently in different media—newspaper, radio and television, direct mail pieces, handbills—you should try to evaluate the relative effectiveness of each.

Measuring the results of advertising is imprecise because of many complicating factors, including the time element, other forces affecting the customers' behavior, changing business conditions, and changes in competitors' advertising.

Merchandising and Sales Promotion

Merchandising denotes the promotional effort made for a product or service in retailing firms, especially at the point of purchase. It includes window displays, store banners, shelf stickers, the label and package of the product, product demonstrations, giving samples, bill stuffers, and special price offers.

Sales promotion consists of activities that have the purpose of making your other sales efforts (e.g., advertising) more effective. Some of the more popular techniques are:

1. Creating special displays.
2. Offering premiums.
3. Running contests.
4. Distributing free samples.
5. Offering free introductory services.
6. Demonstrating products.

It may be directed toward ultimate consumers, the trade, and sales representatives.

If you become a retailer, you may consider using promotions, stamps, "two for the price of one," and premiums to obtain new customers. However, you should determine whether they are really effective or are merely reducing your profits. Your window and counter displays should be changed frequently to help bring the merchandise to your customers' attention. Some manufacturers and wholesalers advise on store layouts and personnel training programs, provide free advertising mats, provide short training courses for sales personnel, and maintain a staff of sales engineers to assist in solving customers' problems.

If you are a manufacturer, you may consider trade shows as an advertising and sales promotion medium. These shows are particularly beneficial when your buyers are widely scattered geographically and when significant innovations in equipment are being made each year.

Your sales representatives should be furnished good sales kits, up-to-date promotional materials, and catalogs. If you are selling two or more products, you should decide whether to promote them jointly or separately.

Every promotional activity should integrate or mesh with every other activity. To illustrate, if you are advertising a certain item, reinforce the advertising by devoting window displays, points of purchase, and direct mail to it. Customers need several reminders before they act.

SUMMARY

In this chapter, we have tried to provide you with some how-to-do-it marketing strategies. Some specific information was provided to help you with your market research and sales forecasting. Several sources of data were mentioned, including published and unpublished material. Concerning advertising and sales promotion, the subjects covered were the types of advertising, the timing of advertising programs, budgeting for this purpose, and measuring the results of advertising.

Personal selling, channels of distribution and logistics, pricing, and the marketing mix are covered in the next chapter.

QUESTIONS FOR FURTHER DISCUSSION

1. What are three areas of marketing research that small business managers should consider?
2. List the steps in market research.
3. Describe briefly sources of market information.
4. What are the benefits of sales quotas in a small company?
5. Give three kinds of information that can best be answered by interviews with a company's customers and distributors.
6. What are three values of analyzing a company's records in performing market research?
7. Describe briefly the stages of a life cycle of a product.
8. Cite three factors that should be considered in setting price strategy.
9. A product costs $16 and the markup is $8.00. What percentage of the sales price is this markup?
10. Define price-lining.
11. Define a marketing channel.
12. Cite three indicators that may be examined to determine whether changes are necessary in marketing channels.
13. What is the use of advertising in a small company?
14. Define institutional advertising.
15. Cite four factors that affect advertising expenditures.
16. Give four types of assistance rendered small companies by advertising agencies.
17. Define sales promotion.

17

Selling Your Product or Service

This chapter on personal selling continues the discussion of the how-to-do-it marketing strategies begun in the previous chapter. It deals with the use of agent middlemen—as well as your own sales force—to sell your product(s) or service.

In spite of all your efforts spent in doing market research, sales forecasting, and advertising and sales promotion, someone ultimately must do some personal selling of your products or services. If you are a manufacturer selling to wholesalers or jobbers, retailers, or industrial users, you should decide whether to use your own sales force or sell through agent middlemen. Without these middlemen, small manufacturers or companies with limited lines would have difficulty competing in the market.

SELLING THROUGH AGENT MIDDLEMEN

Typically, a new manufacturing firm starts as a local or regional operation seeking sales in a limited market. Since it has a small amount of capital, it usually utilizes existing agent middlemen. If the firm succeeds, it may expand to new markets, again probably working through middlemen.

Sometimes, a sequential plan for distribution is adopted by a new manufacturing firm. Having a limited product line and limited finances, the manufacturer may gain access to a geographically dispersed market by using the full-service wholesaler. With growth in financial stability, capabilities, and product line, the manufacturer may move to a limited use of wholesaler services or to a selling agent, or broker, in selected areas. Later, contractual arrangements may be established with manufacturers' agents. Ultimately, the firm may develop its sales force and set up branches. The manufacturer's control over sales increases as this sequence progresses.

Brokers

A broker represents either the buyer or, usually, the seller in negotiating purchases or sales without physically handling the goods. Each broker usually specializes in a limited number of items and sells by description or sample. The broker possesses only limited authority in setting prices and terms of sale. After the sale is arranged, the seller ships the goods directly to the buyer. The broker's commission—usually 1 to 5 percent of sales—is received from the principal who sought the broker's services.

Each transaction of a manufacturer with a broker is considered completely apart from every other one; no obligation exists to maintain a continuing relationship. Firms using brokers are usually buyers and/or sellers of highly specialized goods and seasonal products not requiring constant distribution. Smaller canners, for example, often use brokers.

Selling Agents

The selling agent performs on the basis of an extended contract and negotiates all sales of a specialized line of merchandise or the manufacturer's entire output. Usually the agent has full authority concerning prices and terms, is the sole seller for the line represented, and is not confined to a given market area. Some agents even provide working capital to the manufacturer.

Under this arrangement, the small manufacturer shifts most of the marketing responsibility to an outside organization and can concentrate on production and other nonmarketing problems. The agent advises the manufacturer on styling and design and often carries out sales promotion and advertising—usually on a straight commission.

The manufacturer should recognize the risks involved in yielding too much bargaining power to the agent. The agent may engage in price cutting instead of devoting sufficient effort to selling the manufacturer's output. The manufacturer may also become financially obligated to the agent.

Selling agents are found primarily in the marketing of textiles but also sell coal, lumber, metal products, and canned food. New, highly technology-oriented companies sometimes use sales agents, but the highly speculative nature of their unproven products often dictates contractual requirements highly favorable to the agents, particularly if market success is realized.

Manufacturers' Agents

The manufacturers' agent (or representative) is an independent business person who sells a part of the output of two or more client manufacturers whose products are related but noncompeting on a continuous, contractual basis in a limited or exclusive territory. Manufacturers' agents are used more often than any other type of agent middlemen.

The agent does not take title to the goods, is paid a commission, and has little or no control over prices, credit, or other terms of sale.

Characteristics of Manufacturer Using Manufacturers' Agents. The firm that uses manufacturers' agents usually has one or more of the following qualities.[1]

1. It is financially weak having sufficient resources for production but not for maintaining its own sales force.
2. It produces a single product—or a narrow line of products—on which revenue is insufficient to support its own sales force.
3. Its sales force handles its major product line, which serves an established market, but entrusts the agent with an item designed for a different market.
4. It has its own sales force operating profitably in concentrated territories but wishes to expand to areas where expected sales volume does not warrant use of company sales representatives.
5. It finds the administrative problems of maintaining a sales force to be troublesome and undesirable.
6. It wants to retain primary control of distribution policy while shifting some selling to others.
7. It desires to maintain rigid control of selling costs.
8. It desires rapid establishment of regional or nationwide distribution.

Characteristics of Product Handled by Manufacturers' Agents. The product handled by this type of agent usually:

1. Is being introduced by a new manufacturer, and the manufacturers' agent can lend his or her prestige to the product.
2. May not be handled by wholesale merchants satisfactorily because the latters' salespeople cannot provide some specialized service the product requires.
3. Requires sales personnel with considerable technical knowledge.
4. Involves long periods of negotiating or completing a sale, and the

---

[1] Thomas A. Staudt. *A Managerial Introduction to Marketing*, 2d. ed. (Englewood Cliffs, N.J.: Prentice-Hall, 1970), pp. 364–70.

manufacturing firm desires to avoid large presale costs and expenses of its own sales force.

Characteristics of Market Served by Manufacturers' Agent.   The market most effectively served by manufacturers' agents usually:

1. Is too small to support a manufacturer's own sales force.
2. Is distant, making sales cultivation too expensive.
3. Is thin, with a few geographically dispersed customers and prospects.
4. Is marked by relatively infrequent sales to individual customers, but close contact with them is desirable to avoid possible loss of orders.
5. Is somewhat seasonal, but continuous representation is conducive to sales.

Selecting the Agent.   In making its selection, the small firm should try to select an agent who meets the following criteria:

1. His or her product lines are limited to the extent that aggressive representation may be achieved.
2. Each product within his or her line is closely related to the others.
3. The price and quality of each line handled are compatible.
4. He or she has similar or identical territories for all products so that maximum trade cultivation and continuous representations of all client manufacturers are possible.

The small manufacturer should learn a great deal about the operations of each available agent. No basic conflict should exist between the manufacturer's and agent's distribution policies.

Sources of Information about Prospective Agents.   The small manufacturer can obtain information regarding manufacturers' agents from several sources, including classified ads in trade papers whose readership is geared toward the type of agent sought; editors or sales representatives of trade magazines; and trade associations of manufacturers' agents. Examples of these associations are the Materials Marketing Associates, Inc., which represents principals who market chemical materials and equipment to the chemical industry; and the Manufacturers' Agents National Association (MANA), which includes agents for all types of goods and services, from costume jewelry to foundry facilities, that are sold throughout the United States.

Many small manufacturers learn about and maintain an up-to-date file on potential outlets through direct inquiries from manufacturers' agents who express interest in handling their product lines.

Questions to Be Asked.   Questions that the small manufacturer should pose in selecting a manufacturers' agent are:

What sort of selling skills are necessary for selling our products? Does an agent need technical knowledge and experience in addition to personal selling ability? What marketing functions, if any, does our company need in addition to selling? Must the agent service our product as well as sell it? Is a one-person agency or a larger organization needed? If the latter, how large? What is the agent's record of success in products and territories similar to our company's? How long has the agent been in business? What is his or her reputation and how well can our company trade on it? Will the other lines carried by the agent be compatible with ours? Will the agent's contracts for its existing lines help gain entry for our line? Is the trade the agent specializes in the one our company wants to reach? Does the agent cover the geographical area needed and in what depth? Are the character, personality, values, and integrity of our two organizations compatible? Is the agent the type that merely follows instructions? Does the agent have a reputation for offering constructive suggestions? Which type of agent does our company need? Will we enjoy working together?

Contracts and Advance Preparation. The manufacturer should have a comprehensive contract in writing with its agent. The contract usually includes: definition of relationship; territory and coverage; products to be sold; sales policy; prices, terms, customer credit responsibility; product warranties; invoices; collections; cancellations; change orders; returns; commissions and methods of computation and division; servicing obligations of factory and representatives; sales aids; and rights of principal and representative upon consummation and termination of the contract.

Policies to Consider in Managing an Agent. The small manufacturer should consider these policies: training, merchandising aids and support, commissions, and relationships with agent.

Training. Following appointment, arrangements should be made by the manufacturer to have the agent spend enough time at the plant to obtain a thorough knowledge of the product, manufacturing processes, company policies, and the marketing program. The training period should be brief (because the agent cannot afford to be away from his or her own business very long) and should be planned and conducted with care.

Merchandising Aids and Support. Agents should be supplied with adequate tools to operate effectively. Display stocks, swatch or sample books, other promotional aids, and market data should be integrated with the agent's operations. Engineering and sales assistance should be made available when necessary. Manufacturers should solicit suggestions from agents about the most effective methods of merchandising and make a sincere effort to honor any reasonable requests from them for information, records, and other data.

Commissions. Adequate commissions should be established both to attract high-caliber agents and to promote aggressive representation. Straight commissions of about 6 percent, with a range of 2 to 20 percent, depending on the sophistication of goods, are usually paid.

Relationships with Agent.   Before and while an agent is operating in the field, the manufacturer should try to build an environment of mutual confidence, cooperation, and integrity. The manufacturer should state sincerely that permanent agent representation is anticipated. The manufacturer should keep in personal touch with its agent and develop a friendly personal relationship, but without burdening the agent with too much detail.

Evaluation of Manufacturers' Agent's Performance.   The performance of your agent should be evaluated periodically. Standards of performance should be developed and measurement techniques devised. Sales quotas may be established for each territory, product line, and customer group. Actual performance can be evaluated by continuous examination of orders, invoices, and reseller inventories. Other indices are: reseller and ultimate consumer satisfaction, quantity and quality of advertising performed, promptness in paying bills, and amount of new business acquired.

Risks of Dealing with Agents.   One authority points out that some agents are too powerful for the good of their small company clients.[2] He stresses these disadvantages from the client's viewpoint:

1.   Since the agents have control of sales, they attempt to influence company policy, prices, personnel, and so forth.
2.   The client assumes the credit risk.
3.   The client's investment in sales samples, particularly if there is nationwide distributions, can be high.
4.   The new company begins with the inexperienced representatives of the agent; but when these reps become successful, they substitute large clients for their small original ones.
5.   The top agents may have become order takers and represent the customers rather than the client company. They may also concentrate on their other lines.

USING YOUR OWN SALES REPRESENTATIVES

Having your own sales representatives will require the greatest investment. Yet, in the case of a highly specialized, technical product, this course will probably be most effective.

Selecting Your Sales Personnel

One potentially good source of good salespersons is those who call upon you. You can look them over and watch them in action. If you

---

[2] Gardiner G. Greene, *How to Start and Manage Your Own Business* (New York: McGraw-Hill Book Company, 1975), pp. 129–31.

advertise for them, avoid the "We want" approach. Rather you should use the "We have an unusual opportunity for" approach. Prospective salespersons want to know how you can fulfill their needs. Since good salespersons are hard to find, you may have to overlook some things in hiring them. A mutually agreeable probationary period (perhaps six months to a year) should be set.

You should be wary of the following situations in evaluating applicants as possible sales persons:

1. If they have been recently separated or divorced, there may be too many adjustments to make.
2. If they have held too many jobs (three or more) in the last five years, they may be "floaters."
3. If there are gaps in their employment record.
4. If they have been involved in a recent business failure.
5. If they have had no previous sales experience.
6. If their income has not shown steady advancement.[3]

Some Techniques for Effective Use of Sales People

Effective selling should be built upon a foundation of product knowledge. The sales representative who understands the product's advantages, uses, and limitations can educate the potential customer and may be able to suggest new uses of the product.

The critical part of personal selling is the sales presentation to the prospect. A sales representative should adapt the sales approach to the customer's needs and meet every objection. Enthusiasm, friendliness, and persistence are valued traits of a successful sales representative. A "hard-sell" approach is sometimes advocated for intangible products and services, such as life insurance.

A decision should be made whether your sales representatives should be assigned to industry, government, and institutional customers, or assigned by product classification.

Your firm's sales force should be organized on the basis of decisions regarding these features:

1. Number of accounts per representative and average account size.
2. Compensation plan—salary, commission, salary plus commission, salary plus commission with bonus—and method of payment of expenses.
3. Cost of obtaining new accounts versus the cost of holding old accounts. This comparison determines the amount of time a representative should spend servicing certain-sized accounts.

---

[3] Ibid., p. 131.

4. Use of overlapping or exclusive territories.
5. Orientation of sales representatives as specialists in one of your products or lines, or as generalists who will handle your entire line.

Specialists are easier to train and are more effective in their fields. One generalist representative per customer may be less confusing. A small group of high-quality, highly paid representatives may be preferable to a larger number of less competent representatives. Owner-managers of small businesses often find that only a few customers account for a major proportion of total sales

> The owner of a company distributing supplies to an industrial market analyzed the firm's accounts, and found that 2 percent of the customers accounted for half the total sales and more than half of the gross profits. More than 90 percent of the customers were small, and accounted for less than 10 percent of the sales. An analysis of representatives' call reports showed that they were spending most of their time on the small accounts and that many big accounts with good sales and profit potential were neglected.[4]

Through analysis of your sales records, you may find which products should be promoted, which products should be carried even though their profit margin is small, which products should be dropped, which territories are overstaffed or understaffed, and which customers are profitable.

You should provide for continuous or special training programs for your representatives and hold regularly scheduled meetings with them each year. *Contests* tied into promotions, which stimulate representatives several times a year, are often desirable. The effectiveness of contests may be improved when the rewards include benefits for the representatives' spouses. A guide for improving a representative's performance is presented in the appendix at the end of this chapter.

Need for Harmonious Working Relationships

Your sales organization should be working closely and cooperatively with the manufacturing department. The representatives' delivery promises and production's capabilities and willingness should be matched. Good working relationships between your sales organization and market research should also exist.

You should determine whether your sales organization should place its best representatives in the most lucrative markets to compete with your top competitors, or seek untapped markets. Efficient routing of

---

[4] Warren R. Dix, "Getting Facts for Better Sales Decisions," *Management Aids for Small Manufacturers, no. 12* (Washington, D.C.: Small Business Administration, 1966).

your traveling representatives and the making of appointments prior to their arrival are cost-saving practices that should be adopted.

Your representatives can maximize profits by emphasizing high-margin items. But they should look beyond the immediate sale to build customer good will and to help create satisfied future customers. *High ethical standards are vital.*

In determining whether to enter a territory, you should make a comparison of incremental costs and incremental income. You should drop a territory when its cost contribution exceeds its income contribution.

Either you or one of your top executives should support a representative when he is experiencing difficulties in obtaining a big account. Preferably, he should initially seek and request your assistance. Your representatives should be given an opportunity to be trained and promoted into management positions.

You should utilize sales reports, and stress major facts and trends rather than details. Reports show all variances between budgeted and actual sales. You should immediately investigate all excessive deviations upward or downward in order to find their causes. Long-term sales contracts should have protective escalation clauses incorporated in them, particularly under inflationary conditions.

You should check the progress of every new salesperson within 90 days. If the new representative is not producing half of what you realistically expected, you should consider terminating him or her.

To assist your sales manager in managing your sales force effectively, you should consider using the following techniques or forms: job descriptions for salespersons, market evaluation reports, lost sales reports, product service reports, and sales performance evaluations.

SUMMARY

The material in this chapter has covered the subjects of selling through middlemen and your own sales representatives.

Agents described were brokers, selling agents, and manufacturers' agents. Because of their dominance, the latter agents were emphasized. Their selection, contracts with them, policies in managing them, and evaluation of their performance were covered.

Personal selling by your own sales representatives was also described. The importance of product knowledge, the sales presentation, the sales strategy, training, support and assistance, and sales reports was stressed.

QUESTIONS FOR FURTHER DISCUSSION

1. Describe an appropriate selling (distribution) practice of a new manufacturer.

2. Differentiate a broker from a selling agent.
3. Cite three characteristics of a manufacturer using a manufacturers' agent.
4. What criteria for selection should a manufacturer's representative meet?
5. Describe policies that the small manufacturer should consider in managing an agent.
6. Cite three valued traits of a successful sales representative.
7. What are three components of a basic sales strategy in a small company?
8. Cite three benefits obtained from analysis of a company's sales records.
9. Describe Management by Objectives (MBO) as applied to a sales representative.

APPENDIX: GUIDE FOR IMPROVING A SALES REPRESENTATIVE'S PERFORMANCE[1]

One goal in measuring a representative's performance is to create improvement. The three steps in bringing about improvement are *planning*, *measuring*, and *correcting*.

Planning

Get the representative's agreement about goals to be attained or exceeded in the next year:

1. Total profit contribution in dollars.
2. Profit contribution in dollars for each major product line, each major market (by industry or geographical area), and each of 10–20 target accounts (for significant new and additional business).

Get the representative's agreement about expenses for the next year:

1. Total sales expense budget in dollars.
2. Budget for travel, customer entertainment, telephone, and other expenses.

Have the representative plan the number of calls to accounts and prospects during the next year.

Measuring

Review at least monthly the representative's record for: (1) year-to-date progress toward the 12-month profit contribution goals, and (2) year-to-date budget compliance.

---

[1] From Raymond O. Loen, "Measuring the Performance of Salesmen," *Management Aids for Small Manufacturers no. 190* (Washington, D.C.: Small Business Administration, 1972).

Correcting

Meet with the representative if the record shows a variance of ten percent or more from target. Review the number of calls, plus major accomplishments and problems. In addition, you may need to help the representative in these ways:

1. Give more day-to-day help and direction.
2. Accompany the representative on calls to provide coaching.
3. Conduct regular sales meetings on subjects the representatives want covered.
4. Increase sales promotion.
5. Transfer accounts to other representatives if there is insufficient effort or progress.
6. Establish tighter control over price variances allowed.
7. Increase or reduce selling prices.
8. Add new products or services.
9. Increase the financial incentive.
10. Transfer, replace, or discharge representatives.

18

Some Related Marketing Activities

This last marketing chapter covers some of the problems involved in setting up sales territories and assigning marketing responsibilities for them, planning and controlling the activities of your sales people, and the marketing mix.

SETTING UP SALES TERRITORIES

Small firms can improve their marketing performance by carefully analyzing and controlling their selling activities, especially through assigning specific salespeople clear responsibility for definite territories. Consequently, you and your managers should consider setting up sales territories and establishing routing schedules for your sales representatives.

Why Have Territorial Assignments?

Besides the broad objective of controlling sales operations, more specific objectives would include:

1. To attain a thorough coverage of the market.
2. To assign each sales representative a reasonable overall task to perform.
3. To place definite responsibility on each sales representative.
4. To provide management with a valid criterion for judging sales representatives' performance.

5. To reduce sales expenses by eliminating duplication of effort and by obtaining more effective coverage of territories.
6. To facilitate the budgeting of sales expense and performance of distribution cost accounting.
7. To improve relations with customers.

Assigning Market Responsibilities

Several methods may be used to assign market responsibilities to your sales representatives. One procedure, used frequently by companies having small sales organizations, is to permit sales representatives to handle a personal list of customers. Every salesperson retains the accounts which he/she has obtained and contacts them regardless of their location. When a new salesperson is hired, he/she obtains new accounts wherever they can be found.

After a time, however, your salespeople would follow routes that resemble a poorly designed spider web. Once this method becomes established, it becomes difficult to shift to another approach. Adopting another system of assigned territories disrupts working relationships between sales representatives and customers, endangers the morale of the sales organization, and frequently results in the loss of both customers and salespeople.

A preferable way of handling field assignments from the beginning is to make each sales representative responsible for a particular geographical area. Each salesperson is then responsible for obtaining his/her full share of the potential business in that territory. Appropriate sales quotas and cost controls can be set up by territory. Each salesperson understands the selling problems peculiar to that area.

Some Guideposts You Can Use. Five guideposts that should be observed for setting up territories are:

1. Keep territory size practical.
2. Plan efficient sales-call routes.
3. Use established geographical boundaries—wherever possible, using political or census areas.
4. Group territories by trading areas.
5. Design territories for equal potential.

Steps in Setting up Sales Territories. There are seven principal steps you should follow in establishing sales territories for your firm. They are:

1. Secure information on the distribution of sales by states, counties, metropolitan centers, or trade areas for each product or product class. For example, estimates of total retail sales by metropolitan county areas and by ten store groups (food, lumber, hardware, drug, and so forth)

are made by *Sales Management* annually and published in its June issue, "Survey of Buying Power."

Actual sales data for products and product classes may be secured from the decennial census, U.S. Department of Commerce; trade associations; and other sources. With knowledge of actual past sales by territories, you can prepare an index showing the proportion of total sales made in each territory.

An alternative is to develop an index of potential demand. *Sales Management* prepares annually a "Buying Power Index" by counties, metropolitan areas, and principal cities. Even though this index does not pertain to particular products, the buying power potential for either a state or a county may be determined. For example, a particular county might be expected to take 2 percent of the total sales of a product. These data can be applied to either an estimate of total industry sales or to your company's sales. To illustrate, using a basis of past industry sales and an analysis of business conditions, if the estimate of total sales for the next year is 200,000 units, or $100 million, the county could be expected to take 2 percent, or 4,000 units, or $2 million.

2. Determine, on the basis of past experience and strength of competition, the percentage of potential sales that your company can expect to obtain in each territory. These percentages, when applied to potential industry sales, should provide you with estimates of potential sales for your firm. For example, if it is estimated that you should receive 10 percent of total industry sales in the country, the amount would be 400 units or $200,000 in sales.

A different method—securing individual estimates in terms of physical and dollar units from sales representatives or branch managers—may be used. These estimates are combined to derive an industry sales forecast, company sales forecast, or both.

3. Pinpoint on a map the location of customers and/or potential customers. The latter should be classified in terms of their relative importance. Often it is unnecessary or undesirable to call on all customers every trip.

4. Determine how many calls can be made, on the average, in one day. A rather detailed study of the sales representative's job, covering activities and time, should be made. Travel time required for each call should also be included.

5. Group the customers into logical territories. Start at some geographical point, preferably a major trading center. Fulltime services of one person or even of several people may be needed in a large city.

6. Beginning with the city, bring together contiguous counties that constitute either a complete trading area or an appropriate portion of it. Large sales territories may consist of sections of several cities. Small territories usually include a number of counties around the trading cen-

ter. About 230 metropolitan areas—Standard Metropolitan Statistical Areas (SMSA)—now exist in the United States.

One of the published trading area studies could be used. These studies are maps of the United States on which trading centers are shown, together with boundaries of their trading areas. The studies are of two types: wholesale trading areas and consumer or retail trading areas. Several kinds of trading-area maps are available; for example, the U.S. Department of Commerce has analyzed wholesale trading areas for groceries and dry goods, and the National Wholesale Druggists Association has outlined wholesale areas for drugs. Consumer trading maps are exemplified by "Market Areas in the United States," published by Curtis Publishing Company; "Consumer Trading Areas," published by Dartnell Corporation, and "The New Marketing Map of the United States," published by Hearst Magazines, Inc.

7. Each territory should be rechecked in terms of the total business expected and problems of physical coverage. In determining total potential business available in a given territory, the following publications should be consulted: County Business Patterns; *Sales Management's* "Survey of Buying Power"; the U.S. Census of Business, U.S. Census of Population, and the U.S. Census of Housing; and *Survey of Current Business*.

In addition to past sales and sales potentials, other factors that should be considered include:

1. Variation in product.
2. Extent of market development.
3. Channel of distribution.
4. Nature of the work assigned.
5. Competition.
6. Caliber of sales staff.
7. Changes in business conditions.
8. Possibilities of specialization.

Setting Definite Routes

Should definite routes be set for sales personnel or should they be free to route themselves? Usually no clear-cut answer exists to this question. Salespeople should be consulted about routing patterns, and they should be satisfied that the schedule is workable. Field experience, including the selling job to be done, the call frequency, the ability to follow a regular route, and the caliber of the salespeople will be important. If calls are made irregularly, and if the sales representatives are primarily trouble shooters or service people, a fixed routing schedule probably would have little value. Routing schedules are most useful when calls are regular and frequent and when relatively little time needs to be spent with each customer.

Companies that sell to retailers often make good use of a routing pattern. Firms selling to manufacturers and wholesalers find these patterns less valuable.

The first step in routing consists of making a list of customers, together with the frequency of calls on them. The average length of a call is determined for either each customer group or for each individual customer. Routes are then constructed to cover an area efficiently.

Routes should be tested and revised until both you and your salespeople believe that they are the best that can be developed. They should be followed; reports should be filed by the sales representatives and checked by the sales supervisor.

The owner-managers of many small companies ask their salespeople to plan a route for each trip in advance, make the necessary arrangements for it, and adhere to it rather than following the above procedure.

The Territory Agreement

To assist your sales manager and salespeople in increasing the effectiveness of their sales planning, you may consider using a "territory agreement." The components of the agreement are usually: (1) preamble; (2) specification of markets and customers; (3) specification of products and services; and (4) specification of current targets and objectives.

Since this agreement signifies a contract between the employer and the sales representative for an extended period, it is usually written in semilegal terms. The salesperson should be asked to read the document carefully and sign it.

THE MARKETING MIX

You should develop a marketing mix. Four basic variables in this mix are the "four Ps":

1. Product.
2. Place.
3. Promotion.
4. Price.

The right *product* for the target market should be developed. *Place* refers to the channels of distribution. *Promotion* refers to any method that communicates to the target market. The right *price* should be determined to move the right product to the right place with the right promotion for the target market.

The manufacturer of a line of good-quality costume jewelry sold to retail jewelry stores. The owner wanted his company to grow faster. The company had been advertising in monthly trade magazines, using no sales representatives but employing order-takers, attending trade shows, and having good services, pricing, and packaging.

Owner's Study: Company sales volumes for each area of the country were examined over a three-year period. The southeastern area sales were lagging.

New Marketing Mix: Advertising outlays were reduced in the southeastern area. A sales representative was hired for this area.

Results: Sales in the southeastern area began growing more rapidly than in any other area of the country. The sales representative concentrated her efforts on retail jewelry stores that had the largest growth potentials.

Next Phase: Different types of point-of-purchase displays and advertising mats for retailers were developed. More sales representatives were hired.

Results: Sales doubled in two years and continued to increase substantially.[1]

After developing an integrated marketing strategy, you should check it by getting affirmative answers to these questions:

1. Are all marketing activities—market research, personal selling, advertising and promotion, distribution, and pricing—directed toward selling the same product and product image?
2. Are trade-offs made so that each activity contributes the same net marginal benefit? For example, if money is taken away from the sales organization to be used in market research, are profits likely to fall? Have priorities been established in the use of personal selling, advertising, sales promotions, packaging, and pricing within limits dictated by the volume of sales needed and funds available for the marketing program?
3. Are programs, budgets, and schedules prepared at regular intervals (yearly, quarterly, and so forth)?

SUMMARY

The material in this chapter has covered the subjects of setting up sales territories, planning and controlling the activities of your sales people, and the marketing aspects of your business.

---

[1] Harvey C. Krentzman, *Managing for Profits* (Washington, D.C.: Small Business Administration, 1968).

QUESTIONS FOR FURTHER DISCUSSION

1. Cite three specific objectives of territorial assignments.
2. List three guideposts that should be observed for setting up territories.
3. Cite the seven principal steps that should be followed in establishing sales territories.
4. What are three components of the territory agreement?
5. Cite the four basic variables in the marketing mix.

WHERE TO LOOK FOR FURTHER INFORMATION

Cornwell, Arthur W. "Sales Potential and Market Shares." *Small Marketers Aids no. 112.* Washington, D.C.: Small Business Administration, 1972.

Dix, Warren R. "Getting Facts for Better Sales Decisions." *Management Aids for Small Manufacturers no. 112.* Washington, D.C.: Small Business Administration, 1966.

Dutka, Solomon. "Using Census Data in Small Plant Marketing." *Management Aids for Small Manufacturers no. 187.* Washington, D.C.: Small Business Administration, 1972.

Feller, Jack H. "Keep Pointed toward Profit." *Management Aids for Small Manufacturers no. 206.* Washington, D.C.: Small Business Administration, 1972.

Goodpasture, Bruce. "Danger Signals in a Small Store." *Small Marketers Aids no. 141.* Washington, D.C.: Small Business Administration, 1970.

Grubb, Kenneth. "Are Your Salespeople Missing Opportunities?" *Small Marketers Aids no. 95.* Washington, D.C.: Small Business Administration, 1970.

Krentzman, Harvey C. *Managing for Profits.* Washington, D.C. Small Business Administration, 1968.

Lang, John B. "Finding a New Product for Your Company." *Management Aids for Small Manufacturers no. 216.* Washington, D.C.: Small Business Administration, 1972.

Lewis, Edwin H. "How to Set up Sales Territories." *Management Aids for Small Business, Annual no. 3.* Washington, D.C.: Small Business Administration, 1958.

Lipson, Harry, and Darling, John R. *Introduction to Marketing.* New York: John Wiley, 1971.

Loen, Raymond O. "Measuring the Performance of Salesmen." *Management Aids for Small Manufacturers no. 190.* Washington, D.C.: Small Business Administration, 1972.

McCarthy, E. Jerome. *Basic Marketing.* 6th ed. Homewood, Ill.: Richard D. Irwin, Inc., 1978.

Murdick, Robert G., et al. *Business Policy: A Framework for Analysis.* Columbus, Ohio: Grid, 1972. Credit is given to these authors for the approach used in developing this chapter, and for many of their ideas included in it.

Schabacker, Joseph C. *Strengthening Small Business Management.* Washington, D.C.: Small Business Administration, 1970.

Schwartz, Irving. "Personal Qualities Needed to Manage a Store." *Small Marketers Aids no. 145.* Washington, D.C.: Small Business Administration, 1970.

Small Business Administration. *Why Customers Buy (and Why They Don't).* Washington, D.C.: Small Business Administration, 1972. (Administrative Management Course.)

Sorbert, Elizabeth. "Measuring the Results of Advertising." *Small Marketers Aids no. 121.* Washington, D.C.: Small Business Administration, 1972.

Staudt, Thomas A. *A Managerial Introduction to Marketing.* 2d ed. Englewood Cliffs, N.J.: Prentice-Hall, 1970.

Wikman, Allan, Jr. "Marketing Ideas Make or Break a Company." *Marketing Insights,* January 19, 1970.

cases for part V

V–1   Selecting a Profitable Market[1]

Operating an independent business involves many unsuspected pitfalls. The market opportunity that seems to offer the greatest unit volume sales may not always provide a proportionate share of profits.

James Bard had always wanted to be the owner of an independent business. He had tried a number of ventures, with varying degrees of success. Since the area where he lived was famous for its country hams, James concluded that a commercial country ham business, based on local curing methods, should produce a product with a substantial demand. After checking with nearby university food science experts on methods of curing, packaging, and so forth, and visiting similar operations in nearby states, he obtained the necessary equipment and began processing hams. It soon became apparent that fresh hams for processing should be obtained from one of the national meat packing concerns in order to assure an adequate supply and an appropriate uniform size range.

As soon as the meat was cured and ready for marketing, James began calling on independent grocery stores and general independent wholesale grocers, as well as buyers for some of the major regional supermarket chains. In his calls, James presented the potential customer with sample 12-ounce vacuum-packed slices of country ham.

From the start, the market response was favorable. In a few months,

---

[1] Prepared by Curtis E. Tate, Jr., University of Georgia.

the dominant regional supermarket chain began placing substantial orders for the 12-ounce vacuum-packed ham slices.

Since James was process plant manager, ham buyer, and salesman, time did not permit adequate attention to the preparation of monthly profit and loss statements. As he began to get things under control and had more time to give consideration to the profitability of the business, he soon became aware that while the desired sales volume had been achieved, an adequate profit margin had not. After further consultation with his grocery customers, James concluded his business could survive profitably only if sales to this group were stopped. He had learned that sales to restaurants and other special customers could be made on a profitable basis. The sales volume would absorb the existing capacity, but would not necessitate an additional capital investment.

QUESTIONS FOR DISCUSSION

1. Evaluate James' method of entering business.
2. What does the case show about introducing a new product?
3. What effect does location have on product choice?
4. Should he discontinue sales to his grocery customers? Explain.

V–2   Clearview Optics[1]

The Clearview Optics Company was a producer and seller of sunglasses. Its main competitor was the Not-Brite Eyewear Company. These two firms were dominant in the industry, although there were several smaller producers and there was competition from imports. Together, Clearview and Not-Brite accounted for 70 percent of the industry's sales.

Clearview's prices ranged from $2.50 to $10, and the product line included a clip-on model for prescription glasses. Not-Brite's prices ranged from $5 to $15, and its line also included a clip-on model, which sold for $0.50 less than Clearview's. The products of both companies had polarizing lenses; however, Not-Brite had gained a large advantage in the market by naming its line after the process of treating the lenses. The average consumer generally did not know that Clearview's products had polarizing lenses.

---

[1] Prepared by Robert L. Anderson, University of South Florida.

Clearview sold through the traditional manufacturer-wholesaler-retailer channel of distribution. The company had attempted to establish itself in every type of retail outlet where the consumer would expect to find sunglasses. In addition to the salesmen who called on the drug wholesalers, the firm employed representatives whose responsibility was to contact the retailers at regular intervals to promote Clearview Glasses, check the merchandise racks for out-of-stock condition, and to take orders, which were forwarded to the appropriate drug wholesale house.

The company recently engaged an advertising agency, which developed a television campaign centered on "the many moods of sunglass wearers." The main idea of the campaign was that different styles can change the mood of an individual.

The company had also attempted to use "push-money" as a promotional tool. It offered sales representatives of the drug wholesalers "push-money" to promote its sunglasses to retailers. The company representatives also traveled with the drug wholesaler's own representatives to help familiarize the retailers with the Clearview product line.

John Jones, a senior marketing major at a large southern university, had been employed by Clearview for the summer as a representative. John was 21 years old and had a well-groomed, professional appearance. He worked with Clearview for the summer in the university's co-op program, which allowed students to attend school while gaining valuable experience working for a company. John expected to graduate in one year and was considering going to work for Clearview full-time after graduation.

John's superiors were Mr. Smith, the regional manager in Atlanta, and Mr. Jones, the vice president of marketing in New York. For purposes of supervision and direction, John reported to Mr. Smith in Atlanta.

After a month on the job, John visited one of his marketing professors and said that he was having difficulty selling and promoting Clearview glasses to the retailers. Asked what seemed to be the problem, John stated that the retailers said that "they just don't want to handle Clearview glasses when they can sell Not-Brite." John's usual response was to explain to the retailer that Clearview recently had committed more than a million dollars to a consumer advertising campaign, and further that there was no significant difference between the products of Clearview and Not-Brite, since they both had polarizing lenses.

The following are some of the retailers' comments to John:

> "I have a pharmacy to run and I don't have time to talk to customers about sunglasses."
>
> "I handle too many items to be concerned with just pushing one item."
>
> "Why should I take time to promote your sunglasses when the customers come into my store asking for Not-Brite's?"

"Not-Brite's sell themselves; I don't have to bother with them."

"The previous salesman was too young and dressed too wildly. He didn't even know what my customers are like."

"My customers are older and they want a brand they can trust."

"My customers are older and are not concerned with the 'mod' styles you offer. They want sunglasses for eye protection."

"The Not-Brite Company will swap me good movers for non-movers at no penalty. Clearview will not do this."

John said he often made a sale of 10 to 15 dozen pairs of open stock glasses to replenish a retailer's display rack, but they were never delivered by the wholesaler. Such inaction left the retailer in an "out-of-stock" position, and that in turn created a great deal of ill-will against the Clearview Company.

Asked why the glasses were not delivered after they were sold, John said the drug wholesalers did not want to be bothered filling small, open stock orders from Clearview when they could sell whole racks of the Not-Brite brand. John went on to say that the wholesalers wanted to carry only one company's open stock and that they preferred to carry the Not-Brite brand because it had a faster turnover.

When asked why he did not send his orders direct to the factory, John said the factory would not ship this type of order because they did not want to get involved in the wholesaling function.

John further explained to his professor that he had attempted to obtain information from his superior in Atlanta about Clearview's advertising campaign and had been rebuffed with the comment, "I don't know why we advertise as we do. That's not my job; my job is to sell the product and so is yours."

John recognized some of the problems that he was experiencing in his new job but felt that he had no place to obtain information to help him solve his problems. If he did circumvent the chain of command to point out some of the problems or try to obtain information, he could lose his job.

QUESTIONS FOR DISCUSSION

1. If Not-Brite has capitalized on the polarizing feature of their lenses, why doesn't Clearview also do it in their promotional program?

2. Should the company continue to use "push-money"? Is the practice ethical?

3. Do the promotion and distribution programs complement each other?

4. Should the company attempt to by-pass the wholesaler and sell directly to the retailer?

5. Is it possible to use a more selective method of distribution and eliminate the small retailers?

6. If you were John, would you circumvent established lines of authority to suggest changes in the marketing program to the vice president of marketing?

7. Should Clearview revise its price structure?

V–3   Reach-a-Lamp[1]

The Raymond Johnson Manufacturing Company was formed in Oklahoma City in 1972 to produce and market the Reach-a-Lamp, a device or tool for changing fluorescent and Slimline lamp tubes. Although other devices for this purpose were on the market in several areas, the Reach-a-Lamp, designed and patented by a friend of Mr. Johnson's, was described by Mr. Johnson as easier to operate, more versatile, and more capable than the somewhat unsatisfactory competitive changers. Disappointed with sales results after several months of distribution, Mr. Johnson, a general construction contractor, was studying actions that might be taken.

Constructed of lightweight aluminum, the Reach-a-Lamp consisted of a long shaft with a crossed T "hand" at the upper end. At each end of the "hand" were two rubber-covered "fingers," which could be controlled by the operator through manipulation of levers at the lower end of the shaft. One lever was about one foot from the lower end of the tool. When depressed by the operator's left hand, it caused a chain linkage through the shaft to close the "fingers" firmly around the lamp. Another lever at the lower end of the tool was manipulated by the operator's right hand. It turned the "fingers" to rotate the lamp and remove it from the socket. An attachment that could be added equipped the Reach-a-Lamp to remove and replace the starters found in many lamps. The "fingers" could also grip a sponge or dust cloth for cleaning the lamp and fixture surfaces. In addition, the tool was capable of removing and replacing a number of the diffusers and louvers that covered many types of fixtures. In two lengths, six-foot and eight-foot, the tool could be used on fixtures up to about 14 feet above the floor.

One maintenance man equipped with the Reach-a-Lamp could service

---

[1] Prepared by Dennis M. Crites, University of Oklahoma.

many times more fixtures than before, and could replace the two men and ladder normally required for lamp-changing. The tool permitted changing lamps above machines and desks without an interruption of work, as might be necessary if a ladder were used. The manufacturer portrayed the tool as making lamp-changing faster, safer, less expensive, and less of an interruption. Supermarkets, department stores, offices, and factories where fluorescent or Slimline lamps were used in quantity were seen as markets where the Reach-a-Lamp could be effectively used.

Before setting up for production, Mr. Johnson contacted a number of manufacturers' agents and representatives, calling mainly on electrical goods wholesalers. Agents in several key areas were contacted and agreed to distribute the tool whenever production was begun. A display of the Reach-a-Lamp was also set up at the National Lighting Exposition in New York. High interest in the tool was displayed by many of the manufacturers, distributors, contractors, and dealers in attendance at the exposition; a number of the visitors attempted to place orders. Names of the interested persons were taken in order that they could be contacted when production was started. Based on this reception and distribution prospects, Mr. Johnson concluded a royalty agreement with the inventor and arranged to begin production.

A building large enough for production operations was secured at a rental of $150 monthly. Dies and machinery required an expenditure of over $15,000; materials for production of the first lot of about 1,000 tools resulted in an additional $4,000 outlay. A work force of 10 persons was recruited, and production was begun at a rate of about 200 tools per week. Royalty payments were $1.38 per tool sold.

Manufacturers' representatives were obtained to carry the line in nine territories covering most of the area from the Atlantic Coast to the western plains region. Carrying noncompeting electrical goods lines for a number of different manufacturers, these representatives called on most of the leading electrical goods wholesalers in the territory they covered. At times, they might also make calls upon industrial buyers and purchasing agents. They received a commission of 20 percent of the selling price. Through the services of a local advertising agency, catalog price lists, instruction sheets, and advertising folders were prepared. (See Exhibit 1). Over 20,000 mailings were made to electrical supply houses, grocery chains, and a selected list of manufacturing companies. New product news releases were sent to leading journals and papers serving the electrical goods trade, including *Maintenance, Southwest Electrical,* and *Contractors Electrical Equipment.* Descriptive announcements of the product appeared in several of these publications.

Retail or user prices were set at $27.50 each for the six-foot tool and at $29.50 for the eight-foot model. Wholesale discounts were established at 40 percent for lots of one to 24 and at 50 percent on larger quantities.

EXHIBIT 1
Front and Back of Advertising Folder

Shipments of one to 24 were designated as F.O.B. factory while larger shipments inside the U.S.A. were shipped prepaid.

After several weeks of distribution, sales were running far below the rate of production. Representatives reported a number of difficulties. The length and shape of the device made it somewhat awkward for salesmen to carry, yet customers were reluctant to purchase without seeing the tool and observing it in operation. Some interested firms found that some of their lamps or fixture diffusers were of a type that could not be serviced by the Reach-a-Lamp. Some of the representatives failed to follow-up on the leads that were sent to them by Mr. Johnson,

EXHIBIT 1 (*continued*)
Inside of Advertising Folder

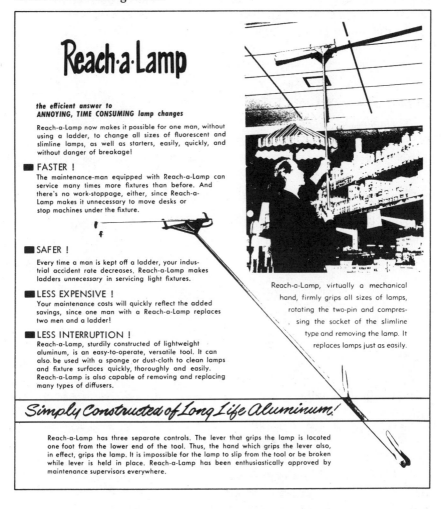

Reach·a·Lamp

the efficient answer to
ANNOYING, TIME CONSUMING lamp changes

Reach-a-Lamp now makes it possible for one man, without using a ladder, to change all sizes of fluorescent and slimline lamps, as well as starters, easily, quickly, and without danger of breakage!

■ FASTER !

The maintenance-man equipped with Reach-a-Lamp can service many times more fixtures than before. And there's no work-stoppage, either, since Reach-a-Lamp makes it unnecessary to move desks or stop machines under the fixture.

■ SAFER !

Every time a man is kept off a ladder, your industrial accident rate decreases. Reach-a-Lamp makes ladders unnecessary in servicing light fixtures.

■ LESS EXPENSIVE !

Your maintenance costs will quickly reflect the added savings, since one man with a Reach-a-Lamp replaces two men and a ladder!

■ LESS INTERRUPTION !

Reach-a-Lamp, sturdily constructed of lightweight aluminum, is an easy-to-operate, versatile tool. It can also be used with a sponge or dust-cloth to clean lamps and fixture surfaces quickly, thoroughly and easily. Reach-a-Lamp is also capable of removing and replacing many types of diffusers.

Reach-a-Lamp, virtually a mechanical hand, firmly grips all sizes of lamps, rotating the two-pin and compressing the socket of the slimline type and removing the lamp. It replaces lamps just as easily.

Simply Constructed of Long Life Aluminum!

Reach-a-Lamp has three separate controls. The lever that grips the lamp is located one foot from the lower end of the tool. Thus, the hand which grips the lever also, in effect, grips the lamp. It is impossible for the lamp to slip from the tool or be broken while lever is held in place. Reach-a-Lamp has been enthusiastically approved by maintenance supervisors everywhere.

who was receiving several dozen mail inquiries weekly in response to the publicity and advertising released.

Mr. Johnson made a number of sales calls himself and found that demonstration of the Reach-a-Lamp almost invariably aroused interest on the part of those who saw it work. Sales were difficult to close, however, and in a number of instances, the representative was referred to someone else in the firm who had more knowledge or authority in the purchase of equipment for lighting maintenance. Some persons were enthusiastic about the need for a tool of this sort. As one electrical contractor expressed it, "This is something for which the lighting industry has had a real need for years." Other persons who might be customers saw the tool and admitted its ability and advantages, but believed that their existing method of handling lamp-changing was sufficient for their needs. For example, some supermarket operators contracted their entire lighting maintenance with electrical service contractors. Others had clerks or stock-boys change the lamps after the store was closed.

QUESTIONS FOR DISCUSSION

1. Would the favorable comments and reactions about Reach-a-Lamp indicate better sales than those attained?
2. Was there really a need for the Reach-a-Lamp on the part of the users visualized as markets by Mr. Johnson?
3. If you were a salesman selling the Reach-a-Lamp, on whom would you call?
4. How would you evaluate Mr. Johnson's choice of sales representatives?

V–4   Graham's Pet Food[1]

The Pet Food Institute reported that dog and cat food sales in the United States, including canned, dry, semi-moist, and snacks, had grown at a rate of about 10 percent per year from 1962 to 1970. Sales had risen from $600 million to $1.16 billion. Of the $1.16 billion market, canned dog food accounted for 36 percent of the sales and canned cat food accounted for 20 percent.

Canned dog and cat food sales had increased from $354 million in 1965 to $680 million in 1970. Canned pet food sales in the Pacific Northwest, primarily Oregon and Washington, were about 1.4 million cases, with a value of $8.4 million.

A National Can study predicted that by 1979 the dollar volume for all pet foods would reach $2.1 billion, an increase of 91 percent over 1970. Volume grocery products were expected to increase only 19 percent in the same period.

It was estimated that in the United States about 54 percent of the households owned a dog, cat, or both. In the western states, ownership of cats and/or dogs was higher than the national average. In addition, the 1969 Brand Rating Index showed that western families used about

---

[1] Prepared by Louis C. Wagner, University of Washington.

40 percent more canned pet food on a per-household basis than the United States as a whole.

COMPETITION IN SEATTLE-TACOMA MARKET

The one dog food canner in the Seattle-Tacoma market produced a quality product in the medium-priced field that retailed for 22–28 cents a can in 1973. In Portland, Oregon, there were four pet food canners. In California, the San Francisco Bay area had four, and the Los Angeles area had six pet food producers. Most of these firms shipped their brands or supplied private brand products that were sold in the Seattle-Tacoma market. Some of these producers packed a canned product aimed specifically at dogs, while others attempted to appeal to both dog and cat owners.

In spite of the fact that several national brands were heavily advertised, two regional brands, "Blue Mountain" (Portland) and "Tyrells" (Seattle) led in local popularity. Exhibit 1 shows the sales of canned pet food by brand in the Seattle-Tacoma market for 1973.

EXHIBIT 1
Dog Food Sales by Brands: Seattle-Tacoma Market, 1973

Brand	Percent	Brand	Percent
Blue Mountain	20	Kal Kan	4
Tyrell's	17	Ken L. Ration	3
Skippy	15	Recipe	2
Vets	10	Others	2
Friskies	10	Private Label	8
Alpo	9		

In 1973, about 40,000 cases of private label dog food were sold in the Seattle-Tacoma market. Most of this dog food was produced by California canners. The only Seattle producer, Tyrells, was not interested in producing a private-label product.

There were three quality levels of canned dog food sold—economy, medium-grade, and high-meat. In addition, a few plants packed economy and medium-grade dog food in large 26-ounce cans as well as in the more popular 15-ounce size. The volume of dog food by these varieties in the Seattle-Tacoma area, as well as prices at which these varieties were sold, is shown in Exhibit 2.

In the economy line, two California firms producing Vets and Skippy dominated the market. In the medium-price field, two regional brands, Tyrell's and Blue Mountain, led the market. Although competition was increasing in 1973, Alpo secured over two thirds of the high-meat segment.

EXHIBIT 2
Volume of Canned Dog Food by Types: Seattle-Tacoma Market, 1973

Size and Type	Price, Cents per Can	Percentage of Volume
15-oz. Economy	15–16	25.0
15-oz. Medium grade	22–28	42.0
14-oz. High meat	31–38	13.0
26-oz. Economy	27	7.0
26-oz. Medium grade	34–37	5.0
15-oz. Private label (economy)	14	8.0
26-oz. Private label (economy)	23	

GRAHAM'S PET FOOD

A Seattle resident, Mr. Graham, who had extensive experience in the canned food industry and had worked for canning companies with a dog food line, believed that there was a good opportunity for a new high-quality dog food producer in the Seattle area. After considerable experimentation with varying dog food formulas, he developed and tested three qualities of dog food that he believed were ready to be introduced to the consumer market in the Pacific Northwest. All three grades were used by a number of kennels raising and boarding dogs in the Seattle area. He received excellent reactions from kennel owners, and had several letters from them endorsing his product. In both the economy and medium-grade fields, Mr. Graham was using 25 percent more meat products in his dog food than were his competitors. This additional meat made the product more appealing to the pet as well as to the owner.

Mr. Graham believed that locating in the Seattle area would provide him with advantages over other packers shipping into the Seattle-Tacoma market. Freight per case from Oregon producers amounted to 15 cents, and California producers paid about 40 cents to ship their products to the Seattle area. In addition, there were adequate supplies of low-cost raw materials, particularly meat by-products and grain. Some Oregon and California producers obtained meat by-products in the state of Washington to fill their needs.

GRAHAM'S MARKET MIX OBJECTIVES

Mr. Graham planned to adopt the following market mix:

1. Introduce three qualities of dog and cat food in the Pacific Northwest.
    For My Love—economy pet food
    Town N'Country Ration—medium-grade pet food
    Town N'Country Super Ration—a 100 percent meat product

2. Introduce beef, pork, liver, and chicken flavors in the economy and medium-priced varieties.
3. Pack pet food in the economy and medium-priced varieties in the 26-ounce (large) can as well as the more popular 15-ounce size. No regional brands were packed in the larger size.
4. Obtain a portion of the local private label business, which was being supplied entirely by out-of-state firms.
5. Push the economy and medium-priced pet food as suitable for cats as well as dogs.

By providing a complete product mix—three quality grades, two can sizes, and private brands—Mr. Graham hoped to obtain a 10 percent penetration of the Seattle-Tacoma and Portland markets. Since the variety of his product mix would not severely dislocate any one segment of the market, he believed this strategy would preclude aggressive retaliatory moves by competitors already well established.

To assist in getting food stores to stock and push his line of pet food, Mr. Graham planned to offer retailers higher margins than competitors. Most manufacturers were providing retailers with margins of 18–28 percent, with 24 percent being most common. Mr. Graham planned to offer retailers margins of 36 percent for the 60-day introductory period and 28 percent later.

INTRODUCTORY OBJECTIVES

To secure sufficient volume to operate efficiently, Graham planned to introduce his line of canned pet foods in both the Seattle-Tacoma and Portland wholesale markets. He was considering allocating from $12,000 to $24,000 for the first year's promotion. Since the Seattle-Tacoma wholesale market had a population of 1.450 million compared with a little over 1 million for the Portland wholesale market, he was considering putting more of his promotional funds into the Seattle-Tacoma market.

QUESTIONS FOR DISCUSSION

1. Does Graham have a good opportunity to enter a field with several well-established national and regional brands?
2. Evaluate his proposed product and brand mix.
3. Should Graham attempt to introduce his pet food in both the Seattle-Tacoma and Portland markets at the same time?
4. Develop a promotional plan for a two-month introductory period in the Seattle-Tacoma area including
   a. Determine the level of expenditures needed for product introduction.
   b. Recommend a promotional plan and media mix needed for product introduction.

V–5   The Stair-Chair[1]

A wheelchair that would climb curbs and stairs has been the subject of inventors' efforts for decades. None has been really practical, and none has reached the market on a commercial scale. Excellent motorized chairs have been available for many years, and stairway-mounted elevators could be purchased to overcome a specific stairway barrier. However, the combination of a motorized chair that would permit paraplegics, quadriplegics, and others to overcome curbs, stairs, and other architectural barriers that deny those in wheelchairs much desired independence (from being assisted, chair and all, over these barriers) had not been developed.

Recently, Eugene Richison, an inventor from Kinta, Oklahoma, was discussing his patented design for such a chair with Gary Keel, owner of East Side Machine Shop in Broken Arrow, Oklahoma. Mr. Keel believed that such a product would be in great demand, and suggested that he could further refine the design and perhaps market the product from his shop. Mr. Richison shared Mr. Keel's faith in the invention, but was not certain he could devote the necessary time and money to its further development. Nevertheless, a patent assignment contract was worked out between them, and within another year Mr. Keel had a prototype model, called the Stair-Chair, ready for a public showing.

The first demonstration was for the Tulsa newspapers. The resulting feature story, complete with a picture of the Stair-Chair being maneuvered up a stairway by a pretty girl, produced a strongly favorable response. Mr. Keel's telephone rang frequently for the next couple of weeks with inquiries from individual wheelchair users and also from wheelchair manufacturers who wanted to purchase rights to manufacture the Stair-Chair, now covered by the original and subsequent patents. But Mr. Keel did not want someone else to manufacture the product; he wanted to do it himself.

At that point in the series of events, principals from a Tulsa firm beginning to diversify its investments suggested that their organization would be interested in a joint venture wherein they would provide the financial backing for producing and marketing the Stair-Chair. The offer was accepted by Mr. Keel, and two initial steps were agreed upon. First, a design and production feasibility study was undertaken by an outside consultant. The results were "very satisfactory"; the Stair-Chair received high marks as to sound design and performance capability. Next, a marketing forecast was requested. These results, summarized in

[1] Prepared by Howard A. Thompson, Eastern Kentucky University.

the Appendix, were also "highly encouraging" to Mr. Keel and to the investors.

Mr. Keel immediately began work on building nine of the now improved prototype models of the Stair-Chair. (See Exhibit 1 for a picture and description.) These were to be placed in strategic locations in order to gain actual experience under diverse operating conditions and also to gain approval of important centers of influence. A list of recommended locations was provided by the marketing study.

As with any complex product, ideas for further modification and improvement occur constantly. This was true of the Stair-Chair experience. For instance, the problem of transporting a heavy (185–200 pounds) motorized chair of this type was partially resolved in that it could now be folded to a height of 25 inches, permitting it to fit into the trunk of most "full-size" cars or into the rear of a station wagon. With the aid of a ramp it could be driven into the trunk of a car, eliminating the need to lift it. Actual running time had also been extended to 4½ hours (constant use) without a battery recharge. A plug-in battery recharge device was standard equipment on all models. Expansion of plant facilities permitted installation of a more efficient production line to replace the job-shop arrangement that was used to produce the nine prototypes. Actual layout and installation of the production line would be delayed pending results from tests of the nine Stair-Chairs, which would be completed in six months.

Mr. Keel engaged a consultant to design a marketing plan and budget for introducing the Stair-Chair following the test market. He was instructed to make the following assumptions:

1. The basic patent rights, good for 17 years, would not be successfully infringed or circumvented by any of the present wheelchair manufacturers such as Everest and Jennings. This assumption was based on a statement by a patent attorney engaged by Mr. Keel. The patented feature that was especially unique was the seat positioning device, which permitted the operator to remain seated vertically while the Stair-Chair climbed or descended.
2. Sufficient development and working capital existed for producing an initial inventory of Stair-Chairs and for a modest $25,000 promotional budget administered by a marketing manager and full-time secretary-assistant.
3. The sales goal was a total of 50,000 Stair-Chairs over the first three years of operation.
4. The estimated cost of producing the basic Stair-Chair with average accessory equipment (most orders would require some special fittings) was $650–750. Learning-curve experience was expected to

EXHIBIT 1

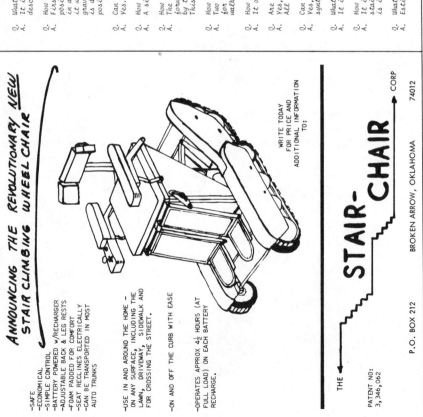

ANNOUNCING THE REVOLUTIONARY NEW STAIR CLIMBING WHEELCHAIR

- SAFE
- ECONOMICAL
- SIMPLE CONTROL
- BATTERY POWERED w/RECHARGER
- ADJUSTABLE BACK & LEG RESTS
- FOAM PADDED FOR COMFORT
- SEAT RECLINES ELECTRICALLY
- CAN BE TRANSPORTED IN MOST AUTO TRUNKS

- USE IN AND AROUND THE HOME – ON ANY SURFACE, INCLUDING THE LAWN, DRIVEWAY, SIDEWALK AND FOR CROSSING THE STREET.

- ON AND OFF THE CURB WITH EASE

- OPERATES APPROX 4½ HOURS (AT FULL LOAD) ON EACH BATTERY RECHARGE.

WRITE TODAY FOR PRICE AND ADDITIONAL INFORMATION TO:

THE STAIR-CHAIR CORP

PATENT NO: 3,346,062

P.O. BOX 212   BROKEN ARROW, OKLAHOMA   74012

Q. What is it?
A. It is an electrically powered wheelchair that is capable of ascending and descending stairs, both normal and circular.

Q. How does it climb?
A. First, a switch is provided to lower the seat (tilt backward) to a semireclining position. This is done for two reasons, the first being to place the occupant in a more comfortable position when ascending and descending the stairway; i.e., it would be a neat normal sitting position; and secondly it shifts the center of gravity backwards on the chair base, which is necessary for climbing. Climbing is done in reverse, descending is done forward. The occupant attains the same position climbing and descending.

Q. Can it cross a street?
A. Yes. It will climb normal height curbs forward and abnormally high curbs backward.

Q. How is it controlled?
A. A single switch to go forward, backward, right and left.

Q. How is it steered?
A. The chair is moved through two identical motor driven tread-belt mechanisms. In forward or reverse movement both belts move at the same speed. Steering is done by turning off the belt on the side of the direction you wish the chair to move. This is done automatically in high or low speed by the control switch.

Q. How fast does it go?
A. Two speeds. Slow for ascending and descending stairs and a second faster speed for movement under normal conditions. The faster speed is comparable to a normal walking pace.

Q. How does it run?
A. It operates by two electric motors powered by two 12 volt batteries.

Q. Are the batteries rechargeable and if so, how?
A. Yes, it can be recharged with a built in recharger to replenish one day's running. All it requires is 115 A.C. power source.

Q. Can it be used in the home?
A. Yes, it will pass through any standard 2 foot 6 inch door. It also has nonmarking synthetic rubber treads and wheels.

Q. What are the dimensions?
A. It is 25 1/2 inches wide and 45 inches long. It weighs approximately 185 pounds.

Q. How safe is it on a stairway?
A. It is so designed that complete loss of power will immobilize the chair on a stairway. Safeguards will be built in to permit climbing only when the chair is in a safe position.

Q. What will be the cost?
A. Estimated in the $1500 range.

reduce this cost to approximately $500 per unit after the first few thousand Stair-Chairs were produced.

5. Maintenance problems would be relatively simple and well within those that a dealer or regional service center could manage.
6. The Stair-Chair would not compete directly with regular or with other nonclimbing wheelchairs, but would be desired as a second chair.
7. The Stair-Chair would not be prices-sensitive within a reasonable range up to $1,500.

APPENDIX: SUMMARY OF MARKETING FEASIBILITY STUDY

Secondary Research of Market Potential

Estimate of population needing wheelchairs in the United States is 500,000. The annual sales of all types of wheelchairs are approximately 20,000. Wheelchairs in constant use require replacement or major overhaul about twice each year. Assuming that users are well pleased with the product, a conservative estimate of the United States market for this type of chair would seem to be 25,000 to 50,000 Stair-Chairs per year.

Statistics concerning the number of hospitals, nursing homes, retirement villages, and so forth, are not as meaningful as originally anticipated, because such centers are usually designed to reduce architectural barriers to the use of wheelchairs to a minimum. Therefore, the Stair-Chair would not offer significant advantages on the premises. Many of the larger hospitals, however, do have physical therapy departments where such a chair might be kept on hand to demonstrate its potential use to patients. Whether or not this is probable was not resolved. Even more likely would be the purchase of one or more Stair-Chairs for demonstration to potential users at rehabilitation centers. Often it is in such centers that the suggestion of a special type of prosthetic appliance is first made and the confidence in its use first acquired.

The Veterans Administration would likely be interested in evaluating the Stair-Chair for possible inclusion on the approved list of products that could be submitted to the VA in New York for their testing and approval, without charge. At least one year should be allowed for this procedure before approval could be obtained. Approximately 50,000 disabled veterans required wheelchairs in 1973.

A basic wheelchair without accessories can be purchased from $100 to $300. Accessories can double this cost. Motorized wheelchairs can be purchased in a range from $750 to $1,500. Eight firms list wheelchairs in *Thomas' Register*. The largest wheelchair manufacturer, Everest &

Jennings, produced 90,000 wheelchairs in 1970, according to a 1971 *Barron's* report. The entire industry produced an estimated 200,000 wheelchairs in 1972.

Results of Demonstration to an Invited Sample of Tulsa Area Residents

The statistics concerning airports serving scheduled airlines may become more meaningful than first anticipated. Respondents representing airlines (American, Braniff, and Continental) suggested that the Stair-Chair might be used .to load nonambulatory passengers in areas not having second-level loading bridges. Nearly every airport, regardless of size, has some passenger loading areas requiring boarding stairs. Airlines prefer to use their own passenger loading equipment rather than to use airport-owned equipment. The Stair-Chair would eliminate the frightening experience for non-ambulatory passengers of being carried by unfamiliar persons up and down the boarding stairs. Assuming the prototype placed with American Airlines is well received, a conservative demand by all airlines would appear to be 500 to 1,000 Stair-Chairs per year for this use.

Respondents representing various nonprofit organizations interested in the treating or rehabilitation of wheelchair users saw the Stair-Chair as overcoming barriers not negotiable with a regular or motorized wheelchair. Some wanted to be convinced further regarding specific points, such as maneuverability and fitting into the trunk of car (in spite of claim on advertising material).

Wheelchair users and their relatives were especially pleased with the Stair-Chair's mobility and the added independence from other architectural barriers and uneven outdoor terrain. They were quick to point out the need for many special fittings and accessories, not all of which have been anticipated by the inventors but that are not difficult to incorporate.

Miscellaneous Comments from Participants in Stair-Chair Demonstration

When asked where they would purchase wheelchairs, some thought they would purchase direct from the manufacturer. Institutional users possibly would want to purchase direct in order to obtain a lower cost. Some individuals also thought they would like to be able to purchase direct from the manufacturer. When questions of service, adjustments, parts, and so forth, were raised, some thought perhaps the chair should also be sold through a dealer, even though this would add 40 percent to the total cost. Dealers who attended felt that they could handle the chair without any conflict of interest. None of the dealers indicated a franchise agreement that would prohibit him from carrying this make of chair.

When asked how potential users would learn about a chair and decide to try one, almost everyone indicated that users would have to learn through the rehabilitation center. The endorsements of the rehabilitation center and of the Veterans Administration were considered important. Certainly the VA endorsements would be a requirement if they were to assist veterans by purchasing the chair for them. The endorsement and recommendation from the therapist, physiatrist, orthopedist, internist, and neurosurgeon were seen as important in inspiring the confidence of the prospective user of a chair. Therefore, it was believed essential that such chairs be available as training devices in physical therapy areas at hospitals and rehabilitation centers. The physical therapist would be the first contact at such centers. It was thought also that perhaps even the physical therapy department might assist the person in ordering the chair direct from the manufacturer or through a dealer.

When asked how one would learn of the Stair-Chair, they thought the center of influence—the therapist, physiatrist, etc.—would learn through sales representatives, journals, conventions, and publicity. The individual would probably learn through the *Paraplegic News* or *Accent on Living*.

QUESTIONS FOR DISCUSSION

1. What target markets should be reached first?
2. What is the consumer adoption process for those target markets?
3. Should the marketing plan be national or regional?
4. What channel(s) and price margins are appropriate?
5. What promotional strategy will reach the target markets selected?

V–6 Unique Lamps, Inc.[1]

Unique Lamps, Inc., was established in September 1974 to manufacture household goods. Management consisted of Mr. Jerry Fornay, president; Mr. Samuel Lytle, vice president; and Mr. Artis Satterfield, secretary-treasurer.

---

[1] Prepared by Lyle R. Trueblood, University of Tulsa.

Four months later they applied for a loan of $100,000 from a Tulsa bank, to be arranged by the Business Development Center of the Tulsa Urban League. The proceeds of the loan were to be used for manufacturing lighting fixtures.

BACKGROUND OF THE COMPANY

Messrs. Fornay, Lytle, and Satterfield each had over three years of successful sales experience in other fields. Mr. Satterfield had also served as operations manager for a materials handling equipment manufacturing firm for three years.

Mr. Fornay was artistic and engaged in creative photography in mid-1974. Deciding that the office walls of his photography shop needed a lift, he obtained some gunny sacks, mounted them in frames on the walls, and used them as background for sample portraits. His customers liked these creations and wanted something similar for themselves.

Mr. Fornay and Mr. Lytle toured old feed mills in the South and developed complete lines of products—lamps, pillows, aprons, wall decorations, and planters—using old original designs of feed and flour sacks.

Mr. Fornay then contacted an interior designer, who believed that these products had good market potential. The lines were taken to the Dallas Trade Mart, and though the market was slow, they were popular with retailers. Manufacturing of the products, except planters, was subcontracted for four months. In January 1975, in order to satisfy demand and to increase earnings, management decided to purchase materials in quantity, manufacture, and distribute lamps. Pillows, aprons, wall decorations, planters, and women's clothing were planned ultimately for production and distribution.

LAMP LINES

Three lines of lamps were manufactured and sold: Yesterday's Bag, New Collection, and "Le Gallery." Each of the lines had about 100 styles.

Management recognized that because of the coming Bicentennial, citizens were nostalgic and were eagerly seeking either antiques or replicas that reminded them of the "Good Old Days." The Yesterday's Bag line was based upon this nostalgic theme. Original designs from burlap and unbleached muslin feed and seed sacks were to be used. Many designs were taken from the late 1800s or early 1900s. Antique glass and art work were also characteristic of this line. Management believed that no other lamp manufacturer had comparable lines.

The New Collection line used a peppy, brightly colored material.

Traditionally, lamps and shades had been neutral, functional pieces, but this line made the lamp a focal point. Its bright colors and design could be coordinated with draperies, wall coverings, pillows, shades, and wall hangings.

The "Le Gallery" series featured original art work in five categories and, with the use of light, produced a striking art form. Because selected textile dyes were used, the colors were permanent. The line was offered as signed and numbered originals or unsigned copies. The number of copies of a single design was limited, a feature that increased the value and desirability of the pieces. This line was the highest priced. Custom work was also accepted at prices believed appropriate.

All of the lines were composed of swag and table lamps. Swag lamp shades used the larger feed and staple sacks. Table lamp shades used the smaller sacks in conjunction with components from the past, such as milk cans and glass jars.

MARKETING

Retailers of lighting fixtures in the United States numbered 50,000 and accounted for about $2 billion in sales annually. There were about 700 lamp manufacturers, including four large ones, in this country.

Unique's marketing plan called for Messrs. Fornay and Lytle to cover the United States, attempting to attract manufacturers' representatives who would sell the lines in their respective territories. Photographs and demonstrator samples were used extensively by the two entrepreneurs, who planned to display the lamp lines at major buyers' markets and trade shows, select and work with the "reps," and make direct calls on major potential accounts.

The marketing strategy specified that products would be changed every two years. The idea was to "hit the market hard," capture a large market share before competitors caught on, and then introduce a new line of products.

An article stressing the salability of these types of lamp lines was published in the trade magazine, *Lagniarre*. Through the assistance of a customer, the management hoped to get another article in another trade magazine for promotional purposes.

Unique's selling price was $27 for the Yesterday's Bag and New Collection lines (for payment within ten days, the price was $22 a lamp). The price range for "Le Gallery" was $28 to $36. Sales representatives received a 10 percent commission.

The company was scheduled to exhibit its products at the home furnishings shows in Los Angeles, Chicago, Atlanta, Dallas, and High Point and Charlotte, North Carolina. Manufacturers distributed to national retail outlets through these shows. In order for them to exhibit at these shows, they had to be represented by a sales organization or manufacturers' representative. The latter sold other products to retailers attending the shows and in their day-to-day calls to retailers in their areas throughout the year.

Unique Lamps had received several testimonial letters from retailers. Three of them are quoted below:

"I have just become aware of your lamp and swag line and find it most impressive. I hope you realize what you have with these ideas. If you market them correctly, you should sell thousands. The national markets could sell several hundred a day . . ."

"We've recently placed our first order of your unique lamp line, and I'm very excited about the potential in Louisville. Not only are the designs great, but the historical significance is a big factor in a state very much involved in its tradition. We are looking forward to a long and successful association."

"In our opinion the lamps are unique. We feel that they will be very much a conversation piece in any home. We are anticipating very good business from this fresh new look in swag lamps."

PRODUCTION

In manufacturing the lamps, all labor was being performed by Mr. Satterfield. However, as production increased, unskilled workers (women, students, etc.) were hired and trained. Efforts were made to obtain employees under the sponsorship of federal employment programs. It was anticipated that learning to operate the equipment would take about one day. One person could produce about 40 lamps a day. Using production line methods, two persons could produce 90 lamps a day. Mr. Satterfield estimated his labor cost at $2 a lamp.

Fabric materials used included burlap sacks, flour sacks, unbleached muslin sheets, and draperies. Other materials included polystyrene for the shade interliners, lamp bases, metal and ceramic-metal hoops, electrical cords and sockets, glue, tape, paint, etc.

Fabric materials were purchased from two manufacturers who had sufficient materials to meet Unique's production needs. Unique had adequate inventories on hand to produce 600 swag lamps and 600 table lamps.

Some machinery and lamp parts (bases, cords, etc.) were purchased from two lamp manufacturers who had recently failed. The two failures were caused by the collapse of the mobile home market and uncontrolled overhead. Mr. Satterfield evaluated the equipment as being simple, complete, and the best in Oklahoma for their business.

LOCATION

Unique Lamps operated at newly completed warehouse facilities in North Tulsa. The site was selected because of lower costs and availability of labor. The "image" factor was also important. Desiring an Indian and "Old West" image, management planned a Sequoyah street address, a Comanche post office box address, and a picture of an Old J Rig oil well. A picture of the rig, in conjunction with the street and mailing address on the company's letterhead, envelopes, labels, and cartons portrayed the desired image.

The new warehouse had an area of about 10,000 square feet but had poor access from Sequoyah street.

SHIPPING

A Tulsa paper company designed a special carton to minimize shipping damage to lamps and shades. Shipping costs were $13 per 100 pounds, and the United Parcel Service's maximum limit was 100 pounds. Each lamp weighed nine pounds.

LEGAL ASPECTS

Mr. Satterfield did not foresee any legal problems because the product was relatively simple and should not create any liability difficulties. Even though Underwriter Laboratory (UL) materials were used for construction, the lamps were not approved by the UL. Mr. Satterfield also stated that wholesale selling eliminated many problems related to retail selling.

FINANCING

The proceeds of the $100,000 loan were to be used for: acquisition of machinery and equipment, $7,250; and working capital, $92,750. Mr. Lytle also contributed about $15,000 equity capital. The percentages of ownership were: Mr. Fornay, 45 percent; Mr. Lytle, 45 percent; and Mr. Satterfield, 10 percent.

Mr. Arnold and his staff in the Business Development Center of the Tulsa Urban League assisted management in establishing Unique Lamps, Inc. Assistance was provided in securing financing, site and facility selection, developing business plans and pro forma statements, and providing community contacts.

A certified public accountant was retained for keeping the company's books and records. Mr. Satterfield stated that he had lost $18,000 in a prior business venture because the books were bungled.

He also stated that $2½ to $3 million additional financing would be sought in the next three years. Attempts were to be made to secure these funds from large banks in financial centers such as Chicago.

EXHIBIT 1

UNIQUE LAMPS, INC.
Pro-Forma Income Statements
1975, 1976, and 1977

	1975	1976	1977
Total Sales (Note 1)	$282,200	$379,200	$600,000
Cost of Goods Sold (Note 2)	126,990	170,640	270,000
Gross Profit	155,210	208,560	330,000
Expenses			
Wages and salaries (Note 3)	21,600	50,000	95,000
Rent	4,800	4,800	6,000
Utilities	2,900	3,600	5,000
Taxes and licenses	100	100	100
Supplies	10,000	11,000	20,000
Repairs and maintenance	1,200	1,500	2,000
Legal and accounting	2,000	3,000	4,500
Loan interest (11½%)	2,840	2,149	1,376
Advertising	10,000	10,000	15,000
Freight	3,275	4,000	7,500
Bad debts (Note 4)	9,982	13,400	24,000
Donations	250	250	300
Depreciation	1,000	1,000	1,000
Total Expenses	71,547	106,399	183,776
Profit	83,663	102,161	146,224
Less owner withdrawals	36,000	40,000	50,000
Net Profit	$ 47,663	$ 62,161	$ 96,224

Note 1: Gross sales are based upon the assumption of the monthly sale of 900 swag lamps at $22 each and 100 table lamps at $37 each. The maximum capacity of the production equipment is 500 units daily in three shifts. The daily production required to meet this level of sales approximates 65 units daily. The broad marketing approach and enthusiasm with which initial shipments have been met indicates this is a conservative sales estimate. Second and third year sales would benefit tremendously from the bicentennial activities with sales tending to be limited only by plant capacity.

Note 2: Cost of Goods sold is calculated at 45 percent of sales. The product is relatively labor intensive and this ratio represents a conservative viewpoint.

Note 3: Wage and salary expense is based upon the first year employment of two (2) individuals engaged in production and assembly and one worker in shipping and receiving under the direct supervision of the company production manager.

Note 4: Bad debts are estimated at 3.5 percent of gross sales during the first year and 4 percent thereafter.

Exhibit 1 consists of pro-forma Income Statements for 1975, 1976, and 1977. A pro-forma cash flow statement, fiscal year March 1, 1975 through February 28, 1976, is presented in Exhibit 2. Each of these exhibits was prepared by the Business Development Center.

EXHIBIT 2

UNIQUE LAMPS INC.
Pro-Forma Cash Flow Statement
Fiscal Year March 1, 1975 through February 28, 1976

Item	March	April	May	June	July	August	September	October	November	December	January	February	Total
Beginning balance........	$35,783	26,700	15,485	15,595	11,008	9,709	2,235	6,675	16,170	16,348	27,177	25,736	—
Collections...............	203	5,222	10,601	14,561	19,920	25,000	27,900	29,300	28,900	26,900	20,800	23,800	$233,107
Purchases*..............	—	(11,930)	(3,510)	(10,800)	(13,050)	(13,500)	(13,500)	(12,600)	(11,250)	(6,750)	(12,600)	(13,500)	(122,990)
Cash expenses and officers' salaries†..............	(9,286)	(4,507)	(5,278)	(8,348)	(8,169)	(12,806)	(9,960)	(7,205)	(10,780)	(9,321)	(9,641)	(11,246)	(106,547)
Income taxes...........	—	—	(1,703)	—	—	(6,168)	—	—	(6,692)	—	—	(3,722)	(18,285)
Cash balance...........	$26,700	15,485	15,595	11,008	9,709	2,235	6,675	16,170	16,348	27,177	25,736	21,068	—

* Assumes purchases are paid in full 30 days after receipt.
† Excludes reserve for depreciation.

RECENT EVENTS

In early April 1975, Mr. Satterfield surmised that Mr. Fornay was not devoting sufficient effort to selling for Unique Lamps. Mr. Fornay became interested in other products including bedspreads, and was selling them and arranging for manufacturing them.

Mr. Fornay attempted to complete the arrangements for Unique Lamps' loan with the bank's loan officer. Financial statements for the company were not available. On April 15, the loan officer was to submit his recommendation to the bank's loan committee as to whether Unique should be granted the loan.

QUESTIONS FOR DISCUSSION

1. What was the competitive edge of this company?
2. How should the marketing plan and strategy of this company be evaluated?
3. Was management's experience appropriate for managing and operating the company? Why or why not?
4. Was the location appropriate? Why or why not?
5. Do you agree with management's evaluations of the legal aspects of the business? Why or why not?
6. How should the pro forma income statement and cash flow statement be evaluated?
7. If you had been a consultant for Unique Lamps, what guidelines for the management and operations of the company would you have prescribed?
8. If you were the bank's loan officer, what recommendation would you have made to the loan committee?

part VI

Profit Planning and Control

No business is stronger than its financial strength and vitality. Today, among the greatest requirements for success in small business are an appreciation of the importance of financial management, an understanding of financial relationships, and the devotion of time, energy, and initiative to this difficult activity. The rewards are worth effort, though, for this is how your firm will not only survive, but grow and develop.

In this part, you will study the procedures for analyzing and evaluating your financial operations and position in Chapter 19; the "how to" of maintaining adequate and accurate records in Chapter 20; the need for, and methods to use in, planning your profit in Chapter 21; how to budget and maintain financial control in Chapter 22; and what you can do to safeguard your assets in Chapter 23.

19

Evaluating Your Financial
Position and Operations

The material in this chapter should help you to understand better some of the financial aspects of running your own company.

The main purpose of the chapter is to help you learn how to set up an accounting system for your firm and how to read, evaluate, and interpret the accounts and resulting profit (or loss) figures. A secondary purpose is to serve as a guide in evaluating, or estimating, your firm's financial position. The material should also aid you in determining the value or worth of your firm. Finally, the chapter covers some important ratios that can guide you in forecasting whether you will have successful or unsuccessful operations.

HOW YOU CAN EVALUATE YOUR FINANCIAL
OPERATIONS AND POSITION

The operations of your firm result from decisions you and your staff make and the resulting activities performed by your employees. As decisions are made and operations occur, your firm's financial position is constantly changing. Cash received for sales increases your bank balance. But, then you spend it for materials, thereby increasing your inventory. At the same time, machines are decreasing in value, goods are being processed by employees, and utilities are being used. The value of your firm is constantly changing.

Through it all, the important question is whether your company is improving its chances of attaining its objectives. One objective is to make a profit, but there are many problems involved. Some companies have made a profit, and still have failed. Profits are not necessarily cash. Profits may be reflected in accounts receivable, and those accounts may not be collectible. Too much money may be tied up in other assets and not available to pay your bills.

You may have had this trouble in your personal finances. Your salary or income may be adequate to pay for your food, clothing, and other operating expenses. However, you may need a new house or car, for which you must make a down payment in the form of cash. Your funds are invested in a fixed asset, and they are not available for you to use to pay your bills.

Your accounting records must adequately and accurately reflect the continual changes in your *assets, liabilities,* income, expenses, and *equity.* You must make certain that the interrelationships between these accounts remain "satisfactory." For example, what amount of cash reduces your income-producing possibilities? An increased investment in building and equipment reduces your ability to pay your operating expenses. Increases in liabilities increase your obligations and monthly payments. Therefore, you need to study your firm's financial structure to assure its being able to do the things that it needs to do. The continued operation of your company depends upon maintaining the proper balance between its investments, expenses, and income. These subjects are discussed in the balance of this chapter, and are divided into two parts:

1. The meaning of each of the accounts and how it affects the company's operations.
2. Methods of evaluating a company's financial condition, and important ratios and their meanings.

We will use The Sample Company as an illustration as we go through the financial analysis.

FINANCIAL ACCOUNTS OF THE FIRM

The financial structure of your firm is reflected in its assets, liabilities, and equity. These accounts are interrelated and interact with each other. See Figure 19–1 for location of the accounts on the balance sheet.

Assets

As has been stated, assets are the physical, financial, or other values that your company has. Assets are divided into *current* and *fixed* assets.

Current Assets. Current assets are those that turn over—that is, they change from one form to another—within one year. For example, it is expected that accounts receivable will be paid and converted into cash within one year and that inventory will also be converted into sales within that period.

The first item of current assets is *cash*. It includes the currency—bills and coins—you have in the cash register, the deposits in your checking account in the bank, and other noninterest-bearing values that you can convert into cash immediately. When cash is available, it means that you can pay today's bills. It is the most liquid of any of the accounts.

FIGURE 19-1

THE SAMPLE CO.
Balance Sheet
December 31, 19 —

Assets

Current Assets:

Cash...	$ 3,527	
Accounts receivable..............................	30,242	
Inventory.......................................	40,021	
Prepaid expenses................................	523	
Total Current Assets.......................		$74,313

Fixed Assets

Equipment......................................	$50,250	
Building.......................................	20,475	
	$70,725	
Less reserve for depreciation......................	8,450	
Net Fixed Assets...........................		62,275
Total Assets...........................		$136,588

Liabilities

Current Liabilities:

Accounts payable...............................	$25,674	
Accrued payables................................	1,530	
Total Current Liabilities....................		$27,204

Long-Term Liabilities

Mortgage payable..............................		10,354
Total Liabilities.......................		$ 37,558

Net Worth (Equity)

Capital stock...................................	$80,000	
Retained earnings...............................	19,030	
Total Net Worth.......................		99,030
Total Liabilities plus Net Worth......		$136,588

A certain level of cash is necessary to operate a business. However, cash does not produce income. Having accumulated too much cash means that the company has reduced its income-producing capacity. Yet, you cannot pay your bills if you do not have cash. Therefore, a certain level of cash must be maintained, but not too high a level.

Accounts receivable is a current asset that results from giving credit to customers when they buy your goods. Your company may sell entirely on credit, which should help it maintain a level of sales volume. This is a service that your customers will usually want. While extension of credit implies future payment by the customer, some customers—fortunately, only a few—do not pay their accounts. Care must be exercised to select customers who will pay within a reasonable period of time. Policies should be set on the terms of payment and how much credit will be extended.

Credit is a cost to the company. Until the *cash* has actually been. received, the money cannot be used for paying your own expenses or buying other goods. Several means are used to circumvent this, including the following:

1. You may factor your accounts receivable. Under this arrangement, your company sells its accounts receivable and receives cash less a fee.
2. Your company may honor one or more of the many kinds of credit cards.

Note that both types of transactions make it easier for you to pay your company's obligations, but they also result in an expense to the company. This expense may be offset by increased sales (or maybe not a loss in sales) and a reduction in the amount of assets needed.

Too large an investment in accounts receivable will place your company under considerable financial strain. Your investments of financial resources in the company must be increased, and the chance of your incurring a high expense because of bad debts is increased.

Inventory is an asset that provides a buffer between purchase, production, and sale of the product, as discussed in Chapter 14. A company must maintain some level of inventory to serve the customers when they demand, or request, a product. Some sales are made on the basis of availability. On the other hand, a customer may want a special item and be willing to wait until it is ordered and delivered.

However, there are costs resulting from carrying inventory. Your money is tied up, space is used, products must be maintained and can become obsolete, and so forth. Also, inventory, as such, is not an income-producing asset. The amount of inventory to carry depends upon a judicious balancing of costs. In addition, too high a level of inventory places a financial burden on the firm.

Other current asset accounts might include *short-term investment, prepaid items,* and *accrued income.* Usually, these are only a small percentage of the current assets and need little attention.

Fixed Assets. *Buildings, machinery, store fixtures, trucks,* and *land* are included among fixed assets. The company expects to own them for considerable time and writes off part of their cost each period as a depreciation expense.

Different types of fixed assets have different lengths of useful life. Land is not depreciated; buildings are usually depreciated over a period of 20 years: machinery, over 5–10 years; and store equipment, 2–10 years. The amount of fixed assets should be related to the needs of your company. Idle fixed assets are a financial drain and are usually avoided when possible.

Some companies find it advantageous to rent fixed assets instead of owning them. A retailer rents a store to reduce his need to make a large investment.

Whether you decide to rent or own your fixed assets will depend on the cost of rental, the period cost of owning, the availability of capital, and the freedom to operate.

Liabilities

A company obtains its funds by borrowing (creating an obligation to pay) and by owner investment. The first results in a liability to pay someone; the second results in owner's equity. *The total of the liabilities and the owner's equity always equals the total of the assets.* A company is wise to maintain a proper balance between the higher risk of investment by creditors and the investment by owners. The investment by creditors is divided into current liabilities and long-term liabilities.

Current liabilities are obligations that are to be paid within one year. They include *accounts payable, notes payable,* and *accrued items* —such as payroll—which are services performed for the company, but are not yet paid.

Accounts payable are usually due within 30 or 60 days, depending on the credit terms. The delay in required payment is the service a vendor provides to the buyer. A company maintains current assets to pay these accounts. A check should be made to determine whether early payment is beneficial. Some companies offer a cash discount, such as 2 percent if paid in 10 days, for early payment. Maintenance of a high level of accounts payable requires a high level of current assets.

Notes payable, which are written obligations to pay, usually give the company a somewhat longer period before payment is required and usually require payment of interest. An example is a 90-day note.

Bonds and *mortgages* are the usual types of *long-term liabilities.* A company contracts these when it purchases fixed assets but its owners do not have sufficient equity to pay for the assets. Also, *long-term loans* may be used to supply a permanent amount of *working capital,* which is current assets less current liabilities. Small businesses use long-term borrowing as a source of funds much less frequently than do large businesses. This type of borrowing requires regular payment of a fixed amount on the principal and a smaller amount for interest. The necessity of making these payments during slack times increases the risk to a company of being unable to meet its obligations.

Owners' Equity

Equity is the owners' share of the company after the liabilities are subtracted from the assets. The owners receive income from the profits of the company in the form of dividends or an increase in their share of the company through an increase in the retained earnings. They also absorb losses, which decrease the equity.

Capital stock is the value the owners invest in the company. A share of stock is issued in the form of a certificate and has a stated value on the books of the company. Additional shares can be sold or issued in place of cash dividends.

Retained earnings are the accumulation of the profits that are not distributed to the owners in cash dividends. *Cash dividends* reduce current assets. Since a company usually does not pay out all its profits in dividends, some earnings are retained as protection for the firm or to provide for its growth. Many small firms have failed because the owners paid out the profits as dividends too quickly. A long-range plan for paying dividends should be established.

The assets, liabilities, and equity accounts form the financial structure of a company at a point in time, but they tend to change from one period to the next. At regular intervals, a *balance sheet* is prepared to show the value of the company and how the funds are distributed.

The financial structure of a company is changed by the profit-making activities of the company. These activities are reflected in the revenue and expense accounts. (Net income = Revenue − Expenses.) During a given period, the company performs services for which it receives values. The financial values exchanged are shown by the profit and loss statement. (See Figure 19–2.)

FIGURE 19–2

THE SAMPLE CO.
Profit and Loss Statement
January 1 through December 31, 19—

Net Sales.................................		$231,574
Less cost of goods sold.....................		145,631
Gross Profit........................		$ 85,943
Operating Expenses:		
Salaries..................................	$41,569	
Utilities..................................	3,475	
Depreciation.............................	5,025	
Rent.....................................	1,000	
Building services.........................	2,460	
Insurance................................	2,000	
Interest..................................	1,323	
Office and supplies.......................	2,775	
Sales promotion..........................	5,500	
Taxes and licenses........................	3,240	
Maintenance.............................	805	
Delivery.................................	2,924	
Miscellaneous............................	875	
Total Expenses......................		72,971
Net Income before Taxes...................		$ 12,972
Less income taxes.....................		3,242
Net Income after Taxes...........		$ 9,730

Revenue and Expenses

Revenue is the return from services performed. Revenue is usually called sales income, and is received by the company in the form of cash or credit—an obligation of the customer to pay. Many companies also have other income, such as interest from investments.

Expenses are the costs of performing services. They include material, wages, insurance, utilities, transportation, depreciation, taxes, supplies, and sales promotion. These items become deductions from the revenue as they are used.

Profit

Profit is the difference between revenue and expenses. Profit is often defined as gross, operating or net before or net after taxes—depending on the type of expenses deducted.

The values of these items are related to each other and to the structure of the company. Earlier, it was stated that a company has fixed assets that are income-producing. Are these assets being used efficiently? To find this, the relationship between the volume of sales income and the value of the fixed assets is determined and evaluated.

METHODS OF EVALUATING THE FIRM'S
FINANCIAL CONDITION

Now that we have considered the financial structure and operations of a company, we should consider the methods of evaluating its financial condition. Look at Figures 19–1 and 19–2, which present the financial statements of The Sample Company. Is the company in a good financial position?

In Chapter 21, we will consider a method of analysis called *profit planning*, which can be used to anticipate the position for the coming year. Now, however, we would like to evaluate the company on a broader basis. Out of this evaluation, changes can be made that may lead to a strengthening of the company's financial structure and to an improvement in company operations.

The evaluation of the financial condition of a company is based upon establishing relationships between two or more variables. For example, the amount of current assets needed depends on other conditions of a company such as the size of the current liabilities. So, the *current ratio* —current assets divided by current liabilities—shows how easily a company can pay its current obligations. Another comparison can be made by subtracting current liabilities from current assets, with the resulting value called *working capital*. Unfortunately, no standard figures have been determined to be best for you to use, nor have any of them been found that can assure your success. Yet, a reasonable evaluation is necessary. Two sets of values that can be used for evaluation purposes are:

1. A comparison of the current value of ratios with those of the past.
2. A comparison of the ratios of your firm with other similar ones.

Values of Each Ratio in the Past

A change in the value of selected ratios for a firm indicates a change in its financial position. For example, suppose the current ratio for The Sample Company has moved gradually from a value of 1.0 to 3.0. The firm apparently has moved to a more liquid position and, therefore, looks good. However, this improvement may be due to keeping old uncollectible accounts on the books. In that case, the company would not be more liquid. While the trend does indicate a change, only in-depth analyses can determine the causes.

Values of Other Like Companies

Average and range of values for the ratios are published for a large variety of small to large companies. Some of these firms will fail, but the averages are ranges that provide a guide to what other companies are doing. Suppose the current ratio of companies with assets of $250,000 or less is found to be 2.3 to 1, while The Sample Company has a ratio of 3.0 to 1. Again, the company's ratio looks good. However, it may be losing income by maintaining too many nonproductive assets.

In the past, a ratio of 2 to 1 has been used as a rule of thumb for the current ratio. However, no one value of a ratio is optimum for all companies.

IMPORTANT RATIOS AND THEIR MEANINGS

The ratios and percentages are valuable in answering a number of questions that you may ask yourself about your company. By obtaining answers to these questions, you can make plans to correct deficiencies in the operations and structure of your company. When a ratio is mentioned, look at Figure 19–3 for the method of computation of the ratios. Spaces are provided for you to compute the ratio for The Sample Company using the data provided in Figures 19–1 and 19–2. Comparable figures for the industry are provided for comparative purposes.

Are you making an adequate or reasonable return on your investment? The *ratio of net profit to net worth* [often called return on investment

FIGURE 19–3
Financial Ratios

Ratio	Formula	The Sample Company	Industry Average
1. Net profit to net worth....	$\dfrac{\text{Net profit before taxes}}{\text{Net worth}}$ =	—————	18.4%
2. Net profit to net sales.....	$\dfrac{\text{Net profit before taxes}}{\text{Net sales}}$ =	—————	3.1%
3. Net sales to fixed assets....	$\dfrac{\text{Net sales}}{\text{Fixed assets}}$ =	—————	5.8
4. Net sales to net worth.....	$\dfrac{\text{Net sales}}{\text{Owner's equity}}$ =	—————	7.5
5. Current ratio.............	$\dfrac{\text{Current assets}}{\text{Current liabilities}}$ =	—————	1.3
6. Acid test.................	$\dfrac{\text{Current assets} - \text{inventory}}{\text{Current liabilities}}$ =	—————	1.0
7. Receivables to working capital................	$\dfrac{\text{Accounts receivable}}{\text{Working capital}}$ =	—————	1.2
8. Inventory to working capital................	$\dfrac{\text{Inventory}}{\text{Working capital}}$ =	—————	0.4
9. Collection period..........	$\dfrac{\text{Accounts receivable}}{\text{Average daily credit sales}}$ =	—————*	43.0 days
10. Net sales to inventory.....	$\dfrac{\text{Net sales}}{\text{Inventory}}$ =	—————	22.0
11. Net sales to working capital................	$\dfrac{\text{Net sales}}{\text{Working capital}}$ =	—————	10.0
12. Long-term liabilities to working capital.........	$\dfrac{\text{Long term liabilities}}{\text{Working capital}}$ =	—————	0.7
13. Debt to net worth........	$\dfrac{\text{Total liabilities}}{\text{Net worth}}$ =	—————	1.6
14. Current liabilities to net worth................	$\dfrac{\text{Current liabilities}}{\text{Owner's equity}}$ =	—————	1.1
15. Fixed assets to net worth..	$\dfrac{\text{Fixed assets}}{\text{Owner's equity}}$ =	—————	1.2

* If 80 percent of sales are on credit: Average daily credit sales $= \dfrac{\text{Annual sales}}{365} \times 0.80 = \dfrac{\quad}{365} \times 0.80 = \underline{\quad}.$

(ROI)[1]] is used to evaluate this, but several other ratios should be considered to aid in profit planning and to make decisions.

How much return is your company making on its sales dollar? The *ratio of net profit to net sales* provides this information. Suppose The

[1] The term "return on investment" may be misleading. In reality, it is "return on equity" (ROE).

Sample Company makes four cents per dollar of sales. Is the trend up or down? How does it compare with other like companies? If it is dropping, why? Your costs may be increasing without an increase in price. Your competitors may be keeping their prices low and you need to keep yours low in order to compete. You may be trying to obtain a large sales volume at the expense of profit. An increase in sales volume with the same investment and net profit per dollar of sales will increase your ROE, but if you reduce the return on a dollar of sales, your ROE may decrease.

Does your company obtain enough sales from its producing assets? This is reflected in the *ratio of net sales to fixed assets*—your fixed assets representing the producing units of the company. This is only a general guide, for so many variables exist—such as leasing instead of owning fixed assets—that the ratio can change with changes in policies. Still, trends and good use of industry data make this a valuable ratio.

Does your company have enough sales for the amount of investment? The *ratio of net sales to net worth* provides a guide to this evaluation. Note that this ratio can be combined with the profit to sales ratio to obtain the ROE.

Can you pay your current obligations? A number of ratios can be valuable to you. The best known is the *current ratio,* that is, the ratio of current assets to current liabilities. You may be making a good profit, but not be able to pay your debts, for cash does not necessarily increase when you make a profit.

The *acid test ratio,* that is, the ratio of current assets minus inventory to current liabilities, is used to make a further check.

Another check is obtained by using *working capital,* or current assets less current liabilities, as a basis. Working capital is the margin of safety your company has in paying its current liabilities.

The *ratios of accounts receivable and inventory to working capital* provide an insight into the riskiness of the company's ability to make current payments.

How good are your current assets? Cash in hand is the best current asset. Accounts receivable represent what the company will receive in cash from customers some time in the future. However, the older an account is, the greater the expectation of loss. The *collection period ratio,* that is accounts receivable to average daily credit sales, provides a guide as to the "goodness" of your accounts receivable. Suppose The Sample Company has set a 30-day payment period for its customers and its collection period ratio is 50 days. Many accounts are less than 30 days old, so many other accounts must be over two months old. Apparently, Mr. Sample is not adequately checking on those to whom he extends credit, he is carrying bad accounts, or he is not exerting enough effort to reduce the slow payments of accounts. Periodically, each account in accounts receivable should be reviewed for its collectibility. A system of control of accounts receivable is discussed in the next chapter.

Inventories can be evaluated in about the same way as accounts receivable. Goods in inventory become obsolete if not sold within a reasonable time. Therefore, inventory should be "turned over" during the year. The turnover rate is expressed by the *ratio of the net sales to inventory*. A turnover of inventory of six times each year for a company is good if turnover for the industry is five. If your company is turning over its inventory too slowly, you may be keeping obsolete goods. Too high a ratio may result from so low an inventory that it is hurting production or not providing necessary customer services.

To obtain an idea of the support that a company is receiving from its current assets, *the ratio of net sales to working capital* may be computed. Accounts receivable and inventory should increase with an increase in sales, but not out of proportion. Payroll and other expense increases require a higher level of cash outflow. On the other hand, too low a ratio indicates surplus working capital is available to service the sales.

How much equity should your company have? Assets are financed by either equity investments or the creation of liabilities. Retained profits are part of equity and can be used to increase your assets or decrease your liabilities. You can maintain a high level of equity with a relatively low level of risk, or a relatively high level of liabilities with a higher expected return on equity.

Most small companies do not like to maintain a large amount of long-term debt. The risk is too great. The common ratios used for checking the company's source of funds relationships are:

1. *Long-term liabilities to working capital.*
2. *Debt to net worth.*
3. *Current liabilities to net worth.*
4. *Fixed assets to net worth.*

If any of these are extremely high, the company is in a risky situation. A bad year decreases the income, but the obligation to pay continues.

More questions can be asked, and you can develop more relationships to guide you in analyzing your company's financial strengths and weaknesses. Each ratio is an indicator of only part of the company's position. The ratios overlap because a company is a complex system so that a change in the size of one of the accounts, such as cash, will change other values.

The financial ratios for the items on the profit and loss statement are usually expressed in percentages of sales. This information is usually hard to obtain from competing firms, but when it can be, it can point to any out-of-line costs. High cost of goods sold as a percentage of sales income may indicate a poor choice of vendors, inefficient use of material or labor, or too low a price. A high percentage of salaries may indicate an overstaffing of the company.

SUMMARY

This chapter has provided a set of tools for analyzing your company's financial condition and operations. The next chapter presents some methods for maintaining your accounting records. These will help you in your profit planning and control activities discussed in later chapters.

QUESTIONS FOR FURTHER DISCUSSION

1. Compute the ratios listed in Figure 19–3 for The Sample Company.
2. Evaluate the financial condition of The Sample Company.
3. What might be some recommendations you could make to the owner of The Sample Company?
4. Make an evaluation of your personal financial structure and operations. What steps can you take to improve them?

20

Maintaining Adequate—and Accurate—Records

Have you ever considered how many records you possess or generate? You probably have in your possession a driver's license, credit cards, student activity card, social security card, and/or checkbook.

Without these records, you would be unable to transact much of your business. When you use one of these, records—or entries in the records—are generated. For example, suppose you use a credit card. This generates a sales slip, an account for you, a bill, and a record of payment. You use the bill to write a check and to deduct the amount from your bank balance. At the same time, you keep some information in your head to save time in filling out forms. While this informal method may be all right for you as a student, it is not sufficient for you as a small business manager. Instead, you need a system of records to aid human memory. A business has a much more extensive set of records than an individual, because it has many more transactions and more people are involved.

After finishing State University, Tobe Jackson and his wife decided to use their savings to open an independent trucking firm. Things progressed to the point that he was operating seven tractor-trailer rigs under contract to a major national corporation to haul eggs to New York and/or Chicago. In addition, he had obtained a special certificate to enable him to "back haul" other agricultural products.

When Tobe's business became strapped for funds, he felt that if he could just get an SBA loan all would be well! The SBA referred Tobe to one of his former professors, who was a member of

SCORE, for counseling. The professor asked Tobe to bring his most recent balance sheet and profit and loss statement.

The debt of $185,000 shown on the statements seemed an awesome sight, especially as the statements were three months old and the income statement revealed a substantial loss on operations. The professor suggested that Tobe raise the gross contract prices by 10 to 15 percent, acquire a small bookkeeping machine to expedite accounting processes—in order to obtain current operating cost data, and cut costs.

Tobe's response was, "I can't raise my prices, for my customers will give their contracts to someone else and I will be out of business." To this, the professor retorted, "Tobe, you aren't in the charity business. The other companies don't care if you go broke."

As Tobe and the professor parted, it was obvious that Tobe wouldn't raise his prices.

Several months later, Tobe was no longer in the trucking business.

IMPORTANCE OF RECORDS KEEPING

You have already read about the information needed to make personnel, production, marketing, and financial decisions. Much of the information needed for decision making is carried around in the owner's, manager's, or employees' heads. Certain types of information, however, are more valuable if brought together from a variety of sources, related in a systematic way, kept accurately, recorded permanently, and made available to the people who need them. A procedure is needed to provide the needed information in the proper manner.

Accuracy and completeness of accounting information seem to become increasingly important as the economy and business operations become more complex. We prefer to think of these data as "management information."

While the increasing complexity of business has expanded the amount of paperwork, records still need to be kept in as simple and inexpensive a manner as possible—while providing the required information. How can this be achieved? By knowing what information is needed, by obtaining and storing information with little copying and recording, and by storing information for easy retrieval, you may achieve this.

Historically, accounting data have been developed for purposes of satisfying the needs of tax reporting and reporting the condition of the firm to the owners. The emphasis has been placed on gathering and using historic data rather than projective data to be used in the future. Yet, each category has its role. In addition to the traditional accounting approach, in contemporary times, decision making is becoming more important. Thus, you need to ask questions of yourself and of your associates such as, "What are the decisions that I need to make?" "What information do I need to make these decisions?" "How can I best record and retrieve this information?" The answers to these questions should serve as guidelines for establishing an accounting system, and that is the objective and rationale of this chapter.

WHAT INFORMATION IS NEEDED

In determining what information is needed, you should ask: For what purposes do I want the data? The usual answers are:

1. To plan ahead. Past information can be used for planning the future. Examples might be past sales trends, sales per salesperson, output from a machine, delivery time for a purchase, quality of output of an employee, payment experience from a given customer, and demand for a particular product at a given time.
2. To meet obligations. For example, money is borrowed, material is purchased on credit, delivery is promised for a certain day at a certain price, and taxes are due.
3. To control activities. Many activities are routine, but vital, to the firm and can be checked by a clerk. For example, material ordered has not arrived, inventory has reached zero, losses in supplies are occurring, and too much time is being spent on routine work. By having guidelines and "warning flags," a clerk saves the manager time by performing the control function.
4. To satisfy the government. For example, the government collects taxes; requires conformance to safety, fair employment, and price control standards; and checks on ethical standards of business practice.
5. To evaluate performance. Evaluation is obtained from review of selected records and reports.

In addition to determining the information needed, you must know how to use it. This involves classifying it into a usable form. The information for accounting purposes has been classified in Chapter 19 as follows:

1. Assets.
2. Liabilities.
3. Owners' equity or net worth.
4. Revenue and expenses.
5. Profit.

Many other pieces of information are needed, including economic and market conditions, personnel history and capabilities, sources of material, and specifications for products. Systems and procedures need to be established to assure the availability of critical information. This area is beyond the scope of this book.

FIGURE 20–1
Accounting for Sales

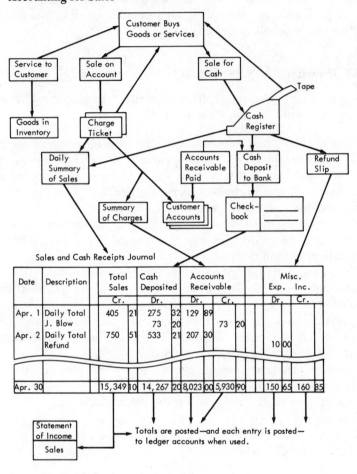

Sales and Cash Receipts Journal

Date	Description	Total Sales Cr.		Cash Deposited Dr.		Accounts Receivable Dr.		Cr.			Misc. Exp. Dr.		Inc. Cr.	
Apr. 1	Daily Total	405	21	275	32	129	89							
	J. Blow			73	20			73	20					
Apr. 2	Daily Total	750	51	533	21	207	30							
	Refund										10	00		
Apr. 30		15,349	10	14,267	20	8,023	00	5,930	90		150	65	160	85

Totals are posted—and each entry is posted—to ledger accounts when used.

Records of Service to Customers

These transactions provide both the income and an expense of doing business. When you perform a service—such as the sale of a product, repair of an auto, or rental of an apartment—cash, a check, or a IOU is received in exchange for goods and/or labor. Recordings on slips and tapes are used to accumulate the changes in the affected records. For example, the cash sale of a pair of socks increases your cash. Yet, it creates the obligation to pay sales taxes and reduces your inventory of socks. See Figure 20–1 for a flowchart of the transfer of data, cash, and goods. A credit slip is used to reverse the above transaction when goods are returned.

FIGURE 20–2
Accounting for Purchases

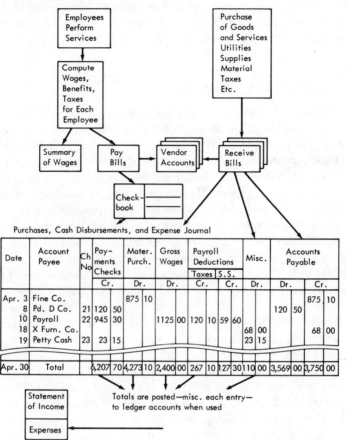

Purchases, Cash Disbursements, and Expense Journal

Date	Account Payee	Ch No	Pay-ments Checks	Mater. Purch.	Gross Wages	Payroll Deductions		Misc.	Accounts Payable	
						Taxes	S.S.			
			Cr.	Dr.	Dr.	Cr.	Cr.	Dr.	Dr.	Cr.
Apr. 3	Fine Co.			875 10						875 10
8	Pd. D Co.	21	120 50						120 50	
10	Payroll	22	945 30		1125 00	120 10	59 60			
18	X Furn. Co.							68 00		68 00
19	Petty Cash	23	23 15					23 15		
Apr. 30	Total		6,207 70	4,273 10	2,400 00	267 10	127 30	110 00	3,569 00	3,750 00

Totals are posted—misc. each entry—
to ledger accounts when used

Records of Services Performed for You

These transactions originate your expenses of doing business. Materials, parts, and finished products are purchased to be transformed or sold. Employees are paid for work performed. Electricity is consumed, taxes are paid, advertising promotes the products, and supplies are used. Also, the service performed may increase the assets of the company—such as equipment and machine purchases, building construction, and stock investments. A somewhat different type of service fitting this category is the floating of bonds to obtain cash or credit. All these types of transactions generate obligations and initiate transfers of data within an accounting system, as shown in Figure 20–1 and Figure 20–2.

Records of Other Activities

Many matters of a nonaccounting nature initiate other records. Sources for these include inquiry letters, agreements on sales, complaints, and implementation of controls over physical units.

RECORDING THE INFORMATION

All transactions involving accounting information must be recorded. Some very small firms use a single-entry system for its simplicity. This type of system records a transaction only in one place—a sale for cash is recorded as cash income. This type system does not provide much needed information or control. Your use of a double-entry system of accounting requires that your accounts will be in "balance" by entering a transaction in two places. When a sale is made for cash, income is increased and cash—an asset—is increased by the same amount; conversely, inventory is decreased and material expenses increased. When material is purchased on credit, inventory—an asset—is increased and accounts payable —a liability—is increased by a like amount. A machine wears out. So periodically, depreciation is deducted from assets, and expenses are increased by the same amount. Notice in all of these transactions that the changes are made so that the *sum* of Assets + Expenses = the *sum* of Liabilities + Equity + Income. The amount of the totals may change, but they change by the same amount.

The accounting system starts with the tapes and other items discussed under *sources*, and includes journals and ledger accounts. The journal is the original book of entry, and records the daily transactions in chronological order. To group like items together, the chronological entries are entered individually or as totals in ledger accounts. A ledger account might be set up for each of the accounts listed in Figure 19–1. The amount of detail depends on the needs of your company and its other records. For example, journals and statements may be used to show the income and expenses, whereas only the profit—the difference between income and expenses—is shown in a ledger account. Under all circumstances, the ledger accounts must balance.

Figures 20–1 and 20–2 diagram the flow of data for some of the more common entries in the accounting records of a small business. The following sections discuss some transactions and entries to help you to understand the system of recording information. (The month is used for the time period for adjustments to emphasize the need for frequent review of the results of your operations. Some of the formal accounting illustrated may be performed only once a year, often by an accountant. But the examples illustrate the concepts.)

Sales

The sale of your products or the service you perform is the source of profit. In every company, a record must be kept of each sale made. The auto repair shop makes a record of the charges to the customer for labor hours and parts used. A *sales slip* is completed when a radio is sold. The number, type, unit price, and total price of the radio should be entered on the slip. On all items sold, the sales tax must be recorded. Cash sales, when cash registers are available, can be recorded on a tape to be used as the sales slip.

Information on the sales forms is used to accumulate the sales income, to reduce inventory, to make analyses for future plans, and—in the case of a credit sale—to enter in the *accounts receivable record* for the customer. To eliminate the totaling of sales slips, cash registers can be used that total the daily sales. When many different items and people are involved, the registers can total by variables, including type of product, sales person, or department. The classification should be aligned with the types of analysis you will make and with the controls to be exercised.

Sales are entered in a *sales journal*. This shows the daily summary or the individual item depending on the detail desired. The sales journal can be multi-columnar paper to provide additional information, such as how much was sold for cash (or credit card and account) in each department, of each type of product, and by each salesman. If you analyze this sheet, it can provide information on sales trends, where the major volume is, or who is selling the most. Figure 20–1 provides an illustration of a sales and cash receipts journal.

The totals of the columns of the sales journal are transferred to the income statement and/or the sales income ledger account.

Cash Income and Outgo

When services are sold, the total of the recordings for cash, credits, and other values must equal the sales income recorded in order to balance the accounts. The accounting for cash is most important, as cash is negotiable anywhere. The person handling cash can mishandle it so that losses will occur. The recording system for cash should be designed and established with care so as to minimize losses.

When sales are made for cash, the goods sold and the cash received should be recorded independently of each other—if possible. Also, in order to maintain control, only certain people are allowed to handle company cash, and only on an individual basis. Each person starts with a standard amount for change, and the cash balance is reconciled each day or more often. The reconciliation checks that the cash on hand equals the beginning cash on hand plus cash sales less cash returns.

The waitress makes out the bill for a customer at a restaurant and a cashier receives the money. The gas pumps record the total gallons pumped, the price, and the total amount of the sale, and the gas station attendant collects the cash. The cash register, placed in view of the customer when he pays his bill, allows the customer to check the cash recording.

Checks are not as negotiable as cash, but are handled with the cash. One extra step is required. To guard against losses from bad checks, a method of identification of the person presenting the check is established. Past experience with payment by check often determines the policy to follow. Some companies accept only cash; some require identification such as driver's license and social security card, the number of which is recorded on the check; and some accept the check without formal identification. A proper balance between safeguarding against losses and making the customer feel that a personal service is being performed should be maintained.

At the end of each day, standard amounts of money are retained to make change the next day and the rest is deposited in the bank. *Deposit slips* are forwarded to the bank with the money and the amount deposited is added to the checkbook stub balance.

Payments are made by check or, if for small items, from petty cash. The *checkbook* can be used as a ledger account by adding bank deposits and deducting each check on the checkbook stubs. Each check is entered in the *cash journal* to show the account to which it is charged.

It often becomes too expensive to pay small bills by check, as for example, payments of $5 and under. A *petty cash fund*—say, $25 or $50 in cash—can be used to pay these bills. Each payment should be recorded on a form to keep track of the account and amount paid. The sum of the amounts on this record, plus the cash in the account, should always total the figure set for the size of the fund. Periodically, the fund is replenished by check to the set figure, and the expenditures recorded transferred to the appropriate accounts in the *cash journal*.

Accounts Receivable

When your customers buy goods using *credit cards* or *open accounts*, each sales slip either is entered on a customer account record or is filed under the customer's name. These records are details of the *accounts receivable account* and are totaled periodically to compare with the account. Any differences should be investigated. At the end of each period—usually a month—each customer's account should be totaled and a bill sent to the customer. As payments are received, the amounts of the checks are recorded in each customer's account and totaled for entry in the *sales and cash receipts journal*. A discussion of the decisions regarding credit is included in Chapter 22.

Periodically, a review of the individual *accounts receivable records* provides information about the status of the accounts, who is slow in paying, and which accounts need follow-up. The follow-up methods include delinquent notices, personal contact, and use of a collection agency. Some should be written off by charging them to *bad debts* when they cannot be collected. Other information can also be obtained, including identification of your large customers, what kinds of items they buy, and who has stopped buying your services.

Credit card sales are totaled by each credit card company and, after service charges are deducted, are processed through the bank. Gross sales are entered as sales income, as are accounts receivable and cash sales; the service charge is charged to that account; and the accounts receivable or cash account posted, depending on the procedure.

Some transactions—such as installment sales, damaged or lost goods, and income from insurance of damaged equipment—require more complex accounting procedures than are being presented. For these, we recommend consulting with an accountant or studying an accounting text.

Accounts Payable

An operating business incurs many obligations for material and equipment purchases, wages, utilities, taxes, and notes payable. These are reported in a *purchase and cash disbursements journal*. Practically all purchases are paid by check, and the number of individual payments is relatively small.

Bills and *invoices* can be filed by date to be paid, and when paid, filed as a history of *accounts payable*. As each initiating record is received, it is entered in the purchases and cash disbursements journal, as shown in Figure 20–2. Notice the columns used to classify the expenses and the "Miscellaneous" column used for expenses or assets for which there are few bills each month. Columns are used for accounts in which many entries occur during a month. For example, each month many purchases are made of a variety of materials, products, parts, and supplies for which one or more columns are provided. Few purchases of office equipment are made in a year, so they are handled in the miscellaneous column. Utilities might warrant a separate column. As a payment is made, the bill is marked and filed and the amount is entered on the check stub and in the purchases and cash disbursements journal.

As with accounts receivable, there are complex transactions about which you should consult an accountant or an accounting book.

Inventory

One of the troublesome records to keep is that for inventory. The problem of inventory was discussed in Chapter 14. A number of methods are used to assist the manager in maintaining records of his stock. All are based on a systematic method of spotting a low inventory item—that is, there are some methods that help "wave a warning flag" when the inventory is below a predetermined standard. These methods include setting aside the standard amount, setting aside an amount of space, making a regular physical count of the items, and for bulky material, flashing a light. A business selling a high volume of many items, like a grocery store, depends on visual inspection of the number of items on the shelf by several people, each assigned to certain items. For slower-moving and fewer items, the paper work is not increased very much by keeping a *perpetual inventory record*. (See Figure 14–4.) All the methods require establishing the amount of the minimum or standard amount left in inventory before ordering.

A record is made of the sale and the physical movement of an item when it is sold. The recording of the removal to expense is handled in two ways. First, for high-volume and a multiplicity of other items, the purchased items are charged to expense directly and adjusted at the end of the period for the inventory obtained by a physical count of the items. This reduces the volume of transfer recordings out of inventory into expense required of the second method. The second method uses perpetual inventory recordings described above, with added columns in the form for dollar values of units. The total cost of units used is the material expense. This method is usually used by manufacturing companies.

Expenses

Your business will purchase services from other people, and these will become expenses as they are used. Material is transformed and sold, electricity is used, machines decrease in value, and insurance protection is based on time. The bases of payments for these costs of doing business vary from daily to over five years, and an item's use may be delayed for years. In order to determine your true profit, income and expenses must be determined for the same period, say for each month.

Many small businesses compute their profit on a cash basis rather than on the accrual basis. The *accrual basis* makes adjustments to align income and expenses. The *cash basis* charges the items as they are actually paid. The cash basis is used for simplicity and, as will be seen, is not a pure cash procedure. The cash basis assumes that payments and use occur in the same period or that payments do not vary from one period to another. The analysis of the method to choose should balance the validity of the result against the cost of getting a more accurate picture.

Procedure for Using Accural Method.   The procedure for obtaining the expenses by the accrual method is:

1. Obtain the values for all assets, payments, and obligations.
2. Determine how much of each has been used during the period.
3. Transfer the used portion to expense, reduce the asset, or increase the obligation.

Examples of the Procedure.   A number of examples of this procedure are shown below. (See Figure 20–3 for sample recordings of each.)

1. *Material for sale in a retail store.* The expense of material = Beginning inventory + Purchases − Ending inventory.
2. *Insurance.* Insurance may be paid monthly, quarterly, or annually for the period ahead. Usually, annual payments reduce the cost and, by spreading the payment of different policies over the year, payment can be distributed to different months. Insurance is usually charged to expenses when paid and, for monthly statements, one-twelfth is charged to expenses and the remainder of payments placed in an asset account for prepaid insurance. This adjustment is not necessary when the monthly payment is close to one twelfth the annual cost (the latter is a cash-basis type of accounting).
3. *Wages and salaries.* These expenses are paid regularly after the employees have performed a service for the business. By paying salaries for a month at the end of the month, salaries are the expense of the month and need no adjustment. When wages are paid, say every two weeks, the payment is for the past two weeks, which often covers work in the previous month. At the end of the month, wages have not been paid for part of the month, so a liability exists for accrued wages. Adjustments between labor and accrued wages are made. Subsidiary records are usually kept to compute the wages, salaries, employee benefits, and company payments for social security and so forth.
4. *Machinery, equipment, and buildings.* These are used up over a period of years. On a monthly basis, the expense of a machine may be calculated according to the following expression:

$$\frac{\text{Cost of machine} - \text{Sale value at end of expected life}}{\text{Expected life (in months)}}.$$

This figure remains constant until the assets are sold, added to, or used up.

FIGURE 20-3

Examples of Recordings and Adjustments of Transactions

1. Receive order for material X, $100, entered when received.
   Used $80 of material X, entered at end of period.

Cash	Material Purchase Expense		Material Inventory	
$100 ◄	► $100	$20 ◄	► $20	
(decrease)	(increase)	(decrease)	(increase)	

or

Cash	Material Inventory		Material Expense	
$100 ◄	► $100	$80 ◄	► $80	
(decrease)	(increase)	(decrease)	(increase)	

2. Paid insurance policy, $75, entered when paid.
   Monthly expense of insurance, $50 (1/12 of annual $600), entered
   at end of period.

Cash	Insurance Expense		(cash basis)
$75 ◄	►$75		
(decrease)	(increase)		

or

Cash	Prepaid Insurance		Insurance Expense	
$75 ◄	► $75	$50 ◄	► $50	
(decrease)	(increase)	(decrease)	(increase)	

3. Paid wages, $2,400 (160 hours x $3.00 per hour x 5 workers) (from
   payroll book). Wages paid for last month's work, $480 (32 hours
   x $3.00 per hour x 5 workers). Work not paid this month, $600 (40
   hours x $3.00 x 5 workers).

Cash	Wages Expense	(cash basis)
$2,400 ◄	► $2,400	
(decrease)	(increase)	

or

Cash	Wages Expense		Accrued Expense	
$2,400 ◄	► $2,400	$480 ◄	► $480	$480 (from last
	600 ◄		► 600	600 month)
(decrease)	(increase)	(decrease)	(decrease)	(increase)

4. Have machine which cost $1,300. From machine records, machine
   expense, $20—machine cost, $1,300 less estimated scrap value,
   $100—divided by estimated life, 5 years (60 months).

Reserve for Depreciation		Depreciation Expense	
$20 ◄		► $20	
(increase)		(increase)	

Maintaining the original cost of machinery and equipment in the records is valuable. The cost of using the machine, which is called *depreciation,* is an estimate and the reduction in value for depreciation is kept in a separate account, called *reserve for depreciation.*

Many other items of expense and income need the same types of adjustment as just discussed. The main points to determine are: How much of the cost is used up during the period? How much is an asset?

How much is a liability? Find the easiest way to assign the proper values to expenses, income, assets, and liabilities. These records can now be used for analysis and for making reports.

Financial Statements

During each period—say on a daily or weekly basis—a check should be made of a few critical accounts, such as sales, for trends and other changes that are occurring. This enables you to anticipate changes that may be needed. Shortages or overages of stock may be detected.

Financial statements are prepared from accounting records to aid management in its analyses. They are a *profit and loss statement* and a *balance sheet* (see Figures 19–1 and 19–2). The accounts are grouped so that a financial analysis can be performed, as discussed in Chapter 21. Profit and loss statements should be prepared monthly, and balance sheets less often, perhaps semi-annually.

Tax reports are completed for the various government divisions many times during the year. These include reports for income, sales, social security, and excise taxes. As reporting requires an understanding of the regulations, which change periodically, you are advised to see the Internal Revenue Service, accountants, or one of the appropriate tax pamphlets on these reports.

PROCESSING AND STORING INFORMATION

Methods of processing and storing data have been changing rapidly during recent years. In the past, increased use of machines for accounting, reproducing, and other business activities has resulted in reduced costs, improved service, and more management planning and control. More recently, some small businesses have used service bureaus and time-sharing networks for large computer processing of payroll, cost data, and sales data. At present, capabilities and reduced prices of mini-computers have increased management's interest in the benefits of computer use. The increase in the number of alternative methods of processing all kinds of data requires investigation to keep a company competitive.

High-speed collecting and processing of accounting and other data are major uses of computers. Other uses are for controlling machines (numerical control) and improving productivity (composing in printing). Choice of owning or leasing a machine or having the processing done outside depends on the volume and type of work to be done, personnel, and costs. Computers vary as to types of inputs, logic systems for processing, and outputs. Decisions must be made as to whether a new accounting or other system must be designed and whether standard

FIGURE 20–4
Job Cost Record

JOB COST RECORD

FOR _____ ORDER NO. _____

PRODUCT _____ QUANTITY _____

DATE WANTED _____ DATE STARTED _____ DATE COMPLETED _____

DIRECT MATERIALS			DIRECT LABOR			APPLIED OVERHEAD		
DATE	REQ. NO.	AMOUNT	DATE	TIME CARD NO.	AMOUNT	BASIS	RATE	AMOUNT

SUMMARY FOR ORDER NO. _____

DIRECT MATERIALS _____

DIRECT LABOR _____

APPLIED OVERHEAD _____

TOTAL FACTORY COST _____

FACTORY COST PER UNIT _____

From R. Lee Brummet and Jack C. Robertson, "Cost Accounting for Small Manufacturers," *Small Business Management Series, no. 9,* 2d ed (Washington, D.C.: Small Business Administration 1972).

or specially designed programs are to be used. You are advised to obtain help from technically qualified people such as consultants, accountants, and/or sales representatives in revising or initially installing a system for processing your data. Continual review is necessary.

Information that has future use should be properly stored. Critical records should be stored securely such as in safes so as not to be lost, stolen, burned, or otherwise destroyed. Other information accumulated for daily decision making should be stored for easy and quick access such as in the memory system of a computer. Systematic arrangements for keeping records can save time and money.

JOB COSTS

You not only should know the costs for a period, but should know the cost of units or jobs to determine how profitable each is. Estimates and/or standards of material, labor, and overhead are used to establish planned costs for bidding and pricing of a product. Actual data are collected from material requisitions and time tickets, and costs for a job or product are calculated on a job cost record (Figure 20–4). Comparison of the planned and actual costs provide a basis for analyses of operations and prices.

SUMMARY

How we hate records keeping! Yet, it is now essential for survival as a small business or even as an individual, especially at income tax preparation and auditing time.

Considerable detailed, specific, and practical material was furnished in this chapter that should be of help to you in coping with this problem. Specifically, we made suggestions for dealing effectively with: (1) deciding what information is needed; (2) locating sources where information can be found; (3) recording information in appropriate places; (4) choosing the processing equipment; and (5) storing it where it can be retrieved when needed.

We also provided tables, figures, journals, and statements to serve as guidelines for you to use in your business.

QUESTIONS FOR FURTHER DISCUSSION

1. What management decisions do you need to make?
2. What information do you need to make those decisions?
3. For what purposes does a business want information?
4. How can the needed information be classified?
5. What are some sources of information you need?
6. Discuss the recording of information.
7. Discuss the following: sales account, cash income and outgo, accounts receivable, accounts payable, inventory, and expenses.
8. What information did Tobe Jackson not have (in the mini-case)?

21

Planning for a Profit

Profit should not be left to chance. All too frequently, however, that is the way it actually occurs. We have observed in the past that even in those rare circumstances where an effort has been made to plan for profit, it has been on a summary basis. It has been assumed that historical relationships are fixed and, therefore, profits willl continue.

It is now becoming increasingly important that the independent business owner-manager recognizes the need to identify *all* the cost factors. If profit is to be made, then it becomes essential that each item be broken out and costed with a final increment of profit added.

A recurring problem among independent business owners, as well as others, is the lack of accurate cost information, which usually results in "profits" of unknown quantity—or even of a loss. Many times there is also the illusion that the amount of "profit" is greater than it really is. Such was the status of things in the two examples that follow.

A phone call from "Children's Party Caterer" to a professor of small business set in motion a series of conferences concerning the catering business.

During the first interview, the caterer said she had "around $400 of party materials" in her pantry at home. But, when discussing the amount of time that was involved, or the cost of materials used in preparing for each party she was vague. The professor gave her a "homework assignment" to determine the time she spent preparing for and giving each party, and the cost of materials. Her homework findings were revealing, if not pleasant. She found she spent 19–20 hours per party; the cost of materials per party ranged from $20–

$25; she had not computed transportation costs nor the $5–$6 baby sitting cost for her two children. Yet, the average fee charged per party ranged from $20–$25.

When it was suggested that she raise her prices to cover these costs—plus a profit, her response was, "People won't pay it." When the professor responded, "You aren't in the charity business," her exuberant reply was, "Oh! but I like to do it."

For several years, the owner of a compounding company expressed great satisfaction over the profitability of one of his products. His pricing policy was to add 67 percent to raw material costs in order to find the selling price.

When an outside consultant questioned the validity of this practice, the owner became emotionally defensive. The matter was discussed periodically over an extended period until a thorough operating cost analysis was made of that particular product. The facts confirmed that the pricing concept was, in fact, in error. While raw material costs were $1 per pound and the selling price was $1.67, the true costs were $1.83.

Because of the changing nature of our economic environment, all goods and services should be priced for profit. Only in so doing will there be an assurance of profit. This chapter will aid you in planning what profit you desire and determining how you can achieve it.

HOW TO PLAN FOR PROFIT

When you study the profit and loss statement in Figure 19–2 you may tend to read the statement in the following order: "The Sample Company received $231,574 in sales, expended $145,631 for cost of goods sold, had $72,971 of other expenses, and had $12,972 left over as profit." It seems that profit was a "leftover."

Neither you nor Mr. Sample, owner-manager of The Sample Company, can do anything about the past, but you can do something about the future. Since one of your goals is to make a profit, you should plan your operations so that you attain the profit you feel you should make from the business.

Steps for Profit Planning

The steps you need to take to achieve this goal during the coming year are:

1. Establish your profit goal.
2. Determine your planned volume of sales.
3. Estimate your expenses for the planned volume of sales.

4. Determine your estimated profit based on plans reached in Steps 2 and 3.
5. Compare your estimated profit with your profit goal.

If you are satisfied with your plans, you can stop after completing Step 5. However, you may want to check further to determine whether improvements can be made—particularly if you are not happy with the results of Step 5. The following steps may help you understand better how certain changes in your business activities may affect your profit. They are:

6. List possible alternatives that can be used to improve your profit position.
7. Determine how costs vary with changes in sales volume.
8. Determine how profits vary with changes in sales volume.
9. Analyze your alternatives from a profit standpoint.
10. Select changes in your plans, if any, and implement the changes through the use of budgets.

You should be realistic when going through these steps; otherwise you may not be able to attain your goals. You may feel the future is too uncertain to make such plans, but the greater the uncertainty, the greater the need for planning.

> The president of a company said that his forecast was too inaccurate to use, so he had stopped forecasting. The company was not very successful, and he had to sell out.

> Recently, the owner of a small business complained that she could not forecast next year's revenue within 20 percent of actual sales. However, she continued to forecast and plan, because she needed plans from which to deviate as conditions changed.

An Example of Profit Planning

The following material deals with the use of the above steps in a company, using The Sample Company as the example. The details are shown in Figure 21–1.

Place yourself in Mr. Sample's shoes as he plans for the coming year. He should start making his plans several months ahead of the time to put them into effect, say starting in October for the coming calendar year. In order to present a systematic analysis, we will assume he is planning for the first time. Actually, he should be planning for each month at least six months or a year ahead. This can be done by dropping the past month, adjusting the rest of the months in his prior plans, and adding the plans for another month. This planning will give him time to anticipate needed changes and do something about them.

FIGURE 21–1

THE SAMPLE COMPANY
Planning the Profit for the Year, 19—

Step	Description	Analysis	Comments
1.	*Establish your profit goals*		
	Equity invested in company...........	$ 80,000	
	Retained earnings....................	20,000	
	Owner's equity......................	$100,000	
	Return desired......................	$ 15,000	15% × $100,000
	Estimated tax on profit..............	5,000	20%
	Profit needed before income taxes......	$ 20,000	
2.	*Determine your planned volume of sales*		
	Mr. Sample's estimate of sales income...........................	$250,000	8% increase over last year
3.	*Estimate your expenses for planned volume of sales*		

Item of Expense	Actual Last Year	Estimate 19—
Cost of goods.......................	$145,631	$159,100
Salaries............................	41,569	44,000
Utilities...........................	3,475	3,600
Depreciation.......................	5,025	5,025
Rent...............................	1,000	1,000
Building services....................	2,460	2,500
Insurance..........................	2,000	2,000
Interest............................	1,323	1,500
Office expenses......................	2,775	2,900
Sales promotion.....................	5,500	6,100
Taxes and licenses..................	3,240	3,400
Maintenance.......................	805	850
Delivery...........................	2,924	3,200
Miscellaneous......................	875	900
Total...........................	$218,602	$236,075

Step	Description	Analysis
4.	*Determine your profit based on (2) and (3) plans*	
	Estimated sales income..............	$250,000
	Estimated expenses.................	236,075
	Estimated net profit before taxes.......	$ 13,925
5.	*Compare your estimated profit with your profit goal*	
	Estimated profit before taxes.........	$13,925
	Desired profit before taxes...........	20,000
	Difference.........................	−$ 6,075

STEP 1: ESTABLISHING YOUR PROFIT GOAL

Your desired profit must be a specific value that you set as a target. Since you are managing the business, you are paying yourself a reasonable salary. Also, as the owner, you should receive a return on your investment, including your initial investment plus prior earnings left in the business. In order to determine your desired profit, you can compare what you would receive in salary for working for someone else, plus the income you would receive if you invested the same amount of money in a savings and loan association, house loans, bonds, or stocks.

Each of these investments provides a return with a certain degree of risk—and pleasure. Say you could invest at a 7 percent return with little risk, what do you feel the return on your business should be? Peter Drucker states that profits are:

> . . . the "risk premium" covering the costs of staying in business.
> . . . the source of capital to finance the jobs of tomorrow.
> . . . the source of capital for innovation and for growth of the economy.
>   Profit planning is necessary. . . . The minimum needed may well turn out to be a good deal higher than the profit goals of many companies, let alone their actual profits.[1]

Originally, Mr. Sample invested $80,000 in his company and has left $20,000 of his previous profits in the business. He made about 10 percent on investment this past year. He could make about 8 percent if he invested his money in a good grade of bond. He judges his return has been too low for the risk he is taking and feels that about a 15 percent return is reasonable.

In Figure 21–1, Step 1, he enters his investment, his desired profit, his estimate of income taxes (from the past and after consultation with his accountant), and determines he must make $20,000 before taxes, or a 20 percent return on his investment. Having set his goal, he next turns to the task of determining what his profit before taxes will be from his forecast of next year's plans.

STEP 2: DETERMINING YOUR PLANNED VOLUME OF SALES

A forecast of your sales for next year is based on your estimate of factors including market conditions, the level of your sales promotion, your estimate of your competitors' activities, and forecasts of business activity made by business managers, by magazines such as *Business Week*, by government specialists, and by people specializing in forecasting. Talks with your banker, customers, vendors, and others provide added information.

Mr. Sample has been gathering this information and has been watching his company's sales trend. From these, he estimates he can increase his sales about 8 percent. Thus, he enters $250,000 (1.08 × $231,574) in the figure as Step 2.

---

[1] Peter F. Drucker, *Management Tasks, Responsibilities, Practices* (New York: Harper & Row, Publishers, 1974), p. 114.

STEP 3: ESTIMATING YOUR EXPENSES
FOR PLANNED VOLUME OF SALES

To estimate the expenses for next year, you collect the company's costs for the past years. Mr. Sample has listed these for the past year in Figure 21–1, Step 3. (He also has them for the previous years if he needs to refer to them.) These expenses must be adjusted for the planned sales volume, for changes in economic conditions (including inflation), for changes in sales promotion to attain the planned sales, and for improved methods of production.

Mr. Sample has figured that about 63 percent of his income is expended on purchased material and the labor used directly on the goods he sells. He uses this figure (63 percent), adds a one percent increase in the unit costs for inflation, and enters the result, $159,100, for cost of goods. He estimates the value of each of the other expenses, recognizing that some expenses vary directly with volume changes, others do not change at all, and still others have small changes. Each figure for expenses is entered in the appropriate place.

STEP 4: DETERMINING YOUR PROFIT FROM
STEPS 2 AND 3

In this step, he deducts the figure for his total expenses from the sales income, and adds the total of any other income, such as interest. Mr. Sample calculates this amount, and finds that his estimated profit before taxes is $13,925 ($250,000 − $236,075). This amount is slightly better than the $12,972 made last year. (See Figure 19–2.) However, he had thought that the increased volume of sales would increase his profit more than $953.

STEP 5: COMPARING YOUR ESTIMATED PROFIT
WITH YOUR PROFIT GOAL

Mr. Sample then compares his estimated profit with his desired profit. He enters the value for these profits in Figure 21–1, and finds that his plan will result in a profit figure that is $6,075 ($20,000 − $13,925) lower than his goal. After pondering what he should do, he decides to follow the rest of the steps.

STEP 6: LISTING POSSIBLE ALTERNATIVES
TO IMPROVE YOUR PROFITS

As shown in Figure 21–2, Step 6, there are many alternatives for improving profits available to Mr. Sample. Some of these are:

1. Change the planned sales income by:
   a. Increasing the planned volume of units sold by increasing sales promotion, improving the quality of product and/or service, making the product more available, or finding new uses for the product.
   b. Increasing or decreasing the planned price of the units. The best price may not be the planned one. How will these changes affect the profit? Have there been price changes in the past and, if so,

FIGURE 21–2   (continuation of Figure 21–1)

Step
6. Some alternatives:
    a. Increase planned volume of units sold.
    b. Increase or decrease planned price of units.
    c. Decrease planned expenses.
    d. Add other products or services.
    e. Subcontract work.

7. Determine how costs vary with changes in sales volume

Item of Expense	Total Estimated Expenses	Fixed Expenses	Variable Expenses
Goods sold........................	$159,100	$	$159,100
Salaries.........................	44,000	20,000	24,000
Utilities........................	3,600	2,600	1,000
Depreciation.....................	5,025	5,025	
Rent.............................	1,000	1,000	
Building services................	2,500	2,000	500
Insurance........................	2,000	2,000	
Interest.........................	1,500		1,500
Office expenses..................	2,900	1,500	1,400
Sales promotion..................	6,100		6,100
Taxes and licenses...............	3,400	2,500	900
Maintenance......................	850	450	400
Delivery.........................	3,200		3,200
Miscellaneous....................	900	900	
Total........................	$236,075	$37,975	$198,100

8. Determine how profits vary with changes in sales volume

Total marginal income = sales income − variable expenses
= $250,000 − $198,100 = $51,900

Marginal income per dollar of sales income = $51,900 ÷ $250,000
= $0.208/$ of sales income

Estimated costs and profits at various sales volumes:

Sales Volume	Fixed Costs	Variable Costs	Profit
$175,000	$37,975	$0.792 × 175,000 = $138,600	−$ 1,575
200,000	37,975	0.792 × 200,000 = 158,400	3,625
225,000	37,975	0.792 × 225,000 = 178,200	8,825
250,000	37,975	0.792 × 250,000 = 198,000	14,925
275,000	37,975	0.792 × 275,000 = 217,800	19,225
300,000	37,975	0.792 × 300,000 = 237,600	24,425

what has happened? Have there been changes in the attitudes and economic status of the company's customers? Which products' prices should be changed?

c. Combining (a) and (b). It has been observed, on occasion, that some small business owners become too concerned with selling on the basis of price alone. Instead, you should price for profit and sell quality, better service, reliability, and integrity. Never be entrapped by the cliche, "I won't be undersold," or "I will meet any price." The economic path of life is strewn with many failed businesses whose key to failure was this form of pricing strategy.

2. Decrease planned expenses by:

a. Establishing a better control system. Money may be lost by too many people operating the cash register, by poor scheduling, and by having too much money tied up in inventory. Expenses may be reduced if these areas are spotted and controls are established.

b. Increasing productivity of people and machines by improving methods, developing proper motivators, and improving the types and use of machinery.

c. Redesign of the product. Research is constantly developing new materials, machines, and methods for improving products and reducing costs.

3. Add other products or services:

Costs per unit can be reduced by adding a summer product to a winter line of products, selling as well as using parts made on machines with idle capacity, and making some parts customarily purchased.

4. Subcontract work.

Having listed the alternatives that might be available, Mr. Sample needs to evaluate each of them. Some alternatives may not be good choices now. Their evaluation can be delayed until after deciding on more favorable alternatives. An understanding of cost and volume relationships is important in evaluating the alternatives.

STEP 7: DETERMINING HOW CHANGES IN COSTS VARY WITH SALES VOLUME CHANGES

Mr. Sample planned for changes in his expenses with an increase in sales volume, as shown in Step 3 of Figure 21–2. He used a simple breakeven chart, which is shown in Figure 21–3. Notice that as the volume of sales changes, the costs of doing business also change. Straight lines are used, because costs are estimated and a straight line adequately approximates the costs.

Mr. Sample collected the figures for production volume and costs from

FIGURE 21-3
Breakeven Chart, The Sample Company

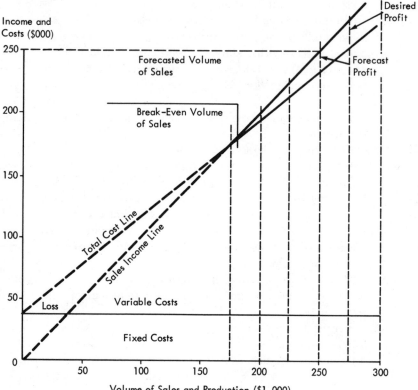

Volume of Sales and Production ($1,000)

his records of the past five years. Production figures and costs for items such as direct materials, depreciation, and office supplies are shown in Table 21–1 and are plotted in Figure 21–4. Note that when the cost of direct materials (A) is plotted in the figure, the cost increases in direct proportion to sales volume, starting at zero cost and zero volume. This is to be expected, as amounts of materials used directly in manufacturing the product increase directly as the volume of products increases.

Depreciation (B) is the loss in value of the machinery and equipment as they are used and as they get older. This is similar to the cost of running your car—its value decreases with time. Businesses usually deduct the estimated resale value of an item from its costs and divide the balance by the life of the item—in years—to obtain its annual depreciation cost. Depreciation is called a fixed cost because its cost per year does not change, regardless of the volume of output, until you buy or sell the fixed asset. Other fixed costs, such as rent, are paid each period.

TABLE 21–1
Data Collected from The Sample Company Records

Year	Production Volume	Direct Materials	Deprecia- tion	Office Supplies
1................	$110,100	$45,900	$3,100	$2,150
2................	139,000	52,900	3,100	2,500
3................	165,200	60,700	3,800	1,900
4................	205,000	74,800	4,400	2,800
5................	231,600	85,100	5,025	2,800
19–(est.).........	250,000	92,000	5,025	2,900

The office expenses account (C) is shown to illustrate what is called a semi-variable expense. When Mr. Sample plots this cost, the line starts at about $1,500 at zero sales volume, and increases from that amount as the sales volume increases. You can use the graphs to help you in your analysis, but be sure to recognize that:

1. The relationships exist only within limited changes in sales volume. Very high sales volumes may be obtained only by such measures as extraordinary sales promotion, added fixed costs for machinery, or in-

FIGURE 21–4
Costs and Volume of Production

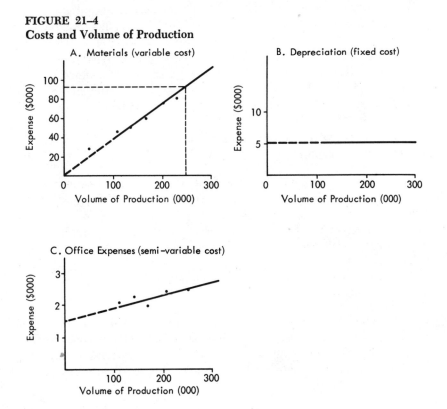

creases in overtime. Low sales volumes result in extra costs of idle capacity, lost volume discounts, and so forth.

2. Past relationships may not continue in the future. Inflation or deflation, changing location of customers, new products, and other factors can cause changes in the costs per unit. Mr. Sample recognized a possible increase in the cost of goods sold for the next year, and increased his cost of goods.

Mr. Sample computed fixed and variable costs for each of his items of expense at his planned volume of sales, and entered the figures in Step 7 in Figure 21–2.

STEP 8: DETERMINING HOW PROFITS VARY WITH CHANGES IN SALES VOLUME

How much does profit increase when you increase sales by $1.00? Mr. Sample planned for $250,000 of sales and $236,075 of expenses. Therefore, each dollar of sales will incur a cost of $0.944 ($236,075 ÷ $250,000). However, if he increases his sales $1.00, the extra sales should not cost him $0.944. The fixed costs will stay constant, and only the variable cost should increase. So his cost should increase only by the variable portion. For $1.00 of sales increase, his cost should increase by only $0.792 ($198,100 ÷ $250,000). His increase in profit per dollar of increase in sales volume, often called *marginal income* (MI), is $0.208 ($1.00 − $0.792). What do you think this means to Mr. Sample?

The marginal income (or gross profit) can be determined for each product, and tells you which product is the most profitable.

STEP 9: ANALYZING ALTERNATIVES FROM A PROFIT STANDPOINT

Mr. Sample can compute his cost and profit at several sales volumes in order to give him a picture of the changes in profit. This is shown in Step 8 of Figure 21–2, and is plotted as a graph in Figure 21–3. Note that the sales volume at which the company still makes no profit is close to $175,000, and it can make the desired profit only if sales increase to $275,000.

Mr. Sample can use the marginal analyses to help him in his decision making, as follows:

1. How much can he reduce his price for a sale to bring in more sales volume? He must not reduce it more than 20.8 percent, for if he does he would be paying out more than the extra sales bring in. Any less reduction would contribute to reducing the fixed-cost charges, or increasing the profit.

2. Is it profitable to increase his advertising $2,000, which, Mr. Sample estimates, would increase his sales $15,000? He should obtain additional profits of $3,120 ($0.208 × $15,000) for the $2,000 he paid out. This would give him an added profit of $1,120 ($3,120 − $2,000).

3. Is it profitable to increase the price 2 percent if he can expect a drop of 5 percent in sales? The price increase would result in a marginal income (MI) of about $0.228 ($0.208 + $0.02), and the profit would change to about $16,175 ($0.228 × 0.95 × $250,000 − $37,975), which would be better than the present expected profit of $13,925.

4. What would a reduction of 5 percent in his variable costs do to profit? The MI should increase to $0.2476 [$1.00 − ($0.792 × 0.95)], and the profit at $250,000 sales volume would be $23,925 ($250,000 × $0.2476 − $37,975). This looks very good if the means can be found to reduce the variable cost without hurting other operations.

5. Which product is the most profitable?

Other alternatives can be evaluated in much the same manner.

Having made these economic analyses, Mr. Sample is now ready to make his final plan for action.

STEP 10: SELECTING CHANGES IN YOUR PLANS

The selection of the changes, if any, depends on your judgment as to what would be most beneficial to your firm. The results of the analyses you have made in the prior steps provide the economic inputs. These must be evaluated along with your other goals. Cost reduction may re-

FIGURE 21–5

THE SAMPLE CO.
Planned Profit and Loss Statement
For the Year 19—

Sales income		$250,000
Less		
Cost of goods sold	$155,900	
Other expenses	76,975	232,875
Net profit before taxes		$ 17,125
Return on investment		17.1%

sult in laying off employees, or a reduction in service to your customers. But lowering prices may satisfy your goal for a larger volume of sales. Higher prices are risky.

Mr. Sample has just read this book, made the case analyses, and has been studying some other management literature. He feels that he can reduce his cost of goods by 2 percent. Figure 21–5 shows a simplified statement of his planned income and outgo for the next year.

SUMMARY

Profits do not just happen! Planning your operations improves your chances of achieving your profit goals. You can achieve more by knowing your goals, understanding the company's sales income to cost relationships, and determining the best operating plan. You should know where your breakeven point is and what the effects of alternative plans would be.

Before making your final plans, you need more information about the financial condition of your company. The next chapter provides you with some more tools for obtaining this information.

QUESTIONS FOR FURTHER DISCUSSION

1. What steps are needed in establishing your future plan?
2. How do you establish your profit goals?
3. How do you determine planned volume of sales?
4. How do you determine planned expenses?
5. What are some alternatives that could improve your planned profit?
6. Explain how you can measure the change in cost because of a given change in sales volume.
7. How can you determine variations in profit because of changes in sales volume?

22

Controlling the Financial Structure and Operations of Your Firm

The underlying theme of this part up to this point has been related to control—in some manner. In this chapter, an effort is made to place control in focus by providing you with sufficient information to understand its nature, its mechanics, and its objectives.

Specifically, it is hoped that you will become aware of some of the causes of poor performance, some characteristics of an effective control system, and suggestions for setting up and operating such a system. In addition, the design and use of budgets are discussed.

WHAT IS INVOLVED IN CONTROL?

Profit planning alone is not enough! Instead, after developing plans for generating a profit, you must then design an operating system to help you carry out those plans. Then, the system must be controlled to see that the plans are carried out and objectives are reached. This material is designed to help you understand the controls that can be used in your small business.

> A machine shop owner, with a reputation as a top-rated, skilled machinist, developed a special machine to produce wooden art-object holders. While there were no comparable American-made machines on the market, there were a number of outstanding machines available from European sources. The machinist arranged to display his machine at a trade show for art dealers in a nearby city.
>
> The reception of this new equipment was good and he received

orders for ten machines. Returning home, he attempted to raise the necessary capital to enable him to produce the machines. After ten months, he was successful in obtaining financial assistance with the aid of SBA. Four months later, the machines were ready for delivery, but his orders had evaporated, having been filled already by the available European machines. As no advance payment had been received, he found himself with ten machines and an additional materials inventory of $18–$20,000.

If he had only obtained advance deposits on the machine orders, and made an arrangement to have received payments as the production of the machines progressed, his dilemma would not have happened.

The Role of Control

As shown in Part II, your managerial functions are planning, organizing, staffing, directing, coordinating, controlling, and evaluating. As shown in Chapter 7, planning provides the guides and standards used in performing the activities necessary to achieve your company's goals. A system of controls is essential if you are to make actual performance conform to the plans you have made. Any deviation from the plans should point to a need for change—usually in performance, but sometimes in the plans themselves.

Each day, we as individuals exercise controls over our activities and also have controls working on us. We control the speed of the car we are driving. Police officers control our traffic flow. Thermostats in our homes keep the temperature within an acceptable range. Controls are everywhere and are established to assure reasonable accomplishment of some set of objectives.

Steps in Control

Regardless of where it occurs, the process of control consists of five steps. They are:

1. Set up standards of performance.
2. Measure actual performance.
3. Compare actual performance with the planned performance standards.
4. Determine whether deviations are excessive.
5. Determine the appropriate corrective action required to equalize planned and actual performance.

The steps are performed in all control systems, even though the systems may be quite different. This chapter covers in detail these five steps of control. The following subjects are discussed:

1. Characteristics of control systems.
2. Causes of poor performance.
3. Establishing standards of performance.
4. Obtaining information on actual performance.
5. Comparing actual performance with standards of performance.
6. The design and use of budgets.

CHARACTERISTICS OF CONTROL SYSTEMS

Almost all control systems have the same characteristics. They should be timely, not overly costly, provide the accuracy needed, be quantifiable and measurable, show cause-and-effect relationships, and be the responsibility of one individual.

Controls Should Be Timely

To keep them timely, checks should be made frequently and as soon as practical after they are needed. You cannot wait until the end of the year to find out what your sales are and whether they meet your plans. Some stores check their daily sales for indications that their performance is not meeting expectations. They have many small purchases, and a daily check helps to indicate whether changes are needed. Manufacturers handle fewer transactions on a less regular basis, so that weekly or monthly checks may be sufficient.

The collection of the totals of an activity, such as sales, takes time. Such data collection has been simplified through the use of cash registers with tapes, mini-computers, and other office machines.

A system for fast checks is valuable. The old adage, "It is too late to lock the barn door after the cow has left," applies well to your controls.

Controls Should Not Be Costly

All controls require the time of a person or of some equipment. Often, paperwork is involved. The cost of the control system needs to be balanced against its value to you. It is not economical "to spend a nickel to save a penny."

Also, some systems are simple and others are complex and costly. Therefore, you should try to reduce the time of employees, the amount of paper, and your time in collecting information. A systematic, simple inspection of what is on the shelves may give enough information for control without a clerk providing a written or tabulated summary of what has been removed from the shelves. At selected times, extra cost may be justified to provide for more detailed controls.

Controls Should Provide the Accuracy Needed

Inspection for control of quality can take two forms. Either it can test every unit of product or only a sample of the units. Statistical techniques can be applied to many areas of control in order to reduce cost and, in many cases, to improve quality. You can periodically check the output per hour of workers, cleanliness of the stock room, and the cost of paper to obtain a good check of performance.

Performance can vary above as well as below standard. Also, part of the variance from standard cannot be controlled, while part can. But, should you do it if you can? The correction of a variation of a few cents in a $10,000 figure may not be desirable or justified, but may be very significant in a figure of $0.05 per unit.

Controls Should Be Quantifiable and Measurable

The choice of measuring sticks for control is vital. Sales can be measured in dollars, pounds, tons, barrels, gallons, grams, kilograms, meters, or other units of product. Which will give you the information you want for control? Which is the least costly? You should choose the unit that will give you the needed control for the least cost.

Controls Should Show Causes, When Possible

A report that the costs of a manufactured product are higher than past costs may indicate the actual situation, but not explain why. On the other hand, a report that the cost per unit of purchased goods is higher than planned, shows not only the actual situation, but also identifies the source(s) of the higher costs.

Controls Should Be Assigned to One Individual

Because you do not have time to control all activities yourself, you need to delegate the authority for those actions to a subordinate. Give that person authority, provide the necessary resources, and then hold the person responsible for accomplishments.

Selected controls that have these characteristics, and that enable you to meet your plans, will be invaluable to you in managing your business.

CAUSES OF POOR PERFORMANCE

Poor performance can result from many factors in a company. A partial list of some of these activities or nonactivities would probably include the following:

1. Customers not buying the company's product.
2. Poor scheduling of production or purchases.
3. Theft and/or spoilage of products.
4. Too many people for the work to be performed.
5. Opportunities lost.
6. Too many free services or donations.

A company oriented toward research and development was found to be providing customers with special R and D service without reimbursement for the thousands of dollars spent in this manner. This policy was changed to the company's profit benefit.

7. Having the wrong objective.

The president of a TV station authorized items such as the purchase of a fleet of sports cars for key personnel. Subsequent low profits resulted in his dismissal and in the elimination of the expensive items.

ESTABLISHING STANDARDS OF PERFORMANCE

Standards of performance are developed from many sources. Some of these are:

1. Intuition.
2. Past performance.
3. Plans for desired accomplishment.
4. Careful measurement of activities.
5. Comparison with other standards or averages. (See Chapter 16 for a discussion of time standards.)

Once the standards of performance are determined, they should be communicated to the people who are responsible for their performance by means of policies, rules, procedures, budgets, and statements of standards. These should be stated in writing.

Statements of standards are norms, stated in writing, for employees to follow. They are usually stated in terms of units consumed or of price paid or charged. Illustrations of these are standard hours per unit to produce a good or service, miles per gallon of gasoline used, and price per part for purchased goods. Standards are used to inform the employee of the time to do a job and to measure how well he or she does it. They are valuable in locating sources of inefficient—as well as efficient—performance.

OBTAINING INFORMATION ON ACTUAL PERFORMANCE

Information on actual performance is obtained through some form of "feedback." It can be obtained by observation, oral reports, written memos or reports, and other methods.

Observation will probably be most satisfying to you, as you are at the scene of action and have direct control over the situation. However, this method is time consuming and you cannot be in all places at one time. Observation time is justified when your knowledge is needed, when your presence may improve the work, or when you are present for other purposes.

Oral reports are less simple, time consuming, and provide two-way communications. They are the most prevalent type of control used in business.

Written memos or reports are prepared when a record is needed and when many facts must be assembled for decision making. These types of feedback are most costly unless they are the original records. A good record system, as discussed in Chapter 20, is a valuable aid and, when designed, should consider the reports needed.

Indirect Control by Means of Reports

The new and very small business usually lends itself to the direct type of controls. But indirect controls may be necessary at later stages of growth. Your best means of this indirect control are the reports just mentioned.

Some *guidelines* that you should follow with respect to reports are:

1. They should cover separate organizational units.
2. They should be designed to be updated as needed.
3. They should be factual and not designed just to make someone look good.
4. They should also be designed to indicate actions that are taken or planned to be taken.
5. They should be designed to highlight comparisons of performance between various organizational units and/or individuals within your company.

These reports should be given to all executive and supervisory personnel concerned. You should operate on the basis of the *exception principle*, which requires an immediate investigation of the causes of significant variations, whether favorable or unfavorable. You should arrange for immediate remedial action to prevent a repetition of bad results or to preserve and continue good results.

Effective Cost Control

Next to providing wanted products, the ability to keep costs low is one of the most important advantages a small company can have. An effective cost accounting system and cost-sensitive controls are vital. As small companies are usually labor-intensive, labor costs typically represent a significant cost area that should be watched and controlled.

COMPARING ACTUAL PERFORMANCE WITH STANDARDS

Information about actual performance, obtained by feedback, is compared to standards to determine whether any changes are needed. This procedure may be simple or complex. Usually it will be simple for the many informal controls used in your decision making. The measures of performance are carried in your head; you make the comparison as you receive feedback; and you make your decisions accordingly. It must be emphasized, however, that this type of control follows the same steps as the more formal types of control. Examples of the use of standards have been discussed in Chapters 12 through 14 and follow the same pattern as control through the use of budgets. The rest of this chapter will cover the design and use of some budgets that are of most value to small business firms.

THE DESIGN AND USE OF BUDGETS

As stated in Chapter 7, a budget can be defined as an itemized summary of probable expenditures and income for a given period of time, which embodies a systematic plan for meeting expenses. The budget system is based on your profit plans for the coming period. As each day, week, or month passes, checks are made to assure progress toward meeting your goals. If actual performances equal the budget, the company is meeting its goals. If they are different, decisions can be made about whether changes are needed. Thus, budgets provide:

1. Guideposts toward your goals.
2. Indications of where trouble exists.
3. Planned actions that need to be taken during the year.
4. At planning time, the feasibility of the plans.

An effective budget system would include close controls in the areas in which poor performance most affects your company. Other areas do not warrant such expense for control, and may be controlled less often. For example, the cost of goods sold by The Sample Company is planned for 63 percent of the sales dollar, and utilities are 1.4 percent. Cost of goods sold may be divided into material and labor, and checked weekly. Utilities might be checked on a monthly basis.

Illustrative budgets presented in this chapter are sales; cash; credit, collections, and accounts receivable; and others.

Sales Budget

The sales budget is the most basic one, for once sales are planned and budgeted, the other budgets can more easily be prepared.

This budget should be the responsibility of a sales manager or you. Let us assume you have a sales manager. You and he/she should have worked up the sales plan for the coming year. Now, how much does the sales department need to sell each day? The plan for The Sample Company call for sales of $250,000 per year. If the firm plans for 203 sales days per year, it must average $1,230 ($250,000 ÷ 203) per sales day. But some days are good days, and some are poor. You may have noticed seasonal, monthly, and even daily patterns in the past. The daily average can be adjusted upward or downward for each day in the week or for the month.

Another method that can be used to obtain daily, weekly, or monthly sales is to modify the figures for the past year. If you think the pattern of sales for the coming year will be the same as that of the past year, merely change last year's daily sales by a given percentage. Mr. Sample planned to increase his sales by 8 percent, as shown in Step 2, Figure 21–1.

How often should you compare actual sales to the budget? A grocery store manager usually makes a daily check, for he finds the daily sales vary considerably from his budget. This is expected, but they should be within range of the budget, and actual sales should range above the expected figure at least as often as below. If they do not, you have a warning signal to do a more complete check or perhaps take some corrective action. Weekly, monthly, and year-to-date summaries provide more stable relationships for control.

Companies may check at longer intervals and may use other types of checks. One owner watches the number and size of contracts at the end of each month. Other managers watch the units of product sold— by product line, by customers and/or by territory. The detail needed for control depends on the nature of the business.

For budgeting purposes, a simple tallying of sales in one column of a control pad, the budget in a second column, and the difference in a third column may be adequate.

Cash Budget

Cash planning is very important if a company is to meet its payments. Cash planning takes two forms: (1) the daily and weekly cash requirements for the normal operation of the business, and (2) the maintenance of the proper balance for all requirements.

Planning Cash Status Monthly-Weekly.   The first type of planning tends to be routine. For example, your company may have a fairly constant income and outgo, which can be predicted. Policies can thus be established for the level of cash to maintain. Therefore, a procedure should be established to control the level of cash. These operating demands represent a small part of the cash needed and tend to remain fairly constant,

Planning Cash Status Monthly-Yearly.   The second type of planning requires a budget for, say, each month of the year. Payments for rent, payroll, purchases, and services require a regular outflow of cash. Insurance and taxes may require large payments a number of times each year. A special purchase, say of a truck, will place a heavy demand on cash. It takes planning to have the *right* amount of cash available at all times.

Procedure for Cash Planning.   Figure 22–1 shows one form of a cash budget for three months ahead. Each month is completed before the next month is shown. Lines 1–3 are completed for the cash estimated to be received. The Sample Company expects to receive 20 percent of its monthly sales in cash. A check of its accounts receivable budget (presented in the next section) can provide estimates of the expected cash receipts in January. Other income might come from interest on investments or the sale of surplus equipment.

Expected cash payments, lines 5–12, should include items for which the company pays cash. The Sample Company might list salaries and utilities separately, and combine advertising and selling expenses under sales promotion. Cash is often paid in the month after the service is performed. Examples of this are payments for electricity and for material purchases. Some cash payments can be made at any one of several times. For example, payments on a new insurance policy can be set when your other cash demands are low. The cash budget shows when payment is to be made.

The cash balance on the first of January, plus the month's receipts, less the month's cash payments, provides you with an expected cash balance at the end of January. A negative balance will require an increase in cash receipts, a decrease in payments, or the "floating" of a loan. In addition, a company should have a certain amount of cash to take care of contingencies. Line 17 is used to show the desired amount needed as a minimum balance. Lines 18–22 show alternative means of maintaining a reasonable cash balance.

A three-month projection is probably the practical minimum estimation for a cash budget. If your company is seasonal or you expect heavy demands on your cash balance, longer periods may be necessary. Also,

FIGURE 22–1

THE SAMPLE COMPANY
Cash Budget Form

CASH BUDGET (for three months, ending March 31, 19—)						
	January		February		March	
	Budget	Actual	Budget	Actual	Budget	Actual
EXPECTED CASH RECEIPTS:						
1. Cash sales..........................						
2. Collections on accounts receivable.....						
3. Other income.......................						
4. Total cash receipts..................						
EXPECTED CASH PAYMENTS:						
5. Raw materials......................						
6. Payroll............................						
7. Other factory expenses (including maintenance).......................						
8. Advertising........................						
9. Selling expense....................						
10. Administrative expense (including salary of owner-manager)............						
11. New plant and equipment...........						
12. Other payments (taxes, including estimated income tax; repayment of loans; interest; etc.)......................						
13. Total cash payments................						
14. EXPECTED CASH BALANCE at beginning of the month..............						
15. Cash increase or decrease (item 4 minus item 13)..........................						
16. Expected cash balance at end of month (item 14 plus item 15)..............						
17. Desired working cash balance........						
18. Short-term loans needed (item 17 minus item 16, if item 17 is larger).........						
19. Cash available for dividends, capital cash expenditures, and/or short-term investments (item 16 minus item 17, if item 16 is larger than item 17)........						
CAPITAL CASH:						
20. Cash available (item 19 after deducting dividends, etc.).....................						
21. Desired capital cash (item 11, new plant equipment)...................						
22. Long-term loans needed (item 21 less item 20, if item 21 is larger than item 20)...........................						

Source: J. H. Feller, Jr., "Is Your Cash Supply Adequate?" *Management Aids no. 174* (Washington D.C.: Small Business Administration, 1973).

as you approach the end of January, your performance should be checked and a month added. In Figure 22–1, the budget for February and March is reviewed toward the end of January, and April is budgeted.

Rationale of Cash Budgeting. The cash budget is a technique for controlling your cash flow so that you can make needed payments and not maintain too high a cash balance. Many small business people do not recognize the importance of moving money through their system as quickly, effectively, and efficiently as possible. Everything else being equal, the faster you can move your money, and turn it over in sales and income, the greater should be your profit.

Credit, Collections, and Accounts Receivable

As previously stated, the extension of credit increases the potential for sales. In Chapter 21 you may have found that the amount in accounts receivable for The Sample Company was large relative to its credit sales. It is potentially dangerous to wait until the end of the year to find this out. Checks should be made often enough to identify customers who are slow in paying and determine the reason(s) for the slow payments. It is believed that the average retailer loses more from slow accounts than from bad debts.

The best control of losses on accounts receivable starts with their prevention. You will enhance your position if you investigate the customer's ability and willingness to pay and provide clear statements of terms. The level of risk is balanced against the gain from giving credit. Then, establish surveillance of past-due accounts each month so that a slow account will be followed up promptly. As time passes and an account is not paid, the probability of collection decreases. You can expect to collect only about one quarter of the accounts over two years old and none of the accounts over five years old.

A first check should be made of the total amount of your accounts receivable. Chapter 19 discussed the ratios used to evaluate the amount of receivables to sales (collection period). Then a comparison of your planned figures and the actual amounts indicates if the situation is satisfactory overall.

Next, the accounts can be "aged." This is a tabulation of the accounts receivable by their age. Thus, The Sample Company's accounts receivable might be something like the following:

	Age of Accounts					
	30 Days or less	*30–60 Days*	*2–6 Months*	*6–12 Months*	*Over One Year*	*Total*
Amount...........	$17,150	$8,102	$2,500	$990	$1,500	$30,242

What should be done? Particular attention should be given to accounts over 60 days past due, and then to the 30–60 day accounts. Remember that most customers are honest, and that you want them to be willing and able to pay.

Mr. Sample's analysis may lead him to write off some accounts as an expense of bad debts and to provide some incentive for earlier payments by slow-paying customers. Bad-debt adjustments should be made at or near the end of the fiscal year. *Uncollectible accounts* receivable create a misstatement of income, and therefore an unjustified increase in your business income tax liability. Unless there exists a reasonable expectation of collecting the account, a good rule of thumb is to write off all accounts six months old or older at tax time. Mr. Sample should examine next year's profit plans for the extra cost of bad debts and for a review of his credit policy.

Other Budgets

Many other budgets can be used to control the activities and investments of your company. Each expense can increase gradually without your noticing the change. Have you noticed how fast the cash in your pockets disappears? You know you need to control this, but it is so very hard to do. Some call it being "nickeled and dimed to death." A company has similar problems. Such diverse situations as the following may contribute to this creeping increase in your firm's costs. A clerk is added to take care of the added paperwork, a solicitor comes in for donations, a big customer wants a special delivery, some of the employees use company stamps for personal letters, and inflation increases costs. While it may be unpleasant to do, these costs must be controlled if your firm is to survive.

Detailed control of inventory has been discussed in Chapter 14. An inventory budget can be established for weekly or monthly checks, based on the level of your expected sales. Purchases may be budgeted on the basis of the demand for materials. The budget can then be coordinated with the inventory and cash budgets. Analysis of a similar nature can be performed for other expenses.

Control over current liabilities is tied to expense and cash plans. Fixed assets and long-term liabilities usually change on a fixed basis, except for infrequent changes of equipment and other needs. Capital stock changes are infrequent, and retained earnings change as a result of the operations of the company. Budgets for fixed items can be maintained through a quarterly set of planned financial statements.

SUMMARY

Controlling is measuring and correcting actions of subordinates in order to ensure that your objectives and plans are achieved. It involves the following steps:

1. Setting up planned standards of performance for you and your employees.
2. Measuring your actual performance.
3. Comparing the actual performance with your planned performance.
4. Determining whether variations between actual and planned performance are excessive.
5. Taking the appropriate action to bring actual and planned performance together.

Controls in a small company need to be simple, yet effective. While a small firm cannot spend much money for controls, it cannot afford the risks of any out-of-control activity. Therefore, it must establish at least a basic control system.

Direct control by an owner is possible for a very small business. As the company grows, however, the owner must depend increasingly on subordinates, and must use policies, rules, procedures, and budgets to help control operations. The owner always uses some type of standards of performance, either formally or informally. Also, as the business grows, more information is recorded rather than being remembered. The art is to keep paper work and cost low, and yet maintain effective controls.

QUESTIONS FOR FURTHER DISCUSSION

1. List the steps in the process of control.
2. List the guidelines to effective use of reports.
3. Define the exception principle.
4. Make a cash budget for your personal use over the next four months.
5. Make recommendations to Mr. Sample for control of his operations.
6. Should a company use a budget for inventory? Explain your reasoning.
7. How should a company with many products, say a drug store, design its sales budget?
8. Who should be made responsible for variances from the budget? Give examples.

23

Safeguarding Your Assets

This final chapter of this Part deals with the many risks that you face in managing and operating your company. The more common risks that are emphasized are: fire hazards; flood, hurricane, and tornado losses; business interruptions; liability; death or other loss of a key executive; business frauds; and crime.

Insurance provides one of the surest and most effective methods of safeguarding yourself from extremely large losses from these risks. In addition, there are many security measures you can take that will further reduce your chances—or at least the magnitude—of loss.

The first part of the chapter discusses how you can use insurance to minimize your losses. The second part looks at a security system you might use to deter losses from crime.

SAFEGUARDING YOUR ASSETS WITH INSURANCE

In deciding what to do about your business risks, you should ask yourself: Without adequate insurance, what happens to my company if:

1. I die or become suddenly incapacitated?
2. A fire destroys my firm's building and/or inventories?
3. A customer is awarded a liability judgment for an accident?
4. There is pilferage by customers or employees?
5. An employee embezzles company funds?
6. A robber "hits" my firm?
7. A customer is awarded a whopping settlement after bringing a product liability suit?

Often, when these disasters occur in small companies whose insurance protection is inadequate or nil, the owners are forced to the wall and operations are severely restricted. Therefore, you need to understand as much as possible about the nature of insurance and how you can use it for your protection.

The Nature of Insurance and Its Limitations

Pure risk always exists when the possibility of a loss is present, but you do not know the possible extent of the loss. To illustrate, the consequences of a fire, the death of a key man, or a liability judgment cannot be predicted with any degree of certainty. Yet it is probably impossible to handle the full burden of pure risks through insurance, because the premiums would be so great that they would leave you nothing, or almost nothing, to operate your business.

The principal value of insurance is its reduction of pure risk. In buying insurance, you are trading a potentially large but uncertain loss for a small but certain cost (the expenditure for the premium.) Briefly, you are trading uncertainty for certainty.

You should not attempt to insure situations that should be handled in other ways, such as:

1. Trivial losses. If the potential loss is trivial, you should not insure against it.
2. Unnecessary coverage. If the insurance premium is a substantial proportion of the value of the property, you should not buy the insurance. For example, if the annual premium for a $50 deductible automobile collision insurance policy is $35 greater than the premium for a $100 deductible, the insured would in effect be paying $35 for $50 additional coverage—70 percent of the possible recovery if a single collision occurred during the policy term.

A well-designed insurance program not only provides for losses, but also can provide other values, including reduction of worry, freeing funds for investment, loss prevention, and easing of credit.

Alternatives to Commercial Insurance

Methods other than commercial insurance for dealing with risk include: noninsurance, loss-prevention, risk transfer, and self-insurance. Perhaps you can reduce costs related to risks in your company by using one or more of these methods, or by combining them with commercial insurance.

Noninsurance is used by most firms, for they must inevitably assume some risks. You should use this method only when the severity of the potential loss is low and for risks that are more or less predictable, preventable, or largely reducible.

Loss prevention programs involve reducing the probability of loss, such as preventing fire and burglary. These programs usually result in reductions in insurance premiums.

Risk transfer involves transferring the risk of loss to others, as in leasing an automobile under a contract whereby the lessor buys the accident insurance.

For *self-insurance* to be considered, you should have adequate finances and broadly-diversified risks. Often, these requirements cannot be met in small companies. Self-insurance plans should be actuarially maintained with a cash reserve accumulated to provide for losses.

Types of Coverage

Some of the major types of insurance you should consider are:

1. Fire.
2. Casualty.
3. General liability.
4. Workers' compensation.
5. Business life.
6. Business continuation life insurance.
7. Fidelity and surety bonds.

The standard *fire insurance* policy, excluding endorsements, insures you for only fire, lightning, and losses due to temporary removal of goods from your premises because of fire. In most instances, this basic policy should be supplemented with an extended-coverage endorsement that insures against windstorm, hail, explosion, riot, and aircraft, vehicle, and smoke damage. Business interruption coverage should also be provided through an endorsement, because frequently "indirect" losses are more severe in their eventual cost than are direct losses. To illustrate, while rebuilding after a fire, you must continue to pay salaries of key employees and expenses such as utilities, interest, and taxes.

Casualty insurance consists of automobile insurance, both collision and public liability, plus general liability, burglary, theft, robbery, plate glass, and health and accident insurance. Automobile liability insurance is necessary because firms are often legally liable for the use of trucks and passenger cars, even though they do not own any vehicles. For example, an employee may use his own car on behalf of the employer. In case of accident, the employer is liable. Automobile physical-damage insurance, covering perils such as collision, fire, and theft, is also essential.

General liability insurance is particularly important because, in conducting your business, you are subject to common and statutory laws governing negligence to customers, employees, and anyone with whom you do business. One liability judgment could easily result in the liquidation of your business.

Worker's compensation and *employer liability* insurance are related to common law requirements that an employer provide his employees a safe place to work, hire competent fellow employees, provide safe tools, and warn his employees of any existing danger. Damage suits may be brought by employees for failure of employers to perform these duties. State statutes govern the kinds of benefits payable under workers' compensation policies, which typically provide for medical care, lump sums for dismemberment and death, benefits for disablements by occupational disease, and income payments for a disabled worker or his dependents.

Business life insurance can be used in several ways in small firms. A firm can buy, or help buy, group life insurance and health insurance policies for its employees. (See Chapter 10.)

Business owner's insurance is an important coverage consisting of:

1. Protection of an owner or dependents against losses from premature death, disability, or medical expenses.
2. Provision for the continuation of a business following the premature death of an owner.

Business continuation life insurance, which is related to (2), is used in sole proprietorships, partnerships, and closely-held corporations. Advance planning involves the provision of ample cash and its use. Life insurance often provides the cash, and a trust agreement, coupled with a purchase-and-sale plan, provides for its use. The cash can be used to retire the interest of a partner or to repurchase the stock of a closely held corporation. As for life insurance, partners or stockholders may buy sufficient insurance on each other's lives to retire each other's interest in case of death. Or the firm may buy the necessary insurance on the lives of its principal owners.

Fidelity and surety bonds are issued by insurers that guarantee to another firm that your employees and others with whom your company transacts business are honest and will fulfill their contractual obligations. Fidelity bonds are purchased for employees occupying positions that involve the handling of company funds in order to provide protection against their dishonesty. Surety bonds provide protection against the failure of others to fulfill contractual obligations.

Guides to Buying Insurance

In buying insurance, the two most important factors are:

1. Financial characteristics of the insurer and the insurer's flexibility in meeting your requirements.
2. Services rendered by the agent.

Financial Characteristics and Flexibility of Insurer.   The major types of insurers are: stock companies, mutual companies, reciprocals, and Lloyd's groups. While mutuals and reciprocals are cooperatively organized and sell insurance "at cost," in practice their costs may be no lower than those of profit-making companies. In comparing different types of insurers, you should use the following criteria:

1.   Financial stability.
2.   Specialization in types of coverage.
3.   Flexibility in the offering of coverage.
4.   Cost of protection.

Only after you are satisfied with the first, second, and third should you consider the fourth of these.

While you ordinarily rely on your insurance agent to judge the financial stability of insurers, *Best's Insurance Reports* are reliable sources of financial ratings and analyses of insurers if you want to check for yourself.

Some insurers specialize in certain types of coverage and offer you the advantage of greater experience in these lines. For example, Lloyd's groups often underwrite "dangerous" risks that other insurers will not assume.

Some insurers offer you great flexibility by tailoring their policies to meet your needs. Tailoring can be accomplished through the insertion of special provisions in the contracts and/or the provision of certain services to meet particular requirements.

In making cost comparisons, you should not confuse the *initial* premium with the *net* premium. Some insurers have a lower initial rate (deviated rate), while others have a higher initial rate but pay a dividend to the insured.

Valid comparisons of insurance costs are difficult to make, but insurance brokers, independent insurance advisers, or agents may assist you. In general, you should avoid an insurer who offers a low premium.

Services Rendered by Agent.   You should decide which qualifications of agents are most important to you, and then inquire about agents among business friends and others who have had experience with them. In comparing agents, some of the things to look for are contacts among insurers, professionalism, degree of individual attention, quality of "extra" services, and help in time of loss.

You should determine whether the agents' contacts among insurers are sufficiently broad to supply all the coverage you need without undue delay and at reasonable cost. Professionalism is indicated by the agent's possession of the *Chartered Life Underwriter* or *Chartered Property and Casualty Underwriter* designations. You want an agent who is willing and able to devote enough time to your individual problems to justify his commission, to survey your exposure to loss, to recommend adequate insurance and loss-prevention programs, and to offer you alternative methods of insurance. He should also be known for serving his clients well in time of loss. The quality of the agent and the companies he represents may be validated by checking with the insurance commissioner of your state or his representative.

Product Liability

In our contemporary legal and societal environment, the liability of the producer or seller of a product or service is increasingly significant. A recent Supreme Court Decision holding a manufacturer liable for a piece of equipment sold to the Navy during World War II and subsequently sold to a series of purchasers has reverberated through both the business and casualty insurance community. Premiums for product/service liability coverage were already becoming exorbitant. Since many small and independent business managers/owners are unaware of the potential liability they may incur in offering their products or services, we urge you to give thoughtful consideration to your possible liabilities. We counsel you to seek the guidance of your attorney and the assistance of your insurance agent/broker to minimize your cost and maximize your protection from product/service liability-claim. Since legislative action and court decisions are regularly occurring in this field, we suggest that you stay current on the legal status.

SAFEGUARDING YOUR ASSETS WITH SECURITY SYSTEMS

It is important that small business owners be aware of crimes that may be committed against their businesses. We, as you, are aware of incidents of criminal acts that have forced small—as well as large—businesses into insolvency.

It is our intention to make you aware of the potential dangers, and to make suggestions that will help you minimize the risks involved and deter those who would harm you. You will note that we said "deter," not "prevent," for it seems impossible to have a security program that will prevent all criminal acts against your business. All you can hope for is to minimize their occurrence and severity.

Nature of the Problem

Armed Robbery.   In recent years, the incidence of armed robbery has increased significantly. A person—or persons—enters the premises armed and with the intent of obtaining cash as quickly as possible and then departing. Since time is of the essence in these circumstances, locations that afford easy access and relatively secure escape routes seem most vulnerable to being "hit." This type robber usually wants to be in and out of the location in three minutes or less in order to minimize the risk of identification or apprehension. The pressure of the situation tends to make the robber "trigger-happy." The high price of drugs has encouraged the addict to fund the habit in this fashion, and the effects of the drugs further add to the danger of physical harm during the robbery and lessen the likelihood of talking the culprit(s) out of the act. Those businesses that use the same person, schedule, and route to take the deposits of cash to and from the bank are increasing their vulnerability to armed robbery.

Armed robbery is not always confined to cash; it may involve the taking of high-value merchandise such as diamonds, watches, drugs, electronic components, finished products, TVs, digital computers, cameras, radios, and stereophonic and high fidelity equipment. We are becoming more aware of areas particularly susceptible to crime. The nature of the crimes seems to fit a pattern—there may be a given neighborhood where armed robbery occurs frequently; there may be another one where pilferage is the problem; or there may be an area where both categories are problems. Because of the increasing incidence of this type problem, you—as a prospective business owner—need to evaluate the potential site with this problem in mind.

Pilferage.   Pilferage has become a serious problem for businesses, and the reasons are numerous. One of the many reasons is *inflation*. As incomes have not kept abreast of inflation, people resort to pilferage to maintain the standard of living to which they have become accustomed. Many national merchandising businesses add a factor of 2 to 3 percent pilferage cost to their prices, but even this may not be enough to compensate for the total loss. Another reason is the recent high level of *unemployment*. In order to survive, some of the unemployed have resorted to pilferage. In other instances, pilferage is a game; a challenge—"Can I get away with it?"; and unfortunately, in some circumstances, it occurs for peer approval.

Types of Pilferage.   There are essentially two types of pilfering— that done by *outsiders*, which is usually called "shoplifting," and that done by *employees*.

Shoplifting may be done by the amateur, the kleptomaniac, or the professional.

The *amateur* may be a thrill-seeker who takes an item or two— experimenting to see whether he or she can get away with the act—or one who may not be able to purchase the item and the desire overcomes self-control. The *kleptomaniac* is the individual with an uncontrollable urge to take things, whether it is needed or not. The *professional* is a person who may wear specially prepared or large garments to conceal stolen merchandise. Instead of special garments, the thief may carry a large handbag to accommodate stolen merchandise. Other professionals may ask you for an empty box, or boxes, which will then be used to facilitate removal of merchandise. Another one may walk in with an air of confidence as if he or she were a delivery person or clerk, pick up merchandise, and proceed out of the store. Some examples of pilferage are:

> A convenience food store was forced out of business by pilferage losses. Customers concealed prepackaged cheese, luncheon meats, and other high value items in regular garment pockets and hand-bags.

> The manager of an independent supermarket, near a major university campus, caught a young man with four hams hidden under a large sport shirt.

> A well known matron was at the checkout counter. Upon inspection, her large purse was found to contain several prepackaged steaks and packages of luncheon meat. The store owner was heard to observe, "I thought she was one of our good customers. She has been coming in here for years. I wonder how much she has taken?"

> An independent supermarket kept its empty boxes at the front of the store, outside of the checkout counter. A man entered the store during the rush hour, walked to the pile of empty boxes, and selected a large one. He moved to the cartoned cigarette display, filled the box with cartons of cigarettes, hoisted it on his shoulder, and proceeded to pass through the checkout as if he had an empty box. After clearing the checkout counter, but before reaching the door, the box separated and 30 cartons of cigarettes fell to the floor. The culprit departed in haste.
>
> Not easily discouraged, the culprit returned the following day with a well-taped box. Being immediately recognized, he was invited from the premises.

Employee pilferage may range from the act of an individual who takes only one or two small items to the raids of groups that remove truckloads of merchandise. An individual employee, operating independently, may steal from the employer. Frequently, this is the person least likely to be suspected of such an act. The "loner" may take anything from an inconspicuous item to anything he or she can get out the door.

Two or more employees may conspire to cheat their employer by stealing. Some merchants have thought if they required employees to purchase merchandise from other employees that they would be less likely to steal. Instead, employees sometimes may conspire to report a much smaller amount for the sale on the sales ticket.

Employees sometimes conspire with outsiders to steal from their employer. It may occur several ways, by charging a lower price or by placing additional merchandise in the package. Some examples are:

> A service station attendant serviced a friend's car by changing the oil, lubricating it, and putting in $4 worth of gasoline. He charged the friend only $1.

> A tire dealer's service attendant sold four first-line tires to a customer for $50 and pocketed the cash.

Areas of Special Consideration.   Some areas needing special attention are pilferage of construction materials, removal of supplies and inventories, and white-collar crimes.

Construction materials may be pilfered by either employees or outsiders. A lack of controls, looseness of accountability, and the minimal —or nonexistent—security at storage yards and job sites lead to this type of pilferage. Some examples are:

> Workers loaded material to take to a job site, but no tally sheet identifying the quantity or kind of material was filled out. The trucks were detoured to the site of a side job being done after hours by the employees, and a portion of the material was unloaded.

> Some workers took a special route to a job, stopping at a place where some pipe, rolls of electric wire, conduit, and electrical switch boxes were left for later retrieval and sale.

> Unattended job sites or storage areas have been raided on weekends and whole truckloads of materials have been removed.

> Many builders and contractors fail to identify and enumerate the materials required for specific jobs. This makes control and accountability difficult and seems to invite the thieves to come and help themselves.

The *removal of supplies and inventories,* such as raw materials, finished goods, maintenance supplies, tools, equipment, parts, and so forth is not an uncommon practice by employees in small plants. Some examples follow:

> A batch mixer in a small baking plant carried away sugar, flour, and shortening in 25-pound metal cans in which other materials

were received. Supposedly, he was taking some empty cans home. The loss was indeterminate, but significant.

A fast food place lost $20,000 of raw chicken in a six-month period, not by the piece, or even whole chickens, but by the case—out the back door.

A chemical compounder wrote off 50,000 pounds as inventory shrinkage in six months. He said, "It costs too much to take physical inventory each month."

White-Collar (employee) Crimes.   Another category of serious abuse against business is white-collar crime. Possibly, the "take" is greater than the totals in other categories. White-collar crimes include the removal of cash; falsification of accounts; fraudulent computer manipulation; bribery of purchasing agents and various other employees; collusions that result in unrecorded transactions; sale of proprietary information; sabotage of new technology, new or old products, or customer relations; and so forth.

Preventive Measures

Armed Robbery.   There are several measures that can be taken to reduce the chances of being robbed. They include modifying the layout of your store, securing entrances, using security dogs, varying the methods used to make deposits of cash, and redesigning the surrounding area.

Modifying Store Layout.   *Location of the cash register* or cash is important in preventing armed robbery. If the perpetrator(s) is not able to dash in, scoop up the cash, and dash out again within a short time, he or she is not as likely to attempt the robbery. *Visibility from the outside,* or being able to see all over the customer area, is also important.

One convenience food chain removed all material from the windows that would impair the view into the store. In addition, it encouraged crowds at all hours by using various gimmicks, and attracted policemen by giving them free coffee. The average annual robbery rate dropped from ten to one per unit.

Securing Entrances.   Security of entrances and exits is extremely important in preventing robbery. Rear doors should be kept locked and barred. Windows should be kept secure by bars and locks. In high crime neighborhoods, many businesses have found it advantageous not to use glass in their windows, but to use Lexan,* a tough, shock-resistant, transparent material, or some other material of similar characteristic. Safes are

---

* A trademarked product of General Electric Corporation.

not infallible. Many businesses no longer allow access to the safe's combination by more than one or two people. It is not uncommon for a sign to be posted on the safe, or in its vicinity, advising that the person on duty does not have access to the combination.

Dogs.   You may obtain security dogs from people who specially train vicious dogs to respond to command. These animals have been found to be effective deterrents against armed robbers. The animals may be purchased outright or rented. Even if you purchase a dog(s), it may be advisable to have them periodically run through a refresher course to keep them effective. However, health and sanitation regulations, in some jurisdictions, may prevent the use of dogs.

Varying Routine for Depositing Cash.   *Daily deposit of cash* is highly recommended. Banks and other businesses are rigidly enforcing minimum cash rules for cash drawers. In order to reduce the loss in the event of an armed robbery, some business people have found it desirable to keep only *minimum cash on hand* and to use safes with unobtrusive hiding places.

> Several businesses we know have found it advantageous to use lock boxes with a sign posted for all to see: "Notice: Cash in drawer does not exceed $50."

> Other stores we have seen use a locked cash box and accept only correct change or credit cards during certain hours. (The locked cash box usually has an accompanying sign saying that no employee on duty has a key to the box.)

The Schedule for Making Bank Deposits Should Be Varied Frequently.   Different people, different vehicles, and different times should be used to make the deposits. Routine and easily recognized people and vehicles involved with the deposit invite the would-be robber and make it easier to plan and carry out the robbery.

Redesigning the Surroundings.   Well-lighted parking lots help deter robbers. If possible, try to keep vehicles from parking too near the entrance of your business. Anything that reduces the convenience of access, or creates the possibility of a foul-up, reduces the probability of armed robbery.

> A convenience foodstore parking lot had concrete pre-cast bumper blocks so dispersed in the lot that they deterred fast entry and exit from the lot.

It is advisable for some businesses to use video cameras to photograph the crime in action from several different camera angles, or to use video cameras tied to TV monitors in a security office.

Pilferage.   There are several techniques that can be used by retail establishments and contractor/construction firms.

Retail Merchandising Establishments.   These firms have found the following measures effective in reducing pilferage.

1. *Wide-angle mirrors* placed strategically about the store expand the opportunity to observe employee or customer behavior that indicates pilferage.
2. *One-way mirrors* have been used by some retail outlets with secret passageways to observe activities in various parts of the store. Perhaps their effectiveness as a deterrent is more psychological than real.
3. *Electronic noise activators* are also used. There are several types of gadgets that can be attached to the merchandise, some visible, some not, that will activate an alarm if the merchandise is removed from the area without first detaching the warning device.
4. *TV cameras* are frequently tied to monitors that allow one person to observe a large portion of the store.
5. *Security guards* may also be used. If your business is large enough and if pilferage is sufficiently serious, you may wish to employ a full-time security person. All too frequently, however, such people are poorly trained and are ineffective. Therefore, you may wish to obtain the service of an independent security organization. There are local and national organizations that provide this type of service.
6. *Security audits* are also effective. *Unannounced spot checks of cash register activity* may be advisable. Check to see if appropriate amounts are rung up. Be sure that correct change is returned and that all items are accounted for by the clerk or cashier.

    Unannounced spot checks may be made of employees' packages, car trunks, lunch pails, or other personal effects, and rest rooms. Check garbage or waste disposal holding areas for concealed materials that may be removed later.

    Visible security surveillance may be used. It is important to observe employees in the normal work activities for indications of criminal acts.

    Monthly or quarterly physical inventory checks may be made. In many situations this serves as a deterrent. On occasion, it has been found even more effective to conduct weekly inventory checks.
7. *Polygraph tests* may be used before and after hiring—if legal requirements are met. While the use of this device is questioned by unions and others, it is considered by many business people to serve as an effective deterrent against employee pilferage activities. Some firms require that such a test be taken by *all* employees periodically. In the event of questionable circumstances, it may be administered specially to accommodate the immediate situation. Also, it is used,

on occasion, in screening new employees. *A word of caution:* you should thoroughly investigate the background of persons or organizations responsible for administering the tests. We would go one step further and suggest the *counsel of your attorney* before using them.

Construction Contractors, Home Builders, and so Forth. These firms need to take special care to prevent or minimize pilferage.

Planning and control are important. You need to develop a schedule of materials needed for each job, including both the correct quantities of materials and the time they will be used on the job. This will facilitate ordering the appropriate quantity of material, and the delivery can be timed with need. Delivery of material far in advance of need increases the opportunity for loss.

> One contractor found that by running his material inventory down near the end of the week and not replacing it until early Monday morning, he could substantially reduce his losses.

Purchasing procedures may be improved by ordering dimensional lumber and other materials and by determining the exact material requirement as specified in the project plans. These improvements reduce the opportunity for waste in the construction process and make it more difficult for removal of material from the job site without detection. This also helps you maintain more effective control over your costs.

Other security measures that you can take include:

1. *Storage yards* should be *fenced and well-lighted.* There should be a cleared area adjacent to the fence on all sides.
2. *Dogs* may be used to *patrol construction areas.* Robbers sometimes use tranquilizer dart guns or live ammunition to overcome the dog(s). In spite of this, dogs are one of the most effective and economical deterrents to after-hour losses.
3. If the project is large enough, you may wish to hire your own *security guards.* For small projects, you may want to procure the services of private security patrols. In recent years, vandalism at residential project sites, and the removal of plumbing fixtures, lighting fixtures, carpeting, and so forth have underscored the need for on-site security patrols.
4. *A combination of security dogs and security guards* is more effective than either used individually.
5. *Locks that are difficult to "jimmy"* seem to provide additional security. A visit to your locksmith or your building hardware dealer may provide you with the latest complementary lock systems. No system is foolproof, however, so you may discourage only the amateurs with some of these systems.
6. You need a *receiving clerk* or some employee who is *sufficiently knowledgeable* to *assume the responsibility for checking materials*

into the job site. Unfortunately, too many people fail to recognize the importance of this activity and permit it to be dealt with haphazardly. They say, "Put it over there and when you've finished unloading, check back with me." Unannounced rotation of the person responsible for receiving materials may serve as a deterrent to collusion with the delivery person.

White-Collar Crimes.   Special measures must be taken to minimize crimes by white-collar personnel.

Purchasing agents may take bribes, not always in cash, but in various gratuity forms. Audit of inventory levels and prices on a comparative basis may uncover undesirable circumstances. This requires a much more thorough and detailed audit in this area than is sometimes carried out.

Cashiers and disbursing agents have been known to prepare bogus or forged invoices, purchase orders, receiving reports, and so forth. Spot audits of documents and of actual receiving areas should help in reducing this type of loss.

Sales adjustments should be handled by an officer of the company. No salesman should be permitted to make the adjustment, for that practice allows collusion and cash compromises to the customer and salesperson's advantage. Appropriate reports showing adjustments made on each customer's account should aid in revealing any misdeeds.

Computer crimes are increasing in frequency and severity. If you use a computer in your business, you need the services of a CPA firm with computer security expertise.

Special Note.   You should be aware of your white-collar employees' work habits. They may all be open and aboveboard, but they deserve being checked. You should ask yourself questions such as: Do they work nights regularly? Do they never take a day off? Do they forego their usual vacation? Standards of living, dress, car, housing, entertainment, and travel that seem to be excessive in terms of income are often signals of economic misconduct.

Fraud.   Another crime requiring special measures is fraud involving check cashing, the use of credit cards, and trade documents.

Check Cashing.   Proper identification along with a device that takes pictures of the check and the person cashing it tend to discourage bad check artists. Your bank may assist you in developing effective identification procedures.

Credit Cards.   Since credit cards are frequently stolen, you or your cashier should require additional identification. You should be sure that the signature corresponds to the one on the card.

Recently a professional thief removed a credit card from a home. The card had never been used by the owner, but the thief used it to purchase an airline ticket, some personal items, and a new set of burglar tools. He signed the purchase tickets by crudely printing the name that was on the card. The carelessness in accepting the card needlessly cost the airlines and merchants $750.

Trade Documents.   As in the case of credit cards, be sure to ascertain the validity of these items. Each year, millions of dollars are lost by business people through carelessness that allows others to pawn off on them bogus documents. A careful check with the appropriate bank or company would have prevented many of these losses.

Document Security

Our recent personal experiences in working with small businesses—as well as press releases in recent years—have made us aware of the importance of document security.[1] *Information is a vital factor in directing and controlling business activities.* Its management and maintenance are significant in assuring the continuation of the business. Since the life of an organization is dependent on the appropriate recording of information and its transmission to the appropriate person, it is essential to have a storage facility that will protect the information from unauthorized persons, as well as from loss by fire or other hazards of nature.

In the discussion that follows, the connotation of "document security" will be very broad. Not only will the term concern the physical document, but it will address itself to the need for documentation of information and the routing of the documents to the appropriate person(s) in the organization.

The proprietary nature of business records and various documents make their protection from unauthorized eyes and hands essential. The trade secrets and competitive advantage of the firm may be aborted by the passage of this information into the wrong hands.

In an effort to preserve the sanctity of information records—as well as business documents—it may be necessary to arrange a restricted area where information and documents may be processed and stored. An unbending rule should be that *under no circumstance will you permit the removal of this material from the restricted area or* from the business premises. We have known instances where the business owners thought they were able to gain an economic advantage by permitting material to be carried to an employee's residence where the employee would work on the firm's records after hours and at his or her convenience. The opportunity for loss, the opportunity for access by unauthorized persons, and the risk of a charge for inadequate compensation makes this practice inexcusable.

---

[1] See the case in Part III entitled "Holly Springs Food" for an example of the importance of document security.

In order to minimize the space requirements, it may be desirable to have older, inactive records transferred to microfilm or microfiche. This requires a workable classification and cataloging system in order that the material may be retrieved for study or reference when needed.

In designing and maintaining a document security system, it is desirable to make a list of personnel who are authorized to have access to these records and documents. This list should be frequently updated and provided to the person or persons responsible for the document security.

QUESTIONS FOR FURTHER DISCUSSION

1. Discuss the different methods that are available to reduce the chances of being robbed.
2. Discuss four alternatives to Commercial Insurance.
3. Discuss the criteria one should use when comparing different types of insurers.
4. What are some measures which have been found effective in reducing pilferage?
5. Should a manager insure the business against all possible losses? Discuss.

WHERE TO LOOK FOR FURTHER INFORMATION

Anthony, R. N., and Reece, James S. *Management Accounting: Text and Cases.* 5th ed. Homewood, Ill.: Richard D. Irwin, Inc., 1975.

Anthony, Robert N., and Welsch, Glenn A. *Fundamentals of Management Accounting.* Homewood, Ill.: Richard D. Irwin, Inc., 1974.

Brummet, R. L., and Robertson, J. C. "Cost Accounting for Small Manufacturers," 2d ed. *Small Business Management Series no. 9.* Washington, D.C.: Small Business Administration, 1974.

Crowningshield, Gerald R., and Gorman, Kenneth A. *Cost Accounting: Principles and Managerial Applications,* 3d ed. Boston: Houghton Mifflin Co., 1974.

Greene, Mark R. "Insurance Checklist for Small Business." *Small Marketers Aids no. 148.* Washington, D.C.: Small Business Administration, 1971.

Gruenwald, A. E., and Nemmers, E. E. *Basic Management Finance.* New York: Holt, Rinehart, and Winston, Inc., 1970.

Hedrick, F. D. *Purchasing Management in the Small Company.* New York: American Management Association, Inc., 1971.

Horngren, Charles T. *Cost Accounting: A Manager's Analysis,* 3d ed. Englewood Cliffs, N.J.: Prentice-Hall, Inc., 1972.

Katz, B. *Happiness or Misery.* Alexandria, Va.: Overlook Company, 1971.

Kenney, Donald P. *Minicomputers.* New York: Amacom, 1973.

Kreutzman, H. C. *Managing for Profits.* Washington, D.C.: Small Business Administration, 1968. (Management and Financial Control Series.)

Miller, D. E. *The Meaningful Interpretation of Financial Statements,* rev. ed. New York: American Management Association, Inc., 1972.

Mockler, Robert J. *The Management Control Process.* New York: Appleton-Century-Crofts, 1972.

Moran, Christopher J. "Preventing Embezzlement." *Small Marketers Aids no. 151.* Washington, D.C.: Small Business Administration, 1973.

Niswonger, C. Rollins, and Fess, Phillip E. *Accounting Principles,* 11th ed. Cincinnati, Ohio: South-Western Publishing Co., 1973.

Sanzo, Richard. *Ratio Analysis for Small Business,* 3d ed. Washington, D.C.: Small Business Administration, 1970.

Welsch, G. A. *Budgeting: Profit Planning and Control,* 3d ed. Englewood Cliffs, N.J.: Prentice-Hall, Inc. 1970.

Welsch, Glenn A., and Anthony, Robert N. *Fundamentals of Financial Accounting.* Rev. ed. Homewood, Ill.: Richard D. Irwin, Inc., 1977.

Woelfel, B. L. "Financial Audits: A Tool for Better Management." *Management Aids, no. 176.* Washington, D.C.: Small Business Administration, 1972.

Zwick, Jack. "Handbook of Small Business Finance." *Small Business Management Series no. 15.* Washington, D.C.: Small Business Administration, 1965.

cases for part VI

VI–1   Money Is Not Enough[1]

It is not uncommon for owners of independent businesses to think that if additional funds were available "everything would be fine" with the business. Such was the case with the president and major stockholder of a veneer and custom plywood plant, which was a labor intensive operation.

Initially, he obtained a $100,000 SBA guaranteed loan from a local bank. The funds were to be used for purchasing a woodchipper (for converting the residual veneer cores to chips that could be sold to a paper mill) and for working capital. For a short time, things seemed to improve after the chipper was installed—at least, bills were kept current. However, after operating the chipper for a week, it was shut down, resulting in an accumulation of residual cores. This, plus the scrap veneer, necessitated the expansion of the two steam boilers' fireboxes.

In time, things were again in a state of financial crisis. An approach was made to the SBA to increase the guaranteed loan from $100,000 to the maximum of $350,000. An SBA representative called at the plant and reviewed the operation. He concluded that by replacing the veneer peeling knife machines with four new machines the labor force could be reduced by 12 workers, down to a work force of 212 people.

It was apparent that the operation involved too much manual labor

---

[1] Prepared by Curtis E. Tate, Jr., University of Georgia.

and too little mechanization. The excessive use of labor combined with the aging state of the plant created a burden of excessive cost, which, in time, placed the company in another financial crisis and the banker and SBA in an uncomfortable position.

QUESTIONS FOR DISCUSSION

1. What does the case illustrate about the need for balancing the use of resources?
2. Referring to Figure 21–3, what did the investment in new equipment do to the breakeven point?
3. What would you do if you were the banker? SBA adviser?

VI–2   Ruth's Dashiki[1]

Bill was a finance major at a large university located in a major Northeastern city. He was registered for Finance 559, an independent study course in which each student was given the assignment of studying a small business firm and recommending courses of action the firm should take. The course was a cooperative effort between a professor at the university and the Small Business Administration. The SBA identified those firms needing assistance, and the faculty member assigned, guided, and evaluated the student "consultant."

After being told what was expected of him in terms of a final report, Bill had been assigned to Ruth's Dashiki. From the meager information he had been given, he learned that Ruth's Dashiki was a small firm owned and operated by a black woman who specialized in designing and making Afro-American clothing.

He found Ruth's Dashiki in a small, somewhat run-down business district in the south side of town. The store was located next to a rather run-down pawn shop. Small display windows on either side of the door contained several brightly patterned garments.

The business had grown out of Ruth's sewing hobby. She had always made most of her family's clothing, and relatives frequently asked her to sew something for them. She possessed an obvious talent for selecting fabrics and designing garments and, through family and friends, developed a reputation as a skilled seamstress.

---

[1] Prepared by Donald DeSalvia and Allan Young, Syracuse University.

After she accepted the offer of the deacon of her church group to pay her to make several choir and ministerial robes, she began to take the prospect of forming a business more seriously. She purchased some equipment and material, and took orders from people referred to her by friends and relatives. She operated on a part-time basis.

She felt the business could be expanded sufficiently to warrant her full-time attention, and left her job. At the same time, she applied for a Small Business Administration loan. After an investigation, the loan was approved, and an initial installment of $2,000 was granted in April 1971. A major portion of this installment was used to cover the debts she had contracted in setting up and running her business to that time.

A new storefront location was found with a rental of $125.00 per month. The relocation, extensive renovations, and installation of equipment cost the firm several months' output and absorbed a good share of a second $7,000 installment of the SBA loan.

A seamstress was hired at $1.85 per hour, one-half of which would be paid for fifteen weeks by the New York State Department of Labor under an On-The-Job-Training Contract. Ruth believed the contract could be extended to cover additional employees as needed.

Bill was impressed with the product line and the quality of craftsmanship embodied in the finished garments. The dashiki was the primary item in the line. A dashiki is a loose-fitting type of shirt made in a variety of styles and patterned fabrics. Although a small inventory of finished garments was available, most items still were made to order. Their retail price varied from $17 to $20, depending upon the fabric and the amount of decoration on the garment. Vests sold from $12 to $15, and women's floor-length robes varied from $30 to $35. Ruth also carried some purchased accessories and jewelry. In the past, choir and ministerial robes had been made, but no orders had been received for them in several months.

Sales were entirely dependent upon word-of-mouth advertising. The firm was located in a low income area with a high proportion of welfare families and with little consumer traffic.

Bill could find no direct competitors, but wondered if a sufficient market could be developed for the product. There were about 200,000 residents in the city with approximately 250,000 in the surrounding area.

The store consisted of an 1,800-square-foot showroom/salesroom and production room. Equipment used in making the garments consisted of five sewing machines, a hand iron, an ironing board, a cutting table, a clothes rack, one electric scissors, seven manikins, several pairs of scissors, and sales display and office equipment.

The production process was fairly simple. One person carried out all the operations needed in making a garment. These included cutting, sewing, and pressing. There was sufficient work space and equipment to greatly expand output. An item was seldom completed without frequent interruptions, making it difficult for Bill to ascertain how long it took to make each item. He estimated the average dashiki could be made in three or three and one-half hours. Vests took four to five hours, and robes took about five hours. A dashiki required one and one-fourth yards of material as compared with three and six yards for vests and robes respectively. Ruth purchased fabrics from the Fabric Center at prices that varied from $2 to $3 per yard.

EXHIBIT 1

RUTH'S DASHIKI
Balance Sheet
November 1, 19 × 1

Assets

Current Assets

Cash............................	$ 53.40	
Accounts receivable................	548.26	
Finished goods inventory...........	245.00	
Materials inventory................	780.82	
Prepaid expenses...................	75.00	
Office supplies.....................	124.16	
		$ 1,826.64

Fixed Assets

Machinery and equipment..........	2,669.00	
Improvement in property...........	2,315.65	
		$ 4,984.65
Total Assets.............		$ 6,811.29

Liabilities

Accounts payable..................	$1,672.43	
Taxes payable.....................	60.53	
Notes payable—SBA...............	9,000.00	
Notes payable—Other.............	128.10	
Total Liabilities.........		$10,861.06
Equity.................		($ 4,049.77)

Bill also was concerned with the management of the firm. Friends and relatives frequently spent hours visiting the store. During these visits, little work was accomplished. Ruth occasionally hired people for one or two days to "straighten up a bit." When asked about this practice, Ruth explained that those employed were relatives who were out of work and "hard up" and she had to help them if she could.

Bill found that although the business had been operating for some time, there was no system of record keeping. Therefore, he found it difficult to make sense of the assortment of paid and unpaid bills, receipts, scraps of paper, and notes Ruth kept. She had both a personal and a business checking account, and used them interchangeably. Deposits seldom were recorded. In addition, she frequently used bank checks to make withdrawals without recording them in either account, with the result that the true balance was uncertain. With some guesswork and a great deal of estimating, Bill was able to construct an estimated balance sheet as shown in Exhibit 1.

He was able also to rough out a tentative profit and loss statement for October (Exhibit 2). October, however, was not a typical month, since renovations were still in process at that time. The figures also were incomplete, for depreciation was not included. A salary for Ruth was also omitted, although the student learned that she drew out an

EXHIBIT 2

RUTH'S DASHIKI
Profit and Loss Statement
October, 19 × 1

Sales..........................			$609.81
Cost of goods sold			
Labor........................	$184.78		
Materials....................	121.96		
	$306.74		
Shop Overhead			
Rent........................	$125.00		
Debt service.................	105.00		
Utilities.....................	10.58		
	$240.58		
Total costs..............		$547.32	
Less OJT*.............		−85.87	
Net Cost.............			$461.45
Net Profit.............			$148.36

* State Department of Labor reimbursement for on-the-job-training.

average of about $150 per week. For subsequent months, the costs of telephone service and insurance would have to be included. He estimated these at $30 and $20 respectively. On the more positive side, sales could be expected to increase. The $609.81 of sales had been achieved while renovations were going on and without any promotional activities at all.

Bill knew the firm was seriously short of cash, but Ruth expected to ask the SBA for a third installment. He wondered how large a loan would be necessary and how much more the SBA would be willing to advance.

Credit sales were frequent and informal. Ruth often allowed people to take garments without a down payment and without specific provisions for payment. As a result, accounts receivable were high. The age distribution of accounts receivable is shown in Exhibit 3.

EXHIBIT 3
RUTH'S DASHIKI: Age of Accounts Receivable

12 Months and over......................	$ 90.20
9–11 months.............................	65.00
6–8 months..............................	100.78
3–5 months..............................	0.00
0–2 months..............................	292.28
Total accounts receivable.............	$548.26

QUESTIONS FOR DISCUSSION

1. What do you consider to be Ruth's objectives? Are there indications that she is following these objectives? Not following them?
2. What kind of planning has she done? What should she do? (Remember that this is a very small business.)
3. Examine the financial statements that Bill developed. Would you make any changes? If so, explain.
4. What kind of a financial record keeping system do you advise for Ruth?
5. Can a reasonable level of profit be obtained in the future? Show the breakeven point for the company and your estimate of the volume of sales needed for a reasonable profit.
6. How much of a loan would you advise Ruth to ask for? What other sources of funds might be available?
7. How would you advise Ruth to determine her prices? Do present prices appear to be reasonable?
8. What financial analysis tools can be used to determine the condition of the company? What do they show?
9. Evaluate the credit policy of the company.

VI–3   Chaney Operations[1]

Chaney Operations consisted of four corporations—Chaney Creations; Chaney, Inc.; Jingle-Jangle; and Jewelry Displays, Inc.—and two franchises. The first three corporations were engaged in manufacturing and wholesaling, while the fourth one was solely active in retailing.

---

[1] Prepared by Leon C. Megginson, University of South Alabama, and Terence A. Oliva, Louisiana State University.

In 1974, Chaney Operations reported $1 million in sales and no profits. According to Mr. Chaney, Jr., "no profits" meant no increase in cash flow. Mr. Chaney attributed the lack of profits to:

1. The failure to maintain proper accounting records.
2. The lack of inventory control (as an example of this, he mentioned the fact that great amounts of inventory were embezzled by previous employees.
3. The slow turnover of accounts receivable, which he said sometimes took as long as 90 days to be paid.

In February 1975, he incorporated Jewelry Display, the retail operation. He hired a new bookkeeper, a college graduate with experience in handling accounting systems of small businesses. He decided to reduce his wholesaling operations and go into retailing, which did not involve troublesome accounts receivable.

In October 1974, Chaney opened its first retail store, Jewelry Displays, in the Fairview Mall in Central City. The retail store consisted of a kiosk equipped with display counters and cash registers, and was manned by four employees. The kiosk was a small, light structure with four open sides. Utilizing all available counter space, the earrings were displayed on revolving stands on all four sides of the kiosks, with the 14-karat gold and silver earrings kept under small glass counters on the two long sides. The displays were placed in such a way that the costume jewelry was easily accessible to customers or passers-by.

The kiosk was located in the main walkway of the mall, which was a highly trafficked area. The merchandise inventory of the kiosk was supplied by the wholesaling end of the business.

The goal of Mr. Chaney for 1975 was to put into operation four additional Jewelry Displays in different areas of the south. At the time of this case, two had just been opened—one in Nashville, Tennessee, and the other in Tallahassee, Florida. Two additional proposed locations were in Tampa, Florida, and Columbus, Georgia. According to one manager, "Current operations provided enough working capital to finance the construction and equipment of the outlets and the payment of operating expenses." Mr. Chaney's accountant supplied an estimate of the operating income for each kiosk (Exhibit 1).

Accounting personnel consisted of a bookkeeper and clerk in charge of accounts receivable. The bookkeeper was authorized to sign checks, cash them, send checks to creditors, and select accounts to which charges were made. Inventory records were kept for incoming items and amounts and items sent to kiosks. Estimates were made of the expected amount of revenue for items sent. "If the figures seem 'too far off' at the time of accounting for total revenues generated by inventory, something will be

EXHIBIT 1

JEWELRY DISPLAYS, INC.
Pro-Forma Statement of Operating
Income for Each Kiosk
For One Year of Operations*

Gross Revenues		$135,000
Less cost of goods sold (approximately 37 percent)		50,625
Gross profit		84,375
Operating Expenses		
Labor (approximately 12 percent)	$16,200	
Lease (approximately 10 percent)	13,500	
Advertising (approximately 3.7 percent)	4,050	
Supplies, insurance, miscellaneous	4,000	
Depreciation expense (straight-line on 6 years' useful life—primary term of lease and 1-year renewal, $9,500 base w/$2,000 salvage value)	1,250	
Total Expenses		39,000
Net income before taxes		$ 45,375

* Based on management's estimations.

done," said the same manager. These records were kept by the available person in the office. One employee estimated that around 30 to 40 percent of inventory shrinkage was attributable to employees.

QUESTIONS FOR DISCUSSION

1. How would you improve the organization of the firm?
2. What managerial policies should be established?
3. What accounting system would you set up, especially to control assets?

VI–4   Tanner's Book Store, Inc.[1]

Late Thursday morning, July 24, 1975, Ralph Blake, sole owner of Tanner's Book Store, Inc. (TBSI), sat in his office contemplating his present

---

[1] Prepared by Lynn E. Dellenbarger, Jr., and Emit B. Deal, of Georgia Southern College.

predicament and wondering what his next step should be. Mr. Blake had just returned from the local bank, where he had been informed that the bank could not grant his request for a $45,000 loan increase. Mr. Blake had submitted this request in June to provide cash for operations during the slack summer months and for building the textbook inventory prior to the fall quarter sales rush. In his analysis, Mr. Blake intended not only to review his past financial statements (Exhibit 1) but also to study some recently acquired industry ratios developed by the National Association of College Stores, Inc. (Exhibit 2).

EXHIBIT 1

TANNER'S BOOK STORE, INC.
Balance Sheets
April 30

Assets	1975	1974	1973	1972	1971
Current Assets:					
Cash.............................	$ 96	$ 5,011	$10,969	$ 7,907	$ 7,455
Accounts receivable...............	7,075	4,406	1,315	2,058	18,006
Merchandise inventory............	112,876	84,410	59,255	54,178	63,402
Prepaid assets...................	NIL	1,850	28	60	NIL
Total Current Assets........	120,047	95,677	71,567	64,203	88,863
Investments (land):..............	13,078	750	NIL	NIL	NIL
Property (at cost):					
Furniture and fixtures............	30,547	23,771	16,044	16,044	15,289
Automobile and trucks...........	2,245	2,245	2,875	2,875	2,875
Total...................	32,792	26,016	18,919	18,919	18,164
Less Accumulated Depreciation.....	17,684	12,827	12,507	10,017	7,230
Property—net..............	15,108	13,189	6,412	8,902	10,934
Other Assets (loans to shareholder)..	33,603	10,541	NIL	NIL	NIL
Total.................	$181,836	$120,157	$77,979	$73,105	$99,797

Liabilities and Shareholder's Equity

	1975	1974	1973	1972	1971
Current Liabilities:					
Accounts payable.................	$ 89,138	$ 67,305	$39,272	$36,474	$27,180
Payroll taxes withheld and accrued...	4,012	292	769	455	382
Notes payable—bank..............	86,347	11,250	171	245	30,000
Total Current Liabilities......	179,497	78,847	40,212	37,174	57,562
Long-term Liabilities (equipment)					
Note payable (less current portion)...	1,875	3,229	NIL	NIL	NIL
Total Liabilities.............	181,372	82,076	40,212	37,174	57,562
Shareholder's Equity:					
Common Stock....................	28,000	28,000	28,000	28,000	28,000
Paid-in surplus...................	8,645	8,645	8,645	8,645	8,645
Retained earnings (deficit).........	(36,181)	1,436	1,122	(714)	5,590
Total Shareholder's Equity..............	464	38,081	37,767	35,931	42,235
Total.............	$181,836	$120,157	$77,979	$73,105	$99,797

EXHIBIT 1 (*continued*)

TANNER'S BOOK STORE, INC.

Statement of Income
For the Years Ended April 30

	1975	1974	1973	1972	1971
Sales	$237,959	$255,391	$231,676	$218,285	$258,022
Cost of Goods Sold	163,169	172,894	177,462	166,605	203,365
Gross Profit	74,790	82,497	54,214	51,680	54,657
General and Administrative Expenses:					
Officers' salaries	24,950	19,189	5,600	5,200	5,200
Salaries and wages	22,681	22,176	20,775	21,602	22,057
Payroll taxes	3,785	2,048	1,742	1,744	1,793
Office supplies	109	282	689	649	495
Operating supplies	1,751	615	(352)	1,430	637
Utilities	3,280	1,713	1,206	1,291	1,389
Professional fees	3,152	2,322	1,545	1,220	1,375
Telephone	4,576	2,666	854	1,028	1,144
Miscellaneous services	311	458	34	52	84
Sales and operating taxes	8,082	7,477	6,939	7,143	7,173
Property insurance	3,367	1,476	737	NIL	968
Depreciation	4,857	3,045	2,490	2,807	2,500
Repairs and maintenance	607	856	112	63	423
Automotive expense	2,372	1,270	451	407	563
Rentals	15,808	9,902	7,600	7,867	7,099
Advertising	2,724	3,317	1,846	2,073	1,099
Contributions	248	194	10	20	49
Dues and subscriptions	721	426	130	155	380
Travel and entertainment	1,000	515	204	363	141
Freight	423	NIL	NIL	2,118	1,355
Bank charge	578	193	105	124	132
Interest	6,699	1,342	1,327	1,195	1,422
Cash short (over)	84	466	NIL	NIL	NIL
Miscellaneous expenses	166	170	50	88	NIL
Total	112,331	82,118	54,094	58,639	57,478
Net Income (loss) from Operations	(37,541)	379	120	(6,959)	(2,821)
Other Income—Interest	66	10	42	26	9
Net Income (loss)	$(37,475)	$ 389	$ 162	$(6,933)	$(2,812)

GENERAL BUSINESS BACKGROUND

TBSI was located in rented facilities adjacent to a college campus in a southern town with a population of approximately 20,000 people. Enrollment at the college had been about 6,000 students for the last two years, and Mr. Blake expected it to remain at this level for the next few years. Mr. Blake estimated that 95 percent of the store's business was generated by students and faculty, and he believed the store's sales volume was tied very closely to the enrollment at the college.

Mr. Blake estimated that the 1975 sales volume (TBSI operated on a

EXHIBIT 2
Statistics of College Stores

A. Operating Summary*

Item	Percentage of Net Sales
Net sales......................	100.0
Cost of sales..................	76.0
Gross margin..................	24.0
Operating expense.............	20.2
Operating income..............	3.8
Other income, net.............	0.2
Other expense.................	0.2
Net income before income taxes and profit distribution.........	3.8

B. Breakdown of Operating Expense†

Item	Percentage of Net Sales
Personnel.....................	13.9
Occupancy....................	4.2
Advertising...................	0.2
Telephone and other communications.............	0.3
Stationery and supplies.........	0.6
Data processing (other than salaries)....................	0.4
Furniture, fixtures, and equipment...................	1.0
Professional services............	0.2
Travel and entertainment........	0.2
Insurance.....................	0.1
Other taxes...................	0.2
All other operating expenses......	1.6
Total operating expense.......	22.9

C. Sales Distribution, Space Allocation, and Turnover Ratios

Category	Sales (dollars per sq. ft. of occupied space)‡	Space Occupied§‡		Stockturn
		Selling	Storage	
Course books.................	123.1	151.1	583.6	3.9§
General books.................	21.8	21.8	0.0	2.1§
All books.....................	102.7	124.7	449.0	3.2§; 3.7‖
Student supplies...............	43.8	55.6	192.8	1.9‖
All departments...............	64.7	82.6	278.7	3.1‖

* Average of 35 stores with net sales below $250,000.
‡ Average of 25 stores with net sales below $250,000.
‡ Average of 22 stores with net sales below $250,000.
§ Average of 15 stores with net sales below $250,000.
‖ Average of ten stores with net sales between $500,000 and $1 million.
Source: The ratios in this exhibit are reproduced with the permission of the National Association of College Stores, Inc.

fiscal year ending April 30th) involved the following amounts (in thousands):

Art supplies	$ 15	
Engineering supplies	2	
Gift items, soft goods, and fraternity and sorority supplies	25	
Supplies such as paper, calculators, and pencils	15	
Books other than textbooks	5	
	$ 62	(26%)
Textbooks	176	(74%)
Total sales	$238	

Mr. Blake believed the drop in sales in 1972 resulted from the college's opening its own book store directly across the street from TBSI.

EMPLOYEES

Permanent employees consisted of Mr. Blake, who worked full time at the store, and two women who had been employed at TBSI at the time Mr. Blake acquired the store. One woman was the bookkeeper, and the other handled operating details such as ordering. All other employees were college students who were paid 85% of the minimum wage under a special exemption for student personnel. The number of students employed varied from 1 to 2 during slack periods up to 15 during the two rush weeks at the beginning of a quarter, when the store might be operating 6 cash registers.

LEASED FACILITIES

TBSI occupies 5,150 square feet of leased space in a building directly across the street from the college campus and the college book store. When TBSI first opened for business in this location it occupied 1,800 square feet of space. In 1969 it added 450 square feet for storage space. In 1971 it added 900 more square feet, and in September 1974 it added 2,000 square feet formerly occupied by a men's clothing store. Before the expansion in 1974 the monthly rental was $700. Upon the expansion in 1974 a new five-year lease was negotiated, and the monthly rental was increased to $1,100. When Mr. Blake realized he was in financial difficulty in 1975 he immediately attempted to renegotiate the new lease, but the out-of-town bank was unwilling to consider any changes in the lease terms.

ACQUISITION BY MR. BLAKE

Mr. Blake, who had had experience working in book stores, purchased the stock of TBSI in March 1973 for $45,000, supplying $8,500 of his own cash, borrowing $22,500 from the local bank, and giving the former owner his note for $14,000. In addition to the $22,500, the local bank also loaned TBSI $2,500 on the same terms as the larger loan to provide the initial cash for operations.

In the acquisition of TBSI Mr. Blake received merchandise inventory, valued at cost, of $59,000 plus fixtures, a car, and other personal property valued at $6,500. Mr. Blake also assumed accounts payable on the corporation's books of $39,000.

At the time of the acquisition Mr. Blake anticipated that increased sales and an improved gross margin would provide the means for debt reduction. He believed that promotion and advertising would provide the increased sales and that better management of used textbooks would provide the improved margin.

MARKET STRUCTURE

Mr. Blake recognized the importance of nontextbook items both because of the high margin involved and because of their somewhat non-seasonal nature. Textbook sales were highly seasonal with the bulk of the sales falling in the four months in which the college quarters started (see Exhibit 3).

There are no returns allowed on nontextbook merchandise items, and the suppliers do not set a suggested retail price as is done in the textbook

EXHIBIT 3
Tanner's Book Store, Inc.: Monthly Sales and Book
Repurchases From Students*

	Sales	Purchases from Students
1974		
Month		
August	$ 3,080	$1,902
July	5,718	576
June	22,604	5,226
May	8,644	2,322
April	12,272	1,047
March	43,354	9,408
February	8,023	654
January	62,885	1,750
1973		
December	4,376	9,356
November	6,374	932
October	11,172	1,035
September	73,998	206
August	2,646	2,980
July	4,597	620
June	26,892	2,122
May	5,182	9,870

* Summarized from cash reports.

field. In general Mr. Blake prices such items to provide a gross margin of 40%. TBSI sells less than $5,000 of nontextbook merchandise.

Mr. Blake visualized the market for TBSI's textbooks as illustrated in the following example based on a new textbook with a retail list price of $10.00:

Condition and Source of Book	Cost to TBSI	Sales Price
New		
From publisher............	$8.00	$10.00
From wholesaler...........	7.00	10.00
Returned by student........	5.00	7.50
Used, in current demand		
From wholesaler...........	5.00	7.50
From student.............	3.75	7.50
Used, not in demand		
From student.............	4.50–4.75	Cost plus 10–15%*

* Sold to wholesaler.

TBSI receives a weekly bulletin published by the National Association of College Stores, Inc. (NACS), which lists books for sale by various stores and wholesalers throughout the country. Some books are obtained from this source.

Textbooks left on the shelf after the regular quarterly rush period may be returned for full credit to publisher, kept in inventory for sales at a later date, or sold to wholesalers.

FINANCIAL REPORTING PROBLEM

At the beginning of fiscal 1975 Mr. Blake forecasted sales of $280,000 and undertook the previously noted expansion. Sales reports for the first four months of fiscal 1975 (see Exhibit 3) convinced Mr. Blake that the increased sales forecast was sound.

From the time of the acquisition in 1973, Mr. Blake normally received monthly cash statements of sales. In April 1974, Mr. Blake's regular accountant moved to another town, and Mr. Blake switched his business to another local firm. Because of a backlog of work at the new accounting firm's office, Mr. Blake received no monthly cash sales reports from September 1974 through February 1975. In March 1975, suspecting his business was in trouble, Mr. Blake switched the work back to the original accountant. The data developed at this time indicated that the business had lost approximately $30,000 in the period from January to March 1975.

BANK FINANCING

In addition to what Mr. Blake termed permanent financing, TBSI normally borrowed short-term money from the local bank to acquire textbooks for the large sales volume at the beginning of each quarter. These funds were normally repaid shortly after the rush period, but in January 1975 TBSI was unable to repay the short-term loan made to finance the inventory buildup for the September 1974 sales peak.

As of April 1975 indebtedness to the local bank was roughly as follows:

Purpose of Loan	Loan Balance	Interest Rate (percent)
Initial loan............................	$22,600	10
Expansion, September 1974 (furniture and inventory)..............	8,000	10
Purchase of printing machine..............	3,100	12.5
Purchase (1974) of one acre of land next to a college in Florida............	11,500	10
Short-term loan for inventory buildup......	43,000	10
Total.............................	$88,200	—

All assets of Tanner's Book Store, Inc. are pledged as collateral on the above notes.

CURRENT SITUATION

Mr. Blake approached the local bank in early June 1975 to borrow $40,000–$45,000 more to finance operations during the summer and to provide funds for the textbook inventory buildup for the September sales rush. At this time accounts payable to the publishers had aged to the point that they refused to send more textbooks unless payment was received. The last week in July the local bank informed Mr. Blake that they would not advance the requested funds.

QUESTIONS FOR DISCUSSION

1. List the reasons for and against Mr. Blake purchasing TBSI. Would you have purchased it?
2. Evaluate Mr. Blake's financial activities. Were they sound?
3. Should Mr. Blake have expanded his floor space? What were the sales per square foot before, during, and after expansion?
4. Forecast future cash flows and financial condition.
5. How do TBSI's financial condition and operations compare with the trade?

6.   What alternatives does Mr. Blake have now?

7.   What steps would you recommend to Mr. Blake if he wanted to continue in business?

VI–5   Ideal Sheen Cleaners, Inc.[1]

Mr. William E. Miller, a respected black businessman of Cleveland, Ohio, had been engaged in various aspects of the laundry and dry cleaning business since 1939. His first business venture as a laundry route operator was financed with an investment of less than $200, of which $50 was obtained from a loan shark. The assets of the business consisted of a small amount of cash and an automobile, which was used to pick-up and deliver laundry between customers and a commercial laundry. He paid the laundry 60 percent of the revenue collected from customers for the washing service. Over the years his business grew and expanded.

HISTORY

1939—Self-employed laundry route operator. Started with $200, including $50 borrowed from a loan shark.

1943—Purchased a dry cleaning and tailor shop.

1952—Purchased a dry cleaning machine to eliminate using outside commercial cleaning services.

1955—Purchased more modern pressing machines.

1956—Leased next-door property for expansion.

1960—Took over store next to existing property for storage use.

1963—Incorporated as Ideal Sheen Cleaners, Inc.

1968—Acquired property for an up-to-date cleaning plant. Converted old plant to a shirt laundry.

1969—Completed dry cleaning plant expansion.

1971—Introduced cleaning by the pound to provide for different categories of dry cleaning.

1972—Added easy-care service, which used steaming process in place of pressing.

---

[1] Prepared by Donald W. Scotton, Jeffrey C. Susbauer, and A. Michael Sibley, The Cleveland State University.

In 1973, Ideal Sheen operated (1) a shirt laundry, (2) a dry cleaning plant, (3) three retail outlets, and (4) several dry cleaning sales and delivery routes. Mr. Miller expected that the business would continue to grow.

Recent financial history of the organization is described in Exhibits 1 and 2, which contain income statements and balance sheets for the years 1969–72. An examination of these statements reveals that the business had grown substantially in both sales and total assets.

During 1973, Mr. Miller was considering a number of additional expansion plans designed to increase the firm's long-run profitability and return on investment. These plans included: (1) an increase in the

EXHIBIT 1

IDEAL SHEEN CLEANERS, INC.

Consolidated Profits and Loss Statements
For Fiscal Years Ending June 30, 1969–1972

	1969	1970	1971	1972
Net Sales...........................	$184,400	$244,400	$262,800	$236,700
Cost of production.................	82,300	139,800	128,200	116,900
Gross Profit from Operations.......	$102,100	$104,600	$134,600	$119,800
Expenses:				
Sales and delivery................	$ 58,000	$ 73,300	$ 78,800	$ 71,700
Administrative...................	27,700	31,300	30,000	39,100
Total.......................	$ 85,700	$104,600	$108,800	$110,800
Operating Income..................	$ 16,400	$ 0	$ 25,800	$ 9,000
Other Income......................	$ 1,400	$ 1,400	$ 1,300	$ 200
Less Other Expenses...............	$ 3,000	$ 10,000	21,200	$ 18,900
Net Other Income..............	($ 1,600)	($ 8,600)	($ 19,900)	($ 18,700)
Net Profit before Taxes......	$ 14,800	($ 8,600)	$ 5,900	($ 9,700)
Reserve for Income Taxes....	$ 2,800	—	—	—
Net Profit after Taxes.....	$ 12,000	($ 8,600)	$ 5,900	($ 9,700)

variety of services available at the existing dry cleaning plant, and (2) the opening of a retail outlet in Park Center, a large apartment-shopping complex under construction in the downtown area.

Expansion plans at the existing plant called for (1) opening a coin-operated laundry, and (2) the addition of drapery and carpet cleaning services. Additional plant and equipment would be needed. Land was available for purchase adjacent to the existing dry cleaning plant. The existing plant had 3,300 square feet of space, and an additional 4,000 square feet of space would be necessary. This would include space for (1) the coin-operated laundry, (2) new equipment to clean rugs, draperies and upholstered furniture, and (3) some replacement equipment to be used for traditional dry cleaning services. This expansion was anticipated to cost approximately $164,900. A breakdown of the costs follows:

Land; building	$ 97,000
Drapery and carpet cleaning equipment	13,000
Laundromat equipment	45,900
Traditional dry cleaning equipment	9,000
Total	$164,900

It was hoped that the addition of the coin-operated laundry and the carpet and drapery cleaning service would draw new customers to the retail store in the existing plant and thus increase sales for traditional garment-cleaning services. The existing dry cleaning plant was operating at only 50 percent of capacity because of limited area sales, the popularity of wash-and-wear garments, and the adoption of the casual look.

The second part of the expansion plan was the opening of a new retail outlet in the Park Center Apartment complex, an urban redevelopment project that would contain 1,000 apartments, a 75-store shopping mall, business offices, and recreational facilities. In addition to Park Center, several other apartment buildings were located within a two-block radius and were thought to be sources of potential customers. Mr. Miller estimated that annual sales through the Park Center outlet would probably be around $80,000 for the first two years, and might become as high as $200,000 after five or six years.

Mr. Miller had talked with the rental agent for the Park Center, and had tentatively agreed on a 10-year lease with the following terms:

1. For the first 30 months, the base rent would be $1,000 per month, plus 10 percent of all sales volume over $84,000 annually.
2. After 30 months, the base rent would be $1,000 per month, plus 10 percent of all sales volume over $100,000 annually.
3. Other features were estimated to cost about $100 per month, including:
   a. Payment for air-conditioning, heat, and utilities on a metered basis.
   b. Payment of a prorated share of maintenance for the common area of the mall.
   c. Mandatory membership in the Mall Merchants Association, for purposes of joint advertising and promotion of the mall.

The immediate investment required by the Park Center outlet was estimated to be $27,000, mostly for leasehold improvements and equipment. It was estimated that improvements and equipment would have a useful life of approximately ten years and a negligible salvage value. The outlet would be open 12 hours a day, six days a week. Initially,

EXHIBIT 2

IDEAL SHEEN CLEANERS, INC.

Consolidated Balance Sheets

For Fiscal Years Ending June 30, 1969–1972

	1969	1970	1971	1972
Assets				
Current Assets:				
Cash on hand...............	$ 7,600.00	$ 1,400.00	$ 8,700.00	$ 8,900.00
Notes receivable..............	–0–	–0–		
Accounts receivable...........	10,200.00	9,000.00	7,800.00	8,200.00
Finished clothes..............	14,300.00	21,300.00	19,700.00	32,000.00
Other......................	6,100.00	15,000.00	24,600.00	29,500.00
Total...................	$ 38,200.00	$ 46,700.00	$ 60,800.00	$ 78,600.00
Fixed Assets:	$117,100.00	$212,800.00	$219,200.00	$227,800.00
Less reserves for depreciation....	18,200.00	33,100.00	48,500.00	61,500.00
Total................	$ 98,900.00	$179,700.00	$170,700.00	$166,300.00
Other Assets................	$ 12,300.00	24,500.00	$ 6,100.00	$ 6,100.00
Total Assets................	$149,400.00	$250,900.00	$237,600.00	$251,000.00
Liabilities				
Current Liabilities				
Accounts payable.............	$ 10,500.00	$ 29,900.00	$ 27,200.00	$ 16,600.00
Notes payable................	21,900.00	37,900.00	12,600.00	8,400.00
Miscellaneous taxes payable.....	8,600.00	18,100.00	11,100.00	23,800.00
Other......................	3,500.00	5,100.00	5,300.00	3,900.00
Total...................	$ 44,500.00	$ 91,000.00	$ 56,200.00	$ 52,700.00
Fixed Liabilities:				
Long-term notes..............	$ 62,100.00	$128,100.00	$ 87,800.00	$108,600.00
Mortgage payable............	–0–	–0–	50,000.00	49,100.00
Reserve for income tax........	2,800.00	–0–		
Loans from stockholders........	–0–	1,000.00	8,900.00	15,700.00
Total...................	$ 64,900.00	$129,100.00	$146,700.00	$173,400.00
Net Worth:				
Capital stock.................	$ 8,000.00	$ 8,000.00	$ 8,000.00	$ 8,000.00
Earned surplus...............	32,000.00	22,800.00	26,700.00	16,900.00
Total...................	$ 40,000.00	$ 30,800.00	$ 34,700.00	$ 24,900.00
Total Liabilities and Net Worth..........	$149,400.00	$250,900.00	$237,600.00	$251,000.00

only one person would be on duty at any time. Salary expense under these circumstances was estimated at approximately $12,000 to $13,000 a year. As business increased, additional staff might be required, and salary expense would then increase.

With a few exceptions, ordinary garment cleaning handled by the Park Center store would be processed at the existing dry cleaning plant. Because excess capacity for this type of cleaning service was available, no new machinery or additional help would be required during the first few years. In the past, the cost of production for garment cleaning averaged about 50 percent of sales. This rate was expected to continue in the future, and was thought to be an appropriate estimate of the cost of processing sales made through the new Park Center store. The annual cost of transporting clothing between Park Center and the plant was estimated at approximately $3,000 per year. Office and administrative expenses would also increase by approximately $5,000 per year.

Mr. Miller made contact with the Shaker Savings Association about financing part of the proposed expansions through the United States Small Business Administration "502 Loan Program." It was his understanding that if the loan was approved, the bank could loan 50 percent (and receive a first mortgage lien or SBA loan guarantee), the Small Business Administration would loan 40 percent, and a local development company would provide the remaining 10 percent. Local Development Companies were specified as an integral part in Section 502 of the Small Business Investment Act of 1958, as amended. The savings association was receptive to such a loan, because it held the mortgage of the existing dry cleaning plant and owned the property Mr. Miller had wanted to buy.

Mr. Miller planned to finance the needed equipment from other sources. He was considering applying for a loan from a commercial bank and a local MESBIC (Minority Enterprise Small Business Investment Corporation). These investment corporations were made possible under the Small Business Administration Act of 1958 and under the first specialized application of the Small Business Investment Corporation for minority enterprise in 1968. He estimated that the average cost of borrowed funds from all sources would be approximately 7.6 percent per year.

Mr. Miller was optimistic that his plan for vitalizing and expanding his business would work. He was equally optimistic that his past record as a businessman would enable him to receive the financing required.

QUESTIONS FOR DISCUSSION

1. Evaluate the profitability of Ideal Sheen Cleaners for the period 1969 to 1972. For this period, what was the average rate of return after taxes on (1) assets and (2) equity? Is any trend in profitability apparent?

2. Discuss the plan to expand the services offered at the existing dry cleaning plant, considering that current facilities are operated at 50 percent of capacity. What information would be helpful to Mr. Miller in making an expansion decision of this type? How could this information be obtained?

3. Identify the fixed and variable costs associated with the Park Center retail outlet. What level of sales would be necessary to break even (produce zero profit)? What level of sales would be necessary to produce an annual pre-tax profit of $5,000?

4. In light of its present financial condition, does it appear that Ideal Sheen Cleaners will have any difficulty financing the proposed expansions? If you were a banker, under what conditions would you loan the necessary funds to Mr. Miller?

VI–6 Am I a Tough Guy?[1]

A friend of mine recently said that 1975 is going to be the year of the tough guys, and that's right. It's for the guys and gals who care enough to put everything they've got into what they're doing, and do their best. It's not the year for sitting around and letting everyone else do it for them. It's a good year for challenge and productivity because there is still money there, and there are still people who are ready to spend it. It's up to the tough guys, to the ones who merit being the ones with whom that money is spent![2]

Dorothy Barton, sitting at her desk in the small office just off the Style Shop sales floor, pondered this quotation, which happened to catch her eye as she leafed through the latest edition of the *Dallas Fashion Retailer*.

The year 1974 was a rough one in the women's ready-to-wear business, as it was in many businesses. It was particularly rough, however, for the attractive, energetic Style Shop owner. Wife, and mother of four teenage daughters, Mrs. Barton saw her sales fall 12.5 percent from 1973 to 1974; but more significantly, her net profit plunged 62.5 percent over the same time period. Untold hours she spent on the sales floor catering to her customers' eye for quality and fashion; in the office appealing to manufacturers to ship the next season's orders even though the current ones were yet to be paid; and at the Dallas Apparel Mart buying just the fashions she hoped would fit the needs and desires of her customers. At the same time, she was spending many hours each week in an effort to help her husband get his infant construction business off the ground.

She remembered hearing one "expert" say, "This is not a time for pessimism, nor a time for optimism. This is a time for realism." And an economic prognosticator had indicated that he saw a good future in the industry, despite the economic slowdown. Buyers, he noted, are working

---

[1] Prepared by Janelle C. Ashley, Stephen F. Austin State University.

[2] "Merchandisers Must Provide Leadership," *Dallas Fashion Retailer*, June 1975, p. 17.

a little more cautiously right now. They are still buying—just looking at things a little more carefully.

"What is 'realism' for me?" she asked herself. "Am I one of the tough guys who can stick it out and 'merit being the one with whom that money is spent'?"

COMPANY HISTORY AND DEVELOPMENT

The Style Shop opened its doors on February 12, 1954, at 121 South First Street, Lufkin, Texas. A city of approximately 12,000, Lufkin had a need at that time for a first-rate women's specialty shop. The Style Shop filled that need. With an emphasis on quality merchandise and friendly service, the Style Shop immediately established a reputation as "the place to go" for fashionable wearing apparel for all occasions.

Helen Barton and Dana Young founded the original partnership; Mrs. Young left the business after four years of profitable operation. Dorothy Barton, daughter-in-law of Helen Barton, began with the Style Shop as a part-time accountant in March 1962. As her children entered school she assumed more responsibility at the store and started work on a full-time basis. She worked not only in the financial area, but in the buying and selling phase as well.

By the mid-60s, Helen Barton began to feel that she was reaching a saturation point in her present location. Sales had continued to climb steadily, but there was no room to expand. The opportunity for expansion came in 1968, when a totally enclosed, air-conditioned mall was put in the planning stages. The Angelina Mall, located at the intersection of Highway 59 and Loop 287 in Lufkin, rests at the hub of a trade area extending over a radius of more than 100 miles. The move to the air-conditioned mall was made in July 1969. The Style Shop, with a floor space of 3,183 square feet, joined 16 other retail operations, including a major discount chain store.

Helen and Dorothy Barton organized a new partnership, sharing ownership in the Style Shop, commencing on the date the new shop was opened. In January 1974, Dorothy Barton purchased the 50 percent of the business belonging to her mother-in-law and proceeded to operate the business as a single proprietorship.

THE STYLE SHOP UP TO 1974

The Style Shop employed four full-time clerks, one alteration lady, and a maid. One former employee and the teenage daughter of Mrs. Barton were frequently called in for part-time work during peak seasons. The Style Shop operated with no formal, written policies. Personnel were paid wages and benefits comparable to other workers in similar capacities in

EXHIBIT 1

The Style Shop
Consolidated Statement of Income

	1970	1971	1972	1973	1974
Sales..............	$200,845.43	$213,368.15	$216,927.31	$217,969.59	$190,821.85
Cost of sales......	132,838.30	133,527.91	131,900.84	138,427.14	121,689.74
Gross Profit....	68,007.13	79,840.24	85,026.47	79,542.45	69,132.11
Expenses.........	60,727.46	70,051.29	67,151.58	69,696.93	65,438.20
Net Profit........	7,279.67	9,788.95	17,874.89	9,845.52	3,693.91

the city. They enjoyed a great deal of freedom in their work, flexibility in hours of work, and a 20 percent discount on all merchandise purchased in the shop.

Among cities its size, Lufkin had an average number of retail outlets carrying ladies' ready-to-wear. Several department stores and other specialty shops carried some of the same lines as did the Style Shop, but they were all comparable in price.

Inventory Control. The Style Shop used the services of a consulting firm to prepare monthly inventory control reports. These were broken down into 23 departmental groupings such as junior dresses, swim wear, hosiery, and jewelry. They showed beginning retail inventory for the month, plus purchases for the month and year to date. Sales were broken into monthly and year-to-date figures with percentage changes also indicated. The summary next itemized mark-downs for the month and year to date. Initial mark-up percentage for the current and past year was followed by maintained mark-up percentage, also for the current and past year. Ending inventory was given at both cost and retail, complete with percentage change. Finally, the monthly report showed the month's supply on hand, department percentage to total sales and department percentage to total inventory. Provision was also made to indicate merchandise on order at the end of the month at retail and an adjusted open-to-buy column at both retail and cost. In February, the consultant prepared an "Actual Fall and Winter" summary sales report and in August

EXHIBIT 2

The Style Shop
Consolidated Statement of Financial Condition

	1970	1971	1972	1973	1974
Current Assets.........	$38,524.93	$70,015.11	$66,749.78	$58,530.44	$68,458.34
Fixed Assets..........	7,314.58	86,504.94	83,924.45	80,534.06	63,943.67
Total Assets.....	45,839.51	156,520.05	150,674.23	139,064.50	132,402.01
Current Liabilities......	35,892.81	19,586.45	20,161.93	31,587.57	55,552.70
Long Term Liabilities...	0.00	39,042.90	33,680.07	26,841.76	20,003.45
Total Liabilities..	35,892.81	58,629.35	53,842.00	58,429.33	75,556.15
Net Worth............	9,946.70	97,890.70	96,832.23	80,635.17	56,845.86

an "Actual Spring and Summer" summary sales report. Each of these included a "Projected Sales and Inventory" breakdown for the ensuing period. Cost for this service was $110 per month.

Financial Position. It is often quite difficult and sometimes next to impossible to evaluate the "true" financial position of a single proprietorship or a partnership due to the peculiarities that are either allowed or tolerated in accounting practices for these forms of ownership. This is evident in looking at the following five-year summary Statements of Income and Financial Condition plus the complete statements for 1974 of the Style Shop (see Exhibit 1–4).

Two explanatory notes should be added to these statements. The jump in fixed assets between 1970 and 1971 and the subsequent changes were due in large part to the inclusion of personal real estate on the partnership books. The long-term liability initiated in 1971 was an SBA loan. Caught in a period of declining sales (due in part to the controversy over skirt length and women's pantsuits) and rapidly rising expenses in the new mall location, the Style Shop owners found themselves in that pro-

EXHIBIT 3

The Style Shop
Statement of Income
Year Ended December 31, 1974

Sales:....................................		$190,821.85
Cost of Sales:		
Beginning inventory......................	$ 36,923.00	
Purchases...............................	119,994.74	
	156,917.74	
Ending inventory........................	35,228.00	121,689.74
Gross Profit........................		69,132.11
Expenses:		
Advertising.............................	3,034.63	
Auto expense............................	1,509.63	
Bad debts...............................	(439.83)	
Depreciation............................	1,580.49	
Freight, express, delivery.................	2,545.90	
Heat, light, power, and water..............	1,847.96	
Insurance...............................	1,431.80	
Interest.................................	4,064.25	
Legal and accounting.....................	2,034.74	
Rent....................................	11,220.40	
Repairs.................................	528.98	
Salary..................................	26,227.69	
Supplies................................	5,138.11	
Tax		
Payroll.............................	1,656.18	
Other..............................	604.62	
Telephone..............................	784.67	
Dues and subscriptions....................	601.89	
Market and travel........................	1,066.09	65,438.20
Net Profit...............................		3,693.91

EXHIBIT 4

The Style Shop
Consolidated Statement of Financial Condition
December 31, 1974

Assets

Cash on hand and in banks...................	4,923.92
Accounts receivable.........................	21,306.42
Inventory..................................	35,228.00
Cash value—life insurance...................	7,000.00
Total Current Assets...................	68,458.34

Fixed Assets:

Furniture and fixtures and		
leasehold improvements...................	$27,749.94	
Less allowance for depreciation...............	9,806.27	17,943.67
Auto and truck.............................		9,500.00
Real estate................................		20,000.00
Furniture..................................		10,000.00
Boat and motor............................		2,000.00
Office equipment...........................		2,500.00
Jewelry....................................		2,000.00
Total Fixed Assets...................		63,943.67
Total Assets.....................		$132,402.01

Liabilities and Capital

Current Liabilities:

Accounts payable...........................	$ 30,413.12
Accrued payroll tax.........................	825.64
Accrued sales tax...........................	1,193.94
Note payable—due in one year...............	9,420.00
Note payable—lot...........................	10,700.00
Note payable—auto.........................	3,000.00
Total Current Liabilities...............	55,552.70
Note payable—due after one year............	20,003.45
Total Liabilities...................	75,556.15
Net Worth.................................	56,845.86
Total Liabilities and Capital.......	$132,402.01

verbial "financial bind" in late 1969 and 1970. They needed additional funds both for working capital and fixed investments. Since a big jump in sales was anticipated in the new location, additional working capital was necessary to purchase the required inventory. The new tenants also desired fixed-asset money to purchase display fixtures for their new store. This money they obtained through a local bank in the form of a Small Business Administration-insured loan.

THE STYLE SHOP, 1975

"Certainly there is no longer an arbiter of the length of a skirt or the acceptance of pantsuits," Mrs. Barton mused. "The economic picture is looking brighter. The experts tell us there will be more disposable personal income and a lower rate of inflation. Yet this is a time for 'realism.' Am I a 'tough guy'?"

QUESTIONS FOR DISCUSSION

1. What is Dorothy Barton receiving as a return on her investment? What do you believe would be a reasonable rate of return?
2. What changes might be made to provide a reasonable rate of return? Using the figures provided, make an estimate of a breakeven chart for the company.
3. How do the Style Shop's financial operations and condition compare with the industry? Estimate the sales Dorothy Barton could obtain from the floor space available.
4. If Mrs. Barton should decide to sell the business, what price should she ask? What are your recommendations on this?

VI–7   Solomon Foods[1]

Early in 1970, the management of Solomon Foods was faced with the problem of the financial feasibility of constructing a larger, more competitive retail food store. Management felt it could improve the company's sales and profits by moving from the 3,000-square-foot building. Bernard Solomon especially realized that with the limited parking area and poor location it was only a matter of time before annual sales volume of $250,000 would decline below the break-even point of $248,000. And even if sales remained the same, stagnation was as bad as death in the city's competitive retail market. Bernard Solomon believed that an optimum-size store and parking area located in a highly traveled area would afford economies of scale plus the psychological advantage of low prices. After management reached an agreement, it was time to sway would-be creditors to its way of thinking.

Solomon Foods was owned and operated as a partnership by Maurice and Bernard Solomon. Maurice T. Solomon had been, for 30 of his 64 years, managing this business. He worked 70–80 hours per week planning, organizing, staffing, directing, and controlling the business.

Bernard M. Solomon, Maurice's son, was a 38-year-old businessman

---

[1] Prepared by Robert Crayne, Stephen L. Woehrle and B. D. Perkins, University of South Dakota.

who had expanded the business to its present size. Through his drive and enthusiastic determination, he had been able to persuade his father to risk everything in order to achieve progress. But convincing Maurice to risk the business was achieved only by his son's threat to quit, which he made twice.

After many heated discussions with individuals experienced in the retail food industry, and after a determination of the extent of the keen competition in a city of 100,000, it was felt that a 6,000-square-foot building would provide the optimum floor space. A store of that size could be built at a cost not greater than $7.50 a square foot.

Fortunately, an ideal spot not far from the present location could be purchased (on the going-home side of the street) for $11,000. This location was large enough to give a proper ratio of parking area to store floor space (four to one was the suggested ratio, while at their existing location it was only one to four). Also, planned street changes

EXHIBIT 1

SOLOMON FOODS
Balance Sheet
December 31, 1964 to December 31, 1969

	1964	1965	1966	1967	1968	1969
Assets						
Current Assets:						
Cash	$ 3,954	$ 4,657	$ 3,153	$ 8,377	$ 4,982	$ 7,840
Accounts receivable	4,238	3,267	1,699	1,316	1,384	1,749
Notes receivable	12,398	12,398				
Inventory	16,503	15,614	13,794	14,077	15,279	14,783
Total Current Assets	$37,093	$35,936	$18,646	$23,770	$21,645	$24,372
Equipment—net	22,027	20,010	16,924	13,916	10,766	8,075
Total Assets	$59,120	$55,946	$35,570	$37,686	$32,411	$32,447
Liabilities						
Current Liabilities:						
Accounts payable*	$ 8,824	$ 8,430	$ 5,101	$10,647	$ 8,121	$ 6,721
Wholesaler payable	2,725	1,450				1,465
Taxes payable	1,517	1,499	1,523	1,402	1,350	1,444
Total Current Liabilities	13,066	11,379	6,624	12,049	9,471	9,630
Long-Term Liabilities:						
John Hancock Note	$ 800	$ 800	$ 800	$ 800	$ 910	$ 800
N. Bank Note	1,000	2,620		1,000	1,400	1,000
S. Bank Note	8,322	6,456	4,412			
Total Long-Term Liabilities	$10,122	$ 9,876	$ 5,212	$ 1,800	$ 2,310	$ 1,800
Total Liabilities	$23,188	$21,255	$11,836	$13,849	$11,781	$11,430
Equity						
Total Capital Invested	$35,932	$34,691	$23,734	$23,837	$20,630	$21,017
Total Liabilities and Equity	$59,120	$55,946	$35,570	$37,686	$32,411	$32,447

* Purchases are paid for by the last day of the week on which they were bought.

were expected to increase the traffic of homeward-bound workers. With the possible increased traffic in mind, a store plan was drawn so that future expansion to 10,000 square feet would be relatively easy.

After talking with several equipment dealers, management decided that the new store could be completely equipped, exclusive of building costs, for $10.00 a square foot. Existing equipment was close to being fully depreciated, but was still in good condition. Only 50 percent of the required equipment needed had to be purchased. No additional working cash was needed, and only $5,000 more inventory had to be acquired. It was estimated that equal payments over 20 years would require total payment of twice the cost—half to principal and half to interest, taxes, and insurance.

Much thought was given to just how to finance the total cost of the project. It was determined that a loan from the SBA would be most appropriate. But because the SBA had not as yet been approached, management was still faced with the problem of raising long-term capital.

The financial statements for the company are shown in Exhibits 1 and 2. Competition had been increasing in the retail food business in the past ten years. In moving to the new location, sales (only cash sales would be made) were expected to increase to $9,625 per week. This volume was extremely conservative in view of the fact that the national

EXHIBIT 2

SOLOMON FOODS
Income Statements
December 31, 1964 to December 31, 1969

	1964	1965	1966	1967	1968	1969
Net Sales....................	$260,378	$275,328	$268,132	$265,442	$241,602	$251,747
Cost of Goods Sold...........	215,542	233,725	228,491	228,093	202,055	211,034
Gross Profit...........	$ 44,836	$ 41,603	$ 39,641	$ 37,349	$ 39,547	$ 40,713
Expenses						
Outside labor.................	$ 370	$ 184	$ 183	$ 127	$ 92	$ 176
Operating supplies............	1,843	1,825	1,875	2,045	1,932	1,902
Gross wages*.................	8,979	8,031	8,098	8,458	8,103	6,943
Repairs and maintenance......	556	675	319	534	879	353
Advertising...................	3,603	3,777	3,193	2,947	3,028	4,163
Bad debts....................	477	409	301	216	67	248
Administrative and legal.......	626	560	600	600	600	600
Rent........................	3,420	3,900	3,900	3,900	3,900	4,100
Utilities.....................	3,199	3,116	3,131	3,117	3,415	2,933
Insurance....................	1,881	1,411	925	520	587	559
Taxes and licenses............	974	996	1,129	1,214	1,215	1,241
Interest......................	384	1,222	648	449	120	121
Depreciation.................	3,268	3,254	3,238	3,338	3,150	2,784
Miscellaneous expense.........	1,052	922	906	610	315	300
Total Expenses.........	$ 30,632	$ 30,282	$ 28,456	$ 28,075	$ 27,403	$ 26,423
Net Profit.........	$ 14,204	$ 11,321	$ 11,185	$ 9,274	$ 12,144	$ 14,290

* Owners' salaries are not included in expenses.

EXHIBIT 3

SOLOMON FOODS
Pro-Forma Income Statement
December 31, 1969

	Percent of Total Sales
Sales...	100.00
Cost of Goods Sold........................	83.83
Gross Profit.......................	16.17
Expenses:	
Wages and labor*.........................	6.36
Operating supplies.........................	1.25
Repairs and maintenance....................	0.20
Advertising...............................	1.00
Bad debts................................	0.02
Administrative and legal...................	0.26
Miscellaneous and other...................	0.05
Utilities.................................	1.17
Insurance................................	0.37
Taxes and licenses........................	0.78
Depreciation.............................	1.65
Interest, taxes, insurance on loan...........	0.91
Total Expenses.....................	14.02
Net Profit.....................	2.15

* Owners' salaries are not included. In the past Maurice and Bernard Solomon have withdrawn $75 and $125 respectively each week.

sales average for retail food stores was $2.50 a square foot per week. It was anticipated that sales could be increased to the national average by the third or fourth year of operation in the new location. When sales reached the average, the store would be expanded to 10,000 square feet.

A percentage breakdown of the projected income statement for the first year appears in Exhibit 3. The gross margin was expected to increase to 18 percent when proper departmental controls were established. But in line with the conservative approach throughout the forecast, it was reasonably safe to assume that the margin would not decline below its existing level.

QUESTIONS FOR DISCUSSION

1. Do you feel that management has considered all the factors it should consider before determining whether to relocate?
2. Do you feel the estimates are reasonable? Explain.
3. What are the possible causes for the "total capital invested" to decline? Explain.

4. What sort of profit potential do you feel exists? How do you think break-even points would compare for the present and proposed locations?

5. Do your analyses show the company to be financially sound? Would you loan the company money? How much?

6. How much money should Solomon borrow?

7. The value of income received today is greater than that received, say, five years from now. A present cost is greater for a company than the same cost in the future. Why are these statements true?

8. Would you recommend that the company make the proposed move?

part **VII**

Some Special Considerations
in Managing
an Independent Business

Most of the general aspects of managing a small or independent business have been covered in the preceding parts. However, there are several special considerations that need looking at before we are through.

First, there is the question of whether you will create and operate your own business or whether you will operate a franchise. This problem is explored in relative detail in Chapter 24.

There is also the need to provide for management succession. We have found that the vast majority of business owners do not want to talk about this question—in fact, they almost refuse to discuss it. Yet, if you are realistic, and if you want to assure the continuance of your firm, or if you want to provide a going concern for your children to operate, then this question must be looked at analytically. To help you do this, we have presented some material in Chapter 25 that should make you think about this question.

Finally, in addition to the functional cases at the end of this part, there are several that integrate all of the material covered in this text.

24

Operating a Franchise

Franchising has effectively existed for many generations. However, through time, its structure, organization, characteristics, operations, and total being have been evolving in response to a changing environment. Many new activities have begun to be franchised.

Our concern is to deal with the subject as it has most recently evolved and seems to exist in the last half of the 1970s, for it is within this context that your interests lie. There continue to exist many franchising opportunities, as seen in the daily paper (see examples in the want ads, business opportunity section, block ads in the business section, and so forth), and various business publications, including the magazine *Franchising*. Yet, the fact that franchising opportunities exist does not mean that the probability for success in each situation is good, for the spectrum ranges from the "gyp" to almost guaranteed economic success. You should be cautious in dealing with franchisors who promise you a guaranteed return on your investment. Often, contracts with these elusive or vanishing organizations have proved worthless.

We want you to become aware of what it means to be a franchisee and how you can best proceed in selecting the franchise that is right for you. Perhaps, after giving analytical consideration to the matter, you may conclude franchising is not for you.

IMPORTANCE OF FRANCHISING

Franchising has been one of the most rapidly expanding areas of business activity in recent years. The large percentage of new businesses

479

that fall in this category explains its prominent treatment in this part of the book. A discussion concerning aspects of franchising considered to be most important to the prospective new owner is presented below.

While service stations are considered a form of franchising, government documents separate service station franchises from other types. We will include a discussion of them in this chapter, however, from a practical point of view.

Franchise activities are growing, as can be seen by Tables 24–1 and 24–2. As shown in Table 24–1, the total number of franchise establishments grew 20 percent from 1969 to 1977; the number of company-owned

TABLE 24–1
Number of Franchise Establishments, 1969–1977

Year	Total Number of Establishments	Company-Owned Establishments	Franchisee-Owned Establishments
1969	383,908	68,863	315,045
1970	396,314	71,934	324,380
1971	431,169	74,721	356,448
1972	445,281	77,539	367,742
1973	453,632	78,850	374,782
1974	440,701	78,680	362,021
1975	434,538	80,561	353,977
1976*	445,624	83,294	362,330
1977*	463,482	87,127	376,355

* Data estimated by responses to authors' questionnaire.
Source: Department of Commerce, *Franchising in the Economy, 1975–1977* (Washington, D.C.: U.S. Government Printing Office, 1977), tables 7–9, pp. 30–32.

establishments grew 26 percent; while the number of franchisee-owned establishments grew only 19 percent. It is estimated that franchising accounts for about $177 billion in annual sales.[1]

Table 24–2 shows the average sales per establishment from 1974 to 1976. Of particular interest is the volume of sales by the kinds of franchise business. But also of interest is the fact that usually the average sales in establishments owned by a franchiser are greater than in those owned by the company.

WHAT CAN A FRANCHISE DO FOR ME?

In our survey of the field, we have generally concluded that a franchise can take your money, or it can make you financially independent—depending upon which franchise you choose. At this point, your con-

---

[1] Charles Swayne and William Tucker, *The Effective Entrepreneur* (Morristown, N.J.: General Learning Press, 1973), p. 150.

TABLE 24–2
Average Sales per Establishment, 1975–77 ($000)

Kind of Franchised Business	1975			1976*			1977*		
	Total	Company-Owned	Franchisee-Owned	Total	Company-Owned	Franchisee-Owned	Total	Company-Owned	Franchisee-Owned
Total—All Franchising	420	356	434	476	388	496	515	414	539
Automobile and truck dealers[1]	2,843	18,933	2,690	3,509	23,477	3,319	3,998	26,763	3,781
Automotive products and services[2]	105	377	74	113	391	79	120	397	86
Business aids and services	63	73	60	64	77	61	69	80	67
Accounting, credit, collection agencies, and general business services	47	103	46	44	103	43	46	105	45
Employment services	203	330	166	207	367	167	205	377	165
Printing and copying services	74	91	72	70	89	69	69	91	68
Tax preparation services	21	24	18	22	25	20	23	26	21
Miscellaneous business services	60	190	57	59	206	57	69	198	67
Construction, home improvement, maintenance, and cleaning services	59	181	56	59	176	56	60	178	58
Convenience stores	289	260	340	295	270	337	306	282	344
Educational products and services	132	129	133	122	99	129	108	78	118
Fast food restaurants (all types)	285	344	263	295	358	271	303	363	280
Gasoline service stations	232	232	232	257	257	257	287	287	287
Hotels and motels	839	1,301	720	861	1,396	731	888	1,477	747
Campgrounds	60	176	57	62	283	58	66	356	61
Laundry and drycleaning services	68	98	66	68	104	67	70	111	68
Recreation, entertainment, and travel	48	430	41	47	383	42	54	348	49
Rental services (auto–truck)	227	520	110	235	527	121	242	537	128
Rental services (equipment)	109	339	88	115	371	94	118	412	97
Retailing (Nonfood)	243	328	220	246	319	225	249	317	228
Retailing (food other than convenience stores)	123	604	100	128	649	102	134	672	106
Soft drink bottlers	2,918	3,047	2,914	3,346	3,368	3,346	3,678	3,579	3,682
Miscellaneous	153	383	137	183	383	167	184	393	167

* Data estimated by responses questionnaire.
Source: Department of Commerce, *Franchising in the Economy, 1975–1977* (Washington, D.C.: U.S. Government Printing Office, 1977), Table 13, p. 36.

sideration and focus should be: What can a franchise do for me that I cannot do for myself? In some instances, the answer may be "Nothing," while, in other circumstances, depending upon who you are, a franchise can lead to success.

At this point, we want to mention some of the things that are offered by the more successful franchisors. They tend to provide:

1. A training program that will equip you to manage your unit.
   (The more successful ones have their own special training schools. for example, McDonald's Hamburger University and Holiday Inn's Holiday Inn University.)
2. A standardized accounting and cost control system. These records are audited periodically by the franchisor's staff. In many instances, standard monthly operating statements are required. The franchisor develops a set of standard performance figures based on composite figures of reporting franchisees and return a comparative analysis to the franchisee as a managerial aid.
3. Financial assistance, in some instances, when minimum equity requirements are met by the potential franchisee. This financing would cover land, building, equipment, inventory, and working capital.
4. Site selection and a "turnkey" facility. This would include the purchase of site and the construction of a standardized structure identified as a part of the trademark of the franchise.
5. Counsel and specifications for erecting and equipping the facility.
6. A local, regional, or national image.
7. A well-planned and implemented national or regional advertising programs, establishing and maintaining a uniform image.
8. A set of customer service standards. These are established by the franchisor and professional staff, who make regular inspection visits to assure compliance by the franchisee.
9. Continuing management assistance, training, and guidance.
10. A sensitivity and responsiveness to changing market opportunities.

An example of franchisors' responsiveness to market opportunities is an article in the April 26, 1976, issue of *The Wall Street Journal* about the success "fast food" franchisors are achieving by moving into the small town market. In many instances, they have developed a smaller size unit to accommodate this market.[2]

11. A possible buyer advantage of a larger corporation. (It is important to check on a comparative basis.)
12. An operations system that time has proven successful.

---

[2] "Companies," *Business Week*, August 31, 1974, p. 75.

The information to this point should have led you to where you can make the choice of whether to be independent or to operate a franchise.

WHAT CLASSIFICATION OF FRANCHISE WILL YOU CHOOSE?

Recognizing that there are many categories of franchises, we have selected seven whose track records make them worthy of your consideration. These are: fast foods, motels, automotive, service stations, auto tune-ups, convenience markets, and real estate. We do not intend to imply that all franchises in these categories are of a quality worthy of your selection. Nor do we imply they are the only ones worthy of your consideration.

Some of the more currently active areas of franchising are shown in Figure 24–1.

FIGURE 24–1
Some Currently Popular Franchises

Type of Business	Examples
Auto brakes	Brako, Tuffy Brake Service Centers
Auto mufflers	Midas, Scotti Muffler Center, HODCO Muffler Centers
Auto parts	Western Auto
Auto transmissions	Mr. Transmission, AAMCO, Auto Man
Auto tune-up shops	(Activity in this field just getting underway)
Convenience markets	7–Eleven Stores, Radio Shack, Craft Shack
Fast foods	McDonald's, Hardee's, Sambo's, Wendy's, Captain D's, Kentucky Fried Chicken, H. Salt Fish, Church's Fried Chicken, Burger Chef, Burger King, Pizza Hut, Pizza Inn
Motels	Holiday Inn, Ramada Inn, Days Inn
Real estate	Century 21, Red Carpet
Retail hardware	Ace, American, True-Value
Service station	Amoco, Gulf, Crown

Fast Foods

The success of fast food franchises is related to many factors. One of these is the demographic environment evidenced by the higher percentage of young adults in the population; the large number of singles, both male and female; the increasing percentage of working housewives; and the lack of available domestic help. Other factors that seem to have had a positive influence on the course of events are: a product appealing to

TABLE 24-3
The Top Ten Fast-Food Chains and a Rising Star

Chain	U.S. Food Sales, 1976* ($millions)	Increase from 1975 (percent)	Market Share 1976 (percent)
McDonald's............................	$2,730.0	21.0%	19.6%
Kentucky Fried Chicken...............	1,165.0	16.6	8.4
Burger King..........................	741.6	20.7	5.3
International Dairy Queen.............	684.0	10.4	4.9
Pizza Hut............................	374.2	38.2	2.7
Howard Johnson's.....................	358.0	0.8	2.6
Sambo's..............................	348.4	32.4	2.5
Hardee's.............................	324.3	8.9	2.3
Jack-in-the-Box......................	323.4	17.8	2.3
Burger Chef..........................	305.0	7.0	2.2
And No. 18—coming up fast			
Wendy's..............................	187.0	151.1	1.3

* Includes sales of franchise and company-owned stores
Source: Data: © Maxwell Associates; market shares based on Commerce Dept. data; chart from "The Fast-Food Stars: Three Strategies for Fast Growth," *Business Week*, July 11, 1977, p. 56.

the palate of a significant segment of the market; fast service; a sanitary environment; and a structure with a trade mark image that is easily recognizable.

Wendy's International, Inc., is one of the fastest growing fast food franchises primarily because it appeals almost exclusively to young adults, who make up the fastest growing segment of our population. It specializes in made-to-order, quality hamburgers served in a stylish and comfortable decor.

McDonald's Corporation continues to expand its share of the market by catering to new clientele—such as the occupants of the Water Tower Place in Chicago, a complex of expensive condominiums and elite shops. The wealthy customers have enjoyed this food so much that McDonald's had to double the size of its restaurant in nine months.[3] It has also expanded its product to include new products such as its "Egg McMuffin" breakfasts.

Pizza Hut, Inc., is now appealing to the "ethnic" fast-food market, and finding its sales increasing tremendously.

Some of the personal attributes that franchisors give significant consideration to are: a record of stability; pleasant and personable attitude;

---

[3] "The Fast-Food Stars: Three Strategies for Fast Growth," *Business Week*, July 11, 1977, pp. 56ff.

an organizational outlook, that is, that of a person who can accept operating within the organizational framework, not the innovative, entrepreneurial type who adapts things to personal wishes; a "track record" of reasonable success; two years or more of college; and sufficient personal financial resources to satisfy the franchisor's minimum capital requirements. Generally, franchisors are very public-relations oriented. Their paramount interest is to maintain the company image of quality service and product which contributes to the financial success of both the franchisors and the franchisees. Table 24–3 shows that the top four fast food franchises are McDonald's, Kentucky Fried Chicken, Burger King, and International Dairy Queen.

Motel

During the past three decades the motel industry has had phenomenal growth. We have seen it grow from "mom and pop" units with an often questionable image to an industry dominated by large corporate complexes. These corporations have both company-owned units and a franchise division operating units under the company trade name.

A pioneer in the change has been Holiday Inn. It set standards of consistency and uniformity of accommodations, service, and rates. Its success through providing a uniform image, complemented by its free Holidex* reservation system, became a model for a new fledging segment of the old hostelry industry. The advent of the interstate highway system and the affluence and mobility of the American public created a market with great potential. Almost every interstate highway interchange became a potential motel site. In the early years, success seemed assured. Perhaps, in part, the earlier successes may have been responsible for what became an industry with excess capacity. No one heeded the few who foresaw the energy crises and its ultimate effect on gasoline prices and American life styles. Nevertheless it came, along with a changing mood and customer interest in the amenities a motel should provide. The upshot of all of these events has been such that all of a sudden the motel industry has achieved maturity. Many of the existing properties are now as obsolete as the "mom and pop" motels became with the coming of the national motels. The architecture, location, amenities offered, market, or finances of these properties do not make them suitable for modification. Instead, they are scheduled to be phased out by the franchisor—so beware!

Old Motel Opportunities. In considering the acquisition of an existing franchise motel property, whether new or old, you should make a careful determination of its status.

---

* The credit card arrangement with Gulf Oil Corporation, as well as the use of other national credit cards, further contributed to their success.

In determining an old motel's status, you should study the current and projected *traffic patterns and densities*. Also, you will need to identify the *travelers* and the *types of accommodation* they use. (State Tourist Bureaus or Departments of Transportation often can provide this information.) You need to also look at the occupancy rates for at least the past three years to see trends and relationships to the *breakeven rate*. You will need to identify all of the cost factors to see whether the current rate structure is adequate to cover all of the costs plus an adequate profit.

You will need to make a visual inspection of the facilities to determine the condition of the structure, both external and internal. Be particularly careful in checking to see that there are conference rooms and facilities that have adequate lighting, cooling, heating, and sound equipment and superior acoustical properties. The lobby and office space—and equipment and furnishings—should also be inspected. In looking at the exterior, you should check the ramps, passageways, elevators, roof and gutters, stairways, swimming pool and deck area, grounds and shrubbery, and the drainage, parking, and fire protection systems.

New Motel Opportunities.   There seems to be a concensus that the industry may be overbuilt and some properties are obsolete and should be phased out. This does not mean that new properties are not going to be developed. From a review of the present status and the future of the franchise motel business with some of the recognized people in the business, certain facts seem to stand out; they should be given careful consideration by you if motels are your field of interest. You should give consideration to the following:

1. The number of units operated by the more reputable motel organizations will tend to remain constant.
2. New units will generally be in the 300–500 room size.
3. Most new units will be constructed in metropolitan locations designed to serve a segment of the convention market.
4. Some major motel companies are going to increase the percentage of units that will be owned and operated by the company.
5. There continues to exist an opportunity for new franchisees to develop new properties that will be good revenue producers, but greater care is demanded in site selection than in the past.

Automotive Franchises

Automotive franchises have been around for some time. The franchises have historically been retail outlets for parts and accessories. Some of the units have been affiliated with nationally known tire manufacturers. Others have been related to national automotive parts manufacturers. A comparatively recent entry into the automotive franchise field has been the specialty service shop. Some examples are: those specializing in transmission repairs and parts; those specializing in muffler and shock absorber repairs and parts; the speed shops providing technical assistance, modification, and specialized parts; and diagnostic centers with their gradations of sophisticated electronic, computerized equipment.

Studies of the qualifications that automotive franchisors seek in their franchisees reveal that requirements are significantly different from those desired by other franchisors. One of the outstanding differences is that automotive franchisors tend to look for the male chauvinist. They prefer that the franchisee's wife and family not be associated with the business. A high school education seems adequate. We think that for the diagnostic centers, technical school training should be required, and possibly some college engineering training would be desirable. It does not seem that friendliness is considered an essential attribute. Since the greatest concern of the franchisor seems to be the ability of the franchisee to pay his bills and carry a sufficient inventory, adequate personal finances are considered very important as well as financial stability.

In summary, while the franchisor gives some consideration to personal attributes of the perspective franchisee, by far, the greatest concern is one of economic ability.

In general, the capital requirements of the automotive franchise are less than for some fast food or motel franchises. This difference seems to be most obvious in what you get by acquiring a franchise. Most of these franchises give little help in terms of management assistance, site location, financial assistance, and training. There may be an advantage in the system and product line and national advertising. Each situation should be carefully considered on its own merits. It is important in this class of franchises to perform a cost-revenue analysis as in other similar situations.

Service Stations

From 1972 to 1975, the number of service stations declined from about 226,000 to 193,000, or almost 15 percent.[4] Some observers of the oil industry have predicted that the number might even dip to 110,000 by 1980. Even though it does not appear that this prediction will materialize, it is evident that the number of entrepreneurial opportunities for service station management and operations is decreasing.

During the same period, the total dollar volume of sales increased over 54 percent; and the average sales per station rose about 77 percent, to

---

[4] The material for this part was developed with the assistance of M. M. Hargrove, *The National Petroleum News,* and from an interview with a major oil company marketing executive.

about $223,000 per year. The net profits of stations, however, have been unattractive.

Other significant factors affecting entrepreneurial opportunities in this area are:

1. Increased number of self-service stations.
2. Increased number of combination stations, such as gasoline retailing and tire center, convenience store, car-washes, and automobile parts and services.
3. Increased number of company-operated stations.
4. Dealers' long hours of work each day and weekend and holiday work.
5. Increased amount of investment in facilities and amount of equity capital necessary.
6. Alleged abuses and discrimination by oil companies.
7. Regulations of the Federal Energy Administration, Environmental Protection Agency, and the states.

The net effect of all these factors is that future independent dealers should be better qualified because the companies have become more selective, fewer stations are available, and broader technical knowledge and skills are required.

In order to be successful, these dealers should provide fast, high-quality, friendly, and dependable service. They should recognize these adverse factors affecting service station management and operations:

1. Changes in traffic patterns produced by such activities as neighborhood transitions, opening of a new shopping center, and the construction of streets, expressways, and interstate highways.
2. Poor service and dirty facilities.
3. Using open-account credit rather than requiring cash or company credit cards.
4. Stocking excessive inventory, including items that have little demand but tie up working capital and reduce cash flow.
5. Poor quality of employees.
6. Pilferage by customers and employees.
7. Poor merchandising, which does not assure adequate volume of TBA (tires, batteries, and accessories).
8. In times of shortages, the lack of products to assure an adequate volume of sales to generate a satisfactory level of revenue and profit.

Many major petroleum companies provide training schools for incoming dealers. In some instances, one might question the quality or effectiveness of these programs. In addition, a number of companies provide "in-house" advisory services to their dealers.

The energy crisis has created an atmosphere of uncertainty around the service station industry. The stronger dealer operated stations have been under pressure to survive. The shortage or absence of the main product, gasoline, has had a major effect on the volume of the stations' sales of TBA and other products. In some areas, the major companies have been accused of terminating dealer contracts and converting to company-operated stations.

The future of independent service station operations seems to be clouded by much uncertainty. Until the petroleum industry achieves stability as to direction, volume of product, methods of retailing, and pricing, you should be cautious before venturing into this type of business.

Auto Tune-Ups

Following the Arab oil embargo of 1973, the big increase in oil prices, and the closing of many full-service service stations, as discussed in the previous section, many stations have converted to self-service. This means that there are fewer places for an automobile owner to get a quick tune-up. Now, franchisers are moving into this vacuum with lucrative franchises that promise profitable operations.

Most of these franchises offer nothing but quick tune-ups, which are defined as working over the car's electrical system and carburetor, installing new points and plugs, and adjusting pollution-control devices.

The franchisers, so far, have been using former service stations for their franchises. The franchisees receive the use of the franchise name, get help in arranging the design and financing of their units, a training program, and other types of support, including legal advice and advertising.

> Insta-Tune, Inc., of Irvine, Calif., is the leader in this movement. It now (1977) has over 130 franchises and grossed around $8 million in 1976. The typical cost of a unit is $50,000, with sales of around $140,000 annually, and a net of around $37,000.[5]

Convenience Markets

While the usual connotation of the term convenience market is associated with food outlets, it may in fact cover a variety of specialty shops. The latter perform a service by assembling merchandise or materials into a single location, making convenient the selection and purchase. Some examples of this type franchise are Seven-Eleven food markets, Craft Shack, and Radio Shack.

---

[5] "Franchisers Tune in to Tune-Ups," *Business Week,* July 25, 1977, p. 136.

Real Estate Franchising

In an era when franchising is being used more frequently in an increasing variety of business activities, one of these is real estate. Franchising is not new to the real estate field. In the past, however, most of the real estate franchises were related to farm real estate. Now, activity is primarily concerned with urban real estate organizations; for example, Red Carpet, Century 21, and so forth. A major selling point in marketing real estate franchises is the benefits of "national referrals." The benefits once restricted to large firms are now available to smaller firms through the franchise system. Basically, the franchise makes the smaller firm more competitive with the larger organization. One national real estate authority sees that, in ten years, a significant majority of the smaller real estate firms will be affiliated with a franchise organization.

While fees are split with the referral firm, in today's mobile society, the selling firm hopes to offset such fees through referrals back to the referring firm. The newness and rapid expansion of real estate franchises indicate that a period of experience is needed before the stability achieved by franchisors and franchisees in other fields will be achieved by the real estate franchisors. In considering a real estate franchise, we suggest that you apply some of the criteria mentioned earlier in fast foods and motels and that you keep up with the changes occurring in this dynamic field.

WHAT FRANCHISE FOR ME?

The purpose of the material that follows is to aid you in selecting the *right* franchise—the one that will help you in achieving your objectives without jeopardizing your resources.

Some Pitfalls

Many franchise situations are loaded with pitfalls. Some of these dangers were pointed out in a Small Business Administration press release[6] of a study done for the U.S. Senate Select Committee on Small Business. Such franchises have left hundreds of disgruntled, disappointed, disillusioned people strewn in the aftermath of their onslaught. Unfortunately, many have naively placed their life savings in ventures that were doomed to failure from the start. There has been a broad array of these activities from gum-vending machines, candy machines, and stamp machines to fast food (fried chicken, specialty food items,

---

[6] See Urban B. Ozanne and Shelby D. Hunt, *The Economic Effects of Franchising* (Washington, D.C.: Small Business Administration, 1971), esp. pp. 1–2.

soft custard, and hamburgers), motels, coin-operated laundries, ice cream parlors, and so forth.

A man put up $2,000, on a guaranteed investment, for gum and candy machines. The franchisors promised to find good locations for the machines. However, these failed to materialize as all desirable locations were already being used. As a result, the man lost his $2,000 because the machines did not produce the projected guaranteed revenue. In the meantime, the franchisor evaporated and the guarantee on the investment was of no value.

A well-known radio-TV entertainment personality became involved with a fried chicken franchise operation. After a lot of fanfare and national publicity, a public offering of stock occurred. The fine print on the front page of the prospectus revealed more "padding" of assets than real value. From the outset, the franchisor did a poor job in assisting the franchisees. Consequently, the franchisees went down along with the company's stockholders.

A flurry of activity in mobile home sales and mobile home park franchises led many people to invest in the stock of the companies and buy their franchises. Many "fast-buck" operators rode to the pinnacle of paper success, but most investors lost substantial sums when the house of paper came crashing down.

Camping park franchises appeared vacant or sparsely populated during the recent energy crisis.

Some Pertinent Questions to Ask

In viewing a franchise possibility, you should probably question the objectives of the franchisor. Here is a simple list of questions you might want to investigate before "putting your money on the barrel head."

1. What is in it for me?
    a. Return on investment.
    b. Salary I can reasonably expect.
2. Is the franchisor just unloading a "white elephant" on me?

An example was a franchisor who tried to sell home swimming pools by requiring the franchisee to purchase a display model at a price comparable to a standard retail price.

3. What services does the franchisor provide the franchisee? Are the services priced at a discount or priced above the benefits they offer?

4. What is the attitude of the existing franchisees? Are they seeking to "unload," or are they happy with the results they are achieving?
5. What is the attitude of your banker, CPA, Better Business Bureau, chamber of commerce, and the community toward the franchisor and existing franchisees?
6. Is there a clause in the franchise contract that permits the franchisor, at will, to purchase the franchise on terms favoring the franchisor?

SOME CONCLUSIONS CONCERNING FRANCHISING

Even in the best franchise situations, the franchisor tends to hold an advantage. Usually, this relates to operating standards, supply and material purchasing agreements, and agreements relating to the repurchase of the franchise. However, franchise operations may offer you an opportunity to derive a satisfactory income on your investment and efforts.

A large number of court cases relating to franchise activities are now being adjudicated. Among the issues involved are territorial rights held by the franchisor and by the franchisee, and the right of the franchisor to require the franchisee to purchase supplies and inventory from the franchisor. Decisions seem to indicate that the franchisee may acquire some advantages and lose some from these legal actions.

While the projections look exceedingly favorable for franchising, there is now a concerted effort being made by several of the nation's largest manufacturers of prepared frozen foods sold in supermarkets to change our eating habits. This is the result of unit sales of food items sold through supermarkets, etc., have not increased since 1972. While the unit sales of food items sold through fast food outlets have increased significantly. In other words, the traditional food stores have not been participating proportionately in the increased consumption of food items. If the manufacturers program succeeds the unit sales of supermarkets will increase and those of fast foods will be slowed.[7]

There are two significant changes underway, at least in the fast food franchising area, that may affect your decision to go into this type operation. First, many of the companies are buying back the franchises from individuals and operating them themselves. Companies find that they can make more money this way, particularly in the more profitable areas. A second trend is to grant a group of franchises to existing franchisees who have a proved record of profitable operations. In many of these cases, the company will sell a franchise to an organization such as Horn & Hardart in New York. Figure 24–2 illustrates this trend.

---

[7] See the excellent article by John Peterson, "The Costly New Campaign . . . To Change the Way You Eat," *The National Observer*, January 29, 1977, pp. 1 and 16.

FIGURE 24-2
Franchising's Big Five

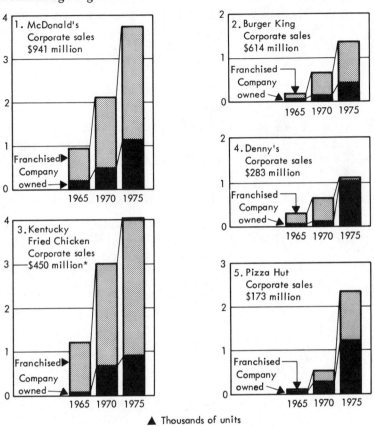

* *Business Week* estimate.
Source: "Fast-Food Franchisers Squeeze out the Little Guy," *Business Week*,
May 31, 1976, p. 46.

SUMMARY

This chapter has given you an overview of some of the advantages and disadvantages of operating a franchise, as well as some of the considerations in choosing the type of franchise you would like to operate.

On balance, the future of franchising seems to be quite favorable, in spite of some slight evidence of a trend away from the practice.

The material in this chapter has seemed to place greater emphasis on fast food and motel franchises, with less in depth discussions on automotive and convenience markets. There exists a rational basis for this, the significant growth in fast foods, which continues, and the growth and size of the motel industry. In both of these categories there are franchises which are sound and solid opportunities for their franchisees. The characteristics of these operations seem worthy to serve as model criteria for evaluating the feasibility of other franchise organizations and the opportunity they pose. In other words these provide a standard by which you may judge others. As always it is our objective to guide you toward the route of success.

QUESTIONS FOR DISCUSSION

1. Present a logical argument for becoming a franchisee.
2. Present a logical argument against becoming a franchisee.
3. Upon what criteria would you make this decision to become a franchisee?

WHERE TO LOOK FOR FURTHER INFORMATION

Department of Commerce, Domestic and International Business Administration, *Franchise Opportunities Handbook,* April 1977.

25

Providing for Management Succession

In Chapter 1, two potential problems were pointed out to you. First, the problems associated with failure were pointed out. The information presented in the intervening chapters has been based upon the assumption that you were going to be successful in the operations of your business. Assuming that your business is not totally successful, however, or if you suspect that you are not doing as well as you would like to, you might want, at this time, to consider the possibility of going out of business rather than continuing operations.

The second problem mentioned in Chapter 1 was what happens when your organization grows too rapidly. We hope that your organization has followed a normal path of growth and development and that everything is in order for you. This may be a good time, however, for you to evaluate your operations to see that you are avoiding the pitfalls of growing too fast.

NEED FOR MANAGEMENT SUCCESSION

If neither of these problems is facing you, you may soon be facing the third possibility, the need to provide for management succession.

An Overlooked Problem

In most small firms, the development of managerial personnel and the provision for management succession are greatly neglected, often until it is too late to do anything about them. Therefore, now that you have your firm operating successfully, you should answer these questions: Who will fill my shoes so that I can retire when I choose? Is there someone to operate the firm so I can take vacations or go to training programs or conventions? If my business is a proprietorship, do I want my spouse or child(ren) to manage it when I leave? If my company is a partnership and I leave it, do I want my spouse or child(ren) to be a partner? How will my death and incapacity affect my small firm?

The premature death of the owner of a family business presented the wife and other family members with a crisis concerning its future management. The eldest son, with a technical degree from one of the nation's leading colleges, was settled into a professional position with a promising future. After much soul-searching, he yielded to family loyalty and resigned his position to return home to become the business's general manager.

After 13 years, when in his early 40s, he called in some consultants to analyze the status of the firm. He had made significant changes in the business, resulting in enviable improvements in revenues and profits. The business included: a plant food, pesticide, and herbicide sales and application business; a cotton gin; a plant for processing certified seed; and a series of warehouses for storing two of the region's major agricultural commodities, as well as drying facilities for one of these commodities and a sizable acreage of farm land, some belonging to the original family and some to the general manager and his immediate family.

As he was describing the business to the consultants, he was interrupted with a question, "Do you mean that this business is not incorporated?" The response was that the business was operated as a partnership. A quick reply from one of the consultants was, "Man, it scares h_____ out of me when I look at all the potential liability around here." (His thoughts were centered, especially, on the two anhydrous ammonia tanks adjacent to the railroad and highway.)

The consultants concluded that at least two corporations should be established, one for the family business and one for the general manager's farming activities. Since the general manager had some personal objectives unrelated to the business, a set of immediate short-term and long-range objectives for the business was needed. A well-defined organization chart was needed to assure an effective line of management succession and to provide for more clearly understood responsibilities. This would also enable the general manager to shift his responsibilities to someone else in order for the business not to lose its momentum in his absence.

What Is the *Real* Problem?

You should realize that many children, grandchildren, and other relatives do not have the capabilities—or the interest—to manage your firm. Also, you need to be exceedingly competent to be either a judge of their managerial talent or a teacher to provide management training. The following discussion is offered for your benefit.

SOME PROBLEMS IN MANAGING A FAMILY-OWNED BUSINESS

When close relatives work together in a business, emotions often interfere with business decisions. "It's our business," is the motto in a family enterprise. Conflicts sometimes arise because relatives look at the business from different viewpoints. For example, relatives who are furnishing the capital or are the "money-men" may consider only income when judging capital expenditures, growth, and other major matters. Relatives engaged in the daily operations judge money matters from the viewpoint of securing the production, sales, and personnel necessary to make the firm successful. Clearly these two viewpoints may conflict.[1]

Individuals' Interests Conflict with Firm Objectives

Many times in a family business, the individuals' interests take precedence over centralized objectives and a supporting organizational structure. Such was the case of the Chapman family, as described in Chapter 4.

> The Chapman House grew like Topsy into a profitable chain of restaurants, motels, and textile industries. In time, the second generation took over more and more from the "matriarch," and the third generation began their entry into the business. It soon became evident that there were too many "chiefs," with a resulting proliferation of activities and increasing internal conflicts and decreasing profitability.
>
> The passing of the "matriarch" was followed by 90 days of internal strife. At the end of this period, a third-generation family member, with an MBA from State University and outside employment experience in a major industrial corporation, was able to hammer out some centralized objectives. This settlement was to be followed by the development of an appropriate organizational structure to reach the objectives. Fortunately, in this case, the family members recognized that their individual economic advantage was in keeping the business intact and expanding only in those areas offering the best return on investment.

Difficulty of Making *Rational* Decisions

The firm's top manager should recognize the extent of the emotions involved and make objective decisions. It is often hard for the manager and other relatives to make rational decisions about the skills and abili-

---

[1] Robert E. Levinson, "Problems in Managing a Family-Owned Business," *Management Aids for Small Manufacturers no. 208.* (Washington, D.C.: Small Business Administration, 1971).

ties of each other. Also, quarrels and ill feelings of relatives may spread to nonfamily employees. Or, family quarrels may carry over into the firm's operations and interfere with its effectiveness. The manager should not permit the business to become divided into factions. It is necessary to convince nonfamily employees that their interests are best served by a profitable company rather than by allegiance to any particular family member. Another complication that often occurs is that nonfamily employees tend to base their decisions on the family's tensions. They know how their bosses react, and they react accordingly.

Incompetence of Family Members—or Worse

Some family-owned companies are handicapped with high turnover among their most capable nonfamily employees. Relatives are sometimes to blame, for they may resent outside talent and make things unpleasant for nonfamily managers. Or, key managers may resign because the lines of promotion are closed to them. A troublesome relative may be discharged (with difficulty), assisted in starting another business in a noncompeting line, exiled to a branch office, or assisted in obtaining a job elsewhere.

Another problem is the family member who has occupied one job after another without being successful in any one of them. But now this person has a job, a title, and a salary—with you. A "ghost," or a lesser manager who knows the job and knows how to perform it, is doing work for which the other person is getting the credit. If the business is incorporated, perhaps the "floater" cannot be discharged because of a major stockholder's complaints. However, the useless manager may be shifted to some newly-created menial position with title and salary, but have no actual job to perform. The "ghost" may be promoted and given proper recognition.

Perhaps the manager is "in a bind" because of emotional involvement. For example, it may be necessary to clear routine matters with family members, because they have not let the manager forget past mistakes— particularly if the person is young, an in-law, or a distant relative.

Another difficulty may be that relatives indulge in excessive family talk during working hours, which hampers their performance as well as the performance of others. The manager should set the example and insist that other relatives refrain from family talk while on the job. If the company can afford it, one way to obtain objective control in a family-owned business is to hire an outside professional manager to handle day-to-day operations.

A common problem is the hiring of relatives who lack talent. Perhaps such a relative can be assigned to a job that permits contributions without disturbing other employees.

A relative can demoralize an organization by loafing, avoiding unpleasant tasks, taking special privileges, or making snide remarks about the manager and other relatives. The manager should assign such a relative to a job involving minimum contact with other employees and requiring no important decisions.

A more devastating aspect of this type of activity is that shown by one of the family members who "spies" on other employees.

> In a retail clothing store, the aunt of the owner-president is notorious for making life miserable for other workers, especially females. She "sneaks" into the ladies room and reports anyone found smoking. The employees always look behind clothing racks before they say anything personal or derogatory of the family to see whether she is listening. They refer to her as "the Gestapo." Needless to say, the morale is constantly low. Turnover is far greater than for comparable stores.

Definite Authority

Definite lines of authority and responsibility are an absolute necessity. The responsibilities of family members should be specified, and the extent of the authority, duties, and activities of each should be clearly stated. A nonfamily employee should be influential enough in the organization to be involved in operations and assist in smoothing out any emotional family decisions.

The manager's authority to suspend or discharge flagrant violators of company rules should also be specified. Control is weakened if the manager must make special allowances for "family employees."

Often the owner-manager may believe an expenditure should be made in order to improve efficiency; yet, other family members may oppose it because they consider it to be only an expense and money out of their pockets. To overcome this tendency, the manager might base arguments for the expenditure on information that nonfamily employees have derived. Perhaps it is possible to show the relatives that an investment can be recovered in a few years. Outside business advisers—including bankers, accountants, attorneys, or consultants—may assist the manager in convincing the relatives of the merits of the expenditure.

When some relatives in a family-owned business grow older, they frequently develop a desire to maintain the *status quo*. They can block, or at least hamper, company growth. These relatives may be given an opportunity to convert their common stock to preferred stock or to sell some of their stock to younger relatives. Perhaps they can be "gradually retired" through salary reductions over several years and induced to relinquish some of their interest in the firm.

Sharing of Profits

Provisions for paying family members and dividing the profits equitably among them can also be difficult. If the business is a corporation, stock dividends may be appropriate.

The salaries of family members should be competitive with those paid others of comparable rank and ability in the same area. Fringe benefits—such as deferred profit-sharing plans, pension plans, insurance programs, and stock purchase programs—can be useful in dividing profits equitably.

Some Sources of Help for You

If you are the manager of a family-owned business, you are not alone. Other individuals managing family companies in the same community may provide a source of information and assistance to you. You should exchange ideas with them and learn how they have solved problems similar to yours. Also, if you manage a small corporation, the presence of outsiders on the board of directors can be of benefit to you.

SOME DIFFICULT PROBLEMS WITH MANAGERS

You will have many problems with your managers, whether they are members of the family or not. You should be familiar with three staffing problems, which are particularly difficult in small firms: (1) the managers who thinks only in terms of "the past," (2) the one who "makes work," and (3) the one guilty of work duplication.

Incompetence

The first of these managers retains the old ways and refuses to learn and adopt new methods of management, regardless of how effective they may seem or how badly needed they are. Either dismissal or transfer to another assignment is appropriate in this case.

The make-work manager may have been hired to perform a specific job—such as doing a market survey—but the need for his/her services no longer exists. Dismissal or transfer to a more productive position may be appropriate.

The problem of work duplication may exist because two managers are both supervising the same project. Their duties should be reappraised.

If you are faced with similar staffing problems in your company, you should start with one or two changes at a time and see how they work out. You should also try to make changes before they become a dire necessity.

Replacing a Key Executive

You may be faced with another type of staffing problem when one of your key executives leaves. Some dislocation will inevitably occur, but you usually have some latitude in the kind of replacement you seek. You could consider reorganizing your management, redistributing the present assignments, and using present managers more effectively. The job specifications for a new manager could be written less narrowly, and the range of choice broadened. Your managers should participate in this planning because they will feel that they have contributed to the decision and will accept the newcomer more readily.

Often, your managers will prefer that an individual *from within the firm* replace a key manager who has left. This attitude usually appears not only in the manager who expects to be promoted, but also in other employees. If you decide upon an outsider, you should discuss the reasons with the manager who expected the promotion and with other managers prior to filling the vacancy.

If you recruit someone *from the outside*, you should have your people who will be working with the new manager meet and talk with candidates. You should observe their reactions and ask for their evaluations of the prospect. You should seek answers to these important questions: Will the prospect fit into the community? Will the family be able to make the adjustment? You should give the prospective manager ample opportunity to consider your situation carefully before deciding.

You can *appraise a prospective manager's ability* by considering several kinds of information: records of past performance, personal statements, and evaluations by others. Perhaps a prospective sales manager provides data that show a 60 percent increase in sales volume over the last five years while the sales force rose only 20 percent. The candidate's personal statements may reflect an interest in high-quality, custom-built products with low volume and high margin. You should determine whether there are inconsistencies in the candidate's statements. If you have doubts, you should ask more questions. Concerning others' evaluations, you should not automatically reject the prospect because of a poor reference. The latter may result from a personality conflict, circumstances of resignation, or some other situation that does not affect the prospect's suitability for your company.

In *determining compensation*, you should review the remuneration of your present managers to see whether it is adequate and equitable, whether it is properly related to their contributions to the firm, and whether it is comparable to that of the new manager. You should probably have a five-year compensation plan in mind for a new manager. Keep in mind that if your offer is too high now you may limit your ability to increase rewards for improved performance in the future. However, you should not drive too hard a bargain. To help make the new manager's interests coincide with yours, you should consider offering a share of ownership in your firm.

When you hire a manager you should discuss with him or her *how the relationship can be terminated.* There should be some penalty for termination, but it should not be so great that you keep an unsatisfactory manager rather than pay the penalty. You also want to avoid giving the manager a bonus for taking a better job elsewhere. You should not conceal any unpleasant conditions that must be confronted soon after the new manager reports for work.

Some turnover in your middle management group can be beneficial if it does not happen too often. If you have a young manager with ability and ambition, you should be frank about the opportunities you can offer. If such a person should desire to move, you should offer help in finding a better position. This assistance is preferable to his job-hunting without your knowledge.

> One of us was on the Panama Limited train going from Chicago to New Orleans with the owner-manager of a large office in the latter city. He was reading the *New Orleans Times-Picayune* want ads. Suddenly he exclaimed, "That's my telephone number!"
>
> When asked what he meant, he indicated a "Position Wanted" ad that gave one of his office phones for prospective employers to call. Needless to say, he was very upset with the young man who had placed the ad.

Replacing a manager can sometimes benefit you. For example, suppose a production manager who has excelled in plant layout, tooling, and production methods leaves you. In replacing this person, you might want a manager with a different mix of skills—perhaps including labor relations, employee productivity, and quality of supervision.

TAXES, ESTATE PLANNING, AND THE FUTURE OF YOUR BUSINESS

In planning the future activities of your business, you should always give consideration to the influence taxes will have on your profits and your business's capital structure. Since tax laws and regulations change frequently, it is important that you stay current in your knowledge of these matters. (It is recommended that you have an annual conference with a CPA well versed in business tax matters.)

Surely, in projecting the future of your business, it is essential for you to plan to minimize your estate taxes and, at the same time, make provisions for their payment should the need arise. It is a simple matter for your business and its assets to appreciate in value to a much greater extent than you may be aware. Therefore, it is in your best interest to review your estate plans, on a frequent basis, as well as your possible estate tax liability and the provisions you have made for its payment.

There are a number of reference sources you may use as an aid to your tax planning.[2] We recommend that in the final analysis, however, you use the services of a professional.

PREPARING FOR YOUR SUCCESSOR

What preparations should you make when you are planning to retire, acquire another business, or otherwise turn the business over to someone else? Too often, a small company suffers under these circumstances. Sales may decrease or production may lag. These difficulties can be prevented by preparations that will enable the new manager to pick up where you leave off. The key is to make available to your successor the specialized knowledge that you have accumulated over the years.

Providing Him or Her with Adequate Information

You should create a reference source for a new manager by making an inventory of the various kinds of information used to manage and operate your business. The inventory should consist of three kinds of information:

1. Facts about the general administration of the company.
2. Data concerning the firm's finances.
3. Information about operating and technical aspects.

Examples of these inventories are presented in the Appendix with this chapter. This type of inventory should also help you evaluate your firm at any time, so you might want to do it periodically.

You should set down some information about goals and objectives you hope to see the company reach, both before you leave and afterwards. An illustration of this type of objective might be the accumulation of funds to replace an old plant. This program should be supplemented with profit and loss and cash flow projections. These long-range goals should be described in two parts:

1. Steps to be accomplished before you leave.
2. Steps to be accomplished after you leave.

Starting Early!

Even though your top assistant should have the same capabilities as you, you should also try to find someone who complements your

---

[2] William H. Hoffman, Jr., ed., *West's Federal Taxation: Corporations, Partnerships, Estates, and Trusts* (St. Paul, Minn.: West Publishing Co., 1977).

abilities. Two dynamic and aggressive individuals often clash. "The capable assistant is usually one whose strengths match your weaknesses, rather than one whose strong points match yours."[3]

In order to facilitate a smooth transition, you should bring in the new manager as early as possible. The length of the transition period varies according to your plans, the type of business you are in, the new manager's experience and knowledge, whether the person is a relative or a hired outsider, and the size of your firm. The period may vary from three to five years.

The "Moment of Truth"

Ultimately, the moment arrives when you must turn over to someone else the business you have created with your own ambition, initiative, and character. If you have built well, it will survive as testimony of your creativity.

> A salesman in the rubber industry and an experienced and technologically competent production man in his early sixties formed a business to produce a component used in the shoe industry. The production manager owned two thirds of the firm and the salesman, one third.
>
> The salesman was weak in his management abilities, so that the real management burdens rested on the production manager, who, in fact, was the general manager.
>
> After four years of operations, the general manager was in his late sixties, and they were still short of the profit objectives. The general manager had planned to retire at 70, but now he began to wonder how he could achieve it. It seemed that not only was his time needed in the plant, but more and more of it was spent in the field; and when he was away from the plant, its efficiency suffered. The nagging question was, as is so often the case in similar circumstances, "What can you do when there is no one to whom you can delegate some of your activities?"

A MANAGEMENT AUDIT

You have now come to the point where you are probably asking yourself, "How well am I actually doing?" All of us like to know how we are doing. Possibly, to determine your individual situation, you should use the questionnaire, General Management Audit, found in Appendix B at the end of this chapter. This material has been field-tested and has proved useful in aiding business owners/managers to take an objective

---

[3] Med Serif, "Pointers for Developing Your Top Assistant," *Small Marketers Aids no. 101.* (Washington, D.C.: Small Business Administration, 1972).

look at their managerial status and the managerial status of their business.

SUMMARY

Because of the time, effort, and money you have expended to make your small business a success, it is important that you do everything possible to provide for effective management succession. In order to do this, you must make adequate provisions for the selection, development, and motivation of competent professional managers to succeed you and assure your firm's continuation. Some ideas to make this possible have been presented in this part.

QUESTIONS FOR FURTHER DISCUSSION

1. What are some staffing problems an owner-manager should be familiar with?
2. What problem will face an owner-manager when a key manager leaves?
3. Discuss the problems involved in managing a family-owned business.
4. How should a manager prepare to leave and turn the business over to a new manager?
5. Why are some family-owned companies handicapped with high turnover among their most capable non-family employees?
6. How should an owner-manager try to resolve a disagreement between family members, when it concerns business expenditures?

APPENDIX A: INVENTORY OF INFORMATION USED TO MANAGE AND OPERATE A COMPANY[4]

Inventory of Facts about General Administration

Company history:
Date organized, key founders, and major events.
Clippings of stories from newspapers and trade journals concerning your company.
Brochures concerning new products, processes, sales personnel, etc.

Company organization:
Organization chart.
Job specifications.
Description of key employees, including your evaluation of their potential.

___

[4] Source: Frederick E. Halstead, *Preparing for New Management* (Washington, D.C.: Small Business Administration, 1972), Management Aids for Small Manufacturers, No. 183.

Report of studies made by your employees or an outside consultant on your company.

Policies:

Information on credit and selling terms, vacations, retirement plans, employee loans and advances, etc.

Legal matters:

Patents, licenses, and royalty agreements.
Note where each formal document is filed.
Employment and labor agreements.
Leases.
Contracts with suppliers and customers.
Outcome of past law suits, and pending suits.

Outside services:

List and brief description of outside professional people who work with your company, including bankers, accountants, insurance agents, advertising agencies, consultants, etc.

Inventory of Financial Data

Profit and loss statements for past ten years.
Copy of most recent balance sheet.
Copy of most recent budget.
Brief description of company's working capital turnover trends, return on investment trends, operating ratios, etc.
List of current bank accounts, including average balances and name of bank employee who handles accounts.
List of prior banking connections, indicating the line of credit and bank officers who arranged it.
List of paid tax bills.
List of insurance policies, including a description of coverages and premiums and name of agent.
Copies of your financial and control reports, with notation about frequency of preparation and distribution.
Copies of procedures or procedure manuals.

Inventory of Operating and Technical Information

Marketing:

List of company's products or services, and notes concerning customer acceptance, profitability, and future potential.
List of geographical areas in which each product is sold, types of customers, and the largest customers.
List of distribution channels.

Brief outline of advertising program, including how it is coordinated with other sales efforts.

Brief descriptions of sales training programs.

Brief description of how prices are set for current and new products.

Brief description of competitors, including a list of their products, location and size of their plants, share of the market, pricing policies, and channels of distribution.

Production:

List of major pieces of equipment. Brief appraisal of efficiency of the plant and equipment.

List of product and manufacturing specifications and process procedures.

List of studies made to improve layout and quality control, replace existing equipment, etc.

Brief description of how production is scheduled and controlled (orders on hand or for stock).

Brief description of standards used for measuring performance and methods for eliminating waste.

Purchasing:

Lists concerning: (1) major materials purchased; (2) names of suppliers; (3) present contracts with suppliers; and (4) procedures for buying, including kind of approval needed for various types of purchases.

Other areas:

Inventory of knowledge in special areas, including research and development, engineering, quality control, etc.

APPENDIX B: GENERAL MANAGEMENT AUDIT

You should now have successfully completed reading and studying the material in this text. We hope it has been of help to you in deciding whether to become an independent business owner-manager, or to continue as one if you are already in that position. For those of you who currently own a small or independent business, you may wish to complete the following form to do a self-audit of the general management of your organization.

As with the other appendixes, you should answer the questions as completely, objectively, and honestly as possible. When you have completed this, you may want to go over it again, objectively evaluating how you are doing. An alternative is to submit this to someone you trust—a consultant, banker, or friend—and have him or her evaluate how you are doing.

Good luck to you!

A. Organization
    1. Do you have a Board of Directors?
        Yes _____ No _____

    2. Who constitute your board? _____
        _____
        _____

    3. How often do you meet? Monthly _____
                               Quarterly _____
                               Semi-annually _____
                               Yearly _____

    4. Are these meetings of any actual benefit?
        Yes _____ No _____

    5. Does any action result from suggestions made in board
        meetings? Yes _____ No _____

B. President—function and status
    1. How old are you? _____

    2. What is the state of your health? Excellent _____
                                          Good _____
                                          Fair _____
                                          Poor _____

    3. Do you have any specific health problems? _____
        _____
        _____

    4. What do you do in running your company? _____
        _____
        _____
        _____

    5. Who looks after things when you are away? _____
        _____

    6. Are you satisfied with what goes on in your absence?
        Yes _____ No _____

    7. If, for some reason beyond your control, you are not able
        to be there to run the business, what would happen?
        _____
        _____
        _____
        _____

8. Could your business continue if you were killed in an automobile accident? Yes _____ No _____

9. Are you training someone to assume your managerial responsibilities? Yes _____ No _____

10. How long have you been training this person? _____

11. Why did you select him or her? _____
   _____
   _____
   _____

12. How much consideration have you given to detailing the activities that take place in your company?
   _____
   _____
   _____
   _____

13. Have you assigned specific people to be responsible for specific activities? Yes _____ No _____

14. Are you happy with everybody's performance in his or her assigned role? Yes _____ No _____
   Who? 1 _____ 2 _____ 3 _____ 4 _____ 5 _____
   _____
   _____
   Why? _____
   _____
   _____
   _____

15. Do you ever go through your organization and evaluate the performance effectiveness of those people assigned to some type of managerial responsibility?
   Yes _____ No _____

16. Do you expect these people to do the same thing of the people they supervise? Yes _____ No _____

17. Construct an organization chart of your business—first do it by functional activity without the people. Now add the people.

C. Management information
   (Purpose: to provide information that reveals what actually
has occurred in a specific time frame. This information should
be utilized to determine accurate costs, to plan more effectively
for profits, and to determine asset and liability status.)

D. Paper-flow analysis
   1. What happens when an order is received? _____
   _____
   _____
   _____

   2. How is it recorded? _____
   _____
   _____
   _____

   3. If it is recorded on a sales order, what is the sequence
      of events that follow? Who handles it (step-by-step
      through production and shipment)? At the end, who takes
      final action and files?
      _____
      _____
      _____
      _____
      _____
      _____

   4. How do you maintain a file of orders? _____
      _____
      _____
      _____
      _____

   5. Who is responsible to see that orders are filled and
      shipped?
      _____
      _____
      _____

   6. Are the sales orders dated and numbered?
      Yes _____ No _____

   7. Are purchase orders issued on prenumbered forms?
      Yes _____ No _____ Trace the paper flow.
      _____

_____

_____

_____

_____

How are purchase orders initiated? _____

_____

_____

_____

What system of record keeping exists for purchases? Do you check invoices against purchase orders?
Yes _____ No _____

8. Do you have receiving reports? Yes _____ No _____
    Who gets them?

    _____

    _____

    Are they matched against purchase orders and incoming invoices? Yes _____ No _____

9. Do you invoice your orders on prenumbered invoice forms? Yes _____ No _____

10. How many copies of invoices are made? _____
    Who receives them? _____

    _____

    _____

11. When are invoices issued? _____

12. In sending invoice to customer do you send copies of all appropriate documents, B/L, other related information?
    Yes _____ No _____

13. What procedures control sales invoices? Are they transferred to Accounts Receivable, Accounts Receivable Aged, etc?

    _____

    _____

    _____

    _____

    (Is it possible that a sales person or other person might make up an invoice, collect for it, and not turn in such receipts?)

14. Do you keep a record of adjustments? Yes _____
    No _____ Who is authorized to make adjustments?
    _____
    _____

    Do you permit sales people to make adjustments?
    Yes _____ No _____ (There is danger of collusion
    between salesperson and customer in making adjust-
    ment.)

15. Do you get sales reports on calls activity, information
    obtained, indication of expected activity or lack of it?
    Yes _____ No _____
    Do you develop a monthly sales expense, salesman by
    salesman? Yes _____ No _____

16. Do you develop a production order? Yes _____
    No _____ For what time period?
    Daily _____   Semi-annually _____
    Weekly _____   Quarterly _____
    Monthly _____   Yearly _____
    Every 6 weeks _____

E. Paper Flow
   1. Sales orders → Who → What happens → Where?

   2. Credit approval? _____

   3. Collection cycle? _____

   4. Cost breakdown:
      a. Overhead _____
      b. Operating
         (1) People _____
         (2) Equipment
             Power _____
             Depreciation _____
             Maintenance _____

   5. List audience paper flow distribution by time through
      operating period. _____
      _____
      _____
      _____
      _____
      _____

6. How do you *price* your product? _____
   _____
   _____
   _____
   _____
   _____

7. How do you plan for profit? Bottom line? Pricing formula?
   Explain: _____
   _____
   _____

F. *Marketing.* What plans and what activities are taking place in your organization to assure a future market?
   1. Are you replacing retiring dealers with younger people? Yes _____ No _____

   2. Are you promoting the development of new customers to assure a continuing market? Yes _____ No _____

   3. How are you approaching the market to accommodate the changing age distribution in the population? Are you developing products with special appeal to the younger generation? Yes _____ No _____

   4. Other: _____
      _____
      _____
      _____
      _____

WHERE TO LOOK FOR FURTHER INFORMATION

Halstead, E. Frederick. "Preparing for New Management." *Management Aids for Small Manufacturers no. 183.* Washington, D.C.: Small Business Administration, 1972.

Levinsen, Robert E. "Problems in Managing a Family-Owned Business." *Management Aids for Small Manufacturers no. 208.* Washington, D.C.: Small Business Administration, 1970.

Robinsen, Joseph A. "How to Find a Likely Successor." *Management Aids for Small Manufacturers, no. 198.* Washington, D.C.: Small Business Administration, 1968.

cases for part VII

VII–1   Floyd Bean Bonanza Steak House[1]

Bonanza International is a franchised chain of over 200 family steak restaurants with headquarters in Dallas. The concept is a limited menu of steak dinners that a family of four can eat for less than $10. Service is modified cafeteria with no tipping, and guests are invited to "come as you are."

In July, 1971, Mr. Floyd Bean signed an agreement with Bonanza International to open up the Bonanza Sirloin Pit #590, at 1111 East Ledbetter Drive, Dallas, Texas.

MR. FLOYD BEAN

Mr. Floyd Bean is 37 years old, married, with two daughters. His health is excellent. Mr. Bean was born in Galveston, Texas, where he graduated from Central High School. He went to Southern University in Baton Rouge, Louisiana, and majored in Sociology with a minor in Physical Education. He graduated from Southern University in the top ten of his class after playing four years of college football.

---

[1] Prepared by Sydney C. Reagan and Calvin W. Stephens, School of Business Administration, Southern Methodist University.

Upon finishing college he returned to Galveston, Texas, and worked as a substitute teacher in the Galveston School System for seven months.

In 1962, he went to work for the Falstaff Brewery in Galveston, Texas, as a Field Sales Representative and Chief Tour Guide. During this time he had four men working under his supervision. His main responsibility was to book parties for the hospitality room, which was used every night. He and his men guided groups on tours of the brewery, then to the hospitality room for a beer party.

In 1963, Floyd Bean was promoted to the Branch Sales Department. He was responsible for the sales of three route men in the Galveston County area.

In 1964, Mr. Bean was promoted to a Special Division Sales Representative covering five states for Falstaff. His duties then were to assist the distributors in these five states. He called on each account in the salesmen's market with the salesmen and made recommendations to the distributor on how he could improve his sales.

In 1969, he resigned from Falstaff to take a position with Bonanza International as Director of Minority Franchising. As a part of his training, he attended the Bonanza School of Management. His duties were to find qualified minority people to go into business as owner-operators of Bonanza Steak Houses. Mr. Bean, in that capacity, temporarily took over the management of several of the Bonanza Sirloin Pits that were having problems. There he proved that he had managerial talent, and there he developed a taste for running a business of his own.

In May 1971, Mr. Bean decided to resign his position at Bonanza International to pursue the ownership of a Bonanza franchise. He had two reasons for this move. He wanted to go into business for himself; he also felt that he would have more opportunities.

THE FRANCHISE DEVELOPMENT

Floyd Bean's ability and his desire to have a business of his own were not enough. He found that going into business takes money, and before bankers and others would lend to an entrepreneur they wanted to know that the entrepreneur or someone was going to be putting enough equity, or ownership money, into the enterprise to have something at stake—enough to make the entrepreneur work hard to make it succeed. So Floyd Bean's first problem became one of how to raise the necessary money.

Everyone who knew him well said that one quality Floyd Bean had was tenacity. He absolutely refused to quit trying. And through months of negotiations and many a disappointment, even after one financing effort turned out to be all wrong, he would not give up.

"I wanted to operate my own business," Bean now says, "and I've got to admit, I got a little sore against the establishment because I thought they were playing games with me. But I told them I'm not going to quit."

Bean also found some people who could help him put his project together. Mr. Hal Gordon of the Chica Corporation of Dallas, the area distributor of Bonanza, had seen an old church on Ledbetter and thought it could be rebuilt into a good Bonanza location. Mr. Gordon was able to purchase the property after seeking and obtaining a loan, and was able to offer a long-term lease to Bean. This required that a lease guarantee be built into the financing package.

The major target service area for the Bonanza Steak House was comprised of low-income, lower-middle and middle-income families. Of these families, approximately 20 percent owned their homes. The average number of persons per occupied dwelling unit in the target service area was approximately 3.89.

The target service area was an integrated neighborhood with blacks comprising about 78 percent of the total, whites comprising 21 percent, and other ethnic groups making up the remaining one percent. (See accompanying table for additional information on the site and neighborhood.)

Walter J. Sodeman, Director of Franchise Development for Bonanza, Bean's former boss, saw a lot of potential business within the black community. Sodeman cited a recent article in *Sales Management* magazine, which pointed out that, while the total population of Dallas in-

Site Information

1.	Address:	1111 East Ledbetter, Dallas, Texas 75216
2.	Location:	Southwest Dallas on State Highway Loop 12, one mile east of Interstate 35.
3.	Size:	87,590 square feet; frontage 335 feet; depth 300 feet
4.	Building:	The building to be converted to a Bonanza Steak House is an old church located on the back side of the property about 150 feet from Loop 12.
5.	Access:	State Highway Loop 12, known as East Ledbetter in this portion, is four lane and is the loop around Dallas. Traffic count at this location is 20,330 in a 24-hour period (1969). Traffic moves at between 40 and 50 miles per hour, with a speed limit of 45 miles per hour.
6.	Major businesses within one mile:	South Park shopping center (85 acres) with all major stores; K-Mart; Target; Gibson; Jack-in-the-Box.
7.	Market area:	There are 3,200 homes in the immediate area, and they range in price from about $6,000 to $25,000. The residential areas just south of Loop 12 are known as Glenview, with a population over 19,000, and Singing Hills, with a population over 15,000. The restaurant would serve a population in a three-mile radius of over 150,000 persons.

creased 25 percent from 1960 to 1970, the black population increased 63 percent; blacks went from 19 percent of the Dallas population in 1960 to 25 percent in 1970. Sodeman contended that the food service business, a service business with high profit potential and large turnover of inventory compared to other capital-intensive businesses, was a good one for black enterprisers to get into.

Also among the people who helped, was Mr. Tony F. Martinez, an Indian from Taos, New Mexico, who was the first Indian to get a Master's in Business Administration from Baylor and was senior analyst for the Dallas Alliance of Minority Enterprise (DAME). With documented experience of other restaurants, with pro-forma cash flow statements, with estimates of the cost of equipment in hand, and everything else needed to sell the project, Martinez helped Bean find the sources of funds he was looking for.

SOURCE OF FUNDS

The first $5,000 was provided by University Computing Corporation Venture Corporation, a Minority Enterprise Small Business Investment Company (MESBIC), on a five-year, $7\frac{1}{2}$ percent subordinated note. Another $5,000, later increased to the needed $15,000, was similarly provided by Motor Enterprise of Detroit, a MESBIC created by General Motors to help minority enterprisers find capital. The Oak Cliff National Bank then provided $45,000 on a five-year note, with the restaurant's equipment pledged. The Small Business Administration of the federal government provided $20,000, on a five-year, $6\frac{1}{4}$ percent unsubordinated note, under the Equal Opportunity Loan Program. And finally the SBA also provided a 15-year lease guarantee totaling $261,000.

Thus, the package was put together to cover the needed lease guarantee, organizational expenses, and working capital for Floyd Bean to get his business started.

Mr. Bean began operations on October 1, 1971.

During the first two months after Floyd Bean opened Floyd Bean Steak House in December 1971, he had difficulty finding the right combination of black and white employees to attract a diverse clientele. His initial problem was to get enough customers—both black and white—to maintain enough sales to make a profit, or even to break even. In January 1972, he hired a white assistant manager who had previous experience in the management of restaurants. Mr. Bean now feels he has a complementary combination of staff and management that will satisfy all his customers.

Another problem Mr. Bean faced was how to increase his sales from Monday through Thursday. During these days he lost a significant percentage of his black customers. He says that the reason for this was

EXHIBIT 1

FLOYD BEAN BONANZA STEAK HOUSE
Statement of Operations
June 1972 and Year to Date

	June 1972		January–June 1972	
	Amount	Percent of Sales	Amount	Percent of Sales
Sales............................	$15,762	100.0	$67,045	100.0
Cost of Sales:				
Beginning Inventory...............	$ 3,678		$ 5,037	
Purchases........................	5,825		26,106	
	$ 9,503		$31,142	
Less: Ending Inventory.............	3,478		3,478	
Total......................	6,025	38.2	27,664	41.3
Gross Profit.............	$ 9,737	61.8	$39,381	58.7
Expenses:				
Cash, over and short...............	(6)	0.0	36	0.1
Advertising.......................	552	3.5	2,285	3.4
Depreciation......................	413	2.6	2,066	3.1
Interest..........................	429	2.7	2,079	3.1
Insurance, general.................	250	1.6	1,250	1.9
Insurance, officers life.............	208	1.3	208	0.3
Insurance, employees...............	142	0.9	142	0.2
Legal and audit...................	250	1.6	1,250	1.9
Office............................			94	0.1
Maintenance......................	359	2.3	1,980	3.0
Rent, building....................	1,490	9.5	7,453	11.1
Rent, equipment..................	283	1.8	849	1.3
Salaries and wages................	3,249	20.6	14,895	22.2
Supplies.........................	171	1.1	977	1.5
Security.........................	76	0.5	424	0.6
Payroll taxes.....................	169	1.1	778	1.1
Telephone........................	25	0.2	179	0.3
Utilities..........................	573	3.6	2,488	3.7
Franchise royalty..................	375	2.3	1,606	2.4
Rubbish removal...................			282	0.4
Uniforms and laundry..............	89	0.5	1,415	2.1
Total Expense...............	9,097	57.7	42,664	63.6
Net Profit (Loss)........	$ 640	4.1	$(3,283)	4.9

that black families in general do not eat out as a family unit except on the weekends.

In 1970, 25 Bonanzas topped $400,000 in sales. Average sales of all Bonanzas were $278,000. Mr. Bean expected to do at least $300,000 a year and hoped he would exceed $400,000 with the added help of a party room he planned to add. Bonanza #572 at 3515 Inwood Road in Dallas, without a party room, had net sales of $416,644 in 1971.

At the time of this case, however, Mr. Bean's actual sales were running behind his predictions. For the first six months of 1972, his projected gross sales were $94,309. His actual gross sales for that period were

EXHIBIT 2

FLOYD BEAN BONANZA STEAK HOUSE
Balance Sheet
January 1, 1972 and June 30, 1972

Assets	*January 1, 1972*	*June 30, 1972*
Current Assets:		
Cash in bank.............................	$15,354	$ 6,245
Cash on hand.............................	700	800
Receivables...............................	(55)	560
Inventory.................................	5,037	3,479
Prepaid insurance.........................	1,606	2,377
Deferred advertising.......................	447	851
Total Current Assets..................	$23,089	$14,312
Property and Equipment:		
Furniture and fixtures......................	$49,585	$50,312
Less accumulated depreciation...............	413	2,479
Total Property and Equipment.........	$49,172	$47,833
Other Assets:		
SBA lease guarantee.......................	$ 7,267	$ 7,065
Total Assets.....................	$79,528	$69,210
Liabilities and Investment		
Current Liabilities:		
Accounts payable...........................	$ 5,167	$ 8,371
Note payable—insurance....................	991	1,419
Payroll taxes payable.......................	992	602
Sales tax payable...........................	902	1,478
Accrued payroll............................	1,304	1,409
Total Current Liabilities..............	$ 9,356	$13,279
Long Term Debt:		
South Oak Cliff Bank.......................	$44,619	$40,838
SBA..	20,000	18,787
Motor Enterprises..........................	15,000	15,000
UCC Venture..............................	5,000	5,000
Total Long Term Debt.................	$84,619	$79,625
Investment:		
Floyd Bean, Investment.....................	($ 7,861)	($14,447)
Net Profit (Loss) for year to date...........	($ 4,911)	($ 3,283)
Less: Withdrawals.........................	1,675	5,964
Total Investment.....................	($14,447)	($23,694)
Total Liabilities...................	$79,528	$69,210

$67,045—some $27,264 short of his goal. For the same six-month period, his projected net profit was $743.50. He actually had a net loss for the period of $3,282.66, which was $4,026.16 short of his projection. However, Mr. Bean was still very optimistic that he would eventually increase his sales and meet his earlier projections. See Exhibits 1 and 2 for statements of operations and balance sheets, and Exhibit 3 for projections by Mr. Bean. The effect of cooperative advertising by all Bonanza Steak Houses in the Dallas area was considered to be highly beneficial to each.

EXHIBIT 3

FLOYD BEAN BONANZA STEAK HOUSE
Pro-Forma Income and Expense Statement
1972

	January–March	April–June	July–September	October–December	1972 Total
Sales..........................	$43,341	$50,968	$60,260	$63,480	$218,049
Cost of Sales.................	16,475	20,650	24,500	25,650	87,275
Gross Profit............	$26,866	$30,318	$35,760	$37,830	$130,774
Expenses:					
Cash short (Over)............	$ 150	$ 150	$ 150	$ 150	$ 600
Advertising..................	1,225	1,535	1,811	1,905	6,476
Depreciation.................	1,239	1,240	1,240	1,239	4,958
Interest.....................	1,374	1,361	1,348	1,334	5,417
Insurance....................	558	558	558	558	2,232
Legal and audit..............	750	750	750	750	3,000
Office.......................	60	65	75	85	285
Maintenance.................	250	150	150	150	700
Rent building................	4,350	4,350	4,350	4,350	17,400
Rent equipment..............	531	531	531	531	2,124
Salaries and wages...........	8,517	10,320	10,350	10,500	39,687
Supplies.....................	1,378	1,735	2,031	2,151	7,295
Service......................	1,020	1,020	1,020	1,020	4,080
Payroll taxes................	619	720	720	729	2,788
Other taxes.................	555	555	555	555	2,220
Telephone...................	120	120	120	120	480
Utilities.....................	1,321	1,841	1,839	1,932	6,933
Franchise royalties...........	1,943	2,449	2,897	3,048	10,337
Miscellaneous................	460	570	755	830	2,615
Total Expenses........	$26,420	$30,020	$31,250	$31,937	$119,627
Net Profit...................	$ 446	$ 298	$ 4,510	$ 5,893	$ 11,147
Less estimated income taxes................	$ 190	165	910	1,180	2,445
Net Profit (AT).............	$ 256	$ 133	$ 3,600	$ 4,713	$ 8,702
Less withdrawals.......	2,499	2,499	2,499	2,499	9,996
Profit (Loss) for loan payment..	($ 2,243)	(2,366)	$ 1,101	$ 2,214	($ 1,294)
All loan payments...........	$ 2,872	$ 3,185	$ 3,198	$ 3,212	$ 12,467

Mr. Bean was considering all his problems and trying to decide how to proceed.

QUESTIONS FOR DISCUSSION

1. Was Floyd Bean's decision to start a business of his own a wise decision?
2. If the answer to Question 1 is positive, did Mr. Bean select the right business to enter?
3. Was the choice of location a good one for Mr. Bean? Is this location a desirable one for this type of franchise?
4. How could Mr. Bean make his restaurant more visible to the people who pass by when driving on Ledbetter Street?

5. Evaluate the following sources of financial support for minority businesses:
   a. Commercial banks.
   b. Small Business Administration (SBA).
   c. Office of Minority Business Enterprise (OMBE).
   d. Economic Opportunity Loans (EOL).
   e. Minority Enterprise Small Business Investment Corporations (MESBIC).
   f. Insurance companies.
   g. Churches.
   h. Friends and/or mentors.

6. What role should the federal government play in the development of more viable minority businesses?

7. How can large corporations and major lending institutions help minority businesses?

8. How can universities and colleges help develop managerial and technical expertise in minority businesses?

9. Can Floyd Bean afford the assistant manager?

10. What alternatives does Mr. Bean have to increase his weekly sales during the Monday–Thursday lag? Can he afford these alternatives?

11. What steps do you suggest Mr. Bean take to stop the drain on cash reserves?

12. By analyzing the financial statements, what would you say are Mr. Bean's major financial difficulties, other than low sales?

13. Should Mr. Bean reduce his monthly withdrawals of $833 ($10,000 a year)?

14. What do the analyses of the statement of operations, the balance sheet, and the projections of the pro-forma income and expense statement reveal?

15. What adjustments should Mr. Bean make in the pro-forma projections, based on operations from January through June 1972?

VII–2   Lamm-McLaughlin Realty, Incorporated[1]

Lamm-McLaughlin Realty, Incorporated, is a small real estate brokerage company located in Central City, Texas. The company was started as a

---

[1] This case was prepared by Carle M. Hunt, Oral Roberts University, and Richard C. Johanson, University of Arkansas.

partnership in October 1970 by Mr. John Lamm and Mr. Ken McLaughlin with an initial investment of $500.00 each.

In the spring of 1976, the board of directors was facing a decision whether to enter into an agreement with one of several national residential real estate franchise organizations.

Members of the board of directors were concerned about recent franchising trends. One of the national franchisors had recently begun soliciting franchises in Central City, an event that set off numerous formal and informal discussions and debates concerning the advantages and disadvantages of franchising. A prevalent concern among the owners of the company was the distinct possibility that Lamm-McLaughlin Realty could not survive in the increasingly intense competitive market in Central City unless it tied in with a national franchise organization.

BACKGROUND

John Lamm, a native of Central City, met Ken McLaughlin at the local college where both men were studying business and majoring in real estate. In addition to going to school, both held full-time jobs: John as a real estate and insurance salesman and Ken as a real estate appraiser for the local office of the Veteran's Administration. It was a combination of graduation plus dissatisfaction with their jobs that caused John and Ken to start their own real estate brokerage company in October 1970. By this time both principals had obtained their broker's licenses. Their first office was very small, and working conditions were difficult. Mr. McLaughlin said that many of the first deals were worked out and contracts signed in the donut shop across the street because the privacy of a booth offered better working conditions than their small office. Since that time the firm grew, working conditions improved, the firm incorporated (1973), and there evolved a natural and workable division of responsibilities between Mr. Lamm and Mr. McLaughlin.

THE FRANCHISE SITUATION

Both John and Ken had agreed that since business had begun picking up from the 1974–75 recession, time was becoming a problem. Both were feeling time pressures as they were preparing for the spring 1976 board meeting.

They decided to put a concentrated effort into collecting information about the franchise question. The following list represents their findings to date on the advantages of franchising.

1. Being associated with quality firms that have a prestigious image will enhance our reputation. You have to evaluate the type of brokers who have joined already.

2. If it does not join a franchise, then the intermediate-sized firm (7 to 25 associates) with two or more offices will go out of business.

3. Pooled advertising offers more "bang for the buck." It is important to determine who controls the advertising expenditures, locally and nationally.

4. Franchising is a very good way to improve the market share and reduce the risk of failure for firms that are relatively new in the real estate industry.

5. Franchise operations increase the firm's ability to hire qualified sales personnel (because of their desire to be associated with big firm) and to train salespersons (with specialized sales training programs).

6. Franchising affords a stronger position to negotiate with mortgage financing institutions in acquiring lower discount points and lower interest rates for customers.

7. The image of a large business organization (the franchisor) brings more business in the form of both listings and sales because customers who had done business with a member firm often looked to another member firm when moving to a new community.

A few disadvantages came up; the main one was that brokers were afraid of losing their individual identity, which many think is the only thing that provides professional stature.

It is now up to them to recommend a course of action to the board of directors' meeting. John Lamm made a long-distance telephone call to Jim Summers, a good friend who was a national officer in their real estate trade association. Their conversation proceeded as follows:

JOHN: Hello, Jim! This is John Lamm in Central City. I need your advice on how to analyze the question of franchising that our firm is facing.

JIM: John, you're in the middle of a very important issue. Are you familiar with the advantages and disadvantages?

JOHN: Yes, I think so. But how do you analyze all the information and put it in proper perspective? You can't rely on friends and associates since about as many think franchising is the only way to go as those who think it is a mistake. I'm confused.

JIM: Well, let me send you an outline developed by one of our fine staff members who worked closely with the Committee on Franchising. The first thing you must do, John, is to make sure you understand what is happening in the industry and in your community—the so-called external environment. Second, you need a plan of action—i.e., where do you and your firm want to go? Only after these two steps can you evaluate and decide the franchising question.

JOHN: I'm beginning to see how to approach the problem, Jim. Would you please send that outline? And thanks!

Two days later John Lamm received the Franchising Analysis Outline in the mail (see Appendix A). John Lamm and Ken McLaughlin began to review the information in order to present a concise recommended course of action to the board of directors. Their attention focused on the sample Memorandum of Agreement, which the representative of a national franchisor had left with them a few days before (see Appendix B).

APPENDIX A: FRANCHISE ANALYSIS OUTLINE

A. Where to Look
   1. Franchise directories.
   2. Franchise shows.
   3. Franchise consultants.
B. Checking the franchise
   1. The company (Franchisor).
      a. Solid financial position.
      b. Satisfactory credit rating.
      c. Good reputation.
      d. Length of time in business sufficient to prove ability and evaluate competitiveness of its service/product.
      e. Detailed histories of the background of principals.
      f. Number and names of other franchisees in operation.
      g. Dun & Bradstreet rating.
      h. Supplier and bank references checked.
   2. The company representative.
      a. One who evades questions is suspect.
      b. One who pressures under guise of "losing territory if you don't sign" is suspect.
   3. Costs of franchising.
      a. Should be spelled out in detail.
      b. What is included in franchise fee?
      c. What does down payment cover?
      d. Is equipment reasonable in price and of good make?
      e. Who pays for extensive delays in getting started?
      f. Is the continuing percentage on sales a reasonable amount that can be afforded once business is going?
      g. What services does the franchisor provide in return?
      h. Any "hidden costs?"
   4. Legal aspects of franchising.
      a. Violations of local building, sign, and zoning codes.
      b. Talk the offer over with local attorney, one who is independent.
      c. Examine lease and equipment purchase agreements.
      d. Examine financial instruments.
      e. Understand and be willing to accept the restrictions involved in any particular franchise.

f. Important part is the circumstances under which the contract can be terminated.
g. Length of franchise contracts.
h. Beware of contracts that, under threat of cancellation, impose unreasonable obligations such as minimum purchase levels (of materials/equipment) or unrealistic sales quotas.
i. Check provisions with regard to transfers, goodwill, and restrictions on opening another business after termination.

C. Sources of help
1. Local Better Business Bureau.
2. Regional office of Small Business Administration.
3. Federal Trade Commission field offices.
4. Bureau of Consumer Protection.

D. Sources of Information
1. The International Franchise Association
7315 Wisconsin Avenue
Washington, D.C. 20014
2. *Directory of Franchising Organizations*, published in 1975 by Pilot Industries
347 Fifth Avenue
New York, New York 10016
3. *Franchise Opportunities Handbook*, published in 1972 by the U.S. Department of Commerce. For sale by
The Superintendent of Documents
U.S. Government Printing Office
Washington, D.C. 20402

APPENDIX B: ELEMENTS OF THE FRANCHISE AGREEMENT

The following paragraphs capture the sense of various elements of a typical franchise agreement submitted to Lamm-McLaughlin Realty by a national franchise organization.

1. Lamm-McLaughlin agrees to pay an initial franchise fee of $5,000.
2. Lamm-McLaughlin agrees to pay national franchisor a continuing service fee of five percent (5 percent) of gross revenue (excluding capital gains or regular income for the principal's own account).
3. Lamm-McLaughlin will have the right to use national franchisor's name and participate in joint advertising, educational, promotional, and other available staff services programs.
4. Lamm-McLaughlin is entitled to operate one office, which shall be located at. . . .
5. National franchisor shall not locate another franchised office within a one- (1-) mile radius of. . . .

6. Lamm-McLaughlin shall not sell, transfer, relocate, or assign the franchise without prior written consent of franchisor.

7. Lamm-McLaughlin may terminate the agreement at any time after one (1) year from date of agreement upon 90 days' written notice.

8. Lamm-McLaughlin understands and agrees that it is important to use the trade name, trade marks, and various "staff services" (i.e., educational, promotional and advertising services).

9. Lamm-McLaughlin agrees to cooperate with other local, regional, and national franchisees of this national franchise organization.

10. National franchisor will furnish franchisee an illuminated sign, not to exceed $500 in cost, which meets all local sign codes.

11. National franchisor shall assist Lamm-McLaughlin in locating sources of supplies and other materials that aid in the marketing of real estate.

12. National franchisor shall make available to Lamm-McLaughlin advertising, promotional, and educational methods and techniques developed by franchisor.

13. National franchisor reserves the right to prohibit the use of all other advertising, promotional, and educational material unless Lamm-McLaughlin receives prior written approval.

14. National franchisor shall provide Lamm-McLaughlin from time to time with appropriate operating and administrative manuals designed by the national franchisor.

15. National franchisor will establish a local coordinating board, which is made up of all local franchisees and which is authorized to act on behalf of all local franchisees on matters affecting their joint interest including legal matters, educational, advertising, and promotional programs. Local coordinating board has authority to make assessments for its operations and activities.

16. National franchisor agrees that 50 percent of the continuing monthly service fees received from each local franchisee will be credited to the local coordinating board for use to offset operating expenses and various educational, promotional, and marketing programs.

17. Lamm-McLaughlin shall not engage in any other real estate brokerage operation during the term of this agreement.

18. Lamm-McLaughlin shall use supplies approved by the national franchisor.

19. Lamm-McLaughlin shall have an office that is of adequate size and maintain the decor, both exterior and interior, which reflects favorably upon the image of the national franchisor.

20. Lamm-McLaughlin recognizes that the success of their real estate office is dependent upon the management of their office and therefore agrees to participate in the management of the office on a day-to-day basis.

21. Lamm-McLaughlin agrees to use their best efforts to operate their office in accordance with the laws, regulations, customs, and practices of the local real estate sales industry.

22. Lamm-McLaughlin agrees that their failure to earn total commissions during any one- (1-) year period that are not at least 50 percent of the average earned by other local franchisees during said one year period, shall constitute a material breach of this agreement.

VII–3   Bill's Service Station[1]

Bill's Service Station was a full-line service station owned and operated by Bill Richardson and located in a medium-sized southeastern metropolitan area. The city had a population of 75,000, of which 35 to 40 percent were black. The metropolitan area (SMSA) population was approximately 120,000. The local economy was based partly on agriculture with heavy emphasis on timber and wood pulp operations. This was supplemented by several manufacturing firms (chemicals and rubber), which employed several thousand people. The economy received an additional boost from 14,000 students attending a state university located in the town. A small four-year college, several hospitals, and state and federal government offices added a sizable service base to the economy.

Bill started the business in 1962 and located it in a concrete block building that he converted from earlier use as a car wash operation. In front of the station were three gasoline pumps situated on an unpaved driveway that led into two open bays for automobile servicing. Inside the station was an office for customer service and accessory displays and a back room used for storage and rest room facilities. An enclosed area at the side of the office, originally the car wash tunnel, had been remodeled for use as a community meeting room.

A station wagon and a half-ton pick-up truck with road service equipment were used to provide full road service to customers. The station operated daily, including holidays, from 7:00 A.M. to 8:30 P.M. In addition to the owner, who was a qualified mechanic and a graduate of a vocational training school where he specialized in auto repair, there were two other full-time mechanics and six part-time employees. The full-time employees were both partially disabled veterans who had worked in a

---

[1] Prepared by Joseph Barry Mason and Morris L. Mayer, University of Alabama.

motor pool while in the Korean War, and the part-time workers were high school students in need of financial support. Bill's wife provided the bookkeeping and accounting services for the station. She was an accounting graduate of a local vocational training school.

The service station offered a wide range of products and services. Tire service, both at the station and on the road, mechanical services ranging from minor tune-ups to major overhauls, and maintenance services, including oil changes and air filter replacement, were all available through the station. The accessory line was limited to high-turnover items, such as automotive chemicals. Although facilities were available, no car washes were performed. A 30-day credit service was also provided for selected customers who did not have credit cards. Bill's merchandising policies were a result of attending a dealer sales school and of having helped his father operate a service station while he was in high school.

FINANCIAL POSITION

The financial records indicated that the business was highly successful. The entire facility, including land, building, and all equipment associated with the business, was purchased by Bill on a ten-year mortgage of $40,000. Gross income per month ranged from $8,700 to $9,000, while expenses, including cash payment for inventory items, ranged from $7,500 to $7,600, which yielded a gross profit of $1,100 to $1,500 per month—from which the owner's salary, depreciation, and periodic expenses such as tax payments must be deducted. The first year of operation resulted in a loss of $3,000, but since then the profitability of the business had improved to such an extent that the mortgage was paid off in 1970, two years ahead of schedule.

In terms of individual product lines, the gross margin on gasoline was 5¢ per gallon, 30 percent on oil, and 40 percent on automotive chemicals. However, the service aspects of the business were the most profitable. Tire changing, for example, produced about a 90 percent margin—providing that modern equipment was used to hold down labor costs.

GEOGRAPHIC AND SOCIO-ECONOMIC MARKET CONDITIONS

The business was located in a primarily residential neighborhood of one-family homes with a few local businesses dispersed throughout the area. The station was one-half mile from the nearest main highway and was situated on the second lot from an intersection and fronted on a street of residences.

Surrounding the station was a totally black residential area. Living conditions in the immediate vicinity ranged from "extreme poverty" to "relative affluence." Within two blocks of the station there was a relatively new subdivision of brick homes that sold in the $25,000 range. A few blocks east was a federally-funded housing project for low-income families. Many of the residents of the housing project were unemployed and on welfare, but the immediate area around the station was comprised of one-family residences in the moderate to low-income class.

BACKGROUND INFORMATION ON THE OWNER

Bill was a native of this city. He became involved in community affairs and civil rights while he was in high school in 1948, when he participated in a move to get the black vote franchised. After high school he joined the Army, served in Korea, and returned home in 1956. At that time, he became involved in the unionization of local industries while he was employed as a mechanic in a local heavy industry. Several strikes occurred in the following period, and during a strike in 1958 he was fired from his job. His case was appealed to the National Labor Relations Board where he argued his own case and won a decision after three years of litigation. During the 1958–1962 period, he worked for the city in the municipal garage.

Since the early 1960s, Bill had been politically active and was currently serving on the city school board, the board of the Veteran's Hospital, and was Chairman of the Community Advisory Board, which functioned primarily in the area of race relations.

In 1968, he sought election as Police Commissioner of the city, but was defeated by the white incumbent. However, he continued to have political aspirations and planned to enter other municipal elections.

CONSUMER INFORMATION

Bill stated that the losses suffered by his business during the first year of operation were due to his efforts to attract customers who were middle-income professional people and white-collar workers. Problems arose from offering credit to middle-income customers, including ministers and other self-employed individuals, and those he knew through his involvement in community affairs.

After the first year, an improvement in profitability followed Bill's efforts to concentrate on customers with lower incomes. Most of his customers were city employees and blue-collar workers (laborers, etc.) with annual incomes between $4,500 and $7,000. A large number of industrial shift workers lived in the area, but relatively few of these were customers. He consciously avoided encouraging their trade because of layoffs and strike problems and the resulting pressure for credit.

Bill made a major effort to make his customers feel comfortable at the station. All customers were asked to address him simply as Bill. Employees and owner alike wore plain work clothes. Since his home was only half a block away, customers regularly visited him at home. The house was modest and unassuming in appearance. It was furnished with comfortable furniture, few pieces of which were new or expensive.

Bill drove an older model station wagon, while his wife drove a newer full size, but low priced, automobile.

BUSINESS PHILOSOPHY

Bill worked hard at establishing a reputation for honesty, speed, and dependability among his customers. If a customer called for road service, a truck was immediately dispatched. If it was not possible to reach the customer within a few minutes of the call, the customer was advised of the delay so that he might call another station. Likewise, employees were sent home if they arrived for work in such a disagreeable mood that "they might lower the quality of service rendered, or if they arrived at work under the influence of alcohol."

All advertising was done through three local radio stations. Spot announcements were used on musical radio shows that presented either rock or spiritual music. Initially, the advertising budget was $100 per month, and the strategy was to inform potential customers of the business. As the business became established, however, the advertising budget was reduced to $40 per month, with less money going to radio, and more money being spent in community activities, such as providing shirts for ball teams, and in similar community involvement projects.

Before extending personal credit to a person, Bill used the services of a credit bureau and also did some personal investigation. He did not extend any credit to the clergy or to self-employed people. If credit was approved, he used a rule of thumb of 35 percent of the customer's weekly salary to establish the upper limit on the amount extended. By such attention to detail, he reduced his loss on bad debts to 3.5 percent. To avoid loaning money to customers, Bill did not carry money on his person and had himself bonded so that he could explain to a customer why he could not take money out of the cash register.

The station kept maintenance records on the automobiles of regular customers and reminders were sent to the customer at specified intervals. The strategy had been highly successful.

DISCUSSION

The mortgage on the business was now paid off, and money was available for capital improvements and expansion. Bill was in a quandary as to what direction the business should take in the future. His wife desired to move to a home out of the neighborhood and into one more in keeping with their new affluence. Bill was afraid this would endanger the success of his present business. He did not have sufficient capital for a major new investment elsewhere but could engage in a modest expansion program. Money was available through the white financial structure, but he had stated that "any time I tie myself to the white banks, I lose my independence in supporting causes I believe in." He was unsure as to how a change in his present method of doing business would affect his effectiveness in the community as a leader, apart from the economic viability of the business.

QUESTIONS FOR DISCUSSION

1. What do you think of Bill's philosophy of doing business?
2. Evaluate Bill's credit policy.
3. Evaluate Bill's policy of market segmentation, i.e., establishing specific groups as customers to be sought and those customers to be avoided or rejected.
4. Given Bill's two major concerns of the moment, the future course of his business and satisfying his wife's wishes to leave the neighborhood for improved housing more in keeping with their present economic status. What action would you recommend? Why?

VII–4   Hummel Maid, Inc.[1]

Many years ago, Mrs. Lucile Hummel moved into a new house and busied herself making it into a home. It was located in a campus community. There was no dining room rug, but there were several football jerseys of rich gold and brown colors. With characteristic ingenuity, she converted the jerseys into a beautiful braided floor covering.

Many people admired the braided rug, and several wanted to know how it was made. Mrs. Hummel—Lu to friends—helped them, and even casual acquaintances, make braided rugs for their own homes. The rugs were handsome and inexpensive. As more and more women tried to acquire the skill, it became evident that most failures were due to the use of poor materials. Soon Lu Hummel was in business selling wool to homemakers. A maid cut the wool into strips by hand in the basement.

---

[1] Prepared by M. M. Hargrove, University of Tulsa.

Lu's hobby-business was interrupted for several years while she completed her education and became a professional teacher. She was well on her way to receiving her Ph.D., with only her dissertation unfinished, when World War II broke out and her husband was sent to the Southwest. Lu found a teaching position at the University of Tulsa, and soon became the head of the Office Administration Department. She was an enthusiastic, understanding, patient teacher, admired by her students and fellow professors. Her husband returned after the war, and both seemed destined to have separate professional careers—she as a professor and he as an oil company executive.

But her career was again interrupted when the oil company decentralized and transferred her husband to Oklahoma City. In her new home, she reassembled her interests and planned again for her future. She considered an offer to teach at a nearby state university, but decided not to accept. This was her opportunity to revive her rug business.

Wherever she traveled, Lu looked for braided rugs. She found them in the show cases at the Smithsonian Institution, the national shrines of historical Americans, and old homes of colonial origin. She read all available materials written about braided rugs, and she collected hundreds of pictures showing them used with furniture of all periods.

With free time on her hands and her enthusiasm bubbling again, Lu Hummel consulted with her banker and a lawyer recommended by a friend. The banker suggested, "We'll get you some money," and the attorney added, "Let's make a big thing of this." Feeding her high spirits on these bits of professional advice, Lu continued to consider various aspects of her proposed business. Gradually, her thoughts crystallized. She found 20 women willing to buy $20,000 of stock. She incorporated under the name of Hummel Maid, Inc., with common stock totaling $50,000. The women all wanted to help. Fifteen agreed to serve as members of the Board of Directors. They were well known and held responsible positions in the major companies of the city. Lu Hummel retained 52 percent of the stock.

LOCATION

At an early meeting of the Board of Directors, after they had voted themselves a salary of $10 per meeting, the women considered the problem of finding a good location for Hummel Maid, Inc. Lu thought incoming travelers emerging from the Turner Turnpike would want to stop and relax before tackling the traffic of the city by-passes and congested throughways. Or, if traveling toward the East, the drivers would want to stop before entering the turnpike for relaxation, gas and oil, or to get a bite to eat. Near a proposed site, three large service stations cared for the needs of cars. A beautiful new unit of a large chain of motels was across the divided highway. A tourist attraction, "Frontier City," was to be located nearby. Here restless children and fatigued adults were invited to watch snatches of life of the old West re-enacted with exciting realism. Tourists were also invited to visit the modern, attractive training school of one of the nation's largest automobile manufacturers.

The directors decided to locate in this vicinity. A contact was made with Mr. A. C. Brown, part-owner and operator of the motel. Mr. Brown owned land along the highway, and offered to sell for $100 a front foot. The lots were 300 feet deep. For the site chosen with 100 front feet, he wanted $10,000 and would hold the deal open for $100 earnest money. After practically no discussion, the directors accepted Mr. Brown's offer and called for $10,000 on unpaid stock to cover the purchase cost.

An attractive building was erected well back on the site so as to allow for parking. The building served as a retail display room, home office, training center for workers, and shipping center. The original cost of the building was $27,500. Furnishings were purchased to enhance the merchandise to be displayed. These appointments eventually cost $10,000. A loan was secured on the real property calling for an annual payment of $2,000 plus interest.

There were many other necessary items. An appropriate sign was acquired. Insurance coverage was provided. Taxes and utilities bills were submitted and seemed high when related to the income of the infant business. Then more help and more inventories were needed, and it appeared obvious that the anticipated increased production must soon get under way.

PROPOSED OPERATIONS

Lu Hummel outlined her proposed operations to her board members. Production would not be done by factory methods. The work would be done in the worker's home. In this way, there would be less capital invested and operating costs would be minimized. Workers would be recruited among housewives and unemployed women of the community who would work during their spare time. Lu Hummel would teach them how to make the rugs. Excellent designs and beautiful woolen materials would be supplied to the workers. Hummel Maid, Inc., would market the rugs for the workers. It would advertise and promote the sales. The Board of Directors approved the program as outlined.

TRAINING

In arranging the teaching room, Lu Hummel used the vestibule school idea, and in this way introduced her workers to the ideals of the good home workshop. At first the lessons were free to all comers, but a $10 charge was made after many women learned the art only to quit after making a single rug. The learners met at 9:30 each Friday morning. These group meetings started with a 20-minute lecture advising the workers what was expected of them, the time they should take to produce a rug, the size and layout of the ideal production room, the size of the work table, what treatment would help if they were affected by wool and dust allergies, transportation procedures, the problems caused by small children being around the work center, and similar items of information. After the lecture, the workers were taught how to make small circular rugs. They developed skill in the proper use of the thumb, which was the key to successful rug making, and proper stitching, which made the rugs lie flat. The necessary time was given for each learner to become expert.

WORKERS

For the most part, the workers took unusual pride in their work. They were able to fit their rug work into their family schedules. Generally, farm women were better producers than suburban women. The farm women had fewer distractions. Age of the workers had little to do with the quality and quantity of production. Some young mothers with small children were slow in getting the rugs produced, while others did fast work of acceptable quality. Often, several workers were in one family group. No special physical attributes were needed, but outside interests did interfere. Many women felt a sense of accomplishment from creating a beautiful and useful product, and all agreed that money was only one of their motivators. One woman inherited a substantial estate, but continued to maintain her production schedule. Another worker, almost 90, sold her land to the federal government because it was to be inundated by the waters of a flood control dam. With plenty of money to care for her and being too old to make the big, heavy rugs, she continued to make "mockups," which were sold to dealers.

A distinctive cloth label was signed by each woman and attached to her rugs. The label stated that the rug was an original heirloom rug designed by Lu Hummel, hand braided for the designated customer, the handiwork of the designated worker, specifying the pattern and size, and recorded the register number. The pattern was registered by number so that in years to come the customer could duplicate the order if desired.

PRODUCTION

In production, wool strips were braided first and then sewed by hand with a special concealed stitch. For sewing thread, a heavy grade of waxed linen warp was used. The rugs were heavy, weighing about one pound per square foot. A nine- by twelve-foot rug weighed approximately 100 pounds.

More than a hundred color shades were available, and all were vat dyed. If the right color for the customer's decoration scheme was not on hand, a special dye lot was run for a charge of $10 or less.

Standard designs called for circle or oval shapes. Special shapes were available at higher cost, and included rectangular, square, three-circle, multicircle, and half-circle rugs. The customer was asked to provide the color scheme desired. While standard color patterns were ordered by name, custom color patterns were available at no extra charge. Even the standard color patterns could be altered to meet customers' needs and without extra charge.

Five easy specifications to aid the customer in ordering included (1) size; (2) shape; (3) general effect, including light, dark, predominating color, and accent colors (when possible, the customer was asked to send swatches of furniture fabric or wallpaper); (4) pattern; and (5) price. After the order was received, a chart was submitted to the customer with colors attached showing what was to be used in each row. The chart was returned to indicate approval.

The office work connected with each order was no simple task. Acknowledgment of the order was mailed, the shipping date was scheduled, the design of the rug planned and approved, many letters were written to be certain that the customer was satisfied, rug charts were kept, labels recorded, and wool poundages estimated for each color. The colors selected for each rug then had to be dyed in proper quantities. And good records were kept. Lu Hummel once remarked, "Cost accounting is a must. We simply have to know where we stand with our costs."

Lu had learned that she had to be certain about all of her costs of operating, especially before she entered a new market. If her cost records were inaccurate, she made decisions from false information. She knew the close relationship between cost and sales prices. When sales prices were increased, she had to have justification for herself, her dealers, and her customers. She tried never to raise all prices at the same time and to have as few increases as possible. She found that she could raise prices on odd sizes and shapes with little or no objection.

PRODUCTION PROBLEMS

To avoid confusion, workers were asked to notify the office at least three days before they returned a finished rug, so that the next rug could be readied. Workers were scheduled so that not more than two were in the shop at the same time, to keep from wasting time for both the workers and the office staff. The workers were given the following suggestions to help ensure efficiency in the shop when they called:

1. Tie each color of unused wool together to make it easier to put up.
2. Bring sacks of unused wool into the large teaching room for weighing, and be sure your name is on the sack.
3. Take small rugs to back shipping rooms, and large rugs to front.
4. Keep small scraps in a paper sack and short lengths of 1 to 2 feet in another sack so we can put them in our hit-and-miss barrels. Scraps have value!
5. Check in the office to get the materials for the rug inspector to use.
6. While your rug is being inspected, put your colors on the chart for your next rug.
7. The inspector will talk to you privately about the rug and help you with any problems.
8. Take your check sheet and materials from the finished rug to the office and sign your slip.
9. Now get checked out with wool, charts, and supplies for the new rug.
10. Place the due date on your chart. If you feel you can't make it, tell us now! If something comes up later while you are at work on the rug, tell us in time to have someone else take over.

Within two years after moving into the new building, sales poured in and production was increased repeatedly. A group of nearly 100 workers was trained and producing. More workers were needed, and Lu Hummel appealed to trained producers to help find the right type of women. She explained that they could not use a producer who, after she had learned to make small rugs, could not make a nine-by-twelve or larger. And with so many workers, the money invested in wool increased so substantially that some control was necessary. Lu decreed that only one half the wool needed for a large rug would be issued initially, and the remainder issued only when needed. On rugs up to six-by-nine, all the wool needed was issued with the work order. When it became apparent that special dye problems would delay the production, Lu Hummel gave to the braider a "no-rush" order on which to work if her production should be stopped.

When an order was received for a set of several rugs, all were produced by one person. It was found easier to give the total order to one woman so that all the rugs would be alike. If an order for a set involved unusually large rugs, it was given to two women who lived close together for joint production.

Lu Hummel knew the answers to problems brought to her. She showed the women how to make the firm, even braid necessary for a beautiful rug. A tight braid was difficult to sew and not handsome. She demonstrated how to braid different weights of wool together. She determined that every row put on a rug should add two inches to the size. With this standardization, production control and uniform quality were possible. Through experience, she found that there were several techniques for improving the color beauty. For example, when it was necessary to change shades, it was best done in the corners.

Lu Hummel recalled vividly the crisis precipitated by the regional head of the Wage and Hour Administration. Hummel Maid, Inc., had been reported to the Administration by an unknown informer. A heated discussion ensued about the relationship of the braiders to the company. Lu claimed that the women were independent contractors and that she had no control over their hours of work or their production schedules. She gave the agent the names of 24 braiders with the request that he visit their work centers and learn first-hand about this relationship. From his inspection, he determined that the braiders were, in fact independent contractors and could easily make the minimum wage or more per hour. His ruling simplified Lu's relationships with them and with the government.

If an adverse recommendation had been made by the agent, Hummel Maid, Inc., would have had to hire more accounting services, pay more taxes, and incur more office expenses. Actually, the company had operated one year under Social Security. This was discontinued.

The better braiders made substantial supplementary incomes for their families. They averaged $1,200–$1,500 per year. One woman made in excess of $4,000 annually, and another built a $10,000 home from her rug money. Many had added rooms and other improvements to their homes or purchased new appliances.

FINANCES

The original five-year loan had to be refinanced. The loan holder died in April and the loan was due the following September. When the lender's estate was probated, it showed that the principal had been reduced to $19,000. The Southwestern Life Insurance Company was asked for a loan. The company refused to deal with a group of women. However, the company did offer to make a personal loan to Lu Hummel. Lu owned 52 percent of the stock at the date of organization, and four years later she had increased her share of ownership to 83 percent of the 351 shares outstanding.

Occasionally, differences of opinions occurred among the stockholders. On one such occasion, Lu had to pay almost double per share to get a few directors out of the company. This price was substantially more than the book value of the stock. After a series of attempted negotiations, Lu acquired the land and building on her personal credit, and Hummel Maid paid her rent for their use.

MARKETING THE RUGS

At first, all rugs that could be produced were sold without much effort. One satisfied customer told another, and this word-of-mouth advertising absorbed the limited production. Since the rugs were made of heavy wool, thickly braided, and lasted almost a lifetime with reasonable care, there was little repeat business.

Lu Hummel was astounded at the free publicity her rugs received in *House Beautiful, Better Homes and Gardens, Interior Design, The Wall Street Journal,* and many other publications. She managed a modest advertising program, run in home magazines that she considered helpful in selling the rugs. Chatty, friendly, informative letters sent to current and prospective dealers were effective. Prospective dealers were urged to invest in a sales kit and stock-rugs which, when purchased, entitled them to be listed as official dealers. Kits were sold to dealers at less than half of the actual cost, because experience had shown how much a sales staff needed information and aids in order to present the line. A 30- by 48-inch stock rug made sales efforts even more effective. A few dealers who had sufficient floor space bought sizes ranging up to nine by twelve feet for display.

The themes repeated frequently in dealer contacts were (1) your profit for each sale is much greater on our rugs; (2) the customer knows the rug was made for her, and when pleased, she becomes an active sales force for your store; and (3) the rugs are "right" for the casual living of today. On special price lists prepared for dealers, prices were stated at retail and the dealer's discount was 40 percent.

The number of dealers increased until there were more than 500 department and furniture stores, carpet shops, and decorators all over the country, including New England, the home of the braided rug. With this expanded sales organization, it was difficult to keep a production-sales balance. Lu recognized these growing pains. Hummel Maid rugs sold too well! What should have been a sweet experience proved to be a major problem of production. Her workers were unable to speed up, so she tried to turn the operation into factory-type production. This didn't work because she could not get workers who took pride in their work. Delivery dates were delayed. Lu philosophized, "You know that the people of Oklahoma talk slowly, and they work the same way; but the beauty of the finished product is well worth the waiting time." After returning strictly to home production, she appealed to her dealers to help her keep high standards of quality and to be understanding if deliveries were slow. Lu explained that if the homemaker had wanted a machine-made braided rug with limited colors, no special design, and a stereotyped look, she would not have ordered a Hummel Maid rug.

MARKETING CHANNELS TRIED

Hummel Maid, Inc., tried many channels of distribution. Word-of-mouth advertising was sufficient during the early years. As production mounted, an attempt was made to combine the retail business with some wholesale activities. This program was gradually replaced by exclusive distributors. It was hoped that these distributors would develop their exclusive territories and would push the rugs more diligently than the wholesalers, who often carried them as a sideline. The dealers provided all customer services and billed their own accounts. Hummel Maid was the supplier and had little customer contact under this arrangement. But sales through these exclusive distributors were disappointing, so the company tried to operate as a wholesale mail-order business. Later, sales representatives replaced the mail-order program. These sales representatives emphasized the wholesale business and did only casual retail business. They tried to get stores with good showrooms as customers. For example, the rugs were displayed in the showroom of Sullivan's on Fifth Avenue, New York, and in the showroom of the Trade Mart in Dallas, Texas. Sales representatives were paid 10 percent commission, which was considered good by the trades people.

ADMINISTRATIVE PERSONNEL

Mrs. Elsie Shidell, Office Manager, started with Hummel Maid two years ago. She learned to design some of the rugs, and worked with independent contractors when needed. She assumed much of the routine work of processing orders, invoicing, preparing materials, keeping records on the workers, and general office work. Her husband worked for an oil-field equipment firm. Mrs. Shidell had worked for 12 years in a retail grocery that she owned jointly with her husband. Prior to the grocery venture, she spent five years as office manager of a tool company and three years as a partner in a small company selling oil field equipment. She had also had a little experience selling in a retail gift shop.

Charles Irvin Springer, Jr., son of Lu Hummel, was 30 years old and married. He had completed three and one-half years of college study in business administration. During his college years, he worked closely with Lu, helping especially with the cutting of wool and the supervising of rug makers. For several years he had created authentic hand-made stage coaches for dude ranchers, movie producers, and other customers. Recently he had been giving his full time to the rug business. He was mechanically inclined and creative.

LU HUMMEL

Lu Hummel drove herself hard in all that she did. Her enthusiasm and optimism were contagious. She liked people, and they responded. About six months ago, she had a severe case of the flu. She had a continuous cold, and knew she was run down. Her hands and feet became swollen and painful. When they turned red and became of major concern, her family physician referred her to Dr. H. C. Johnson, Chief of Staff at a large, new Baptist hospital.

One morning at breakfast, Charles Springer called Elsie Shidell and said, "Dr. Johnson has told mother she has Raynaud's disease and that she will be a convalescent for an indefinite period of time. She doesn't know when, if ever, she can return to the business. Raynaud's disease is not fatal, but she is unable to use her hands, and her feet are also affected. She must be unusually careful because in her exhausted condition she has little resistance to infections and other diseases."

QUESTIONS FOR DISCUSSION

1. How did Lu Hummel combine education and experience to provide a promising and interesting career? Evaluate experience as education.
2. Would men have added to, or detracted from, the operations?
3. The "farming out" system predates the "factory" system. How could it succeed in a contemporary business?
4. What qualities of leadership did Lu Hummel possess? What weaknesses?
5. How strong was the organization? The board? The office manager?
6. What should the company do now that Lu Hummel is ill? What short-range actions should be taken? Long range?
7. Are all managers teachers? Explain.
8. How important is an adequate cost accounting system to a manufacturer? What costs must be controlled?
9. How should braided rugs be marketed?
10. Evaluate the financial strengths and weaknesses of Hummel Maid.
11. Evaluate the attempt at "factory-like" production. Why did it fail?

VII–5   Bell Associates[1]

Mr. E. N. Bell, founder, owner, and president of Bell Associates, estimates he spends 80 hours per week overseeing the company's construction jobs, supervising the Tank Lining, Industrial Services, and Construction divisions, preparing bids for upcoming construction projects, making economic feasibility studies, generating new work, inspecting and signing daily work orders, handling personnel problems, and planning the company's expanding activities.

Bell evidenced entrepreneurial characteristics while still in high school and college, and started his own company in 1956. Exhibit 1 summarizes the company's developmental history. At present, Bell Associates has about 90 employees engaged in constructing metal buildings, maintaining building grounds, making pallets, and lining tanks. The company's scope of activities and organization structure are depicted in Exhibits 2 and 3.

GENERAL CONSTRUCTION

During 1972, Bell Associates completed 12 general construction jobs, the largest of which grossed $200,000. Mr. Bell spends considerable time working up bids and estimates, and he obtains 10 percent of the jobs on which he bids. He prefers jobs in the $150,000 range that can be completed within 90 days, are within a 100-mile radius, and require only one crew. However, Bell is currently involved in bidding on a job that has mushroomed unexpectedly to about $700,000.

Bell maintains that the company's success in bidding on government jobs is attributable to his willingness to put up with extra paper work and to accept close inspection—both of which tend to deter other contractors from bidding on government jobs. Bell ferrets out most of his leads on new projects from published listings, but he also gets repeat business from previous customers and inquiries from potential customers.

BUILDING GROUNDS MAINTENANCE

For eight years, Bell Associates has had a crew maintaining part of the Warren Company grounds and buildings, and has recently added a crew to maintain the grounds of two other local companies. This work includes grass cutting, weed killing, making small repairs, and performing miscellaneous maintenance work. For each of these crews Bell Asso-

---

[1] Prepared by Charles R. Scott, Jr., Alonzo J. Strickland III, and Arthur A. Thompson, University of Alabama.

EXHIBIT 1
History of Mr. Bell and Bell Associates

Early 1950s	Organized grass mowing teams and earned, in summers, $75 to $85 per week. Repaired mowers and cycles, and helped father build houses.
1954	Obtained contract from Warren Company for $15,000 to supply 6" to 30" plywood disks to seal tank openings. Netted $7,700 for college payments.
1956	Interviewed for job after graduation, but decided he could make more money by starting his own business. Rented a building, hired a manager and sold and repaired mowers and cycles. Received a B.S. degree in Business Administration.
1958	Bought a 5,000-sq. ft. building, and added golf cart sales and repair.
1960	Sold mower, cycle and cart business. Entered into a partnership arrangement with Mr. Rum to manufacture wood plugs for cores on which paper is rolled. Designed, made and sold cricket boxes.
1962	Dropped the manufacture and sale of cricket boxes. Designed an "indestructible" 5' × 5' wooden pallet. Received orders from the Warren Company for these. Took on the management of his father's house construction company. Started making cabinets and related wood items for commercial firms.
1965	Obtained a contract for part of maintenance of building and yard, for waste disposal, and for small construction jobs from Warren Company. Began constructing commercial metal buildings.
1968	Discontinued managing father's business because of heavy workload, and incongruity of managing both union and nonunion work forces.
1969	Moved into a 20,000-sq.-ft. building. Sales about $340,000 per year. Incorporated Bell Associates.
1971	Discontinued the company's cabinet and millwork operations. Purchased the tank and pipe lining operations from the Warren Company, and added 10,000 sq. ft. to Bell Associates Building.
1972	Redesigned pallets—steel channels welded to rectangular tubing with wood slats.
1973	In process of dropping waste haulage at Warren Company due to new environmental regulations requiring a $25,000 to $50,000 investment in compacting equipment.

ciates receives gross revenue of $150 per day, and from this Bell nets about $10. Also, Bell has used this work as a contact point for learning about and securing other more profitable maintenance related jobs, including cleaning up after major plant changes and performing field engineering services.

EXHIBIT 2
Organization Chart and Personnel Information

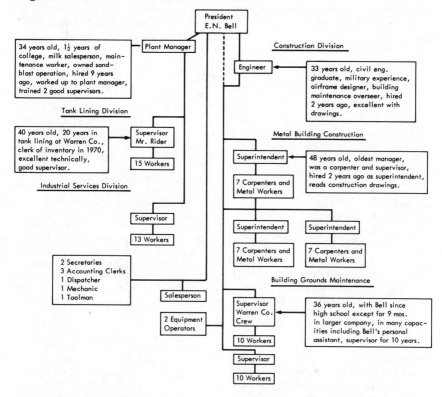

INDUSTRIAL SERVICES

Since 1962, Bell Associates has made about 4,000 pallets for the War-ren Company and, last year, started manufacturing redesigned pallets to replace the old "indestructible" ones. The local unit of the Warren Company is changing to the new pallet, and Bell expects to raise production from 73 per day to 100 per day as soon as Bell Associates completes the repair of the old pallets. He has trial pallets in several other plants of the Warren Company and also has made contact with several other potential users of the new pallets. Mr. Bell plans to increase the sales of pallets so that he can reduce the price below their current level of $30 per pallet.

TANK LINING

In 1970, Bell bought the machinery and the rights to use the Warren Company's tank lining operation. The Warren Company had been lining

EXHIBIT 3
Product, Work, and Financial Information

Metal Building Construction (40%)*

Product:
Buildings made of concrete and metal
During 1972, largest four jobs between
$100,000 and $200,000
Subcontracts plumbing, electrical and
masonry work.

Volume:
10 years ago, 15% of the company
revenue
1970, 70% of the revenue
1972, 50% of the revenue
1973, 60% of the revenue (estimated)

Net income:
Estimated to be 2½% of revenue

Industrial Services Division (10%)*

Products:
5' × 5' pallets steel welded frame, with
wood slats and 4 vertical pipes.
Stairs, braces, and small support sections requiring welding, drilling, bending, etc. usually for the construction
division.

Production facilities:
Bell-designed roller conveyor line fitted
with jig to hold and move parts of
pallet as they are assembled, welded
and bolted. Maximum production is
100 pallets/day.
Job shop arrangement of machines for
other work.

Pallet price: $30 each

Buildings Grounds Maintenance (40%)*

Work Description:
Grass cutting
Weed killing
Small building repairing
Storm sewer cleaning
Fence painting
Waste hauling

Income: $150/day/crew

Wages: 70% of income

Net income: $10/day/crew

Tank Lining Division (10%)*

Products:
Rubber-lined tanks which can be filled
with liquids, gases, etc., such as acids,
with no corroding effects. Sandblasting and painting of many items such
as concrete mixers, buses, wash pots
and bedsteads is performed to keep
machines busy.

Production facilities:
In the yard:
Sandblaster
Refrigeration building for rubber
In building:
Rubber sprays
Autoclave to cure rubber. One is the
largest in the market area (12 ft.
dia.)
Hand steam units to cure large tanks.
Paint spray for outside of tanks.

Purchase cost from Warren Co.:
$100,000

Sales income:
1971—$96,000 (8 mos. oper.)
1972—154,000 (12% net income)
1973—150,000 (first 3 mos.)

---

* Bell's estimate of his division of time.

tanks since early 1950, but started to phase out the operations in 1965 when its sales were about $300,000 per year. By 1970, Warren had reduced its tank lining output, stopped replacing equipment, and transferred many men to other operations. Bell made the purchase for $100,000 with the provision that the Warren Company allow its tank lining supervisor, Mr. Rider, to join Bell Associates and furnish necessary technical knowledge. Bell hoped to raise tank lining sales to $250,000 by 1972, though he was aware that demand for tank lining is linked to economic conditions in the textile industry and, further, that improved methods of chemical storage are reducing the number of lined tanks needed.

Bell Associates has been sandblasting storage tanks and many other small items for many years. In addition, it has purchased painting equipment for $7,000 to paint the outsides of tanks and selected small items. Sandblasting and small painting jobs gross $5 to $50 each.

ACCOUNTING

The cost system of Bell Associates is designed to collect costs by job and division. Each day, each construction supervisor records the hours worked on each job by each worker in his crew. Labor rates are applied to the hours to compute the payroll and job and division costs. A computerized payroll system has been considered, but as many as seven wage rates (reflecting regular and overtime hours, union and nonunion, job, and other variations) may be used for a single worker during a given day. The use of computers was deemed impractical. Material and supplies, subcontracting, and job-identified financing costs are assigned to the jobs and divisions. Other costs are collected and prorated over the entire operation, using rates that are determined annually. In working up costs and estimating new jobs, Bell customarily applies a 7½ to 8 percent charge for overhead and profit, and expects a profit of 2½ percent of the bid price. However, Bell states that even with this detailed accounting system he has to "wait until the end of the year to know just where we stand."

In addition, costs must be collected in such a manner that bonuses of 25 percent of division profits can be distributed to five key managers. These bonuses ranged from $1,800 to $3,800 per manager and totaled $10,000 in 1972. However, these managers have questioned the application of the company's indirect costs in determining their profit bonus.

MR. BELL AND THE COMPANY

Mr. Bell attributes his long work hours to his inability to delegate. For example, he assigned management of building construction to one of his superintendents. But after a trial period, the superintendent asked to be relieved of that responsibility and returned to the supervision of only one crew. Bell has transferred the superintendent's responsibility to the engineer, but bypasses him when Bell feels the decisions go beyond the engineer's fairly limited experience and knowledge. It is Bell's policy, however, to urge each supervisor to train someone to provide a backup for the position.

Bell says he needs to keep in contact with all work, as he is best equipped to deal with the more serious and urgent matters. To facilitate communications, he has located his office in the center of the building in view of the operations and the equipment dispatch board, and has installed radio equipment in company trucks for contact with workers on the jobs.

The company, despite Bell's watchful eye, has experienced several operating incidents that Bell feels should not have occurred. In one recent case, a job had passed final inspection of the architect, but Bell felt it was shoddy and ordered some of the work redone. Although Bell realized this caused some resentment among the work crew, he said, "I cannot have perfection in all things, but I want more than the minimum."

EXHIBIT 4

BELL ASSOCIATES
Income Sheet
For the Year Ending December 31, 1972

Income		
Construction...		$1,007,747
Rubber lining...		154,006
Industrial...		104,259
Rental..		18,784
Total..		$1,284,796
Direct Costs.......................................		1,090,448
Gross Profit.......................................		$ 194,348
Indirect Costs.....................................		89,314
Gross Profit after Indirect Costs...............		$ 105,034
General and Administrative Costs....................		32,404
Operating Profit.............................		$ 72,630
Other Income...................................	$5,868	
Outgo..	9,002	3,134
Net Profit before Taxes......................		$ 69,496
Provision for Income Taxes........................		13,097
Net Profit after Taxes.......................		$ 56,399

Indirect Costs		*General and Administrative Costs*	
Auto and truck expense.......	$ 6,723	Salaries.....................	$21,600
Depreciation................	18,513	Payroll taxes................	1,169
Employee insurance..........	8,016	Employee insurance..........	264
Insurance—other.............	9,404	Advertising expense..........	1,595
Maintenance.................	2,497	Bad debts....................	1,776
Supplies....................	2,458	Depreciation................	374
Payroll taxes...............	19,166	Donations...................	209
Rent.......................	11,950	Dues........................	984
Utilities...................	7,823	Legal and accounting........	808
Taxes and licenses...........	2,764	Office supplies..............	1,545
Total................	$89,314	Rent.......................	1,200
		Taxes and licenses...........	150
		Utilities....................	400
		Miscellaneous...............	330
		Total................	$32,404

In another case, a concrete mixer that had been improperly stored and recorded was stolen and subsequently found not even to be insured. Additionally, several daily work sheets for the Warren Company were found in error, which caused Bell some embarrassment. Now, he inspects and signs each daily work sheet.

Mr. Bell finds himself forced to spend many hours each week resolving personnel problems. Among these are problems of general supervision, lack of job descriptions, interfacing with union and nonunion employees, and the seasonal nature of construction work which interferes with scheduling and manning of work crews. On a recent day, a supervisor waited an hour to talk to Mr. Bell about having to come 15 minutes early each day to thaw out some rubber in order not to delay production. The supervisor hinted about being entitled to extra pay, but Mr. Bell felt it was more a case of frustration than concern with pay. One of Bell's superintendents just left the company to accept an offer of $20,000 per year— $3,000 more than the salary at Bell Associates.

A number of situations involving company equipment also consume much of Bell's time. He finds it hard to turn down small jobs for his idle millwork equipment. He is considering purchasing a van to avoid paying the travel costs for employees on out-of-town jobs. He feels renting equipment is high-priced financing, and so he owns many pieces of equipment, including air compressors and trucks, which are rented to others when not in use.

EXHIBIT 5

BELL ASSOCIATES
Balance Sheet
December 31, 1972

Assets

Current Assets

Cash..............................	$ 18,074	
Accounts receivable...................	195,916	
Inventory..........................	24,794	
Prepaid expenses.....................	3,146	$241,930

Fixed Assets

Building, machinery, equipment.........	$185,046	
Less reserve for depreciation...........	41,570	143,476
Total Assets...................		$385,406

Liabilities and Stockholder's Equity

Current Liabilities

Accounts payable.....................	$129,343	
Notes payable.......................	28,625	
Accrued payables.....................	20,562	$178,530
Long-Term Liabilities.................		92,772

Stockholders Equity

Common stock.......................	$ 30,000	
Retained earnings....................	84,104	114,104
Total Liabilities plus Equity......		$385,406

Last year, Bell states, he budgeted too low by 30 percent, and this year it appears that the difference will be even greater. Yet, his net income increased from $15,000 in 1970 to $56,000 in 1972. (See Exhibits 4 and 5 for 1972 financial statements.) Even though estimating the future is perplexing, he plans to continue planning and budgeting his operations.

Bell recognizes that his company has expanded and that he has fallen short in defining duties, training new people and keeping up with the company's changing character. As Bell closed up the office, he expressed the thought that "there are so many opportunities for me to improve my business, but I just do not know where to start."

QUESTIONS FOR DISCUSSION

1. How would you evaluate Bell's managerial capacities? What are his strengths and weaknesses?
2. What would you say are the goals of the company? Are they the same as Mr. Bell's?
3. Evaluate the history of the company. Do you believe Mr. Bell made the best choice when he graduated from college? Estimate Bell's salary.
4. Should Bell Associates continue to engage in all its current activities? If not, what should it drop and why?
5. Can Mr. Bell delegate some of his time-consuming activities? If so, what and how? Would it be economical?
6. Evaluate the organizational structure of Bell Associates. Would you recommend a reorganization of the company's divisions? Does Mr. Bell need a general manager to help him oversee the firm's activities? Can he afford to hire such a person?
7. Make a financial analysis of Bell Associates. Is the company in a sound financial position? How profitable is the company?
8. Do you recommend that Bell Associates continue to expand? Should the company bid on the $700,000 job, which will surely increase the company's sales?
9. What will happen to the company if Mr. Bell becomes incapacitated?

VII–6   Harold Motors, Inc.[1]

Jerry Harold is concerned with the current business situation. "It's been a hard go from the beginning," he said. "It seems that we've had to invest $2 for every $1 we made. I want to keep the business and really build it up, but I'm simply not getting enough return for my investment."

---

[1] Prepared by Philip W. Ljungdahl, Larry Gene Pointer, and Harold Prasatik, Texas A&M University.

BACKGROUND

Jerry and Rose Harold organized Harold Motors in May 1972 when they purchased a small Datsun agency in a city where a major university is located. Jerry has about 20 years experience with automobiles, including five years in a military motor pool, ten years in sales and management, and five years as owner and operator of a used car lot in California prior to his move to Texas.

Net assets of the agency were purchased for $20,000 cash and a note payable for $10,000. Of the $30,000 purchase price, $10,000 was for parts inventory (which upon actual verification was determined to be $2,300), and $20,000 was for furniture, fixtures, tools, and equipment. At the time of purchase there were 11 new Datsun automobiles that were floor-planned under a $35,000 limit, 10 percent interest arrangement at a local bank.

Immediately upon acquisition of the Datsun Agency, Jerry transferred the assets to Harold Motors, Inc., in exchange for a $20,000 long-term note from the corporation, and corporate assumption of the $10,000 note payable for the parts inventory. Jerry also loaned the corporation an additional $10,800 for working capital, making a long-term note payable to Jerry Harold of $30,800.

EXHIBIT 1
Loan Conditions Required by Lender and SBA

1. First security interest in all machinery, equipment, and furniture now owned and to be acquired.

2. First security interest in parts and used cars inventory, accounts receivable, and proceeds, to be serviced as Lender, in its discretion, may see fit.

3. Lease agreement on leased premises occupied by Borrower with conditions satisfactory to Lender, with landlord's subordination to Lender's security interest to be obtained prior to disbursement.

4. Semi-annual financial statements to be submitted to Lender/SBA, with interim figures to be furnished upon request.

5. Before disbursement borrower to assume to SBA loan on Jerry Harold's used car business in California.

6. Hazard insurance sufficient to protect Lender/SBA position, with Lender shown as loss payee.

7. Life insurance policies with face value of $52,000 and $50,000 on lives of Jerry and Rose Harold, respectively, assigned to Lender, may be reducing term insurance.

8. Personal guarantees of Jerry and Rose Harold secured by pledge of stock owned in applicant.

In January 1973, Harold changed to a new bank which offered a $75,000 floor-plan limit at 10 percent interest. In August 1973, Harold Motors obtained a $50,000, five-year, 8.75 percent SBA loan. Exhibit 1 shows the loan conditions. The SBA loan was primarily to finance expanded operations required under an American Motors Corporation (AMC) franchise, which the company was obtaining in September 1973. However, as specified in the loan conditions, Jerry had to use $12,508 of the proceeds to repay part of the long-term note to him so that he could repay an outstanding SBA loan on his used car business in California. Also, in obtaining the SBA loan, Jerry was required to transfer into paid-in surplus the balance of the long-term note payable to him. At the time Jerry obtained the AMC franchise, the bank raised Harold's floor-plan limit to $125,000.

EXHIBIT 2
Organization Chart

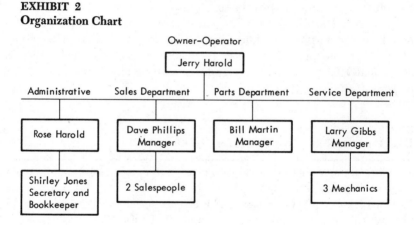

Exhibit 2 shows an organization chart for the company. Jerry Harold is president and general manager. In this capacity he handles some administrative duties, functions as a salesman, periodically acts as a sales manager, and works in the service department. Jerry is aided in the administrative duties by Rose. Rose's salary is included in the clerical salaries and is equal to the wages drawn by Shirley Jones, the bookkeeper, cashier, and secretary for Harold Motors. Shirley has sole responsibility for maintaining the accounts and is the only employee who fully understands the financial system.

Exhibits 3 and 4 show the income statements for 1974 and 1973, Exhibit 5 shows the comparative statements of financial position, and Exhibit 6 shows selected data about the company.

EXHIBIT 3

HAROLD MOTORS, INC.
Income Statement (by Department)
For Year Ended December 31, 1974

	All Depts. Totaled	New Vehicle Dept.	Used Vehicle Dept.	Service Dept.	Parts and Accessories Dept.	Indirect Expense
Sales	$1,012,307	$716,799	$133,760	$64,955	$96,793	
Cost of Sales	840,756	626,909	113,692	34,516	65,639	
Gross Profit	$ 171,551	$ 89,890	$ 20,068	$30,439	$31,154	
Selling Costs:						
Salesmen compensation and incentives	$ 19,893	$ 15,371	$ 4,522			
Delivery and freight	2,531	1,539	47		$ 945	
Policy adjustments	3,516	2,524	422	$ 436	134	
Demonstration expense	1,176	1,027	149			
Advertising	7,058	6,308	310	106	9	$ 325
Interest—Floor Plan	11,440	11,440				
Other Operating Expenses:						
Salary—owner	18,200	2,150	2,150	2,150	2,150	9,600
Salaries—supervision	21,326	2,724	2,712	8,286	7,604	
Salaries—clerical	15,442	3,606	3,606	3,606	3,606	1,018
Other salaries and wages	5,815	1,279	528	1,387	2,460	161
Company vehicle expense	1,486			1,296	190	
Stationery and office supplies	1,622	168	110	197	303	844
Supplies, small tools, and laundry	2,855	77	73	2,188	322	195
Travel and entertainment	2,414	49		29	5	2,331
Memberships, dues, and publications	1,500	176	150	118	98	958
Legal, auditing and outside service	1,128	85	15	247	25	756
Telephone	2,655	572	229	728	1,009	117
Bad debts	150					150
Rent	13,572	2,965	4,925	3,940	1,564	178
Repair and maintenance—real estate and equipment	705	39	44	383	59	180
Depreciation and amortization	7,050	524	1,425	4,340		761
Taxes—Other than income	7,560	16	6	3		7,535
Insurance	5,930	1,863	81	1,111	80	2,795
Employee Benefits	2,580			309	100	2,171
Utilities	2,230	833	495	714	159	29
Total Expenses	$ 159,834	$ 55,335	$ 21,999	$31,574	$20,822	$ 30,104
Net Income (Loss) from Operations	$ 11,717	$ 34,555	$ (1,931)	$(1,135)	$10,332	$(30,104)
Other Income and Deductions	(6,049)					
Net Income (Loss) before Taxes	$ 5,668					
Net Income (Loss)	$ 4,051					

EXHIBIT 4

HAROLD MOTORS, INC.
Departmentalized Income Statement
For Year Ended December 31, 1973

	All Depts. Totaled	*New Vehicle Dept.*	*Used Vehicle Dept.*	*Service Dept.*	*Parts and Accessories Dept.*	*Indirect Expenses*
Sales	$912,726	$695,000	$98,945	$42,581	$76,200	
Cost of Sales	750,118	582,862	86,571	25,995	54,680	
Gross Profit	$162,618	$112,138	$12,374	$16,586	$21,520	
Selling Costs:						
Salesmen compensation and incentives	$ 21,377	$ 17,452	$ 3,925			
Delivery and freight	1,770	688	13	478	1,069	
Policy adjustments	4,769	3,786	497		8	
Demonstration expense	701	591	110			
Advertising	5,221	4,751	282	55	9	$ 124
Interest, floor plan	5,568	5,568				
Other Operating Expenses:						
Salary—owner	11,910					11,910
Salaries—supervision	13,831	1,810	1,450	5,179	5,392	
Salaries—clerical	14,045					14,045
Other salaries and wages	3,564	451	227	622	2,237	27
Company vehicle expense	577	78		455	43	1
Stationery and office supplies	1,089	47	38	119	126	759
Supplies, small tools, and laundry	2,446	51	8	2,119	31	237
Travel and entertainment	2,165			104		2,061
Membership dues and publications	1,027		52	22		953
Legal, auditing and outside services	739					739
Telephone	1,894	256	106	505	328	699
Bad debts	581	193		193	195	
Rent	14,435	2,540	5,887	4,747	841	420
Repair and maintenance—real estate and equipment	330	30		244		56
Depreciation and amortization	3,288		473	2,587		228
Taxes—other than income	8,599			3		8,595
Insurance	5,799	2,056	24			3,719
Employee benefits	1,559			235		1,324
Utilities	1,789	380	439	713	130	127
Total Expense	$129,073	$ 40,729	$13,531	$18,380	$10,409	$ 46,024
Net Income (Loss) from Operations	33,545	71,409	(1,157)	(1,794)	11,111	(46,024)
Other Income and Deductions	(3,219)					
Net Income (Loss) before Taxes	$ 30,326					
Income Taxes	6,802					
Net Income (Loss)	$ 23,524					

EXHIBIT 5

HAROLD MOTORS, INC.
Comparative Statements of Financial Positions

	12/31/74	12/31/73	12/31/72	5/31/72
Current Assets				
Cash..................................	$ 7,220	$ 16,393	$ 1,567	$ 9,671
Accounts receivable.....................	6,798	3,201	1,377	
Inventory: New vehicles..................	167,585	88,060	32,492	35,260
Used vehicles.................	8,192	13,339	6,009	1,150
Parts and accessories...........	26,770	23,097	9,838	8,000
Other.......................	7,660	5,342	846	
Other Current Assets....................	2,678	1,508		4,000
Total Current Assets...............	$226,903	$150,940	$52,129	$58,081
Fixed Assets (Net)				
Bldgs. and Improvement..................	$ 21,816			
Mach. and shop equipment...............	12,877	$ 17,013	$17,788	$20,307
Parts and accumulated equipment.........	280			
Furn. and fixture.......................	3,350	4,029	1,237	1,125
Service units...........................	546	1,263		
Leaseholds.............................	5,963	6,139	934	
Signs..................................	2,492	2,449		
Net Fixed Assets..................	$ 47,324	$ 30,893	$19,959	$21,432
Total Assets...................	$274,227	$181,833	$72,088	$79,513
Current Liabilities				
Accounts payable........................	$ 6,537	$ 9,321	$10,455	$12,486
Notes payable..........................	183,738	77,941	31,296	35,260
Accrued liabilities.......................	712	3,681	553	265
Total current liabilities.............	$190,987	$ 90,943	$42,304	$48,011
Long-term debt.........................	40,406	49,513	30,856	30,856
Total Liabilities...................	$231,393	$140,456	$73,160	$78,867
Owner's Equity				
Capital stock...........................	$ 1,000	$ 1,000	$ 1,000	$ 1,000
Paid-in surplus.........................	18,348	18,348		
Retained earnings......................	23,486†	22,029*	(2,072)	(354)
Total Net Worth..................	$ 42,834	$ 41,377	$(1,072)	$ 646
Total Liabilities and Net Worth	$274,227	$181,833	$72,088	$79,513

* There was a direct credit to retained earnings for $577 from a reduction in the note payable for parts.

† There was an adjustment subsequent to closing for inventory adjustments in the parts department in the amount of $2,619 and $25 extraordinary adjustment.

SALES AND MARKETING

Harold Motors enjoys the advantage of being the only AMC and Datsun dealership within a 100-mile radius. There are, however, 11 new car dealers and 22 used car dealerships in the city.

Dave Phillips, sales manager, has been with the company since August 1972. He has about eight years of sales experience in auto dealerships. As

EXHIBIT 6
Selected Data About Harold Motors, Inc.

		1974		1973	
		Sales	Gross Profit	Sales	Gross Profit
1.	**Parts and Accessories**				
	Parts–car–R.O.*–mech.........	$18,521	$ 7,276	$13,162	$ 4,896
	Parts–truck–R.O.–mech........	6,387	2,613	3,773	1,566
	Parts–warranty claims.........	6,803	1,349	2,992	602
	Parts–internal................	4,934	702	1,645	345
	Parts–counter–retail...........	17,846	8,505	6,908	2,588
	Parts–wholesale...............	7,029	2,054	5,646	1,844
	Inventory adj.–parts...........	—	2,445	—	—
	Accessories–counter...........	4,608	1,484	3,937	1,293
	Tires and tubes...............	4,499	841	3,380	924
	Accessories–internal...........	22,744	4,423	31,303	6,148
	Gas, oil, and grease...........	3,422	1,909	3,454	1,314
		Revenue		Revenue	
2.	**Service Dept.**				
	Car labor....................	$30,636		$19,570	
	Truck labor..................	11,773		6,625	
	Warranty labor...............	3,781		2,030	
	Internal labor................	10,027		7,738	
	Sublet labor (includes body, electrical system, valve, head, alignment work, etc.)........	8,738		6,618	
	Total....................	$64,955		$42,581	
	Revenue less labor cost.......		$30,439		$16,586

3. Car Unit Sales and Gross Profit per Unit by Manufacturer

	Unit Sales	Gross Profit per Unit	Unit Sales	Gross Profit per unit
Datsun......................	116	$543.89	186	$532.80
AMC........................	71	377.44	28	465.46
Used Retail..................	58	327.15	51	249.31
Used Wholesale..............	50	21.86	45	(7.58)

4. Monthly Sales and Inventory of Autos by Manufacturer, 1974

	Units in Inventory			Units Sales			Inventory, December	
	Average	High	Low	Average	High	Low	Units	Costs
Datsun.............	20	36	6	10	22	1	20	$ 58,002
AMC...............	24	30	14	6	10	3	30	109,584
Used Retail.........	12	17	8	5	7	3	9	8,194
Used Wholesale......	—	—	—	4	10	1	—	—

* R.O. = Repair orders.

EXHIBIT 7

HAROLD MOTORS, INC.
Income Statement (total of departments)
For Eight Months Ended December 31, 1972

Sales..	$284,058
Cost of Sales...................................	228,632
Gross Profit.............................	$ 55,426

Expenses

Salesmen Compensation and Incentives............	$ 4,955
Advertising—new and used Vehicle...............	6,531
Interest—Floor plan...........................	3,612
Other Operating Expense	
Salaries—supervision............................	9,017
Stationery and office supplies.....................	1,139
Supplies, small tools and laundry..................	1,689
Travel and entertainment........................	468
Memberships, dues and publications...............	668
Legal, audit and outside services..................	2,489
Telephone.......................................	1,200
Employee training...............................	(70)
Rent...	6,093
Repair and maintenance—real estate and equipment.	206
Depreciation....................................	2,825
Taxes—other than income........................	12,435
Insurance.......................................	3,780
Utilities..	554
Total Expenses:..........................	$ 57,591
Net Income (Loss) from Operations................	$ (2,165)

sales manager, Dave draws a $700 monthly salary and also receives the normal sales commission of 25 percent of gross profit (sales price minus cost of the vehicle sold) on all cars that he sells. On the average, there have been two salesmen. Salesmen are generally paid on a straight commission basis of 25 percent of gross profit.

In explaining the operation of the sales department, Dave Phillips indicated that determination of the proper inventory mix and quantities is a major consideration of the sales department. According to Dave, a 2½-to-3 inventory-to-sales ratio is a good benchmark. Local sales have dropped, a trend that Dave attributes to rising new car prices. At the present level of sales, Dave figures that two salesmen, including himself, can handle the sales traffic. Jerry thinks that with four salesmen, he can keep them on their toes and have them greeting customers as they come onto the lot.

In addition to local advertising expenses, Harold Motors is charged for national advertising by AMC. Nissan, on the other hand, has developed a co-op advertising program. When Harold Motors purchases a Datsun from Nissan, $25 of the purchase price is placed in an advertising co-op, to which Nissan contributes an additional $25. When Harold advertises solely a Nissan product and sends a sample of the ad to Nissan, the cost is paid by funds in the co-op.

Nissan also requires that Harold Motors participate in a direct mailing, in which Nissan sends letters to all customers, thanking them for their patronage. Harold is charged $3.50 per customer for this mailing.

About the future, Mr. Harold said, "I think we have to wait for the economy to change. You can't force the public to spend money. When national employment and the economy get back to normal, we can expect to see a change overnight in car sales. Until then, we'll just have to try to sit it out."

PARTS AND ACCESSORIES

In January 1974, Bill Martin was hired as parts manager, and since taking over the parts department, Bill has increased sales by almost 27 percent and the gross profit by nearly 44 percent. However, net income from parts has decreased from $11,111 to $10,332. Considering the general efficiency with which the parts department operated and the inventory control system that Bill utilized, management was somewhat perplexed by the reduction in income.

Parts prices were determined by the manufacturer's suggested retail price lists, which were updated quarterly. According to Rose Harold, prices were 35 to 40 percent above cost on retail parts sales, from which dealers received a 15 to 20 percent discount; whereas parts used by the service department for repairs generally had a 20 percent markup (see Exhibit 6 for sources of revenues and their related gross profits). Parts and accessories operations have been profitable.

SERVICE

In June 1973, Larry Gibbs was employed as full-time service manager, Larry's duties are writing customer repair orders, scheduling service work, preparing the customer's invoice for service work, and customer relations.

Since operations began, ten mechanics have been employed, three of whom are currently employed by the firm. Of the three currently employed by Harold Motors, two are experienced mechanics and the other is a trainee.

Mechanics were paid on a salary basis until October 1974, at which time they went to a 50 percent commission basis. All other local dealers had been paying their mechanics on a 50 percent commission basis. Mechanics are required to repair all of their own comeback jobs without pay. Mechanics are also compensated by a Nissan bonus program under which the two mechanics that work on the largest number of repair orders each month are given stamps with which they can purchase items from a catalogue. This program costs Harold Motors $7.50 per mechanic per month. Labor is billed at $10 per hour with the number of hours being derived through the use of flat rate books from Datsun and AMC.

Along with his other activities, Jerry Harold occasionally spends some time preparing new cars for customer delivery. Jerry feels that he is capable at almost any type of service work.

FINANCE

Harold Motors' new car inventory is floor-planned at a local bank with a limit of $125,000. Under the floor-plan arrangement, Nissan and AMC draft directly on the bank for the cost of Harold's new cars. When a car is sold, Harold pays the bank. The bank has not always adhered to the stated limit, and in September 1974, there was $180,000 under the floor plan. At the end of 1974, however, the bank informed Harold that the $125,000 limit would be enforced.

When AMC and Nissan ship a new car order to Harold Motors, they mail a notice to Harold's bank in order to begin floor-planning before Harold receives the cars. AMC has realized this inequity and automatically pays for 20 days' worth of floor-planning on all cars regardless of when Harold receives or sells them.

All used cars in inventory are owned by Harold Motors, and at no time have used cars been financed.

QUESTIONS FOR DISCUSSION

1. "I'm simply not getting enough return for my investment." What is Mr. Harold receiving as a return on his investment? What do you believe would be a reasonable rate of return?
2. How do Harold Motors' financial operations and position compare with the industry?
3. Should anything be done about the losses in the used vehicle and service departments? Are the departments contributing to the company profits?
4. Go through the process of planning Harold Motors' profits for the next year. What steps might Mr. Harold take to improve the company's profit? What do you recommend he do first?
5. Explain the change in profit in the parts and accessories department from 1973 to 1974. What appears to be the mark-up used? How would you determine if the average mark-up is adequate?
6. What financial information should department supervisors receive?
7. Might Shirley Jones' position cause some problems? What controls would you establish?

REFERENCES

American Marketing Association. *Marketing Definitions: A Glossary of Marketing Terms.* Chicago: American Marketing Association, 1960, pp. 9–23.

Bach, G. L. *Economics: An Introduction to Analysis and Policy,* 2d ed. Englewood Cliffs, N.J.: Prentice-Hall, Inc., 1957.

Ballentine, J. A. *Ballentine's Law Dictionary,* 3d ed. San Francisco: Bancroft-Whitney Company, 1969.

Corley, R. N., and Black, R. L. *The Legal Environment of Business,* 3d ed. New York: McGraw-Hill Book Company, 1973.

Donnelly, J. H.; Gibson, J. L., and Ivancevich, J. M. *Fundamentals of Management,* 3d ed. Dallas, Texas: Business Publications, Inc., 1978.

Gist, R. R. *Marketing and Society.* New York: Holt, Rinehart, and Winston, Inc., 1971.

Gross, Harry. *Financing for Small and Medium-Sized Business.* Englewood Cliffs, N.J.: Prentice-Hall, Inc., 1969.

Meigs, W. B., and Johnson, C. E. *Accounting: The Basis for Business Decisions,* 2d ed. New York: McGraw-Hill Book Company, 1967.

Myer, J. N. *Accounting for Non-Accountants.* New York: New York University Press, 1957.

Samuelson, P. *Economics,* 8th ed. New York: McGraw-Hill Book Company, 1970.

Still, J. W. *A Guide to Managerial Accounting in Small Companies.* Englewood Cliffs, N.J.: Prentice-Hall, Inc., 1969.

Weston, J. F., and Brigham-Holt, E. F. *Essentials of Managerial Finance.* New York: Holt, Rinehart, and Winston, Inc., 1968.

Whiteside, C. D. *Accounting Systems for the Small and Medium-Sized Business.* Englewood Cliffs, N.J.: Prentice-Hall, Inc., 1961.

Glossary of the Most Frequently
Used Business Terms*

The following glossary should help you understand the terms used in the text and the exhibits.

ABC inventory control   An inventory classification system which breaks down the inventory into similar unit values.

Absolute liability   Liability for injury resulting to another where no account is taken of the standard care exercised. Liability of a principal as distinguished from that of a guarantor.

Accelerated depreciation   Depreciation expense which offers an allowance for the wear and tear (including an allowance for obsolescence) of tangible property used in business or held for the production of income.

Accruals   Continually recurring short-term liabilities, such as accrued wages, accrued taxes, and accrued interest.

Affirmative action   Guidelines of the Office of Federal Contract Compliance program state that contractors must take "affirmative action" by actively recruiting members of minority groups being underutilized, thereby avoiding unlawful discrimination in employment.

Agent   A business unit which negotiates purchases and/or sales but does not take title of the goods in which it deals.

Amortize   To liquidate on an installment basis. An amortized loan is one in which the principal amount of the loan is repaid in installments during the life of the loan.

Annuity   A series of payments of a fixed amount for a specified number of years.

---

* Prepared by Frank White, University of Georgia.

Balloon payment   When a debt is not fully amortized, the final payment is larger than the preceding payments.

Better Business Bureau   A community organization which is sponsored by the local businessmen which acts to police unfair business practices.

Bill of lading   A written acknowledgment by a carrier of the receipt of goods described therein and an agreement to transport them to the place specified therein and deliver them to the person specified therein.

Bond   A long-term debt instrument used to provide external funds for business.

Bonding   An obligation made binding by a money forefeiture, such as an insurance agreement pledging security for financial loss caused by an act or default of a person or by some contingency.

Book value   The accounting value of an asset.

Broker   An agent who negotiates contracts of purchase or sale but does not take control of the goods.

Bureaucracy   A form of organization which has many of the characteristics of the classical organizational design; i.e., it is highly structured and centralized, with narrow spans of control.

Business cycle   A definable pattern of changes in business activity which is periodically repeated. Particular cycles do not correspond to any accounting period.

Capital   See Owners' equity.

Capital asset   An asset with a life of more than one year that is not bought and sold in the ordinary course of business.

Capital budgeting   The process of planning expenditures on assets whose returns are expected to extend beyond one year.

Capital gains   Profits on the sale of capital assets held for six months or more.

Capitalization rate   A discount rate used to find the present value of a series of future cash receipts. Sometimes called the discount rate.

Carrying costs   Costs associated with holding inventory, such as interest charges or funds invested in inventory; storage costs; and costs of storage devaluation due to physical change, obsolescence, or market changes.

Cash   A broad classification of easily transferred negotiable assets, such as coin, paper money, checks, money orders, and money on deposit in banks.

Cash cycle   The length of time between the purchase of raw materials and the collection of accounts receivable generated in the sale of the final product.

Caveat emptor   "Let the buyer beware." A maxim of common law expressing the rule that the buyer purchases at his peril. Implied warranties in the sale of personal property are exceptions to this rule.

Caveat vendor   "Let the seller beware." This means that it is the seller's duty to do what the ordinary man would do in a similar situation.

Chattel mortgage   A mortgage on personal property (not real estate), such as as mortgage on equipment.

Civil Rights Act of 1964 Federal law that was passed to eliminate job discrimination based on race, color, religion, sex, or national origin, and to insure due process and equal protection under the law.

Clayton Act Prohibits certain practices in commerce if they might substantially lessen competition or tend to create a monopoly. It also exempts labor unions and farm cooperatives from the provisions of the Sherman Antitrust Act.

Commercial bank An ordinary bank of deposit and discount, with checking accounts, as distinguished from a savings bank.

Compensating balance A required minimum checking account balance that a firm must maintain with a commercial bank. The required balance is generally equal to 15 to 20 percent of the amount of loans outstanding. Compensating balances can raise the effective rate of interest on bank loans.

Conditional sales contract A method of financing new equipment by paying it off in installments over a one- to five-year period. The seller retains title to the equipment until payment has been completed.

Consideration One of the prerequisites for a contract which makes it clear from the contract's terms that each party has incurred a detriment in exchange for the other party's doing so also. Something given in exchange for a promise.

Consumer Product Safety Commission This commission has primary responsibility for establishing mandatory product safety standards where appropriate, to reduce the risk of injury to consumers from consumer products. It can also ban consumer products found to present an unreasonable risk of injury.

Cooperative The joining together of independent producers, wholesalers, retailers, consumers, or a combination thereof to act collectively in buying or selling or both.

Cost-benefit analysis An analytic technique of weighing the specified costs of a project or investment against the benefits derived from the project or investment.

Credit union An organization, usually by labor groups, to provide financial services for employees. Credit unions offer low-cost loans and sometimes cooperative buying power to employees who participate by buying stock in them.

Decentralization A method of organizing a business so that separate parts are designated as divisions or organized as subsidiaries of the parent company. Thus, each division or subsidiary will function almost *autonomously* under conditions of controlled competition among the groupings. Each is responsible for its production, procurement, personnel, and other needs as they fit into the overall picture of company profits.

Depreciation The accounting procedure for apportioning the cost of fixed assets as a part of the expense of each period. Thus, the cost is amortized over a defined period of time.

Depression   The bottom of the overall business cycle, marked by a low level of production, a widespread unemployment of resources, especially labor, and a sharp drop in price levels due to decreased demand. (See Recession.)

Detail man   A company's salesperson who is responsible for direct selling of products to retailers or to the ultimate consumer without the use of an agent. Often he is responsible for setting up point-of-purchase displays and other special promotional materials.

Disposable income   Personal income remaining after the deduction of taxes on personal income and compulsory payment, such as social security levies.

Dow-Jones industrial average   An unweighted arithmetic average of 30 stock prices, adjusted for splits, which represented, in 1970, approximately one third of the value of all stock on the New York Stock Exchange.

Drop shipment   The delivery of goods directly from a producer to the consumer, while the sale is handled by an agent for the producer, such as a middleman or a company representative.

Dun and Bradstreet   A mercantile agency which offers credit ratings, financial analysis, and other financial services, usually on a contractual basis. A well-respected source of credit information about businesses and businesspersons in the United States and elsewhere.

EBIT   Abbreviation for earnings before interest and taxes.

EEOC (Equal Employment Opportunity Commission)   The federal administrative agency which is responsible for enforcing the provisions of the Civil Rights Act of 1964 and promoting voluntary action programs to put equal employment opportunities into actual operation.

Employee turnover   The rate at which employees are hired and terminated. It is usually represented as the percentage of the total work force which is hired on payroll and later taken off payroll within a year.

EOQ   Economical ordering quantity, or the optimum (lowest cost) quantity of merchandise which should be purchased per order.

EPA (Environmental Protection Agency)   An administrative agency set up to protect and improve the quality of the environment. Most of its work has been in the area of air and water pollution.

EPS   Abbreviation for net earnings per share of stock after interest and taxes are provided for. It is computed by dividing the number of shares outstanding into the net earnings.

Equifax   The world's largest consumer credit rating service. It provides credit investigations on a contractual basis for anyone having a legitimate business need.

Equity   The net worth of a business, consisting of capital stocks, capital (or paid-in) surplus, earned surplus (or retained earnings), and occasionally, certain net worth reserves.

Escrow   Placing in the hands of a third party the property, money, or assets of a firm which are to be released to a grantee only upon the fulfillment of a condition.

Excise tax   A tax on the manufacture, sale, or consumption of specified commodities.

Factoring   A method of financing accounts receivable under which a firm sells its accounts receivable (generally without recourse) to a financial institution (the factor).

Fair Labor Standards Act of 1938   This act (commonly called the Wage and Hour Law) was the original wage and hour law. It and its amendments cover minimum wages, maximum working hours per week, payment of overtime, and restrictions on child labor.

Fair Trade Act   An amendment to the Federal Trade Commission Act which permits minimum price levels for products for resale in states with fair-trade laws, without violating any antitrust laws.

FDA (Food and Drug Administration)   A part of the Department of Health, Education, and Welfare which acts to protect the nation against impure and unsafe foods, drugs, and cosmetics, and other potential hazards.

Federal Reserve Bank   The national banking system which acts as a reserve and discount for affiliated banks in its 12-member system. Its purpose is to provide an elastic currency, to afford a means of rediscounting commercial paper, and to establish a more effective supervision of banking in the United States.

Field warehousing   A method of financing inventories in which a "warehouse" is established at the place of business of the borrowing firm.

Fixed assets   Assets of a business which are of a relatively permanent nature and are necessary for the functioning of the firm, such as buildings, furniture, equipment. See Capital Assets.

Fixed costs   Costs which do not vary with changes in output, such as interest on long-term loans, rents, or salaries.

Franchise   An agreement by a retailer to sell only the produce manufactured or distributed by the seller.

FOB (free-on-board)   This refers to the point at which the title of goods transfers from the producer to the buyer. "FOB-origin" means that the title is transferred upon leaving the loading dock of the producer and that the shipping costs are paid by the buyer.

FTC (Federal Trade Commission)   This commission is an independent administrative agency that assists in the enforcement of the Clayton Act and other laws for maintaining free competitive enterprise as the keystone of the American economic system.

Good faith   Acting with a sincere belief that the accomplishment intended is not unlawful or harmful to another. The antithesis of fraud and deceit.

Goods-in-process   Goods in the midst of production or manufacture such that they are neither in a raw materials state nor finished and ready for sale.

Goodwill   Intangible assets of a firm established by the excess of the price paid for the going concern over its book value.

Gross national produce (GNP)   A measure of the economic performance of the economy as a whole.

Holding company   A corporation operated for the purpose of owning the common stock of other companies.

Hurdle rate   The effective capitalization rate which must be met or exceeded before a project or investment will be made. Any rate of return on assets above this rate assures that a profit is being made.

Implied warranty   A guarantee arising from contract law which implies that goods for sale are reasonably fit for their ordinary and intended purpose or are fit for a particular purpose.

Inflation   The injection of more money into the economy relative to the volume of goods and services. It results in generally rising prices for goods and factors of production.

Intrinsic value   The value which, in the mind of the analyst, is justified by the facts. It is often distinguished from the asset's current market price.

Inventory   The total of items of tangible personal property which (1) are held for sale in the ordinary course of business, (2) are in process of production for sale, or (3) are to be currently consumed in the production of goods and services to be available for sale.

Investment tax credit   A credit from federal income taxes that is computed as a percentage of the initial cost of certain capital assets.

IRR (internal rate of return)   The rate of return on an asset investment. This return is calculated by finding the discount rate that equates the present value of future cash flows to the cost of investment.

Jobber   A synonym for wholesaler or distributor.

Job cost   The aggregate cost of direct labor, material costs, and indirect manufacturing expenses associated with a specific order or job.

Leverage   The use of external funds (as opposed to equity) to generate profits. For example, borrowing funds at 8 percent and making a net return on the funds of 12 percent constitute a use of leverage.

Line of credit   An arrangement whereby a financial institution commits itself to lend up to a specified maximum amount of funds during a specified period.

Line and staff   A descriptive term which defines the structure of an organization. Line refers to jobs or roles which have direct authority and responsibility for output. Staff personnel contribute indirectly to production. Usually they advise line personnel.

Liquidity   Refers to a firm's cash position and its ability to meet maturing obligations.

Loss leader   A product of known or accepted quality priced at a loss or no profit for the purpose of attracting patronage to a store.

Management by Objective (MBO)   A management technique of defining attainable goals for subordinates through an agreement of the supervisor and the subordinate. It offers continual feedback to subordinates in terms of their contribution to the organization's total performance.

Manufacturer's agent   An agent who generally operates on an extended contractual basis, often sells within an exclusive territory, handles noncompeting but related lines of goods and possesses limited authority with regard to prices and terms of sales. He or she may be authorized to sell a definite portion of the principal's output.

Marginal contribution   The contribution by an additional unit of production sold to the fixed and/or variable cost of a firm.

Marginal cost   The cost of an additional unit. In production, it is the cost of producing one additional unit.

Marginal revenue   The additional gross revenue produced by selling one additional unit of output.

Markdown   A reduction in selling price. An item priced at $1 would have a 20 percent markdown if it were discounted to a special price of 80 cents.

Market segmentation   A marketing strategy consciously developed to produce a product or service that embodies characteristics preferred by a small part of the total market for the product or service—for example, compact autos.

Markup   The percentage change in price from the purchase price or the cost of goods sold to the selling price. An item costing 80 cents to produce and sell would have a 25 percent markup if it sold for $1.

Merchant   A business unit that buys, takes title to, and resells merchandise. Both retailers and wholesalers are considered middlemen or merchants.

Missionary salesman   A salesperson employed by a manufacturer to call on the customers of distributors, usually to develop goodwill and stimulate demand, to help or induce them to promote the sale of the manufacturer's goods, to help them train their salespeople to do so, and often to take orders for delivery by such distributors. Also used to introduce a new product or service.

Motivation   The inner state that activates or moves, including inner strivings, such as drives, desires, and motives.

National brand   A manufacturer's or producer's brand, usually enjoying wide territorial distribution.

NLRB (National Labor Relations Board)   An administrative board set up to protect labor's right to organize and bargain collectively and thereby encourage the "friendly adjustment of industrial disputes" by restoring equality in workers' bargaining positions with employers.

Opportunity cost   The rate of return on the best investment *alternative*. It is the highest return which will *not* be earned if the funds are invested in a given project.

OSHA (Occupational Health and Safety Act)   This act established specific safety standards requiring the installment of safety appliances by employers and the use of safety equipment by employees. It develops and issues regulations and conducts investigations and inspections to determine the status of compliance.

Owners' equity   Those assets left over after all creditors have been paid off. The two sources of equity are owner investment and prior earnings from profitable operations.

OTC   Stocks which are sold over the counter rather than through an organized stock exchange.

Overhead   All the costs of business other than direct labor and materials. Overhead costs include such items as maintenance, supervision, utility costs, and depreciation.

Payback period   The length of time required for the net revenues of an investment to return the cost of the investment.

PERT/CPM   Management aids that place the separate activities of a project on a schematic network to view the interrelationships of each project. The technique is used to cut costs by planning, scheduling and monitoring, and control of the overall project.

Peter Principle   A humorous book by L. J. Peter and R. Hull which examines the "Peter Principle" in hierarchial organizations. The principle states: "In a hierarchy every employee tends to rise to his own level of incompetence."

Pledging accounts receivable   Short-term borrowing from financial institutions where the loan is secured by accounts receivable. The lender may physically take the accounts receivable but typically has recourse to the borrower.

Price/earnings ratio   The ratio of price per share to earnings per share. Most growing firms have high P/E ratios.

Private brand   A brand sponsored by a merchant or agent as distinguished from brands sponsored by manufacturers or producers.

Product line   A group of products that are closely related because they satisfy a class of needs, are used together, are sold to the same customer groups, are marketed through the same type of outlet, or fall within given price ranges.

Progressive tax   A tax that requires a higher percentage payment on higher incomes.

Promotion   A blend of the three following sales activities: (1) mass, impersonal selling efforts (advertising); (2) personal sales; and (3) other activities, such as point-of-purchase displays, shows or exhibits, and other nonrecurring sales efforts.

Proxy   A document giving one the authority or power to act for another.

Purchasing power   The amount of goods and/or services which money can purchase. During times of inflation, the purchasing power of money declines.

Rack jobber   A wholesaling business unit that markets specialized lines of merchandise to certain types of retail stores and provides the special services of selective brand and item merchandising and arrangement, maintenance, and stocking of display racks. Usually rack jobbers place merchandise in a store on a consignment basis.

Recession   The downturn or a fluctuation in the aggregate business cycle recognized by a decrease in the growth in GNP for two successive quarters. It is characterized by changes in inventory levels, increased unemployment, changes in government spending, and attempts by the Federal Reserve Board to control inflation by tightening credit.

Retailer A merchant or agent whose main business is to buy goods for resale to the ultimate consumer.

Robinson-Patman Act The Robinson-Patman amendment to the Clayton Act gave the FTC jurisdiction to eliminate quantity discounts and to forbid brokerage allowances, except to independent brokers, and to prohibit promotional allowances, except on the equal basis. Any discrimination of this kind has to be based upon a cost justification.

Salary A fixed compensation paid regularly for services.

Salvage value The value of a capital asset at the end of a specified period. It is the current market price of an asset being considered for replacement.

Savings and loan bank A bank which accepts and pays interest on deposit savings, subject to whatever conditions may be prescribed as to the time such savings remain on deposit. Chartered by the Federal Home Loan Bank Board to encourage thrift and promote home ownership by making loans for home financing.

Sherman Antitrust Act The first law passed by the U.S. Congress to preserve competition in the "free-market" system. It outlawed monopolies and all combinations to restrain trade or commerce.

Soldiering A term which was used during the scientific management era to refer to the observed practice of output restriction. Employees were observed to be producing at a lower than expected rate.

Standard The basic limits or grade ranges in the form of uniform specifications to which particular manufactured goods may conform, and uniform classes into which the products of agriculture and extractive industries may or must be sorted or assigned. The expected employee performance upon which product costing and employee pay are determined.

Stock dividend A dividend paid in additional shares of stock rather than in cash. It involves a transfer from earned surplus to the capital stock account; therefore, stock dividends are limited by the amount of earned surplus.

Stock-out A situation in which the supply of an item in a firm's inventory is found to be used up. This is usually the consequence of poor inventory management.

Stock split An accounting action to increase the number of shares outstanding. This action involves no transfer from surplus to the capital account.

Stock turnover The rate at which the minimum order quantity purchased is sold. It may be calculated by dividing the cost of goods sold by the average inventory for the accounting period.

Surtax A tax levied in addition to the normal tax. The normal corporate tax rate is 22 percent, but a surtax of 26 percent is added to the normal tax on all corporate income exceeding $25,000.

Target market The segment of the total market which is selected for a concentration of promotional effort.

Theory X A set of assumptions about the nature of man which, according to Douglas McGregor, underlies classical management theory. The assumptions stress the indolence of man.

Theory Y An approach to management which is based on precepts exactly opposite to those of Theory X. They are: (1) workers do not inherently dislike work; (2) workers do not want to be controlled and threatened; (3) workers under proper working conditions seek out additional responsibility; and (4) workers desire to satisfy other needs besides those related to job security.

Time-motion study The process of determining the appropriate elapsed time for the completion of a task or job. This was a technique used by scientific managers to determine a fair day's work.

Trade association An organization formed to benefit members of the same trade. Nationally it works to inform its members of issues and developments within the organization and about how changes outside the organization will affect the members.

Trade credit Interfirm debt arising through credit sales and recorded as an account receivable by the seller and as an account payable by the buyer.

Trademark A brand or part of a brand that is given legal protection because it is capable of exclusive appropriation; because it is used in a manner sufficiently fanciful, distinctive, and arbitrary; because it is affixed to the product when sold; or because it otherwise satisfies the requirements set up by law.

Uniform commercial code A comprehensive code of practices drawn up by various legal and commercial associations to simplify, clarify, and modernize the law governing commercial transactions; to permit the continued expansion of commercial practices through custom, usage, and agreement of the parties; and to make uniform the law among the various jurisdictions.

Value added The part of the value of a product or a service to the consumer or user which results from the change from one form to another, for example, the conversion of a raw material into a *finished* product for sale.

Voluntary group A group of retailers, each of whom owns and operates his own store and is associated with a wholesale organization or manufacturer to carry on joint merchandising activities, and who are characterized by some degree of group identity and uniformity of operation. Such joint activities have been largely of two kinds: cooperative advertising and group control of store operation.

Wages A payment usually of money for labor or services, usually according to contract, and on an hourly, daily, or piecework rate.

Wholesaler A business unit which buys and resells merchandise to retailers and other merchants and/or to industrial, institutional, and commercial users but which does not sell in significant amounts to ultimate consumers.

Working capital Refers to a firm's investment in short-term assets—cash, short-term securities, accounts receivable, and inventories.

Index

Index

This book has been set in 10 and 9 point Caledonia, leaded 2 points. Part titles are 18 point Goudy oldstyle italic and chapter titles are 18 point Goudy oldstyle. Part numbers are 24 point Goudy oldstyle italic and Goudy Bold and chapter numbers are 42 point Weiss, series I. The size of the type page is 27 by 45½ picas.